A Complete Chronological Bible Co[mpanion] Guide
Read the Bible in a Year in the Order th[at it is] Presented

Written by Gary Torborg
Portions ©2003, ©2005, ©2010, ©2011, ©2012, ©2013, ©2014, ©2015. ©2016
Copyright ©2016 by Gary Torborg

Introduction

For the Christian believer, there are few things as important to your daily walk with Christ than spending time in the Word. For the seeker or the person born into a different faith, the Word becomes the guidebook for becoming a believer. But for both groups of people, there is nothing more rewarding in terms of Bible reading and study than reading the *entire* Bible, as opposed to reading just some portions. The importance of reading the whole Bible cannot be emphasized enough.

The problem is, reading the entire Bible is a very daunting task, even for good readers.

Of course, what you need is an organized plan to guide you through reading the Bible. There are many plans available for reading the Bible in its entirety, all with their pros and cons. The plan that is correct for you depends on your goals and reading ability, as well as personal preference. The duration of plans ranges from 90 days to 3 years, but the most common is one year. Some plans try to include a Psalm, a few verses from Proverbs, and at least one other Old and New Testament reading each day in a devotional style. Some just go from Genesis to Revelation, breaking up the entire Bible in 365 chunks of as close to equal length as can be obtained. The possibilities are endless.

This reading plan, and the commentary that I give you with it, is a chronological reading plan designed to get you all the way through the Bible in one year. That is, the events are presented in the order in which God presented them Himself.

There are chronological Bibles available in Christian bookstores and online, but this is different. You can also look up a variety of downloadable reading plans that you can use with the Bible edition of your choice (which is *basically* what I did here) but that's still not what makes this read-through different. My search for a truly great chronological reading plan began in 2002 with a few online searches. I found several chronological plans, but they almost all suffered from one or more of these problems:

1. Most plans simply presented the complete books of the Bible in a roughly chronological order, without regard to the way in which the Kings books, Chronicles, and the prophets are

supposed to be blended together. Problems with this included reading Chronicles about 2 months after the completion of the nearly-exact parallel story in Kings, and the reading of books by the prophets (particularly Isaiah and Jeremiah) weeks or even months after their stories were told in Chronicles.
2. Many plans made the bogus assumption that the Psalms were written entirely or almost entirely by David. Although David can be credited with a *majority* of the Psalms, there are still about 70 Psalms written by a large variety of other Psalmists, ranging from Moses to Ezra. As a result, some plans that *did* actually blend the prophets and the Kings/Chronicles books simply stuck all or most of the Psalms between the end of 2 Samuel and 1 Kings.
3. What all the plans have in common, even the one that formed the basis for this book, is that the read-through went all the way through the Old Testament before beginning even a single New Testament reading. In the strictest sense, this is correct for chronological reading. But in terms of a year-long plan to read the entire Bible, this means spending only 3 ½ months in the New Testament, taking in a larger amount of New Testament information per day than what is appropriate for good studying.

One innovative plan I encountered had both an Old and New Testament reading each day, but it suffered from problem #1 above in two ways: not only was there no blending of Old Testament history from the various books, but the Gospels weren't blended either. The harmony of the Gospels is one of the reasons why we *can* rely on the Bible as true history, and so there is no good reason *not* to blend the Gospels.

There are many Bible reading plans that make no pretense about chronological order. These plans are all good because of their focus on getting you to read the entire Bible in one year's time (or so). But, Bible reading plans that simply start with Genesis and end with Revelation are also among the least effective because of the risk of losing the reader's interest. By unfolding God's salvation plan in the order in which God Himself did so, one gets a true sense of the weight and importance of scriptures.

In spite of the fact that the Old Testament is about 3.5 times the size of the New Testament, it is the New Testament that contains the most important words regarding our salvation. Often, a great deal more can be said in a shorter number of verses in the New vs. the Old Testaments. So, the Bible chronologies (note the plural) should have New and Old Testament read side by side. But it should also be done with the correct and proper blending of books for the sake of accurate history.

In 2005, I found a reading plan online that featured the best overall blending of Kings, Chronicles, prophets, and writings such as Psalms. Alas, I regret that the original website from which I obtained it is no longer running, and therefore I can't give credit to the scholarship of the chronology. In 2008, I found another website called Realms of Faith (http:// faith.propadeutic.com/schedules/schedchron.html) containing a chronological reading schedule very similar to the one on which this book is based, but it, too, has since been taken down (it still shows up on Google search). To the best of my knowledge, there is currently no website containing a chronological reading plan for the Bible that comes close to this book or to the websites on which they were based.

Neither website was perfect, though, as both schedules suffered from problem #3 above, but I decided this was a fixable problem (see below). Using the 2005 online schedule (downloaded to a spreadsheet), I built the foundation for my chronological reading plan, and the result is this book.

The only significant fault shared by both websites was their strict chronology that had the New Testament starting in late September (problem #3). But, starting with this "base," here is what I did with it:

- I separated the Old and New Testaments
- I lined up John 1:1 with Genesis 1:1 on January 1
  - This placed several days' worth of readings in the NT prior to January 1, so the chronology actually begins on December 21. This was done so that the birth of Jesus (Luke 2) would be read on the most appropriate date possible, December 25.
- I began the process of "stretching" the reading plans.
  - The New Testament definitely had the larger chore, as it's original length, in days, of about 100, had to be stretched by a factor of over 3 times. The Old Testament needed some stretching, too, but not nearly as much. The chore was made all the more difficult by the fact that there were

some minor but annoying errors in the original listing that left a few gaps and overlaps. In order to make sure the final chronology didn't have any such gaps or overlaps, each day's readings had to be "graphed" in a spreadsheet and then carefully analyzed to determine its correctness.

Thus, you have in your hands the reading plan that resulted from this work. Not only do I present the chronological plan I came up with, but I offer a brief commentary on each of the passages. Some of the commentaries are longer, others shorter, mainly to reflect their relative importance to each other.

If you decide to follow this reading plan, you are about to embark on a journey that is as satisfying and worthwhile as it is (occasionally) lengthy and difficult. This chronological reading plan hopefully makes that reading more enjoyable as well as easier to understand.

Tips:

1. Although any English-language translation of the Bible will do, you should pick one "main" translation and stick with it. Read the next section for a comparison of several translations and why you should use one for the entire read-through.
2. This reading schedule is designed to start on December 21; however, this is by no means strict. Although you should start with the reading scheduled for December 21, especially when doing this for the first time, this reading plan can actually be started on any date.
3. The amount of scriptures read each day with this plan varies somewhat. Some days, the total amount of reading time will only be about ten minutes. Other days, you'll spend as much as a half-hour. The average will be about 15 minutes.
4. Obviously, you can "read ahead" if your schedule permits, and thus finish this read-through in less than a year's time. Or, if things get particularly difficult, this schedule can be stretched beyond a year's time.
5. The Apocrypha, or Deuterocanonical books (as Roman Catholics call them) of the Bible are not included as part of this plan, though references are made to them in some daily readings.
6. It is suggested that you do your Bible reading at approximately the same time of day each day, if possible. This kind of

schedule fits neatly with an evening devotion just before or after prayer. However, don't choose a time that is too late at night or too early in the morning. Remember, this is a study guide and you need to have an alert mind in order to get the most out of each day's Bible readings.
7. Most of all, cherish and enjoy the Bible. Savor the "ah ha!" moments that will come more frequently than you might think. Let the Holy Spirit work within you and deepen your faith.

Peace be with you.

Pros and Cons of different Bible translations in English

An important question, sure to be asked by readers attempting this plan for the very first time, is "which Bible translation should be used when going through this chronological reading plan?" The answer, basically, is whichever translation you like the best. Here are some guidelines.

In writing this chronological study guide, I deliberately did not include a Bible or simply publish a Bible with chronological study notes. Part of this is due to the practical matter of securing permission from the publishers of the various Bible translations that aren't in the public domain. Part of this is due to my belief that you should choose whichever Bible version/translation you prefer or is called for by your church.

I cannot make any comment on Bible translations in other languages such as Spanish or French; this commentary is only about English-language translations. The only reason this whole translation business is an issue at all is that the Bible's 66 books were not only not written in English, but were written in languages that are either hardly ever spoken today or not at all: classical Greek, Hebrew, and Aramaic.

Each language presents its own unique set of problems, based mainly on how *different* the language is compared to English and also its similarities or lack thereof to modern versions of the same languages. For instance, classical Greek is similar to modern Greek, but someone from Greece today would actually have considerable difficulty reading an original manuscript of, say, one of Paul's Epistles. It would be similar to the problem of an English-speaking person in the United States trying to read an Old English document written in Britain circa 1300. Hebrew *is* spoken in modern Israel and in Jewish synagogues around the world, but nearly nowhere else. Aramaic and Hebrew are "brother" languages; that is, both were developed from a common root (Semitic) in Old Testament times and probably haven't been spoken by anyone outside of a few Biblical quotes since the fall of the Roman Empire.

Thus, in order to do what I advocate in this book (that is, to read the entire Bible), it needs to be translated into a language that can be understood by English-speaking people in the 21st century. The work of translating the Bible into English has been going on for over 500 years, and each effort has been met with a varying degree of success.

Numerous factors influence the net worth of any Bible translation efforts, far too numerous for this commentary to mention. Among them, however, are factors such as which copies of which manuscripts were used, whether or not the translation went through another language between the original and English, whether or not the translation is merely an update of a previous one or a genuinely new translation, denominational bias, and the differences in the English language at the time of translation vs. now.

As a result, every translation available to us today has some pros and some cons. In the vast majority of cases, the pros outweigh the cons, and thus nearly any translation will do when embarking upon this chronological read-through. For some of you, the choice is already made for you by whichever Bible you happen to already have. For others, with or without a Bible, there may be some very strong inclinations towards one particular translation vs. another coming from the denomination to which you belong. For some of you, reading level will be the primary factor in choosing a Bible. The plethora of different translations makes the choice more difficult, though, so a comparison of them is in order, in roughly chronological order.

Geneva Bible (GEN, 1560 and 1599), **Douay-Rheims** (D-R, 1609), and **King James Version** (KJV, aka the "Authorized Version", 1611) - The earliest efforts at translating all or part of the Bible into English were made at a time when 1) the Church prohibited the practice, 2) there was no printing press to make mass copies of the translated work, and 3) the English language of the time bore very little resemblance to the English language of today. John Wycliffe is credited with doing the first *complete* translation of the Bible into English in the late 1300s, but his translation was based on another translation (in Latin, called the "Vulgate", translated from Greek to Latin by Jerome in 400 A.D.) rather than the original tongues. It wasn't until the 1500s and the work of William Tyndale that copies of the original manuscripts in their original languages were used for direct translation into English. Tyndale's translation philosophy was to translate each and every word, leaving out none, though occasionally adding or rearranging words for the sake of English grammar and readability. We call this "word for word" translation today, and more translations follow this model than any other. It's also known as the *"Tyndale tradition."*

Among the early examples were the Geneva Bible (GEN) and the King James Version (KJV, also known as the "Authorized Version"). Whereas the Geneva Bible was brought to America by the Puritans, and the KJV gained rapid popularity among English-speaking Protestants in Europe (and, much later, in America), English-speaking Roman Catholics stuck with translations based on the Latin Vulgate. At about the same time as the Geneva Bible, the Douay-Rheims (D-R) Bible was produced as the first "official" translation of the Bible into English for Catholics. It would maintain that official status for nearly 350 years.

Despite the older age of the Geneva Bible, it is actually considered easier to read than the KJV. All three of these older translations are still in print, with the Geneva being brought back just in the last decade. The main differences between them, besides some minor translation differences, are the footnotes/margin notes, cross-references, book introductions, and commentaries. Here, they each reflect biases towards Catholicism (D-R) or Protestantism (GEN, KJV), pro-monarchy (KJV) or anti-monarchy (GEN, D-R). All three are beautiful examples of Elizabethan English (sometimes mistakenly referred to as "Shakespearean English"), but that's also their primary drawback. Although there once was a time when people actually spoke in that dialect, people simply don't talk like that today. Many passages require at least a college-level reading ability. Due to the sometimes-archaic terminology compared to language today, some misinterpretation is possible even by excellent readers.

There is no doubt, however, that the KJV has stood the test of time. Year after year, the KJV remains near the top in total sales, and is the all-time best seller overall. Other advantages of the KJV include widespread endorsement by some denominations and individual churches, the fact that it's in the public domain so it can be freely quoted or copied without royalty or permission, and the availability of *numerous* study aids such as the Ryrie, Dake, Thompson Chain and Scofield references whose availability in other translations is limited (or, in the case of Dake, non-existent). Many common prayers spoken aloud communally (such as the "Our Father") are direct quotes from the KJV. So renowned is the KJV that it has spawned a movement best labeled as "King James Only-ism."

The KJV-Only ("KJO") claim is that the process that led to and resulted in the King James Version was, itself, inspired by God just as the original manuscripts were. Therefore, no other translation was ever or will ever be considered the true Word of God. Well beyond simply being a statement of preference, KJO devotees are often quite passionate about their belief, which is based on a *mostly*-justified perception of high accuracy in the translation of the original languages, word for word, into English.

But, the KJV is not without its problems. There *are* errors in translation, and the translation itself was based on Greek manuscripts that were anywhere from 600 to 1000 years newer (later) than the manuscripts used for other, modern translations. *The result is that some of the KJV translators translated errors.* A notable error is the "extra Canaan" in the genealogy of Jesus in Luke 3. This error is found only in a small number of relatively new (late 8th to early 11th century) Greek manuscripts, and not in the earliest copies. Another error, with the same cause, is the use of the phrase "through His blood" in Colossians 1:14, which is simply not in the early Greek manuscripts (despite some loud and angry remarks about this from some KJO people), but rather, is a copy from a parallel passage in Ephesians 1:7.

Despite these problems, along with the steep learning curve necessary to read them, the pros still outweigh the cons by a considerable margin. The KJV underwent a number of revisions as the English language evolved over the next 300 or so years, but none of the revisions were extensive enough to call them anything but newer "editions" of the KJV. One of the changes in the later editions of the KJV was the eventual dropping of the books known as the Apocrypha (known as the Deuterocanonical books by Catholics), which were present in the original 1611 edition of the KJV. The D-R, meanwhile, continues to have them. The KJV and D-R remained basically unchallenged until the late 19th century.

American Standard Version (ASV, 1901) – The most notable revision of the KJV was the ASV, even though it is out of print, because nearly all "Tyndale" translations that have come since can "trace their roots" back to it. It's available online and is in the public domain, but has no advantages over any other translation except for its historical significance. It has as high a reading level as the KJV on which it's based.

Revised Standard Version (RSV, 1952) – The RSV improved on this quite a lot, and became the most popular pew Bible for the 1950s through 1970s. The RSV came under criticism because the translation team that did it, being made up primarily of Methodists, Presbyterians, and Episcopalians, gave it a "liberal bias" according to some evangelicals. Versions of the RSV were available with the Apocrypha and published as "Catholic editions" until the late 1970s.

Starting in the 1960s, well before the first attempt at revising the RSV was made, several attempts were made at improving the readability of the Bible in English while retaining the accuracy of Bibles in the Tyndale tradition. Translations like the **Berkeley** (Modern Language Bible, 1959), **Bible in Basic English** (BBE, 1965), the **Amplified Bible** (1965), and the **Jerusalem Bible** (1966) each became very popular but only for a very short period of time. The Berkeley translation was used for numerous New Testaments placed by the Gideons in hotels in the 1960s. The Jerusalem Bible was a Catholic work translated first into French and then English and contains the Deuterocanonical books (the Apocrypha) in the Catholic sequence. A "New Jerusalem Bible" has since superseded it. The BBE can still be found on virtually all Bible software programs because it was entered directly into the public domain.

About the only one of these translations that remains of note is the Amplified Bible. Using the ASV as a basis, and cleaning up the language to fit modern usage, the Lockman Foundation put together a Bible in which alternate translations of many tricky or obscure words or phrases appear embedded in brackets immediately after the questionable word or phrase. Some argue that this makes it easier to understand when doing an in-depth study, while others are bothered by the interruptions to the flow of the text when doing a more casual reading.

Good News Bible (aka Today's English Version, 1976) – The 1960s also saw the start of an entirely new method of translation. My first complete read-through of the Bible was made using a (Good News) Bible that utilized a completely different translation philosophy than the Tyndale tradition. All Tyndale Bibles, then and now, suffer to some degree from a common problem: they're still difficult to read, particularly by children. In response, the American Bible Society came out with what was first called "Good News for Modern Man," (1966) a translation of the New Testament using a new method:

dynamic equivalence, better known as "thought for thought." The entire Bible was finished in 1976 and initially published as "Today's English Version."

The Good News Bible has a tremendous history, being the first widely accepted English-language translation of the Bible to use dynamic equivalence. Even the Roman Catholic Church made a formal endorsement of the New Testament when it was published prior to the publication of the NAB (see below) in 1970. But, the people concerned with Biblical accuracy were not happy with the Good News Bible. Despite strong sales, there was a lot of very loud criticism of the Good News Bible from conservative churches, the KJO people, and mainline Protestants who felt that the sometimes-strange wording of familiar passages ruined their meaning rather than expressed it. The people who most favored it were those involved in education. To this day, the successor to the Good News Bible, called the **Contemporary English Version** (CEV, 1995), is among the most widely used Sunday School Bibles due to its easy readability even by children as young as the 3rd grade. There have been other attempts besides this at creating a very "easy English" Bible, with mixed results.

New American Bible (NAB, 1970) – At about this same time (the 1960s), the Second Vatican Council was ending and changes to the liturgy and doctrines of the Roman Catholic Church were being implemented. One of the changes was a greater endorsement of Scripture, and thus was commissioned a replacement for and an update of the aging D-R Bible for English-speaking Catholics. The result was the NAB, and it immediately became the *official* Bible for use in Scripture readings at Mass where English is spoken. It still relies on the Latin Vulgate as its basis, though original-language manuscripts were also consulted. The style is still word-for-word, and it is among the better choices for Catholics embarking on a complete chronological read-through of the Bible.

The Living Bible (LB, 1971) – As popular as was the Good News Bible, there were some that thought that the Bible could be made even more readable and thus reach an even larger group of people. This third major effort at producing an "easier to read" Bible is called "paraphrasing." Though some consider this to be an example of dynamic equivalence taken to its extreme, I (as do many others) place this as a third category of Bible translation. The LB is the oldest of these paraphrases. Translator and writer Kenneth Taylor didn't make any pretense about its paraphrased nature. That didn't make some conservative Christians any less vocal in their opposition to his efforts, however. One criticism was that the "Bible was too sacred to paraphrase". But there is no doubt about the beauty and easy readability of it. A New Testament edition was released in 1968 under the name "Reach Out."

New American Standard Bible (NASB, 1971) – Despite all the efforts at dynamic equivalence and paraphrase in the 1960s, the Tyndale tradition was by no means dead as that decade ended. Criticisms of over-simplification leveled at the Bibles using dynamic equivalence and paraphrases, and the liberal bias of the RSV led the Lockman Foundation (already mentioned as publishers of the Amplified Bible) to create their own revision of the ASV called the New American Standard Bible. The NASB isn't a revision of the Amplified (though the language is nearly identical). Like several other translations, it was also compared to a number of manuscripts in the original languages that have been found recently, including the Dead Sea Scrolls. Thus we have what many consider the most accurate word-for-word translation in *modern* English. As one might expect, the NASB is much more popular in the conservative Evangelical churches (Baptist, Assembly of God).

The main "pro" of the NASB is its perceived level of accuracy, which is said to exceed that of the KJV (though the KJO crowd disputes this very loudly). The only "con" of the NASB is the fact that the formal language and style make it a Bible with a learning curve that is still somewhat steep. A big pro is that the NASB was the first translation other than the KJV to become available in popular reference editions such as Ryrie, Scofield, and Thompson-Chain. All NASB editions have extensive footnotes and cross-references, the latter more so than nearly any other translation besides the KJV. With its acceptance by many churches, its literal accuracy, and consistently high sales, **it is the translation that I personally recommend most highly overall**. It has been updated recently (1995) to reflect further changes in the English language as well as improvements in archaeology that have revealed more and older original-language manuscripts.

New International Version (NIV, 1978) – Long before the 2011 revision of this overall most-popular modern translation, the NIV became the most controversial of the modern translations. Due in part to its status as the #1 selling Bible of each of the last three decades (though the KJV remains right behind it), and despite largely using the same manuscripts as the far-less-controversial NASB, the NIV has been deemed everything from the crowning achievement in English-language Bible translations on down to a heretical perversion of the Word of God… and everything in between.

The appeal of the NIV is largely from its easy to read (about 7th grade level) format that is markedly free of sectarian (denominational) bias. The intent of the translators was to create a version that was as accurate as the KJV but was as easy to read as the Good News Bible. It is unashamedly thought for thought (dynamic equivalence), but strikes a closer balance than perhaps any other Bible translation between accuracy and readability.

The controversy over this translation comes almost entirely from the KJO people. The claims include allegedly "missing verses" or phrases, and the fact that the NIV, like nearly all modern translations, has a copyright on the translation, which means that you can't freely quote any more than just a small amount of the NIV in a written work without permission of (and royalty paid to) Zondervan Publishing. At best, critics refer to the NIV language as "weak". The NIV and the NASB use mostly older manuscripts that I (and many others) believe to be closer to the original autographs, and thus the "missing verses" issue is actually a case of the KJV using manuscripts such as the Textus Receptus that contain *added* verses and phrases and copies of marginal notes. In other words, to me there really is no controversy.

In 2000, the NIV was updated and released as "Today's New International Version." After good sales initially, the tNIV faded in popularity while the original (1978) edition remained a consistently top seller. The next revision came in 2011 without a new title, and generated new controversy over the use of gender-inclusive language much like other newer translations (see NRSV and ESV below for more details).

New King James Version (NKJV, 1982) – The controversy over the NIV's "weak" language led a team of translators to produce a new translation following the Tyndale tradition, and name it for the best-selling Bible translation of all time. The NKJV was produced as a direct response to translations that were considered not accurate enough (the paraphrases, Good News, etc), too liberally biased (RSV,

NIV), or *still* too hard to read by the layman (NASB, Amplified). The goal was to produce an edition that has the same overall style and accuracy of the KJV without the archaic terminology and the sometimes excessively formal sentence structure.

In my opinion, they fell far short of this goal. Despite strong sales (it consistently outsells the NASB), its accuracy amongst other Tyndale translations has been questioned by many, and not just people in the KJO group. Their attempts at making a Bible with the same style as its namesake but in modern English makes many passages sound *very* clumsy when read aloud. Despite being named for King James, the manuscripts used to produce the NKJV *aren't* the same ones used in the original KJV (i.e. not the Textus Receptus). This might be considered an improvement by some, since modern archaeology has brought us increasingly closer to the original scriptures, but it has made the KJO people more loudly critical about the NKJV than they are about any other modern English translation of the Bible except the NIV.

New Revised Standard Version (NRSV, 1989) – Whereas there were several translations, of three different types (Tyndale, dynamic equivalence, paraphrase) made in *response* to the RSV, it wasn't until 1989 that a true "revision of the revision" came out. The NRSV's language is much more up-to-date, containing **no** "Thee" or "Thou" words at all, and was among the first word for word translations to use "gender neutral" substitutions. This is the practice of using terms like "brothers and sisters" in place of just the masculine, such as "brethren," in the older translations (more about this in HCSB, below). It is now the standard Bible for the Lectionary for the Evangelical Lutheran Church in America. A Roman Catholic edition of this Bible that includes the Apocrypha has been widely used in religious education classes, and is increasingly gaining acceptance for readings during Mass and in Scriptural references in the Catechism of the Catholic Church.

The Message (1993 and 2002) – The 1990s saw a pair of paraphrases make their debut. Eugene Peterson wrote The Message as a direct translation from Hebrew and Greek (like the NLT, see below) but paraphrased it according to the "street language of today much like the originals which were written in the street language of their day". He updated it further in 2002. Questionable accuracy, along with some very awkward-sounding passages makes this one of the least-recommended translations.

The New Living Translation (NLT, 1996) – The other major 1990s paraphrase isn't a revision of the LB in the same sense as the NRSV is a revision of the RSV. Rather, it is a completely new translation from some of the oldest Greek and Hebrew manuscripts directly into a modern English paraphrase. It has many stylistic similarities to the Living Bible, though it is completely separate. It is also among today's most popular translations, frequently selling in the top 5.

God's Word (GW, 1995) – God's Word seems to be one the best compromises between the (arguably) over-simplification of Scripture found in most paraphrases and the too-literal approach of the word-for-word versions. It has a style that feels very much like the more popular NLT, but because it isn't as well known suffers from a severe lack of supplementary materials (concordances, study guides, etc.). Some consider GW a paraphrase, others put it in the dynamic equivalence category; I place the GW translation somewhere in between (as do the publishers themselves).

Holman Christian Standard Bible (HCSB, 2004) – Of the various things about newer translations (particularly paraphrases and dynamic equivalence) that are controversial or are criticized by the KJO people, perhaps the greatest is the tendency toward "gender neutral" renderings. Most paraphrases and thought-for-thought translations (after the NIV) seem to go out of their way to not use the masculine pronouns "he," "him," or "his". Even some that follow the Tyndale tradition (NRSV in particular) started eliminating what were perceived as words with an excessive masculine bias. The accusation, of course, is that these other translators are trying too hard to be "politically correct," to which I agree. The publishers of the HCSB have put together what is arguably the best recent attempt at a balance between the Tyndale tradition and dynamic equivalence while using an absolute minimum of gender-neutral language.

The "Holman" name comes from part of the publisher's name, not one of the translators. The project that resulted in the HCSB was actually started by Arthur Farstad, who was one of the editors of the NKJV. Farstad died in 1999, but his work lived on with the team he had assembled. The result feels more literal than other thought for thought translations like the NIV (to which it feels most similar) but is quite a bit *less* literal than other Tyndale translations like the NASB. It has managed to successfully skirt the controversy generated by other modern translations by using the Novum Testamentum Graece 27th edition as the basis for its New Testament, which is a text based on the Textus Receptus, the same used for the KJV.

English Standard Version (ESV, 2005) – This revision of the NRSV (which was a revision of the RSV) has similarities to several other modern translations, seeking to achieve an even better compromise between readability and accuracy. Like its predecessors, it is word for word (Tyndale), but utilizes even more gender-inclusive language than the NRSV. But like the competing HCSB, it uses a mix of Greek manuscripts for the New Testament that includes a lot more material from the Textus Receptus than most modern translations. Like the NASB (to which it feels most similar), it is now available in a large variety of study editions for which most modern translations are not. It is considered to be easier to read than the NASB, but not quite as easy as the NIV.

There are others besides those mentioned in this commentary, but I've included only those that are or were in the sales top 10 or get a "lot of press." Which is best? That's going to be largely a matter of personal preference, but hopefully this section gives you the tools by which to make an intelligent choice. The tips at the end of the previous section are also important, the first one being to pick a version you can enjoy at your reading level and stick with it for the entire journey as your "main" Bible. Recommendation number two is that you have at least one other Bible available for occasional comparison. In choosing the two, I also recommend that at least one be a newer and one be an older translation. For instance, one of my complete read-throughs (yes, I've done it more than once) was done using the NRSV as my "main" Bible, with both a God's Word and a KJV as comparisons.

I've already mentioned my number one choice, the NASB. Also highly recommend are the NIV and HCSB (dynamic equivalence). Honorable mention would have to go to the ESV, NRSV and NAB (newer word for word), KJV and GEN (older word for word), GW (dynamic equivalence), and the highest-ranking paraphrase in my list, the NLT (though some would argue the GW is a paraphrase, too).

Among those that I recommend less are the LB and Message (paraphrases of questionable accuracy), the D-R (unless you're a

Traditional Catholic), the Good News family (outdated dynamic equivalence), NKJV and Amplified (awkwardly rendered word for word), and any translation completely out of print (ASV, RSV, etc).

The only translation that I openly tell people to never use is one that isn't described above – the New World Translation used by the Jehovah's Witnesses. It has a history and lineage similar to the RSV, but uses renderings that have been in some cases deliberately distorted to reflect Jehovah's Witnesses doctrines that are contrary to orthodox Christianity. The most notable of these changes is the wording of John 1:1 which denies the deity of Jesus, making Him sound like just another created being.

But the main thing is that you choose a translation you can actually *enjoy* reading and you can comprehend. The goal here is simply to get *all of God's Word* read in a year's time, regardless of the language or style.

December 21
Luke 1:1-25
The Birth of John the Baptist Foretold

And so our journey through the Bible begins; not on January 1 and not with Genesis 1 (which will, however, start on January 1), and not even in the Old Testament. For the next 11 days beginning here and ending on December 31, our journey will span only the earliest *New* Testament history, beginning in the Gospel according to Luke.

We know little about Luke, and even less about the Greek man named Theophilus (1:3) to whom Luke's Gospel, in its original letter format, was written. Luke is believed to be the same Luke who traveled with Paul on at least one missionary journey (2 Timothy 4:11, Philemon 1:24) and was, by profession, a doctor (Colossians 4:14). Beyond that, we only know Luke by his attention to detail in writing what most people would argue is the most complete human biography of Jesus.

Why begin our chronological Bible read-through here? Several reasons. Besides the practical application of placing the Christmas story on December 25th, Luke's is the only Gospel to go into any detail regarding events prior to Jesus' birth. Sure, John goes all the way back to "in the beginning…" (John 1:1) but gives no biographical detail there. Luke is not the only Gospel writer to give details about John the Baptist, but is the only one to detail his birth.

Luke's Gospel actually starts with John's parents, and an encounter with the angel Gabriel in the temple by Zechariah, John's father. Gabriel proclaims a miraculous promise to Zechariah (1:13-15), similar to the promise made to Abraham some 2400 years earlier (Genesis 17:19). But Zechariah not only expresses doubt about his wife's being able to have child, but justifies his doubt with an excuse (1:18). For this, Gabriel does not withdraw the promise, but does inflict a penalty on Zechariah, rendering him speechless until "the proper time" (1:20).

As promised and prophesized, though, Zechariah's wife, Elizabeth, does become pregnant (1:24) and thus is prophesy fulfilled, that there would be one to come before Jesus.

December 22
Luke 1:26-56
The Birth of Jesus Foretold

The next segment of the pre-Christmas story is commonly known as "the visitation," and we once again encounter Gabriel, this time speaking directly to the person to whom a miraculous promise will be fulfilled.

The promise to Mary is even more miraculous than the one to Zechariah and Elizabeth, for although Elizabeth is of "advanced age," (1:36) she is a married woman who, unlike Mary, *has* had relations with a man. Mary has not, and she points this out (1:34) to Gabriel, but displays a very different attitude than Zechariah did and so does not incur any penalty. Mary does not so much express doubt as she does curiosity when she asks "how can this be?" (1:34), and Gabriel answers her question (1:35). Mary accepts this willingly (1:38) and thus will Jesus be born, some 6 months after John.

The Roman Catholic prayer called "Hail Mary" has its origin in today's passage. The prayer begins with a paraphrase of verse 28, and then verse 42. Verses 39 through 45 have Mary visiting Elizabeth, with them both now pregnant, and the as-yet-unborn John leaps for joy *in Elizabeth's womb* at the encounter of the as-yet-unborn Jesus!

Finally, versus 46 to 56 make up what is commonly called The Magnificat, Mary's song of joy. Following the meeting with her relative Elizabeth, Mary breaks forth in song, singing the praises of God who fulfills all his promises.

December 23
Luke 1:57-80
The Birth of John the Baptist

Three days into our one-year journey, and we only now come to the end of a single chapter. Today's reading begins with the birth of John the Baptist, as promised. As per Jewish custom, the boy is circumcised on his 8th day, and this is the apparent "proper time" foretold by Gabriel, as Zechariah regains his speech after writing to the astonished observers that "his name is John" (1:63).

What follows is Zechariah's great turn of words, as he prophesies a great Psalm-like oratory about the coming Messiah, thanking God for his coming and praising Him for the salvation He is to bring. He also declares his own son to be a prophet (1:76) and makes references to "preparing a way for Him" and guiding "our feet into the path of peace" (1:79).

Today's reading ends with the only pre-ministry statement about John the Baptist in any of the Gospels, that he grew "strong in spirit" and lived in the desert (1:80).

December 24
Matthew 1:1-25
The Family of Jesus

On Christmas Eve, we take a break from Luke and get our first look at Matthew's account of Jesus. Matthew is believed to be the same tax collector who would be called by Jesus himself to be an Apostle. Most believe Matthew to be one of the earlier Gospel writers but not the earliest; however, Matthew's would also (if he is indeed the Apostle, one of the twelve) be one of only two eyewitness accounts of the four (the other being John).

Matthew's Gospel is not as detailed as Luke's in terms of pure biography, but it does contain some things found in no other Gospels, and is (by a narrow margin) the longest of the four. And although Luke also contains a genealogical record of Jesus (Luke 3:23-38, December 26), Matthew actually *starts* with it. For the first 16 verses, Matthew takes us up the family tree through David and up to Abraham, and meticulously lists the bloodline all the way from Abraham, through David, to Jesus. Though a long string of kings are in Jesus' bloodline, only David is mentioned by Matthew as "*King David*" (1:6). The genealogy ends with an interesting and often-pondered numerical coincidence, that there are exactly 14-generation lines from Abraham to David, then David to the Babylonian exile, and then from the exile to Jesus (1:17).

Matthew then goes on with his brief account of the birth of Jesus, giving the only detail of Joseph's visit by an angel prior to Jesus' birth. It is here that we also get the first notice of what the Messiah's name is to be (1:21). In verse 23 we get the first of dozens of quotes by

Matthew of prophets (he was particularly fond of Isaiah) to show that Jesus was the fulfillment of these many prophesies, as he quotes Isaiah 7:14 in foretelling the virgin birth.

December 25
Luke 2:1-20
The Birth of Jesus

Christmas Day, as traditionally celebrated, and back to Luke for one of the most quoted passages of scripture of the entire Bible, the birth of Jesus in a Bethlehem manger. Luke is very careful to set the time exactly by mentioning the Roman Emperor of the day and the Syrian Governor. Following the birth, Luke goes to account for early reaction by shepherds who were told by an angel of the birth.

A popular song of praise used in the liturgies of the Roman Catholic Church as well as many others starts with a paraphrase of verse 14 of today's reading.

Verses 8-14 are quoted in an unlikely place that still resonates with me every time I hear it. Near the conclusion of "A Charlie Brown Christmas," as the Peanuts gang is bemoaning the commercialization of Christmas while rehearsing a Christmas program, Linus steps onto the nearly empty stage and recites Luke 2:8-14, Revised Standard Version, from memory, and then goes back to Charlie Brown and tells him "*that's* what Christmas is all about." Amen to that.

December 26
Luke 3:23-38
Jesus' Family Tree

In our chronological readings, I have placed the two genealogical accounts as brackets around the nativity itself. We read Matthew's version on Christmas Eve, we now have Luke's. The first difference between the two is the order – Matthew, starting from Abraham, goes forward to Jesus; Luke, in today's reading, starts with ("as was thought") Joseph, Jesus' stepfather, and works backwards all the way through Abraham back to Adam and to God himself. But starting with the very first name after Joseph, it is obvious he is using a different family tree.

From Abraham to David (or David to Abraham, depending on which one you're reading), the listings are identical. At this point, the genealogies split. Where Matthew takes the royal bloodline, starting with King David through Solomon, Luke takes the bloodline of one of David's other sons, Nathan, and proceeds from there. In the end, not only do the genealogies diverge after David but they disagree as to the total number of generations from David to Joseph (and thus, to Jesus). This is the subject of very intense debate and too often results in ridicule of Bible scholars who insist (as I do as well) that the Bible itself contains no errors. There are, however, a number of explanations that could account for the differences in Luke's version of the family tree vs. Matthew's. The explanation I favor is the one that seems to appear most in most listings of "harmony of the Gospels;" namely that of Luke's genealogy is actually being traced through Mary, not Joseph.

December 27
Luke 2:21-38, Matthew 2:1-12
The Infancy of Jesus

Today's reading is the first to feature passages from two different books, one from Luke's Gospel, the other Matthew's. In both cases, it is the earliest telling of events in Jesus' childhood.

Only one verse is devoted to the circumcision of Jesus (Luke 2:21), and thus his naming, but a much longer section is devoted to the presentation to the Lord in the Temple. Luke quotes two Old Testament verses (Exodus 13:2 and Leviticus 12:8) when explaining the rituals Mary and Joseph went through at the time, which drive home the point about Jesus being a Jew, notable since Luke was believed to have been Greek, and not Jewish.

Luke then tells of the encounter with Simeon (Luke 2:25-35) who was waiting for his time to see the Messiah face to face. At some earlier time, Simeon prayed to be able to see the Christ before his death. God answered his prayer by sending the Holy Spirit to tell Simeon when Jesus would be in the Temple. There, Simeon burst forth in a great song of praise (2:29-32). But in vs. 34-35, Simeon concludes his visit with a bleak warning for Mary, which is one of the earliest NT prophesies that Jesus would have to die in order to carry out His saving work.

At this point, the sequence of events becomes a matter of controversy, as the next verse after today's passage in Luke (2:39) explains Jesus' family's return to their home in Nazareth. But this event could not have taken place immediately after the Presentation if the account in Matthew of the visit of the Magi is true, particularly regarding the historically backed-up Slaughter of the Innocents by Herod following this visit.

Matthew is alone in describing this mysterious and beautiful event that is commonly (and mistakenly) referred to as the visit of the "Three Kings." Largely due to a popular Christmas song of that title, people have had some interesting pictures of this visit. Variously referred to as astrologers, wise men, and kings, we aren't even told by Matthew how many visitors made up this group of men. The assumption that it is three is based solely on the presentation of three gift items (Matthew 2:11) to the infant Jesus.

The sequence of events is presented this way mainly due to what happens next (see tomorrow's reading).

December 28
Matthew 2:13-23, Luke 2:39-52
The Wrath of Herod; the Flight to Egypt; Jesus in the Temple

Only a small portion of the Bible is backed up by extra-biblical sources. Today's reading is one such portion. Herod (sometimes referred to as Herod the Great) is an historical figure of some note. His appearance in both Luke's and Matthew's Gospels makes it somewhat of a curiosity that Luke didn't go into any detail of the events surrounding the event known as The Slaughter of the Innocents. (One interesting theory I heard is that Luke was considerably younger than Matthew and received his information on Jesus' early life second hand, most likely from Mary).

In Matthew's account, Herod, after discovering he'd been duped by the Magi, went into a rage and demanded the deaths of all boys younger than 2 years of age. This also fulfills prophesy, as Matthew quotes Jeremiah 31:15. As Joseph was warned to take his family and flee in a dream (Matthew 2:13), this event is believed to have taken place very shortly after the visit of the Magi, possibly within a few days. Thus, this could not have taken place prior to Jesus' presentation in the temple, which was described as taking place when Jesus was 8 days old. Luke's account, then, of returning home to Nazareth (Luke 2:39) must have followed not only the presentation, but also the flight to Egypt and their return approximately 1 year later (according to tradition as well as Roman records that mark the date of Herod's death).

The remainder of today's reading is the Epiphany, from Luke's Gospel. Long before the commencement of His active ministry in Galilee, Jesus was aware of his role, maybe not all the way up to and including his crucifixion, but at least in terms of who His real father was. In this well-known passage, Jesus stays behind at the Temple after His parents return home to Nazareth. Jesus was a mere 12 years of age at the time, and his frantic parents return to Jerusalem only to find him *teaching in the Temple*! From a parent's point of view, one can certainly understand the combination of relief and anger Mary and Joseph must have felt when they asked him "why have you treated us like this?" (Luke 2:28, NIV). But Jesus silenced their fear and anger with his response, revealing to everyone including Joseph that He was fully aware of who his father really was, and that he was in His father's house (2:49).

Jesus returned home with Mary and Joseph, and was purported to be an obedient child (2:51) who grew up in wisdom as well as stature (2:52). An interesting note about stature: if the Shroud of Turin is the authentic burial cloth of Jesus, our Savior would have stood 5 feet 9 inches tall (1.75 meters). By typical Middle East standards of the day, this would have been quite tall, proportional to someone standing 6 feet 2 inches today.

December 29
Mark 1:1-8
John Prepares the Way in the Jordan

Unlike the seemingly conflicting reports of what took place during Jesus' early life, there is very little doubt about the nature and order of events once Jesus reached the age of about 30. The roughly 18-year gap between when we last encounter the boy Jesus (in the temple, Luke 2:41-52) and John's appearance in the Jordan River, "making straight the way" for our Lord, leaves us with some puzzling unanswered questions. All of these, of course, constitute the ultimate in unprovable trivia. None shed any light on Jesus' reason for existence. The truth about these events would have no bearing on His ministry, and should therefore have no impact on His Church. Starting with the event covered during the next three days, however, these events have sometimes huge impact on our very lives today.

Our first look at the Gospel according to Mark reintroduces us to His cousin John, now a grown man, just prior to the beginning of His ministry. Mark quotes Malachi 3:1 and Isaiah 40:3 in introducing us to the Gospel and to John the Baptist. It is the first we hear about John since he was born, and the picture is the familiar and simple one of the man clothed in camel's hair (Mark 1:6) proclaiming a baptism of repentance (1:4) and prophesying of the baptism by the Holy Spirit (1:8) yet to come.

Mark's account is the shortest of the 4 gospels, as is the rest of his Gospel. But where it is short it is also concise and to the point. Mark doesn't waste words in his account of Jesus, as he emphasizes the works of Jesus, especially his miracles.

December 30
Matthew 3:1-12
John Prepares the Way

Another account of John baptizing in the Jordan, Matthew's story has many elements in common with Mark's. Matthew also quotes Isaiah 40:3, and describes John's odd attire and diet and methodology. But Matthew goes on to an encounter with some Pharisees and Sadducees in which he has some sharp words against them (Matthew 3:7-12) not found in Mark's account.

December 31
Luke 3:1-18
John Prepares the Way

The third telling of the work of John the Baptist prior to Jesus' active ministry is also the longest of the three. Luke begins his account by describing in extreme detail the exact time when John was baptizing (Luke 3:1-2) and thus when Jesus' ministry was about to begin (presumably shortly after His baptism, a few days after this account).

Like Mark and Matthew, Luke quotes Isaiah, this time going 2 verses farther (Isaiah 40:3-5) than the others in showing how John's baptisms were the fulfillment of prophesy. Then, Luke tells of the same harsh words as Matthew tells of, only this time not specifically directed at Pharisees and Sadducees, but "at the crowds" (Luke 3:7). This pattern would repeat itself several later times. Also different is the dialog between members of the crowd and John that only Luke describes (3:10-17).

January 1, Old Testament (OT)
Genesis 1:1-3:24
From The Creation through the Fall of Man

Today we begin side-by-side readings from both the Old Testament and the New. We begin with a pair of readings that each start with the words "In the Beginning." It may seem like a lot to cram into a single day's reading, particularly when you consider the relative importance of the passages, but the OT is nearly 3.5 times the length of the NT, and we would be stretching our reading plan considerably beyond one year if we didn't, to begin with, take in 3 whole chapters of the first book of Moses, called Genesis.

Although Moses is believed to be the writer of Genesis, as well as Exodus, Leviticus, Numbers, and most of Deuteronomy, this is held more by tradition than any proven authorship. Very likely, the creation account given in today's reading was passed on through oral tradition, generation after generation, until Moses finally wrote it down some 1400 years after the events themselves took place. This has led many people, even devout Christians, to believe that the Genesis account of creation is either symbolic, a myth, or allegorical, instead of the historical (as well as spiritual) truth I believe it to be.

(I could write an entire book on the subject of Creationism alone but I choose not to take up too much space in this commentary on this controversial but important topic. Suffice it to say that I am a staunch young-Earth Creationist who believes wholeheartedly that the universe, and thus the world, is only a little over 6010 total years old (Ussher's chronology) and that the Genesis account is literal history).

The creation itself is summarized in chapter 1 and the first 3 verses of chapter 2. The writer (Moses?) uses the Hebrew word *Yom* to note each of the days of creation. This is significant, as Hebrew words don't have multiple meanings like many English words do, and the only meaning for *Yom* is a single 24-hour Earth day. Thus we have one small part of the reason I believe in a young Earth: that creation took place in 6 regular days, just like it says here. Then, what many consider a second account of creation (2:4-2:25), is actually a *detail* of day 6 of "creation week." It does not, as some suppose, contradict the story given in chapter 1. It simply explains in much more detail the creation of man, including intimate details of both the "how" and the "when" of the creation of woman to be with man. The key to recognizing the harmony of the two creation stories is carefully reading the tense, not the sequence, of each detail given in chapter 2.

We don't know how much time passed before the events of chapter 3 occurred, but we do know that these events changed all of history forever. Our first encounter with Satan in the Bible shows him, as a serpent, making the oldest and most common of all temptations: planting doubt in Eve about God's word and giving her the idea that it really *is* all right to do whatever you want. Of course, we know this to be the first Sin, which Adam repeats soon after, and the result is The Fall of Man. God pronounces a curse on creation, starting with the serpent (crawling on belly, eating dust, and the prophesy that he would be defeated in the end – see below), then the woman (pain in childbirth, desire for her husband who shall have authority over her), the Earth itself (man would have to work the land in order to get food), and then the most chilling curse of all – the curse of death (3:19). Death had now entered the world, all because of Sin.

The late comedian Robin Williams once did a stand-up routine in which he did a parody of God looking down on the Earth and saying, "…you know, I gave you this nice planet and you went and [messed] it up." Though told as a joke, and using a completely inappropriate expletive, there is a very important fundamental truth in what he said. Though the Curse was pronounced by God on His creation, it's important to note that He wouldn't have done anything of the sort were it not for the rebelliousness of man. Had man not sinned, we would still be living, today, in a "garden of Eden." It would be a perfect world if only man hadn't ruined it, *and we have no one to blame but ourselves.*

But God's mercy is already evident in this passage; even as He is pronouncing the Curse, as He gives the eerie and cryptic prophecy in 3:15. When God tells the serpent that his head will be crushed by the offspring of a woman, He is referring to a savior, who will be a person, not just a spirit or concept, and that Satan will be able to do no better than strike at His heel. In this pronouncement, Satan is made the forever enemy of mankind, and is already a defeated foe. God would fulfill this prophecy some 4000 years later in the person of His son, Jesus Christ.

January 1, New Testament (NT)
John 1:1-18
The Pre-existence of Jesus

John, the last of the four Gospel writers, begins his Gospel with the same words that Moses did in describing the creation: "In the Beginning." From here John goes on to give us one of the most striking and beautiful passages in the entire Bible.

John's Gospel differs from the other three in a number of ways. There is ample evidence that this was the last one written, and perhaps John had seen one or more of the previous Gospels before writing his own, and thus may have felt it unnecessary to simply repeat all the biographical data found in Mark, Matthew, and Luke. John does not write of Jesus' birth or early life at all, and does not provide a human genealogy like Luke and Matthew both did. What John does provide, however, is the most striking pronouncement about Jesus of all, a theme John would carry throughout the Gospel: ***Jesus is God*** and was with God from the very beginning of creation. Mark emphasized the power of Jesus over death and disease, Matthew emphasizes how Jesus' coming is the fulfillment of prophecy, and Luke's biographical attention to detail and genealogy all the way back to Adam shows his emphasis on Jesus being the savior of *all* people, not just a select group. Though all 4 Gospels make Jesus out to be both human and divine, only John makes Jesus' divinity the central theme of the entire work.

Here, just like with Genesis, the sheer weight of importance of this passage is such that even a verse by verse commentary would not do it justice. A whole book could easily be written on the first 18 verses of this Gospel, as it is a true summary of the Good News of our salvation. The key verse is 1:14, as it states "the Word became flesh (human) and dwelt among us." God indeed came to visit us *in person* through his son, Jesus.

January 2, OT
Genesis 4:1-5:32; 1 Chronicles 1:1-4; Genesis 6:1-22
The Generations from Adam to Noah

Today, passages from more than one OT book will be read as part of a single day, as we get our first look at the Chronicles.

Genesis 4 gives us the beginning of the next generation after Adam and Eve with the births of Cain, and then Abel. It should be noted that although these were Adam and Eve's first two sons, they were not necessarily Adam and Eve's first two children. Ancient Hebrew writings seldom mentioned the women in family trees except when it became necessary to clarify something in the patriarchal line, such as two men with the same name who lived in the same generation. Thus, by the time Abel was born, Adam and Eve may have already had a number of daughters.

Genesis 4 is also the story of the first *murder* mentioned in the Bible. Cain, in a jealous rage, murders his brother Abel when Abel's sacrifice is accepted by God while Cain's isn't. Thus it is that sin increased even further in the world.

From here on, we get a fairly detailed account of the generations from Adam to Noah, which would later be repeated in Luke to show Jesus' lineage. The Chronicler (the title we give to the writer of the two Chronicles books, as we do not know for certain who it is) gives a less detailed but equally precise account of the generations from Adam to Noah (and his sons) in just the first four verses of Chronicles. (There is some speculation that Ezra is the Chronicler.)

Returning to Genesis, we take time out from the genealogies and chronologies to focus on one of the most important characters of the Bible, Noah.

January 2, NT
John 1:19-34
The Lamb of God

Before we meet Jesus in person in John's Gospel, John the Baptist prepares the way and makes clear the fact that he (John) is *not* the messiah, nor is he Elijah, just as was stated in all three other Gospels. John doesn't go into the details about fulfilling Isaiah's prophecy or of the baptist's wardrobe and the encounter with the Pharisees and Sadducees doesn't contain quite so harsh a tone. Nevertheless, the stage is set for the beginning of Jesus' ministry to follow shortly.

John's Gospel doesn't have an exact telling of Jesus' baptism. But some time after the event, John the Baptist described the event to others in a post-Baptism testimony that includes the famous title ascribed to Jesus, the Lamb of God (John 1:29) used in numerous prayers and hymns in the Christian churches today.

January 3, OT
Genesis 7:1-9:29
Noah, the Ark, and the Flood

Whether you refer to it as the Great Deluge, Great Flood, Noah's Flood, or just The Flood, few can argue that the account of God's great judgment upon the Earth and all it's inhabitants except for a single family is among the most exciting and dramatic events described in the Bible. Genesis chapter 7 begins that story.

Some who attempt to discredit the story of Noah's Ark cite the fact that 40 days and nights of rain would be nowhere near sufficient to cause a worldwide flood, even if the rain itself was worldwide. This comes from people who didn't first read Genesis 7:11, which I believe is a reference to underground water beneath what was originally a single continent (evolutionary geologists believe in a single continent called Pangaea that supposedly existed millions of years ago). Genesis 1:9 is a good supporting verse for the idea that there was, at the time of creation, only a single continent: "And God said let the waters under the heaven be gathered together *into one place*, and let the dry land appear, and it was so." [Emphasis mine].

As far as the reference to covering all the mountains to heights exceeding 20 feet above the peaks (7:19-20) goes, there is another group that attempts to discredit Noah and the Ark by stating that this, too, is impossible. However, a careful examination of Earth's water volume and the volume displacement in water of our present mountains would show that if the volume of all of the world's mountains above 6000 feet altitude were placed in what is currently the deepest sea trenches, the amount of water displaced would cause the entire globe to be covered with water to a *minimum* depth of over 300 feet (100 meters). Since even the evolutionists believe that most of the world's mountains were formed during the shifts of tectonic plates, and that such shifts could certainly take place in a worldwide flood, this is not beyond the realm of possibility.

Today's OT reading concludes with a most curious story about Noah and his sons. Despite God's finding Noah to be the only righteous man before the Flood, God also recognizes the universal depravity of man, and Noah was no exception. Noah plants a vineyard, harvests the grapes, makes wine, drinks it, and gets himself thoroughly drunk, passes out naked in his tent and gets covered up by two of his sons, Shem and Japheth (9:21-23). When Noah sobers up, he doesn't repent of his own sin but instead curses his grandson Canaan (9:25-27), son of Ham, who was first to report Noah's nakedness to his brothers. This has puzzled me for years, but a classic Commentary has shed some light on this:

Ham, when discovering his father's shame, didn't do the right thing right away. Instead of telling his brothers (and possibly others, as tradition holds) about it, and possibly making a mockery of the situation (according to *two* classic commentaries), Ham should have covered his father himself instead of it being done by Shem and Japheth. At the very least (assuming it required two people to do this job), Ham should have participated in covering his father along with perhaps one brother. It should also be noted that Ham was the only brother to actually *see* his father naked, and this has led centuries of believers to believe that nudity is among the greatest of shames. The cursing of more than one generation was a common practice in Noah's day, and was reserved for only the most heinous of crimes. Thus was Canaan, the next generation *after* Ham, the object of Noah's wrath, which also became where the phrase "sins of the father" originated.

January 3, NT
Matthew 3:13-17, Mark 1:9-11, Luke 3:21-23
The Baptism of Jesus

John's Gospel may not have had an explicit account of the baptism of Jesus, but all three of the other Gospels did, and that's today's New Testament reading.

The three passages that describe this event are as brief as they are similar. Of note is the exchange between John the Baptist and Jesus, recorded only in Matthew's Gospel.

January 4, OT
Genesis 10:1-5; 1 Chronicles 1:5-7; Genesis 10:6-20; 1 Chronicles 1:8-16;
Genesis 10:21-11:26; 1 Chronicles 1:17-27
The Generations from Noah to Abram

The flood is past and the primeval history continues with the generations from Noah to Abram (later, Abraham). Jumping back and forth between the accounts in Genesis and the first book of Chronicles, we trace the bloodlines of Shem, Ham, and Japheth, the sons of Noah, and many branches of the family from each.

To get the full effect, these passages, though jumpy, should be read in the order above. Later, in Chapter 11 of Genesis, we get the fascinating tale of the Tower of Babel. In the history leading up to this event, we get some geography lessons about the directions these families scattered, the cities they founded, etc. Notable is that even those that are mentioned as going a great distance away from Ararat, the farthest reaches of humanity prior to Babel only got as far east as modern-day Iraq, as far west as the Mediterranean, as far north as (maybe) Greece, and as far south as modern-day Ethiopia. This does not mean that some others hadn't ventured further yet, such as the ancestors of modern day Australian Aborigines. But the great scattering of people didn't really take place, at least not en masse, until the Tower of Babel was built (Genesis 11:8). This story is dismissed as myth by a large number of Christian churches, which is a shame because it would actually explain the existence of not only mankind's many languages but also the existence, prior to Europe's "discovery" of the "new world" of many of the Native American nations, Inuit (in both northern Siberia and northern Alaska), and other indigenous peoples in many parts of the world that cannot be explained simply through evolution, millions of years, or ice ages.

The history lesson concludes with the tracing of the family line from Noah's son Shem through Abram, and the exact ages of each patriarch, which later gave rise to Bishop Ussher's chronology that determined, by his calculation, the age of the earth (a little over 6000 years for us young-earth creationists.)

January 4, NT
Matthew 4:1-11, Mark 1:12-13, Luke 4:1-13
The Temptation of Jesus

Some time shortly after Jesus' baptism in the Jordan, and prior to His ministry in Galilee, Jesus was led into the desert where He fasted for 40 days and was tempted by the devil.

Mark's version of the temptation begins with the word "immediately," implying that there was no gap of time between Jesus' baptism and his departure to the desert. The verse also states that the Spirit drove him into the desert, i.e., He was compelled to do so. Then, in just one more verse, the duration of this desert excursion is mentioned, Satan is mentioned by name and Jesus' being with wild beasts and ministered-to by angels is all mentioned.

What isn't mentioned in Mark is significant: Mark does not actually describe the encounter between Jesus and Satan. Mark also does not indicate that Jesus was fasting during this time. Both of these things are, however, mentioned by Matthew.

Matthew doesn't say that Jesus' temptation took place *immediately* after the baptism, as Mark's does, but he does go into more detail about the encounter itself. Satan first makes a temptation of turning stones into bread to appease His hunger (Matthew 4:2) and Jesus refutes the first temptation with a quote from Deuteronomy 8:3. The second temptation has Satan quoting scripture, this time Psalm 91:11-12, which Jesus counters with Deuteronomy (again) 6:16. Satan offers Jesus the world in exchange for worship, but Jesus' final comeback quotes Deuteronomy (for the third time) 6:13. It is then only after Satan departs (at Jesus' command) that Matthew mentions the angels ministering to him (Matthew 4:11) and no mention is made of wild beasts.

Luke's account of the temptation starts almost verse for verse identical to Matthew's account. The first temptation, right down to the quote from Deuteronomy 8:3, is identical to the Matthew version. The second and third temptations are in reverse order, but outside of that use the same lines of dialog and same Scripture references. With that reversal, Luke's account doesn't have Jesus commanding the devil to leave. Rather, the passage ends with the devil's somewhat more quiet departure and no mention of wild beasts or angels at all.

It is notable that the Roman Catholic Church uses this passage as justification for *not* using the Bible as the supreme authority in the Church, due to the devil's use of Scripture to make the temptations. I am of the opinion that this hollow argument is simply a cover for centuries of unjustifiable Papal authority, especially in interpreting Scripture.

January 5, OT
Job 1:1-3:26
Job Loses It All but Doesn't Lose His Faith

With the genealogy from Adam to Abram traced in Genesis and Chronicles (and Luke), we now depart from the primeval history to take in the story of one of the Bible's most thought-provoking Old Testament characters, Job. Job's story is considered one of the oldest books of the Bible, likely written prior to Moses' writing down of the Torah. The story itself (which, again, some churches regard as legend) takes place in the land of Uz, which would be in the northern part of present-day Syria. The timeline is uncertain, but with no mention of any post-Abraham covenant or practices, it is assumed by most scholars, to take place around the time of Abram, or just prior.

The first two chapters of Job contain the "cosmic wager" between God and Satan that sets up the entire rest of the book. God allows Satan to greatly afflict Job to see if Job will renounce his faith in God. He doesn't, even as the visit of his three friends (Eliphaz the Temanite, Bildad the Shuhite and Zophar the Naamathite) begins.

All 26 verses of chapter 3 of Job is a pitiful lament by Job cursing the day he was even born. Job's despair is so profound that if Job were here today, he would probably be carted off to a psychiatric hospital. His friends listen in silence, though, letting Job rant (rather graphically at times) about his condition, without interruption.

January 5, NT
John 1:35-51
The Call of the First Apostles

Each Gospel writer has a different take on the call of the first disciples. There are some similarities, but the differences (especially the timing or sequence of the "calls") are very controversial. Because of the placement of the call of the first apostles, there is some room for speculation as to whether it happened before Jesus' ministry in Capernaum began or after. Looking at three different harmonies of the Gospels, I have decided to place the first apostles *prior* to the Galilean ministry in Capernaum.

Thus, we open the account of the first apostles in John where John (the Baptist) points Jesus out to a crowd that includes Andrew and Simon, brothers who become the first apostles in John's Gospel. When Andrew gets his brother and introduces him to Jesus, He then calls him "Cephas" which translates as "Peter."

The passage concludes with a prophecy directed at all of them (the word "you" is used plural throughout) that they "shall see heaven open, and the angels of God ascending and descending on the Son of Man" (1:51). This prophecy is found only in John's Gospel.

January 6, OT
Job 4:1-7:21
Eliphaz Speaks, Job Responds

After sitting patiently with Job and joining in his sorrow, Job's three friends begin a series of speeches in which each tries to explain Job's loss. The first to speak is Eliphaz the Temanite.

Eliphaz's speech is centered on the idea that the righteous never get destroyed the way Job apparently has been; therefore, Job must not be righteous (Job 4:6-21). Despite the harsh words, though, Eliphaz goes into a beautiful and lengthy description of God's mercy (5:8-16) that Job is allegedly in dire need of. Job questions his responsibility for his condition, but never curses God.

Job does complain to God, however. He justifies his complaint against God and pleads with Him on the basis that he doesn't deserve this kind of punishment (7:20) but then turns right around and acknowledges his own sin as being the cause of his condition and begs God for forgiveness (7:21).

January 6, NT
John 2:1-12
The Miracle at the Wedding at Cana

The sequence of events in the life of Jesus, if any one of the Gospels is simply read chronologically following the temptation, yields a different and seemingly conflicting sequence of events. In examining three different "Gospel harmonies" and two different chronological reading plans, of which no two were the same, I took the major events at the beginning of Jesus' ministry and see if I could reconcile them myself. What I came up with is a sequence that continues, after the temptation and the call of the first Apostles, with His first miracle.

Jesus' first public miracle takes place in the Galilean city of Cana. Despite a stated reluctance, He performs the miracle, and the wine he produces is better than the wine served at the beginning of the wedding. In short, he "saved the best for last", a metaphor for what will eventually happen to believers when they die.

Gospel writer John then points out that this is Jesus' first "sign" and that the disciples believed in him after this. Today's reading concludes with Jesus' trip to Capernaum with his mother, brothers, and some of His disciples.

January 7, OT
Job 8:1-10:22
Bildad Speaks, Job Responds

Round 2 of the debate between Job and his friends opens with the second friend, Bildad, speaking to Job. Bildad's words are even harsher, especially at first, than Eliphaz's, even telling Job that his now-dead children got what they deserved because of their sin (8:4). Bildad uses a different approach than Eliphaz, in that Eliphaz used ordinary logic to convince Job of the error of his ways, whereas Bildad uses an unusual metaphor to describe how Job wound up in his predicament (8:9-13).

Job's reply contains one of the most profound truths ever spoken (9:2) about how a mortal can never truly be righteous before God. But Job arrives at this truth by emphasizing man's insignificance before a mighty and infinite God (9:3-19), and as a result, falls into error.

Job then resumes his complaints directed at God, questioning God about His motives and demanding an explanation (10:3-19) and finally repeating his wish for death on the assumption that his life is nearly over anyway.

January 7, NT
Luke 4:14-30
Jesus Debuts His Ministry in Nazareth of Galilee

Jesus' first miracle occurred before He had formally begun His ministry, because His reputation preceded Him (Luke 4:14) as he was about to make His debut. Widely regarded as Jesus' first *real* public appearance, and thus the beginning of His earthly ministry, Jesus starts His ministry by entering a synagogue in his old hometown and declaring himself to be the fulfillment of prophecy. Jesus reads Isaiah 61:1-2 to the enraptured congregation, but stops short of finishing verse 2 (which speaks of God's vengeance) and instead declares that the prophecy, which he did read, has been "fulfilled in your hearing."

Jesus goes on to make comparisons of himself, as a prophet, to other prophets in the Hebrew Scriptures. This does *not* go over well with the congregation, and they incite a riot and attempt to kill Jesus, only to have Him slip out of their hands. I sometimes wonder if first-time preachers feel like they're in the same situation as Jesus when they deliver their first unpopular sermon. Jesus' first sermon can be read aloud in fifteen seconds, and they ran Him out of town for it!

It would be a long time before Jesus returned to Nazareth, and that subsequent visit (we read about it on February 12) doesn't go any better than this one.

January 8, OT
Job 11:1-14:22
Zophar Speaks, Job Responds

The third of Job's three friends begins the third round of debate. Zophar the Naamathite takes Job to task for the previous reply but then changes his tone as he (correctly) points out that some of Job's sins have already been forgotten by God (11:6). Job's response in chapter 12 is an attempt to prove that his wisdom is at least the equal of his friends. He accuses his friends of contempt instead of sympathy, expressing his dismay at probably losing his life because he doesn't know how many sins he has committed. Most of all, though, he puts a greater value in his faith in God than in his own life.

Job then spends a chapter and a half in open prayer to God, basically giving up any hope that he will survive this ordeal, and asking God only for one thing: an explanation. He eventually gets it, but not until his friends have another series of words with him.

January 8, NT
John 3:1-21
The Meeting of Jesus and Nicodemus

The Gospel within the Gospel: that sums up the famous meeting of the Pharisee Nicodemus and Jesus on a night in Galilee. It is from this passage we get, among other things, the references to being "born again" (John 3:3), Jesus' question of being able to believe heavenly things when they don't even believe the earthly things (3:12), and the most-often-quoted verse in the entire New Testament, "God so loved the world," 3:16.

(Notice that this chronology skips John 2:13-25 for now. I am one of those who believe there was only a single "cleansing" of the temple, and that it occurred at the time and sequence presented by Matthew, Mark, and Luke. More about this on April 19.)

In this meeting, there is an interesting and important shift of focus regarding salvation. Jewish history and Old Testament prophecy is filled with references to a Messiah who will come to save Israel and restore the Kingdom. Jesus' early ministry has Him proclaiming that the Kingdom of Heaven is near, repeatedly. Most of his early disciples, even those who acknowledging Jesus as the Messiah, would have believed that Jesus was the savior of the nation of Israel, thus making him more of a political savior or military leader. Jesus changed all that in front of a leader of the Jews (as John puts it here) who should have known better. Jesus explains what the salvation he brings *really* means: that it is not a group thing but an individual relationship between God and man, with the gap bridged by the savior sent from God who was telling them right then of the need to become "born again" or "born of the spirit" (depending on translation).

But the most important line concerns the *reason* why this salvation is nigh. God is sending this salvation not out of any sense of duty or responsibility, not even just because He promised it years before, but out of a sense of *love*. The greatest promise in the Bible is made out of the incredible and unfathomable love that God has for each of us, though we are all stuck in sin. But if we believe, we get to live forever, just like God originally intended for the original creation. What an uplifting promise!

January 9, OT
Job 15:1-18:21
Eliphaz and Bildad Speak Again

Eliphaz sat out a couple of rounds in the debate while Job's other two friends had their turn. Now, Eliphaz comes back with a scathing indictment of Job in response to Job's open lament before God. Basically, Eliphaz tells Job that he's wrong to be angry with God, wrong to have been open about his (Job's) feelings before God, and wrong to think that his friends *don't* have superior wisdom to his.

Job counters with a sarcastic remark (16:1) and goes on to defend his complaining, while at the same time arguing in favor of his suffering being the results of God's wrath (16:9). Then, in verse 18, he goes back to prayer, and prays for (among other things) death (17:1), victory in his debate (17:4), and an end to his friends' falsely cheerful words.

Bildad then returns to the debate for his second round. In Bildad's speech (18:1-21), the increasing hostility of Job's friends starts to really show. Eliphaz, Bildad, and Zophar came with sympathy and had tried to cheer Job up. Now, tensions are increasing as Job seems to agree with *nothing* his friends say, and his friends (especially Bildad) are getting frustrated to the point of anger. This is made all the worse by the fact that, in the end, God points out that Job really was in the "right" in this whole debate. However, that wouldn't happen until near the end of entire book.

January 9, NT
John 3:22-36, Luke 3:19-20, Matthew 4:12, Mark 1:14
Jesus, John, and Disciples Baptizing

This period, still early in Jesus' ministry, appears to be one of the calmer times, in spite of the arrest of John the Baptist. These four brief passages show, in one sense, an earthly "passing of the torch" from John the Baptist to Jesus and His disciples. This is the first of the few days in this chronological reading in which a portion is read from all four Gospels. However, note that two of these passages encompass a single verse each. By actual total verses, this is among the shortest New Testament readings. This is necessary as a setup for the next big event in the life of Jesus in tomorrow's reading.

January 10, OT
Job 19:1-21:34
Job Replies to Bildad and then to Zophar

As Job's friends turn up the heat of frustration with him, thinking that Job is basically "not listening," he responds with the best defense so far since his infliction. And just as his words "hit bottom" in terms of negativity, he expresses some of the strongest words of hope so far in the entire debate (19:23-27). How prophetic are Job's words in verse 23 when he says that he wishes his "words were written down"! Needless to say, he got his wish.

In chapter 20, Zophar begins his second round of speeches by saying, in so many words, that Job's criticisms of his (Zophar's) assessment are an insult to his intelligence (20:2-3) and spends the next 25 verses accusing Job of great wickedness. Job counters with an argument that can be paraphrased as: "go ahead and mock me all you want; I'm right and you know it." The highlight of Job's counter-argument is a very insightful passage lamenting how the wicked seem to go unpunished (21:7-15). How many people today, in times of trouble, don't make the same lament?

January 10, NT
John 4:1-26
Jesus Meets the Samaritan Woman, Part One

This New Testament lesson is long enough and important enough to break up into two parts over two days. In the first of three straight days from the Gospel of John, Jesus travels to Galilee via Samaria, and meets a woman who doesn't know Jesus, but He definitely knows her! A popular song by Peter, Paul, and Mary from the 1960s celebrates this encounter.

When the woman points out that Jews worship in Jerusalem and Samaritans worship "on this mountain" (4:20), Jesus' reply foreshadows the fact that the true believers will worship and believe because of the Holy Spirit and the earthly location will not matter (4:21-24). Part of this explanation is Jesus' statement that "salvation is from the Jews" (4:22b), a statement that I believe **proves the case against "replacement theology."**

Replacement theology (sometimes called "Supersessionism") is the idea that all not-yet-fulfilled prophecy about "Israel" refers to the Church, not the Jewish state. According to replacement theology, the promises given to Abraham in the Old Testament that established the Jews as "God's chosen people" are null and void because of the Jews' rejection of Jesus as the Messiah. Christians (like me) who don't believe in replacement theology are sometimes referred to as "Zionists." Unfortunately, Roman Catholics, Lutherans, and several other mainstream Protestant churches officially believe replacement theology as doctrine.

Jesus' explanation about the Holy Spirit is enough to ignite (re-ignite?) the woman's belief in a coming Messiah (4:25). Then, like a good cliffhanger, Jesus ends today's passage by telling her that He *is* the Messiah (4:26).

January 11, OT
Job 22:1-26:14
Eliphaz and Bildad Attack Again

Eliphaz returns to the debate with Job (Job 22:1) with a near repeat of Zophar's statement regarding the (apparent) wickedness of Job, essentially saying that "it's no wonder you're suffering" to Job. Job replies in anger at first; not at Eliphaz, but at God. He is fully ready to take on God and challenge Him, like a defense lawyer in a court of law, firm in his belief that the defendant would be acquitted once the judge "gives heed" (23:6) to his statement.

Job explains that he isn't the wicked person Eliphaz and Zophar say he his by describing where the *real* wickedness is in the world: thieves (24:2), murderers (24:14), and adulterers (24:15), all the while making his point that he is *not* one of them, and is, therefore, righteous.

Bildad then retorts that it is not possible for a mortal, who he likens to a maggot and a worm (25:6), to be righteous before God. In one narrow sense of the word, Bildad is right. We live in a fallen world in which we only have ourselves and our sin to blame. But Bildad's words are nothing more than another attack on Job, and God and Job both know it. In Job's response (*dripping* with sarcasm, 26:1-4), he acknowledges that God's majesty is an unfathomable mystery, but says that the mystery of God can't be used to declare that Job *isn't* righteous.

January 11, NT
John 4:27-44
Jesus Meets the Samarian Woman, Part Two

In yesterday's reading, Jesus meets a Samarian woman at a place called Jacob's Well. Their legendary conversation is told in John's Gospel (and nowhere else).

Here's a woman with a notorious reputation (and deservedly so) who just had a conversation with the Messiah but didn't realize it right away, and now she actually succeeds in convincing some who dwelled in the nearby town to listen to and believe Him. Some of them even invited Jesus into their home to stay for a few days (4:40) where even more believers were made.

A good conclusion to this two-part account is to consider a profound statement made by Jesus in part one, and how it relates to something he said here. Back in John 4:22, Jesus told the woman (who is never named) that salvation is "of the Jews" or "from the Jews" depending on translation. Outside of the obvious facts that Jesus was a Jew and that He was speaking to someone who wasn't, the point was not that Jews were the only to be saved. As He explains in 4:34-38 (to His disciples, not the woman, though she may have heard this part when she returned), He was sent by the One who "sowed" the seed to complete His work. This is another affirmation of Creation by God, and is also a note about how this new faith was going to be spread. Jesus had not yet called all of his apostles, but He let those that He had already called know that they would all be Jews like Him, even though He just evangelized a Samaritan city.

January 12, OT
Job 27:1-29:25
Job Defends Himself and Defends God

By the beginning of chapter 27, Eliphaz and Bildad have each made their last attacks on Job. Zophar (apparently) declines a third opportunity to get his two cents in. We learn that God has won the wager between God and Satan from back in chapters 1 and 2. Though Job has repeatedly expressed dismay and even anger towards God, he never curses Him and never renounces his belief in Him.

Though nearly the entire book is written as poetry, the "poem within a poem" in chapter 28 stands out as one of the most beautiful in all of Hebrew poetry. Young readers, in particular, will question the idea of most of Job being poetry, because the verses do not rhyme or have any obvious meter to them. One has to remember that this book, like nearly all of the Old Testament, was written in Hebrew. This book, when read aloud in Hebrew, still doesn't rhyme, but it does have a noticeable cadence to it; that is, there is a "meter" or "rhythm" to it that becomes increasingly obvious. There are websites where you can listen to the Bible read aloud in the original languages such as http://www.mechon-mamre.org/p/pt/ptmp3prq.htm. If you check out this or one of the other (numerous!) sites, note that the language sounds very strange, but also very beautiful.

January 12, NT
John 4:45-54
The Second Miracle: Jesus Heals the Nobleman's Son

This reading, one of the shorter entries in this reading plan, details Jesus' second miracle. John goes so far as to enumerate each miracle, and thus we know this to have been miracle #2. But like most brief readings in this plan, there is an important reason for it: it is not simply the fact that the next event would make today's reading too long if combined with this miracle; it is the manner in which this miracle occurred.

Jesus' first miracle was done with reluctance, at the behest of His mother, in a (more or less) private setting (a wedding) prior to His official "debut". Jesus had yet to make His ministry known at that point. By the time of this healing, he not only did have his "coming out" in Nazareth, but He also was beginning to get a widespread reputation. And so, we have a nobleman approach Jesus and beg for the healing of his son. Jesus' reply shows a continued reluctance to perform miracles (John 4:48), and it's important to read the verse to know why. Jesus doesn't just want to be known as a miracle worker. Jesus wants people to obtain the gift of *faith,* which is the belief in things *unseen* (Hebrews 11:1). The nobleman pushes anyway, which must have indicated to Jesus that the nobleman really did already believe (John 4:49) because Jesus then did something he seldom did after this: he performed the miracle at a great distance.

The nobleman's faith is evident when his slaves tell him of his son's miraculous healing: he asks only to verify the time of the event (4:52) to solidify his belief that it really was Jesus who made his son well. He doesn't cast any doubt on the fact that it happened. It is with this same mindset that we should approach our examination of the wonders of God.

January 13, OT
Job 30:1-31:40
Job Concludes His Defense

The final section of Job's speech before his so-called friends begins with Job telling them, in so many words, that he would have kicked their fathers out if they had spoken to Job as Eliphaz, Bildad, and Zophar did. It is also revealed here that these three people are all younger than Job (30:1). Job goes on to explain just how worthless his friends' so-called "advice" is to him.

Job finishes his defense by swearing that his words are the whole truth. He even makes repeated references to being cursed by God if any of his words are not true. Neither he nor any of the other men have any clue yet as to exactly why Job is enduring this hardship. They all have theories, and the only common thread seems to be that the afflictions are from God. Little do they know that God allowed Satan to do the dirty deed, not God Himself, with a purpose in mind that hasn't yet been revealed to any of them. Then, just like a good courtroom drama, the story takes a fascinating, almost bizarre twist (tomorrow's reading) after it says "the words of Job are ended" (31:40).

January 13, NT
Luke 4:31-32, Matthew 4:13-22, Mark 1:14-20
"I Will Make You Fishers of Men"

Back on January 5, the New Testament lesson was about the call of the first apostles, told in John's Gospel. Today, we read about these same apostles in Matthew and Mark. Because it is the first appearance of men like Simon Peter and the sons of Zebedee in these two books, most Bible publishers *mislabel* this section as the call of the first apostles or disciples. Here's why it's a mislabeling:

Using Luke's account of Jesus entering the synagogue in Capernaum, we can correctly place the next series of events (in Luke) to take place *after* Jesus' return to Galilee via Samaria (where we earlier read the story of His encounter with the woman at the well) and His first two miracles, both of which must take place *after* the call of the first apostles. Therefore, that makes the event mistakenly called the "call" of the apostles in Luke, Matthew, and Mark a completely separate event!

Matthew's version of events picks up where Luke's leaves off, detailing His arrival in Capernaum. The one unique thing here is that Matthew explains that Jesus' choice of homes is actually the fulfillment of prophecy, and quotes Isaiah 9:1-2 to prove it. From there, Matthew goes on to tell of Jesus' famous words to His first apostles, "I will make you fishers of *men*." These fishermen *were already Jesus' apostles*, as described in John. But in John's version, they had not yet abandoned their occupations as fishermen. Here, Jesus finally "gathers them up" to follow him and take a more active role in His ministry.

Mark's version of the same event is much shorter and to-the-point than Matthew's (or Luke's from tomorrow), and skips over many details between the arrest of John the Baptist and "call" of the fishermen, who were already Jesus' apostles at that point.

January 14, OT
Job 32:1-34:37
A New Voice is Heard, Part One

Up to this point, the book of Job has 29 straight chapters of poetry, encompassing a sometimes-heated dialogue between Job and three younger men who attempt to advise Job on why he is suffering. The speeches are of varying length, from a mere 6 verses all the way up to 4 whole chapters. Some of what is said is correct, some is not. What we don't find out, as readers, until now, is that there was at least one more person present for most, if not all, of this dialog. Silent until now, today is the first of two day's worth of speech from a young man named Elihu.

We know as much about Elihu as we know of Eliphaz, Bildad, and Zophar: almost nothing. It becomes obvious in the first few verses that he stayed silent because he was the youngest of the entire group. Respect for elders was obviously part of the culture of the time, but after all the speeches by Job and his other "friends," Elihu could contain himself no longer. Elihu begins by rebuking Job's friends, not because Elihu believes they were wrong, but because they *didn't* speak up and rebuke Job after Job's last speech! Elihu defends his position by stating that age doesn't necessarily bring with it any more wisdom (32:9). Thus, before Elihu brings any real new arguments to the debate, he defends his relative youth to the four older men, including Job.

Closer to the truth than the other 3 men (though still missing the point), Elihu places the responsibility for Job's suffering on Job himself, but not as punishment for sins. Rather, Elihu argues, God uses pain and suffering as a way of purifying mortal men (33:17-22). Thus, Job's affliction is a *warning*, not a *sentence*. Elihu's proclamation of God's justice is surprisingly insightful, but he stumbles near the end of this first part by saying that a person must be taught what his sins are in order for them to be forgiven (34:31-33) by God, and that Job is adding "rebellion to sin" (34:37) because of Job's anger.

January 14, NT
Luke 5:1-26
"I Will Make You Fishers of Men," Continued

Luke's version of this event isn't a continuation of the Matthew and Mark versions, but it is a more detailed version, and it includes another miracle of Jesus. It also contains what I consider "proof" that this isn't the *"call"* of the apostles, but is actually an early episode in the apostles' life with Jesus.

Skeptics have attempted for many years to discredit the Bible by pointing out *alleged* "discrepancies" or "inconsistencies" in the Bible. The claim is that there are errors in the Bible, and that, therefore, the Bible is **not** the Word of God. My belief is that the Bible is *inerrant*, at least in its original manuscripts (of which we have none). I further believe that 99.9% of all the copying errors that may have crept in since then have been successfully eradicated, especially with improved archaeology, and the discovery of older, intact manuscripts that have validated the claims of many previous translators and copiers. From my past studies of the Bible, I have found that not all human writers in the Bible present events to us in their exact chronological order. In other words, two different human writers could each write about the same event, have some of the details in a slightly different sequence from each other, yet both are "accurate" and acceptable as Truth. Such is the case with the 4 Gospel writers.

Since many events are presented in more than one Gospel, we must assume that they really did happen *even if the sequence of those events is different from one Gospel to another*. There are some events described in only one or two of the Gospels, and these can be used as a frame of reference or "anchor point" to determine the true, correct order. The Gospels according to Matthew, Mark, and Luke are called the "synoptic" Gospels because their sequence is almost the same, and many events are described in more than one of them. John's Gospel stands out as not "fitting" as easily into that harmony. Almost half of John shows up *only* in John. The other half contains a number of events that are either in a radically different order or are described in a completely different way.

Two such events are: the call of the first apostles/disciples, and the "cleansing of the temple." In the reading for January 8, I explained the fact that John's version of the "cleansing" was being skipped until

April. Here's why: John's version, though it appears in a completely different sequence than the other versions, is described almost the exact same way, which makes me believe that it is the same event in all four Gospels. Some scholars believe there were two separate "cleansings" to reconcile the sequences; I disagree because of the similarities in the accounts. The other event, the call of the first apostles, has almost the exact same problem. Not only is John's version *way* out of sequence compared to the others, but the description of how the events unfolded is *completely different*. Therefore, I believe that John's "call" is a completely different, *earlier* event than the "fishers of men" event described yesterday in Matthew and Mark, and today in Luke.

What I object to is that most Bibles still call this event in Luke "the Call of the First Disciples." Skeptics seize on things like this to make it easier for them to discredit the Bible – and harder for believers like me to defend it. Using the above reasoning, we get a sequence of events that *is* reconcilable between *all four* Gospel accounts.

A careful reading of Luke's version, in particular, *proves* that the "fishers of men" event is a later, separate event from the call of the Apostles in John's Gospel. Luke's account begins with "And it came to pass" (or "One day" in some versions), as opposed to something like "And then he...." Luke is indicating that the next event he describes in chapter 5 didn't necessarily follow the one (skipped) in chapter 4 in exact sequence. Another hint that the "call" had already taken place has to do with what happened next: Jesus steps into Simon's boat (Luke 5:3) and begins to preach to the crowds. Simon puts up no objection to this invasion, which seems to indicate that he already knew Jesus. Simon then calls him "Master," (5:5) which indicates that Simon has heard Jesus preach before.

Luke also details a miracle here that is not found in Matthew or Mark's accounts (5:6-7) and follows it with the first addressing of Jesus as "Lord" by Simon. It would be the first of many. Then, Luke tells of two more miracles: the cleansing of a leper (5:12-16) and the healing of a paralytic (5:17-26), both of which are also found in Matthew and Mark. Those versions will be read tomorrow.

January 15, OT
Job 35:1-37:24
A New Voice is Heard, Part Two

Elihu, the young man from whom we first heard in yesterday's reading, continues his only speech to Job and his "friends". He picks up where yesterday's reading left off by accusing Job of engaging in self-righteousness and condemning it.

Through the centuries since the book of Job first became part of the Hebrew Bible, and later our Old Testament, scholars have debated the relative merits of Elihu's speech. Unlike Job or the other three (or, for that matter, God), Elihu is permitted to speak without interruption. Not only was he not interrupted, but neither Job nor anyone else "cross-examined" him at the conclusion. He shows greater insight and wisdom than the other men, which is surprising considering his relative youth. But, how "right" was he?

The best answer is that Elihu was right on some things and wrong on others, but was arguably closer to The Truth than anyone else in that group, including Job. Among the things on which Elihu was wrong was the idea that Job was wrong to argue his case before God (Job 35:14). If that were really true, then we would be doomed after committing a single sin. But after this statement, Elihu spends nearly the next two and a half chapters correctly declaring God's justice (36:5-23) and His majesty (36:24-37:24).

It seems as though Elihu may have intended to go further in his speech, because there is no obvious conclusion to it. There are no notes such as "this is the end of Elihu's speech" the way there is for Job. Job, Eliphaz, Bildad, and Zophar either chose not to respond or weren't given the chance, because immediately after Elihu's last verse, we read God's words to Job and the rest of the group, starting in tomorrow's reading.

January 15, NT
Matthew 8:2-4, Mark 1:40-2:12, Matthew 9:2-8
The Cleansing of the Leper and the Healing of the Paralytic

These two miracles in Matthew and Mark, already revealed in yesterday's reading from Luke, differ from Luke's only in sequence. Matthew has the two miracles a whole chapter apart, with a couple other significant events yet to be read in Mark or Luke occurring in-between. It should also be noted that Matthew has both miracles occurring *after* the Sermon on the Mount, which this chronology says has not yet happened.

Most notable of all is the fact that Mark goes into more detail about the healing of the paralytic than does Matthew, though not quite as much as Luke. Mark's sequence of events also seems to most closely match Matthew's, except for the absence of the Sermon on the Mount in Mark.

January 16, OT
Job 38:1-39:30
The Lord's Answer to Job, Part One

The last time we read about God speaking directly to humans was when the Flood had just ended and He spoke to Noah and his family. His entrance here after the debate between Job and his friends is no less dramatic; as it says He spoke from a "whirlwind." But it's *what* He says that raises the most eyebrows. Instead of answering any of Job's numerous questions, God begins his response with some questions of His own.

Have you ever prayed for something and didn't get it? Everyone has, of course. Has that ever led you to believe that God *doesn't* answer all prayers – or *any* prayers? I think we've all felt that way at one time or another. The truth is that God answers all prayers; He just doesn't always give us the answer we want or expect. God's answer to Job is a prime example.

God goes into a lengthy series of rhetorical questions that seem to almost affirm what Job's friends told him. God's self-answering questions seem to emphasize just how big and important He is versus how small and insignificant Job is. Many verses point out God's work of Creation and are used by creationists like me to defend the position against evolution.

January 16, NT
Luke 4:33-39, Mark 1:21-31, Matthew 8:14-17
Two More Miracles

After an initial reluctance to perform miracles publicly, Jesus went on to accelerate them after getting his first Apostles to leave their boats and follow him. This is another of the reasons for the seemingly goofy sequence of readings, jumping back and forth and from one book to another: the only sequence that works to reconcile the Gospel of John (from which we don't read for nearly a week) and the other three Gospels is the sequence found in this chronological reading plan.

In Luke we go "back" to the 4th chapter and read of two events: Jesus' casting out of an "unclean spirit" from a demon-possessed man, and the healing of Simon's mother-in-law. The casting out of the demon also appears, nearly verbatim, in Mark, albeit in a somewhat different sequence relative to other events. Matthew's Gospel appears not to have this event, but does have the healing of Simon's (here named Peter) mother-in-law. Matthew's Gospel does add, however, some additional exorcisms and healings not mentioned by Mark or Luke that apparently took place in Peter's home. Matthew also uses this opportunity to point out that these miracles are the fulfillment of prophesy; in this case Isaiah 53:4.

I have always heard that there was some kind of debate about whether or not Peter was a married man. Why such a debate exists is beyond me, when the readings from Luke and Matthew are taken plainly. Clearly, Simon-Peter was a married man, at least some time *prior* to his encounter of Jesus, if not concurrent with it.

January 17, OT
Job 40:1-42:17
The Lord's Answer to Job, Part Two; Conclusion of Job

Today, we wrap up the book of Job with the remainder of God's response. At the beginning of chapter 40, God wraps up the first part of his response by informing Job that it is *Job* that must respond to *God*, and not the other way around (Job 40:2b) due to Job's challenge.

God continues with more questioning of Job, including a gem for creationists about two beasts whose identities have been debated for centuries: behemoth (40:15) and leviathan (41:1). If, as I believe, leviathan is a dinosaur (and possibly behemoth as well), then God's speech about the soon-to-be-extinct animal was an *excellent* way of making His point. A lot of the Lord's language in this chapter describes the strength and power of this (apparently) great beast. As one of many creations of God, this beast is described, in the end, as "king over all that are proud," (41:34) which is said not to raise the stature of the creature but to humble the insignificant man. Best of all, *Job gets it*.

When Job gets his chance to respond, he fully humbles himself before the almighty God (42:1-6) and even begs forgiveness for being so bold as to argue before Him. God, of course, already knew Job's heart. God had already won His bet with Satan, and so He answered Job's challenge by the simple act of granting Job something that *very* few humans had ever been (or would ever be) granted – a *direct* encounter with God.

God then rebukes three of Job's friends but decides to not only show them mercy (despite their errors), but He showers Job with a double portion. Everything Job lost was returned and then some. Job lived the remainder of his life as a happy, wealthy man, blessed by God in ways that few other people ever would be (42:11-15). The book ends with Job's eventual death at a ripe, old age (42:16-17), one of the happiest endings to any story in the Bible.

What does it all mean? The book of Job is the answer to all the numerous questions people have about human suffering. In the end, the only true conclusions anyone can draw are that all suffering is the result of sin and The Curse, and that we truly did bring it on ourselves. However, God is in control of everything – in spite of all arguments about our "free will" empowering us to do what we want, nothing would happen without God letting it happen. The world isn't ours; it's His. And, if we go before Him with meekness and humility, God will let the good things happen more than the bad. In the end, it's not up to us – it's up to Him.

January 17, NT
Luke 4:40-44, Mark 1:32-39, Matthew 4:23-25
More Healing, More Preaching

The healings and the preaching tour that follow yesterday's reading are told in nearly identical detail in the three synoptic Gospels. The only significant difference is where Matthew places the event (obviously the same event in all three places), in this case *prior* to the "Sermon on the Mount," which is yet to come in the chronology.

January 18, OT
Genesis 11:27-15:21
The Covenant, Part One

Though Genesis is the first book of the Bible, it is not the first book completed. Yesterday, we completed the reading of the entire book of Job, who is believed to be a contemporary of the man who will become the focus of attention in Genesis for the next 14 *chapters*: Abraham, the "father of our faith".

Abraham's importance in God's salvation history cannot be understated. Matthew's genealogy of Jesus starts with Abraham. Abraham's expression of faith in Genesis 15:6 is quoted three times in the New Testament: Romans 4:3, Galatians 3:6, and James 2:23. God's Chosen People, later known as Israelites, then Hebrews, and later still as Jews, began with Abraham and an important promise made to him by God. That promise, that Abraham would father "a great nation" (Genesis 12:2, 15:5) is called *The Covenant*.

The spelling and pronunciation of the names Abram and Abraham are very similar in English, but are vastly different in Hebrew. They refer, however, to the same person, as will become apparent in tomorrow's reading. Today, we meet a large number of very important Bible characters, including Abram, his father Terah, Abram's brothers, and nephew Lot. Abram's wife, Sarai, also first appears here, as is the fact that she cannot have children (11:29-30). Like Abram, God would later change her name as well, in her case to the more familiar "Sarah".

Another briefly mentioned but important character is Melchizedek (14:17-18) who is listed as a king and a priest. Outside of this information, we know nothing of this man, yet he is later mentioned in Psalm 110 and Hebrews 7:11-17, and thus becomes a very important figure. Melchizedek is the first to use bread and wine in worship (14:18), and his blessing of Abram includes the first-ever mention of tithing (14:20).

January 18, NT
Luke 5:27-39, Mark 2:13-22, Matthew 9:9-17
The Call of Levi / The Question about Fasting

Jesus had not yet gathered up all 12 men who would later be called the Apostles, yet he had performed several public miracles and had uprooted a few of his first followers. He had encountered crowds and several interesting individuals including a Pharisee named Nicodemus (John 3). But as a whole group, Jesus had yet to go head-to-head with the Pharisees. Today's reading talks of two such encounters.

Levi is called Matthew only in Matthew's Gospel. The former tax collector becomes one of the Apostles, and is believed to be the same Matthew for whom the Gospel is named. Some think that this is not so due to the numerous references from here on out of Matthew in the third person, but this practice was actually very common in both Hebrew and Greek writing.

The call of Levi/Matthew is nearly identical in the three synoptic Gospels. It includes the first of many similar encounters with the Pharisees in which Jesus is accused of doing something wrong or even blasphemous because of His association with sinners. Jesus counters with important statements about evangelical work: that He has come to call sinners, not the righteous.

Like the Pharisees, the disciples of John the Baptist equally misunderstood the purpose of Christ's coming. They pressed on with questions about fasting; specifically, why the disciples of Jesus weren't doing so. Jesus' response likens Himself to a bridegroom, and speaks for the first time about the bridegroom being "taken away," a veiled reference to His death. Jesus then told a parable about putting new wine in old wineskins, the first of many parables He tried to use to get the Jews to stop interpreting His coming in terms of the Law of Moses. As important as it was to fulfill the prophecies made hundreds of years earlier, Jesus' coming was not designed to restore the kingdom of Israel and drive out the Romans, as most people then thought. It's also a reference to the eventual spread of this new faith (new wine?) beyond the borders of Judea. Despite its relative brevity, it's a worthwhile parable for family discussion and individual study and is one of relatively few parables that appear in 3 or more of the Gospels.

January 19, OT
Genesis 16:1-18:33
The Covenant, Part Two

The word "covenant" means "agreement" or "promise." In yesterday's reading, God made some lofty promises to Abram about having numerous descendants. Despite Abram's faith and despite how frequently that faith is lauded, today's reading begins with an open act of doubt on Abram's part about those promises.

It was acceptable practice in those days for infertile women to grant their husbands a chance to have a child by another woman. This was neither condemned nor condoned by God, as the laws regarding marriage fidelity and monogamy had not yet been written (though God's intent was clear since the Creation). We don't know how widespread the problem of infertility was except that Sarai's permission to Abram to impregnate their servant Hagar (Genesis 16:1-4) was not viewed as something wrong or unusual. After all, God was still talking about re-populating the earth after the Flood by commanding mankind to "be fruitful and multiply." Sarai's barrenness was, therefore, one of the worst curses a woman could possibly bear. With God promising Abram numerous descendants, Abram and Sarai decided to attempt to "help God out" in this matter. However, there were two consequences to this action that are in today's reading: 16:5-6 and 16:15-16.

The Covenant becomes controversial at this point because Arab Muslims today recognize Abram (actually, Abraham by name) as their father in faith the same way as Jews and Christians do. Most are adamant about Ishmael's status as the first-born of Abram, and therefore the true recipient of God's promises about the land of Canaan, including the modern-day countries of Israel, Lebanon, and Jordan. As shown in Genesis 17 however, God did *not* intend for Ishmael to be the first descendent of Abram. God is very clear about making His covenant with the yet-to-be-born Isaac, *not* Ishmael (17:21).

January 19, NT
John 5:1-47
The Healing on the Sabbath

John's Gospel seldom refers to "Pharisees," instead simply using the term "the Jews" to refer to those who followed (or pretended to follow) the Law of Moses but were blind to the prophecies concerning the Messiah, namely Jesus. Today we read of another miracle, this time in Jerusalem, on the Sabbath, and in front of "the Jews." Not only was Jesus doing, in their eyes, something forbidden, but blasphemous (John 5:16). Jesus did two things differently here: He healed on a Sabbath (5:9) and told the healed man to "sin no more" (5:14). This, coupled with Jesus' answer to their questions, enraged the Pharisees to the point of wanting to kill Him (5:18).

People who belong to one of the more evangelical churches will clearly recognize the verse that forms one of the articles in the Statement of Faith: that there will be two resurrections: one for the good to the resurrection of life, another for the evil to the resurrection of the damned (5:29).

January 20, OT
Genesis 19:1-21:34, Genesis 25:12-18, 1 Chronicles 1:28-31
The Destruction of Sodom and Gomorrah

What is the worst sin? Are any sins really worse than others? All sin is looked at equally badly in God's eyes, but some sins have more severe *consequences* to them than others, as proven in today's OT reading.

The sin of Adam and Eve resulted in the curse of all mankind to follow that all people would eventually die (remember, man was not originally meant to die). The sin of their descendants would result in God's destruction of the world in the Great Flood, with the exception of Noah and his family. The sins they committed aren't specified except by definition of "sin" itself: rebellion against God.

Abraham had already committed a pair of sins that are known today as being particularly heinous: incest (Abraham married his half-sister, Sarah (Genesis 20:12), a relationship that would later be forbidden) and adultery (despite Sarah's permission, Abraham technically committed adultery in having sex with Hagar). Abraham would later be punished for his sin of doubt (and Sarah for giving him the okay to do it) by having to deal with Hagar and their illegitimate offspring. But these consequences paled in comparison to the sins being committed by the citizens of Sodom and Gomorrah.

All sin has consequences, but the ancient city of Sodom was known as quite possibly the *most* evil place in the world, then or since. Despite Abraham's plea in yesterday's OT reading, God could *not* find 10 people for whom to spare the city, so God decided to go through with the destruction. The city's great evil is shown in the form of an attempted homosexual gang rape of the two angels of God, sent to help Abraham's nephew, Lot, escape. (19:5-11) The crime of homosexual rape was considered so heinous, even in the days of Abraham (centuries before the Law of Moses was spelled out forbidding homosexuality), that Lot even offered the rapists his virgin daughters (19:8) in exchange for the men *because that would have been considered a lesser crime.*

And so came one of God's greatest acts of wrath, one of the most violent passages in the entire Bible.

January 20, NT
Luke 6:1-11, Mark 2:23-3:6, Matthew 12:1-14
More Sabbath Incidents

One of the most severe charges the Pharisees had against Jesus was His allegedly blasphemous treatment of the Sabbath. As Jesus Himself points out in today's NT reading, He is the "Lord also of the Sabbath" (Mark 2:28).

Today's reading continues the part of Jesus' ministry where His reputation with the general public was increasing while the Pharisees were, in turn, getting increasingly suspicious of Him. Jesus and His disciples eat fresh grain on a Sabbath, and Jesus performs yet another healing miracle, on the (you guessed it) Sabbath. Just as in yesterday's reading from John 5, the passage ends with the Pharisees anger rising to the boiling point over this apparent violation of the letter of the law. Already at this relatively early stage in Jesus' ministry, they (the Pharisees) were plotting to kill Him.

January 21, OT
Genesis 22:1-24:67
The Command to Sacrifice Isaac, The Death of Sarah, and The Marriage of Isaac and Rebekah

Three important events from the life of Abraham make up today's OT reading.

The practice of animal sacrifice long pre-dates the specific guidelines that were handed down to Moses for the Israelites. So when young Isaac asks his father "where is the lamb for the sacrifice" (Genesis 22:7), Abraham can't give him a straight answer (22:8) because God commanded Abraham to sacrifice his first legitimate *son* as a burnt offering! God eventually stops Abraham from going through with it, but it was close. The whole point was to test the faith and loyalty of Abraham, and he passed the test.

A little math from a passage yet to be read (25:20) places Sarah's age at the time of the birth of Isaac at 87 years! When Sarah died 40 years later, Abraham purchased a large, expensive tomb for his wife (23:4-20) and had her buried there. The site of the tomb, where Abraham himself would eventually be buried as well, is thought to have been recently found by archeologists.

The remainder of today's reading is the story of the marriage of Isaac to Rebekah, as Abraham sends a servant to find a wife for Isaac in his original homeland (24:1-9). Isaac and Rebekah were married according to the custom of the day, which also gave Isaac comfort after the recent death of his mother, Sarah (24:62-67).

January 21, NT
Matthew 12:14-21, Mark 3:7-12, Matthew 4:23-25
The Crowds Follow Jesus

Jesus may have been having problems with the local Jewish authorities (Pharisees) after several miracles and other incidents, but He certainly wasn't having a problem with the general public of the area. Following a recent string of miracles, the "servant Jesus" tried to slow His own progress down by telling them not to "blab it everywhere". Both the miracles and His attempt to halt the too-rapid spread of His popularity were found by Matthew (Matthew 12:17-21) to be fulfillment of prophecy, by quoting Isaiah 42:1-4.

Jesus' reputation continued to spread, to the point where He feared for His own safety (Mark 3:9) at one point. His seaside appearances were all a lead-up to the biggest sermon He would ever give in His entire ministry, as described during the next few days' NT readings. Before that, however, He had one more very important detail yet to take care of (in tomorrow's NT reading).

January 22, OT
Genesis 25:1-4, 1 Chronicles 1:32-33, Genesis 25:5-6, 1 Chronicles 1:34, Genesis 25:19-26
More of the Abraham Family Tree

We pause after the detailed stories of The Covenant and the events that got God's Chosen People started to examine two brief accounts of the top of Abraham's family tree. Today's OT reading is actually quite brief despite the jumping around between Genesis and 1 Chronicles. A careful comparison of the names in the two books will reveal them to be the same family tree.

In one account, Abraham re-marries some time after the death of Sarah (Genesis 25:1), where the other account lists this relationship as being with Abraham's concubine (1 Chronicles 1:32). These accounts don't conflict: though Abraham was not a Polygamist, any wives a man took in those days following the death of the mother of his firstborn was given that negative-sounding label. This further drives home the point that Isaac is considered the legitimate heir (firstborn) of Abraham.

The genealogy then leads up to the firstborn of Isaac and Rebekah: the twin brothers Esau and Jacob (Genesis 25:24), whose stories would dominate the remainder of Genesis.

January 22, NT
Luke 6:12-19, Mark 3:13-19, Matthew 10:1-4
The Appointment of the Twelve Apostles

By this time, Jesus had many disciples. A few had already been named as Apostles, the difference being one of formality: the Apostles, or "followers" were with Jesus all the time; the other disciples believed, and did spend some time with Jesus, but did not live with Him in any formal sense. Despite how much jumping around (in Matthew) is necessary to synchronize the Gospel accounts, no chronology makes any sense without first clearing this hurdle *prior* to the Sermon on the Mount, which begins tomorrow.

And so we have three nearly identical accounts describing Jesus' formal appointment of the 12 Apostles. The very fact that the list of names is identical is significant. It is not known how many of these men were still alive at the time these three Gospels were written; we only know for certain of the death of one of them (Judas) by the time the first one (Mark) was written. That means that Mark, Matthew, and Luke (presumably in that order) received their information about the names of these 12 men either by way of eyewitness account (only available to Matthew and John, 2 of the Twelve), a third-party eyewitness (Luke is assumed to have received most of his data from either Peter, an Apostle, or Mary, the mother of Jesus) or direct inspiration from God. At any rate, it lends an air of authenticity to accounts like this when there is such exact agreement from three different biographers who, presumably, never even met.

January 23, OT
Genesis 25:7-11, Genesis 25:27-26:35
The Death of Abraham and the Beginning of the Longest-Ever Family Feud

We now refocus on the family of Abraham, who dies at the beginning of today's OT reading at the age of 175 (Genesis 25:7). The math reveals that his son Isaac's marriage to Rebekah took place when Abraham would have been 140 years old, making Isaac 75 at the time of Abraham's death. Fifteen years earlier, Isaac's twin sons, Esau and Jacob were born. It was revealed yesterday that Esau and Jacob struggled in Rebekah's womb, and that Esau came out with Jacob's hand around his ankle, indicating that Jacob was, perhaps, struggling to be the real firstborn.

Then, Esau "sells" his birthright as the biological firstborn to Jacob for a meal (25:29-34). Though Jacob had "bought" (swindled?) the birthright from Esau, Jacob had not yet actually formally received it from Isaac. That would require an act of deception on Jacob's part that we don't read about until tomorrow.

Today's OT reading includes a near-repeat of The Covenant, this time to Isaac, as Isaac almost repeats word-for-word the "sister" deception his father Abraham tried to pull (26:7-11) and receives the promises made to his father for himself (26:4-5, 26:24-25).

Esau (also known as Edom, 25:30), meanwhile, goes on to marry two Hittite women (26:34), the first two of what would later be at least three wives, one of whom is a daughter of Ishmael (tomorrow's reading, 28:9). This cousin marriage (which was common in those days) would be another log on the fire of controversy over today's two largest feuding groups of people.

January 23, NT
Matthew 5:1-5:37
The Sermon on the Mount, Part One

The Sermon on the Mount, as it has come to be known, is Jesus' best known and longest sermon. Reading it over the course of three days completes it, but doesn't begin to do it justice. Whole books have been written about just small portions of this marvelous oratory. Nevertheless, it is the next event in correct chronological sequence and contains numerous summaries of the most important teachings on the Christian life and faith.

The Sermon appears in its entirety only in Matthew's Gospel. An abbreviated version appears in Luke, but there is considerable debate as to whether Luke's version is referring to the same event or a subsequent sermon Jesus gave in which He said many of the same things. I personally prefer the latter (as some Bibles refer to Luke's version as the "Sermon on the Plain"), but I also place the two sermons back-to-back, which makes sense in light of Matthew 4:23, which seems to indicate that Jesus was on a large-scale speaking "tour" in Galilee, where both sermons appear to take place.

The Sermon begins with a section commonly called The Beatitudes (Matthew 5:1-11), which is marked by each verse beginning with "Blessed are…." Jesus starts with a detailed description of what is good, before later describing what is sinful. He then compares the listeners to the "salt of the earth" (5:13) and the "light of the world" (5:14) as He continues His positive opening.

Jesus then continues, for the rest of today's NT reading, with a very important clarification of an issue that still gets debated today: how much of the Old Testament law, sometimes referred to as the "Law of Moses," still applies? The reason for the controversy is the *apparent* contradiction between the positive teachings of Jesus with the laws His Father handed down to the Israelites through Moses. Hot-button issues such as Capital Punishment, the Just-War, and Marriage and Divorce, are all part of this debate. Jesus makes it clear that the laws *do* still apply (5:17-18) and then spells out several specific examples.

Jesus' first example is of the commandment to not "kill" (or "murder," depending on translation), in which He states that even ordinary anger falls under the same commandment, and is, therefore, sinful (5:21-26). The commandment to not commit adultery includes even looking at a woman lustfully (5:27-30) or divorcing for any reason other than the one exception given by Jesus (5:31-32). Then, Jesus clarifies the commandment to not use the name of God in vain (sometimes called the "swearing" commandment) in relation to *any* swearing, not just formal "oath-taking" (5:33-37).

January 24, OT
Genesis 27:1-28:9
Jacob, the Con Man

Those who have read any part of the Bible before taking on this chronology know that Jacob would later receive a new name, in much the same way as his grandfather Abraham did. That name is *Israel*. Israel is a Hebrew word for "struggles with God." Today's OT reading might lead some to believe that "Israel" means "con man."

Today's reading includes a detailed account of how Jacob completed his swindle (with his mother Rebekah's help) of the inheritance that was rightfully Esau's because of their real birth order (Genesis 27:1-10). But, Rebekah took full responsibility for this assistance in order to fulfill a prophecy she received from God (25:23).

Does this mean that being a con artist is a good thing? Jacob's trickery can't be blamed entirely on Rebekah because she didn't give Jacob all the details of the prophecy she received. But, after Isaac's questionable birthright and Jacob's birth *after* Esau, isn't Jacob's deception a theological "third strike?" Apparently not, in God's eyes. Let's not forget that the laws regarding even as basic a thing as lying had not yet been written, except for the one very obvious deception that occurred in the Garden of Eden. The big difference is that the earlier lie was an incitement to rebel against God, whereas Jacob's lie was done to make it possible to *fulfill* God's word! Every time this topic is debated, we have to remember that it's God's decision, and not ours, to interpret what is and is not sinful. Who are we to judge Jacob's actions here when, after all, it was a necessary event to continue The Covenant?

January 24, NT
Matthew 5:38-6:34
The Sermon on the Mount, Part Two

Part two of the Sermon on the Mount continues with Jesus' clarification of the Law of Moses, specifically some often-misinterpreted laws. The first two of those points, which we can call "turn the other cheek" and "love our enemies" statements (Matthew 5:38-48), fly in the face of strict, legalistic interpretations of laws written in places like the Torah, but that's the whole point: Jesus' recent encounters with the Pharisees revealed that the real problem was not the law itself, but the interpretation thereof. Those who defend the "letter of the law" without noting the "spirit of the law" are the ones who are hypocrites.

Jesus' attack on hypocrites continues in a thinly veiled jab against those who would "sound a trumpet before thee… in the streets" (6:2), an obvious reference to the Pharisees. Jesus advocates almsgiving and prayer in secret, and praying directly to "Our Father" (6:6). What follows is the best-known prayer Jesus taught us (6:9-15), known as the "Lord's Prayer" or the "Our Father."

He then talks about fasting (6:16-18), "treasures in heaven" (6:19-21), an interesting metaphor about the human eye (6:22-23), and the fact that one cannot serve two masters (6:24), all of which are or contain familiar sayings of Jesus. Today's NT reading concludes with His advice to not worry (6:25-34).

January 25, OT
Genesis 36:1-43, 1 Chronicles 1:35-54
The Descendants of Esau

Today's OT reading takes a break from the narrative of the Patriarchs (the name given to Abraham, Isaac, and Jacob) to focus on the family of Esau. Many of the names are hard to read and pronounce, but they are worth a look. Remember, these people are the ancestors of modern Arabs. Though the Muslim holy book, the Koran, contains no genealogies, there are many Muslims who can trace their family tree all the way up to Esau and, by extension of one of his wives, all the way up to Ishmael. The Bible, on the other hand, contains quite a lot of family history, and it's found in several books, most prominently in Genesis and 1 Chronicles. We read from both today.

The serious student of the Bible would do well to compare the two genealogies of Esau, noting the places where they differ. There are diagrams of all the family trees available online at sites such as http://www.d.umn.edu/~jbelote/bible2.html and http://bible.ort.org/books/gened2.asp.

January 25, NT
Matthew 7:1-8:1
The Sermon on the Mount, Part Three

The final segment of Matthew's version of the Sermon on the Mount picks up where He left off, expounding on laws *other* than those in the Ten Commandments.

Matthew 7 starts with the "mote and beam" argument (Matthew 7:1-5). Besides being an interesting metaphor about not judging others, it is yet another example of Jesus' war on hypocrisy. This is followed by an argument against profaning what is holy ("pearls before swine," 7:6) and the "ask, search, and knock" advice (7:7-11).

The Golden Rule (7:12) appears in both Matthew and Luke's versions of the Sermon, with nearly identical wording. This is followed by the familiar "narrow gate" statement (7:13-14) and "tree and its fruit" statement (7:15-20). But Jesus, not wanting to emphasize a person's good works as a means of attaining salvation, makes it very clear in the next passage that doing these good things will not get you there (7:21-23). Rather, what is required is a relationship with Him so that He cannot say that He "doesn't know you."

The Sermon on the Mount concludes with a message that has been given the title "the solid rock" (7:24-28). Hymns and whole sermons have been built around these wise words that liken the building of one's faith and relationship with God to the building of a house. Jesus' words are that right kind of foundation, the solid rock, upon which to build one's faith.

January 26, OT
Genesis 28:10-30:43
Jacob's Ladder and the First Eleven Sons of Jacob

A lot of ground is covered in the first two chapters of today's OT reading. Highlights include Jacob's dream known as "Jacob's Ladder" (Genesis 28:10-12), confirming the fact that he really was the true heir to God's Chosen People (28:13-15). Then, the detailed and occasionally humorous account of Jacob's courtship and marriage to Rachel, and how the stumbling blocks set in his way resulted in his fathering 11 sons through *four* different women: Leah, her sister Rachel, and each of their handmaids. In this order and with the following women, Jacob became father to these sons:

Number	Mother	Name	Genesis reference
1	Leah	Reuben	29:32
2	Leah	Simeon	29:33
3	Leah	Levi	29:34
4	Leah	Judah	29:35
5	Bilhah (handmaid of Rachel)	Dan	30:6
6	Bilhah	Naphtali	30:8
7	Zilpah (handmaid of Leah)	Gad	30:11
8	Zilpah	Asher	30:13
9	Leah	Issachar	30:18
10	Leah	Zebulun	30:20
11	Rachel	Joseph	30:24

These eleven sons would become the first 11 of eventually 12 sons who would bear the title "the Twelve Tribes of Israel." In addition, at least one daughter was also born (to Leah, 30:21 just after Zebulun) named Dinah.

January 26, NT
Luke 6:20-49
The Sermon on the Plain (?)

We know that Matthew's Gospel contains the entire Sermon on the Mount. Today's NT reading sounds, at first, like another account of the same event, told by Luke. Many scholars still believe this, and there is evidence both ways in the debate. But as I mentioned three days ago, I favor the position that the sermon delivered by Jesus here in chapter 6 of Luke's Gospel is a separate event, likely shortly after the sermon told in Matthew.

The two distinguishing features of this sermon are its relative brevity (less than one third the length) and the fact that it doesn't contain anything that *wasn't* said in the Sermon on the Mount. Jesus begins with a short version of The Beatitudes (Luke 6:20-26) in which he reverses some of the blessings to express them as "woes." (This is part of the reason I believe this was a separate event.) This is followed by the passages on loving one's enemies (6:27-36), not judging others (6:37-42), "a tree and its fruit" (6:43-45), and building upon the "solid rock" of God's word (6:46-49).

January 27, OT
Genesis 31:1-32:32
Jacob Escapes Laban, Prepares to Meet Esau, and Wrestles with God

The three parts in today's two chapters follow Jacob after he pulls his latest stunt to gain an advantage or escape a bad situation. Part one is his and his family's "escape" from Laban, his father-in-law (Genesis 31:1-55). Laban seems more concerned about the "idols" (or "household gods") that were stolen than the cattle-breeding swindle pulled by Jacob or saying a proper goodbye to his daughters.

After Jacob and his caravan resume their journey, we read part two as Jacob prepares for the inevitable confrontation with his brother Esau, whom he had not seen in 21 years, and who was also the victim of one of Jacob's swindles (32:3-21). This leads to the third, and most unusual, part in today's reading: Jacob's encounter with an unknown opponent who wrestled with him through an entire night (32:24-30). The opponent is not identified; in fact, the word "he" is not capitalized to indicate that the man is actually God. Yet the consensus among virtually all Bible scholars is that it was God who wrestles with Jacob in this passage, thus clarifying his new name "Israel," which means "struggles with God."

January 27, NT
Luke 7:1-17; Matthew 8:5-13
Miracles in Capernaum and Nain

In Luke's part of today's NT reading, two miracles are described: the healing of the Centurion's slave, and the raising of a widow's son from the dead. Matthew's portion contains only the healing miracle.

Luke is the only Gospel writer to describe the raising of the widow's son. The widow and her son are not named. Chronologically, this event would have to have occurred a fairly long time *before* the miracle of Lazarus, which is told only in John. Furthermore, there are many believers who think that the Lazarus incident was Jesus' only miracle of resurrection before His own. This is not the case, of course, as today's reading bears out. The account is so brief as to sometimes get buried in amongst those passages that appear only in one Gospel, particularly when it is sandwiched by two other passages that are better known and appear in other Gospels.

One of those is the healing of the Centurion's servant, which is found in two Gospels: Luke and Matthew. Luke's account goes into more detail than Matthew, but both contain the same basic information, including an important piece of dialog. The Centurion's (Roman soldier's) statement about not being worthy of Jesus' healing gift (Luke 7:6-7, Matthew 8:8) is an amazing proclamation of faith, considering from whom it was coming. Jesus was astonished enough at this profession of faith that He declared that He had not found such faith even among the Jews!

Roman Catholics reading today's NT lesson will easily recognize the Centurion's words as being used for a communal prayer immediately before Eucharist at Mass: it is a near verbatim recital of Matthew 8:8.

January 28, OT
Genesis 33:1-35:29
Jacob Meets Esau, The Rape of Dinah, The Deaths of Rachel and Isaac

Like yesterday, today's OT reading is in three parts, but this time it is spread over three chapters. Considering what must have been incredible hatred and animosity between Esau and Jacob, their reunion (Genesis 33:4) seems rather anticlimactic. Despite being cheated out of his inheritance, Esau welcomes his returning brother with open arms.

Today's part two is known by the title "the Rape of Dinah," Jacob's daughter. Though the rape itself isn't described in much detail, the vengeful aftermath is, as Jacob's sons (Dinah's brothers) get deadly revenge on the rapist and the rapist's family. This violence gets no punishment from God, and only a few words of dismay from Jacob (34:30), which has puzzled scholars for centuries. Were Jacob's sons' actions justified (34:31)? Is God ok with taking vengeance of this kind? Here, we are not yet told.

Today's OT reading concludes with a happy occasion surrounded by a pair of tragedies: the birth of Benjamin (35:16-18) to Rachel, who dies in childbirth (35:19). After this (we're not told how long), Isaac dies (35:28-29) and is buried by Esau and Jacob.

January 28, NT
Luke 7:18-35, Matthew 11:2-19
A Message from John the Baptist

It is human nature to doubt the supernatural. After all, if we can't experience it using our senses, we can't prove it exists. Such was the case with the greatest Messianic prophet and preacher, prior to the arrival of Jesus, in the Bible: John the Baptist. Not only did John "pave the way" for Jesus' ministry, up to and including baptizing his own savior, but John's own arrival was foretold by prophecy (Malachi 3:1), and it was Jesus Himself who clarifies that in today's NT reading.

The rendering of this passage is nearly identical in both Luke and Matthew. Both accounts take place with John having been thrown in prison, though we're not told in either case how long he'd been there.

His request about whether or not Jesus was the One they were waiting for was an expression less of doubt and more of confusion. John needed clarification on whether or not Jesus was the promised Messiah or if another was to come. John may have thought that Jesus was the prophet foretold in Malachi, instead of himself. Jesus clarified this for not only John but also the crowds who witnessed this query.

John need not have worried. As you can read in today's passage, Jesus had very high regard for John. He concluded His speech in praise of John with a comparison between Himself and John designed to make people wonder why so many people couldn't see the connection between John and Himself.

January 29, OT
Genesis 37:1-38:30, I Chronicles 2:1-27, Genesis 39:1-23
Joseph and the Coat of Many Colors

We now turn our attention for the last 14 chapters of Genesis on primarily one of Israel's 12 sons: Joseph. Today's OT reading starts with the familiar story of young Joseph, beneficiary of his father's favoritism, who is sold into slavery by his furiously jealous brothers. His brothers, meanwhile, made this look as though Joseph had been killed by wild animals (Genesis 37).

As significant as Joseph is in salvation history, it isn't Joseph who is mentioned in the genealogies of Jesus in Luke and Matthew amongst Israel's sons, but *Judah*. Genesis 38, a significant one-chapter break in the narrative of Joseph, is the story of Judah's first two sons: Er and Onan, who were put to death by the Lord (38:7-10) for wickedness. The complex chain of events that follows results (among other things) in Judah's fathering of a son named Perez. Though born out of a combination of Tamar's treachery and Judah's weakness, *this illegitimate child was the next "heir" to the Messiah, Jesus.* We jump momentarily to I Chronicles to examine the Judaite bloodline through several generations to and through Perez. As before, reading genealogies can be a bit boring and difficult until one remembers how important family records were back then, and the fact that this particular family line eventually leads to Jesus. A good exercise for serious Bible study would be to diagram these genealogies as a family tree on paper or using genealogy software on a PC. There are websites where you can view these Biblical family trees, such as http://marshallgenealogy.org/bible/pafg01.htm.

The narrative then returns to Genesis as we read more about Joseph's rise and fall in Egyptian society up to and through his imprisonment.

January 29, NT
Matthew 11:20-30
Three Rebukes and a Prayer

Matthew's version of the reply to John the Baptist continues beyond what Luke recorded, as Jesus continues his speech to the crowd with a strong, frightening rebuke – a rebuke directed at three cities: Chorazin, Bethsaida, and Capernaum. We know of two of these cities as being the sites of some of Jesus' early miracles. Presumably, Chorazin is another such city, because His wrath is directed towards people who have not "repented long ago" after witnessing His "deeds of power" (Matthew 11:21). The scary part is when He compares the three cities to Sodom, the city destroyed in Genesis 19 along with Gomorrah, in one of God's most frightening displays of wrath.

Jesus then changes to a much gentler tone, presumably still in front of the crowd (though this isn't certain). Jesus says a prayer of thanks to His Father that, so far, the real truth about Him has not yet been revealed. It is a curious-sounding prayer until one realizes the point: Jesus is expecting people to commit to Him through faith, not simply by those things He has directly revealed to them using His powers. His prayer concludes with a great statement of comfort that has been used for numerous hymns and prayers written in the centuries since, summed up in the verse "…for my yoke is easy, and my burden is light." (11:30).

January 30, OT
Genesis 40:1-41:57
Joseph, the Dream Interpreter

In today's OT reading, Joseph uses his gift of dream interpretation (one of the things that got him sold into slavery in Egypt in the first place) to eventually get out of an Egyptian prison and reclaim his position in Egyptian society. Most importantly, his release is the result of an interpretation of a dream for Pharaoh that is also a prophecy of seven years of plenty and seven years of famine yet to come (41:25-32). His prophecies all came true (41:46-57), leading to the climax of Joseph's story.

January 30, NT
Luke 7:36-50
Jesus Forgives a Woman's Sins

Jesus had many encounters with the Pharisees, few of them pleasant. Yet, this encounter begins with Jesus accepting the invitation to have dinner with a Pharisee named Simon (not to be confused with Simon Peter or Simon the zealot, both Apostles). Jesus had also publicly forgiven the sins of other people prior to this incident, including some well-known incidents in front of Pharisees. What's different or special about this particular encounter?

Considering the reputation Jesus had with the Pharisees by now, it was highly unusual that He would be invited to the home of one. Jesus' acceptance of this invitation was not unexpected, however. In those days, most everyday tasks took place outdoors in close proximity to one's dwelling. This includes the simple act of having a meal. Thus, it wasn't unusual for someone "off the street" to observe another eating, and possibly join or attempt to join the meal. The repentant woman fills this role in today's NT reading.

The woman, who is never named, doesn't seem to have any connection with the Pharisee, Simon, except that Simon apparently knows that she is a sinner. That usually meant, in the culture of the time, that she was either a prostitute or some other kind of adulteress. The Pharisee doesn't comment on this—he only thinks it to himself. Jesus knows the thoughts of people, and answers the Pharisee's thoughts with a parable.

The parable, Simon's response, and Jesus' teaching afterwards make up one of the most important lessons in all of Jesus' teachings: the inseparable connection between forgiveness and love. The woman's act of complete humility and surrender to Jesus showed her repentance, and was the basis for Jesus' forgiveness. Jesus' forgiveness of the woman showed His great love for repentant sinners like her, even more so than His love for someone whose sins are less but are unrepentant of them. Years later, Paul would clarify this sometimes misconstrued teaching in his letter to the Romans to show that it isn't about the number or magnitude of one's sins that matter; rather, it's the depth of God's love for us when we repent.

January 31, OT
Genesis 42:1-44:34
Joseph Meets His Brothers

If you believe in divine providence the way I do, you then realize that there can be no such thing as coincidence in God's eyes. Such is the case with today's OT reading, in which 37-year-old (do the math) Joseph, managing the citizens of a foreign nation through a famine that he predicted would happen gets paid a visit from 10 of his 11 brothers whom he had not seen in 20 years.

You can imagine the mixed feelings Joseph had when he recognized his brothers upon arrival but they did not recognize him (42:7-8). With Joseph knowing that one younger brother remained at home and with the brothers unaware of Joseph's knowledge of the Hebrew language, Joseph's brothers inadvertently confessed their crime right in front of him (42:21-23). Rather than simply reveal his identity to them, he let the situation be used to accomplish the twin tasks of punishment *and* reconciliation. This combination of justice and mercy is a huge foreshadowing of Jesus.

January 31, NT
Luke 8:1-3, Matthew 12:22-37, Mark 3:20-30
The Unforgivable Sin

Women were an important part of Jesus' life and ministry, as shown in today's brief verses from Luke. This mention of Jesus' female followers is followed by the next encounter with the Pharisees. Matthew (with more detail) and Mark both describe an encounter that starts with another demon-oppressed person being relieved of the demon in front of a crowd of people. This time, the reaction of the Pharisees was to accuse Jesus of being in league with Beelzebul, the ruler of the demons. (This accusation appears again at a later time in Luke). Jesus responds that He could not be using "Satan to cast out Satan," among other things. The exchange gets particularly heated when He calls the Pharisees a "brood of vipers." This comes just after

His explanation of the only unforgivable sin: *speaking against the Holy Spirit*.

Jesus' tirade seems to contradict His own teachings, but only if it is taken out of context. Numerous passages in the Gospels and Paul's epistles point to the fact that God doesn't consider any sin worse than any other. God hates all sin; the only thing that matters is the repentance of the sinner. So what is Jesus getting at here with an "unforgivable" sin? Remember, He is talking to Pharisees. Pharisees look only at the strict "letter" of the law without regard to the "spirit" of the law. Jesus' rebuke of the Pharisees is a rebuke against the legalism that many people practice, even today. This passage is thought to be responsible for the old Roman Catholic concept (overturned in Vatican II) of sins being either "venial" or "mortal," the latter being the kinds of "eternal" sins (Mark 3:29) that would send someone to Hell even if confessed before a priest.

The Pharisees, as Jesus points out, are guilty of this eternal sin, not because of their words against the Son of Man, but because of their words against the Spirit.

February 1, OT
Genesis 45:1-46:9, 1 Chronicles 5:1-6
Joseph Brings the Family of Israel to Egypt

With the new month of Bible readings comes the dramatic, emotional climax (though not the conclusion) of the biography of Joseph. His elaborate back-and-forth ruse accomplished its purpose in punishing his brothers for what they had done to him 20 years earlier. Now it was time to show his brothers mercy, reunite the family and ride out the famine that had spread well beyond the borders of Egypt.

What follows at the end of today's OT reading is the first part of a detailed enumeration of the family of Israel. He did, after all, have 12 sons! Beginning here, we detail the family tree of Jacob/Israel with Jacob himself, and his firstborn son Reuben (46:8) and Reuben's children (46:9), which is echoed in the reading from I Chronicles 5.

February 1, NT
Matthew 12:38-50, Mark 3:31-35, Luke 8:19-21
The True Kindred of Jesus

Today's NT reading picks up where yesterday's left off, with Jesus' latest encounter with the Pharisees. In it, Jesus answers a question posed by a Pharisee asking to see a "sign". (Matthew 12:38) Jesus answers by repeating the statement that true believers live by faith and not by sight, and condemns those who need some kind of sign as hypocrites. He then prophesies His death and burial using the metaphor of "the sign of Jonah."

To this, Jesus adds a warning about what happens when a demon is driven from someone without safeguarding against the return of the demon *and seven others* (12:43-45). This was mainly for the Pharisee's benefit, but applies to everyone at any time who think they are doing themselves good by "going through the motions" of their religion, and perhaps even reforming themselves for a time, but winding up "worse than the first" because of their lack of real faith, real repentance.

At the conclusion of this encounter with the Pharisees, we have the only part of this event that appears in all three synoptic Gospels: the arrival of Jesus' mother and brothers. To this day, after extensive study of the Bible as well as study of the Catechism of the Roman Catholic Church, I cannot see how the RCC continues to stubbornly hold to the idea that Mary remained a virgin her entire life after giving birth to Jesus. The RCC maintains that Mary was *ever* virgin" and that the references in the Gospels to his "brothers" (and "sisters" in Matthew) refer to other relatives such as cousins. In one sense, it can be argued from the point of view that the word "adelphos," here translated as "brothers" or "brethren," is one of those several Greek words that can, like in English, have multiple meanings. "Brothers" can mean a biological brother or half-brother or can also mean any fellow man meaning other countrymen. But refuting this are two facts about Jesus' statement: one is that Jesus would not have spoken these words in Greek, but in Aramaic, where there is much less ambiguity regarding the word He would have used for "brother." Second, Jesus uses the words "mother" (all 3 Gospels) and "sister" (Matthew only) in the same statement. In both of the latter cases, there is no ambiguity, even in the Greek: the word "meter" in Greek can only mean biological mother, and the word "adelphe" can only mean biological sister (also note the similarities to the word "adelphos" earlier). Even though it is by way of fallible human reasoning that Protestants believe that Mary had to have had normal relations with her husband Joseph, this reasoning is backed up by Jesus' own words, even though He was trying to make a point that went *far* beyond his immediate nuclear family.

That point is, simply, that all who hear the word of God and act upon it are part of His family, and therefore have the right to be called His "brethren" or "sisters" or "mother". Notice the one metaphor He does *not* use in this instance, however: He makes no mention of "Father". But, the reasons for that should be obvious, when one considers who His Father is and how He is all of "Our Father."

February 2, OT
Genesis 46:10-12; 1 Chronicles 2:28-55
The Family of Israel: Simeon, Levi, and Judah

Our break from the narrative of Israel's (Jacob's) journey to Egypt to join Joseph continues with the family trees of Simeon, Levi and Judah. The account in Genesis is quite brief, whereas the family tree in Chronicles goes into much greater length and detail. Today's reading from the Chronicles is, in fact, focused solely on Judah, and it continues in tomorrow's OT reading as well. Yesterday, the family tree of Reuben was explored in chapter 5 of 1 Chronicles; today, we jump back to a point mid way through chapter 2 where we left off from January 29 having already explored part of the family tree of Judah.

Confused? Don't be. The Chronicler (Ezra?) wrote his account of the family tree of Israel hundreds of years after Moses (presumably) wrote the account in Genesis which is, in turn, some hundreds of years after these people actually lived, in many cases. The remarkable consistency, even after all these centuries, is something at which to marvel.

February 2, NT
Luke 8:4-18
The Parable of the Sower, version 1

The observant reader will notice that today's NT reading immediately *precedes* yesterday's passage from Luke; but, according to the chronology followed here, it is believed that Jesus told this parable some time shortly *after* the encounter with the Pharisees chronicled the past two days.

The parable of the sower is one of the few parables found in all three synoptic Gospels. In all three versions (one each over the course of the next 2 days), He also offers a detailed explanation of the parable (Luke 8:11-15) and then continues with another metaphor for evangelism: the lamp that should be placed where all can see it. Both metaphors serve the purpose of explaining not only how the Gospel will or should be spread, but the effect it will have on "anyone with ears to hear" (8:8). In some cases, this is then followed by some other parables that appear only in either Matthew or Mark.

February 3, OT
1 Chronicles 4:1-23; Genesis 46:13; 1 Chronicles 7:1-5
The Family of Israel: Judah and Issachar; The Prayer of Jabez

The family tree of Israel continues with a lengthy description of the descendants of Judah and then a small passage about Issachar. Remember, King David came from the Judah branch of the Israel family tree, and Jesus later was born into the same family.

In the midst of the genealogy is a curious verse that was adopted into a book that affirms what I consider to be a false doctrine. I Chronicles 4:10 is commonly called "The Prayer of Jabez," referring to a great-grandson of Judah who made a simple petition on the "God of Israel" that included enlarging his borders and keeping him from evil (or "harm" in some translations) and not cause pain. His prayer was granted. This obscure passage was ignored for centuries. None of the classic commentaries seem to notice it. Its "discovery" by Dr. Bruce Wilkinson has, unfortunately, been abused by those who hold the doctrine often called "name it and claim it" or the "prosperity gospel".

The prosperity gospel predates the popularity of Dr. Wilkinson's book by quite some time. I have a bookmark for my Bible that I received as a gift which has the prayer of Jabez inscribed on it. Certainly, Jabez's prayer is as sincere as it is bold, and the fact that God granted Jabez what he asked for means that we are *not* forbidden to make the same petitions. But although the prayer of Jabez didn't start the "name it and claim it" movement, it certainly stoked the flames of it. Sure, God loves us and wants the best for us. Sure, God is available any time you ask Him for a conversation; it's called *prayer*. But we must never forget that it was Jesus who later came to teach us how to pray, and one of the most important parts of any prayer is to remember that *God's* will is what counts, not ours. It is not our place to impose our will upon God. God hears all prayers and answers them, though His answer is sometimes "no."

February 3, NT
Mark 4:1-34
The Parable of the Sower, version 2

Mark's Gospel is noted for showing the fewest parables, and only one that *doesn't* appear in other Gospels. Nearly all of Mark's output of Jesus' parables is found in this one chapter that makes up today's reading.

Mark's version has Jesus telling the parable to a crowd and then explaining it in private to His disciples (Mark 4:1-20) just as it does in Luke. This is followed by a similar metaphor to Luke's version of the lamp parable, with Mark being more explicit about its undesirable placement under a "bushel basket." But where this is the point in which Luke's version ended, Mark's continues with the parables of the growing seed (4:26-29) and the well-known parable of the mustard seed (4:30-32). Luke does have the mustard seed parable, but in a separate incident at a much later date. Matthew's version is like Mark's in that the mustard seed parable follows the parable of the sower, but Matthew's version lacks the lamp parable.

February 4, OT
Genesis 46:14-18; 1 Chronicles 7:30-40; Genesis 46:19-25
The Family of Israel: Zebulun, Gad, Asher, Joseph, Benjamin, Dan, and Naphtali

Seven more of Israel's son's families are chronicled (pardon the pun) in today's OT reading as we continue the break in the narrative of the Hebrew's journey to Egypt to ride out the famine. Not only do we get more details from more family members, both in Genesis and in I Chronicles, but Genesis even provides an explanation as to the unusual order (so it seems) in which these family records are displayed. In several verses, the narrator pauses to point out that the sons of Israel are grouped according to their four different mothers. Thus, the first parts of these records were of those sons of Israel born to Leah, with whom Israel first had relations. Then came the sons born to Leah's handmaiden, Zilpah. Then, the sons born to Rachel (Joseph and Benjamin), and finally the sons born to Rachel's handmaiden Bilhah, even though these sons predate the sons born to Rachel.

Harmonizing the Chronicles with Genesis is almost impossible to do without dragging these genealogies out to a ridiculous length before getting back to the narrative. You will notice that some of Israel's family tree as written in I Chronicles is not yet read even after today or tomorrow's OT readings. This, however, is due to the role that some of Israel's grandsons would play in future events told in both Genesis and elsewhere.

February 4, NT
Matthew 13:1-53
The Parable of the Sower, version 3

The third and final version of the parable of the sower is read in Matthew today. Despite slightly different lengths (Matthew's being the longest), this parable is very close to identical in all three Gospels.

Its length, along with what follows it, is the reason for breaking it up into three separate days' NT readings.

Matthew has Jesus explaining the parable in private, just as Luke and Mark, but then has a parable found only in Matthew after that. The parable of the weeds among the wheat (Matthew 13:24-30) is also explained by Jesus (13:36-45) later, in private. Matthew also has the parable of the mustard seed (13:31-32) and four others that each comprises only a single verse (or two) apiece. All four of the brief parables begin with a line like "the kingdom of heaven is like…" Though brief enough to not be given names in most Bibles, one of them (13:45-46) is well known as the parable of the "pearl of great price."

If this chronology is correct, the final parable of this set is Jesus' first public warning about Hell in the afterlife (13:47-50) where the evil will be thrown into a "furnace of fire". It would not be His last.

February 5, OT
1 Chronicles 7:6-13; Genesis 46:26-47:12
The Family of Israel Arrives in Egypt

Today, we complete the genealogies of the immediate family of Jacob/Israel with the I Chronicles version of the family trees of Benjamin (Israel's youngest son) and Naphtali, and then bring the great migration to Egypt to a close in Genesis. Israel's reunion with Joseph in Egypt (Genesis 46:28-30) is nearly as emotional a scene as was Joseph's reunion with his brothers a short time earlier.

February 5, NT
Luke 8:22-39
The Storm at Sea and the Exorcism of Legion

Like the parable of the sower, the story of Jesus' miracle of calming the storm at sea and driving out the legion of demons from the man from Gerasene is told in all three synoptic Gospels – and just differently enough to warrant telling on three separate days. As was done for the parable of the sower, we begin with Luke's version.

All three versions tell the two stories in the same order with nearly the same details. Luke's version of the storm at sea is the briefest of the three, emphasizing the reaction of the disciples after first seeing the miracle and then being rebuked by the very Master who performed it.

Following this is the account of why they (Jesus and the disciples) were in the boat in the first place, as they were headed to the other side of the Sea of Galilee to a place called the Gerasenes (or Gadarenes or Gergesenes depending on translation). The name is a transliteration of the original Aramaic that is found in the various Greek manuscripts any of the three different ways. Luke details the fact that the demon-possessed man was naked and living in a graveyard (Luke 8:27). The man begs Jesus not to torment him but Jesus realizes that it is the demon, and not the man, that is speaking. Jesus confronts the demon by asking its name, to which it responds with the frightening name of Legion "for we are many" (8:30). Jesus responds to the demons' request to not be sent to the abyss by driving them out of the man and into a herd of pigs (8:32-33).

Obviously, the Gerasenes weren't Jewish, since they were swine herders. And how did they react to this exorcism? They were scared enough to tell Jesus and his disciples to leave (8:34-37), except for the healed man. He asked to go with Jesus, but He told the man to return and tell the others what He had done for him (8:38-39). This is a turning point in Jesus' earthly ministry, since Jesus mostly told people previously to *not* tell everyone about His miracles. Obviously, He saw something different in the reaction of the Gerasenes that told him that their faith, or lack thereof, was different.

February 6, OT
Genesis 47:13-50:26
From the Famine to the Last Days of Jacob and Joseph

Today's OT reading takes us from the point where Israel and his family settle in Egypt to the end of Genesis and the deaths of Israel, Joseph, and possibly others among Israel's sons. Except for genealogies in the Chronicles and references to them as being the beginning of the "tribes" of Israel, this is the last we hear, by name, of the 12 sons of Israel while they were alive.

The highlight of the reading is the string of events 17 years after Jacob/Israel's arrival in Egypt. Realizing he is near death (at the age of 147), Israel makes Joseph swear to bury him in his homeland

(47:29-31). (Joseph and his brothers later did just that (50:1-14).) Then, starting with Reuben, each son is brought before the dying Jacob in roughly age-order for final blessings, which in the cases of some sons became a curse. Reuben's blessing as firstborn is cursed due to an earlier sexual indiscretion (49:3-4). Simeon and Levi's messages are combined (49:5-7) and prophesies the eventual lack of a specific land for the tribe of Levi. Judah's blessing (49:8-12) becomes a Messianic prophecy. Zebulun gets a single verse (49:13) that explains his eventual position as leader of a people by the sea. Issachar's blessing (49:14-15) includes mention of becoming slaves at forced labor. Dan is prophesied to be a judge and a warrior (49:16-17). Gad, Asher, and Naphtali get a verse apiece (49:19-21), followed by Joseph's blessing (49:22-26) which is the longest overall, and is arguably the most positive though it doesn't seem to contain a Messianic prophecy in the same sense as Judah's. Benjamin's blessing (49:27) seems hardest to interpret until you realize that Saul, first king of Israel, comes from this tribe. You will understand this cryptic prophecy when you read about Saul in I Samuel (starting April 16).

The Bible's third longest book (behind Isaiah and Psalms) concludes after this with Joseph's formal spoken acquittal of his brothers (50:15-21) for the harm they intended to do to him, and finally Joseph's death at the age of 110 (50:24-26).

February 6, NT
Matthew 8:18, 23-34
The Storm at Sea and the Exorcism of Legion (version 2)

Matthew's version tells of these two events in the same manner as Luke's except for the interruption to note an encounter Jesus has with a scribe (note the missing verses starting with verse 19), which will be read in March. From there, the actual event is described along with the disciples' reaction and rebuke by Jesus about having little faith.

Then, just as in Luke, Jesus and the disciples cross the Sea of Galilee to a place spelled "Gadarenes" in Matthew's Gospel (though some manuscripts spell it the same as Luke's version). In Matthew's version of events, there are *two* demoniacs instead of one, and they don't speak as much with Jesus as the one mentioned by Luke. They don't identify themselves as "Legion," and in fact the story jumps ahead to the plea to be cast out to the nearby swineherd. From this point on, the event is identical except for no mention of the healed man asking Jesus if he could accompany them back across the Sea of Galilee.

February 7, OT
Exodus 1:1-4:17
Moses, From Birth to Burning Bush

With Genesis completed, we begin Exodus whose 40 chapters focus largely on a single person: Moses. Exodus is believed to have been written by Moses just as was Genesis, even though Moses is referred to in the third person throughout the book. Some scholars, especially Roman Catholics, doubt Moses' authorship of the book partly for this reason, but most everyone else believes it was Moses who wrote it, dismissing the "third person" claims as irrelevant (since most writers of that day did the same thing).

Today's OT reading covers a period from 350 years prior to Moses' birth up to approximately 80 years after, including the oppression of the Israelites in Egypt (Exodus 1:11-14), the slaughter of Hebrew boys under age 2 (1:16,22), Moses' birth and rescue (2:2-10), his deadly revenge on an Egyptian (2:11-12), and his escape to Midian (2:13-15) where he got married and had a son (2:16-22). It was at this place and time that Moses then has the famous (and important) encounter with God at the Burning Bush (3:2-4:17) that began Moses' time as the leader of the Israelites.

February 7, NT
Mark 4:35-5:20
The Storm at Sea and the Exorcism of Legion (version 3)

Mark's version of these two events more closely parallels Luke's than Matthew's, including the spelling of the name of the region (Gerasene), the fact that there was only a single demoniac, and the aftermath when the now-healed man asked to accompany Jesus and His disciples (to which Jesus declines). One minor difference is the additional detail Mark goes into regarding this final conversation.

Overall, though by a narrow margin, Mark's account of these two events is the longest of the three synoptic Gospels. Considering Mark's overall brevity, this is surprising until one realizes the different writing styles employed by each of the Gospel writers. Mark was consistent in his emphasis on the works and deeds of Jesus to show the almighty power of the Lord vs. expounding on the teachings or divinity of Christ.

February 8, OT
Exodus 4:18-6:27; 1 Chronicles 6:1-6:4a; Exodus 6:28-7:13
Moses and Aaron Confront Pharaoh

Today's OT reading takes us from the end of the commissioning of Moses by the Burning Bush up to just prior to the sending of the first plague. On the return journey to Egypt, Moses has a near-death experience at the hands of the Lord Himself! Exodus 4:24-26 is considered one of the most difficult passages in all of Exodus. My interpretation of this enigmatic event is the one of most common consensus: Moses was being punished for having not circumcised his son, but was then "let go" when his wife performed the circumcision for him.

After this we have Moses' reunion with Aaron and the first confrontation with Pharaoh. As expected (and foretold), the meeting doesn't go well and even appears to backfire against the Israelites. But, this leads to God's preparation of Moses and Aaron for the next confrontation.

A break in the narrative then appears to cover some genealogical ground. Exodus contains portions of the family trees of Rueben and Simeon, and then several generations of detail on the family tree of Levi to explain the fact that Moses and Aaron belong to that tribe. The passage from I Chronicles echoes that portion of the genealogy.

When the narrative resumes, Moses and Aaron go to Pharaoh for a second confrontation, but today's reading ends with Pharaoh's heart still hardened.

February 8, NT
Luke 8:40-48
One and a half Miracles

The odd title given to the passages that will be read over the next 3 days is because of how the account of one particular miracle (the raising of Jairus' daughter) is split on either side of another complete miracle, told in all three synoptic Gospels. Our exploration of this event begins, just as the last two events in this chronology, in Luke.

Luke's version begins immediately after the return of Jesus and his disciples from their trip to Gerasenes. Luke briefly details the encounter with Jairus falling at the feet of Jesus and begging Him to come heal his daughter, age 12. Minor differences between this version and the other two will be examined over the next 2 days. All three Gospels have Jesus agreeing to go to the house of Jairus and having to go through a crowd of people along the way, but in all three cases, this is interrupted by another miracle: the healing of the woman with a bleeding problem. Luke's version has the woman touching Jesus' clothes, being healed immediately, and Jesus asking, "who touched me?" After denials, Peter tries to explain what happened but Jesus knows better, as He states that He felt the "power gone out from Me." The now-healed woman admits to Jesus what happened, and Jesus assures her that it was her faith that healed her.

February 9, OT
Exodus 7:14-9:35
The First Seven Plagues

Moses and Aaron needed to convince a hostile pharaoh to let the Israelites (his main source of cheap labor) leave Egypt. Pharaoh stubbornly refused to grant this wish, and the Israelites suffered even more because of it. Moses and Aaron needed something to convince both Pharaoh and their fellow Israelites of their authority and God's superiority in freeing the Israelites. God provided this in the form of ten plagues, the first seven of which are described here in today's OT reading.

Each plague follows a similar formula: Moses and Aaron repeat their appeal to Pharaoh, in some cases pointing out a previous plague. Pharaoh refuses and the plague is brought on. The plagues affected the Egyptians with increasingly severity while affecting the Israelites little if at all. In some of the cases, Pharaoh appeared to partially soften his stance and grant part of what Moses and Aaron wished, but always returned to his stubborn heart-hardened position in the end.

The seven plagues of today's reading are, in this order, turning the Nile to blood (7:14-25), frogs (8:1-15), gnats (8:16-19), flies (8:20-32), deadly pestilence in their livestock (9:1-7), boils (9:8-12), and thunderstorms with hail (9:13-35). Each one increased in severity over its predecessor, and there were still three left to come.

February 9, NT
Matthew 9:1,18-22
One and a half Miracles, version 2

Matthew's Gospel contains a similar, though not identical, account of the miracle split on either side of another complete miracle, thus the title "One and a half Miracles".

In Matthew's version, Jairus is not named but does actually get quoted (unlike Luke who only summarized what he said). Jairus tells Jesus that his daughter has actually died, but will live if Jesus touches her (Luke's version said she was dying, not dead). As in Luke's version, Jesus' trip to do this healing is interrupted by the encounter with the woman with the bleeding problem.

In this version, though, Jesus turns around immediately after being touched, instead of asking, "who touched me". The Matthew account doesn't contradict the Luke account if you take Matthew's version as simply going into a great deal less detail than Luke's. The account ends as the other versions: with Jesus telling the now-healed woman that it was her faith that made her well.

February 10, OT
Exodus 10:1-12:51
The Passover

Today's OT reading tells of the most important event in Jewish history, "The Passover." After the eighth and ninth plagues, locusts (Exodus 10:1-20) and darkness (10:21-29), God certainly got Pharaoh's attention, but Pharaoh's heart was still hardened. It would take a frightening, colossal, and deadly tenth plague to finally turn things around. That tenth plague was the death of all firstborn.

In order for the Israelites to come out of this plague unharmed and be able to use this as their "ticket out," Moses passed along God's detailed instructions to prepare for the plague: they were to take an unblemished lamb, slaughter it and have a meal of freshly roasted lamb, unleavened bread, and bitter herbs (12:3-10). Most importantly, they were to smear the doorposts with the blood of the lamb (12:7) so that when God saw it, He would then "pass over" that house (12:13). It served its purpose; Pharaoh finally relented and granted the Israelites their departure.

Thus did the people of Israel spend their last night of their 430-year stay in Egypt. They left in haste, with the help of many of the Egyptians themselves, 600,000-plus along with their belongings, to begin their journey to the Promised Land (12:33-42).

February 10, NT
Mark 5:21-34
One and a half Miracles, version 3

In spite of the fact that Mark's Gospel is the shortest of the three synoptic Gospels, Mark's account of the "one and a half Miracles" is nearly as detailed as Luke's.

Mark's version of events surrounding Jairus combines elements of Luke and Matthew: Jairus is named here, like Luke, but speaks, like Matthew, and states that his daughter is "at the point of death," which is closer to Luke's version. Jesus agrees to go to Jairus' home, but is interrupted along the way by the woman with the bleeding problem.

After this, Mark's version reads almost identical to Luke's. Given the belief that Mark's Gospel was written first and that Matthew and Luke may have drawn parts of their works from Mark, the differences seem to make sense between the three synoptic Gospels. One curiosity is that it is also believed that Mark got most of his information from Peter, but the only Gospel writer to mention Peter in this series of events is Luke, not Mark. Given the issue of medicine, where physicians are mentioned especially in Mark's version, and the fact that Luke was a physician, it's entirely possible that Luke was an eyewitness to this event.

February 11, OT
Exodus 13:1-15:27
Escape from Egypt

Today's OT reading chronicles the first days of the Israelites' exodus from Egypt, a journey that would eventually take 40 years. Joseph and his brothers had earlier made essentially the same trip in only a few weeks in order to fulfill their father Jacob's wish to be buried there. The escaping Israelites were a much larger group, which would have made the going much slower, but even then it should have taken less than one year for the entire population to make this exodus. So why did it take so long? There are multiple answers, and we get only one of them in today's reading: they were led the long way around the land of the Philistines in order to avoid war before being properly prepared (Exodus 13:17-22).

The first major obstacle in their journey is chronicled in Exodus 14, as we read of the Egyptian army's pursuit of the Israelites (14:1-9), the parting of the Red Sea that allowed them to escape (14:10-22), and the defeat of the Egyptian army when the waters of the Red Sea were closed back in upon them (14:23-31).

Exodus 15 is dominated by two songs sung in celebration of this escape (15:1-21), but their joy didn't last long as they had to overcome another obstacle (lack of water except for a source that was poisoned, 15:22-27).

February 11, NT
Luke 8:49-56; Mark 5:35-43; Matthew 9:23-26
"Little Girl, Get Up"

The miracle of the raising of Jairus' daughter is the event immediately following the healing of the woman with the bleeding disease in all three synoptic Gospels. The accounts are brief and similar enough to combine them into a single day's reading instead of spreading them out over three days.

All three of these Gospels have this miracle split on either side of the healing of the woman. The first part (thus the name "one and a half miracles…") is the request, by Jairus, to come heal his daughter. In Matthew's version, Jairus tells Jesus that his daughter has died. In Luke and Mark's versions of the actual miracle, news reaches Jesus that she has died and that He shouldn't be troubled any longer. In all three cases, Jesus dismisses this by telling them that the girl is not dead, but is asleep.

This statement is laughed at in all three accounts, but this is followed by the proof that the girl is, indeed, alive. Jesus then tells someone to get something for the girl to eat. Like several of His early miracles, he commands the witnesses to not tell anyone else about what had happened, but in Matthew's version we know that this is exactly what happened: Jesus' reputation grew even further after this latest miraculous healing.

February 12, OT
Exodus 16:1-18:27
Quails, Manna, War, and Advice from In-laws

A lot of information is packed into the three chapters of today's OT reading. The reading is fairly long, but the commentary is brief. Moving 600,000 people on foot with all their possessions was a monumental undertaking, with many obstacles including lack of readily available sources of water and food. In the case of the latter, God provided quails and later a strange bread-like substance for them in response to their complaints (Exodus 16:1-15). Not knowing what the substance was, they asked, "what is it?" (Hebrew "man hu", transliterated "manna" in English), and the name stuck.

Despite taking the very long way around to avoid war with the Philistines, war was not avoided altogether (17:8-16). Moses' need of some assistance in winning this brief war became important in the final segment of today's OT reading, as Jethro, Moses' father-in-law, met up with Moses and advised him on delegating some of his duties; advice which Moses wisely took up (18:1-27). The best leaders aren't necessarily the ones who actually *do the most* - the best leaders are those that *get the most done*…whether it is by their hands or those that they lead. Moses became proof of this wise adage.

February 12, NT
Matthew 9:27-34; Mark 6:1-6; Matthew 13:54-58
Jesus is Rejected at Nazareth

Today's NT reading begins with a pair of miracles found only in Matthew: the healing of the two blind men (Matthew 9:27-31) and the mute demoniac (9:32-34), which brings on yet another accusation of using the ruler of demons to cast out demons by Pharisees.

The last time we know of Jesus being in Nazareth was when he "announced" His ministry in a synagogue and was virtually run out of town (Luke 4:14-30, read January 7). We don't know how much time elapsed between then and the events described in today's reading from

Mark (and again in Matthew with nearly identical wording), but it is speculated that this "rejection" occurred about a year after the earlier event, making this the beginning, roughly, of His second year of active ministry on earth.

Just like the events we read about on February 1 ("The True Kindred of Jesus"), this reading is a strong case against the Roman Catholic notion that Mary remained a virgin her entire life. In both the Mark and Matthew accounts, the people of Nazareth marvel at Jesus' preaching by bringing up the other members of His family: His mother Mary and His brothers, James, Joseph, Simon, and Judas. An online Catholic encyclopedia tries to show that Mary in this passage is Mary, the wife of Cleophas and sister to Mary, the mother of Jesus (thus, Jesus' aunt), but there is no scriptural evidence to support this. Though I do not doubt the virgin birth in the least, and furthermore do not doubt the existence of Mary wife of Cleophas, there is no evidence that this was not Mary, the mother of Jesus. After all, Jesus is referred to here as the "carpenter's son" (Matthew's version), and the people of Nazareth would have known about His family background.

February 13, OT
Exodus 19:1-20:21
The Ten Commandments

In the hilarious Mel Brooks movie "History of the World (Part One)," Moses (played by Brooks) descends Mount Sinai with *three* tablets and announces "the Lord has given you these *fifteen*..." but is interrupted from saying "commandments" as one of the tablets falls to the ground and breaks. Almost not missing a beat, Moses continues with "Oy... Ten! Ten Commandments...for all to obey!" The Bible, of course, gives us the one true account of the receipt of God's Law in today's OT reading.

Few passages from the Bible are held simultaneously in such high reverence and in widespread ridicule like the passage we now call the Ten Commandments. This ten-point summary of all of God's Law, which is not numerated in the Bible itself (neither here nor in Deuteronomy 5), is quoted extensively by Jesus and by the Apostles. When Jesus refers to Himself as the fulfillment of the Law, it is presumed to be mainly these ten to which Jesus is referring. The Ten

Commandments are also the focal point of numerous "separation of Church and state" controversies today (ironic since these laws are revered by both Jews and Christians). Their importance cannot be emphasized enough.

The commandments themselves are given in what modern Bibles divide into 17 verses in chapter 20. The reason for the difference in numbering of the commandments by Catholics and Lutherans vs. most of the rest of the Christian world is due to the ways in which the verses are combined. A brief numeration with verse numbers looks like this: (shading indicates equivalent commandments)

	Catholics and Lutherans	Other Christians
I	20:1-6 "I am the Lord your God; You shall have no other Gods before Me" (no mention of the prohibition of graven images)	20:1-3 "I am the Lord your God; You shall have no other Gods before Me"
II	20:7 "You shall not take the name of the Lord in vain"	20:4-6 "You shall not have any idols or graven images before Me"
III	20:8-11 "Remember to keep holy the Sabbath day"	20:7 "You shall not take the name of the Lord in vain"
IV	20:12 "Honor your father and your mother"	20:8-11 "Remember to keep holy the Sabbath day"
V	20:13 "You shall not murder" (or "kill" depending on translation)	20:12 "Honor your father and your mother"
VI	20:14 "You shall not commit adultery"	20:13 "You shall not murder" (or "kill" depending on translation)
VII	20:15 "You shall not steal"	20:14 "You shall not commit adultery"
VIII	20:16 "You shall not bear false witness (lie) against your neighbor"	20:15 "You shall not steal"
IX	20:17a "You shall not covet your neighbor's possessions"	20:16 "You shall not bear false witness (lie) against your neighbor"
X	20:17b "You shall not covet your neighbor's wife"	20:17 "You shall not covet anything that is your neighbor's"

The Ten Commandments would not be the only law given to Moses and the Israelites, however. The only reason this list stops at ten is because of the natural break at the end of the command to not covet and the historical narrative which bridges the gap between the Ten Commandments and the rest of the law which follows (20:18-21).

The commandment regarding not "murdering" is controversial because of the Hebrew word "ratasch" which can mean either "murder," "assassinate," or simply "kill." If the intended meaning were the more generic "kill," then all forms of killing would be condemned by this command, including killing in time of war and capital punishment. Most people's objections to capital punishment are based on this verse. As I previously mentioned, I lean towards being in support of it because of my belief that "ratasch" means "murder." This is based on the fact that there are (that I know of) at least five different Hebrew words translated as "kill" in the Old Testament, and "ratasch" is one of two that mention murder whereas the other three do not. I also hold this belief because of the numerous times in which Israelites were told by God to kill in times of war.

February 13, NT
Matthew 9:35-38; 10:5-15
The Evangelization of the Lost Sheep of Israel

Today's NT lesson is the first of two parts, the most detailed of which is found in Matthew. By this time, Jesus had gathered all 12 men that would be called Apostles. He had been on multiple speaking tours of Galilee and surrounding regions. He had preached to crowds in the thousands and had healed dozens of people. He performed a resurrection miracle and made a return visit to His hometown, only to find so much unbelief that He couldn't (or wouldn't) perform many miracles. In Matthew's version of what follows, Jesus left Nazareth and went to other villages in the area, preaching and healing - and coming to an important realization: in His human form, He would never be able to reach all of these "lost sheep" by himself. It was time to get His Apostles into action. It was time to send "laborers into His harvest."

And so, Jesus sends forth His Apostles to spread the Good News, heal the sick, cleanse the lepers, raise the dead, and cast out demons, all of which are things He had done before but had not yet been done by the Apostles. This delegation of authority would become the model for

Christian ministries centuries later. Jesus provided the Apostles with explicit, detailed instructions for going about with this evangelism, including that it is done solely (for now) to the Jews. It is from this passage that we also get the quote regarding shaking off the dust from one's feet after being rejected in these evangelistic efforts. Jesus' instruction here comes with a stern warning: that it would be worse for the rejecters than for those in Sodom and Gomorrah.

February 14, OT
Exodus 20:22-24:18
Social, Religious, and Property Laws

The Ten Commandments are a summary of the laws that God expanded upon in the remaining chapters of the books of Moses. Except for a few passages here and there, the next six weeks' worth of OT readings will contain very little historical narrative. Instead, we get a detailed description of the laws that are still regarded as the supreme regulations by Orthodox Jews. They are known by the name "Torah," the Law of Moses.

They are also one of the two major issues that define the theological conflict between Jews and Christians right up to the present day (the other being the fact that Jesus is the Messiah). Few doubt the applicability of the Ten Commandments, but few of the other laws are taken as seriously. Admittedly, there are quite a few laws and regulations after the Ten that are only ceremonial laws designed for Temple worship, but even those have applicability as a framework for modern worship ("liturgy"). Other laws are more controversial, and are frequently used by those who set out to discredit the Bible.

The first law after the Ten is actually an expansion of the first Commandment (Exodus 20:22-26) regarding the altar used in worship. The next, the law regarding slaves (21:1-11), has caused problems for believers for years. Does the fact that God gave laws regarding the ethical treatment of slaves mean that God endorses slavery? No. God simply recognized the fact that slavery did exist, and set out to make the Israelite form of it clearly distinct from the oppressive Egyptian form. Careful reading of these regulations almost changes the meaning of the word "slave" here to "employees."

The laws concerning violence (21:12-27) make a strong case in favor of capital punishment. But, although not struck completely down by Jesus centuries later, He did clarify when such laws could and could not be enforced. The "property" laws that follow (21:28-22:15) mostly concern restitution in various agricultural situations, but lawmakers would do well to make punishments fit their crimes by modeling laws after these. The miscellaneous laws after these include a few well-known gems, such as the death penalty for witches (22:18) and for bestiality (22:19), not charging interest from the poor (22:25-26) and the consecration of the firstborn to God (22:29b-30).

After a few more laws about judicial matters (23:1-9), we read the laws regarding the sabbatical year and three of the annual festivals (23:10-19, expanded upon later in Leviticus) followed by a reiteration of The Covenant given to Abraham, Isaac, and Jacob years earlier (23:20-33) with the first hint that the people there would have to be driven out ahead of the Israelites.

The only part of today's OT reading containing any real history is Exodus 24, where Moses is given instructions to receive these (and other) laws on the mountain where he had just received the Ten Commandments after making an animal sacrifice that formally set Israel apart as the people of God in a "covenant of blood."

February 14, NT
Mark 6:7-13; Luke 9:1-6; Matthew 10:16-11:1
"Be Not Afraid, I Go Before You Always"

Though today's NT reading is a continuation of yesterday's reading, it warrants the title above that many will recognize as the lyrics to a popular hymn. The passages from Mark and Luke echo the account given in yesterday's reading from Matthew 10, where Jesus delegates a great portion of His ministry to His Apostles. Then, in today's continuation from Matthew 10, we have the basis for the song lyric quoted here.

> You shall cross the barren desert, but you shall not die of thirst.
> You shall wander far in safety though you do not know the way.
> You shall speak your words in foreign lands and all will understand.

> You shall see the face of God and live.
>
> Be not afraid. I go before you always.
> Come follow me, and I will give you rest.
>
> If you pass through raging waters in the sea, you shall not drown.
> If you walk amid the burning flames, you shall not be harmed.
> If you stand before the pow'r of hell and death is at your side,
> know that I am with you through it all.

The songwriter (listed variously as Bob Dufford, SJ or John Michael Talbot) obviously had today's Matthew reading in mind when writing it. (A third verse draws on the Beatitudes.) The reading explains very clearly that the road of true discipleship will not be easy (Matthew 10:16-25), but it is absolutely worth every hardship (10:40-42).

In between is a pair of theological gems. The first is the often quoted verse about those who can "kill the body but cannot kill the soul" (10:28). The other should be required reading for all those who are afraid to speak out in defense of their faith for fear of "offending someone." The verse is Matthew 10:34, some of the harshest-sounding words to ever come out of Jesus' mouth. Jesus clearly states that the Apostles (whom He is addressing at this point) are not to think that Jesus' message is to bring peace. Much as it would be wonderful if all countries could lay down their differences and their arms and put a permanent end to all war, this is just not possible in a fallen, sin-cursed world. Jesus didn't come to bring peace, but "the sword". That doesn't mean "war is good" or some other over-reactionary nonsense. But what it does mean is that all the secular humanists who believe that "inclusion" is the highest virtue and that anything that infringes on this is the greatest sin (or at least "politically incorrect") is simply not paying attention to what Jesus said. Verses 35-39 confirms this and should be a clear warning to those who would compromise the Truth merely for the sake of not offending someone, or worse yet, because of some misguided "separation of church and state" issue.

February 15, OT
Exodus 25:1-27:21
Ceremonial Laws, part one

The three chapters in today's OT reading comprise a detailed set of laws regarding the manner and form of worship, the highlight being the exact specifications of an item that today is one of the most sought-after archeological treasures of the ancient Middle East: the Ark of the Covenant (Exodus 25:10-22). Despite the elaborate nature of the construction of the tabernacle, all of it was to be built for portability, as the Israelites were still in the early part of their desert journey.

One part of note regarding the tabernacle furnishings: the thick curtain that separates the most holy place from the rest of the tabernacle is the curtain that symbolically separated God and man, which was torn from top to bottom when Jesus died, thus also symbolizing the reconciliation that occurred at that moment.

February 15, NT
Matthew 14:1-12; Mark 6:14-29; Luke 9:7-9
The Death of John the Baptist

This is the only event told entirely in flashback form in the New Testament. Each account (Mark's being the most detailed) speaks of how John had already been beheaded by the time Herod started noticing Jesus and His disciples.

In the last two days' readings, Jesus gave detailed instructions to the Apostles for carrying out His ministry. If word of Jesus' activities hadn't reached Herod before, it certainly did now! Instead of just two men (Jesus and John) to deal with, Herod now had 13. It would have been 14, but John had already been executed in prison. The issue was prompted by the fact that the Apostles were preaching largely the same message as John, which led some to believe that John had risen from the dead. He hadn't, of course, but that didn't help ease the fears of the Roman elite. And thus it is told of the past (but presumably recent) imprisonment and execution of John.

We knew from a previous reading (January 28) that John had been in prison and that Jesus was aware of it. What we don't know is how long prior to the events that got Herod's attention was the execution of John or the events immediately leading up to it.

February 16, OT
Exodus 28:1-29:46
Ceremonial Laws, part two

Today's two chapters are actually longer than yesterday's three. The reading continues the detailed set of ceremonial (worship) laws, concentrating today on the vestments (clothes) that were to be worn by the priest (worship leader) and the ceremony that would be followed when ordaining these priests.

February 16, NT
John 6:1-15; Luke 9:10-17
Five Loaves + Two Fish = Lunch for Five Thousand

There are some that believe that this miracle, the only one told in all four Gospels, took place immediately after the Sermon on the Mount. John and Luke's versions, which we read today, seem to bear that out, but Mark's version (tomorrow) and Matthew's version (the next day) prove otherwise.

John's Gospel contains the fewest miracles of any of the Gospels, but the ones he included are doubtless the most spectacular. Jesus' first miracle is recorded only here (water into wine at Cana), as is the raising of Lazarus (read on March 31). Most of the miracles depicted in John appear only in John; this is one of the few exceptions. All four accounts of this miracle are very similar but for a few minor details. John is the only one to make mention of the fact that the Passover was drawing near. Also, John records a conversation with Philip that isn't recorded anywhere else (John 6:5-7).

Luke's version of events starts by stating the city near which the miracle took place (Bethsaida) and speaks of not only a speech/sermon by Jesus but also some healings (Luke 9:10-11). Luke not only doesn't mention the conversation with Philip, but also doesn't give any detail regarding the boy who first provided the five loaves and two fishes. Luke does mention, however, Jesus' command to have the crowd sit in groups of "about 50," which John does not mention.

Both Gospel writers mention the twelve baskets of leftovers after the amazing miracle.

February 17, OT
Exodus 30:1-33:6
Yom Kippur and the Golden Calf

Near the end of the detailed specs for tabernacle, furnishings, and vestments for worship is a detailed specification for the altar on which to offer incense. As part of this, God outlines an annual rite to be performed by Aaron (later, his descendants) called the "rite of atonement" (Exodus 30:10). Thus, the "day of atonement," celebrated to this day by Orthodox Jews, is instituted, called by its Hebrew name, "Yom Kippur."

The historical narrative resumes after nearly 12 chapters of laws and regulations near the end of chapter 31, when Moses was given the stone tablets containing, it is believed, the Ten Commandments (31:18), written by God's own finger. God obviously did not write the entire law He had given to Moses on these tablets; they simply would not have fit. The tablets are called "the two tablets of the covenant," presumably meaning that they are meant to be placed in the yet-to-be-built ark of the covenant, whose specifications were also part of the law given to Moses.

But Moses' descent of the mountain to the waiting Israelites revealed that they weren't waiting patiently. They had grown impatient during Moses' time on Mount Sinai and had made an idol of gold in the form of the Egyptian bull-god Apis, better known as "the golden calf," and they were worshipping it. After preventing God from emptying His wrath on them (32:7-14), Moses vented some anger of his own by smashing the stone tablets (32:19), grinding the golden calf to powder (32:20), and assembling a Levite group to carry out the death penalty for this sin on about 3000 of the Israelites (32:26-29). After all this, the "stiff-necked" Israelites were ordered to leave Sinai and resume their journey to the Promised Land (33:1-6), with God *initially* saying that He would *not* accompany them.

February 17, NT
Mark 6:30-52
Feeding Five Thousand, Walking On Water

Three of the four Gospel writers follow their account of the miracle of feeding 5000 people immediately with another spectacular miracle: Jesus walking on water. Whereas the feeding of the 5000 miracle differs only in minor detail from one Gospel to the other, there are some rather significant differences in the way Matthew, John, and (today) Mark handle this event.

First, though, is Mark's account of the feeding, which seems to combine elements of Luke's and John's versions. Like John, Mark does not mention the name of the city they were near, but like Luke does not mention the conversation with Phillip either. Also like Luke, Mark doesn't mention getting the five loaves and two fishes from a boy in the crowd, but does indicate that Jesus told the crowd to sit in groups; this time, though, it is groups of 50 *or 100* (where Luke only specified "50"). This is followed by the first of the three accounts we will read of Jesus walking on water to the boat on which the Apostles were after the great miracle of the feeding.

February 18, OT
Exodus 33:7-36:7
The Renewal of The Covenant

Following the dramatic and violent events of Exodus 32, the Israelites resume their journey to the Promised Land, even though God warned that He would not be with them. Today's OT reading starts with Moses' intercession on behalf of the sinful Israelites. God agrees to be with His people, and tells Moses to cut two new tablets on which He will re-write the law (Exodus 33:12-34:1), and then formally renews The Covenant (34:10-11) with Moses and the Israelites. Several of the Commandments and other laws are then repeated to Moses, and he then returns from the mountain with his face brightly shining (34:29-35) because he had been speaking with God.

Moses then assembles the people and passes along some of the laws regarding the Sabbath and the tabernacle, and they all prepare for building it. Moses even passes along God's call to two special craftsmen, Bezalel (of the tribe of Judah) and Oholiab (of the tribe of Dan) whom God had chosen for the making of the tabernacle.

February 18, NT
John 6:16-21; Matthew 14:13-33
Feeding Five Thousand, Walking On Water

The last two days have seen John's, Mark's, and Luke's versions of the miracle of the feeding of the five thousand; today we get Matthew version. Yesterday we got Mark's version of the miracle of Jesus walking on water; today we start with John's version (almost identical to Mark's) and then Matthew's.

Matthew's version of the feeding miracle is almost word-for-word identical to Mark's. The only reason for separating it from yesterday's NT reading, besides allowing John's version to be read, is what follows immediately thereafter. Matthew's account of the walking on water starts out very much like Mark's and John's until verse 28. In only Matthew's version, Peter replies to Jesus while Jesus is still walking on the water, and asks Jesus to command him to walk out there himself. Jesus does this and Peter walks out towards Him but begins to sink when he "noticed the strong wind" (Matthew 14:30). Jesus' rebuke in verse 31 is therefore directed at Peter rather than the whole group as in other versions.

In 2005, I was given the immense privilege of being a "substitute Pastor" for a Sunday at worship. I was the co-director of music at a Lutheran church at the time, and the Pastor was out of town at a conference. I had done two sermons previously as a guest preacher but was never actually in charge of an entire worship service from beginning to end, and never on a Sunday (my previous experience was with "Summer Saturdays" and Wednesday night services). On the Sunday in question, the Gospel reading was Matthew 14:22-33 (Matthew's account of the "walking on water" miracle). The Epistle was Romans 10:8-13, which some will recognize as the tail end of the "Romans Road," a string of verses often used for witnessing (which will be read in this chronology on September 12). I called my sermon "Salvation 101" and keyed in on Romans 10:13 which repeats the statement that all who "call on the name of the Lord will be saved." This is, of course, exactly what Peter did in today's NT reading from Matthew.

February 19, OT
Exodus 36:8-38:31
Making the Tabernacle and the Ark of the Covenant

Moses received all the instructions the Israelites would need for the construction of the Tabernacle (Exodus 36:8-38) and the Ark (37:1-9). Today's OT reading chronicles this construction, on which a large portion of the traveling Israelite population participated. A detailed reading of the rest of chapters 37 and 38 show an Israelite enthusiasm for this task that is matched only by their very careful attention to detail, constructing the two objects and the tabernacle furnishings exactly according to the specs laid down by God.

February 19, NT
Matthew 14:34-36; Mark 6:53-56; John 6:22-40
The Bread of Life, Part One

Just as on February 14, today's NT reading contains a passage that has been used in a well-known hymn (John 6:35). The reading starts with two brief accounts of the immediate aftermath of the miracle of Jesus' walking on water. Matthew and Mark each chronicle the visit to Gennesaret (not to be confused with Gerasene, about which we read on February 5-7), where it is obvious that Jesus' reputation preceded him. In both versions, numerous people who had apparently witnessed His previous healing miracles flocked to Him to have their own ailments cured.

Neither Luke nor John described the visit to Gennesaret, but John apparently does describe the event that immediately follows. Recall that the previous day, Jesus had miraculously fed 5000 people with five loaves and two fishes. Then the disciples left by boat followed by Jesus sometime during the night (another miracle). Though John doesn't chronicle the events in Gennesaret, he does describe the events back on the other side of the Sea of Galilee (John 6:22-24). The people who witnessed the feeding miracle chase Him down in Capernaum (which must be fairly close to Gennesaret). Once they catch up, expecting more miracles, Jesus gives them a very important sermon that we read over the course of two days.

Jesus and the crowd start with a dialog in which Jesus acknowledges their earlier presence at the feeding miracle (6:26) and uses it as a metaphor for the food that "endures unto everlasting life" (6:27). The crowd doesn't understand Jesus' divinity and asks first what God is asking of them, and then what sign Jesus would give so that they would believe by pointing out Moses' role in providing the "manna" from heaven. Jesus responds that the bread "that gives life" was given to them by the Father, not Moses, to which the crowd asks to be given "this bread always." (6:28-34)

What follows is the first of a two-part message (today and tomorrow) that is commonly called the "Bread of Life" discourse. The first part, read today (6:35-40) is pretty straightforward to the Christians of today, using the metaphor of bread to describe both the divinity of Jesus and the necessity of taking in this bread. But, the Jewish crowd still doesn't get it, and what Jesus uses for words to explain the metaphor make for one of the most controversial passages in the entire set of Gospels, in tomorrow's NT reading.

February 20, OT
Exodus 39:1-40:38
The Glory of the Lord Fills the Tabernacle

Today's OT reading brings the book of Exodus to a close. After making the Ark of the Covenant and the materials and equipment for the tabernacle, the vestments for the priests are made (Exodus 39:1-31), exactly (again) according to God's specifications. With all the preparatory work completed, the tabernacle was erected and all of its equipment installed (39:32-40:33), and the real completion then came in the form of God filling the tabernacle with His glory (40:34). Whenever this cloud of glory covered the tent, the Israelites would stay put; when the cloud was lifted, they would resume their journey to the Promised Land.

February 20, NT
John 6:41-7:1; Mark 7:1-23
The Bread of Life, Part Two

Proof that the Jewish crowds didn't "get it" when it came to Jesus' message of His own divinity comes when they complain that they know His mother and father (John 6:42) *Joseph*, and object to His statement of coming down from heaven. From there, it only gets more intense.

Jesus responds to their grumbling first with one of the founding verses of the doctrine of election (6:44), then a quote from Isaiah about being "taught of the Lord" (6:45), and then an explanation and contrast of His "bread of life" from heaven with the manna from heaven eaten by their now-dead ancestors (6:48-51). When the Jews object further, Jesus responds with a statement that is still used by the Roman Catholic Church to justify their doctrine of Transubstantiation (6:53-58). (My take on this is that Jesus was speaking metaphorically, predicting His own death and the necessity of believing in it as the atonement for sins, and thus justifying the doctrine of the Lord's Supper, not Transubstantiation, long before He instituted the practice.)

The doctrine of election may not be as much of a stumbling block as Transubstantiation, but it is still controversial. The idea that only those who are "drawn" to the Father can see Him seems to fly in the face of statements that also indicate that God loves everyone in the world, not just some select group. Understanding at least that much of the controversy, some disciples question Jesus further after the "bread of life" discourse (6:59-65) and Jesus explains further. This causes some who were following him to leave (6:66). The disciples don't, however, and Peter sums up their faith in Jesus and His divinity with the well-known statement: "Lord, to whom shall we go? You have the words of eternal life." (6:68)

It is not known how much of a gap there was, if any, between the "bread of life" discourse and the next encounter with the Pharisees told in Mark chapter 7, but the similarity of theme seems to indicate that the gap was short. Jesus and the Pharisees butt heads over issues of traditions of men vs. the real law (Mark 7:1-13), and the inability for things *outside* of someone to defile ("make unclean") him (7:14-23), thus clarifying a huge amount of the Torah for people in New Testament times.

February 21, OT
Leviticus 1:1-4:35
Sacrifices

The next 10 days' OT readings are in a book with almost no historical narrative. It's considered one of the Bible's most difficult books to read and comprehend. A Catholic attending Mass daily in addition to

Sundays would hear from this book an average of only twice per year, never on Sundays, and briefly at that. The book doesn't appear at all for Sunday readings in the Evangelical Lutheran Church in America. Many people who attempt a complete read-through of the Bible get bogged down here and give up. Why all the negatives?

The simple answer is that Leviticus, more so than any other book of the entire Bible, is a rule book. Some of it is just a continuation of the law handed down to Moses as has already been read in Exodus. These laws are more detailed and more complex, though. Scholars have debated for centuries whether any of it really has any meaning to Christians. There are many ceremonial laws (like in Exodus) and laws that were very obviously handed down for the sole benefit of the Israelites on their journey from Egypt to the Promised Land (and no one else). Nearly half the book concerns itself with just one topic: the assorted sacrifices (or "offerings") that had to be performed, mainly by those in the tribe of Levi, thus the name of the book – sacrifices that were all replaced by the one sacrifice made by Jesus on the cross hundreds of years later.

But if you read it with the explanations given in this reading guide, a pattern will gradually emerge that will impart a greater appreciation for Leviticus on you. Just commit to sticking with it all the way through and keep the historical *context* of the sometimes-strange rules and procedures in mind as you read them. For the first day in Leviticus, we get a detailed description of the proper procedure and reasons for performing 4 sacrifices or offerings: the "burnt offering" (Leviticus 1:1-17), the "grain offering (2:1-16), the "peace offering" (3:1-17), and the first half of the "sin offerings" (4:1-35 and beyond).

February 21, NT
Matthew 15:1-20
The Tradition of the Elders

Matthew's version of Jesus' latest encounter with the Pharisees, shortly (immediately?) after the "bread of life" discourse, is almost identical to Mark's, read yesterday. Jesus responds to the Pharisees accusations of being "unclean" with a sharp rebuke for their hypocrisy, and quotes Isaiah to prove His point. He then follows this with the same explanation of how the things that go *into* a person aren't what make him unclean, but rather, what comes *out*.

The commonly spoken idiom "the blind leading the blind" comes from today's reading, in verse 14.

February 22, OT
Leviticus 5:1-7:38
The Barbecue of God's Justice

The tongue-in-cheek title for today's OT reading comes from the emphasis on burning animal sacrifices that continues from yesterday's reading on through today's. The various sacrifices had different purposes, but the one that gets by far the most attention is the one called "sin offering" in some places and "guilt offering" in others. It is here that the need for sins to be atoned via a blood sacrifice was established, which eventually paved the way for the ultimate sacrifice of blood, Jesus' sacrifice.

Detailed instructions as to what constitutes a sin necessitating the sin offering begins today's reading followed by the procedures as to which animals to use, to whom to bring them, method of slaughter, other things that had to be done particularly when restitution was involved, and the exact and detailed rituals that accompanied each of the different kinds of sacrifices, including one that gets more detail tomorrow.

February 22, NT
Matthew 15:21-28; Mark 7:24-30
Throwing Bread to the Dogs

The only thing more astonishing about this encounter between Jesus and a Gentile woman is that it *doesn't* appear in Luke's Gospel. Luke was, after all, the only one of the four Gospel writers known with certainty to have been Greek and wrote in Greek. Yet, he didn't include this fascinating encounter with a Greek woman (listed as Syrophoenician, Canaanite, and Gentile in different places), which is included in Matthew and Mark.

The Matthew version is slightly more detailed, but both include the main points regarding the woman's request to have the demon driven from her daughter. Jesus uses the metaphor of throwing bread to dogs (a commonly used metaphor for Gentiles) to explain His priorities: to tend the "lost sheep of the house of Israel" (Matthew 15:24). To His obvious great surprise, the woman counters Jesus' argument with one of her own, using the exact same metaphor! By saying that "the dogs eat of the crumbs from the Master's table," (Matthew 15:27), she is saying that just because Jesus came for the "lost sheep of Israel" doesn't make the Gentiles any less in need of *or deserving of* the healing power of the Lord.

Jesus agrees, and the woman's daughter is healed, marking at least the second time in which Jesus did such a healing from a great distance.

February 23, OT
Leviticus 8:1-10:20
The First High Priests

Among the detailed and elaborate rituals the Israelites were called upon to perform, one in particular stands out: the ordination of their priests. The priests, who all must be from the same tribe as Moses and Aaron (the tribe of Levi), had to be ordained in an 8-day-long ceremony. The first to be ordained were Aaron and his sons in the first real historical narrative of the book of Leviticus.

Part of the narrative is a great tragedy, told to us as an object lesson in listening to God *exactly*. Two of Aaron's sons, Nadab and Abihu, fail to heed the Lord's warnings about what not to do in connection to ceremonies, and are killed by the Lord right then and there (Leviticus 10:1-3). Moses gets two of Aaron's cousins (10:4) to dispose of the bodies, and anoints Aaron's two remaining sons to take their place as high priests with Aaron (10:5-20).

A misunderstood verse in the middle of it all was humorously used in an episode of the TV show M*A*S*H: Father Mulcahy attempts to preach a sermon on temperance and reads part of Leviticus 10:9 ("do not drink wine or strong drink…lest you die") – in a state of intoxication himself. Though temperance is certainly a virtue and staying sober is a good common sense idea, the verse in question is about Aaron and his sons staying sober when performing their priestly duties, not a general ordinance against alcoholic beverages.

February 23, NT
Mark 7:31-37; Matthew 15:29-31
A Healing Tour of Galilee

Mark and Matthew each note Jesus' return from Tyre and Sidon (where He encountered the Gentile woman with the demon-possessed daughter) with several healings of people who were blind, deaf, or mute. Mark goes into slightly more detail this time than Matthew, in preparation for the next large-scale miracle in tomorrow's reading, which sounds like a repeat of an earlier miracle.

February 24, OT
Leviticus 11:1-13:46
The Clean and the Unclean, Part One

The Old Testament emphasis on things being "unclean" vs. "clean" was just as important to the Israelites as things being evil vs. good. The concepts were so strongly linked that they were still inseparable during Jesus' time. In order to establish the difference, Moses wrote down the better part of five chapters, about half of it today, describing those things.

The first are the dietary laws including the well-known prohibition against pork (Leviticus 11:1-23). Some animals were considered so unclean that merely touching their carcasses made a person unclean (11:24-47). One chapter is devoted to the need for purification of women who have given birth (12:1-8), and is referenced in Luke when Mary undergoes the same ritual (Luke 2:24). The remainder of today's OT reading is a lengthy discussion of the various skin diseases, how to treat them, their different symptoms, all under the banner of "leprosy" (Leviticus 13:1-46).

Many of these strange-sounding laws were a matter of simple practicality. The Israelites were about to spend 40 years essentially outdoors full time. Uncleanness could easily lead to a plague that would wipe out huge numbers of them. Another reason for the unusual regulations was that God wanted to make sure they were different from their pagan soon-to-be neighbors, setting them apart as special. Yet another reason was to keep the Israelites constantly aware of their sinful nature and the need to atone for those sins. By keeping the bar so high that it was nearly impossible to always be "clean," God also made Jesus' eventual atonement on the cross the basis for the doctrine of grace.

February 24, NT
Matthew 15:32-39; Mark 8:1-10
The Feeding of Four Thousand

On February 16-18, we read of an earlier miracle told in all four Gospels (the only miracle of which that is true) where 5000 people were fed from a starting stock of only five loaves of bread and two fish. We know today's NT reading to be a separate event (though probably not long after the earlier one) for three reasons.

One reason can only be ascertained from a careful reading of the details of each event in Matthew 15 vs. Matthew 14; a second reason being the existence of this feeding (the 4000) in two Gospels in which we also read of the feeding of the 5000. If, for example, the earlier miracle was recorded *only* in John and Luke (from which we first read it), one could conclude that the event read today is the same event with a discrepancy in the total number of people fed (as well as a different starting number of loaves and fish). This is, however, not the case. Although Jesus thus repeats a miracle, this by no means diminishes either the importance or the awesomeness of the miracle He performs.

A third reason for this being a separate event from the feeding of 5000 is explained by Jesus Himself in tomorrow's NT reading.

February 25, OT
Leviticus 13:47-15:33
The Clean and the Unclean, Part Two

These two and a half chapters start with the conclusion of the "laws of leprosy" started in yesterday's OT reading. The rules concerning the diagnosis of the various skin diseases falling under the banner of leprosy, who should do the diagnosing, what needs to be done to purify the diseased person and the person's belongings, are many and detailed. In teaching portions of this to a class of 8th graders, the most common reaction I got was "ewww!" But, God had good reasons for imposing these complicated rules, and much of it symbolically foreshadows the atonement for our sins paid for by Jesus.

Chapter 15 shifts to a different but related subject. Still concerned largely with the issues of "cleanness" vs. "uncleanness," the emphasis changes to bodily discharges, particularly those that are sexual in nature. The first half of the chapter concerns rules for men, the remainder for women. The presence of these explicit rules in the Bible will embarrass some younger readers and baffle many others, but the reasons for their inclusion (particularly if you factor in the hygiene issue) will gradually become more and more obvious.

February 25, NT
Matthew 16:1-12; Mark 8:11-26
The Leaven of the Pharisees and Sadducees

In the middle part of Jesus' ministry, He seemed to be particularly fond of using metaphor to teach truths to His disciples. Such was the case with His use of leaven as a metaphor for the teachings of the two largest Jewish religious groups of the day in today's NT reading.

Jesus begins today's NT reading with yet another rebuke of the Pharisees when they ask for a sign. Matthew's version has Jesus repeating His statement about the "sign of Jonah" which we read Him saying back on February 1. Then, He and the apostles travel by boat to Bethsaida, but neglect to bring any bread for the journey (Mark 8:14). Jesus uses this fact in order to warn the apostles about the Pharisees and Sadducees with whom He has been seen frequently arguing. It takes further explanation by Jesus for them to get it, but they do finally understand.

The end of today's NT reading is the only miracle that is recorded *only* in Mark: the healing of the blind man in Bethsaida (Mark 8:22-26).

February 26, OT
Leviticus 16:1-18:30
Yom Kippur, The Kosher Sacrifice, and Sexual Laws

Three distinct parts, divided by chapter, make up today's OT reading. The first is the institution of the special ceremony to be performed once per year on behalf of all the people of Israel. Among other things, this ceremony includes the use of a goat upon which all the people's sins are imparted, followed by the exiling of the goat. This began the use of the expression "scapegoat" in referring to a person or thing that takes the blame for others – yet another foreshadowing of Jesus. The scapegoat ceremony was part of a larger event called the Day of Atonement, or in Hebrew, Yom Kippur.

The first part of chapter 17 is a continuation of the description on what to do and what not to do when slaughtering animals for sacrifice. The rest of that same chapter explains why, and it's another foreshadowing of Jesus: God links blood to life, life to blood (Leviticus 17:11) and prohibits the eating of anything containing blood. Animals killed for food must be bled out completely in order to be "kosher," which means, "clean." The blood atonement of Jesus later became the ultimate kosher sacrifice.

The third part is a detailed list of rules about sexual relations, specifically prohibition against incest. Leviticus 18:1-18 speaks mainly of prohibition against "uncovering the nakedness" of various blood relatives and in-laws. Had these regulations been in place at the time of Abraham, his union with his half-sister Sarah would have been unlawful. Had these regulations been in place at the time of Cain, son of Adam, the human race could not have been propagated, as it was necessary for Cain to marry his sister. An interesting note here is that the prohibition against incestuous relations does not extend to cousins; obviously, these are not considered "too close" even though cousins are blood relatives.

The remainder of that third part contains additional regulations regarding sexual activity, including the prohibitions against homosexuality (18:22) and bestiality (18:23). It's easy to see why some in the homosexual community try to justify their behavior by dismissing these regulations. They're only a verse apiece, and a very large amount of Leviticus was later modified or even revoked by Jesus. What they fail to see is that Leviticus chapter 18 is one of the few sections of The Law that Jesus doesn't ever touch, therefore making the laws still binding. Plus, these laws are echoed elsewhere in both the Old (Deuteronomy) and New (Romans) Testaments.

February 26, NT
Matthew 16:13-28
Peter's Declaration of Faith

The event in today's NT reading is found in three of the Gospels (we'll read the same event in Luke and Mark tomorrow), of which Matthew's account is by far the most detailed. Matthew's version alone contains a quote from Jesus that has since become one of the Bible's most controversial verses: Matthew 16:18, which is used by the Roman Catholic Church to justify the doctrine of the "supremacy of Peter."

In all three versions, Jesus asks His disciples how people have been identifying Him. The responses range from "Elijah" to "one of the prophets" to even a resurrected "John the Baptist." Also in all three versions, Jesus repeats the question to ascertain what the *disciples* say about the Son of Man, followed by Peter's emphatic declaration: "you are the Christ – the Son of the living God!" (Matthew 16:16). Jesus warns the disciples in all three Gospels to not tell anyone else this truth.

But in Matthew's version, Jesus tells Peter in front of the other disciples that he is "Peter" (Greek "petros," meaning "stone"), "and upon this rock" (Greek "petra," meaning "large rock") "I will build my church." It is this play on (Greek) words that gives rise to the controversy, which can be summed up in one (huge) question: *who or what is the "rock" upon which the Church is built?*

Catholic theology states that Matthew 16:18-19 was Jesus' appointment of Peter as the head of the Church, thus providing the foundation for what would later become the Roman Catholic Church. It is believed that Peter later went to Rome and established and led a church there, and his successors (the Popes) continued and sustained that church, using Roman infrastructure, to spread the Gospel long before Christianity was legal in the Roman Empire. The widespread belief in this accounts for such well-known images as St Peter standing at the Pearly Gates like some kind of heavenly receptionist. Peter is believed to have been martyred in Rome and is believed to be buried underneath what is now the Basilica of St Peter in Vatican City. Thus, Catholics believe that Peter was set above all other disciples and crowned the first Pope by Christ Himself.

Protestant Christians deny nearly every point of this. They point to the fact that despite the two Greek words (petros and petra) having similar meanings, they *are* different, and then point out the fact that the Latin Vulgate translates them as the same word, thus resulting in the D-R Bible translation rendering Matthew 16:18 as "thou art *rock*, and upon this rock I will build my Church" (emphasis mine). Protestants believe that this has resulted in centuries of misinterpretation, equating Peter with the rock, and thus making Peter the rock upon which the church was built, rather than Jesus. Furthermore, there is no Biblical evidence that Peter ever went to Rome, leading to the Protestant belief that the RCC wasn't actually founded until *after* Constantine's legalization of Christianity more than 3 centuries later.

Which side is right? My belief is that both sides are partially right: like the Catholics, I do believe that Peter eventually made it to Rome and did lead a church there, in spite of the fact that Paul (who knew Peter) doesn't make any reference to him in his letter to the Romans or his letters from a Roman prison. (I base this on the idea that Peter didn't arrive in Rome until after Paul wrote his letter to the Romans, and was martyred before Paul arrived in person.) The difference in the two words tells me that it is *Jesus*, not Peter, who is the rock on which the Church is based, but that His proclamation of Peter as a "stone" was a prophesy of Peter's role as the first Church leader on the Day of Pentecost, the actual birthday of the Church.

The remainder of this passage is found in all three Gospels, with details discussed in tomorrow's entry.

February 27, OT
Leviticus 19:1-21:24
The Laws of Holiness

God calls us to holiness because God Himself is holy. So says the second verse of today's three-chapter OT reading. This begs the question "what is holiness?" Many people have many different definitions, but there is one common thread to them all: to be holy is to be *set apart* from other people or people groups. In instituting the many and various laws in Leviticus 19, for example, the emphasis is repeatedly on making sure that the Israelites *don't* follow the practice of the Egyptians from whom they escaped, or their new neighbors-to-be in the Promised Land. Some of the laws sound very miscellaneous, such as the numerous one- and two-verse gems about respect for the poor (19:9-10), disabled (19:14), and elderly (19:32), loving your neighbor as yourself (19:18), prohibition against the use of mediums and speaking with the dead (19:26, 19:31), and some strange-sounding agricultural regulations (19:19, 19:23-25). Some of the laws are very obviously intended for only the Israelites and only during their desert journey. Others are more obviously intended to be laws for all time. There are a few that fall in between these extremes, but the next chapter actually helps clarify things.

Chapter 20 goes into some detail about the practice of human sacrifice to a god named Molech, apparently a widespread practice by the people the Israelites had or would encounter. After this, the penalties for violating any of these "holiness" rules, along with the penalties for violating the sexual rules from chapter 18. Some of these include the death penalty by stoning, and is the one area that Jesus *did* touch, such as when he stopped the stoning of the adulterous woman in John 8 by pointing out who could cast the first stone (no one, for we all have sin). This doesn't revoke the laws, but it clarifies who can and cannot enforce the law and how we are actually supposed to atone for such sins.

Chapter 21 is a special set of laws (which continue into chapter 22 tomorrow) regarding the priests – not to be confused with Christian priests today, but the priests of Aaron from the tribe of Levi who was to carry out the ceremonial duties of the people of Israel.

February 27, NT
Mark 8:27-9:1; Luke 9:18-27
Peter's Declaration of Faith

Yesterday we read about Peter's declaration of faith, and the response by Jesus that is only recorded by Matthew (and the controversy that resulted). Today, we read Mark and Luke's version of the same event. In Mark and Luke's version, Jesus responds to Peter's declaration of Jesus being the Christ by simply telling them to tell no one else this. In Matthew and Mark, Peter then follows his highest moment with one of his lowest: Jesus predicts his coming death and resurrection, to which Peter loudly objects. Jesus then rebukes Peter by calling him *Satan* (Mark 8:33) and then explaining how followers must deny themselves, take up their own cross, and "follow me" (8:34).

February 28, OT
Leviticus 22:1-23:44
The Perfection of Sacrifices, The Feasts of Israel

Today's OT reading is only two chapters instead of three due to the great length of Leviticus chapter 23. Chapter 22 is a continuation from yesterday regarding the special holiness laws that apply to priests. Leviticus 22:17-30, in particular, emphasizes the fact that God expects all sacrifices to be *perfect*, without physical defect, and these are spelled out explicitly. In this way, yet another foreshadowing is made of Jesus in His perfect sacrifice for us.

Then in chapter 23, we have a description of how and when to celebrate the seven Hebrew festivals (we learned of 3 of them on Feb 14 in Exodus), still celebrated today by Orthodox Jews. In roughly chronological order according to the Hebrew calendar, and with varying degrees of significance, the seven described feasts are the back-to-back celebrations of Passover (23:4-5) and Unleavened Bread (23:6-8), then the feast of the First Fruit (23:9-14), followed about two months later by the festival of Weeks a.k.a. Wave Offering (23:15-22). Months later are celebrated the feast of Trumpets (23:23-25), the already described Day of Atonement (23:26-32), and the festival of Booths (23:33-44). Additional feasts would be added centuries later, including some that would not appear in the Bible officially; rather, they would appear in a special section described on the next page.

February 28, NT
Matthew 17:1-13
The Transfiguration

The mysterious, glorious, and beautiful event we call The Transfiguration appears in the Synoptic Gospels just as does Peter's declaration of faith, and is believed to follow "six days later" (Matthew 17:1) just as it says here. The vision is essentially a preview of God's Kingdom. As if Peter (one of three apostles to witness this spectacular event) needed confirmation of the deity of Christ, he got it in overflowing measure on the high mountain. Peter would later write about this experience in his second letter (which we will read on November 2).

Common elements of all accounts of The Transfiguration include Jesus' face and garments shining brightly, the appearance of Moses and Elijah, Peter's impulsive offer to build "three tabernacles" (17:4) for the three men of God, and God's word to Peter and the apostles: "This is My beloved Son, with whom I am well pleased" (17:5).

Jesus clarifies an obscure prophecy as they return (minus Moses and Elijah) from the mountain. Malachi said that "Elijah is coming and will restore all things" (Malachi 4:5, read on December 20), which the apostles thought was partially fulfilled by The Transfiguration. Jesus clarifies the partial fulfillment of the prophecy, but not in the Transfiguration but in John the Baptist. The Scofield Reference Bible helps make this even clearer by citing Matthew 11:14 and Luke 1:17 as "backup" for this explanation.

February 29, OT
The Deuterocanonical Books a.k.a. The Apocrypha

Since there is only one February 29 in each 4-year period, this seems an appropriate section to describe and opine about a controversial part of some Bibles. Absent from most Bibles, the Roman Catholic Church calls it the Deuterocanonical books, meaning the "second canon". Protestants call these same books and sections of books the "Apocrypha" which means "secret" or "hidden." Whichever name you call it, these writings are either found only in Catholic edition Bibles or are placed in a special separate section, usually between the last book of the Old Testament (Malachi) and the first book of the New (Matthew).

The Apocrypha is *not* included in this chronological reading plan, so Catholics who want to include these books or portions of books in their readings must do so *in addition to* the schedule given in this book for the rest of it. Protestants are certainly not forbidden to read it, but it can be difficult to obtain without getting hold of a so-called "Catholic Bible."

Why the controversy? There are a number of reasons, some explained below, but they boil down to this: the early scholars who decided which books would become part of the "canon" of Scripture decided that the books we now call the Apocrypha were *not* inspired by God. This doesn't mean that they have no value at all. Each of the books and readings that make up this part of the Bible has some different pros and cons. The "pro" shared by all of them is the additional insight into Jewish history that can be obtained by reading them, particularly since nearly all of it was written in or about the period of time that is commonly thought of as being "between the Testaments," that is, after the prophet Malachi and before the birth of Christ. The biggest "con," other than the lack of consensus on whether or not they are inspired, is that some teachings in some of the books (described below) contradict teachings found elsewhere in the agreed-upon parts of the Old and New Testaments.

Tobit – Called "Tobias" in some Bibles, it is one of the two parts of the Apocrypha for which there is a fragment in the Dead Sea Scrolls written in Aramaic. The rest of what we today know as the book of Tobit is based on Greek manuscripts, and was believed for many years to have been composed in Greek by Hellenistic Jews in the 2nd century B.C. Like nearly all the rest of the Apocrypha, it appears as part of the Septuagint, a translation of the Old Testament from Hebrew to Greek made by 70 (thus the name) Jewish scholars in the 1st century B.C. Tobit is one of the few books in the Bible that even Catholics acknowledge is a work of fiction. Tobit is best described as a fable about a righteous Jew and his family around the time of the Assyrian exile. It is valued for its praise of fidelity in marriage, and teaches respect for elderly parents, reverence for the dead, and the value of intercession of angels. Praying for the dead and having any intercessor besides Jesus are two of the doctrines that make this book controversial, however.

Judith – Another book, this one originally in Hebrew instead of Aramaic or Greek, in which we have what is agreed upon as a fictional tale, though it contains some items of historical significance. The title character is alleged to live at the time of the Assyrian exile just like Tobit, and was written at about the same time. The central part of the drama concerns her beheading of an Assyrian general, an act that either makes her a heroine or a murderer depending upon one's point of view. Some of its historical inaccuracies are believed to have been deliberate, and were written as an allusion to other, real, historical characters (notably Esther) and places and times. Events leading up to the establishment of the Jewish festival of Hanukkah is also mentioned.

additions to Esther – The book of Esther, up to Esther 10:3, is considered part of the canon of scripture by all Christian churches, though there remains considerable dispute over whether it's a work of fiction (like Judith or Tobit) or is actual history. The Apocryphal part is all of which that follows, from 10:4 to 16:24, usually notated as the "additions to Esther." In Catholic Bibles, these chapters are incorporated into the rest of the text to form a single work, in spite of the fact that the canonical portion was written in Hebrew while the additions are found only in Greek with a completely different writing style. Some of the additions appear to even contradict details of the story in the original Hebrew. The parts are believed to have been written as many as 4 centuries apart, though some Catholic scholars believe the entire work was written at about the same time, in the 2nd century B.C. One value of the additions is that it contains a number of references to God, including prayers, which are oddly lacking in the rest of the text.

Wisdom – Also known as the Wisdom of Solomon, it is universally agreed that the author was *not* Solomon despite portions written in the same first-person style as Ecclesiastes and the Song of Solomon. It is the most-used part of the Apocrypha in Catholic Mass readings and contains the only part of the Apocrypha authorized for use in the Lutheran church. It is the only Apocryphal book directly quoted in the New Testament. In style and doctrine, it reads very much like a Greek version of Proverbs, which we know was mostly written by Solomon, and can almost be thought-of as a supplement to it. Whoever wrote it was familiar with the Proverbs, as there are several verses that quote the Septuagint version of some of them word for word. The emphasis or "theme" of the work seems to be the superiority of Jewish wisdom to Greek wisdom.

Sirach or **Ecclesiasticus** – Not to be confused with Ecclesiastes, penned by Solomon centuries earlier, these wisdom writings, which are also in the style of Proverbs, were written by a man named Jesus ben Sirach sometime in the 3rd century B.C, in Hebrew. A few fragments were found amongst the Dead Sea Scrolls. The entire text, in Greek, is found in nearly every codex of the Septuagint. The theme of the work is similar to Wisdom and is in the style of Proverbs, but the emphasis is much more strongly set towards being a manual of moral teaching, with theological explanation that draws upon and quotes from the Mosaic Law and some of the Prophets. There are some claims to the effect that Sirach is quoted in the New Testament just as is Wisdom, most notably by Mary in part of her song called the Magnificat (Luke 1:52), though this is disputed.

Baruch – The controversy surrounding this book's inclusion in the Bible stems entirely from its disputed authorship. According to the text itself, it was penned by the prophet Jeremiah's scribe, Baruch ben Nariah, and actually follows Lamentations (also scribed by Baruch) immediately in Catholic Bibles. It has a writing style very much like that of those parts of Jeremiah known to have been written down by Baruch, and seems to be consistent in its historical detail with the prophet in the early part of the Babylonian Exile. Not one single fragment of this work exists in Hebrew and there is no record of it ever having been in the Hebrew Scriptures, whereas the accepted books of Jeremiah and Lamentations have had copies found of the entire works in the original Hebrew. The only codices of Baruch are in Greek and are believed to have been written in the 2nd century B.C. The sixth chapter, when it exists, is sometimes labeled the "letter of Jeremiah," sometimes as a separate book. It contains some wise teachings, prayers, and a special message "to those in captivity," though it is disputed as to whether this refers to the exiles in Babylon or to Greek oppressors around the time of the Maccabees.

additions to Daniel: the **Song of the Three Young Men** (a.k.a. Song of the Three Children), **Bel and the Dragon**, and **Story of Susanna** - Protestant Bibles that include the Apocrypha separate these into three books, while Catholic Bibles incorporate them into the canonical book of Daniel. The first goes in as an addition to chapter 3 (v 24-90), telling of the song sung by Hananiah, Mishael, and Azariah after being thrown into the furnace, once they realized that God had delivered them. The other two parts or books are believed to be fictional fables involving a different Daniel than the prophet who penned the book of that name. The inclusion of these two stories, which are believed to have been written in Aramaic in the 2nd century B.C., is what makes them apocryphal and controversial: since portions of Daniel were also written in Aramaic, in a style very much like that of Susanna and Bel, there are some who believe the entire book of Daniel was actually written much later than the more commonly accepted 6th century B.C. timetable. Believing this forces a radical change in interpretation of the prophecies of Daniel, and is thus believed by Protestants (especially Dispensationalists) to be written much later than the rest of Daniel.

I and II Maccabees – These two separate books, which bear the distinct writing styles of at least two different authors, contain an account of a known and verified historical event: the Jewish revolt against the Greek ruler Antiochus IV, led by Judas Maccabeus. It would seem a natural to include these books in the canon of Scripture except for two problems: the account of events in the two different books is far too different to be harmonized, and the doctrinal additions in the second book contradict Jewish and later Christian teaching on several subjects. Unlike the four Gospels which are relatively easy to harmonize despite their differences, parts of II Maccabees contradict I Maccabees in such a way that there is uncertainty as to which one is historically correct at all. In most cases, these disputes can be settled by simply assuming the first to be correct, but that renders the second book worthless. There exists an apocryphal III and IV Maccabees as well, but even the Catholic Church denies their credibility.

There are other books besides these that are found in some special Bible editions or online, but they are generally considered to be of such little value as to be virtually worthless, even to Catholics who believe in the above books as being inspired. There's also no way one could read the entire Apocrypha on Leap Day as dated here. Today would, however, be a good day to read portions of the Apocrypha as a break from the rest of the chronology, particularly those writings that are of generally higher value, such as Wisdom or Sirach.

March 1, OT
Leviticus 24:1-25:55
The Lamp, the Law, and the Land

The description of the seven Hebrew festivals is followed by two laws regarding the oil lamp to be used in the tent of meeting and some specifics about a bread offering. After this is a piece of history which includes a set of controversial laws.

The history concerns the son of an Israelite woman and an Egyptian man who blasphemed the Lord's name (24:10-11). The people didn't know what to do about this situation, and so consulted Moses. Moses consulted the Lord who said that the penalty for blasphemy was death by stoning. But that's not the controversial part.

What follows is commonly referred to as the "eye for an eye" passage, and is frequently used by those who favor the death penalty to justify the position. The Lord authorizes the death penalty for the specific crime of murder (a different Hebrew word used for it vs. the word translated as "kill" or "execute" in the case of the penalty) and that justice is only done when the punishment fits the crime. Thus, causing injury should result in the same injury to the guilty party. Hundreds of years later, Jesus would clarify this when a woman who was about to be stoned to death was spared by Jesus' words to the mob that he who is "without sin can cast the first stone." At the end of the section, the man guilty of blasphemy is executed according to the law.

Chapter 25 consists of a five-section description of what is commonly known as the "law of the land." In the first section (25:1-7) the Lord commands the Israelites to give the land itself a one-year break every seven years, called a "Sabbatical year." God answers the obvious question about what to eat during a year in which nothing is planted or gathered in the next section, called the "year of jubilee" (25:8-24). Among other things, God states here that the land to which they are headed is not actually the Israelites', but the Lord's (25:23). Keeping the land in the family is the focus of the third section (25:25-34) and insuring that the poor are sustained and slaves and foreigners are treated properly with regards to the land are the focuses of the fourth section (25:35-46). The fifth section (25:47-55) goes into further detail about the poor man after having been sold into slavery, which sounds very much like a law designed to prevent another incident like Joseph, son of Jacob, from happening.

March 1, NT
Luke 9:28-36; Mark 9:2-13
The Transfiguration

Today we read Luke's and Mark's versions of The Transfiguration, read from Matthew yesterday (or two days ago if this is a leap year). Luke's version lacks the statements of Jesus about how Elijah was prophesied to come but includes mention of Moses and Elijah "speaking of His departure" (Luke 9:31, NASB). Mark's version is closer to Matthew's in that it includes Jesus' explanation of the Elijah prophecy.

March 2, OT
Leviticus 26:1-27:34
Blessings, Curses, and Dedications

Today's two chapters bring Leviticus, one of the Bible's most difficult books, to a close. If the importance of Leviticus, despite its complexity, wasn't clear before, it should be now. The two closing chapters, in particular, contain some things of much greater significance than what most people think.

After all the complexity and apparent illogic of some of the laws, God (through Moses) spells out the blessings (Leviticus 26:3-12) for obeying the laws and the consequences (26:14-33) for not in much clearer language than the previous chapters. Of particular note is a prophecy made at the end of the list of consequences: the desolation of the land brought about by the dispersion of the Israelites (26:32-39). This prophecy was fulfilled more than once since then. But, anyone who believes either in Replacement Theology (read John 4 on study notes for January 10) or believe that the Jews have no historical claim to the Holy Land seriously need to read Leviticus 26:40-45, which spells out the case for the *forever*-fulfillment of the Covenant. God keeps all of His promises!

The concluding chapter of Leviticus describes the guidelines for the valuation of things dedicated ("consecrated") to the Lord. In particular, special mention is made about the firstborn of any animals

(27:26-27) and the fact that anything consecrated cannot be "sold or redeemed" (27:28-29), including any and all tithes (27:30-33).

March 2, NT
Matthew 17:14-27
Death and Taxes

Benjamin Franklin famously said, "In this world nothing is certain but death and taxes." Today's NT reading speaks of both. All three synoptic Gospels contain the account of the casting out of the demon from the boy just after returning from the Mount of Olives (Matthew 17:14-21), but with varying degrees of detail. Matthew's version of this event is actually the least detailed of the three (we read Luke's and Mark's tomorrow). But, common to all three and almost word-for-word identical is Jesus' prediction of His death and resurrection (17:22-23). Depending upon how the various chronologies are viewed, this is at least the second time He does this in front of His disciples. In this, as in all of the cases, the disciples are left grieved, confused, or both.

It is the part at the end of the reading that is unique to Matthew. This section (17:24-27) is not the only time Jesus discusses taxes, but it is the only time in which the payment of the "temple tax" is done miraculously. In one other famous passage, Jesus declares the proper place for taxes in society (Mark 12:13-17, read on April 24), and does so in a similar but not identical manner here. The difference here is the ending, where Jesus tells Peter to pull a fish from the sea (presumably the Sea of Galilee) and extract a shekel coin from it to pay the tax.

Matthew 17:25-26 (Jesus' conversation with Peter) may have been used as the basis for the tax-exempt status enjoyed by churches in the United States.

March 3, OT
Numbers 1:1-2:34
The Census of Israel

The name given to this book, the fourth book of Moses, comes from a census taken at the beginning and again at the end of the book which covers nearly 40 years of Israelite history. An equally good title would be "In the Desert," because it describes the journey by the liberated Israelites from near Mount Sinai to just across the river from the Promised Land. Where Leviticus contains almost no historical narrative, Numbers contains almost nothing but, the exception being the two sections that give the book its name.

The Israelite census was taken near the place where Moses received the Ten Commandments and the rest of the law, which indicates that they moved very little, if any, since that time. However, despite the length of the last few chapters of Exodus and all of Leviticus, this may not have actually been a particularly long time. The census itself was not like the type of demographic survey of today, though it did break out the people by Israelite tribe. The total number counted, 603,550 (Numbers 1:46), does not include women and children; rather, the purpose was to count fighting men in anticipation of war along the way to the Promised Land. The number also excludes any, men or women, from the tribe of Levi, for they were to serve a different purpose.

With the number totaled up, the Israelites were divided up by tribe into camps by compass direction (2:3-32), with leaders from each tribe chosen as well. Little did any of them know at this point that only two men out of 603 thousand would actually make that final crossing to the Promised Land.

March 3, NT
Luke 9:37-45; Mark 9:14-32
Jesus Exorcises a Demon His Disciples Couldn't

The events in today's NT reading are found in the three synoptic Gospels. We read of the exorcism and Jesus' prediction of His death and resurrection in yesterday's reading from Matthew; today we read the same two events in Luke and Mark.

Once again, despite the relative brevity of Mark's Gospel compared to the others, it is Mark's version of the exorcism that has the most detail. (Luke's is very close to exactly the same as Matthew's.) Mark's is the only version to note that the boy *appeared* to have died during the exorcism, though he had not. It was, however, among the most violent of exorcisms performed by Jesus while here on earth. All three Gospels contain the account of how the disciples were first asked to perform this exorcism, but failed, while Jesus was successful, rebuking the disciples for having too little faith to be able to do it.

The conclusion of the readings is the (at least) second prediction (possibly third) made by Jesus of His death and resurrection.

March 4, OT
Numbers 3:1-4:33
The Levite Census

Today's OT reading combines census, genealogy, history, and law. With the "fighting men" numbered, the Levites who were excluded from that count for their priestly duties are now counted, and their duties spelled out. Among other things, this section shows how the Levites were consecrated (see March 2) to the Lord, and we also find out how many males have been born since the exodus.

One of the duties describes the proper handling of the holy objects, lest they be improperly touched and cause death (Numbers 4:15). This was written to prevent a repeat of the unfortunate incident described in Leviticus 10:1-3 (February 23).

March 4, NT
Luke 9:46-50; Mark 9:33-50
Childlike Faith; The Consequences of Sin

The synoptic Gospels all tell of the conversation in which the disciples argued amongst themselves about who was the greatest. In all three cases, Jesus interjects Himself into the argument by presenting a child to them and explaining that "whoever shall receive this child in my name receives Me: and whoever shall receive Me receives Him that sent me: for he that is least among you all, the same shall be great." (Luke 9:48) Jesus next grants permission for others besides Himself and His disciples to drive out demons by stating that those who are "not against us [are] for us" (9:50).

At this point, Luke's version of this event ends. Mark's version is worded slightly differently, but says the same things, adding here that one who desires to be first shall be last, and vice versa (Mark 9:35). Mark also adds that one performing a miracle in His name will not be able to soon speak evil of Him (9:39).

After this is a passage found only in Mark and Matthew (Matthew's version tomorrow) that is basically Jesus' most stern warning about the consequences of sin (9:42-48). Anyone who doubts the reality of Hell as a real place needs to seriously read this passage or its counterpart in Matthew. Here, Jesus explains what should be done in cases of temptation, advocating the cutting off of various body parts because it would be better to enter heaven with such disabilities than to be thrown into hell with all of you intact, where "the worm does not die and the fire is not quenched" (9:48). English translations that are based on younger (newer) manuscripts, such as the KJV, repeat this verse three times, once in its accepted position (verse 48), and once each as verse 44 and 46. Older manuscripts lack this repetition.

March 5, OT
Numbers 4:34-6:27
The Levite Census; Marital Purity; The Nazirites

The counting of men from the tribe of Levi concludes, by family, in the first part of today's reading. Only those between 30 to 50 years of age (Numbers 4:35, for example) were counted, as these were the only men qualified for service as priests. God then commands the people of Israel about what it means to be and remain pure, and what to do about lepers or anyone who is ritually unclean. A lengthy part of this is the section regarding the "fidelity test" for marital purity (5:12-31), which includes an elaborate (and potentially deadly) rite for the accused woman to go through. It is one of the several passages used to justify divorce, though only in cases of adultery.

The Nazirites were a special group consecrated to the Lord with a special oath. They could be either men or women (6:2), and had to "separate themselves" from the rest of the public, refraining from alcoholic beverages or even grapes and grape juice (6:3-4). They were forbidden to have their hair cut, could not ever touch a dead body, and had to make several special sacrifices in order to complete their consecration. The monastic lifestyle practiced and advocated by various religious orders such as the Benedictines are patterned after this Nazirite practice. Famous Nazirites in the Bible include Samson (see OT readings beginning April 2) and John the Baptist.

This section ends with one of the most famous benedictions, beginning with the familiar line "The Lord bless you and keep you…" (6:23-26).

March 5, NT
Matthew 18:1-20
Childlike Faith; The Consequences of Sin; and Discipline Done Right

Matthew's version of the passage read yesterday in Luke and Mark is worded slightly differently, but contains all of the points made in Mark's version plus several more. Like both Luke and Mark, it begins with Jesus' discussion with the disciples about who is "the greatest," to which Jesus responds with the passage about how one who humbles himself like a child is the greatest in the kingdom. Matthew's version does not include the rebuke of the disciples found in Luke and Mark about granting others permission to drive out demons, but continues like Mark's after that, regarding the consequences of sin and what to do to resist temptation.

Here, Matthew's version continues further with a passage that He would later repeat in Luke. I consider it to be two separate events rather than two versions of the same because of the events that occur between Luke chapter 9 (read yesterday) and 17 (where the parallel passage is found). In Matthew's version, Jesus goes on to give instructions for the proper way to carry out discipline in the Church (Matthew 18:15-20).

March 6, OT
Numbers 7:1-89
Gifts for the Levites

In this single but very long chapter, which makes up the entirety of today's OT reading, the elaborate dedication offerings for the Levites and the tabernacle to which they were in charge are described. The gifts included everything from various livestock (for sacrifices) as well as silver and gold dishes used in their priestly duties.

March 6, NT
Matthew 18:21-35; John 7:2-10; Luke 9:51
On Forgiveness

In the Lord's Prayer, first spoken at the Sermon on the Mount, one of the verses asks God to forgive our debts as we also forgive our debtors (Matthew 6:12). In today's NT reading, Jesus explains this further, linking our forgiveness of others with God's forgiveness of us. First to Peter (18:21-22) and then the rest of the disciples, Jesus uses the number "seventy times seven" for the number of times a person must forgive. It's not the number 490 that is important here; Jesus is speaking metaphorically to make a point about forgiving a virtually unlimited number of times. The parable of the Unforgiving Creditor (18:23-35) serves to drive the point home all the more.

After this, two brief passages from John and Luke set up a string of readings after today that will last over a week: after preaching mainly in Galilee and the surrounding area, Jesus decides to take His earthly ministry to Jerusalem. Jesus would make no fewer than three trips to Jerusalem in the last 12-14 months of His earthly ministry, the last being the journey that ended with His death and resurrection. In the passage from John, Jesus was encouraged by his brothers (half-brothers, actually – and another example of the Bible confirming the idea of Jesus having biological brothers by Mary) to go to Jerusalem to attend the Festival of Booths (John 7:2-5). Jesus initially declines this opportunity because His brothers are trying to get Him to go there for all the wrong reasons, and turns the invitation around for *them* to go instead. In the end, Jesus does begin His journey to Jerusalem, but separately and privately (John 7:10, Luke 9:51).

March 7, OT
Numbers 8:1-10:36
The Passover at Sinai; The Journey Resumes

In the middle of today's OT reading, we get the first real indication of just how long the Israelites spent near the base of Mount Sinai, as final preparations are made to the tabernacle (the lamps and lamp stands) and to the Levites to begin their commission as priests (Numbers 8:1-26). The Lord tells Moses to remind the Israelites to observe the Passover at the appointed time in "the first month of the second year"

(9:1, 9:5) of their post-exodus time in the desert. This reminder came from the Lord just days before it was to occur, in the wilderness of Sinai. Thus, we now know that the Israelites spent over a year at the base of the mountain, receiving the law, preparing the tabernacle, and commissioning the priests. So important is the Passover to the Lord that He grants a special exemption to the Israelites in the event of being ritually unclean at the time of the observance (9:6-14).

The Israelites were then given the guidelines as to when to begin moving again and when to stop (9:15-23). With the "cloud of glory" to guide them and silver assembly trumpets to alert them (10:1-10), the Israelites at last resumed their journey to the Promised Land in the second month of the second year (10:11). From Sinai, their next stop was in the wilderness of Paran (10:12).

March 7, NT
Luke 9:52-62; Matthew 8:19-22
Getting Priorities Straight

It's interesting to note how both of today's readings involve journeys. In the case of Jesus' journey, an important lesson had to be taught at the beginning of His journey to Jerusalem to attend the Festival of Booths. Because such trips were taken on foot, the walk from Galilee to Jerusalem would take two or more days, thus making at least one overnight stop a necessity. Today, the trip would take less than an hour by car. The length of the trip in ancient times also meant that many people could become aware of your trip as you made your way. Such was the case here.

Jesus planned to spend a night in a Samaritan village but the Samaritans didn't extend their hospitality to Him. His disciples wanted to retaliate for this apparent insult, but Jesus told them not to (Luke 9:53-56) by explaining the reasons for this journey and His ministry. After choosing a different village in which to stay, other issues of priorities came up, as Jesus even told one man to "let the dead bury their own dead" (9:60), another verse that isn't to be taken literally, but was used to explain where our priorities should lie. Adding to this (in Luke only; all else is also in Matthew), Jesus tells another man that "no one, after putting his hand to the plow and looking back is fit for the kingdom of God" (Luke 9:62), referring to the fact that the man wanted to follow Jesus but only after saying a proper goodbye to his family. This reflects both a misguided priority (family before God) on the man's part and a desire to follow God "on our own terms" instead of God's.

March 8, OT
Numbers 11:1-13:33
Quails, Whiners, and Spies

The Israelites were a whiney lot. On several occasions after their exodus from Egypt, the Israelites complained to Moses to the point where either Moses was ready to throw up his hands in despair, the Lord's anger was kindled against the Israelites, or both. In response to the Israelites' latest complaint about being tired of manna and wanting meat (Numbers 11:1-9), the Lord granted them quails but commanded that the meat be eaten for a whole month until it was coming out of their nostrils (11:19-20)! After Moses and the elders returned to camp and the Lord sent the enormous quantity of quails, the Lord caused the Israelites to get what may well be the Bible's first-ever large scale case of salmonella poisoning, resulting in the deaths of those who ate the largest amounts of the infected meat (11:33-34).

The complaints and the troubles weren't over yet, either. Moses' siblings (younger brother Aaron and older sister Miriam) decided to talk behind Moses' back, complaining about his leadership. The Lord overheard them (doesn't He hear everything?) and chastised them in front of Moses (12:1-9). Miriam, in particular, got the brunt of the punishment when she was made leprous (12:10) and was not granted any preferential treatment in eventually becoming clean (12:11-16).

After this, the Lord told Moses to send spies, one from each tribe, ahead to Canaan and find out about the land and the people there (13:1-20). The spies then went on a forty-day journey to the Promised Land and back (13:21-24), and then gave conflicting reports about it upon their return (13:25-33). The Lord's eventual response, in tomorrow's OT reading, was even more dramatic than the "quails" incident.

March 8, NT
John 7:11-30
Jesus Teaches in Jerusalem

For the next eight days, all of the NT readings are from John during the period of Jesus' longest Jerusalem ministry. This trip to Jerusalem is not to be confused with the much later event where Jesus arrives in Jerusalem to a king's welcome, an event commonly called the "triumphal entry," and celebrated as Palm Sunday in many churches (read on April 16).

As His Jerusalem ministry begins at the Festival of Booths, He goes to the temple and, despite death threats (John 7:13, 7:25, 7:30) and open objections (7:15, 7:20), gives the crowd a very important lesson about His deity (7:16-19, 7:28-29). He also touches on a theme that came up often when confronted by Pharisees: the *real* meaning of the law (7:21-24).

March 9, OT
Numbers 14:1-15:41
The Forty-Year Death Sentence

When the Israelites set out from Egypt, they didn't know they were going to spend, collectively, 40 years wandering in the desert. Some probably knew that it would take only a matter of a few weeks, since the sons of Israel made the trip from Egypt to Canaan and back in a comparable amount of time to bring and later bury their father. They were obviously close enough to the Promised Land, even after a year under Mount Sinai, to send twelve men on a spy mission that they completed in a month and a half! But it was when those very spies returned with their conflicting (and mostly ominous) reports that the Israelites' reaction brought a forty-year "death sentence" upon them.

The Israelites had enough of the bad news and conspired to appoint a new leader to take them back to Egypt (Numbers 14:3-4), but one of the two spies who brought back good news (Joshua) tried to talk them out of it. It nearly got him stoned to death (14:10). The Lord then threatened to dispossess the Israelites (14:12) but Moses skillfully talked Him out of it, this time without being threatened with violence. But the Lord would not just let this one go. The Israelites' whining stoked the Lord's anger once too often, and so He declared this punishment: no one, not even Moses (though he didn't know it yet; see March 11 reading), alive at that time would actually set foot in the Promised Land, except for Joshua (see above) and Caleb (14:22-38). Their children, born in the desert over the course of 40 years, would be the first generation to see God's promise fulfilled.

Some people overreacted to the Lord's discipline and tried to engage a nearby enemy, but without God's help ended up badly defeated (14:39-45). The Lord then clarified laws regarding special sacrifices to be done once they entered the Promised Land that only their sons and daughters would see (15:1-31, 37-41), which the Israelites took seriously this time (15:32-36).

March 9, NT
John 7:31-53
Who is this Jesus?

Jesus' teaching in a Jerusalem temple influenced many people. Many believed Jesus when He explained His divinity, only to be confronted by Pharisees who refused to believe the same way (John 7:31-36). Jesus' invitation at the end of the Festival to "let him come to Me" (7:38) causes even more discussion over the central question: who is this Jesus?

After speculation about Jesus being "the Prophet" and "the Christ," the chief priests and Pharisees get into the argument too. A Pharisee who met Jesus previously, Nicodemus (John 3, read on January 8), came to Jesus' defense, but was then met with scorn himself by being accused of being from Galilee like Jesus (7:52). In the end, the matter is left temporarily unresolved.

March 10, OT
Numbers 16:1-18:32
The Revolt of Korah; The Priesthood of Aaron Confirmed

The Israelites were sentenced to wander the desert for 40 years altogether. No one would see the Promised Land from the "current" generation except for two men. Despite knowing exactly where this discipline came from, some Israelites continued to complain to the point of revolt. Korah, a Levite, and a group of 250 men from among the Levites and Reubenites, decided to openly question Moses' authority as the leader of Israel (Numbers 16:1-3). Moses came up with a plan to have the Lord decide the matter, but the rebels initially refused (16:12-14). But, the Lord sided with Moses and got Moses to gather the rebels together for the Lord to then pass deadly judgment (16:18-35), swallowing the main group into the earth and burning many others with fire.

As if this wasn't enough, the Israelites then accused Moses and Aaron of bringing on the deaths and destruction (16:41) instead of blaming those who actually rebelled against the Lord. Once again, the Lord threatened to smite them with a plague, a threat He partially carried out (16:44-49). The only thing that stopped the threat from taking more lives than it did was the quick thinking of Moses and the quick action of Aaron. The Lord then put on a graphic demonstration for the remaining Israelites that confirmed Aaron and the tribe of Levi as the priests of Israelites and their true leaders (17:2-11), using a budding rod as a way of putting an end to their grumbling. The Lord then reiterates the duties and responsibilities of the priests (18:1-32) to Aaron.

March 10, NT
John 8:1-20
The Woman Caught in Adultery; Another Argument with Pharisees

There is an old joke, in Roman Catholic circles, surrounding the first half of today's NT reading, the well-known story of the woman caught in adultery and forgiven by Jesus. The joke simply relates the event up through verse 7 where Jesus told the crowd that the one who was "without sin" could be the first to cast a stone at the woman. But then, in the joke, this is followed by a 50-ish woman nearby bending down to pick up a stone, throwing it at the woman, and hitting her, to which Jesus groans and says "ah, mom!" The laugh comes from the fact that Catholics believe Mary to have lived her life without sin. Of course, what Jesus *really* says after verse 7 proves the exact opposite to be true.

Jesus simultaneously condemns everyone in the crowd while forgiving the adulterous woman. There is no doubt of her guilt. The penalty is known by all (as read on February 27 in Leviticus 20). Yet, here Jesus publicly commutes her sentence and thus clarifies exactly under which circumstances that part of The Law can and cannot be enforced—this being one of those many places where the law can*not* be enforced because of the lack of a sinless person to carry it out. There is no doubt of the death penalty for sin, but after Jesus' sacrifice on the cross, these penalties for these sins could *all* be commuted the same way.

The passage itself (John 8:1-11) has been frequently debated as possibly *not* being part of John's Gospel. A majority of the "older" manuscripts lack the passage. It appears in the "newer" manuscripts, including those that were used for the translation of the King James Version. However, even most KJV Bibles put the passage in brackets and put in a footnote regarding its disputed origin. The dispute is not over whether or not it belongs in the Bible, but rather, who wrote it. I know of no one who believes the passage is *not* the inspired Word of God. But its absence from the older manuscripts leads some to believe that it was added much later. One of my Bibles even states that there is evidence to suggest that it was written by Luke and actually belongs at the end of chapter 21 of that Gospel, just before the Passion.

The far more likely possibility is that it was written by John and belongs in John just as we see it because of how well it dovetails in with the arguments with the Pharisees on either side of this event (especially the one after). With there being no doubt as to its inspiration, and therefore authenticity, we can conclude that there really was a real woman brought before the real Jesus. In other words, this story is absolutely true. It happened the way it is told here. Among the many people who witnessed this event were some "scribes and Pharisees" (8:3) who were among those who returned after the woman left, and resumed the argument with Jesus about His divinity.

That argument makes up the remainder of today's NT reading (8:12-20), and it continues tomorrow as well.

March 11, OT
Numbers 19:1-21:35
The Journey to Moab

The rather mundane-sounding title for today's OT reading belies the fact that these three chapters are chock-full of important events in the history of the Israelites. In this order and in the following places, this reading includes: the "ordinance of the red heifer" (Numbers 19:1-

13), a new type of sacrifice, the death of Miriam after arriving at the wilderness of Zin (20:1), Edom's refusal to allow the Israelites to pass through their land (20:14-22), the death of Aaron (20:23-29), and the Israelites' victories over the Canaanites (21:1-3), the Amorites (21:21-25), and the king of Bashan (21:33-35).

But it was the event immediately after the death of Miriam (and before the death of Aaron) that is most important to the reading. The Israelites complained of the lack of water (20:2-7), and the Lord gave instructions for Moses to "speak to the rock" and it would bring forth water (20:8), but instead of doing *exactly* what they were told, Moses made two costly mistakes: he took credit for something that the Lord was about to do, and struck the rock with the staff instead of speaking to it (20:10-11). For these errors, Moses' career as leader of the Israelites would end before they reached their destination (20:12-13) and he would die in the wilderness with the rest of them.

March 11, NT
John 8:21-59
"You will know the truth, and the truth shall set you free"

When someone decides to accept Christ as his/her savior, the new Christian is often encouraged to begin their journey through the Bible by reading the Gospel according to John. I used to wonder why this was emphasized so much until I did likewise (though well after I had become a Christian myself). Although Jesus asserts His divinity in all four Gospels, there is no place where He does so better or more often than here in John. This chronological reading guide includes all of John, of course, but not quite in the sequence it appears in the Bible itself. If you ever decide to isolate just this Gospel and read it through (it can be done in a couple of hours' time) from beginning to end, come back to this passage in particular and you'll see exactly why this is the new believer's first stop.

The passage is the remainder of one of the longest arguments between Jesus and the Pharisees, which began in yesterday's NT reading. Jesus tries to both explain and justify His divinity to them, but He is met with either confusion and misunderstanding (John 8:25, 8:27) or rage (8:59). Along the way, Jesus speaks of His crucifixion (8:28a). At one point, he speaks to those who believe Him by saying that they will know the truth "and the truth shall set you free" (8:32). The reply of even the believers reflects the fact that they *still* don't really get it

(8:33). Jesus tries to explain further, but it just extends and intensifies the argument. In the end, Jesus almost becomes a stoning victim (again) when the Jews in Jerusalem become convinced that Jesus has a demon for speaking that way (8:52). He doesn't yet leave Jerusalem, but He does escape the Pharisees, for now.

March 12, OT
Numbers 22:1-24:25
The Prophecies of Balaam

Long before the Biblical books of the prophets, like Isaiah and Jeremiah, long before we read about Elijah and Elisha in I Kings, we read about a prophet, not even an Israelite, named Balaam. Balaam was a "prophet for hire," employed by the king of the Moabites to *curse* the advancing Israelites. He was a magician for a pagan culture, but one who nevertheless went against his king's request after having several direct contacts with God.

Today's OT reading contains one of the most bizarre strings of events depicted in the entire Bible. Among other things, this passage features the only passage in the Bible after the serpent in Genesis 3 with an animal speaking to humans – Balaam's talking donkey (Numbers 22:22-30) that could see an angel (22:31-35) that Balaam couldn't see himself. Instead of cursing the Israelites camped nearby, Balaam chose instead to listen to God and *bless* the advancing nation. Balaam spoke with God seven times, and gave a total of four oracles, each one more exasperating than the last to the furious Moab king. Eventually, the king simply gave up trying to get Balaam to pronounce the curse on Israel.

This wouldn't, however, be the last we hear about Balaam. We read about him again in just 3 more days, and he is mentioned no less than 5 times in the New Testament, where we then get an entirely different picture of this mysterious prophet.

March 12, NT
John 9:1-23
The Healing of the Man Born Blind, Part One

When Jesus made His public debut in a Synagogue in Nazareth, He read a prophecy from Isaiah that proclaimed eyesight to the blind

(Luke 4:18, Isaiah 61:2), and then told the crowd that they were witnessing the fulfillment of that prophecy in Him. Jesus would go on to perform the specific healing miracle of restoring a blind man's sight more than once after that, but today's NT reading is the first instance of this happening in Jerusalem. It is also another example of a miracle found only in John, and it's a big and long enough passage to break into two days' readings.

The miracle itself is done with the same quick dispatch as many of His others, and He gives the man being cured some specific instructions that lock in the location of this miracle as occurring in Jerusalem (John 9:7). The man's neighbors then marvel at the now-seeing man and question how his eyes were opened (9:8-10). Then the Pharisees, from whom Jesus had escaped the day before (or at least one day, anyway, see verse 14) got in on the act and not only grilled the healed man but brought in the man's parents (9:18-22). It was the formerly-blind man's parents who had the line of the day, though, when they rightly told the Pharisees that the man was "of age" and could "speak for himself" in the matter (9:21). But for their cooperation, their son would (in tomorrow's reading) end up being kicked out of the temple anyway.

March 13, OT
Numbers 25:1-26:34; 1 Chronicles 7:14-19; Numbers 26:35-37; 1 Chronicles 7:20-29; Numbers 26:38-65
The Seduction of Israel; The Second Census

Though the end of the book of Numbers is five days away (counting today), we today reach the other "bookend" event that gives the book its name. Back on March 3-5, we read a detailed census of Israel in which 603,550 "fighting men" were counted by tribe. Over the course of the last 10 days, we read of a variety of reasons why only two adult men out of that group would be alive when they reached and entered the Promised Land. One of the numerous reasons for the loss of over 603 thousand men over forty years' time makes up the first part of today's OT reading. The Israelites got the Lord angry again by joining the Moabites in worship of Baal (Numbers 25:1-3). In response, the Lord sent a plague to go along with a series of executions, resulting in the deaths of 24,000 (25:4-9).

They were now very close to their destination and it was time to count the "fighting men" of Israel again (26:1-65). The total number shows a net loss of 1820 men, totaling 601,730 (26:51). The two interludes from 1 Chronicles give some additional detail about the families of Manasseh and Ephraim. In the end, though, that number includes only two men who were counted at the first census at Sinai nearly 40 years earlier (26:64-65).

March 13, NT
John 9:24-41
The Healing of the Man Born Blind, Part Two

There was nothing more humiliating for a Jew living in Jerusalem than to be "put out" of the temple. After not getting a satisfactory answer from the formerly-blind man's parents about how he regained his sight, the Pharisees brought the healed man back in for further questioning (John 9:24).

The questioning reveals an extreme hostility towards the man who did the healing, a Man the Pharisees know but the healed man never mentions by name during the interrogation (9:25-34). In the end, unable to defend himself against the rage-blinded (9:40) Pharisees, he is put out of the temple (9:34).

But where he lost his standing in the community, he gained two other much more important things: 1) his sight and 2) his relationship with God, as he gets his hunch confirmed by Jesus Himself about who He really is (9:35-39). This He contrasts with the blindness (spiritual blindness) of the Pharisees (9:40-41) as He continues into His next lesson to the Pharisees in tomorrow's reading.

March 14, OT
Numbers 27:1-29:40
The Law of Inheritance, The Appointment of Joshua, More Laws of Sacrifice

The emphasis on men in the Bible, particularly with a pair of censuses that counted only men, is often criticized by women who feel unfairly discriminated against by gender. Apparently, there were some women in Moses' time that felt the same way. They asked for, and got, an explanation about the circumstances under which they would inherit their father's name if their father died without sons (Numbers 27:1-11) in the first part of today's OT reading.

Part two of the reading is Moses' forewarning of how and where he was going to die. Moses' response was a reverent request to know who is successor was, and he got his answer: Moses was to appoint Joshua to lead the Israelites across the Jordan and into the Promised Land (27:12-23). The final part of today's OT reading is a summary of the periodic sacrifices that would need to continue to be offered after their arrival there (28:1-29:40).

March 14, NT
John 10:1-21
Jesus, the Good Shepherd

One of the most popular and endearing images of Jesus is that of the Good Shepherd. The metaphor of being a shepherd, laying down His life for His flock (us), is an accurate and comforting picture of the Savior. Numerous works of art depict the Lord in that role. There are hospitals and nursing homes in many places that are called the "Good Shepherd." The often-quoted statement "I have come that they may have life and have it abundantly" (10:10) is found in this discourse to the Pharisees. Yet here, Jesus uses this gentle, comforting imagery on the Pharisees with whom He was arguing earlier. In most of Jesus' conversations with Pharisees, He either spoke out against their hypocrisy or tried to explain His deity. This was one of the few exceptions.

At this point, Jesus had been in Jerusalem long enough to attend the Festival of Booths, save an adulterous woman from execution by stoning, argue about His deity with the Pharisees, heal a man born blind, and return to his argument with the Pharisees again. Here Jesus turns his speech to the Pharisees into a teaching opportunity, using this "figure of speech" (literally "proverb", John 10:6) to explain how anyone who enters through the "sheep gate" (that is, Him; 10:9) will be saved. Everyone else (presumably meaning the Pharisees and those like them) that tries to enter by other ways is a thief or a robber (10:1). Jesus further makes comparison between Himself and others who would pretend to lead ("hired hand," 10:12-13, referring again to the Pharisees) the Jews. Near the end, He also makes a very important but often-missed prophecy regarding "other sheep" (10:16), referring to the Gentiles who would later become the Church.

Like previous encounters, there were some who began to believe (or at least, waver), but most Pharisees rejected this message like all the rest, even calling Jesus "insane" (10:20).

March 15, OT
Numbers 30:1-31:54
The Law of Vows, The War Against Midian, and its Aftermath

Another of the several things told to Moses by the Lord (which Moses then passed along to the Israelites) near the place where he would soon die was the Law of Vows (Numbers 30:1-16). It's a curious set of regulations that serve as an extension of the Law of Inheritance in granting women certain specific rights. Basically, the regulations spell out the fact that women have the same rights and responsibilities as men when making vows. They are just as binding as the vows made by men with two notable exceptions: the vows of an unmarried woman can be annulled by her father and the vows of a married woman can be annulled by her husband. Furthermore, the vows of a widow made while her husband was alive are only binding if she made them without any objection by her husband. If taken literally, this chapter could form the basis for solid contract law.

Part two of today's OT reading is a lengthy chapter concerning what was actually a brief event. After the incident that brought a plague that killed 24,000 Israelites (called "the Seduction of Israel," read two days ago), Moses received the Lord's permission to take vengeance against the Midianites for that seduction (31:2) as what would be Moses' last major event as leader of the Israelites. And so, a brief but fierce war ensued in which Israel routed the Midianites, killing every male (31:7) including Balaam (remember him?) the prophet who refused to curse the advancing Israelites yet fully participated in the pagan worship rites and seduced quite a few Israelites to join him (31:8). After the rout, there was a considerable amount of wrangling done to determine the proper way of dividing the spoils of war, which included 32,000 women and girls who had "not known a man intimately" (31:35). Despite the huge victory, this would not be the last time we read about either the Midianites or the Moabites with whom they were allied.

March 15, NT
John 10:22-42
Jesus Leaves Jerusalem after the Feast of Dedication

Jesus' last encounter with the Pharisees (the "Jews" as John puts it) while in Jerusalem happened during the Feast of Dedication, therefore some time in His last winter on Earth. That places this about four months before the crucifixion. Though slightly more than half of the remaining readings from the Gospels are yet to come in this chronology, this event marks the approximate ¾ mark through Jesus' active ministry on earth.

In this encounter, the Pharisees confront Jesus with more demands that He "prove" His deity (John 10:24). Jesus' efforts, with some of the most forceful preaching of His earthly ministry, almost get him stoned again (10:31-32), but He gets them to stop long enough to explain their rage. It boils down to the fact that the Pharisees absolutely will not accept the idea of a man making Himself out to be God (10:33). After Jesus counters with The Truth, he escaped them again and left Jerusalem (10:40) to a "place beyond the Jordan" where "John was first baptizing." It would be His last time leaving Jerusalem before His crucifixion.

March 16, OT
Numbers 32:1-33:56
Final Preparations for Entering the Promised Land, Part One

The Israelites were now so close to the Promised Land, the land of Canaan, that they could see it. It was across the Jordan River from what would become essentially their last camp. The "fighting men" had been counted; there were presumably another 500,000 to possibly 750,000 women and children with the 600,000 or so fighting men. Along with their belongings, cattle, and of course the Ark of the Covenant, they made for quite the formidable group. After defeating their last pre-Canaan enemy (there would be many more), two of the tribes of Israel make an interesting proposal: the tribes of Rueben and Gad, who apparently had the largest portion of the livestock, wanted to claim land on the side of the Jordan they were currently on as their own instead of crossing the Jordan with the rest of the Israelites

(Numbers 32:1-5). This was, at first, *not* taken well by Moses, as he believed they were trying to renege on their obligation to help defend Israel, as they were about to take the land they had been promised (32:6-15).

The leaders of Gad and Rueben responded that they fully intended to cross the Jordan with the other Israelites and help defeat all of their enemies, and then return to the land east of the Jordan River afterwards (32:16-19). Moses and the tribal leaders agreed to terms according to the wishes of Gad and Rueben, and they built villages for the women and children of those tribes in preparation for this.

Part of the reason for the belief that Moses was the author of Numbers (and the other books of the Pentateuch) is found near the beginning of the second chapter of today's OT reading: it is stated that Moses recorded the journey from the beginning in Egypt right up to the point where today's reading begins (33:2). From there, this recorded journey is spelled out stop by stop, all the way from Egypt to the plains of Moab across from the Promised Land.

At the end of the reading is a passage that would come back to haunt the Israelites long after they entered Canaan. The Lord commanded Israel, when taking possession of the land, to completely drive out the inhabitants of the land and destroy all of their "figured stones" and "high places" (33:50-54), and gave them a stern warning of the consequences of not following this law completely (33:55-56).

March 16, NT
Luke 10:1-37
The Mission of the Seventy; the Parable of the Good Samaritan

New Testament readings for the next two weeks, starting today, are exclusively from Luke. There is no portion of any of the Gospels that is in greater dispute as to its *position* in the chronology, or "harmony" of the Gospels than the section that begins with chapter 10 of Luke and ends with Luke 17. In putting together this chronology, I consulted with a number of different "harmonies of the Gospels" written by several different authors. They seemed to fall into three different camps based on where they placed this, the first of the readings that I claim come from just *after* Jesus' departure from His next-to-last trip to Jerusalem.

One group believes that Luke 10 is parallel to Matthew 10, from which we read just over a month ago. There is some evidence to support this, as several passages from today's NT reading (and several from the next two weeks) are almost word-for-word the same as their counterparts in Matthew and Mark from a period well before Jesus' most recent trip to Jerusalem. But parallel passages alone aren't enough to convince me, in this case, that the two accounts of the events are indeed parallel. We read on several other occasions where Jesus repeated various statements He previously had delivered in sermons. Also, Jesus' words are directed this time to a group of seventy people (72 in some translations) he sends out, not just the 12 as was the previous case. This alone tells me that these are two separate events.

Noting that the "ministry of the seventy" is a separate event, there is a second group that believes this to be part of Jesus' Jerusalem ministry. The group from which I took the bulk (but not all) of my decisions on where things were placed in the chronology is that same second group. That group placed John 10:40 *after* Luke 15, making the bulk of the next two weeks' readings take place in Jerusalem. There are a couple of problems with this. Most notable are His references to places in and around Galilee and Samaria, which in some cases were a long way from Jerusalem. After all, why would Jesus repeat his "statements of woe" about Tyre and Sidon (Luke 10:13-15) to people in Jerusalem? When He previously spoke them, there were people present from each of those communities.

The only logical conclusion is that the ministry of the seventy, their return to Jesus, and the great parable of the Good Samaritan are the first of several events in the life of Jesus immediately *after* His departure from Jerusalem to the "area beyond the Jordan." The only drawback to this interpretation is that it leaves Luke as having recorded Jesus' preparations and departure *for* Jerusalem and the events immediately after he *left* Jerusalem, but *none* of the events that occurred while He was *in* Jerusalem. (But, I can live with that and so can most scholars).

The final part of today's NT reading is the familiar parable of the Good Samaritan. Whole books can be (and have been) written on this topic (10:30-37). My very first opportunity to preach a "guest sermon" in a church was on this passage, and it's a personal favorite of mine. My emphasis in the sermon was on the verse that immediately precedes the parable itself: the lawyer and Jesus conclude their conversation with the lawyer asking, "who is my neighbor?" Jesus' parable, as an answer to that question, emphasizes not simply the good works of the Samaritan traveler or the hypocrisy of the other travelers who saw the injured man but did nothing, but the fact that the man was a *Samaritan* – the most hated group of people, outside of the Romans, to the average Jew of the day.

That's who our neighbor is.

March 17, OT
Numbers 34:1-36:13
Final Preparations for Entering the Promised Land, Conclusion

The conclusion of the Fourth Book of Moses is reached here, starting with a detailed abstract of what was to be the borders of the new land of Israel. Assuming the ability to find all of the locations listed (Numbers 34:1-12), the Promised Land had boundaries that included all of modern-day Israel, and portions of Lebanon, Syria, Egypt, and Jordan. This included the portion granted to Reuben and Gad and the half-tribe of Manasseh east of the Jordan River. The other 9-½ tribes had delegates appointed (34:13-29) to apportion the remaining land, noting that the Levites didn't get a specific portion of land because of their special status as priests. Instead, the Levites were given cities within the boundaries of the other tribes (35:1-5), including the "six cities of refuge" (35:6-29) in which someone guilty of homicide could flee and be sheltered. This form of Jewish judicial mercy is another of the many places in the Bible where a clear distinction is drawn between the crime of murder and other forms of killing, both deliberate and accidental.

The penalty for murder is still death, however (35:30-33), regardless of the refuge cities, but only when there would be *more than one* eyewitness. The book of Numbers concludes after this with a brief chapter with added details regarding the law of inheritance (36:1-12), discussed 3 days ago. At the end of the book, we still read of Moses and the rest of the Israelites on the east side of the Jordan River opposite Jericho, having not yet crossed over to the Promised Land.

March 17, NT
Luke 10:38-11:13
Martha and Mary and the Lord's Prayer

Jesus had many friends, some of them women. Martha and Mary were two of those friends, and He visited them at the beginning of today's NT reading. The comforting passage to "not worry" was delivered with the kind of loving care for which He had become famous. This is followed by one of the several passages in these next two weeks that are sometimes thought to be a parallel version of other passages from Matthew and Mark. But the last time Jesus is found teaching us how to pray, it was at the Sermon on the Mount. Even if you believe that the Sermon on the Plain, recorded in Luke (only) was the same event, the fact that this passage comes well after that should make it plain that this was simply a different event at a different time and place with a different audience – even though the message is the same.

When comparing the Lord's Prayer as found in Matthew to that in today's reading (Luke 11:2-4) it becomes obvious to any Roman Catholic reading this chronology that the church chose the Luke version for use in the liturgy (Mass). Paul and James later echo other verses in this reading in their epistles: James would quote Luke 11:9 and 11:13 and Paul would quote Luke 11:10 and 11:13, both in Romans. Notable, though, is the fact that James may have written his Epistle *before* Luke wrote his Gospel, which would make it Luke that was quoting *James* instead of the other way around.

March 18, OT
Deuteronomy 1:1-3:11
Moses Begins the Second Law

Most people believe that Moses wrote the first five books of the Bible. Deuteronomy is the final book of that set. Doubts exist for the Mosaic authorship because of the exclusive reference to Moses in the third person throughout all five books. But, as previously mentioned, scholars familiar with other ancient Hebrew literature know that this is not a real problem, as it was common practice to write everything that way, even when referring to one's self. The one possible problem with this comes near the end of this book: Moses' death. Someone else had to write that part, but I have a strong idea who it was which I will mention in the commentary for the March 29 reading.

Deuteronomy is the third most-quoted Old Testament book in the Gospels (behind #2 Isaiah and #1 Psalms). When the Israelites returned from exile in Babylon, they found a copy of The Law and had it read aloud in public. This Law is believed to be a copy of Deuteronomy. The name Deuteronomy comes from the Greek title in the Septuagint meaning the "second law".

A great deal of Deuteronomy will sound familiar to you if you have been following the chronology to date. That's because the bulk of the book is a series of discourses by Moses that include a recalling of the history of Israel from the exodus to their final encampment, and a recalling of The Law. The first part of this discourse, making up the entirety of today's OT reading, focuses on the events at Kadesh-barnea, which were read about on March 9 in Numbers 14.

March 18, NT
Luke 11:14-36
More Repeats from Earlier Sermons

The fact that today's NT reading contains no new material isn't meant to demean or reduce Jesus' words or in any way discredit Luke or the Bible. Any good pastor is going to occasionally repeat statements he/she makes, particularly when the statements are *good*. Thus, we have Jesus answering (for the *third* time, actually) those who accuse Him of being in league with demons (Luke 11:15-23), and reusing well-known metaphors to make His points such as the Sign of Jonah (11:29-32) and the parable of the lamp and the basket (11:33-36), among other things.

March 19, OT
Deuteronomy 3:12-5:33
End of First Discourse, Beginning of Second

As indicated yesterday, Moses spoke these things to "all Israel," making this a very large speaking occasion for someone who had complained to God about having a speech impediment! In addition to his discussion of the events that caused the "forty-year death sentence" (read on March 9 in Numbers 14 and yesterday), Moses recalled the events leading up to the brief war with the Midianites. At the beginning of today's part of that discourse, Moses recalls the results of that brief war: their land east of the Jordan (where they already were) was added to the already Promised Land (Canaan) and conditionally granted to the tribes of Gad, Reuben, and the half-tribe of Manasseh (Deut. 3:12-22).

But this was not the end of the "first discourse," as most call it. The continuing sections of the first discourse of Moses are: Moses specifically recalls his offense that resulted in his inability to cross over with the Israelites to the Promised Land (3:23-29) and teaches a new generation the importance of The Law (4:1-40). The three cities of refuge east of the Jordan are established (4:41-43) and the setting for the "dress rehearsal" of The Law (4:44-49) is then set up.

The beginning of the second discourse, though it is another example of something repeated from earlier writings (this time from Exodus), is one of the most important chapters of the entire Bible. Moses received a very large amount of "law" at Sinai and thereafter. The entire book of Leviticus is an example of just how much Law he received beyond just the Ten Commandments. But, the main reason we know that the Ten is the foundation for all law, besides what Jesus said much later, is right here (5:1-33). The Ten Commandments are restated here by Moses and clarified for even today's readers.

March 19, NT
Luke 11:37-54
Pharisees and Lawyers

Jesus' previous words (the last two days) were directed mainly at crowds of increasing size that didn't contain very many Pharisees. But, it's obvious that there were some who overheard Jesus' last few messages, as today's NT reading begins with one such Pharisee, who must have been present for at least part of the last sermon, inviting Jesus to have lunch with him. Jesus not only accepted, but also seemingly baited the Pharisee into a confrontation about the letter vs. the spirit of The Law (Luke 11:37-38). Jesus goes into a familiar tirade against the hypocritical Pharisees.

Luke then makes one of the very few distinctions in the Bible between Pharisees and Lawyers, as Jesus targets one of the latter. Luke is the only Gospel writer to make this distinction, quite possibly because he is believed to have been the only Gospel writer who was not a Jew. In reality, there is little difference except one of degree or emphasis: the word translated "lawyer" in Luke 11:45 and beyond is an "expert in Mosaic law," whereas Pharisee is a formal title, like that of a politician, whose origins are outside of the Bible, given to experts in the law who were also charged with enforcement. In one sense, the distinction, small as it is, between Pharisees and Lawyers is like Law and Order ("two separate but equally important groups…").

March 20, OT
Deuteronomy 6:1-8:20
The Shema

The Shema is the name given to a passage near the beginning of today's OT reading, in which Deut. 6:4-9 is actually recited word-for-word in Jewish prayers to this day. The word "shema" is the first word, in Hebrew, of verse 4. The key verse is 6:5 which translates "you shall love the Lord your God with all your heart and with all your soul and with all your might" (NASB). Everything else in this part of the "second discourse" stems from this statement, sometimes called "The Great Commandment."

Readers will recognize several passages in today's OT reading that are quoted (sometimes more than once) in the New Testament, and the Gospels in particular. The Shema (or parts of it) are quoted by several people in addition to Jesus. Deut. 6:13, 6:16, and 8:3 are used by Jesus in His response to Satan when tempted in the Desert. (Satan's two quotes of Scriptures come from Psalms.)

March 20, NT
Luke 12:1-21
The Parable of the Rich Fool

One of the several clues that this string of passages in Luke is *not* simply a parallel passage to earlier sermons and speeches recorded in Matthew and Mark is the fact that today's NT reading contains a parable found only in Luke that is part of His answer to a man who wanted Jesus to become involved in a family dispute.

Jesus begins today, following His most recent unpleasant encounter with the Pharisees, with a repeat of His warning about "the leaven of the Pharisees" (Luke 12:1-3). He continues with a repeat of His earlier speech about whom to fear (and who not to) (12:4-12) which leads to a man in the crowd asking Jesus to resolve a dispute over His inheritance (12:13). Obviously, the man had heard Jesus' words and was impressed with the obvious power in them, but had missed the point completely. Jesus points this out (12:14-15) and then tells the parable that gives today's NT reading its title (12:16-21).

March 21, OT
Deuteronomy 9:1-11:32
The Just War

The concept of the "Just War" is part of Roman Catholic doctrine, but is based on Scripture. It is an attempt to answer the often-asked questions about when (if ever) it is appropriate to use deadly force against an enemy of any kind. The Israelites had already fought against several enemies by the time of this second discourse by Moses, and they would be fighting many more in their future. But were they justified in fighting these battles? Did the war of invasion in which the Israelites were about to engage fit the criteria for the "Just War?" The answer can be found by comparing Moses' description of the war to come (Deut. 9:1-3) with at least one of the previously fought wars (Numbers 14:39-45). For all of the detail the Catholic Church puts into the Just War Doctrine, it boils down to this simple question: does/did God sanction the war or not? If the answer is "yes," despite the numerous reasons why God might choose to not show favor to His people (Deut. 9:4-29), then the war is justified; otherwise, it is not.

Moses' second discourse continues with a recalling of the making of the second set of tablets containing the Ten Commandments (10:1-11). God's grace and mercy are evident in that passage as well as the remainder of today's OT reading. In fact, God repeatedly grants the Israelites (and by extension, us) favor ("grace") despite weaknesses and rebellion if we only do one thing: love Him in return and thus acknowledge His great love for us.

March 21, NT
Luke 12:22-40
Don't Worry, Be *Ready*

The 1988 Bobby McFerrin tune "Don't Worry, Be Happy" is chock full of sound advice, wrapped up in an infectious a capella pop song. Its lyrics seem to indicate that at least some of it was inspired by Jesus' words in today's NT reading. Following the parable of the rich fool, which Jesus used to explain His reason for refusing to get involved with a family financial dispute, Jesus goes on to give a beautiful description of how God provides for our needs by citing nature (Luke 12:24-27) among other things. Unfortunately, one of the concluding verses of His "don't worry" speech is also one of the Bible's most abused passages: Luke 12:33 has Jesus telling us to "sell your possessions and give to charity," which some unscrupulous televangelists and cult leaders have interpreted as a *command* instead of the advice that it is.

What Jesus is trying to do here is get us to get our priorities straight. We focus far too much attention on earthly things and nowhere near enough on the spiritual. This incorrect focus isn't just bad in the short run. As Jesus explains (and goes into great deal about *later* in Matthew 24), focusing our attention in the right direction is a matter of readiness. Someday, this readiness is going to spell the difference for our eternal destination. The Doctrine of Imminence is based, in part, on the last verse of this passage, which states that the Son of Man is coming "at an hour that you do not expect" (12:40).

March 22, OT
Deuteronomy 12:1-14:29
The Test of True Prophecy (part one); Other Laws Repeated

Moses' second discourse, making up the majority of the book of Deuteronomy, continues with further justification of the war that would have to commence when the Israelites crossed the Jordan River and entered the Promised Land. God's call for war includes instructions to destroy all of the pagan "high places" of worship (Deut. 12:2-12), a statute the Israelites would, to their detriment, ignore later on. Moses also repeats some of the dietary laws (12:13-32) but this time explains why they are there: to separate the Israelites from the pagan, Baal-worshipping inhabitants of the Promised Land who frequently did things that were the exact opposite of The Law.

The key part of today's OT reading, however, isn't any of the repeating of The Law, but the best explanation of what it means to be a true prophet (13:1-5). To understand it properly, the word "prophet" itself must be defined. A prophet isn't necessarily someone who makes predictions, though most prophets do so. Rather, a prophet is someone who speaks for God and has direct contact with Him. That said, there must therefore be some way in which someone hearing a prophecy can discern the truth. Moses brings up two criteria: one is that the prediction made by the prophet must come true (more about this at the end of tomorrow's OT reading). The other, addressed here directly, is that if a prediction comes true but the prophet tries to use this fact to lead people *away* from God or to another god, that prophet is to be rejected as a false prophet. The rest of that chapter (13:6-18) addresses what should be done to such a prophet. Needless to say, the consequences for a false prophet are *not* pleasant.

The remainder of the reading continues with the "why" of the laws regarding clean vs. unclean foods (14:3-21) and regulations concerning tithes (14:22-29).

March 22, NT
Luke 12:41-59
Don't Wait, Decide Today

About two weeks from now, you will read a passage from Joshua in the Old Testament that implores us to chose whom we will serve, ending with the well-known quote "as for me and my house, we will serve the Lord" (Joshua 24:15). The point is to not put off your decision to serve God vs. serving other gods. Jesus makes a similar point in today's NT reading with a parable (Luke 12:42-48). He told this parable in response to a question from Peter about Jesus' sermon (yesterday) about readiness. The two messages go hand in hand.

Jesus continues with a differently worded but equally powerful message about why He came (12:49-53), echoing a statement made earlier in Matthew 10:34. Then, more about the readiness doctrine (12:54-59).

March 23, OT
Deuteronomy 15:1-18:22
Treatment of the Poor; The Test of True Prophecy (part two)

In between a pair of theological gems, Moses' second discourse continues with a further explanation and repetition of the annual festivals starting with Passover (Deut. 16:1-17), guidelines for appointing officers of law enforcement (16:18-20), forbidden forms of worship (16:21-17:13, 18:9-14), and the limitations and privileges of leaders (17:14-20). It is the beginning of the first and end of the fourth brief chapter in today's OT reading that we read the two "gems" of which I'm referring.

The question about how the poor should be treated makes up the first part of the reading, and it contains what some anti-Bible critics refer to as proof that the Bible contains contradictions. In one verse, Moses says that "there shall be no poor among you" (15:4), while saying almost the exact opposite later in "the poor shall never cease to be among you" (15:11). Which is right? Both, of course…but only if each verse is taken in its proper context. Both verses are inside a passage about the Sabbatical Year, a statute first introduced in Exodus (and echoed in Leviticus), in which debts are released as a way of treating rich and poor alike in an equitable manner. The former verse indeed says that "there shall be no poor among you," but this promise is conditional. The rest of that verse and the next (15:4-5) explain that this utopia will only occur if the Israelites *completely* obey the voice of God and all the commandments. Obviously, that wasn't going to happen, and it didn't, and that's why Moses brings up the opposite condition in verse 11. Jesus even brought this up during His ministry (Matthew 26:11, among other places).

At the other end (18:15-22) is the key passage about true prophecy for the entire Bible. Moses makes a great Messianic prophecy in 18:15 when he speaks of how the Lord will "raise up for you a prophet like me from among you…" This is one of the earliest prophecies of Jesus. Later, Moses explains the Test: if a prophecy does not come to pass, it wasn't from the Lord (18:22). This doesn't necessarily mean that all prophesies that *do* come true are from the Lord; only that the converse is true.

People who want to discredit the Bible often use the fact that many prophecies have not yet come true to make their case. Most, but not all, Biblical prophecies have come to pass; the ones that haven't yet are considered to be coming in the future, even when they date from the Old Testament. The only way any of those prophecies could be considered false is if it were *no longer possible* for it to come true. As far as anyone knows, this isn't the case with even one single prophecy, regardless of the symbolic or metaphorical language used in the prediction.

March 23, NT
Luke 13:1-21
Teachings, Healings, and Parables

Rather than focus on just one of the three things Jesus did while on earth, today's NT reading features some of all three, including the well-known (but brief version) of the parable of the mustard seed.

March 24, OT
Deuteronomy 19:1-22:30
Four Chapters of Laws

Nearly all of this part of Moses' Second Discourse was previously stated in Exodus, Leviticus, and Numbers. In several of the cases, Moses makes his summary here in Deuteronomy much more concise and brief than previously. For instance, the first part of today's OT reading concerns the law about the "cities of refuge" that are to be set up in the Promised Land. Here, he explains in 13 verses what previously took 34 verses in Numbers Chapter 35.

That theme of explaining, briefly but concisely, the laws previously established in the Pentateuch, is continued in the ensuing chapters, including the method by which Israel goes to war (which includes a wonderful passage about first making a peace offering) (Deut. 20:10), investigation of a murder (21:1-9), dealing with a rebellious son (21:18-23, which Jesus referred to when teaching the parable of the Prodigal Son in Luke 15), and many miscellaneous laws, mostly from Leviticus, concerning sexual relationships.

March 24, NT
Luke 13:22-35
The Lament over Jerusalem

According to the sequence of events in this chronological reading guide, Jesus departed Jerusalem after a week of readings in which He taught, performed miracles, and had several encounters with Pharisees. So if we assume (and I think correctly) that Jesus spoke of the doctrine of immanency (or readiness) *outside* of Jerusalem, then how is that reconciled, chronologically, with the references, starting in today's NT reading, of His next trip to Jerusalem?

The first verse of today's NT reading has Jesus passing from one village to another "on His way to Jerusalem" (Luke 13:22). We don't know from the readings this past week in Luke just how much time had passed since He left Jerusalem. We assume, from the way other events and festivals occurred, that there was, at *most*, a 4-month gap (and probably only 3) between Jesus' departure to a place "beyond the Jordan" (read last week) and the eventual "triumphal entry" into Jerusalem (read in three weeks) just prior to the Crucifixion. If He did indeed begin His final journey to Jerusalem at this time, then He either 1) took His time getting there and/or had His journey interrupted frequently by groups of people needing teaching or healing, or 2) almost half of all of Jesus' teachings, miracles, and parables occurred in the period immediately before and shortly after the Triumphal Entry. Personally, I believe both of these to be true.

After another parable about readiness, which also answers some questions about the doctrine of Election (Luke 13:22-30), Jesus speaks His 2-verse lament (13:31-32) over Jerusalem. He did not, as some believe, speak this while *inside* the city; rather, He said this while on his way to the city for the last time.

March 25, OT
Deuteronomy 23:1-26:19
Laws Concerning Divorce, Tithing; Conclusion of Second Discourse

Today's OT reading brings Moses' Second Discourse to a conclusion. Like yesterday, Moses recalls a large portion of the laws already spoken of in Exodus, Leviticus, and Numbers. All but one repeated section is explained using fewer verses than its corresponding first appearance in earlier books, yet is just as concise if not more so. In the four chapters of today's OT reading, two passages stand out in particular: the "Mosaic law of divorce" (Deut. 24:1-4) which was later used by the Pharisees in an unsuccessful attempt to trip up Jesus, and an expansion (the only one in the Second Discourse) of the previously 3-verse "law of first fruits," also known as the law of tithing (26:1-15).

March 25, NT
Luke 14:1-24
Two "Feast" Parables

The two parables spoken by Jesus in today's NT reading, though quite different in tone and point, have one very noticeable thing in common.

Jesus starts by deliberately baiting some Pharisees with whom He was eating bread by performing a healing miracle (Luke 14:1-6) on the Sabbath and challenging them to come up with an objection. They could not. It is the dinner setting of this miracle that probably gave Jesus the idea to make that also the setting of the parable he told immediately after that. The first parable is commonly known as the "parable of the wedding guest" or the "parable of the ambitious guest" (14:8-11), which explains true humility (the opposite of pride) and how to show it. It ends with the verse "whoever exalts himself will be humbled and he that humbles himself shall be exalted" (14:11).

The second parable, the "parable of the great feast" or "big dinner," is told in response to one of the men at the table with Jesus. The man with the question was an invited guest in the home of a Pharisee, and responded enthusiastically to Jesus' words at the end of the previous parable (14:12-14) by saying, "blessed is he that shall eat bread in the kingdom of God" (14:15). Jesus then tells the parable (14:16-24) as a cautionary tale, correcting the man and condemning all those who would reject the invitation of the Lord to repent and come to Him. While not denying or contradicting the doctrine of Election, Jesus makes a very strong case *against* the kind of "country club exclusivity" shown by people like the Pharisee and his invited guests.

March 26, OT
Deuteronomy 27:1-28:68
The Third Discourse

The entire Third Discourse of Moses is contained within today's OT reading in the form of two chapters, one of which is among the longest in the entire Pentateuch. The first part is a command to erect an altar on Mount Ebal (Deut. 27:2-8) and write the words of The Law on the stones. Joshua would later obey this command, as we will read in Joshua chapter 8 in just a few days.

Another mountain would then become the focus of a blessing on Israel with six of the tribes "standing" on that mountain to bless the people while the other six would stand on Mount Ebal for the curse (27:9-13). Moses then lists the "curses" for disobeying The Law, specifically citing several from the Ten Commandments, Leviticus 18-20, and Numbers 35 (Deut. 27:14-26). An almost equal number of verses are then devoted to the blessings granted for obedience (28:1-14). The list of blessings is almost the same as that given in Leviticus 26.

The Third Discourse then takes another dark turn when Moses begins to list the curses again, this time echoing Leviticus 26 (Deut. 28:15-68) but with a particular emphasis on the prophesy of future invasion (28:49-62) and dispersion (28:63-68). This prophecy would be fulfilled no less than *three* future times. Moses even prophesied the timetable for this to possibly occur, by stating in verse 36 that the Lord "will bring thee and thy *king* which thou shalt set over thee unto a nation which neither thou nor thy fathers have known" (emphasis mine). Israel did not yet have a king; in fact, the idea of having one had probably not yet crossed their minds. This prophecy could be applied easily to either of the two major exiles suffered by Israel, but the first of them wasn't set to occur until almost 700 years in Moses' future!

March 26, NT
Luke 14:25-15:2
More Parables on Discipleship

Jesus turns his attention from a small group of Pharisees to a much larger crowd in today's NT reading, with three parables (one of which He told previously) on the cost of discipleship.

The first part of the reading is a differently-worded repeat of an earlier teaching against compromising one's faith for the sake of not offending anyone (Matthew 10:35-39), where Jesus adds the verse "whoever does not carry his cross and come after Me cannot be My disciple" (Luke 14:27) to the earlier teaching. Jesus then goes on to use three parables: the building of a tower (14:28-30), the king preparing for battle (14:31-33), and the previously spoken parable of the salt losing its taste (14:34-35). In each, the emphasis is on being prepared to leave one's entire previous life behind when deciding to follow Him; that is, become a disciple.

Though Jesus' attention is then shifted from Pharisees to large crowds and then back to Pharisees again (15:2), the string of readings beginning yesterday and ending tomorrow make up Jesus' longest continuous string of parables, including one of His most beloved.

March 27, OT
Deuteronomy 29:1-31:29
The Fourth Discourse: The Renewal of the Covenant

Moses had spent the last 40 years of his life leading the Israelites through the desert. Only two people to whom he was speaking out of the entire Israelite population with these four discourses were alive at the time of the Exodus. For all the important detail of the commandments, the curses for disobedience and blessings for the opposite, one very important detail had yet to emerge in this great, final speech by Moses: the reasons for it all. None of these people knew firsthand the horrors of the Egyptian slavery or why it had taken them 40 years to make a journey that should have only taken a few weeks. They were headed for a land that none had ever visited, and was populated by people who took over that land generations ago, yet had previously been promised to one of their own ancestors. The Lord, through Moses, tells the Israelites why.

The first part is mainly about several recent (to them) events that led up to the great explanation: in Deut. 29:13, God expresses His desire to re-enter into a covenant (agreement) with the Israelites as they prepare to enter the Promised Land (Deut. 29:1-13). Moses follows this with another round of warnings of the consequences of disobedience (29:14-28), but then explains God's mercy to them in giving the Israelites the option of repentance (29:29-30:10) as a means of restoring the covenant agreement.

The Covenant was always a conditional agreement. For all of the lofty promises set forth to Abraham first, then Isaac and Jacob/Israel and later the whole nation, the agreement to bring these people to the Promised Land was predilected on their observance of the Lord as their God and their obedience to His laws. Moses spelled out the choice before them (30:11-20) in no uncertain terms. Doubters of The Covenant, particularly Muslims and other groups that say that Israel has no historic claim to the land they now occupy, are quick to point out that Israel has never possessed 100% of the land promised to them by God (see Genesis 15 and Numbers 34), but the reasons why can be ascertained right here. Rather than dismissing the promises as being not fulfilled, one should focus on the fact that the promises were and still are conditional.

This concludes Moses' Fourth Discourse but by no means his last words before the Israelites. It's interesting to note that the entire series of discourses may have happened on his birthday (31:2) depending on how the verse is read. But after his final pieces of advice (31:3-13) and warnings (31:14-21) against breaking The Covenant, Moses meets with his successor Joshua to put the finishing touches on his earthly ministry: he wrote a song which will be the focus of tomorrow's OT reading.

March 27, NT
Luke 15:3-32
The "Lost" Parables

Three of Jesus' best-known parables have the word "lost" in their subtitles, and all three were spoken to Pharisees in today's reading. Just as frequently, the third (final, and arguably best) of them uses the word "Prodigal" in its subtitle, known as the Parable of the Prodigal Son, found only here in Luke.

The first of the three parables spoken today is the only one that had already been spoken: the Parable of the Lost Sheep (Luke 15:4-7) was previously told in Matthew 18:12-14 (read on March 5). This is followed by the Parable of the Lost Coin (Luke 15:8-10). This one is told only in Luke, but echoes the theme of the Lost Sheep parable. That theme is repentance, and the fact that it's not how much or what kinds of sins you commit; but rather, the fact the sinner repents and thus is reconciled with God. All three parables were actually told in response to grumbling by the Pharisees (15:1-2, yesterday's reading) in which Jesus was criticized for "receiving sinners" and eating with them.

That third parable is quite possibly Jesus' most famous. The Parable of the Prodigal Son drives home Jesus' point about the value of repentance more so than any other parable. It's also an important treatise on the response to repentance, forgiveness, as many preachers focus on the actions of the father more so than the son. Some, in fact, like to debate which of the two sons mentioned in the parable is the real "Prodigal."

There is some evidence to support either side of the argument, but there is one thing of which everyone agrees: both sons are sinners and are used by Jesus in the parable to represent all sinners (which is, of course, all of us). The big difference is that the younger one is forgiven because he repented. The older son is a sinner too, and is forgiven as well (15:31-32) but in a different way and to a different degree. If the father is the "God" figure in the story, then we also see the universal-ness of God's forgiveness. The older son's anger was both a sin and the consequence of sin. We don't know, nor does it matter, the nature of any of the other sins committed by the older son. It doesn't matter because God loves us all anyway, and will never turn His back on us no matter how hard we might try to turn our backs on Him.

March 28, OT
Psalm 90:1-17; Deuteronomy 31:30-32:52
The Song(s) of Moses

Psalms is the longest book of the Bible in terms of chapters and verses, and second longest in total words. It is the most quoted book of the Old Testament in the New Testament, and is one of the few known to have multiple writers. There is a small minority of people who believe that David wrote all or nearly all of the Psalms. However, the introduction to this very first Psalm in the chronology of this reading plan puts the first kink in the armor of those who believe in the "all-David" theory.

Psalms are hymns. Chronologically, the first one is believed to have been written by Moses, and is thus placed here, written just before his death. The last one is believed to have been written by Ezra, and is numbered as Psalm 147. The book of Psalms is sometimes called "the hymnbook of Israel" and is still the most popular part of the Old Testament read by Jews, Christians, or seekers.

Today's OT reading is the first since March 13 to feature more than one book, and that last time was a book (Chronicles) containing mostly history. Psalms is different: as poetry, there is almost no historical narrative here, but the chronological placement of the Psalms reflects their historical context. It also reveals, in many cases, the true author, which leads to this chronology's count of 79 Psalms (just over half) that can be attributed to David with certainty, with perhaps another 20 going to David as well.

Moses wrote this first one, along with the song sung in Deuteronomy 31-32, very close to his death (some estimate he died later that same day). It was not the first song sung by Moses, but it was his last. In Deuteronomy, the song contains both history and prophecy. At its conclusion, Moses is commanded to ascend Mount Nebo where he would be given his last opportunity to look at the Promised Land from a distance (Deut. 32:48-52). But before he did this, he would make one more great final speech.

March 28, NT
Luke 16:1-18
No One Can Serve Two Masters

Jesus continues teaching in parables, now adding his disciples to an audience that had previously been made up of Pharisees. In one of Jesus' numerous teachings on the proper use of money, the parable (Luke 16:1-13), sometimes known as the Parable of the Corrupt Steward, is hard to understand unless you read the verse that follows (16:14). There it becomes plain that Jesus was referring to the Pharisees, corrupted with greed and improperly gained wealth. The last verse of the parable sums it all up: that one cannot serve both God and wealth (16:13). It is still a confusing parable, since it "seems" to advocate theft and fraud (16:8), but careful study of related passages and the context of this one will make it easier to understand.

After a final rebuke of the sin of covetousness (16:15-17), Jesus concludes today's reading with a one-verse teaching on divorce (16:18) that echoes several previous teachings.

March 29, OT
Deuteronomy 33:1-34:12; Joshua 1:1-2:24
The Passing of the Torch

The lofty-sounding title given to today's OT reading reflects the central theme of what is written there. Moses' two final acts are recorded here, and then his death. This has led some to believe that it was not possible for Moses to have been the author of the Pentateuch. Others believe that Moses wrote down an account of his death in advance, since he knew the exact manner and time of it. My personal theory on this is that Moses had a scribe (as did some other Biblical writers, most notably the prophet Jeremiah) and that the scribe then finished the book we now know as Deuteronomy, where Moses' death is recorded.

First, Moses gives a great, final speech (Deut 33:1-29), in which he gives a blessing to each of the 12 tribes. Some blessings are as short as a single verse; others stretch on for 4 or more verses. Some of the blessings are easy to read and interpret, others are cryptic and strange. Many are echoes of the blessings given to the 12 tribes by Joseph just prior to his death as recorded in Genesis. Following this, Moses gets his chance to glimpse the Promised Land (34:1-4), and after that he died (34:5-7).

The passing of the torch here has a dual meaning. Joshua succeeds Moses as leader of the Israelites (34:9), and here ends the first set of books believed to have been written by one person (Moses). The writer of the next book, Joshua, is known even less certainty than the Pentateuch. Some believe it was written by Joshua himself, which is a reasonable conclusion, but others have doubts. The writing style is subtly different than that of Moses, so it was likely not Moses' scribe (if he had one). With Joshua we begin a whole new *section* of Bible books, called the Historical Books. Despite the fact that there has already been much history in the first five books and elsewhere, the section starting with Joshua contains almost nothing but.

The first two chapters of Joshua contain his formal ascension as leader of Israel and his assuming of the command of the troops that would lead them across the Jordan and into the Promised Land. Part of this is the fascinating account of the spies sent by Joshua and their encounter with a prostitute named Rahab (Joshua 2:1-14), whose family would later be spared when they would conquer Jericho.

March 29, NT
Luke 16:19-17:10
Lazarus and the Rich Man and Other Teachings

If the story of the rich man (who goes to Hades, or "Sheol") and Lazarus is a parable, it would mark the one and only time in which a person in a parable is given a name (Luke 16:19-31). Most scholars believe that this was the story of a real person, though the Lazarus here is not to be confused with the friend of Jesus and brother of Martha and Mary whom we will meet in tomorrow's reading.

In this reading, Jesus concludes his teaching to the Pharisees and redirects his words in 17:1-10 to his disciples, including the use of the metaphor of "the mustard seed" to describe their faith.

March 30, OT
Joshua 3:1-6:27
The Israelites Enter the Promised Land

These four chapters pack a lot of history into a relatively short time frame. Joshua chapter 3 starts with their new leader giving the Israelites instructions for crossing the Jordan River (Joshua 3:1-13), followed by the miraculous parting of the waters, allowing them to cross (3:14-17). This would mark the second time in which a river's waters parted for the advancing Israelites.

The conquest of the Promised Land continues with the "twelve stones memorial" (4:1-14) in the still-dry riverbed. A second memorial, also marked with twelve stones, was put up at Gilgal, east of Jericho (4:19-20) after the waters resumed their normal flow. The Lord then commanded that the Israelites be circumcised (5:2-7), as this had not been observed with the new generation born in the wilderness. During the recovery period, they observed the Passover (5:8-10) and saw the end of the manna from heaven that had been provided every day

(5:12). Joshua then had an encounter with an angel of the Lord (5:13-15) as the Israelites prepared to conquer Jericho.

It is the sixth chapter that chronicles this miraculous conquest (6:1-27) as the climax comes in verse 20, immortalized in song as "the walls came tumbling down."

March 30, NT
John 11:1-29
The Death and Resurrection of Lazarus, Part One

Our first reading from anyone but Luke in over a week, and the first from outside Luke since Jesus left Jerusalem, is the account recorded only here in John of what is perhaps the most astonishing miracle performed by Jesus during His earthly ministry. Today's half of it consists of the events leading up to the miracle; tomorrow we read of the miracle itself.

This is one of the best-known passages in the Bible. Mary and Martha, whom Jesus had previously met, were sisters of His friend Lazarus (not the one spoken of in yesterday's reading). Lazarus was dying, though we don't know of the sickness with which he was afflicted. Despite what was obviously a close relationship (John 11:5), Jesus decided to stay where he was instead of going to visit the sick friend. This was a deliberate move to show everyone, including his disciples, exactly who had the power over death.

Not everyone is happy with Jesus' decision to *appear* to let Lazarus die. Make no mistake: Lazarus did die, but Jesus knew He had the ability to raise him. This wasn't Jesus' first resurrection miracle; but more importantly, it wouldn't be his last or most important one. Martha, though apparently a woman of great faith (11:24), did not understand what Jesus was trying to point out, but Jesus set her (and everyone else) straight with His words about being "the resurrection and the life" (11:25). Martha appears to understand more fully, and today's reading ends with the preparation for the great miracle that was about to occur.

March 31, OT
Joshua 7:1-9:27
Sin and Repentance, Defeat and Conquest

Israel's conquest of the Promised Land did not stop at Jericho. Jericho was but one town of many that needed to be taken. Their success in Jericho was due to their strict obedience of the guidelines given to them by the Lord through Joshua. But just as with nearly everything the Israelites did, there were one or more people who messed things up either for themselves or for all of Israel.

Such is the case in today's OT reading, as we first get a brief account of the theft, by Achan, of some of the spoils of Jericho that were meant to be dedicated to the Lord. The Lord punished all Israel for this crime by first letting Joshua send in an overconfident and undermanned army to attempt conquest of the next city, Ai (Joshua 7:3-5). When Joshua rightly asked for forgiveness on behalf of Israel (7:6-15), God gave Joshua instructions for what to do next and justice was done (7:16-26). After this, the Israelites took the city of Ai by ambush (8:1-23), doing it right this time because they did it God's way. Joshua led Israel in a ritual of thanksgiving for their victory.

The Israelite's next conquest was more anti-climactic, as they were initially tricked into a peace agreement with one of the people groups they were supposed to conquer (9:1-27). When Joshua discovered that Israel had been duped, he got his revenge on the deceitful Gibeonites by making slaves of them.

March 31, NT
John 11:30-54
The Death and Resurrection of Lazarus, Part Two (Conclusion)

Part two of the account of Jesus' resurrection of Lazarus begins with Lazarus' other sister, Mary, making the same plea: that if Jesus had come sooner, their brother would not have died (John 11:32). Like many similar situations, as Jesus now saw the other family members' emotional reactions, He too got emotional (11:33-36). Jesus knew all along that He was willing and capable of raising Lazarus from the dead, but in the Bible's shortest verse (11:35) He reveals His full humanity along with his full divinity by weeping with the family of the deceased man. Then, He went to the tomb and carried out the amazing miracle (11:39-44).

The result was the same as with many other miracles of Jesus: many converted to faith in Him (11:45) but this only increased the Pharisee's zeal in plotting to kill him (11:46-53). It is here that we are first introduced to the name Caiaphas, the High Priest who would eventually be the one to bring the formal charges against Jesus just prior to His crucifixion.

As indicated at the conclusion of the reading, Jesus did not yet return to Jerusalem, though he was "on His way" for the past two weeks' readings. Rather, Jesus stayed in the town of Ephraim (11:54) with His disciples.

April 1, OT
Joshua 10:1-12:24
The Day the Earth Stood Still

After the Israelites bloodlessly conquered the Gibeonites (following the latter's treachery), some of the other yet-to-be-conquered kings decided to fight back by attacking the same Gibeonites. That may have been sound military strategy, but their fate was already sealed: the Lord had already "given them into [Joshua's] hands" (Joshua 10:8). As part of the great battle that ensued in defense of Gibeon, Joshua successfully pleaded with the Lord to make the sun stand still and not set for a whole day and night (10:12-14).

People who insist on mocking the Bible like to use this passage as a way of discrediting Scriptures. This mockery sometimes comes in the form of statements allegedly "proving," through scientific measurement and NASA photographs, the "extra day" in Joshua. The fact that it cannot be proven scientifically to have occurred doesn't mean it didn't, however, and the fact that some would state that it had been either proven or disproved shows the deceitful nature of some non-believers. Believers should believe the event occurred simply on the basis of God telling us so.

The remaining parts of today's OT reading detail the aftermath of Israel's victory over the attacking armies (10:15-28), the military campaigns after that in the north (10:29-43) and south (11:1-15), and a summary of the wars that were fought and the kings that were conquered (11:16-12:24) on Israel's way towards conquest of the entire Promised Land.

April 1, NT
Luke 17:11-37
The Miracle of the Ten Lepers; Predicting the Rapture

Jesus wastes no time after his most recent miracle. Another is performed, this time in the healing of ten lepers (Luke 17:11-16). The key point of this miracle was not any kind of show of power on Jesus' part (none were, anyway), but rather, a seemingly natural compassionate response by Jesus to their situation, for which only one came to thank him (17:17-19). Here, Jesus reminds him and everyone that it was the man's *faith* that made him well.

Jesus then responded to a question by some Pharisees, and then to his disciples, with another prediction (of several He had already made) of His death and resurrection (17:25)…and then, more importantly, his *return*. Jesus makes it clear that when He comes again, everyone will know it (17:24), but that the day will be like all others (17:26-30) by using the examples of Noah and his family and Lot and his wife. He then makes the clearest prediction of the *manner* of that return in a passage many consider to be the most obvious prediction of the Rapture (17:34-36) made outside of Paul's letter to the Thessalonians.

The Rapture, though controversial because of the debate over its timing, is clearly indicated as an event that, nevertheless, *will* occur. Those who believe, as I do, that it will be a so-called "secret" Rapture cite this passage (especially verses 20 and 22) as proof that Jesus predicted this Himself.

April 2, OT
Joshua 13:1-15:63
The Tribal Allocation, part one

The OT readings for the next four days center around a single topic: having conquered most of the land (not completely displacing the former residents…more about that below), the land was now to be divided amongst the 12 tribes according to the promises made and the blessings issued. It begins with God pointing out to Joshua the lands that still needed to be conquered (Joshua 13:1-6), but telling Joshua to go ahead with the tribal allocation anyway (13:6) and then detailing this starting with the conquered portion going to nine and a half of the tribes of Israel (13:7). After noting the portion going to the Ruebenites, Gadites, and the other half tribe on the other side of the Jordan, God detailed the exact geography of each other tribe's territory.

There are two important things to note about this part of the Bible. First, though God promises to "drive them out from before the sons of Israel," (13:6) the fact that Joshua and his armies had not done so already was going to cause many problems for the Israelites down the road. The other is something that would require a very careful study of the Bible as well as an extensive knowledge of Middle East geography and lots of very accurate maps: if the modern state of Israel were drawn according to the boundaries given here in Joshua, Israel would include all of what is now Israel (including the 1967 borders and Gaza strip), nearly all of Lebanon, most of Jordan, and even portions of what is now Syria and Egypt.

April 2, NT
Luke 18:1-14
Two Parables: Don't Quit, Don't Be a Hypocrite

A popular poem begins "When things go wrong as they sometimes will…" and ends with "Rest if you must, but don't you quit!" This is the theme of the first of two parables taught by Jesus in today's NT reading, both of which concern the value of prayer, but from two completely different angles.

The Parable of the Widow and the Unjust Judge (Luke 18:1-5) is used as an example of the value of persistence. Does God answer our prayers? Yes… and always. It sometimes, however, takes a while for someone to realize that a prayer is being answered when one doesn't get the answer one expects. The key here is, as Jesus points out, to not give up – to continue in the manner of the widow in the parable. Jesus makes a contrast between the judge who only reluctantly gives justice to the widow, and a just Lord who will "bring about justice for them quickly" (18:8). But before the Lord does this, we must not give up. The first parable ends with an interesting rhetorical question: will He (meaning Jesus when He comes again) find faith on the earth? Some have used this verse to justify a belief that all true Christians will have died by the time Jesus makes his Second Coming.

The second parable is easier to interpret than the first. It focuses once again on prayer, but this time contrasts two praying individuals, one (a Pharisee, the obvious target of the parable) from the point of view of someone who measures themselves by *self*-righteousness and pride (18:10-12), the other (a tax collector) who enters prayer in humility, begging for mercy (18:13).

April 3, OT
Joshua 16:1-19:9; 1 Chronicles 4:24-33; Joshua 19:10-31
The Tribal Allocation, part two

Further description of the geographical allocation of the Promised Land to the 12 tribes of Israel is given today along with some details from a book from which we haven't read in 3 weeks: an account of the genealogy of Simeon in I Chronicles to go with his tribe's geographical allocation (Joshua 19:1-9).

April 3, NT
Matthew 19:1-12
Pharisees Question Jesus on Divorce, Version 1

Last time we read from Matthew was prior to Jesus' most recent trip to Jerusalem, which we read about nearly a month ago. Now, after He has left and is on His way back (Matthew 19:1-2), Jesus is confronted by Pharisees who use a technique that is still commonly used by *un*believers today: trying to trip up a believer (or in this case, Jesus) by pointing out *apparent* contradictions in Scripture.

Note the italics. All *apparent* contradictions in the Bible are just that: apparent. Jesus responds to the Pharisees question about divorce (19:3) by quoting Genesis 1:27 and 2:24 (Matthew 19:4-5) to show God's plan for marriage. The Pharisees counter with Deuteronomy 24:1-4 as though it contradicted God's plan for marriage. But where the Pharisees have it wrong is in the meaning of the Mosaic Law. The Mosaic Law is in regards to a man's and woman's status after a divorce is completed, not justification for *when* it can legally be done. Jesus points this out (19:8-9) and then fields a question from a disciple regarding celibacy (19:10). Jesus' response (19:11-12) has been used by the Roman Catholic Church to justify the celibacy of priests, but this is a misinterpretation of what Jesus said. Jesus' teaching here states that celibacy is a *good* thing, though it isn't a *necessary* thing in order to find favor with God regarding relations with women.

April 4, OT
Joshua 19:32-21:42; 1 Chronicles 6:54-81; Joshua 21:43-45
The Tribal Allocation, part three

The first part of today's OT reading describes the land allocation to the few tribes not yet described in detail the previous two days, followed by a pair of special twists: Joshua is granted a plot of land of his own (Joshua 19:49-51), separate and independent from all the others, yet within their midst. Joshua 19:51 makes note of the fact that, at this point, they had finished dividing the land, yet no mention had yet been made of the portion that was to be granted to one of the tribes: namely, the tribe of Levi.

But the reason for that is clear if you had been reading each day's OT passage so far this year. The Levites get no land inheritance at all; rather, they are to live in cities among the other tribes of Israel (Numbers 34 and 35). And so, after the allocation to all the tribes is completed, and Joshua's personal portion is granted, we have a description of the six cities of refuge (Joshua 20:1-9), three on each side of the Jordan, as first described by Moses before the conquest. Then, the cities for the Levites are described (21:1-41) in amongst the lands for other tribes. This is also described in the passage from 1 Chronicles.

The reading concludes with the summation that all of God's promises had been fulfilled, thus the title given to the now-conquered "Promised Land" (21:43-45). If Israel had kept their entire end of the bargain, both up to that point and thereafter, this would have been the end of the story and the last of the history to become part of Scripture. But as you will read following this, the story of the Israelites is filled with more ups and downs in the future than even Joshua realized.

April 4, NT
Mark 10:1-12
Pharisees Question Jesus on Divorce, Version 2

We last read from Mark even longer ago than yesterday's reading was from Matthew, with today marking exactly one month since we last heard from the earliest Gospel writer. But in today's NT reading, we get another account of the exact same event, with just a few minor differences compared to yesterday's version in Matthew.

In most respects, this is an identical but abbreviated account of the Pharisees' questions about divorce and their use of scripture to justify their position. They use Deuteronomy 24:1-4, and Jesus uses Genesis 1:27 and 2:24 to back the correct counter position. Here, though, Jesus does not explain the reasons for the *apparent* contradiction. Also in this version, a second question regarding celibacy does not come up. It does say, though, that there were further questions (Mark 10:10), not quoted by Mark, that were answered by Jesus (10:11-12) with the stern warning against divorce and re-marriage, explaining that doing so is actually the sin of adultery.

April 5, OT
Joshua 22:1-24:33
The Tribes Go Home and So Does Joshua

After the tribal allocation was formally completed, the two and a half tribes that had inherited a land east of the Jordan River were sent home to settle their new territory (Joshua 22:1-9). Before their journey was completed, a controversy arose around an altar they had built (22:10-34), but it was resolved before the land was settled.

And so we come to the end of the history of the last of the leaders of Israel who was alive at the time of the Exodus. The death of Joshua at the end of the book marks the end of an era as much so as did the death of Moses earlier. He begins his final words to Israel by reminding them that all good things come from the Lord (23:1-16), including every victory over their conquered foes. He then goes further back and proves his point by recounting a history from Abraham's father Terah on forward to his present day (24:1-13). Then comes what is likely the best-known passage in Joshua: his exhortation to "choose…today whom you will serve," ending with "as for me and my house, we will serve the Lord" (24:15). Although Israel responded to this with a promise to serve the Lord (24:21, 24:24), their future, recorded in the next few books of the Bible, is filled with numerous examples of them ignoring that promise.

Thus it was with a largely *not*-conquered Promised Land and a weak-spirited people who had no king or judge that Joshua died (24:29) at the age of 110.

April 5, NT
Luke 18:15-30
The Little Children and the Rich Young Man

The two parts of today's NT reading are repeated, nearly verbatim, in tomorrow's and the next day's readings from Mark and Matthew. All three accounts begin with people bringing their children to be blessed by Jesus, which draws a rebuke from His own disciples. In Luke's version, Jesus returns the rebuke (Luke 18:16-17) but there is no mention of the actual blessings that are described in both of the other versions.

The encounter with the rich young man that follows is told almost exactly the same way in each version. One of the verses, in this case Luke 18:24, has been frequently used to equate wealth with sin; i.e. that it is a sin to be wealthy because wealthy people will have an infinitely harder time getting into the Kingdom of God. This is a misinterpretation. What Jesus is referring to here is twofold: one is that, admittedly, the vast majority of rich people get that way with selfish or even fraudulent acts, the other is that even many of those who obtain their wealth through "good" means often hoard it and are not generous. Presumably, if someone obtained much wealth but was generous with that wealth and shared it to the point of being "sacrificial," as Jesus even explains (18:29-30), that person would be rewarded for that sacrifice.

April 6, OT
Judges 1:1-3:6; Judges 17:1-13
The Beginning of Post-Joshua Israel

It is not known who wrote the book of Judges, and there is some evidence to indicate that it is the product of more than one writer. Whoever wrote it had to be either a contemporary of Samson or have lived sometime after that.

After Joshua died, the Israelites were left with no leaders except for their military leaders. There was no king, and there were not yet any Judges, either. Judges, in this context, aren't the same as the image we have today of a person who presides over a court of law. Rather, the Judges were people sent by God to deliver Israel during times when they fell away from the Lord.

At first, things seem to go well without Joshua. The tribes of Judah and Simeon went on a campaign to conquer their remaining allotted territories (Judges 1:1-20), mostly with success. The tribes of Benjamin and Manasseh were not so fortunate (1:21-2:5), because they did not fully obey the Lord. By not completely conquering the land, leaving a remnant of the Canaanites and their pagan religions behind, these tribes were essentially abandoned by the Lord and would face much greater obstacles and problems in the future as a result. The fact that Joshua's death is recorded a second time right after that (2:6-9) is an indication that at least part of this history may have occurred before he had died.

Thus did a new generation come about after that in Israel that not only increased in their disobedience to the Lord but also actively became worshippers of the false god Baal and other pagan beliefs held by the people they were supposed to drive out (2:10-15). In response to this, God appointed "Judges" to lead Israel out of this apostasy. Depending on whether you count Samuel as the last Judge and whether you count Deborah and Barak separately or as one Judge, there are between 13 and 15 Judges who presided over Israel over the course of about 300 years. It should also be noted that three of the Judges would not be mentioned in this book, but in Samuel, much later.

Thus are chapters 3 through 16 of Judges an account of that period in Israel's history. Most of it is in its proper chronological order. From chapter 17 (from which we read today) on to the end of the book, Judges shows other points in history that are difficult to place within the rest of the chronology. Thus we jump from the beginning of chapter 3, before the account of the first Judge, to chapter 17 where we read of a man named Micah (not to be confused with the Prophet) who became one of the first to clearly illustrate just how easily a false religion can crop up when it is *not* based on the word of the Lord (17:1-13).

April 6, NT
Mark 10:13-31
The Little Children and the Rich Young Man

Mark's version of the blessing of the children describes the event in more detail than Luke, as it also goes into more detail about the discussion regarding what it would take for a wealthy person to enter the Kingdom of God.

April 7, OT
Judges 18:1-31; Judges 3:7-4:24
The Idolatry of the Danites; The First Five Judges

Today's OT reading is a lengthy one, so the commentary will be brief. The continuation from yesterday's reading from Judges shows the result of one tribe's actions in ignoring God and moving on with actions that are both selfish and blasphemous. One interesting note: the tribe of Dan did indeed get an inheritance (Judges 18:1) but some were obviously not satisfied with this. Thus, they sought to conquer a larger portion than what God allowed, and went after a land that had just as much of a problem with idolatry as they had.

Back to chapter 3, we then see the first of the many cycles of sin – suffering – crying out to God – deliverance – and finally peace that Israel went through as God appoints each judge for Israel. In response to the idolatry of Micah and the Danites, and the rest of Israel, God allowed the king of Mesopotamia to enslave them for 8 years (3:8). But then God appointed the first Judge, Othniel, who led Israel in the ways of God – and 40 years of peace (3:9-11). The cast of characters changed, and the number of years of suffering followed by the period of peace changed as well, but the basic cycle was exactly the same for the second Judge, Ehud (3:12-30), in one of the more explicitly violent chapters of the Bible, and the third Judge, Shamgar (3:31), whose rule is given only a single verse.

Some consider the duo of Deborah and Barak to be a single phase of Judges, but others (including me) list them as the fourth and fifth Judges as if separate. The account of their victory over the oppressing Canaanites is found in Judges 4:1-24.

April 7, NT
Matthew 19:13-30
The Little Children and the Rich Young Man

The third and final version of these two events during Jesus' return to Jerusalem has much in common with both of the other two, though they are not identical. Matthew's account of the blessing of the children is closer to Mark's than Luke's, including a description of the blessing like in Mark, but like Luke's is only three verses long.

Then, also like Mark, the encounter with Jesus and the rich young man goes almost exactly the same, including the aftermath when Jesus uses the metaphor of a camel passing through the eye of a needle, countered with the statement that "with God all things are possible". Matthew does so using fewer verses than either Mark or Luke, but then goes into much more detail about the rewards for sacrifice (Matthew 19:28-30) than either of the other two synoptic Gospels.

April 8, OT
Judges 5:1-7:25
Deborah, Barak, and Gideon

The first part of today's OT reading is the conclusion of the account of Deborah and Barak, and the victory song they sang (Judges 5:1-31) after they defeated the Canaanites. An interesting note is the location of their victory: Megiddo, the large plain between Jezreel and Sharon, known as Armageddon when translated into Greek.

This was also the site of the next Judge's great victory. Often regarded as one of Israel's greatest (if not The Greatest) Judges, Gideon's rise to power after the 40 years of peace that happened under Deborah and Barak was precipitated by the same cycle spoken of yesterday. The Israelites sinned (6:1) and God allowed another army to conquer them for a time (6:1-10). Gideon was appointed as the sixth (fifth if you count Deborah and Barak as one "team") Judge to deliver them from the Midianites (6:11-7:25 and beyond).

April 8, NT
Matthew 20:1-16
The Parable of the Laborers

This parable of Jesus, found only in Matthew, is actually an extension of yesterday's account of the encounter with the rich young man (and Peter's question that followed), and is actually the reason why the three different versions of that event were presented in that order: Luke, Mark, and then Matthew, who goes on for an additional 16 verses in the same conversation in today's NT reading.

One of the most common human reactions to seeing someone else receive a great reward for doing less than we do is jealousy. The reason for this is the prevalence of one of the most common sins:

covetousness. It is the breaking of the 10th commandment (or 9th depending on how you count them). Like many discussions about sin, it needs to be pointed out that God doesn't look at any one sin as being worse than another, and it's also not a matter of how many times you have committed a certain (or total) sins: what matters is that you repent and receive the free gift of forgiveness for those sins. We call that "salvation".

In the context of the previous passage, where Jesus explained the rewards for true sacrifice, this parable goes on to use the metaphor of a day's wages to explain how everyone, no matter at what point in their lives, can likewise receive this same wage (actually gift). The model of the landowner is the evangelist, meaning all of us, who need to go out as the landowner did and gather up ("hire") individuals who need this salvation... and see to it that they are paid. Salvation is an equal gift to all, but the unsaved need to be "hired" to receive it.

April 9, OT
Judges 8:1-9:57
Gideon, Abimelech, and the First King (?) of Israel

Gideon, the sixth (as I count them from here on out) Judge of Israel, is widely regarded as the greatest of the Judges. The Eastern Orthodox Church regards him as a saint, and has even appointed a feast day (October 9) in his honor. Certainly, Gideon's victory over the Midianites, of which we read partly yesterday, has to be regarded as one of Israel's finest hours. Gideon was, without a doubt, a strong and faithful man who did exactly as was expected by God in delivering the Israelites from the captivity of Midian.

But Gideon was a flawed man just as was everyone used by God for His purposes. Many parallels exist between Gideon and Solomon, the third king of Israel, despite Gideon's most wise act (in today's reading). After completing his successful campaign against the Midianites (Judges 8:1-21) and despite the lack of assistance by two other groups, the Israelites asked him, point blank, to be their king (8:22). Gideon refused (8:23) and explained why. But he not only accepted the spoils of victory, but also was specific in his request for them (8:24-30), and had an ephod made. The ephod became an idol for Israel and a snare for Gideon just as the temple would later be for Solomon. Gideon would later take many wives and concubines, and the result was inevitable.

Though Gideon refused to become king, which included refusing to subsequently hand over the "kingdom" to his sons, it was his son who became the de facto next ruler of Israel. The people had already slid into the cycle of idolatry and sin, and Abimelech's ascension to the "throne" (9:4-6) only made things worse. Abimelech's treachery, which included murdering all but one of his brothers, was eventually met with more treachery (9:23-57) after a three-year reign (9:22) that could be referred to as the first kingdom of Israel.

April 9, NT
Matthew 20:17-19; Mark 10:32-34; Luke 18:31-34
Jesus Predicts His Death and Resurrection Again

Depending on how you count it, this is either the third or (as I believe) fourth time in which Jesus has openly predicted his death and resurrection to the twelve Apostles, other disciples, or both. The main difference here is the detail: Jesus makes note of exactly who is going to carry out the execution, the method of execution (in Matthew and Mark) and, in Matthew, how long he would remain dead before rising again.

All three accounts of this are prefaced by Jesus taking his twelve Apostles aside and telling them that they were going to go with him to Jerusalem, suggesting that Jesus wanted to get on with (resume) the journey, which they were already on.

April 10, OT
Judges 10:1-13:25
From Abimelech's Death to Samson's Birth

After the death of Abimelech, who was not a Judge (though he acted as though he was *king*), we now read the accounts of the next six Judges in a one-day OT reading. Some, like Judge #7, Tola, get only two verses (Judges 10:1-2) to describe their time in Judging Israel. The very brief biographies of some of them make one wonder just how much of the cycles of sin – suffering – crying out to God – deliverance – and finally peace happened with each, though some are described in detail.

Starting with Judge #7 and concluding, today, with the birth of the one who would later become the 13th Judge, we read about Tola (10:1-2), Jair (10:3-5), Jephthah (11:1-12:7), Ibzan (12:8-10), Elon (12:11-12), and Abdon (12:13-15).

After Abdon's death, Israel fell into its usual cycle, which included 40 years under the Philistines. During this time, among other things, the events leading up to the birth of the next Judge, Samson, occurred (13:1-25). Before we read about the appointment of Samson as Judge, there are several other events in three different books (Judges, Ruth, and I Samuel) yet to be read about over the next few days.

April 10, NT
Matthew 20:20-28; Mark 10:35-45
The Request of James and John

In the first few verses of today's NT reading, we discover that not all 12 of Jesus' Apostles were with him when He recently predicted his death and resurrection. James and John approach Jesus with a lofty request, differing in Matthew and Mark in who actually speaks the request (their mother in Matthew, the brothers James and John themselves in Mark). In asking to be seated at Jesus' left and right hands, Jesus replies that they don't know what they're asking for (Mark 10:38) because they are misunderstanding Jesus' role in becoming the Savior (Messiah) of Israel. Jesus goes on to reiterate that his role as savior is to actually be the servant, not the served (10:43-44), and to be ransomed for the people He saves (10:45). Jesus points out that they, too, will die martyr's deaths (Matthew 20:23), but that their requests concern a decision that He cannot make.

April 11, OT
Judges 19:1-20:48
The Deepest Depths of Depravity and Debauchery

No one knows for certain if the events in today's OT reading are actual or fiction, nor is it known for sure *when* they occurred, but one thing is agreed on by virtually everyone who reads them: if someone would make a movie about these events, it would have to be rated "R". Note: today's OT reading is most definitely *not* for children.

This chronology assumes the events are real and that they occur between the times of the Judges Abdon and Samson (who was born by this time). Every "character" here is well into the "sin" phase of the cycle spoken of before during the time of the Judges. In fact, this reading begins the same way as the book of Judges itself begins: a statement indicating that this was during the time of the Judges when Israel had no king. That it also occurred during one of the "sin" phases of the sin – suffering – crying out to God – deliverance (by a Judge) – and finally peace cycles becomes plainly obvious once you start reading it.

The account includes a Levite and his concubine (Judges 19:1), the mistress' infidelity (19:2), her father's attempted treachery (19:4-10), a journey to the city of Gibeah (19:11-21) followed by a near-repeat of one of the most horrific events in the Bible, the attempted homosexual gang rape of the Levite and his servant, just like the two angels visiting Lot in the city of Sodom hundreds of years earlier (followed by God's destruction of that city in Genesis 19).

Unlike the prior (and nearly identical, at first) event in Genesis, though, this time the rapists succeeded in their crime, and it is told in shockingly graphic detail (19:22-26, 20:3-6). Their victim here was the Levite's concubine, who died of her injuries (19:27-28) after an all-night rape. The Levite's response (19:29) sparked a war of revenge against the tribe (Benjamin) to which the people of Gibeah belonged (20:18-48), sanctioned by the Lord, and is one of the bloodiest wars ever depicted in the Bible, whose aftermath is read about tomorrow.

April 11, NT
Matthew 20:29-34; Mark 10:46-52; Luke 18:35-43
The Last Miracle Before the Triumphal Entrance

Restoring sight to the blind was one of Jesus' most-often performed miracles, partly because it also serves as a metaphor for "seeing the light," meaning to come to believe in Him and His salvation. The three different versions of his last healing miracle prior to the "triumphal entry" into Jerusalem differ in several, but minor, respects: Matthew's version mentions two blind men, not just one as do Mark and Luke. Furthermore, Mark and Luke mention the blind man by name: Bartimaeus. One clue that can be used to explain the apparent discrepancy is that Mark and Luke both speak of the miracle occurring when they were *arriving* in Jericho; Matthew makes note of the miracles as they are *leaving* Jericho. The conclusion is that there were, indeed, two men healed: the first, Bartimaeus as they arrived, and the second, unnamed, as they were leaving the city. Both subsequently followed Jesus and His disciples as the journey to Jerusalem continued.

April 12, OT
Judges 21:1-24; 1 Chronicles 6:4-15; Ruth 1:1-2:23
Restoration of Benjamin; The Story of Ruth, Part One

The civil war that broke out as an act of bloody revenge on those that carried out the rape of the Levite's concubine very nearly wiped out the tribe of Benjamin. To make matters worse, they took an unlawful oath at Mizpah denying the few remaining Benjamites wives from any other tribes, either (Judges 21:1). The Israelites had to come up with some kind of solution for this problem, lest an entire tribe get "cut off" from Israel (21:3). They found a solution (21:8-23) but it didn't come from the Lord because there was no real repentance from their sin. Obviously, this period of time between the Judges Abdon and Samson was one of the worst periods of the sin cycle between Judges.

Though the Levite whose concubine was raped and murdered is never named, a Jewish tradition states that he *is* named as part of the Levite family tree, of which we read a short excerpt in I Chronicles today. It is still unknown which of these several names, if any of them, is the Levite from this event.

After that is a part of the Bible that many find to be among its most beautiful stories... and one that *is* quite suitable for children, unlike yesterday's reading. The timing of Ruth's biography is as unclear as the horrific events of yesterday and today's readings, though it is made somewhat more clear by a small piece of genealogical information found at the end of the book, in tomorrow's reading.

April 12, NT
Luke 19:1-10
The Conversion of Zaccheus

Although this event technically took place *between* the two healings of blind men described yesterday (Luke 19:1, "passing through Jericho"), this event is separated out to make an important point about another kind of healing: a conversion. Zaccheus, like another tax collector before him, had already converted to belief in Jesus in his heart prior to Jesus' arrival, and was excited to meet Him in person (19:3). He even climbed a tree just to get a better look (19:4), and Jesus recognized him and told Zaccheus to get ready for their supper together (19:5-6).

This brought the usual grumblings from others who witnessed this (19:7) but Zaccheus ignored the others, and told the Lord what he was now going to do about his past bad deeds, now that he had decided to follow Jesus (19:8). Jesus then acknowledges Zaccheus' salvation and repeats the purpose for His presence in saving "that which was lost" (19:9-10).

Zaccheus was a Jew, a "son of Abraham". Luke is the only one to tell of this event, and it is another reflection of Luke's style, showing that anyone can be saved; all that is required is faith in Jesus.

April 13, OT
Ruth 3:1-4:22; 1 Samuel 1:1-28
Conclusion of Ruth; Birth of Samuel

This chronology assumes that Ruth lived during the period between the Judges Abdon and Samson, though we only have two clues in the Bible as to exactly when this beautiful account of faith and loyalty actually took place. The first clue, which we read yesterday, was that it took place "when the judges governed" (Ruth 1:1). But since the time of the Judges was about 300 years long, the only other clue as to when this took place happens at the end of Ruth, in today's OT reading: the obedience, loyalty, and faith of Ruth was rewarded with her marriage to Boaz (4:10) and a son named Obed (4:17) who became the grandfather of King David.

Before returning to the chronology in Judges after we read of Ruth, we jump to yet another book that was originally one of the Bible's largest. The books of Samuel, named for the last Judge and the subject of a large portion of the first book, was originally a single work. The human writer of this history book is not known, nor is it known if the writer was just one person or several. This chronology assumes some additional overlap with the book of Judges, in that we read today of the events leading up to the birth of Samuel (I Samuel 1:1-28) who would later be a prophet and the last Judge, whose life as a youth overlapped that of the next Judge of whom we read, Samson.

April 13, NT
Luke 19:11-27
The Parable of the Minas

The last parable told by Jesus *prior* to the Triumphal Entry is found only in Luke, and serves as a cap to the events surrounding Jesus' visit to Jericho, though it was by no means His last parable. The parable itself is an allegory of Him entering Jerusalem to establish His kingdom. The people must have been aware that Jerusalem was His destination and that the Kingdom of which He frequently spoke was about to appear. Thus, Jesus explained it in parable form.

The nobleman (Luke 19:12) here represents Jesus, and the distant land represents Jerusalem. It could also be a representation of heaven, given what was about to happen to Jesus, even with the promise of His return (19:13). The three servants who were each given charge of his Minas (about 100 day's wages) represent people of different levels of faith. We are all charged with "investing" His word so that it doesn't come back empty (Isaiah 55:11), and even a modest return on that investment would be acceptable to the Lord. They were not told how long the nobleman was going to be gone; only that he would return at some later time. That requires faith, which two of the three servants had (19:16-17; 19:18-19). The third had the same attitude as the other "citizens" (19:14), lacking faith and trust in the nobleman (19:20-21). This can be compared to any number of people today who grow up in Christian families and/or are made aware of the saving message of Jesus but do nothing about it, or at most only "go through the motions," practicing a religion without faith. To those with faith, more faith will be given (19:26), confirming the fact that faith itself is a gift of God.

April 14, OT
1 Samuel 2:1-10; Psalm 113:1-9; 1 Samuel 2:11-21; Judges 14:1-16:22
The Prayer of Hannah; Boyhood of Samuel; Samson and Delilah

Hannah, the mother of Samuel, was barren for much of her childbearing years. But like Sarah, the wife of Abraham centuries earlier, her faith in God was eventually answered with a son. Hannah's prayer to God was that if she could have a son, he would be a Nazarite (I Samuel 1:11, yesterday), a promise she did her part in fulfilling in yesterday's OT reading. Today, following Samuel's presentation in the Temple, we read Hannah's prayer (2:1-10) and what is believed to be a Psalm (Psalm 113) written by her or possibly by the Priest Eli. The prayer of Hannah begins with the phrase "my heart exults in the Lord" which could have been the same phrase, in Hebrew, sung by Mary following the Annunciation. That song, in Luke 1:46-55, is called The Magnificat. We then return to I Samuel (I Samuel 2:11-21) to read further about the boyhood of Samuel as a Nazarite.

Meanwhile, the boy Samson, last read about on April 10, had grown to a man and would become the next Judge of Israel. As we return to the chronologically certain part of the book of Judges, we read of several events in the life of Samson as a young adult, as he was being prepared by God to become the next Judge. Like the much younger Samuel, Samson was also a Nazarite (Judges 13:5-7). Unlike other Judges, Samson's appointment as Judge is told in great detail, as various colorful events in the young adult life of Samson, particularly in his relations to the Philistines, are read today in chapters 14-16 of Judges.

In chapter 16, Samson meets Delilah, a Philistine woman, who would go to great lengths to discover the source of Samson's great strength (16:4-14) and eventually betray Samson to her people (16:15-21).

April 14, NT
John 11:55-12:8
The Anointing at Bethany

The last time we read from John on March 31, Jesus raised his friend Lazarus from the dead, arguably the greatest of His miracles. Nothing more about Jesus' time to Ephraim (John 11:54) and Jericho (all NT readings for the last two weeks) is written in John, but He presumably returns to Bethany, as indicated early in today's NT reading (12:1).

The Anointing is told in three Gospels, but this time Luke *isn't* one of them. Matthew and Mark's versions are told tomorrow. In John's Gospel, Jesus and the recently raised Lazarus are having a meal, and Mary (named only here in John), the sister of Martha, anoints the feet of Jesus with very expensive perfume (12:3). This act is criticized by Judas Iscariot (12:4-5), again named only here in John, to which Jesus responds with His explanation of why the anointing was more than simply not a bad thing, but something very good: the preparation for His burial (12:7-8). Jesus concludes with a paraphrase of Deuteronomy 15:11, in stating that "you always have the poor with you".

April 15, OT
Judges 16:23-31; Judges 21:25; 1 Samuel 2:22-5:12
The Death of Samson; The Call of Samuel

Samson's story, which ends today, is a curious one even for the chaotic time of the Judges. Samson was blessed by the Lord with strength and charisma, but it all went to Samson's head (literally), resulting in the deception and imprisonment of which we read yesterday. In today's conclusion to the book of Judges (remember, we've already read chapters 17-21) we read of Samson's final act: blinded and bound and with the source of his strength shaved off (though it was regrowing, Judges 16:22), and forced to entertain the enemy Philistines, Samson pulled down the building where thousands of Philistines were, but at the cost of his own life as well.

Samson is the last Judge mentioned, chronologically, in the book of Judges, but was not the last Judge. His success in killing many Philistines did not defeat them completely, thus actually not completing the "cycle" mentioned earlier. This was left to the next Judge, of whom we've already read: the priest Eli who raised the young Samuel. Eli wasn't any more successful than Samson in overcoming the Philistines, due in part to his "worthless" sons.
 Samuel, meanwhile, continued to grow in the Lord, and was called to be a priest and prophet (I Samuel 3:11-18). In the end, God's judgment against Eli was carried out when Eli broke his neck in a fall

after hearing about the theft of the Ark of the Covenant (I Samuel 4:18). And so ends the Judgeship of Eli who Judged for 40 years, but died before his work was completely done.

April 15, NT
Matthew 26:6-13; Mark 14:3-9; John 12:9-11
The Anointing at Bethany and Afterwards

In Matthew's version of the Anointing at Bethany, Jesus eats at the home of Simon the Leper (Matthew 26:6) in Bethany. Lazarus' presence is not mentioned. Then, unlike John in yesterday's reading, the woman who pours the perfume on Jesus is not named (26:7). Furthermore, she pours the perfume on His *head*, not his feet, and the criticism comes from "the disciples" (26:8-9) without naming Judas. Jesus' words in response starts out just like those quoted in John, but go on to say that the woman's actions will be remembered wherever the Gospel is preached (26:13). The version in the Gospel of Mark is almost verse-for-verse identical to Matthew's version.

Afterwards, as we read in John, people became aware of Jesus' presence in Bethany, which is near Jerusalem, and came to see Him and Lazarus. The crowd grew as, on the next day, Jesus resumed his journey to Jerusalem (John 12:12).

April 16, OT
1 Samuel 6:1-9:27
The End of the Judges; The Beginning of the Kingdom

More than once, we read a verse in Judges, Ruth, or I Samuel that states that these events took place when Israel had no king. The Judges of Israel, up to and through Samuel, led Israel and delivered them from their enemies repeatedly. The last Judge mentioned in the book of the same name is Samson; Eli and Samuel follow, but are only described in I Samuel.

Though Eli died before the Ark was returned, the eventual return of the Ark (I Samuel 6:1-21) marked the beginning of a revival in Israel (7:1-8) and then, finally, victory over the Philistines (7:9-14) with Samuel as their Judge. Samuel tried to appoint one of his sons to succeed him as Judge (8:1-2) when he got old, but his sons didn't follow his lead. Most consider Samuel to be the last Judge; others think it was, briefly, Samuel's son Joel.

Then came one of the major turning points in the history of Israel: the demand by Israel's elders that the next Judge actually be a *king*. For a number of reasons, this demand was rejected by Samuel, with God pointing out the reasons (8:6-18). Despite Samuel's warning, the people pressed their demand for a king (8:19-20) and God finally agreed to it. We then read about Saul, son of Kish, a Benjamite (9:1-2), and a prophesied meeting with Samuel (9:15-27) that would lead to Saul's appointment as the first King of Israel.

April 16, NT
Matthew 21:1-7; Mark 11:1-7; Luke 19:28-35
The Triumphal Entry, Part One: Preparing to Enter

All three of the synoptic Gospels tell of this event in nearly the same way. If you're paying close attention to the actual chapters and verses, you will notice a couple of occasions where we have read passages that come after this in Matthew and Mark, which would indicate they took place in Jerusalem after the Triumphal Entry. Instead, this chronology assumes at least some of those events, parables, etc., took place prior to this final entrance into Jerusalem. There are likewise some passages, yet to be read, from parts of Matthew, John, and Luke, that appear to fall before this Triumphal Entry that actually take place during what we today call "Holy Week," the period between the celebrations of Palm Sunday and the Resurrection.

Palm Sunday, of course, gets its name from a part of the account of the Triumphal Entry that isn't read until tomorrow. In this first part, the preparations are made to enter the city where Jesus asks his disciples to obtain the donkey on which he'll ride (Matthew 21:2-3, Mark 11:2-3, Luke 19:30-31). Matthew quotes Zechariah 9:9 to show, as Matthew frequently does, that this action is the fulfillment of prophecy (Matthew 21:4-5). The disciples carry out this request, laid their coats on the donkey, and the ride into the city is then set to take place.

April 17, OT
1 Samuel 10:1-13:22
"Be Careful What You Wish For...

...because you may get it." So goes an old adage that applies very well to the events in today's OT reading. As the era of the Judges comes to an end and the Kingdom begins, Samuel, the last Judge, anoints Saul the Benjamite (I Samuel 10:1-16) as King, and then has him publicly installed (10:17-27) with a warning that could be paraphrased as the same adage as this reading's title.

Saul's reign started out well, and God was with him (11:6), up to and through a great battle with the Ammonites. Samuel confirmed Saul's status as King as coming from the Lord (11:12-15). But Samuel also rightly points out that the past 300 years have been filled with a mix of people who Judged Israel rightly and who Judged wrongly or poorly, while they had no King except God himself (12:1-11). Now, as Samuel said, they got what they wanted in the form of an earthly King, but they still need to follow the Lord (12:12-17). The people listening to Samuel realized their error, but Samuel also reassured them that God would not abandon His people, despite this evil (12:20-22). In other words, despite the Kingship of Saul, the Israelites were still supposed to serve the Lord with all their hearts (12:24).

And so begins The Kingdom, and an often-repeated verse structure (13:1) detailing the reign of a King, in this case Saul. But unlike many later kings, this verse doesn't explicitly state if he did, or did not, do what was right in the eyes of the Lord. Instead, we get the first of several chapters detailing the life and career of Saul, starting with an extremely foolish act (13:8-14), ignoring the Lord and His laws, and starting the process of bringing God's wrath down upon him and the people of Israel. Following this is the account of Saul's sending 600 men into a hopeless battle against the Philistines (13:15-22).

April 17, NT
Matthew 21:8-11; Mark 11:8-10; John 12:12-19
The Triumphal Entry, Part Two: Hosanna!

Palm Sunday gets its name from the mention in these three Gospels in today's NT reading (Luke only mentions the coats, not the branches, in tomorrow's reading) of the people placing their coats and "leafy branches" in front of Jesus as he entered the city of Jerusalem on a donkey. In a rare turn for the Gospel of John, John uses the same verse from Zechariah (Zech 9:9) to note this entrance as the fulfillment of prophecy (John 12:15) as did Matthew yesterday, though he uses a different part of the verse.

Another part common to all four Gospels about this event is the shouting of the word "Hosanna" by the enthusiastic crowds of people.

The word is a Greek transliteration of the Hebrew "Hoshana" which means "save us now" or "please save us". Its most notable use in the Old Testament is in Psalm 118:25 where it is translated as the noun "savior." It is accompanied by shouts of praise for the man they saw as king, entering their capital city to take his throne in triumph. Most, however, had no idea about the events that were about to take place.

April 18, OT
1 Samuel 13:23-14:52; 1 Chronicles 8:1-9:1a
Saul and Jonathan

When Israel demanded a King instead of a God-appointed Judge to deliver them, they didn't realize what they were getting into. And even though Saul was chosen by God and anointed by Samuel, it was done so that the Israelites could see the error of their ways. Saul proved to be a selfish coward who had no clue about how to properly lead his people, particularly in times of war. In this latest event, Saul led a group of 600 into battle with the Philistines without sufficient weapons. The results were catastrophic. It took Saul's son Jonathan to turn things around for his father as told in today's OT reading in I Samuel. Jonathan won the latest battle against the Philistines (I Samuel 14:1-20) for Israel, but even then Saul couldn't graciously accept that it was his son, not him, that was responsible for the victory, and made a rash oath (14:24-29) for which the Lord turned away from Saul (14:37) and, increasingly, so did the people of Israel (14:40-45).

A break from the narrative then describes the family of Saul and a summary of his acts during the numerous wars he conducted (14:47-52). The passage from 1 Chronicles shows the genealogy from Benjamin to Saul and beyond.

April 18, NT
Luke 19:36-44
The Triumphal Entry, Part Three: Hosanna!

Luke's account of the Triumphal Entry is very similar to those of Matthew, Mark, and John, differing only in the lack of detail regarding palm branches laid before Jesus and His donkey. It is the immediate aftermath that most differentiates Luke from the other three Gospel writers.

In Luke, Jesus' entrance prompts some Pharisees to ask Him to "rebuke Your disciples," which of course He does not do. Instead, he quotes Habakkuk 2:11 to them (Luke 19:40) and then goes on to express His second lament over Jerusalem (19:42-44). The key evidence that the other, previous lament was spoken outside of Jerusalem (and much earlier, Luke 13:34-35) is contained in the fact that Luke presents it twice while the other Gospel writers present it only once (Matthew) if at all. Furthermore, this lament is much clearer about its prophetic nature, where Jesus clearly predicts the coming fall of Jerusalem, occurring about 40 years in the future.

April 19, OT
1 Chronicles 9:35-44; 1 Chronicles 5:7-10; 1 Chronicles 5:18-22; 1 Samuel 15:1-16:23
God Rejects Saul as King

To God, one of the most infuriating problems with every leader of Israel, from Moses and Joshua through the Judges and now the Kings, had to be the fact that only a few of them up to this point brazenly rebelled against Him, yet *all* of them did the almost-worse thing: obeying the Lord only *partially*. It would be much easier to criticize Saul if he *completely* disobeyed God; instead, he used his pride in his own achievements to only do that part of the Lord's command that he thought was right, and disregarded the rest. Every time this happened, Israel had to suffer the consequences.

Thus we set up today's OT reading, jumping around through three readings in Chronicles before getting back to the narrative of Saul in I Samuel. The reading in I Chronicles 9 is another telling of Saul's family tree, noting his son Jonathan who, though "crown prince" of Israel, never became King. Their family line did continue, at least up to the Exile. The two shorter sections, mostly from the family trees of Reuben and Gad, are presented here because of their mention of Saul, and the partially successful war campaigns that were fought involving those tribes.

But it is back in I Samuel that we see the real problem with the selfish, cowardly King. Through Samuel, the Lord tells Saul to go to war and "utterly destroy" the enemy Amalek (I Samuel 15:1-3). Instead, Saul wages a successful war but allows the enemy king to live (15:8-9), thus only *partially* obeying the Lord. God expresses His regret for making Saul King (15:10-11). Samuel attempted, mostly in vain, to get Saul to acknowledge his sin and partial obedience (15:12-31), but in the end it took Samuel himself to carry out the Lord's wishes, not Saul, in finally disposing of the enemy king (15:32-33).

And so God completely rejects Saul as king, and commissions the same Samuel who anointed Saul as king to go to Bethlehem and anoint Saul's successor (16:1-3). It is at this point that we get introduced to the man who would dominate the remainder of the Old Testament: David, the son of Jesse, who is anointed king (16:12-13). David did not take the throne immediately. His first encounter with Saul was as he was brought in to Saul's court to play music for the king (16:14-23).

April 19, NT
John 2:13-25; Mark 11:11-17; Luke 19:45-46; Matthew 21:12-22
The Cleansing of the Temple; The Barren Fig Tree

According to the vast majority of Bible scholars, the event known as "the cleaning of the Temple" occurs twice: once early on in Jesus' ministry (just after the wedding at Cana, read on January 6) and again shortly after His entrance into Jerusalem on what we call "Palm Sunday" (read during the last three days). Though the matter of chronology is trivial compared to many other Biblical issues, I take very strong issue against this notion for several reasons, and thus believe that the Cleansing occurs only once, at this point in time right here, and is told in all four Gospels.

The controversy concerns the fact that the account of this event in John is so extremely far out of sequence in comparison to the other Gospels. It is, first of all, one of the few events *outside* of Jesus' final week on Earth that appears in all four Gospels. The Gospel of John can be a bit of a challenge to reconcile or "harmonize" with the other three for this reason. But with the exception of this one event, the Gospel of John and the other three Gospels harmonize without significant issue from about "Palm Sunday" onwards. The one major thing that would put John's account into harmony with the other three is if the "cleansing" in chapter 2 was really supposed to be in chapter 12. That is: if you take John 2:13-25 and simply insert it between John 12:19 and John 12:20, you'd have a near-perfect match.

It is thus that we begin with John's account of the Cleansing as the first part of today's NT reading. Of the four accounts, John's is the most detailed, but it harmonizes with the other three, as you will see. Like the other accounts, it is placed chronologically near "the Passover of the Jews" (John 2:13), but does not say which of the Passovers (there would have been three during His active ministry) to which this event refers.

About the only detail John doesn't mention in his account is Jesus leaving Jerusalem for nearby Bethany, where he stayed the night, and encountered the barren fig tree on His return to Jerusalem. In Mark's version, the Cleaning of the Temple (Mark 11:15-17) occurs *after* this sequence of events, thus implying that the Cleansing took place on Monday, not Sunday, but this still could have been true of John's version as well, simply because of his omission of the fig tree event. Luke's version also omits the fig tree encounter, and is actually the least-detailed version of the four (Luke 19:45-46).

It is Matthew's version that has the only significant detail about the sequence of the events, though it contradicts Mark's sequence. Like John and Luke, Matthew implies, without any mention of a time interval, that the cleansing takes place almost immediately after His arrival in Jerusalem on Sunday (Matthew 20:12). The key verse that shows the order of events is Matthew 20:17, where it says that He "left them and went out of the city" *after* the Cleansing, and went to Bethany where He spent the night. In the next verse we have the phrase "in the morning when He was *returning* to the city" (20:18, emphasis mine) where we then get the only other recording of the fig tree encounter (20:19-22), this time with an explanation that Mark's version doesn't have until the next day (read tomorrow).

Thus, the first sequence of events after The Triumphal Entry that makes sense in light of all four Gospels is the Cleansing taking place on the same day as The Triumphal Entry itself, after which He left to spend the night in nearby Bethany, and returned Monday morning where He encountered the barren fig tree on the way back. Only with this sequence, even though you have to reverse a few verses in Mark (and include one from tomorrow's reading), does it harmonize completely.

April 20, OT
1 Samuel 17:1-58; Psalm 144:1-15
David and Goliath

David's famous defeat of the Philistine Goliath is brought about because of two things: the first was God's rejection of the king, Saul. The other was the faith and character of the next king of Israel, David. Saul's incomplete obedience of God made each war campaign a stalemate or a defeat. Israel was constantly at war with the Philistines. Goliath was a champion of the Philistines who used the combination of Saul's weakness and his own great height (either 6' 10" or 9' 11" depending on which version of the cubit is used, I Samuel 17:4) to taunt the Israelites...

...and eventually openly mock the young man (17:42-44) who would slay him (17:48-50). Saul was not yet aware that this youth, his court musician, was going to be the next king, and inquired about him (17:55-58). Thus, the rivalry between Saul and David had begun.

This chronology believes that it was at this time that David wrote his first Psalm, which is numbered as 144 here. The Psalm praises God and promises more praises for further deliverance from "aliens whose mouth speaks deceit," (Psalm 144:11) an obvious reference to Goliath.

April 20, NT
Mark 11:18-26
The Barren Fig Tree Aftermath - Monday

In the brief verses of today's NT reading, the account of the barren fig tree and its aftermath are now more fully explained, and the sequence of events, despite the earlier controversy, is cleared up.

In one of the few places in the entire NT where Mark is the only one to present an event or quote of Jesus, we read first of the immediate aftermath of the Cleaning (Mark 11:18-19), with the chief priests and scribes becoming angry with His actions in the Temple. Mark then mentions the departure from Jerusalem (11:19) where they would go out of the city (to Bethany, though the destination isn't mentioned) and return the next morning. Mark takes what was mentioned as a single event in Matthew and splits it, but showing the now-withered fig tree in the morning after (11:20-21). After this, He gives a much longer and more detailed explanation of this encounter (11:22-26) found only in Mark (though part of it is quoted in I John 5:14-15).

April 21, OT
1 Samuel 18:1-20:42
The Crown Prince and the Next King of Israel

In the vast majority of kingdoms, the "crown prince" is the oldest offspring (usually son) of the monarch(s), and is therefore next in line for the throne. In other words, normally, the crown prince *is* the next king, so these two titles refer to the same person. Not in the case of Israel, however, during the reign of its first king, Saul. In readings leading up to today, Saul, after having been anointed by Samuel, either ignores God or only partially obeys Him, resulting in all sorts of problems for Israel. Most significantly, it results in God's rejection of Saul as king, and a call to Samuel to anoint someone else. That someone else was David, the iconic king who would start the royal line that eventually leads to Jesus Christ.

The crown prince, in this case, is Saul's son Jonathan, who quickly became David's closest friend and ally (I Samuel 18:1) after David slew the Philistine giant, Goliath. Jonathan realized that God had left his father, and that, therefore, he would not be the next king. Knowing that his new "brother" David (18:2) was going to be the next king would have normally caused the opposite reaction in the crown prince. Instead, it began the story of one of the most remarkable friendships in the entire Bible. It also began the first of several episodes of jealous rage on the part of Saul, who tried to kill David no less than five times in today's OT reading alone. Each time, Saul was unsuccessful due mainly to the efforts of his own son, Jonathan. The remainder of today's three chapters is a detail of those attempts, and the covenant between the crown prince and the next king of Israel.

A great amount of controversy surrounds the first four verses of this reading (along with a few other passages) that needs to be addressed here. I'll keep it to a paragraph: I Samuel 18:1-4 is frequently used by men in the homosexual community to justify their sinful lifestyle due to a gross misinterpretation of this passage. Depending on which translation you read, you have variations on the fact that Jonathan's soul was "knit" to David's in the first verse, and "loved him as himself". In one translation, a "homosexual Bible" online which I will *not* credit here, part of the translation for that verse says that Jonathan "fell in love with" David, implying the kind of romantic love relationship that often leads to sexual activity, regardless of whether or not the pair is of the same or different genders. A big part of this misinterpretation and mistranslation stems from the gross misuse of the word "love" which is used in all of the English language translations of this passage. There are so many who equate love with sex that they feel the two cannot be separated, and that's what leads to the misinterpretation and misuse of passages like this. I wrote the equivalent of 8 pages of text in response to a blog about this topic, in response to a *church* (yes, a church) that was engaging in this very misuse of the Bible. I actually had a difficult time (and was ultimately unsuccessful) convincing them that love and sex were two different things, and that the form of "love" spoken of here has more in common with "brotherly love" or love within a family than any other meaning one tries to read into it. The kind of love in today's reading is a strong bond leading to loyalty and mutual concern, not sexuality.

April 21, NT
Luke 20:1-8; Mark 11:27-33; Matthew 21:23-32
The Question of Authority - Monday

Another of the several clues that places the Cleansing of the Temple in John 2 as the same event as told in the other three Gospels is the question asked by the chief priests and scribes shortly (or immediately in John's version) afterwards: "by what authority do you do these things?" (Luke 20:2, Mark 11:28, Matthew 21:23). Not only is the question worded almost exactly the same way in all *four* accounts, but Jesus' answer to the question is also almost identical in the three from which we read today.

Using Matthew's version as a guide, we first note that Jesus' answer, as He does several times to their questions, is another question, using John the Baptist as a point of comparison. By comparing Himself to John, a man most considered a prophet, He places Himself in the same role (Matthew 21:24-25) and puts the questioners into a verbal trap. If they say that John's authority was from heaven (21:25), their faith is called into question. If they say that John's authority was from men (21:26), they invite the wrath of the people who considered John a prophet. Thus, when they answer Jesus with an honest "I don't know" (21:27), Jesus replies that He won't tell them, either.

The issue, as Jesus explains only in Matthew (21:28-32) is the issue of trust. In the parable of the Two Sons, Jesus gets the chief priests and scribes to see their error by using the example of the first son in comparison to the repentant sinner, vs. the second son who made a promise and broke it, breaking the trust relationship between him and his father in the same way as the sinner who refuses to repent.

April 22, OT
Psalm 5:1-12; Psalm 59:1-17; Psalm 133:1-3; 1 Samuel 21:1-15; Psalm 34:1-22;
1 Samuel 22:1-5; 1 Chronicles 12:8-18
David, the Fugitive

It is believed here that David, after leaving Saul and Jonathan at the conclusion of yesterday's reading, wrote the three Psalms that begin today's OT reading. The first (Psalm 5) is a prayer for guidance with several references to his "foes," presumably meaning Saul and his men. Psalm 59 is similar, containing even more detail about David's large number of enemies. Psalm 133 is a celebration of brotherly love; the kind that existed between David and Jonathan.

And so the narrative then resumes in I Samuel as David flees the house of Saul, first visiting Ahimelech the priest (I Samuel 21:1-9) where David ate consecrated bread and obtained the sword of his defeated enemy, Goliath. He then went to Achish, the king of Gath, in an attempt to find refuge (21:10-12) but had to feign madness in order to escape (21:13-15). The subtitle to Psalm 34 refers to this event, which pins it down as a Psalm of David written at this time.

The narrative continues in I Samuel and in I Chronicles as David gathers an army of loyal warriors (from multiple tribes, as we read in the Chronicles).

April 22, NT
Luke 20:9-18; Mark 12:1-12
The Parable of the Vineyard Owner - Monday

It is not known for certain whether this parable was told by Jesus on Monday or Tuesday of His final week on earth, but in all three synoptic Gospels (we read Matthew's version tomorrow), the parable is told to the same group of people who challenged His authority and were answered by Jesus with a question. In Matthew's version, tomorrow, it immediately follows the additional parable of the Two Sons. It is reasonable to assume that this is a continuation of Monday's events.

The Luke and Mark versions of the parable are very close to identical. In each, He uses the metaphor of the vineyard owner as God, the vineyard as Israel. The vine growers are the Old Testament prophets, and the beloved Son who is sent as a final attempt to complete the harvest (and is likewise rejected and killed) is Jesus. The destruction of the vineyard (Mark 12:9) is a twofold prophecy: the destruction of Jerusalem in 70 A.D., and the spread of the Christian faith outside of Judaism; that is, to the Gentiles.

In both versions, Jesus backs up this prophesy by quoting Psalm 118:22-23 to show that this was part of God's plan all along. Also in both cases, the passage ends with the chief priests and scribes (introduced yesterday) understanding that the parable was against **them**, and they then went away without carrying out their planned seizure of Jesus.

April 23, OT
1 Samuel 22:6-23; Psalm 52:1-9; Psalm 109:1-31; Psalm 63:1-11; 1 Samuel 23:1-29
The Wrath of Saul

With God's departure from the king, Saul's jealous rage turned increasingly violent, even murderous. David's flight from Saul is detailed yesterday, which necessitates today's "meanwhile" reading. In the remainder of I Samuel 22, Saul seeks David at the home of the priest Ahimelech, meaning that Saul had nearly caught up with David. Ahimelech tried to protect David, but it ultimately cost him his life and the lives of all but one person in the entire city of Nob (I Samuel 22:6-19) at the hands of an Edomite in Saul's camp named Doeg. Psalm 52 is the first of the Psalms of David to be officially listed as a "Maskil," which is an instructional Psalm, or lesson. It specifically mentions Doeg and what he did in its subtitle.

Increasingly, as we see the effect of God having left Saul, we see how God's protective hand is transferred to David. Psalm 109, a prayer for vengeance, shows David's increasing recognition of this fact. Then, in the narrative, God repeatedly shows David His protection and grace as David is drawn into a conflict against the Philistines (I Samuel 23:1), and inquires of the Lord every step of the way – including multiple instances of Saul discovering David's whereabouts but then giving up the pursuit (temporarily), only to resume the pursuit, forcing David to flee and hide again (23:2-29).

April 23, NT
Matthew 21:33-22:14
The Parables of the Vineyard Owner and the Wedding Feast - Monday

In two different translations of the Bible that I have, this same parable told in Matthew as we read yesterday is called the parable of the "landowner" as opposed to "vineyard owner". But except for Matthew's use of the word "landowner" in the first verse (Matthew 21:33), the parable is nearly word-for-word identical to Luke's and Mark's versions that we read yesterday.

The only significant difference is that the chief priests and scribes don't leave the scene at the end, but that's only because Matthew goes on to show Jesus telling another parable, making it actually a string of three parables when starting from the parable of the Two Sons (as read two days ago). The parable of the Wedding Feast is actually a repeat of a parable told by Jesus to some Pharisees (Luke 14:16-24, read on March 25) with a greater emphasis this time on how it parallels the parable of the vineyard owner, and how they are both metaphors of the kingdom of God.

April 24, OT
Psalm 13:1-6; Psalm 17:1-15; Psalm 22:1-31; Psalm 54:1-7; 1 Samuel 24:1-22
David Shows Mercy to Saul

During this period of constant fleeing and hiding, David continued to consult God. Even though he must have felt, at times, like the Lord had abandoned him, David continued to seek God's guidance as he worked towards taking his rightful place as the king of Israel. The four Psalms that start today's OT reading each reflect this feeling of despair while still relying on God. Psalm 13 starts with an inquiry to God about how long He will "hide Your face from me," but ends with a statement of faith, trusting in God and praising Him because He has "dealt bountifully with me". Psalm 17 is a more prayerful statement of reliance on God, but on a similar vein. Psalm 22 continues this theme and is one of his most famous: not only does the Psalm reflect both David's despair while coming back to his great faith and trust in God, but the descriptions of his own suffering at the hands of Saul's men form a graphic prophecy of a form of torture and execution that wouldn't be seen in Israel until the time of Jesus: crucifixion. Verses 14-18 are particularly noteworthy for their literal fulfillment. Yet, this Roman, not Jewish, form of execution wasn't known to David. Jesus directly quotes the first verse of the Psalm on the cross as one of His last words. Psalm 54 is another Maskil, and is another cry for deliverance.

This reliance on God showed through when Saul caught up with David in a cave (I Samuel 24:1-3) but didn't realize it. Saul and some of his men were using the cave to relieve themselves, and David and some of his men were deep inside. David had a golden opportunity to kill his arch rival, but chose instead to cut off a piece of Saul's clothes (24:4) and then use that to reveal his presence to Saul (24:9-15), promising to let the Lord, not himself, judge between the two. The very astonished Saul responded by acknowledging David's show of mercy (24:16-21) and asking only that David not "destroy [his] name" from his family's household, to which David agreed.

April 24, NT
Luke 20:19-26; Mark 12:13-17; Matthew 22:15-22
The Coin with the Likeness of Caesar - Tuesday

The three synoptic Gospels tell this event nearly the same way. Though it is possible that this took place on Monday of His last week on Earth, it is more likely that this took place the next day, after the chief priests had time to tell the Pharisees who, in turn, told the Herodians (Matthew 22:16) to try to trap Jesus. Luke's version refers to them as spies (Luke 20:20). In all three cases, the trap failed because Jesus rightly points out that we are to (metaphorically) "render unto Caesar what belongs to Caesar, and render unto God what belongs to God."

April 25, OT
Psalm 7:1-17; Psalm 35:1-28; Psalm 57:1-11; Psalm 142:1-7
Four Flight Psalms

Only two of these four Psalms can be dated with certainty to this period in David's life (57 and 142) due to the explicit mention of the time "in the cave" in their subtitles. However, all four share a common theme and are known to be of David. That theme is trust in the Lord while being surrounded by turmoil or one's own enemies, counting on the Lord to take care of business, submitting to His will in all matters.

April 25, NT
Luke 20:27-40
The Sadducees and Marriage in Heaven - Tuesday

After His encounter with the Herodians, Jesus was confronted by a prominent Jewish group who didn't (and don't) believe in the resurrection: the Sadducees. So why would a group that doesn't even believe in an afterlife confront Jesus about the state of marriage in that afterlife (Luke 20:33)? Simple: they were engaged in the exact same kind of trap setting as the spies sent by the Pharisees did in yesterday's NT reading. As usual, it didn't work, because Jesus knew how to use Scripture (in this case citing Moses' encounter with the burning bush in Exodus 3:1-6) to effectively strike down the argument from these so-called religious "experts".

Some scribes who listened to this encounter gave Jesus a compliment on His answer, but did so only because they were afraid to ask Him anything else (Luke 20:39-40).

Mark's and Matthew's Gospels each feature this same encounter, but as you will read over the next two days, each also adds an additional encounter with yet another group, one with whom Jesus was much better acquainted.

April 26, OT
1 Samuel 25:1-44
Death of Samuel, David Marries the Widow of Nabal

The last of the judges and the man who anointed both Saul and David as kings did not live to see David take the throne. In fact, the books that bear his name are only half done at this point. But with the death of Samuel and the brief single verse devoted to it, the era of the Judges truly comes to a complete end.

The remaining verses in I Samuel concern a man named Nabal, his wife Abigail, and the curious sequence of events that led to David marrying Abigail. During this time of fleeing and hiding from Saul, David and his men had to have some way of earning a living to obtain basic needs. It can be extrapolated from I Samuel 25:2-4 that they earned this by acting as protectors for the sheep and the shepherds (25:7), as David was a shepherd as a boy. It would have been customary to pay these protectors at shearing time, so David sends his men to meet and remind Nabal (25:6-8). However, instead of responding in gratitude, Nabal responds with insults and criticisms (25:9-11).

David's response to Nabal's ingratitude was almost disastrous. In his anger, David assembled 600 men to take revenge on Nabal (25:12-13) – just for an insult! But before David could carry out this extreme act of overkill, Nabal's wife Abigail intervenes. She correctly sizes up the situation (25:14-20) and confronts David (25:23-31) in a stunning combination of humility, intelligence, honesty, and logic, wrapped in a firm faith in God. Her effort works, David comes to realize that two wrongs do not make a right (25:32-35), and the situation is resolved without bloodshed.

Nabal's blunder did not go unpunished, however. Abigail waited until Nabal was sober to tell him what she told David (I Samuel 25:36-37), but the news caused what many believe was a stroke or seizure in Nabal, resulting in a 10-day coma and, finally, his death. When news came to David, he said a prayer of thanks (25:39) for having Abigail stop him but also for God's action. Following his proposal, Abigail became David's second wife (25:40-42). There was no word from God at this point regarding this polygamy.

April 26, NT
Mark 12:18-34
The Sadducees, The Scribes, and Marriage in Heaven - Tuesday

Mark's account of the encounter between Jesus and the Sadducees on Tuesday of His final week starts out nearly identically to Luke's version, which we read yesterday. They start with nearly the same question (Mark 12:18-23) followed by Jesus' answer, nearly word-for-word identical to Luke's version (18:24-27). Then, Jesus fielded a question from a scribe regarding the foremost commandment (18:28) to which Jesus answers quoting Deuteronomy ("The Schema") and Leviticus. The scribe then responds by quoting similar verses from other parts of Scripture (18:32-33). Jesus recognizes this as being "not far from the Kingdom of God" (18:34), meaning that this knowledge by the scribe was not far from God and the law that convicts us all and forces the need for a savior.

April 27, OT
1 Samuel 26:1-25; Psalm 18:1-50; 2 Samuel 22:1-51; Psalm 14:1-7; Psalm 53:1-6
David's Final Encounter with Saul

David's reliance on God to guide his actions comes to a head in his final encounter with Saul while Israel's first king was still alive. David saw Saul's pursuit, and hid until night (I Samuel 26:1-5). Realizing that the Lord had effectively delivered Saul into his hands, he once again decided that the best course of action was to show mercy rather than destroy the one whom God had anointed (26:6-11). David decided to use the fact that Saul was left unguarded to make his point and put an end to their conflict. David takes a spear and water jug from the sleeping king (26:12), uses the items to then wake one of the guards and start the encounter (26:13-16), and reveals his presence to Saul (26:17-20). Saul's response, beginning with "I have sinned," (26:21) is the last time Saul speaks to David. In it, Saul effectively releases David from his pursuit and ends the conflict. David acknowledges this in his reply (26:22-25), marking David's last words to Saul.

David was very grateful that he had been delivered from this danger, and wrote what we number as Psalm 18, a lofty song of praise to the God who delivers His own. In a curious jump to near the end of the books of Samuel, that Psalm is recorded a second time (almost word for word) in 2 Samuel 22, likely just a second instance of David singing it near the end of his reign as king. Two more Psalms, 14 and 53, were also believed to have been written at this time by David.

These are also nearly identical to each other, echoing similar themes of praise, contrasting God with the Godless who have become corrupted. Both Psalms feature lines quoted in familiar places in the New Testament, two in chapter 3 of Romans: "the fool has said in their heart that there is no God," and "there is no one who does good, no, not one."

April 27, NT
Matthew 22:23-40
The Sadducees, The Pharisees, and Marriage in Heaven - Tuesday

Matthew's version of this encounter, this time labeling the second group as "Pharisees" instead of "Scribes," is nearly the same as both the Luke and Mark versions from which we read the last two days.

The only two differences of note are the one already mentioned and the fact that Matthew doesn't mention the dialog with the scribe that prompted Jesus to tell him that his knowledge was "not far from the Kingdom."

The purpose of drawing out this passage to three days is more than just a case of "stretching" in this reading plan. There are still two days' readings for what is believed to be Tuesday of "Holy Week". The importance of this passage is in the doctrine of marriage spoken by Jesus, declaring that there is no "marriage in heaven," a clear contradiction against the theology of the Church of Jesus Christ of Latter Day Saints, who believe the exact opposite.

April 28, OT
Psalm 31:1-24; 1 Samuel 27:1-12; 1 Chronicles 12:1-7;
Psalm 56:1-13; 1 Samuel 28:1-2;
1 Samuel 29:1-11; 1 Chronicles 12:19-22; Psalm 40:1-17
David's Deliverance

Though David and Saul would never meet again, David didn't know this for certain at this point, and he knew better than to trust in Saul's word after their final encounter. In Psalm 31, David continues his praise for the God who delivers the faithful while his plea also goes on for protection from his enemies. In response, God must have told David to take concrete action in order to prevent being killed by Saul or his men, and David then reasoned that action should be fleeing to the enemy (I Samuel 27:1-2), the Philistines. It was, indeed, the place Saul would least expect (27:4). David did not flee alone; he took his men and both his wives with him, and proved himself worthy to the Philistines by engaging several enemies, convincing the skeptical king that David really had shifted his loyalties. (27:12)

David's men were fellow Israelites, however, and his real loyalties had *not* changed. He only wanted to make it look that way to the Philistine king in order to hide from Saul. A detail of some of those Israelites who were with David is given in the passage from I Chronicles. Then, in Psalm 56 (which some believe was written much earlier), David sings another song of thanks for the deliverance provided by God, and in particular, the success of this latest idea in hiding amongst the Philistines.

But, the plan almost backfired when the Philistines planned an attack on Israel (I Samuel 28:1-2). In the jump to the next chapter, the narrative shows how David's deception worked with Achish, the Philistine king but not with Achish's men. In the end, David was forced to leave the Philistine camp and return to Israel (29:1-11). The Philistine "lords" were suspicious that David would return his allegiance to Saul when in fact, his plan was to stay with the Philistine army just long enough to defeat Saul in battle and take his rightful place as Israel's new king. Part of the proof of this comes from the brief narrative in I Chronicles 12 that follows, as part of the tribe of Manasseh was preparing to defect and join David against Saul, but was thwarted just as was David himself.

Realizing that it was the Lord who delivered David again, David wrote one of the most joyful Psalms (40) of thanksgiving, which likens his deliverance with the salvation a Messiah will someday bring, thus becoming one of his several Messianic Psalms.

April 28, NT
Luke 20:41-44; Mark 12:35-37; Matthew 22:41-46
Jesus Questions the Pharisees - Tuesday

In the three synoptic Gospels, Jesus' next response to the Pharisees that were questioning Him was to question them back. Using, as was His custom, part of Scripture to trap *them* instead of the Pharisees trying to trap *Him* (using part of Psalm 110), Jesus poses a perplexing puzzle: how can David call his son (literally "descendent") his "Lord?" As it is put in the Matthew version (Matthew 22:46), this put an end to the Pharisees' debate with Him.

Or, as a Pastor once put it in a sermon, "this finally shut them up."

April 29, OT
Psalm 69:1-36; Psalm 86:1-17; Psalm 131:1-3; 1 Samuel 28:3-25
David's Humility; Saul's Pride

In yesterday's reading, the Philistine king turned David away because of the suspicions of his men, and thus forced David to return to Israel, against whom the Philistines were about to engage in battle. Though David was thankful about not having to fight against his own people (writing Psalm 40 as part of this), he must have felt humiliated at this rejection. This was then expressed in Psalm 69 (which some believe was written by Jeremiah, not David), which actually comes off as a grand expression of humility that foreshadows the coming Messiah. Psalm 86 and the brief Psalm 131 continue this same theme; not as a "woe is me, I've been humiliated" statement, but a humble submission to the Lord and His perfect will.

Meanwhile, Saul has become aware of the pending Philistine attack (I Samuel 28:5-6), and instead of responding with humility of his own (remember, Saul was already rejected by God) does the worst possible thing: he consults a medium in an attempt to contact Samuel, the since-deceased Judge of Israel (28:3) who had originally anointed Saul as king. It was Saul himself who had outlawed this kind of spirituality, and the woman he consults (under disguise) points this fact out (28:8-9) but he pushed forth with his desire to contact Samuel, and the Lord permits the contact to take place. The reason the Lord allows this sin becomes obvious when Samuel speaks to the terrified Saul (28:15-19) and confirms Saul's worst fears about the upcoming attack. The woman, realizing that it is Saul making the request to contact the dead, prepares a meal for Saul and his men.

April 29, NT
Matthew 23:1-39
Jesus' Final Rant Against the Proud Pharisees - Tuesday

As we first read more than two months ago, Jesus had many encounters with the Pharisees, both in Jerusalem and outside of it, very few of them pleasant. In this last encounter before the crucifixion, Jesus spells out to both the Pharisees and the listening crowds exactly why most of those encounters were so unpleasant. A common theme throughout virtually every encounter between Jesus and the Pharisees is "hypocrisy," specifically the prideful, know-it-all Pharisees who became the very models of religious hypocrisy. In Jesus' strongest language ever, He spells out seven "woes" upon the Pharisees, and concludes with a lament over Jerusalem (Matthew 23:37-39) spoken *within* the city, unlike His previous laments.

April 30, OT
1 Samuel 30:1-31:13; 1 Chronicles 10:1-14; 2 Samuel 4:4; 2 Samuel 1:1-27
David Rescues Ziklag; The Deaths of Saul and Jonathan

The account of the life of Israel's first king comes to a tragic conclusion in today's OT reading. David came upon the aftermath of a raid by the Amalekites on the city of Ziklag, and set out to rescue those who had been captured, including both of his wives (I Samuel 30:5). Because of David's earlier defection to the Philistines, he was viewed by many as a traitor (30:6). But, instead of either fleeing again or, worse yet, wallowing in self-pity about this, David took action. He obtained an Ephod from a priest and inquired of the Lord for advice in the matter (30:7-8) and set out in pursuit of the raiders. Despite a diminished army because of exhaustion (30:10), this military campaign by David was successful and all who were captured were rescued, including both of David's wives. David even insisted that the spoils be divided amongst all his men including those who stayed behind (30:21-25) over the loud objections of those who fought with him.

Meanwhile, the battle at Mount Gilboa went very badly. Jonathan was killed and Saul was wounded (31:2-3), which led to Saul's request to have his armor-bearer run a sword through him, killing him. The armor-bearer refused, so Saul instead fell on his own sword and, apparently, died. The armor-bearer followed suit. The victorious enemy stripped Saul of his armor and weapons and left his body on the battlefield, where Israelites later came and buried him and his sons (31:5-13). Chapter 10 of I Chronicles gives a condensed version of these same events.

In the aftermath of Saul's death, we first jump ahead (2 Samuel 4:4) to read about one of Saul's grandsons, the son of Jonathan, who was just a little boy at the time of Jonathan's death. The significance of this is that if Jonathan had truly been the crown prince of Israel (instead of David), this little boy would become king due to the deaths of both Saul and Jonathan. Then, we get to read more about the character and Godliness of David as we begin the second book of Samuel. Despite God's abandonment of Saul and the fact that Saul had tried to kill him multiple times, David mourned Saul's death and even had the Amalekite who brought the news put to death because he had allegedly killed "God's anointed" (2 Samuel 1:16). Some claim the account in 2 Samuel 1 contradicts 1 Samuel 31 regarding Saul's death; however, the two versions of this can be reconciled a number of ways. One is to note that Saul's armor-bearer may have assumed Saul was dead after falling on his sword when, in fact, Saul was still barely alive. Another is to note that the news-bringer was an Amalekite – an enemy – who may have been trying to "score points" with the new king, but his effort backfired.

And so, before being formally crowned the king of Israel, David speaks a beautiful and heart-felt elegy for Saul and for Jonathan (1:17-27). Near the end is a verse (1:26) that has been abused by some in the homosexual community to try to indicate that David and Jonathan were gay; however, this is another example (see reading for April 21) of an overreaching assumption that equates love with sex, and attempts to justify sinful behavior by using a Biblical example of one of the most remarkable friendships ever described.

April 30, NT
Luke 20:45-21:4; Mark 12:38-44
The Widow's Two Coins - Tuesday

Where Matthew provides all 39 verses of Jesus' final rant against the Pharisees, Luke and Mark each devote only a few verses apiece, mainly to the very end of that encounter. But what both Luke and Mark then do is tell of the immediate aftermath: the widow giving only two coins into the treasury – far less than most of the others – but far *more* in Jesus' eyes, as it was all she had. Jesus points out this model for giving as a contrast to the Pharisee's hypocrisy.

May 1, OT
2 Samuel 2:1-3:5; 1 Chronicles 3:1-4; 2 Samuel 3:6-4:3, 4:5-5:5; 1 Chronicles 11:1-3
The First Divided Kingdom of Israel

David was already anointed by God, via Samuel, to be the next king of Israel. He survived multiple attempts by King Saul to have him killed and even survived a period of time where he had to live with the enemy Philistines in order to do this. Now, Saul was dead and David had every right to claim his rightful place as king of all Israel. So why doesn't this occur until the very end of today's OT reading, after more than three full chapters, and more than seven years, of events?

The answer is found in the history recorded in chapters 2 through 4 of 2 Samuel. After David eulogizes Saul and Jonathan, he asks the Lord for advice about going to one of the cities of his tribe, the tribe of Judah. The Lord tells him to go to Hebron, where he is then crowned king over the tribe (2 Samuel 2:1-4). He is informed of the identities of those who buried Saul, and he gives them a commendation (2:5-7). Meanwhile, a rebellion is brewing. Saul had many supporters who would be none too pleased to have David crowned as king over all of Israel, so the commander of Saul's army, Abner, had one of Saul's younger sons (Ish-bosheth) installed as king over all of Israel (2:8-11) except Judah.

Thus, almost a century before the so-called "divided kingdom," Israel was already divided and in a state of civil war between the tribe of Judah, led by the real king, David, and the entire remainder of Israel, led by Ish-bosheth. Despite being greatly outnumbered, and despite the deaths of Asahel and other top generals, David's army was winning the war, and his military strength was growing (2:12-3:1)

David's family was also growing at this time, as shown in both 2 Samuel 3:2-5 and I Chronicles 3:1-4, with the first of David's sons born in Hebron. This polygamy remained unanswered by God through these events.

When the narrative resumes, we read the fascinating account of treachery and political intrigue that eventually led to David's formal installation of king over all Israel. First is the defection of Abner, the General of Ish-bosheth's army, because of an internal dispute over a sexual indiscretion (2 Samuel 3:6-26), to David. David's General didn't believe Abner's defection to be sincere, and murdered Abner at the gates of Hebron (3:27). But instead of claiming victory over the opposing General, David lamented the death of Abner (3:28-39) and had him buried properly in Hebron. Despite David's words, Ish-bosheth was then killed as well (4:1-12), and what the murderers thought was positive news ended up being their own death sentences. After this comes the formal crowning of David as king over all Israel in both 2 Samuel 5 and I Chronicles 11.

May 1, NT
Matthew 24:1-31
The Olivet Discourse, Part One - Wednesday

The Olivet Discourse is, perhaps, the most heavily debated part of the synoptic Gospels. The name comes from the location of this last great speech by Jesus before the Last Supper, the Mount of Olives, following a crucial twofold question by one of them (who is not named). Placement of this on Wednesday of "Holy Week" is based on just a single line Jesus says at the very end of the discourse in Matthew 26 (which we will read on May 7). It is told in parts in all three synoptic Gospels, and forms Jesus' longest and most detailed prophecy of future events, including events yet to occur in *our* future, events commonly referred to as the "End of the World" or, simply, the End Times.

The two questions are prompted by Jesus' statement about the coming destruction of the Temple (Matthew 24:2). It is interesting to note that Jesus speaks of the temple's destruction as He is leaving it for the very last time. The questions are, paraphrased, "when will these things (the destruction of the Temple) take place" and "what will be the sign(s) of Your coming" (or in some translations, "Your return") "and the end of the age". Jesus answers the second question first in all three versions.

Entire sermons can be, and have been, delivered on each of the verses that follow. What Jesus explains is the manner and order of events in what has come to be called "Daniel's 70th Week," or the manner of fulfillment of Daniel's prophecies, particularly Daniel 9:27. Without going into excessive detail about Daniel's original prophecy here, Jesus predicts each of the following to occur as the End Times approach: false Christs (Matthew 24:4-5), wars and rumors of wars (24:6-8), persecution (24:9-11), lawlessness (24:12-13), and the preaching of the Gospel to the whole world (24:14). These make up the first half of the "week" predicted by Daniel. Jesus then describes the Abomination of Desolation (24:15-20) at the mid-point of this period, a prediction that should put to rest any interpretations of Daniel's prophecy that people believe was fulfilled during the time of the Maccabees and the Greek takeover by Antiochus IV. This is followed by His description of the latter half of the "week," known commonly as the "Great Tribulation" (24:21-28), and then His return, also known as the "Glorious Appearing" (24:29-31). The discourse continues after this, but this completes His answer, in Matthew, of the second of the two questions.

May 2, OT
1 Chronicles 12:23-40; Psalm 2:1-12; Psalm 78:1-72
The Loyal Men of David

Today's OT reading starts as a continuation and deeper detail of the last 5 verses of yesterday's reading. In yesterday's reading, David was formally installed as king over all Israel, rather than just a single tribe, by "all Israel" including its elders. Today, in almost a census-like format, is the detail of the fighting men, by tribe, who were loyal to David rather than Saul, listed by tribe and count. These were, as one Bible edition puts it, the men who "made David king." Of course, it was *God* who made David king, but this detail describes the formal installation.

David wrote Psalm 2 at this time, emphasizing that he was indeed the current king but that there was a King to come that all the world's rulers would eventually bow to. Psalm 78 is our first to be written by a man named Asaph, a Maskil (that is, instructional Psalm) that would be the first of many (we are introduced to Asaph on May 5). It is one of the longest Psalms, in that it recalls nearly the entire history of the nation of Israel up to the installation of David as king.

May 2, NT
Mark 13:1-27
The Olivet Discourse, Part One - Wednesday

Mark is believed to have written his version of the Gospel before Matthew did, and there are strong similarities between the two, particularly with events such as the Olivet Discourse. In Mark's Gospel, he begins exactly as Matthew (later) did, only this time 4 of the Apostles are actually named: Peter, James, John, and Andrew. It is still not mentioned which of the 4 asks the crucial pair of questions or whether or not the other Apostles were present (Mark 13:1-4).

Basically, though, Mark 13:5-27 (the remainder of today's reading) directly parallels Matthew 24:4-31 with just a slightly different wording to account for the slightly shorter number of verses.

May 3, OT
Psalm 16:1-11; 2 Samuel 5:6-10; 1 Chronicles 11:4-9; 2 Samuel 5:17-21; 1 Chronicles 14:8-12
Jerusalem Becomes Capital of Israel; A War with the Philistines

King David was much more than just a great warrior or conquering king. David was a man "after God's own heart" who gave credit where credit was due. A lot of that credit was delivered via his numerous Psalms, one of them being Psalm 16 which is listed as a "Mikhtam," which is translated as an "atonement Psalm". Psalm 16 is also another of David's great Messianic prophecies, as verses 9-10 predict the resurrection of the eventual eternal King, which David knew he wasn't. That King would, of course, be Jesus Christ.

Two events follow in the narrative, both of which are echoed nearly word for word in 1 Chronicles after being told first in 2 Samuel: the formal taking of Jerusalem to become the "city of David" and the official capital of all Israel, and a brief war with the Philistines after they found out that David, who once appeared to defect TO them, was now king over all of Israel. This, like many others, was one of David's successful military campaigns. He first did the exact correct thing by inquiring of the Lord, before then moving forward to take on his enemy. This fact takes on increasing importance in future military campaigns in the next few days' OT readings.

May 3, NT
Luke 21:5-28
The Olivet Discourse, Part One - Wednesday

Luke's version of the first part of the Olivet Discourse starts out very much the same way as both Mark's and Matthew's, which were, presumably, written prior to Luke's. It begins with Jesus' prediction that the Temple will be destroyed (Luke 21:5-6), and then the two questions by an unnamed disciple or disciples (21:7). It's the same two questions asked in the same order as was read in Matthew and Mark. Jesus begins his response to the questions by, again, answering the second question ("what are the signs") first (21:8-19).

The first significant difference between Luke's account of this and Matthew and Mark's comes at verse 20. At first glance, Luke 21:20-24 would seem to be parallel to Matthew 24:15-28 and Mark 13:14-26 until you look closely at the first and last verses (Luke 21:20, 21:24) of that section. There, you realize that this prediction of the destruction (or siege) of Jerusalem in Luke is a different event than what is described in the other two synoptic Gospels. Luke is quoting Jesus referring to the destruction that was literally fulfilled when the emperor Titus destroyed the Temple in 70 A.D., not the End Times as Matthew and Mark were talking about, ending with Jesus' return. Luke also refers to the return of Christ (21:25-28), but only *after* the key verse, only in Luke, that refers to the *time of the Gentiles* (a.k.a. The Church Age) which must come after the (first) destruction of Jerusalem (21:24).

It is also here in Luke that we get the first hint of "when" these things will occur, in the final verse, when Jesus says that (paraphrased) "when these things begin to happen, lift up your heads for your redemption is near" (21:28). This still doesn't give an exact date, but it does say that all these other prophecies must first come true *before* Christ's return, which places the date of the End Times in *our* future.

Another key prophecy is found in tomorrow's reading that should put to rest any notion of these prophecies having been fulfilled already.

May 4, OT
2 Samuel 23:13-17; 1 Chronicles 11:15-19; 2 Samuel 5:22-25; 1 Chronicles 14:13-17; 2 Samuel 5:11-12; 1 Chronicles 14:1-2; 1 Chronicles 13:1-14; 2 Samuel 6:1-11; Psalm 101:1-8
War Against the Philistines; Bringing Back the Ark

One of the advantages of having the same events chronicled (pardon the pun) by two different writers in the Bible is that one can gain a much better perspective of the sequence of the events. There are a number of passages near the end of 2 Samuel that seem (and are) badly out of sequence compared to the rest of the books of Samuel; the beginning of today's OT reading is a case in point. Although the parallel passage from 1 Chronicles requires a slight jump forward as well, it's a very small jump compared to that in 2 Samuel, and it makes much more sense as a result. Jumping back and forth between 2 Samuel and 1 Chronicles, we read several more important details of the war between Israel and the Philistines just as David was crowned king of all Israel. David's constant consultation with the Lord should be noted, particularly in light of the next part of the reading.

Then, an important post-war event is chronicled that has led quite a number of Bible scoffers to claim that the God of the Old Testament and the God of the New Testament are *not* one and the same God. The reason given is that the God of the Old Testament, as evidenced particularly in 1 Chronicles 13 and 2 Samuel 6, seems like an angry, vengeful God who acts out of pettiness and malice, rather than the merciful God of the New Testament. Nothing could be farther from the truth. The same God of grace who promises eternal life to all who believe and put their trust in Him is also a God of perfect justice, who had previously given a quite clear warning about the proper handling of the Ark of the Covenant. On February 23 in Leviticus 10, we already read God's warning about the proper handling of the Ark and other ceremonial items. At that time, two sons of Aaron paid the ultimate price, just as does Uzzah in today's reading, for not obeying the Lord *precisely*, reflecting a lack of real listening to God and His Word.

May 4, NT
Luke 21:29-36; Mark 13:28-37
The Olivet Discourse, Part Two - The Parable of the Fig Tree - Wednesday

Continuing first in Luke, then in Mark (and then in Matthew tomorrow), Jesus speaks a key prophecy regarding the timing of End Times events in the Parable of the Fig Tree. The metaphor of the fig tree refers to the nation of Israel, which, in the time of Jesus, had not existed for more than 400 years (and wouldn't for another 1900+, though the disciples could not have known this). The disciples hearing this would have understood it immediately, but the key verse in this passage (Luke 21:32, Mark 13:30) likely reinforced the disciples' belief that Jesus was the "conquering Messiah" who would restore the *kingdom* of Israel in their lifetimes. The eschatological view called "Preterism" is based on this same idea that all of the prophecies spoken as part of this discourse (and in Daniel and Revelation) were already fulfilled by the end of the first century A.D., and references to Israel are then transferred to the Church ("replacement theology") - all based on a misinterpretation of what Jesus is talking about here regarding "this generation".

What Jesus refers to here is the generation that will see "these" events (meaning the events leading up to the End Times) is the same generation that will see His return. This has led to centuries of speculation as to what constitutes a generation. It has also, unfortunately, led to a great deal of date setting, which Jesus told the disciples was foolish because it was all going to happen on a date that even *He* did not know (Mark 13:32 and in Matthew tomorrow). He nevertheless tells the disciples to be watchful and alert about the signs, a message that was meant to be passed along to future generations (the doctrine of immanency).

In Luke and Mark, this brings the Olivet Discourse to a conclusion, though Matthew's version goes on much longer, as read tomorrow and the next day.

May 5, OT
2 Samuel 6:12-23; 1 Chronicles 15:1-16:43; Psalm 15:1-5
Dance Naked

I had the pleasure of teaching a group of middle school students about the Old Testament years ago, and this passage proved to be among the most giggle-inducing sections of them all. The reasons for that form the basis for the tongue-in-cheek title of today's OT reading. After yesterday's setback in trying to bring the Ark of the Covenant to Jerusalem, David both explains the execution and what needed to be done about it (1 Chronicles 15:1-2), and then assembles the group of Levites who would then carry the Ark the rest of the way into Jerusalem. It is during this procession that David is seen "dancing with all his might" (2 Samuel 6:14) before the Ark, and his Ephod (a very loose-fitting garment that barely covers anyway) comes loose enough for David to be seen naked in public. The only person *documented* to have seen him naked, though, is one of his wives, Michal (6:16). The 2 Samuel passage goes into more detail about this (1 Chronicles does not though it has more detail about the procession itself), as Michal angrily criticizes David afterwards (6:20), but David justifies his behavior to her (6:21-22).

Notable is the final statement in the 2 Samuel passage that Michal would become the only one of David's several wives who bore him no children.

In the remainder of the 1 Chronicles passage and the Psalm, David successfully completes the transfer of the Ark to its new home, a tent (tabernacle in some translations) built by David himself. Both Psalm 15 and 1 Chronicles 16:8-36 reflect the joy and the reverence of this symbol of the Lord's presence. Just before the Psalm of thanksgiving in 1 Chronicles, we are introduced to the priest Asaph, who is presumably the same Asaph who wrote Psalm 78 (read on May 2) and several others. He is listed here as the Chief of the Priests.

May 5, NT
Matthew 24:32-25:13
The Olivet Discourse, Part Two – Two Parables and the Rapture - Wednesday

The most likely reason that Matthew's version of the Olivet Discourse is (by far) the longest, despite not being the first one written, is that Matthew may have been an eyewitness to it, as one of the Twelve. Luke and Mark were not. Though Mark's and Luke's versions of the Olivet Discourse are now complete, there are two days' worth of readings in Matthew of additional detail, including several more very important passages to anyone's study of the End Times.

In all three synoptic Gospels, as read the past few days, Jesus answers the second of the two questions first. That second question concerns the "what," not the "when," regarding the signs of His coming (or return). Jesus then answers the first question by speaking the Parable of the Fig Tree in all three synoptic Gospels, including Matthew to begin today's NT reading (Matthew 24:32-35), which doesn't give an exact date but gives a very important clue as to when it will occur: not until after Israel exists once again as a nation. That prophecy wouldn't be fulfilled until 1948. Then, also in all three Gospels, Jesus tells the disciples to be watchful for these signs, which establishes what we now call the doctrine of immanency. The disciples could not have known that these things would not have occurred in their own lifetimes; in fact, they likely assumed (at first) that when Jesus spoke of "this generation," (24:34) He was referring to them. It was then, and only in Matthew's version of the Olivet Discourse, that Jesus clarifies this for them by expanding on this "watchfulness doctrine" by way of another prophecy and another parable.

After He says that even He doesn't know the exact day or hour of His return (24:36), He uses the metaphor of the "days of Noah" (24:37-39) to explain what the times would be like immediately prior to then. And then comes what appears to be His most mysterious prophecy: his detail of an event that would occur just before this End Times period (Daniel's 70th week) begins: the Rapture. Though He doesn't use that word nor use any phrase that could be translated as "snatching away," (as Paul would later do in 1 Thessalonians) Jesus describes the event using examples of two men in a field (24:40), two women grinding at a mill (24:41), and a head of a household thwarting a thief (24:43), all to drive home the point about the need for being alert and watchful... all for an event that will happen suddenly and at a time people least expect.

Jesus follows this with another parable, called the Parable of the Ten Virgins (25:1-13) that expands on this further, with another parable and more in tomorrow's conclusion.

May 6, OT
Psalm 24:1-10; Psalm 65:1-13; Psalm 68:1-35; Psalm 110:1-7; Psalm 19:1-14; 2 Samuel 8:1; 1 Chronicles 18:1; 2 Samuel 21:15-18; 1 Chronicles 20:4
The Early Days and Wars of King David

In what is almost a continuation of the OT reading two days ago (May 4), the brief narrative portions of todays OT reading, jumping to more "future" places in 2 Samuel, describe more of the wars (plural intentional) between the Philistines and Israel headed by its newly crowned king, David. The most notable difference here (and for the next few days) compared to previous campaigns against the Philistines is the absence (missed by most people) of direct consultation with the Lord. This is despite the fact that it is believed that David wrote all five of the Psalms (one of which is another of his great "Messianic" Psalms) that start today's reading early in his kingship and around the time he was conducting all of these war campaigns. The passage in 2 Samuel 21 is labeled, in some Bibles, as the "final campaign against the Philistines," but this chronology assumes that the description of the events fits better with one of the earlier "campaigns."

May 6, NT
Matthew 25:14-46
The Olivet Discourse, Part Three - The Sheep and Goats Judgment Prophecy - Wednesday

The final segment of the Olivet Discourse (though not necessarily the final events of Wednesday before the Crucifixion) features another parable and a key prophecy about the events at the conclusion of the Great Tribulation and the very end of Daniel's 70th Week. Though the Olivet Discourse is found in all three synoptic Gospels, it is only in Matthew, yesterday and today, in which we read Jesus' explanation of what these prophecies *mean* regarding his answer to the disciples' question at the beginning. When interpreted the correct way, we find that Jesus predicts many events, including the destruction of Jerusalem in 70 A.D. (only in Luke), the Rapture (yesterday, only in Matthew), and many of the events during the Tribulation. Today's reading starts with another parable (Matthew 25:14-30), found only in Matthew, that isn't just another way of explaining the doctrine of "watchfulness," but a clear prediction of the Church Age and the need for evangelizing beyond just the immediate area of what we now call Israel (because He never actually specifies "when" any of the events will occur except for a few cryptic but important clues).

The cap of the prophecy is the final segment of the Discourse (25:31-46), which is commonly referred to as the "Sheep and Goats Judgment," a prophecy that makes clear that there will be two judgments: one, after the conclusion of the Tribulation, at the time commonly referred to as the "Second Coming" or the "Glorious Appearing," and the other, in heaven, that is not yet prophesied (in several places in Romans, 2 Corinthians, and Revelation). It is a sobering prophecy that should also put to rest any notion that there is no "hell" or that no one will be going to the place "prepared for the Devil and his angels" (25:41).

May 7, OT
2 Samuel 23:8-12; 1 Chronicles 11:10-14; 2 Samuel 21:19-22; 1 Chronicles 20:5-8
More Wars Against the Philistines

If you placed a bookmark in your Bibles at the last place before all the "jumping around" began, you will note that it was left at the end of 2 Samuel chapter 6. Today, we read of more military campaigns conducted by David against the Philistines that *appear* to occur much later in David's life (one of those read today actually is presented after "David's last words") but were actually early battles that occurred at nearly the same time as David's coronation as king. A careful reading of the names of David's fighting men in the first two passages reveals that the sequence of events in David's early days is drawn primarily from Chronicles, not Samuel, by the creators of this part of the chronological reading plan. It represents the best overall compromise between the two different accounts of what are obviously the same events.

Notable amongst these is the mention of the Lord in handing over Israel's enemies to them, despite no detail of David having previously consulted God. When reading these passages chronologically, it seems a trivial thing, particularly considering how David always emerged victorious, regardless. But when we finally get back to 2 Samuel 7 (on May 16), this will all come to a very important head.

May 7, NT
Matthew 26:1-2; Luke 21:37-38; John 12:20-50
Jesus' Final Prediction of His Death - Wednesday

The two brief passages from Matthew and Luke establish the time frame of the just-completed Olivet Discourse as Wednesday just prior to His crucifixion, likely Wednesday evening (Luke 21:37). John's Gospel contains no mention of the Olivet Discourse but does go into detail about the aftermath, which could have equally well occurred on Wednesday as on Thursday, but a clue in tomorrow's reading makes it more likely to have been Wednesday.

In the passage from John, Jesus responds to a request for a meeting with some Greeks (John 12:20-22) by telling His disciples that "the Hour," which He had previously stated had not yet come (several times) had now arrived (12:23) and follows this with one of His most lengthy and detailed predictions of His death and the redeeming nature of it (12:24-36, 44-50). Jesus uses the metaphor of being lifted up (literally fulfilled in His crucifixion) as a judgment upon the world (12:31) to indicate this redemption, as He would soon fulfill the role of taking away man's sins first predicted before He was born. John interrupts the quote of Jesus by using a technique used much more often by Matthew: quoting the prophet Isaiah (from portions of chapters 6 and 53) to further explain Jesus' words (12:37-43). But though this is preceded by a statement about Jesus' withdrawal from the crowds to whom He was speaking (12:36), Jesus' words that follow were presumably heard by at least the Apostle John.

May 8, OT
2 Samuel 10:1-19; 1 Chronicles 19:1-19; Psalm 33:1-22; 2 Samuel 11:1; 1 Chronicles 20:1
The Ammonite/Syrian Campaigns

David was a gracious king, but was very consistent in not putting up with deceit or subterfuge from anyone. In this OT reading, a former enemy of Israel (defeated by Saul) lost their king, and David decided to extend a kindness towards them, given that they had extended some courtesy to David (not recorded in the Bible) in the past (2 Samuel 10:1-2). But David's reputation as a conquering king led them to assume that David's emissaries were actually spies set out to conquer them (10:3), and so abused and shamed them and sent the men back to David (10:4-5). When the Ammonites heard that David's kindness had evaporated, they teamed up with another neighbor, the Syrians, to do battle with Israel on two fronts. But David successfully countered both armies with the help of the leader of his own army, Joab, who proved to be equally as good at military strategy as was David (10:6-11:1). Noticeable in its absence is any mention of David consulting the Lord in this whole affair, in either the 2 Samuel or 1 Chronicles accounts.

The end of these wars was obviously a joyous time for *some* believer in Israel, as reflected in Psalm 33, which is full of praise and recognition of the One who is the true savior of kings. But, we don't know who wrote the Psalm that is believed to come from this period. Most Psalms of David have his name in a subtitle ("a Psalm of

David") or some other obvious and usually first person reference to him.

May 8, NT
Luke 22:1-6; Mark 14:1-2, 10-11; Matthew 26:3-5,14-16
Judas Agrees to Betray Jesus - Wednesday/Thursday

These brief passages from each of the three synoptic Gospels establish the beginning of the events commonly known as "the Passion". For all the plots by the Pharisees and others to have Jesus killed, none came (or could come) to fruition until one of Jesus' own closest followers, one of the twelve, Judas, broke away from the group long enough to tell the chief priests that he would betray Jesus for a price. The chief priests agreed and the string of events leading to the Crucifixion got underway, late on Wednesday (Passover…"two days away", Mark 14:1) or early Thursday.

May 9, OT
2 Samuel 11:2-12:23; Psalm 51:1-19
David's Great Sins and Greatest Moment

David may have been known as a "man after God's own heart," but he was still a man, subject to temptation, weakened by pride, and prone to sin. In one of the best-known events in the life and kingship of David, the king was in Jerusalem while his armies were off to battle, when he observes a beautiful woman bathing on the roof of a nearby building. The woman is Bathsheba, wife of Uriah the Hittite. David sends for her and has sex with her (2 Samuel 11:4) and later finds out that he got her pregnant (2 Samuel 11:5). In an elaborate plot to cover up his adultery, David sends for Bathsheba's husband to come home to make it look like the baby would belong to Uriah instead of David (11:6-8). But, the plot was foiled when Uriah's loyalty to David and Joab's army made Uriah decide not to go home to his wife (11:9-13). Desperate to hide his crime, David then sent Uriah back to the army and sent a note to Joab requesting Uriah's placement on the front lines in order that he would be killed. The murder would be viewed as just another casualty of war. Bathsheba mourned the loss of her husband (11:26) only long enough for David to then marry her (11:27), making her the king's eighth wife and at least the sixth to bear a son to David.

David may have believed that he successfully hid his sins of adultery and murder from everyone, but the Lord knows better. If you assume, as I do, that yesterday's Psalm 33 was *not* written by David, then you have several *years'* worth of events in which David was drifting further and further away from the Lord. David repeatedly neglected to consult the Lord before going into battle, something that he never neglected to do before he became king. And though there is no specific commandment against polygamy, God's design for marriage specified one man and one woman, thus making David's accumulation of wives a violation of that design, at least. And though God doesn't always act *immediately* in judging sin, He does always act, thus there are always consequences to sin even when those consequences are delayed.

Such was the case when the Lord sent a prophet named Nathan to David (12:1). Nathan gave David a hypothetical scenario for David to consider (12:2-4) which was later revealed to be a metaphor of the king's behavior. Nathan's "You are the man!" (12:7) stands as one of the greatest rebukes of all time. His rebuke of the king goes on for another 4 verses, and includes warnings (all of which would come true) of the many consequences of that sin (12:10-11, 12:14) - consequences that would dominate David's kingship and the rest of his life.

But the key verse, and his greatest moment, comes near the end of the encounter with Nathan, when David openly admits to his sin (12:13), and Nathan responds to this act of contrition by informing the king that the Lord has already forgiven him. This statement of the truth of God's grace and mercy superimposed on God's righteous judgment makes clear that we are forgiven based on what we believe, not what we do, *but we cannot escape the earthly consequences of that forgiven sin.*

As prophesied by Nathan, God struck down the child born of the unlawful union of David and Bathsheba (12:15-23), the first of many consequences for David's great sins. During this time, it is believed that David wrote the great penitential Psalm, numbered as #51. This sincere outpouring of penitence is the model prayer for all sinners seeking the grace of God to "blot out my transgressions".

May 9, NT
Luke 22:7-14; Mark 14:12-17; Matthew 26:17-20
The Upper Room is Prepared - Thursday

Thursday afternoon, perhaps just before sunset, Jesus sends the Apostles Peter and John (Luke 22:8) to obtain the room in which they would celebrate the Passover meal. This is recorded in all three synoptic Gospels, though the two who are sent ahead are named only in Luke (Mark only says there were two of them, Matthew doesn't specify the number of disciples). All three accounts then specify that Jesus joined them later, and all twelve Apostles were present.

May 10, OT
Psalm 6:1-10; Psalm 32:1-11; Psalm 38:1-22; Psalm 103:1-22; 2 Samuel 12:26-31; 1 Chronicles 20:1-3; Psalm 21:1-13
David Wins the Crown of Rabbah

Psalm 51 may be David's best-known and loftiest statement of contrition, but it was by no means his only. At around this same time, David also wrote the four Psalms that begin today's reading. The first three are all quoted, in part, in at least one place in the New Testament; number 32 is another of David's Maskils, or "instructional Psalms," and number 103, which is more of a song of praise than it is anything penitential, is the lyrical basis for a widely-known hymn. It isn't known whether or not it is actually because of these Psalms that God granted David and Israel victory over the Ammonites, but a notable aspect of the conquest, as told in 2 Samuel 12 and 1 Chronicles 20, is the apparent *bloodlessness* of the victory. One of David's rewards in this victory was a crown containing a talent of gold and a precious stone, which David then mentions in a Psalm of praise written during this time and numbered as 21.

May 10, NT
John 13:1-20
Jesus Washes the Disciples' Feet - Thursday

Once Jesus and the Apostles were in the Upper Room that Thursday evening, they reclined at the table to celebrate the Passover. What the Apostles there didn't yet fully understand was that this was about to be the Last Supper (pun intentional) they would enjoy together. Portions of the Upper Room events are recorded in all four Gospels, but John records two events that aren't recorded in the three synoptic Gospels while Matthew, Mark, and Luke each record several details of the meal itself (including the part instituted as the Eucharist) that aren't recorded in John. Between the four of them, though, Jesus' final night together with His Apostles can be pieced together with certainty.

The first such part, recorded only in John, is the washing of the Apostles' feet by Jesus. Peter's reaction, and Jesus' response to that reaction, forms the basis for some important doctrines of Christianity including election (John 13:18). Jesus also makes a veiled prediction of His coming betrayal. He would be much more specific during the meal itself (in the May 12 reading).

May 11, OT
2 Samuel 12:24-25; 2 Samuel 8:2; 1 Chronicles 18:2
The Birth of Solomon

Today's very brief Old Testament reading actually tells of two events: the birth of the boy who would later become the next king of Israel, Solomon, and the expansion of David's kingdom boundaries to include the former nation of Moab. This commentary, though still brief, is actually much longer than the verses themselves.

Notable in the rather small amount of space given to the birth of one of Israel's greatest kings is the fact that Solomon, like many others before him in the line to Jesus, was not the firstborn of his father (nor was he the firstborn to David and Bathsheba, who in turn was not David's first wife). Going all the way back to Abraham, the family trees of the great heroes of the Old Testament include numerous instances of the "next one in succession" (for the Covenant or the judgeship or the kingdom) being either illegitimate or being, at the very least, a later child often the result of a polygamous marriage. Abraham's first son was Ishmael, not Isaac, but Isaac was his first *legitimate* son. Isaac's twin sons Esau and Jacob were born in that order, thus making Esau the legitimate heir - yet it went to Jacob as the result of a swindle. And Jacob's twelve sons, the "twelve tribes of Israel," were born of four different women, only two of whom were his wives… yet all are considered "legitimate." How can this be, when God's design for marriage is one man, one woman, for life?

The question answers itself when you realize that in every such case, where polygamy or anything contrary to God's design or will was involved, the decision to go against God's will or otherwise "work around it" resulted in earthly consequences for those involved, while God, always in control, allowed certain things to happen in order to fulfill His perfect will. Sometimes this was recognized and acknowledged by the one being judged, and sometimes not, but God's will *always* prevailed.

May 11, NT
Matthew 26:26-29; Mark 14:22-25; Luke 22:14-20
The Last Supper, Part One: The Institution of the Lord's Supper - Thursday

It is the central sacrament of the Roman Catholic Church. It is one of only two sacraments (the other being baptism) recognized and performed in virtually all Christian churches, and the only one performed in *the same manner* in virtually all churches. Whether you call it Eucharist, Holy Communion, or simply The Lord's Supper, Christians do it today as an act of remembrance for that moment in history, on the night before He was crucified, when Jesus took the all important next step in His Passion: not merely predicting His death but taking the next step towards it, and explaining why it was going to occur. At the end of only one of the versions (Luke's, the most detailed), Jesus adds the command to "do this in memory of me," (Luke 22:19) thus instituting the Lord's Supper.

Jesus' wording of this remembrance ritual in all three synoptic Gospels, coupled with Jesus' use of the term "the bread of life" (John 6:53-58, read on February 20), referring to Himself, in the only Gospel to not have any details of the Last Supper itself, is what has led to the Catholic Church's doctrine of Transubstantiation. As explained on the reading for February 20, Jesus was not telling the Apostles that the bread and wine were literally His body and blood, nor that any of them would be granted the power to turn the elements into His body and blood. Rather, He was speaking metaphorically (some would say "symbolically" but this is inadequate) about the death He was about to endure and what the Apostles (and later, all believers) should do to commemorate that atoning death.

May 12, OT
2 Samuel 8:3-4; 1 Chronicles 18:3-4; 2 Samuel 8:7-8; 1 Chronicles 18:7-8; 2 Samuel 8:5-6; 1 Chronicles 18:5-6
Further Expansion of the Kingdom

The military campaigns conducted (all successfully) by David continued after the birth of Solomon (even though these events appear before that birth in the Bible). In these brief passages, jumping back and forth between 2 Samuel and 1 Chronicles, we read of the next success that, if we assume this chronology to be correct, would have had to happen sometime after the adultery/murder incident, but more importantly, after David's repentance as well. The key line is found at the end of the 2 Samuel passage, where it now says that "the Lord helped David wherever he went" (2 Samuel 8:6b, NASB), which may be a direct result of David's acknowledgement of his sin.

May 12, NT
Matthew 26:21-25; Mark 14:18-21; Luke 22:21-23; John 13:21-35
The Last Supper, Part Two: Jesus Predicts His Betrayal - Thursday

The next event during the Last Supper is found in all four Gospels. After washing the feet of the disciples and instituting the Lord's Supper as a specific and formal remembrance ritual, Jesus not only predicts His betrayal, but also exposes His betrayer, Judas. Matthew and Mark's accounts of this are within one word of being identical, Luke's is slightly more abbreviated. John's account, despite being the Gospel containing the least detail about the meal itself, actually contains the most detail about Jesus' prediction of betrayal. Part of the reason for this might be a clue in John's Gospel (John 13:23) not found in the other three: the mention of the one sitting closest to Jesus, who is listed, repeatedly, as the "Apostle Jesus loved." Most scholars believe this is a reference to the Apostle John, and therefore the writer of the Gospel bearing his name. Contrary to some Bible-deniers, John's more detailed version of Jesus' prediction of betrayal does not contradict the other three; rather, John decided to explain Jesus' words and add more detail that previous Gospel writers chose not to include.

May 13, OT
Psalm 124:1-8; Psalm 108:1-13; Psalm 60:1-12
Giving Credit Where Credit is Due

All three of these Psalms, written by David, reference the recently-won (in this chronology) battles for the expansion of the territory of Israel. All three give credit to the Lord, as they should, for those victories. This is a sharp and appropriate contrast to the way things had been going for David prior to the adultery and murder incidents, in spite of the fact that David's armies were victorious both before and after that time.

May 13, NT
Luke 22:24-30; Matthew 26:31-32; Mark 14:27-28; Luke 22:31-32
The Last Supper, Part Three: The Fate of The Apostles - Thursday

With the betrayer now exposed (and departed from them), the Apostles present at the Last Supper made a new inquiry amongst themselves: this time not asking which was the traitor, for they now knew this, but who was the "greatest". This was not the first time this question had come up. Jesus' answer, beginning in Luke, continuing in Matthew and Mark, and concluding in Luke, goes into some significant detail about the future fate of the Apostles, including how their future worth to the not-yet-instituted Church would *not* be like (Luke 22:25) and the reward in being able to "judge the twelve tribes" (22:30), rather than any kind of worldly grandeur.

Jesus also predicts the scattering of the Apostles after His death in the Matthew and Mark passages. The verses in Matthew and Mark are almost identical, and are listed as being quoted after Jesus and the Apostles had left the upper room for the Mount of Olives. This chronology makes the contrary assumption that Jesus said these things near the end of the meal, before the Upper Room Discourse had begun (which Matthew and Mark don't quote at all).

It is assumed that the main question that was asked of Jesus in this part of the Last Supper came from Simon Peter, as Jesus directed the conclusion of His answer directly to Simon (Luke 22:31). But this part of the answer must have certainly been troubling to Simon Peter, as evidenced in tomorrow's NT reading.

May 14, OT
2 Samuel 8:9-14; 1 Chronicles 18:9-13; Psalm 44:1-26; Psalm 20:1-9; 2 Samuel 23:18-19; 1 Chronicles 11:20-21
Dedicating the Spoils of War

When read in chronological order (using mainly the sequence in the Chronicles, though even there we do some jumping around), one can easily see a pattern in the life and military campaigns of David, king of Israel. After being anointed, but prior to becoming king, David always consulted with the Lord as to what to do before each successful battle. This was carried forward to at least the early part of his kingdom. But then, he gradually fell away and neglected to keep the Lord first and foremost. And though he continued to have military success, his backsliding led to pride, polygamy, adultery, and conspiracy to commit murder. It was only after being confronted with this by Nathan that David turned things around - in a big way. David continued to have military success, but now he was giving credit to the Lord for each victory. Yesterday's three Psalms and one of today's (Psalm 20) reflect this. Psalm 44 was written by someone else, but references the things that David dedicated to the Lord after acquiring them in battle.

May 14, NT
Luke 22:33-34; Matthew 26:33-35; Mark 14:29-31; John 13:36-38
The Last Supper, Part Four: Jesus Predicts Peter's Denial - Thursday

Though the question by Peter is worded differently in John, all four Gospels make note of Jesus' prediction that "before the rooster crows twice, you (Peter) will deny Me three times". John's Gospel excludes the word "twice". Matthew and Mark's version are exactly alike; Luke's different by only a couple of words. Peter's statement that prompted the prediction is actually in response to something Jesus said in only Matthew and Mark's version from yesterday: when Jesus mentioned the "falling away" of the Apostles, Peter makes the claim that he never will do that. Jesus lets it be known that Peter, leader though he may be, is not immune to this form of human frailty. This denial is not to be confused, of course, with the betrayal. Both events had yet to occur, but Jesus predicted them both and both came to pass.

May 15, OT
2 Samuel 23:20-39; 1 Chronicles 11:22-47
David's Mighty Men

Today, we read for the last time, a roll of David's top warriors in his army. In 2 Samuel, this account appears after the section called "David's Last Prophetic Words," but is placed in this chronology according to its appearance in 1 Chronicles, prior to the accounts of most of the battles that defined David's kingship. It is readily admitted that reading long lists of names such as this can be difficult and boring. But it's still important for both scholarship and apologetics that these things are covered and continue to be included in the Bible and in Bible study. It will especially make more sense when, as previously stated, all these events in the life of David come to a head in tomorrow's OT reading.

May 15, NT
Luke 22:35-38; John 14:1-21
The Upper Room Discourse, Part One: Words of Warning and Comfort - Thursday

Today begins a five-day, five-part reading of Jesus' most important (arguably) private speech to His Apostles, commonly called the Upper Room Discourse. It is named, of course, for the location where Jesus and eleven of the twelve had just finished the Passover Meal, which would become the Last Supper. There is some debate among scholars as to whether all of it, or even *any* of it, took place in that same Upper Room, or if at least some of it took place (as this chronology assumes) on the Mount of Olives on the way out to the Garden of Gethsemane. This chronology assumes that today and tomorrow's readings took place in the Upper Room, and the remainder (John 15-17) took place as they were walking, even though it is still called the Upper Room Discourse in this reading plan.

Though more than 90% of the Upper Room Discourse is told only in John, the speech actually begins in Luke, where Jesus starts by giving the Apostles a warning about the persecution to come, by referencing the time when He sent them out to evangelize early in His ministry (Luke 22:35). In mentioning the "money belt," (22:36), He makes a veiled reference to Judas, who was the treasurer of their group. Then, and most importantly, He makes clear that it is He who is referenced by Isaiah (in Isaiah 53) as the suffering servant (22:37); it is He who is the fulfillment of prophecy. Though it's obvious by the Apostles' response that they still didn't fully understand (22:38), Jesus' warning of the conflict to come had the desired effect: the Apostles were now on their guard. This then prompted Jesus to utter the words of comfort that follow, as recorded in John.

John chapter 14 contains numerous verses that form the basis for many of the most important Christian doctrines. Among them is Jesus' answer to Thomas' question about "the way" to get to where Jesus was "going," when referring to the place He was preparing in His Father's house: that Jesus *himself* is the Way, the Truth, and the Life, and that no one comes to the Father without Him (John 14:6). It is believed to be the second-most quoted verse in the entire Bible, after John 3:16. Jesus also defines His divinity by declaring that He and His Father are one and the same (14:10-11).

A pair of verses in this discourse also makes for one of the most badly *abused* parts of the Bible. Followers of the "prosperity Gospel" or "name it and claim it" often refer to John 14:13-14 to justify their distorted theology regarding prayer. When coupled with the prayer Jesus himself taught us to pray, known as The Lord's Prayer, a much more correct understanding of these verses emerges, which is that all sincere prayers are answered, though we will not always get the answer we expect.

Rounding out part one, Jesus adds one more very important promise to those He had already made: that a *third* part of the Trinity, referred to here as a Helper, would be sent (14:16-17) along with a promise of His own return (14:18). No clearer definition of our Triune God is made anywhere in the Bible, as the Son of God gives us the promise of the Holy Spirit.

May 16, OT
2 Samuel 8:15-18; 1 Chronicles 18:14-17; 2 Samuel 7:1-29; 1 Chronicles 17:1-27; Psalm 138:1-8
The Davidic Covenant

Beginning in Genesis and continuing throughout the Old Testament, God made covenants with His "chosen people," known first as the Hebrews, later the Israelites, and much later, the Jews. These agreements, or "covenants," were eternal but also conditional. That is, God's promise with each version of the Covenant was an eternal, never-ending agreement to "make a great nation" or deliver His people from some form of destruction or oppression. But, the Israelites had their end of the bargain to keep up, and they rarely did. They were usually asked little more than to obey certain laws or commandments or follow some simple directions. And as previously stated, on more than one occasion, one of the most maddening things, to God, about any of this was the manner in which His people Israel would only *partially* obey His word. This breaking of their end of the Covenant frequently brought them to the brink of destruction, sometimes even at the hand of God himself (see Genesis 19, nearly all of Judges, and the reign of Saul the king in 1 Samuel). But though the Israelites were frequently chastised, they were never destroyed, and this latest version of the Covenant affirmed that their kingdom would be eternal and would lead eventually to a King from David's royal line that would rule the whole world forever.

With David's kingdom finally *fully* established, as told in the two brief passages in 2 Samuel and 1 Chronicles, David expresses his desire to build a house for the Ark of the Lord, rather than the more temporary tents that had been used in the centuries since the exodus (2 Samuel 7:1-3). Though Nathan, the prophet that recently chastised the king for the sins of adultery and murder, approved of the idea, it was through Nathan that God delivered His twofold message: that David was *not* going to be the one to build the Temple (1 Chronicles 17:4), but rather, one of his sons (Solomon), who would be the first of a long line of descendants in a royal line that is established forever (2 Samuel 7:16). This prophecy would be fulfilled literally with Jesus, born in the direct line of descent from David through His stepfather Joseph who was descended of David's son Solomon (Romans 1:3), thus legally receiving "the throne" even though the Israelite kingdom had ceased to exist 400 years before Joseph was born. Likewise, Mary the mother of Jesus was descended of David as well, but through the non-royal line of Nathan (not the prophet) (Luke 3:23). The reasons for God forbidding David to build the temple aren't specified here, but God obviously did tell David, and David would later pass this reason on to his son Solomon (in I Chronicles 22, read on May 29). David's role in establishing this eternal kingdom was just as it was from before he was king: a shepherd gathering his flock and ruling over them. In other words, David was the warrior king, or conquering king, that got the kingdom started, but the Temple would have to wait for a descendant.

David responded with a prayer of praise and thanks (2 Samuel 7:18-29, 1 Chronicles 17:16-27) that is also echoed in Psalm 138.

May 16, NT
John 14:22-31; Matthew 26:30; Mark 14:26
The Upper Room Discourse, Part Two: The End of the Last Supper - Thursday

Jesus continues His words of assurance to His Apostles in response to another question by one of them, this time from Judas (not Iscariot, the betrayer) (John 14:22). Among other things, He clarifies the sending of the Holy Sprit (14:26), and the clear separation of the three Persons of what we now call The Trinity (14:28). But despite these positive things, Jesus also warns them that the "ruler of this world is coming" (14:30), and that He would not therefore "speak much more with you". This meant that the time was short before His time to die at the hands of this "ruler," whom we know to be the spirit of Satan.

The end of the Last Supper also marks the end of events that are believed to have taken place on Thursday, but this was by no means the end of this great final speech by Jesus. At the end of today's NT reading, Jesus tells them to "get up, let us go from here" (14:31), whereupon they sang a hymn and left for the Mount of Olives (Matthew 26:30, Mark 14:26), and Jesus continued His discourse along the way.

May 17, OT
Psalm 139:1-24; Psalm 145:1-21; 2 Samuel 21:1-14; 2 Samuel 9:1-13; Psalm 8:1-9
Bringing Closure to the House of Saul

Part of the Davidic Covenant (read yesterday) had God telling David (through Nathan) that He would not withdraw His loving-kindness from David's kingdom the way He did from Saul's (2 Samuel 7:15). But though that meant that David was the true beginning of the eternal kingdom instead of the actual first king of Israel, David was adamant about making sure that all agreements he made with Saul's family were still fulfilled (a bit of somewhat misguided loyalty that would come back to haunt David in the reading for May 20). Thus it came to be that a famine was ravaging the land, and David assumed that it was due to a previous grievance by Saul against the Gibeonites (2 Samuel 21:1). When the king asked them what could be done in restitution, the Gibeonites responded with a request to execute seven of Saul's men (21:5-6). David complied with the request (21:8-10), but specifically spared Meshibosheth, son of Jonathan and grandson of Saul (21:7), because of a prior agreement. After the executions, David buried the bones of Saul and Jonathan with the bones of the 7 executed by the Gibeonites (21:11-14), and granted the entire remainder of the inheritance of the family of Saul to Meshibosheth (9:1-13), and brought closure (or so he thought) to that entire chapter of Israelite history.

David's next Psalm, numbered as #8, is one of David's great Messianic Psalms.

May 17, NT
John 15:1-27
The Upper Room Discourse, Part Three: Jesus' Great Commandment - Friday

Though the last three parts of what is called the Upper Room Discourse take place *outside* of that upper room, there is almost universal agreement among scholars that these parts all belong together. At the end of yesterday's NT reading, there was a brief interruption in His speech, when He declared an end to the meal and got everyone up to leave, where they all then sung a hymn and departed for the Mount of Olives. In John, there is no interruption at all except for Jesus' remark about getting up to leave. We can thus assume that most of what He says in today's NT reading was spoken on the way out to that destination. Whether it took place before midnight (Thursday) or after (Friday) is anyone's guess, but this chronology assumes that the day known as "Good Friday" began some time during or just after the Upper Room Discourse.

In this chapter, the main theme (though not the only) is Jesus' metaphor of the vine and branches, with Jesus referring to Himself as the "true vine". By analogy, Jesus expresses the love the Father has for Him in the same terms as His plea for "abiding in Me," so that His "joy may be made full" in them (John 15:11). This all leads up to His Great Commandment, to "love one another just as I have loved you" (15:12).

May 18, OT
2 Samuel 5:13-16; 1 Chronicles 14:3-7; 1 Chronicles 3:4-9; 2 Samuel 13:1-15:6
The Consequences of David's Sin

There are *always* consequences for sin.

So says three different pastors from three different Christian denominations that I've personally heard preach on the topic. The topic is frequently broached when speaking of the relative difference in the *severity* of sins; the correct theological position is that God does not view any sins (or their quantity) as being more or less severe than another. The misconception about certain sins being more serious than others stems from a Roman Catholic doctrine concerning "venial sins" versus "mortal sins," which, in turn, stems from the fact that different sins have different types and levels of *earthly* consequences (along with a misinterpretation of 1 John 5:15-16). When we are saved, all of our sins are forgiven. But, this does *not* mean that we are exempt from the *penalty* we must pay for that sin here on earth.

Such was the case with King David. David's best-known sins are chronicled at great length in the Bible, lest anyone believe that one must be perfect or sin free in order to be used for God's purposes. David's finest hour (as read on May 9) occurred when he repented of his sins of adultery and murder before Nathan the prophet. David was told that his sins were forgiven, but that didn't mean that he didn't have to still pay a penalty for those same sins. Thus, David's sins of adultery and conspiracy to murder were punished by the death of the child born from that illegitimate union. But, there were more consequences to come, along with the consequences for other sins David committed, no matter how contrite he was about any of them. Those sins and their consequences dominate the remainder of the history of King David.

One of those sins and the consequences for them can only be understood in light of the first two brief passages in today's OT reading. For the final time in the Bible, 2 Samuel 5:13-16 (and its mirror in 1 Chronicles) lists the wives and children of David, this time showing those children born to him in Jerusalem (see readings for May 1 for children born in Hebron). Combined, the various passages can be compiled into the following list of wives (in chronological order) and the children born to each:

1. Michal, daughter of Saul. She had no children.
2. Ahinoam, mother of **Amnon**.
3. Abigail, mother of Chileab (aka Daniel). There is no mention of Chileab or Daniel outside of the various lists of offspring, which leads some (including me) to believe that he was not a biological child of David.
4. Maacah, mother of **Absalom**.
5. Haggith, mother of Adonijah.
6. Abital, mother of Stephatiah.
7. Eglah, mother of Ithream.
8. Bathsheba, mother of Shammua, Shobab, Nathan, and Solomon.
9. Unknown wife or concubine(s) became the mother of Ibhar, Elishua, Elpelet, Nogah, Nepheg, Japhia, Elishama, Beeliada, Eliphelet, and **Tamar**

The three names in **bold** would play a very prominent role in today's OT reading, as David and his family would struggle through a number of horrific events that formed the consequences for his sin of polygamy. As mentioned in previous comments, there is no specific prohibition against polygamy in the Bible, though it is made plain (in several places) that **mono**gamy is the *intended* design for marriage by God. It is sometimes difficult to tell whether any of the consequences David faced here were due to his violation of this intended design or if they were due to other sins he committed, but it is obvious that God allowed these things to happen as a result of some sin of David's.

The horrific events that begin here start with **Amnon**, the presumed crown prince, conspiring with a friend to rape his half-sister, **Tamar** (2 Samuel 13:1-19), after which **Absalom** commanded his servants to murder Amnon in revenge (13:20-30). Absalom made sure it looked as though he had killed *all* of the other sons of David, even though he was now the new crown prince. (Absalom did not yet know that young Solomon was the next king.) After the friend that plotted with Absalom set the record straight for the king (13:31-36), David mourned the losses of both Amnon and Absalom, though Absalom was still alive. The king was later convinced to bring Absalom back from exile (13:37-14:18), but the rest of Israel began to plot a revolt that would make the handsome prince king. After finally getting to see his father face to face, the king forgave Absalom for the revenge (14:33). But the growing rebellion would become another of David's great consequences for sin, as Absalom's following increased (15:1-6).

May 18, NT
John 16:1-33
The Upper Room Discourse, Part Four: The Work of the Holy Spirit - Friday

Jesus continues his discourse on the way out to the Garden of Gethsemane by first giving another very stern warning about the persecution that is to come (John 16:1-6) but, just as He had previously done, also comforting those same Apostles with an explanation of how His work would be carried on, even after His death, resurrection, and ascension into Heaven, by the Helper who we know to be the Holy Spirit (16:7-28). Even though Jesus used several figures of speech and metaphors in His explanation, the Apostles responded by saying that they finally "got it" because Jesus was "speaking plainly" (16:29). Jesus, in turn, finished this part of the discourse with another warning, this time speaking of how they would be "scattered" and how they would abandon Him (16:32), but that He would never be completely alone because of the continuous presence of His Father. He then concludes his words to the Apostles with one of my favorite verses in the entire Bible, wrapping things up with both a warning of tribulation to come, but to fear not for "I have overcome the world" (16:33).

May 19, OT
2 Samuel 24:1-25; 1 Chronicles 21:1-30; 2 Samuel 15:7-36
The Unauthorized Census; The Rebellion of Absalom

The history of David's sins and their consequences continues here with a series of events that appear at the very end of the books of Samuel (though assumed to occur during the early days of Absalom's rebellion in this chronology). If you ask 10 Biblical scholars to explain why the census taken by David (2 Samuel 24:1-10) was such a great offense to the Lord, you'll likely get 10 different answers, 2 of which will be variations of "I don't know". What matters is that the census (possibly because it was a repeat of an earlier one) was indeed an offense to the Lord, and David recognized it as such. His conscience bothered him so badly that he actually *invited* the consequences on himself. Those consequences came in the form of a choice: David was given three options of possible punishments (24:13-14), choosing the pestilence (24:15) on the assumption that it would be the easiest to deal with since it was from God and not man. But after seeing 70,000 Israelites die as a result, David pleaded with God to lift the plague (24:17). God did so, and David made a series of sacrificial offerings (24:18-25) in exchange.

The next event is a matter of some, albeit minor, controversy because of a number mentioned at the beginning of the passage. In most Bible translations, 2 Samuel 15:7 is rendered as "Now it came about at the end of *four* years…" whereas the King James Version and a few others render the number as *forty*. If the number is truly forty years as counted from Absalom's return to Jerusalem, the events that follow would have occurred after David's death. Even if you back it up and count it from the beginning of David's reign as king, that makes the "Absalom rebellion" occur at the end of David's reign as king rather than in the middle. The much more likely explanation is that the number truly is *four* years, which also makes much more sense in the overall chronology, and that the number forty is a copying error that was perpetuated in some later manuscripts.

From this point forward, however, it becomes increasingly difficult matching up David's sins with the punishments doled out to him and to Israel. The attempted coup by the presumed crown prince of Israel was, without a doubt, a consequence of one or more of David's sins, possibly a continuation of the punishment for polygamy discussed yesterday. But David, after fleeing Jerusalem (15:13-23), rightly suspected that there was more to this rebellion than just his oldest son's desire to impatiently usurp the throne. After sending the Ark of the Covenant back to Jerusalem (15:24-29), David was informed of other conspirators who were behind the rebellion (15:30-31), and responded by sending back a spy named Hushai back to Jerusalem (15:32-36) as well.

May 19, NT
John 17:1-26
The Upper Room Discourse, Part Five: Jesus' Great Priestly Prayer - Friday

Jesus prayed frequently in front of the Apostles and on behalf of them. Jesus even taught them the proper method of prayer (on two occasions according to Luke). This final part of the Upper Room Discourse does not take place in that Upper Room and, unlike the previous parts, doesn't involve Jesus speaking *to* the Apostles; rather, Jesus speaks on behalf of the Apostles in the presence of all of them, in a great priestly prayer of intercession. It would mark the final words spoken in front of all 11 of them prior to the Crucifixion.

In the prayer, Jesus makes seven distinct petitions of the Father: that Jesus would be glorified as the Son would glorify the Father (John 17:1-5), for the safety of believers from "the world" (17:11), for the safety of believers from "the evil one" (17:15), for the sanctification of believers (17:17), for the spiritual unity of believers (17:21-23), that "the world" would believe (17:21), and that believers would be with Him in heaven to see His glory (17:24). Some of these overlap and/or are repeated. Jesus concludes the prayer with praise to the Father who gave Him the Apostles who "have known that You sent Me" (17:25-26).

May 20, OT
Psalm 3:1-8; Psalm 4:1-8; Psalm 11:1-7; Psalm 23:1-6
Taking Refuge in the Lord

The four Psalms that make up the entirety of today's OT reading, including what is arguably David's best-known Psalm, were believed to have been written during this period of waiting while Hushai was sent to Jerusalem. No matter how severe the punishment, no matter how much despair David would have justifiably felt, David always knew who was really in charge, and took comfort and refuge in the Lord. Psalm 3 actually mentions the flight from Absalom in its subtitle. Psalms 4 and 11 show how David continued to encourage his loyal men to likewise take refuge in God. And of course, Psalm 23's 6 verses are among the first Psalms memorized by Bible readers, and for good reason: David uses the metaphor of his own former occupation (shepherd) to make the ultimate statement of trust and comfort in the Lord.

May 20, NT
Matthew 26:36-46; Mark 14:32-42; Luke 22:39-46; John 18:1
The Agony In The Garden

From this point forward, the marker showing the day of the week in which the events of the Passion occurred is dropped, knowing that all of the rest of them until the Crucifixion took place on the day now known as Good Friday.

Thus, all four of the Gospels mention the event immediately following the Upper Room Discourse. The name "Agony in the Garden" comes mainly from one part of the event, described only in Luke (Luke 22:44) in which Jesus' fervent praying, that the "cup be lifted from [Him]," caused his sweat to become "as drops of blood". Though this detail is found only in Luke, Luke's account of this event is shortest except for John's single verse. Mark and Matthew (the longest) go into considerably more detail about the dialog between Jesus and the three disciples He took with Him into the garden: Peter, James, and John (the latter two being listed as the "two sons of Zebedee" in Matthew 26:37). Without mentioning the blood sweat, both Matthew and Mark then go on to tell of Jesus' distress as He entered the garden to pray.

The slight variations in the number of times Jesus prayed and returned to find the three disciples sleeping can be best explained by reading the four different accounts in the order shown here. Matthew's is the most complete and detailed version; Mark's is more like a briefer summary; Luke's even shorter. At the end of two of them (Matthew and Mark), Jesus announces the approaching betrayal and arrest.

Mel Gibson's movie "The Passion of the Christ" begins with this event, but also contains what is believed to be an error. Some believe the darkness that occurred when Jesus was crucified was caused by an eclipse. If God did indeed use this method, astronomically, to cause the darkness, then the night of the Agony would have been a New Moon. In the motion picture, a Full Moon is seen illuminating the garden where Jesus is praying.

May 21, OT
Psalm 26:1-12; 2 Samuel 16:1-14; Psalm 12:1-8; Psalm 36:1-12
The Real Conspiracy is Revealed

The Psalm that starts today's reading was actually more likely written *after* the events of 2 Samuel 16:1-4, but it serves as a terrific introduction to the narrative. In Psalm 26, David prayerfully petitions God for protection from a frightening threat. This is presumably the threat posed by Absalom and his conspirators who are revealed to be some of the members of the family of Saul in the narrative's two encounters. On the assumption that David wrote this Psalm after at least the first of the two encounters, then one can conclude that David was getting desperate to see an end to the rebellion, and was seeking the Lord's protection despite his numerous sins and the consequences that were already delivered. David points out his "integrity" in always following the Lord "without wavering". This is neither arrogance nor is it exaggeration, particularly in light of his encounter with Ziba (2 Samuel 16:1-3) and his previous acts of kindness to the remaining members of the family of Saul.

Though I've read at least one scholarly argument about David's acts of kindness towards the family of Saul (especially as read on May 17) being a case of misguided loyalty, it's not certain if this was ever considered an actual sin by God. However, David certainly ended up having his kindness answered with betrayal! The first encounter, with Ziba, was a meeting with the servant of Mephibosheth, the grandson of Saul helped by David in the May 17 reading. Ziba was sent to David's men with numerous gifts while Saul's grandson was on his way to Jerusalem *to join the rebellion*. David granted Ziba the remainder of Saul's inheritance that he had previously granted to Mephibosheth (16:4).

Thus was the conspiracy to install Absalom as king revealed, reinforced all the more with the second encounter. David and his men were cursed and stoned by Shimei, another relative of Saul (16:5-8). David was accused of being responsible for the death of Saul, thus making *David* (the "man of bloodshed") the usurper. When given the opportunity to retaliate for Shimei's attack, David declined and went on his way with his men (16:9-14). The reason for David's decision here is not explained in the narrative, but might be in the two Psalms (#12, #36) at the end of the reading. In the two Psalms, David contrasts the true word of the Lord with the slanderous words of men (like Shimei, though he is not named), knowing that he will be vindicated just as he requested in Psalm 26 because of whose Word David is following.

May 21, NT
John 18:2-3; Luke 22:47-48; John 18:4-9; Matthew 26:47-50; Mark 14:43-45
The Arrest of Jesus, Part One

Jesus' betrayal by Judas and arrest at the hands of the crowd Judas brought with him is told in all four Gospels. However, the accounts differ enough to where Bible scoffers like to use this as yet another example of *alleged* Biblical contradictions, and thus discredit the Bible. But also yet again, a careful reading in chronological order solves the problem, as indicated by the unusual amount of jumping around found in the series of brief readings above. In fact, to do an even better job of reconciling the four different accounts, there would have to be even more jumping from one Gospel to another than shown. The list above forms the best overall compromise for the first part of this event.

After first noting Judas' approach (in all four), Jesus first questions Judas (Luke 22:48) about what he is about to do, and then asks the crowd brought with Judas "Whom do you seek?" (John 18:4-9). When they answer, and Jesus responds, Judas approaches and kisses him (Matthew 26:49, Mark 14:45), to which Jesus then tells Judas (only in Matthew) to "do what you [Judas] have come for," which they then do (Matthew 26:50). Reading in at least roughly this order gives both a clear and reconciled picture of the arrest of Jesus.

May 22, OT
Psalm 37:1-40; Psalm 9:1-20; Psalm 10:1-18; 2 Samuel 15:37; 2 Samuel 16:15; Psalm 27:1-14
David's Confidence

Where does David's confidence come from? King David was facing some incredible odds against being able to reclaim his kingdom. He knew his sins were numerous and was likely even second-guessing his kind acts towards the family of Saul, now that it was revealed that part of the rebellion led by his son Absalom was actually an uprising by the former royal family. But through it all, David remained confident that the kingdom would be restored to him. How did he know this? The three Psalms that start today's OT reading answer that question. David's confidence was with the *Lord*, not himself or his army. David acknowledged the promise (covenant) God made with him (particularly in Psalm 9:7-8) and knew that God would never break this promise, despite his own sin.

An interesting note of trivia regarding two of these Psalms: Psalms 9 and 10 are a single Psalm in old Catholic Bibles, causing the entire remainder of the Psalter to be numbered differently. This isn't necessarily an error, but merely a dispute about the separation of the Psalms in the Septuagint (the Greek translation of the Old Testament, also known as the LXX), which was used as the basis for several early translations including the Latin Vulgate (and future translations based on it). The Masoretic text, the "original Hebrew," makes the separation whereas the Septuagint did not. Nearly all modern Bibles follow the Masoretic numbering, including modern Catholic Bibles.

Today's OT reading includes only two verses of narrative, marking the point in time where Absalom, Hushai (David's spy), and the principal conspirators arrived in Jerusalem, presumably discovering that David had already fled. But during this time of exile, David continued to place value on faith in God as the basis for his confidence, reflected in yet another Psalm (27).

May 22, NT
Luke 22:49-54; Matthew 26:51-56; Mark 14:46-52; John 18:10-12
The Arrest of Jesus, Part Two

The actual seizing of Jesus at the end of Part One is echoed here in the second part (Mark 14:46), as we read the account of the immediate aftermath of Judas' betrayal of Jesus. Like yesterday, it is important that the passages be read in the order presented so that it makes the most chronological sense, and best harmonizes the four seemingly different accounts, though it would be even better if there was even more jumping around.

Luke's account begins with someone (presumably one of the three disciples who were with him, but this is not known for sure) asking whom he should strike with a sword, but then proceeds to cut an ear off of the high priest's slave without waiting for an answer from Jesus (Luke 22:49-50). Luke goes on to describe the healing miracle that follows (22:51) and then both Luke and Matthew present the words Jesus says to the crowd, getting them to stop the violence (including an oft-quoted line in Matthew about those who "live by the sword," Matthew 26:52) and chastising them for coming for Him with weapons, since He had never been violent to *them*. Mark's version reads very much like a very brief version of Matthew's but includes a detail (the man who escaped naked) not found in the others. John includes only a brief comment made by Jesus to Peter after a one-verse version of the striking of the high priest's slave's ear.

And so, Jesus was led away, while Peter followed at a distance (Luke 22:54) and the rest of the disciples fled (Matthew 26:56).

May 23, OT
Psalm 28:1-9; Psalm 39:1-13; Psalm 41:1-13; Psalm 42:1-11; Psalm 43:1-5; 2 Samuel 16:16-17:23
Hushai Thwarts the Counsel of Ahithophel

During this period of exile during Absalom's rebellion, David's Psalm-writing was at its most prolific. Although only the first three of the five Psalms in today's OT reading can be positively attributed to David (and in fact, Psalm 42 is known to have been written by someone else), they all reflect this common theme of trust in the Lord in the face of traitorous enemies. In particular, Psalm 41 speaks of a "close friend in whom I trusted" who has "lifted up his heel against me." (Psalm 41:9) In the context of the rest of the Psalm and the narrative in 2 Samuel, this is an obvious reference to Ahithophel, last mentioned in 2 Samuel 15 (on May 19), as being one of Absalom's co-conspirators, and the principal reason David sent Hushai to Jerusalem as a spy.

In the narrative, Hushai first gains Absalom's confidence (2 Samuel 16:16-19), making it sound as though he had left the camp of David. Absalom asked for Ahithophel's advice, and was told to have sexual relations with David's concubines in order to make it look as though Absalom was completely "odious" to his father David (16:20-23). Ahithophel further advised Absalom to give him 12,000 men to carry out an attack on David (17:1-4). But having gained Absalom's trust, Hushai was also consulted, and he gave Absalom contradictory advice (17:5-14), which Absalom took instead of Ahithophel's. This, in turn, allowed Hushai to send a message to David warning the king of the attack (17:15-22). David heeded this warning and escaped. Ahithophel, meanwhile, realized that his advice had not been followed, resulting in David's escape, and he committed suicide after "setting his house in order" (17:23), thus bringing one of the conspirators to an unfortunate end.

May 23, NT
Luke 22:55-57; Matthew 26:57-58; Matthew 26:69-70; Mark 14:53-54; Mark 14:66-68; John 18:13-24
Jesus Before Caiaphas, The First of Peter's Three Denials

Matthew and Mark both have the account of Peter's first denial split several verses apart from the first part of Jesus' testimony before an unnamed "high priest," though this is assumed to be the same Caiaphas who *is* named in John's version of the event. In the end, all four Gospels have all three of Peter's denials before the rooster crows (after the third denial, read tomorrow), but in slightly different levels of detail and in a different sequence, except for the first, which is almost identical in all four Gospels. For continuity, John's version of the testimony before one of the other high priests is shown in its entirety here while the remainder is read in Matthew and Mark at a later date.

May 24, OT
Psalm 55:1-23; Psalm 58:1-11; Psalm 61:1-8; Psalm 62:1-12
Four More Psalms of Trust

All four of these Psalms were written by David, and are all believed to have been written shortly after David's successful escape from the planned attack on him, following the thwarting of Absalom's plans by Hushai. The first two make references to the fear that David must have still felt, despite the successful escape, and make references to "false friends" as do a few other previous Psalms. Psalm 58, in particular, features some of David's most violent imagery as he prays for vengeance against the enemies that forced him into exile.

May 24, NT
Luke 22:58-62; Matthew 26:71-75; Mark 14:69-72; John 18:25-27
Peter's Second and Third Denials

As predicted by Jesus, and as told in all four Gospels, Peter denied knowing Jesus two more times before the rooster crowed. Luke and Matthew's version of this join the earlier prediction in John's Gospel, in dropping the "twice" from the number of times the rooster crowed. Mark is the only Gospel writer to match the "rooster crowing twice" (Mark 14:72) prediction, made in the three synoptic Gospels, with the actual event.

May 25, OT
2 Samuel 17:24-26; 1 Chronicles 2:17; 2 Samuel 17:27-18:18
Absalom's Rebellion Comes to an End

Considering what Absalom's rebellion meant to the people of Israel at the time, the conclusion of that rebellion seems really quite anticlimactic. When we last read any real narrative (two days ago), Absalom's first attempt at completing his takeover was thwarted by one of David's spies. Today, we first read of Absalom's response: he decides to pursue David, his father, himself. After a single brief verse describing the family of Absalom (the significance of which won't become apparent for a few days), the narrative resumes with David and his people preparing for battle. Most significantly, it contains a verse spoken by David in which he tells his people to "deal gently, for my sake, with the young man Absalom" (2 Samuel 17:5). In other words, though David clearly wanted his kingdom back, he wanted to *defeat* his son in this battle without *destroying* him. His people, including Joab, the General of his army, agreed.

After the battle began, what happened next put an end to it without David ever meeting Absalom on the battlefield. Absalom gets caught in a tree by his neck (17:9) and would have died anyway if he had not been discovered. Rather than "dealing gently," though, he was discovered by someone who then told Joab, who then ignored what David had said and pierced the heart of Absalom with 3 spears (17:14), with several of his men joining in to finish the job (17:15) of killing the prince. As today's reading ends, David had not yet been informed of this.

May 25, NT
Luke 22:66-71; Mark 14:55-65; Matthew 26:59-68; Luke 22:63-65; John 18:28
Jesus Before Caiaphas and the Sanhedrin

While Peter was outside denying his knowledge of Jesus, Jesus' trial continued before the chief priests and elders. Noting the unusual order of verses read and the splitting of the portion from Luke, the climax of the trial comes after the numerous conflicting testimonies and, finally, Jesus' only words spoken at trial at all. Although the first part of it is quoted differently in all 3 synoptic Gospels (and doesn't appear in John at all), the second part, where He alludes to the Son of Man seated at the right hand of the power of God, itself partially a quote of Psalm 110:1, is identical in Luke, Mark, and Matthew. He is then beaten and mocked and sent off to Pilate for the next part of the trial.

May 26, OT
Psalm 64:1-10; Psalm 70:1-5; Psalm 141:1-10; Psalm 143:1-12; 2 Samuel 18:19-33; Psalm 84:1-12
David Learns of His Son's Death

Before David became aware that the rebellion led by his son was over, he prayed for guidance in the conflict. Four prayerful Psalms that begin today's OT reading reveal David's state of mind during this time. Then, after Absalom has been killed, Joab and his men attempt to get news to David in such a way as to "soften the blow," but only end up making David's state of mind even worse, as the narrative ends with David's cries of grief over the death of his son (2 Samuel 18:33). But while David is mourning the death of the crown prince, his people (including the writer of Psalm 84) are celebrating the end of the rebellion.

May 26, NT
Matthew 27:1-14; John 18:29-38a; Luke 23:1-7
Judas' Remorse, Jesus' First Appearance Before Pilate

Today we read the first of actually two accounts of the death of Judas Iscariot, who committed suicide out of remorse for what he had done in betraying Jesus. The other account was written by Luke, but appears as a sidebar of sorts in the Acts of the Apostles when they were deciding on a replacement for Judas. Following this is Jesus' first of two appearances before Pontius Pilate, the Governor of the region.

Jesus' appearances (note the plural) before Pilate, found in each of the four Gospels, would seem as if they are quite contradictory unless you do two things: the first is to realize He appears before Pilate *twice*, not once, even though only one of the four Gospel writers (Luke) actually mentions the interruption between the two appearances. The second is to note that John merges the two appearances and make them sound as if they were one (though a particularly careful reading of John's version, today and two days from now, might make you think otherwise). John's account of the appearances are by far the most detailed though he doesn't directly mention sending Jesus off to Herod, as Luke does. When read in the order presented in this reading plan, it seems to make the most sense, overall.

Though it must certainly be a matter of opinion, the most arguably chilling line in this passage is when Pilate asks Jesus "What is truth?" in John 18:38a, a clear sign of someone who does not believe in any absolute authority (God) or morality.

May 27, OT
2 Samuel 19:1-43
The Kingdom is Restored to David

Today is the first day in over a month in which the OT reading comes entirely from a single book (except for Psalms). The first part of the reading could easily have the title "Get a Grip". David's mourning over the death of his son, Absalom, was so excessive that it caused him to lose sight of what was really important: the kingdom entrusted to him and now restored to him. No one would begrudge David the need to grieve; but his grieving took what should have been a day of great celebration and instead turned everyone's mood foul (2 Samuel 19:1-3). It took the very person who violated the king's trust, Joab, to turn things around by rebuking David (19:4-7), rightfully pointing out David's loss of perspective in the whole matter. David didn't respond to Joab the way he responded to Nathan's rebuke (similar but for a completely different reason), but he did take Joab's suggestion at the end, and "snapped out of it" in order to appear before the people and acknowledge the restoration of the kingdom.

David showed great wisdom in working his way back into his role as king, knowing that the rebellion and his victory over it created a dispute in the minds of the people. The rebellion was very deep and very widespread, and it took a nuanced approach, including even negotiations with various tribes and public pardons to people like Shimei (19:18) and Mephibosheth (19:24-30), who had earlier done great wrongs to David, including being the principal co-conspirator with Absalom. David also made a public show of thanks to Barzilli (19:31-39) for his help when he fled from Absalom.

But despite David's careful and correct words, the division caused by the rebellion and some northern tribes' perception that David was leaving them out of the celebration became the first hint that the now-united kingdom of Israel wouldn't stay that way forever (19:40-43). In fact, a civil war was about to break out, as we will read tomorrow.

May 27, NT
Mark 15:1-5; Luke 23:8-12
Jesus Appears Before Pilate and Herod

As mentioned yesterday, Jesus actually makes two appearances before Pilate, though only Luke actually mentions what happened between the two appearances. In today's reading, we begin with Mark's account of the first of those two appearances, by far the least detailed of the four accounts. Then, we read Luke's account of what Pilate did at the conclusion of the first appearance: he sent Jesus off to Herod, realizing that Jesus, a Galilean, belonged in Herod's jurisdiction. Of course, this was another of the several things Pilate said or did that indicated his willingness to "pass the buck" when it came to this matter. Herod, after obtaining no testimony from Jesus either, sent Him back to Pilate, now wearing a regal robe. Pilate and Herod, previously enemies, became good friends because of this incident.

May 28, OT
2 Samuel 20:1-26; Psalm 140:1-13
Sheba's Rebellion

David's reinstallation as king of Israel was marred by yet another rebellion. Like the very beginning of his kingship, David became king of only one tribe (Judah) initially (2 Samuel 20:2), but this time because of a man named Sheba. Unlike the revolt under Absalom, this one did not involve his family directly, so David became more decisive about what to do about it. He ordered Amasa, a former general in his son Absalom's army, to gather the men of Judah against Sheba, the leader of the new revolt (20:4-5). Amasa wasn't a competent general, however, and David instead sent Abishai, leader of his royal guard, to do the job, which included summoning Joab, the commander, to pursue Sheba (20:6-7). Along the way, Joab met up with Amasa and executed him for his incompetence (20:8-13).

Joab and his men then caught up with Sheba, putting the city in which he was hiding under siege (20:14-15). A woman in the city convinced Joab to stop the wanton destruction they were causing by promising the head of Sheba. The woman delivered on this promise (20:16-22) and the brief rebellion was over.

David, meanwhile, wrote the Psalm numbered as 140, a prayer of deliverance (again) in the face of the endless wars and revolts David was forced to face.

May 28, NT
Luke 23:13-25; Matthew 27:15-26; Mark 15:6-15; John 18:38b-40
Barabbas Released Instead of Jesus

Pilate's decision to release a robber named Barabbas instead of Jesus is told in all four Gospels, but slightly differently in each. However, the differing accounts can be reconciled when read in the order specified here, though an even greater mixing of verses from each, jumping back and forth, would help more. In Luke's version, Pilate makes his decision to release Jesus (after "punishing Him" first) as part of the tradition at the time of the festival (Luke 23:15-16) without first consulting the crowd, but then gives in to the crowd's desire to have Barabbas released instead and Jesus crucified. Matthew's account begins with Pilate asking the crowd whom to release, and receiving a note from his wife about a dream she had, in which she was warned to spare Jesus (Matthew 27:15-19). After this, Pilate repeats the question, to which the crowd responds as they did in Luke's version, and Pilate caves to their request.

Mark and Matthew's version are identical except for Mark not mentioning the note from Pilate's wife. In the portion read from John today, Pilate queries the crowd and gets his answer but does not actually make the final decision. That part, for reasons explained then, is in tomorrow's NT reading.

May 29, OT
1 Chronicles 22:1-19; Psalm 29:1-11; Psalm 30:1-12
David Prepares Solomon for the Building of the Temple

With the last of the wars and rebellions now, apparently, behind him, David found the ability to get back to the business of being king. Part of the reason this chronology assumes that Absalom's rebellion and the events that followed it were at the approximate mid-point of David's reign as king (as opposed to near the end; see reading for May 19) is the mention of "young Solomon" (1 Chronicles 22:5) in today's OT reading. The preparations, recorded only here in 1 Chronicles, include David's material order for a temple that he was told he could not build ("The Davidic Covenant," May 16) and his encouraging words to his son Solomon (22:6-19) that explain, at last, the reason why David was forbidden to build it.

When Nathan first told David that he would not be the one to build the temple, we weren't told then exactly why this was so, except for a couple of hints. The full explanation is found here in 1 Chronicles rather than 2 Samuel, and spells out the different roles the two iconic kings of Israel each had.

The two Psalms, both written by David, express praise and thanks for deliverance from enemies, and an optimistic look ahead to the days of the temple.

May 29, NT
Matthew 27:27-30; Mark 15:16-20; John 19:1-17
The Mocking, the Beating, and the Crowning with Thorns

Three of the four Gospels (all except Luke) give an account of the beating and mocking and crown of thorns that Jesus endured before His crucifixion. Luke mentions the purple, regal robe placed on Jesus, but this is mentioned as part of the return from Herod before facing Pilate the second time. The order of events is also slightly different in the three Gospel accounts in today's reading, as Matthew and Mark both have these events occurring only after Pilate pronounces his final judgment. But as mentioned two days ago, John's account of the entire encounter with Pilate is the most detailed, by far. John does not mention the interruption in sending Jesus off to Herod as Luke does, but John does include a great deal of dialog between Pilate and Jesus not mentioned anywhere else, including most of what is said in today's reading. In John, Jesus is sent to be punished as in Matthew and Mark, but is then brought before the crowds to make one final appeal for Him to be spared instead of Barabbas (John 19:4-7). The final appeal still does not work, and he even makes an attempt at appealing to Jesus Himself, but is told that this is the way things are supposed to work and that those that handed Him over are guilty of the greater sin (19:11). After this, Pilate gives in to the crowd's demands, just as he did in all three other Gospels, and Jesus is sent off to be crucified.

Mel Gibson's movie "The Passion of the Christ" does, in my opinion, a masterful job of blending two of these four accounts (Matthew's and John's) of Jesus' meetings with Pilate and the beating and crowning with thorns. It's also, of course, the thing that makes this movie version of the Passion so controversial, as much time is spent on the scourging, in particular.

May 30, OT
1 Chronicles 23:1-23
More Preparations for the Temple

David did a great deal to help prepare his son Solomon for the kingdom and for the temple that was going to be built under his rule. One of those things David did was actually "make his son Solomon king over all Israel" (1 Chronicles 23:1). This doesn't mean that David abdicated the throne; rather, it is a declaration of his son's kingship that would become his son's as soon as David died. After all the rebellions and wars, it's no wonder David wanted to make sure that the transition to his son's power was a smooth one.

The remainder of the reading is the first of a multi-part declaration by King David defining the revised duties of various groups and tribes (the Levites today), also having to do with the temple yet to be built.

May 30, NT
Luke 23:26-32; John 19:17; Matthew 27:31-34; Mark 15:20-23,25
The Crucifixion of Jesus Christ, Part One: The Road to Golgotha

One of the few parts of the life of the Lord agreed upon by all 4 Gospel writers is Jesus' death on a Cross. The only differences lie in levels of detail, mostly concerning the last few things actually spoken by Jesus. Between the final condemnation by Pilate and the actual crucifixion, a number of events took place that are found in more than one (and in some cases all 4) of the Gospel readings today. Among them is the carrying of the Cross, at least part of the way, by Jesus. The 3 synoptic Gospels each mention the pressing into service of a man named Simon of Cyrene to help carry the cross part of the way. Today's reading stops just short of the actual Crucifixion, focusing on the events on the way to Golgotha.

Catholics reading today's events will recognize these events as belonging to a portion of the Traditional Form of the Stations of the Cross (or "Way of the Cross"). The Traditional Form contains a number of events not supported in Scripture, though none actually contradict the Biblical account. Nevertheless, the 14-station devotion, observed by Catholics and some Anglicans and Lutherans, contains all of the events found in the Biblical account, the first 9 of the 14 in today's NT reading. If you are an observer of the newer "Scriptural Way of the Cross," in which all 14 events are backed by Scripture, then the first 6 events were depicted in previous days' readings, events 7-9 come today, and the remaining events continue tomorrow.

May 31, OT
1 Chronicles 6:16-30; 1 Chronicles 23:24-24:31
More Preparations for the Temple

More of the family trees of the Levites are presented here to complete that portion of David's preparations for the kingship of his son Solomon and the temple that would be built. David was getting old; he knew he was not far from death. These preparations were as necessary as they were timely, as David knew that once the temple was built, well after his death, the Levites would "no longer need to carry the tabernacle" (1 Chronicles 23:26).

May 31, NT
Luke 23:33,38,34-37,39-43; John 19:18-27; Matthew 27:38,37,35-36,39-44;
Mark 15:27-28,26,24,29-32;
The Crucifixion of Jesus Christ, Part Two: Jesus is Crucified With Two Criminals

The large and unusual amount of jumping around from verse to verse within each of the 4 Gospels is necessary to point out the fact that although the verses are in a slightly different sequence, the events found in today's NT reading are found in all 4 Gospels, with only a slight difference in level of detail to reconcile them. Once you read through 2 of them, you'll even see the possibility of blending them in such a way as to have even more jumping around; yet all are in perfect harmony.

A long-running tradition says that Jesus said seven distinct things after he was nailed to the Cross. Those seven sayings are given the title

"The Seven Last Words of Christ," and are depicted in several works of Classical music and in devotions used during the season of Lent in many churches. The first three of those seven are found in today's reading; the first two are in Luke: "Father, forgive them, for they know not what they do" (Luke 23:34) and "Truly I say to you, today you will be with me in paradise" (Luke 23:43). The third is actually two things: the first to His mother, Mary, the other to "the disciple Jesus loved," "Woman, behold your son," and "behold your mother" (John 19:26-27). Each of the seven "last words" is Scriptural, and the remaining words are found in tomorrow's NT reading.

June 1, OT
1 Chronicles 25:1-31
The Temple Musicians

David's continued preparations for the Temple yet to be built includes a detailed list of the musicians and singers who would serve there under King Solomon. Among them is a name that should be recognized by those of you who have read the Old Testament according to this plan daily: Asaph. Specifically, the sons of Asaph, writer of several Psalms, are numbered among the musicians.

June 1, NT
Matthew 27:45-47; Mark 15:33-35; John 19:28-30; Matthew 27:48-50; Mark 15:36-37; Luke 23:44-46
The Crucifixion of Jesus Christ, Part Three: Jesus Dies

In the traditional order of the Seven Last Words of Christ, there is only one quoted in the original Aramaic, and it appears in Matthew and Mark. The words translated as "My God, My God, why have you forsaken ["abandoned" in some translations] me" is also a quote from Psalm 22, written by David, about 1000 years earlier (Matthew 27:46, Mark 15:34), and makes up the 4th of the Seven Last Words. Some observers thought Jesus was calling for Elijah here (Matthew 27:47, Mark 15:35), at which point Jesus speaks again, saying "I thirst" (John 19:28), the 5th of the Seven Last Words of Christ. In 3 of the Gospels (John, Matthew, Mark), someone did indeed get something for Jesus to drink. There is some debate as to whether the last thing Jesus said on the Cross was "It is finished" (John 19:30) or "Father into Your hands I commit my spirit" (Luke 23:46), but tradition holds that these last two things were spoken in this order. The Seven Last Words are sometimes called words of 1. Forgiveness, 2. Salvation, 3. Relationship, 4. Abandonment, 5. Distress, 6. Triumph, and 7. Reunion.

Then, He died, fulfilling the Law and the Prophets, and finishing, for all time, the work of salvation.

June 2, OT
1 Chronicles 6:31-53; 1 Chronicles 26:1-32
The Musicians and the Gatekeepers

For the 5th straight day (with one day remaining), the OT reading consists entirely of David's preparations for the Temple to be built by his son Solomon when he assumes the throne, all from the first book of Chronicles. This time, a portion of yesterday's list of musicians is repeated – from an earlier section of the same book. After this, another list: the gatekeepers of the Temple.

Tomorrow's reading concludes the list of people and tribes/families listed by David with their roles in the Temple. Many find these readings to be at least as difficult as the genealogies found in Genesis and here in Chronicles, but they carry with them an important truth about Scriptures: few of these historical details has been proven by archeology, but more importantly, ***none*** *have been disproven or debunked*, either. That means that if you start from the point of view that the Bible, including 1 Chronicles, is the inspired Word of God, then what you have in these past 5 days' readings is an incredibly detailed piece of history, worth every word and every name.

June 2, NT
Matthew 27:51, 54-56; Mark 15:38-41; Luke 23:45,47-49; John 19:31-37
After Jesus' Death, Before Jesus' Burial

The immediate aftermath of Jesus' death on the Cross is told in the 3 synoptic Gospels in nearly the exact same way and in the same sequence (if you read the verses in the order above): the tearing of the veil in the Temple, the observation by the Centurion that this was "the Son of God" (in Matthew and Mark) or was "innocent" (in Luke), and then noting the presence of Mary Magdalene, Mary the mother of Jesus, and other women. John doesn't mention these three things, but does mention two others: the breaking of the legs of the two criminals crucified with Jesus along with the discovery that Jesus was already dead (John 19:31-33) and the piercing of Jesus' side from which came blood and water (19:34).

June 3, OT
1 Chronicles 27:1-29:22
The Officials of the Temple, Anointing of Solomon as the Next King

In 1 Chronicles 27, David concludes his enumeration, by tribe, of the officials of the Temple that would take over when his son Solomon becomes king. Then, starting in chapter 28, he gives a great speech that both answers a number of questions as well as passes the torch, for all intents and purposes, to his son Solomon prior to his death.

In "The Davidic Covenant," read on May 16, the prophet Nathan tells David that he will not be the one to build the Temple; rather, it would be one of his sons. However, it wasn't specified at that time who that son would be. Readers of this history in its proper chronological sequence might first assume that this honor was meant for whoever was the crown prince: Amnon first, then Absalom after Amnon's death, etc. But if you went into this reading plan with even a tiny amount of pre-knowledge of Biblical history, you know that neither of these men actually becomes king. In the speech given by David here, we get the first official word that the next king of Israel would be his son Solomon, and we are finally told why: we are told that Solomon was chosen, *by name*, to be the one to build the Temple, that David had been referring to for the past 6 days' OT readings.

And so, after all the preparations made by David, he passes this all to Solomon publically (1 Chronicles 28:9-19) and gives words of encouragement (28:20-21). David's speech continues into chapter 29 and the people respond with joy and gifts. David prays publically and leads the crowd in worship (29:10-22), which finished with the formal anointing of 12-year-old (according to tradition) Solomon as king. No mention was made here about the fate of the several sons of David who were older than Solomon (but see tomorrow's reading for more about this).

June 3, NT
John 19:38-42; Mark 15:42-47; Luke 23:50-56; Matthew 27:57-66
Jesus is Buried

Unlike yesterday's reading, the event told in today's NT reading is very close to identical in all 4 Gospels (including John), differing only in slight level of detail. Matthew adds one detail the others leave out, regarding the call to have the tomb sealed out of fear that the body would be stolen to make it look as though He had risen.

June 4, OT
1 Kings 1:1-27
Another Attempt to Take the Throne of David

Today introduces the first "new" book in quite a while in the Old Testament. The first and second books of the Kings were once originally one book (scroll), though we don't know who the human writer was for this any more than we did for the first and second books of Samuel, first introduced back on April 13. Like the books of Samuel, there is some evidence to suggest that it was the work of more than one writer. Older Catholic editions of the Bible have the two books of Samuel and the two books of Kings named as a set of *four* books of Kings, thus making this the *third* book. Newer Catholic editions use the more commonly accepted naming convention.

The beginning of this book overlaps the end of the books of Samuel, but only slightly. First and Second Kings provides a framework, along with Second Chronicles, for most of the remainder of the Old Testament history. It begins with the last days of King David and ends with the fall of Jerusalem and the end of the kingdom of Judah after Israel was divided. Where Chronicles focuses only on the unified kingdom and the kingdom of Judah after the division, the books of the Kings contain the history of both the Northern kingdom of Israel and the Southern kingdom of Judah.

In today's reading, we get both a leap forward and a flash back. We don't know exactly when the preparations made by David for the temple to be built (read during the past 6 days) by his son Solomon were made, except that it was sometime between the end of Sheba's rebellion and the first mention of David's advanced age (1 Kings 1:1). This reading is the first and only mention since the May 18 reading of one of David's sons that, at this point, would have been in line for the throne ahead of Solomon (in bold face below). Here's a chronological list of David's sons, with their *known* fates:

1. Amnon – murdered by Absalom's men

2. Chileab (aka Daniel) – possibly not one of David's biological children, though this is not proven
3. Absalom – killed at the end of the rebellion that he started
4. **Adonijah** – David's oldest son as of today's OT reading
5. Stephatiah - ???
6. Ithream - ???
7. Shammua - ???
8. Shobab - ???
9. Nathan – not to be confused with the prophet of the same name - ???
10. Solomon
11. At least 9 others

What happened to those with question marks after their names? We don't, *and never do*, get an answer regarding them. They are never mentioned again after the May 18 readings except for Nathan, who isn't mentioned until Luke notes him as an ancestor of Mary, the mother of Jesus. We don't even know if any of them are alive at this point. One can assume, though there is no proof, that the massacre that resulted in Amnon's death also resulted in the deaths of David's other sons born in Hebron, thus answering the question of what happened to Stephatiah and Ithream, but we are never told this. Were those other sons killed in one of the wars? We are not told. After the deaths of Amnon and Absalom, and knowing that Adonijah was still alive, why, then, did David make all the preparations on behalf of Solomon? Yesterday gave us part of the answer to that question; today gives us the rest.

Adonijah was the oldest surviving son from among those born to David in Hebron (i.e. before he married Bathsheba in Jerusalem), and so he did have some basis for assuming that he was the heir apparent. But Solomon became the *real* crown prince, thus making any attempt by Adonijah (as told in today's reading) to become king another *usurping*, no different than what Absalom did years earlier.

The difference was that Adonijah's attempt to assume the throne wasn't accompanied by a widespread rebellion, and David was notified of this attempt in its earliest stages (1 Kings 1:24-27).

June 4, NT
Matthew 28:2-4,1,5-8; Mark 16:1-8; Luke 24:1-12; John 20:1-10
The Resurrection of Jesus Christ

Though Jesus would say the words "It is finished" while on the Cross, thus saving the world from spiritual death, it was His rising from the dead on the third day (day one was Friday, day two was the Sabbath or Saturday, and the third day was the "beginning of the week," or Sunday) that completed His conquest of *physical* death. There are no recorded accounts of the Resurrection itself, only its aftermath as various people discovered that He was no longer in the tomb. But if you read these four passages in the verse order (note the jumping around in Matthew) shown here, you get a completely reconcilable account of Jesus' rising from the dead.

June 5, OT
1 Kings 1:28-40; Psalm 25:1-22; 1 Kings 1:41-2:9
David's Last Days, Part One

In most kingdoms, the new king is not crowned until after the previous king's death. Not so with David and the kingdom of Israel. The numerous wars, rebellions, and attempted usurpations of the throne that David had to endure no doubt left him both weary and wary. Thus, he made it a point to have his son Solomon formally installed as king (1 Kings 1:28-40) *before* he died to ensure a smooth transition of power. This is also reflected in what is believed to be David's last Psalm, numbered as #25, a prayer for guidance and providence with the nation of Israel, and not himself, at the fore.

The coronation also serves the purpose of ending the final attempt at usurping the throne by Adonijah (1:41-50), and it is thus that we read the first of the many recorded words of Solomon (1:51-52) as the new king forgives his older brother for the attempt on the throne.

The reading concludes with David's specific instructions to Solomon regarding how to deal with several different people (2:1-9).

June 5, NT
John 20:11-18; Mark 16:9-11; Matthew 28:9-15
Jesus Appears to Mary Magdalene and Others

The sequence of the post-resurrection appearances of Jesus is a matter of some considerable controversy. Bible scoffers have used the *apparent* inconsistencies to "prove" that the Resurrection never happened, or to debunk the entire Bible. But just as with several other events near the end of Jesus' earthly ministry, a careful reading of passages in their correct chronological sequence leads to the only possible conclusion: the Gospels DO contain a harmonizable account of the life of Jesus on earth. Though we don't get any description of the miracle itself, much is said about its aftermath, particularly as people begin discovering Jesus' absence from the tomb.

June 6, OT
2 Samuel 23:1-7; 1 Kings 2:10-11; 1 Chronicles 29:26-30; 1 Kings 2:12; 1 Chronicles 29:23-25
David's Last Days, Part Two

We return to 2 Samuel for the final time in today's OT reading to read the last words of David. Then, he dies (1 Kings 2:10-11) after a total of 40 years on the throne, at the age of 70. We know this from the fact that he was crowned at the age of 30 (2 Samuel 5:4). Today is also the last time we read from the First book of Chronicles, as we get another summary of the life and reign of king David and the accession of Solomon to the throne as king.

June 6, NT
Mark 16:12-13; Luke 24:13-32
Jesus Appears to Two Disciples on the Road to Emmaus

Many believe that the well-known account of Jesus' first appearance to any of the 11 disciples, known as the "Road to Emmaus" for the location of the encounter, is told only in one Gospel: Luke. However, a careful reading of Mark, in a section that doesn't appear in the earliest manuscripts, reveals that the same two disciples, only one of whom is named, are the ones to whom Jesus appeared on the road to the village about 7 miles from Jerusalem. Mark simply omits nearly all the details of the encounter itself while Luke goes into his usual high detail.

At first, of course, the two disciples don't know that it is Jesus walking with them; thus they explain to the man whom they don't yet know all about the events of the past few days including the fact that several women had visited the now-empty tomb (Luke 24:13-24). Jesus, still not revealing Himself to them, explained how all these things were actually the fulfillments of prophecy (24:25-27). When they were going to part ways, the disciples urged him to stay for supper, which He did, revealing His identity in the breaking of the bread (24:28-31).

Mark's brief version of this encounter ends with the two returning to tell the others. Luke's version of the same is told tomorrow, along with His first appearance before the whole group of 11.

June 7, OT
1 Kings 2:13-3:15; 2 Chronicles 1:1-13; 1 Kings 3:16-28; Psalm 72:1-20
Wise Solomon Begins His Reign as King

Solomon's first days as king of Israel were marked with several instances, some public, some private, in which he displayed an uncommon level of both Godly wisdom and human ruthlessness. Today's OT reading, the first devoted to the kingship of Solomon, describes these instances in some considerable detail.

The first was the first attempt to usurp Solomon's throne, by the same person (Adonijah) who made the last attempt while their father David was king, to take the throne he thought was rightfully his. Adonijah's request to marry one of his father David's companions with his stepmother's (Bathsheba's) permission, was a last attempt at taking that throne (1 Kings 2:13-18), but Solomon wisely saw right through the charade. Solomon's response was to not only to not grant the union, but to have Adonijah executed for his treasonous attempt (2:19-25). He then banished, rather than executed, a priest named Abiathar back to his home per instructions given him by his father (2:26-27), had his father's former army general Joab executed (2:28-35) according to a warning given him by David (2:5, cf 2 Samuel 3:17-30 and 20:4-11), and sentenced Shimei to the equivalent of a house arrest for crimes against his father David, but Shimei violated the terms of the sentence and was then executed (1 Kings 2:36-46). With his kingdom now established, Solomon married an Egyptian princess, the first of what would eventually become 700 wives taken by the king (3:1-2).

But these public displays of wise choices and decisive actions were far less important than a hugely important encounter with God in a dream that affirmed young Solomon's role as a wise king. In 1 Kings 3:3-15 and our first reading from the Second book of Chronicles (a continuation of 1 Chronicles, as they were once one scroll, human author unknown but thought to possibly be Ezra), God asks Solomon for his greatest desire. Solomon's humble (and grateful) reply was to be able to govern His people with an "understanding heart" (3:9). In other words, Solomon asked for wisdom.

Pleased by this request, God granted him not only the wisdom he desired, but also that for which he didn't ask: riches and honor (3:13-14). Solomon responded when he woke by making burnt offerings (3:15).

Solomon's first public display of this newly imparted wisdom (3:16-28) is the well-known story of his judgment in a dispute between two mothers, one of an infant who had died, the other of a living one. This is, most likely, what prompted Solomon to write his first Psalm, numbered here as #72.

June 7, NT
Luke 24:33-43; John 20:19-29; Mark 16:14
Jesus Appears to The Eleven

Chronologically, Jesus' next appearance was to his closest followers, whom we call the Apostles. After the encounter with two of them on the road to Emmaus (read yesterday), those two returned to the place where all but one of the others were gathered. There, Luke, John, and Mark each record Jesus' subsequent appearance in their midst, with varying degrees of detail.

Most noticeably, John is the only one of the Gospel writers to record the fact that Jesus' first appearance before the gathered group of Apostles was without one of them: Thomas, known as the twin. But then, John also records that second appearance, with Thomas present, that affirms the need to come to believe *without* seeing, an important concept we call *faith*.

June 8, OT
Psalm 50:1-23; Song of Solomon 1:1-3:11
The Song of Songs

The Psalm that opens today's OT reading was written by Asaph, a musician appointed by David to be one of the Temple Musicians (read on June 1). He had written some Psalms when David was king; now he continues that work with his first under Solomon. Given its theme, it may have been the inspiration for Solomon to write the next book from which we read in the Bible, the Song of Solomon.

If the writer of the Song of Solomon was indeed Solomon (as there is some doubt about the human authorship), then Solomon was also a man of music, presumably acquiring this talent from his father. Alternate titles for the SoS include the Song of Songs and the Canticle of Canticles largely for this reason. Even if it could be proved that Solomon is the writer, there is further conflict among scholars as to its placement, chronologically, among his writings. Solomon would pen only a handful of Psalms (some say as few as 2), but would write nearly the entirety of Proverbs and all of Ecclesiastes. I personally believe that SoS is indeed written by Solomon, and that it is among his earliest writings.

Despite appearing in every ancient copy of the Old Testament scrolls and translations, there is no doubt about why this is the most controversial book in the OT. However you interpret the "dialog" between the young bride and the handsome king (and the "chorus" that interjects), as an allegory of God's love for His people Israel, or as Christ's love for His Church (despite being written more than 900 years before Jesus was born), or (as I believe) as a romantic love song celebrating the marriage of a man and a woman, the Song of Solomon contains the most explicitly erotic language in the entire Bible. Solomon was, after all, a young (between 14 and 17 years old, by most estimates) and just-married man.

Most modern Bibles include a label to identify who is "speaking" in the various parts of the Song. If you lack one of those guides in your Bible, here is a guide to the portion we read today, after the first introductory verse:

She: 1:2-4a
Chorus: 1:4b
She: 1:5-7
He: 1:8-10
Chorus: 1:11
She: 1:12-14
He: 1:15
She: 1:16-2:1
He: 2:2
She: 2:3-3:11

June 8, NT
John 21:1-23
Jesus Appears at the Sea of Tiberias

The next post-Resurrection appearance of Jesus takes place at the Sea of Tiberius, where a miracle and an important dialog take place.

Several of the Apostles decided to do some fishing but came up empty. Meanwhile, Jesus arrived and stood on the beach (John 21:4) while they were on the boat and did not recognize Him. Jesus directed them to cast their nets on the opposite side of their boat as they got close, and this resulted in a massive catch (21:6). Recognizing that the command and the resulting miracle came from Jesus, they returned to shore to find a meal being prepared by Jesus himself (21:9-10).

During the meal, Jesus engages Peter in the famous dialog in which Jesus asks Peter three times "Do you love me?". Peter answers "yes" all three times, and this is always followed by Jesus' admonition to "tend [or feed] My lambs" or "shepherd my sheep" (21:15-17). This dialog is used in the Catechism of the Catholic Church as a further reinforcement of the "supremacy of Peter" in justifying the doctrine of the Papacy. However, the purpose of the dialog can be found by first realizing the two *different* Greek words, both translated as "love" used by Jesus and Peter, and the words of Jesus after this dialog. The first two times the question is asked, Jesus uses the word "agapao" when asking "do you love me?". This is a much deeper form of love than that of the first two replies by Peter, as the Apostle uses the word "phileo" when he says "Yes, Lord, you know that I love you." This was perhaps said this way as a gesture of humility. The last time prior to this that Jesus and Peter had any kind of dialog was when Jesus told Peter that he would deny the Lord three times before the cock crowed on the morning of His Crucifixion. When Jesus asked the question the third time, He then used the same less-strong "phileo", and Peter responded in kind, adding "You know all things; You know that I love you [more than the other Apostles]".

It is after this that Jesus reveals the time and manner of Peter's death. Knowing that Peter would be a leader in His church, Jesus makes it clear that Peter would eventually grow old and "stretch out your hands" and bring him "where you do not wish to go," indicating Peter's eventual martyrdom by crucifixion.

June 9, OT
Song of Solomon 4:1-5:16
The Proposal

These two chapters of the Song of Solomon center on the proposal by the bridegroom and her acceptance of it. Again, whether taken as a literal celebration of the love between a man and a woman or as symbolic of the relationship between God and His people or Church, both interpretations work. There is less jumping around in these two chapters compared to the first three, but this helpful guide will assist the reader:

He: 4:1-15
She: 4:16
He: 5:1a
Chorus: 5:1b
She: 5:2-16 except for verse 9, which is Chorus

June 9, NT
John 20:30-31; John 21:24-25
Conclusion of Gospel of John

As mentioned when we first read from John on January 1, John's Gospel is very different in style and substance than the other three, which are called the "synoptic" Gospels. John goes into the least amount of biographical detail on Jesus, and even concludes his Gospel without any mention of the Great Commission (Matthew and Mark) or the Ascension (Luke, Acts, and Mark). But what John does accomplish in his inspired work is the most definitive treatise on the divinity of Jesus. Chronologically, he not only wrote it after the other three (Mark, Matthew, Luke, in that order), but also after most if not all of the Pauline Epistles and the Epistles of James and Peter. Thus, when he refers to the "many other things which Jesus did," (John 21:25), he is referring to the many biographical details that he deliberately left out, and concluding then that those details would fill more books than could fit in the entire world. John himself would, however, go on to write 3 Epistles of his own, plus the book that concludes the New Testament, Revelation. Thus, the inspiration from God to write more would continue for many years.

June 10, OT
Song of Solomon 6:1-8:14
The Lovers Sing Each Other's Praises

In today's OT reading, we conclude the Song of Solomon, as the dialog continues and then draws to a close between the bride and bridegroom. The emphasis in this final section is the praise *for each other* expressed by the two lovers in the dialog, presumed to be Solomon, the King, and his new bride, who were married when we last read the narrative in I Kings 3. Here is the final guide to who is "speaking" in each part:

Chorus: 6:1
She: 6:2-3
He: 6:4-7:9a except 6:10 and 6:13a, which are Chorus
She: 7:9b-8:4
Chorus: 8:5a
She: 8:5b-7
Chorus: 8:8-9
She: 8:10-12
He: 8:13
She: 8:14

June 10, NT
Matthew 28:16-20; Mark 16:15-20; Luke 24:44-53
The Great Commission; Jesus Ascends to Heaven

Whereas we read the conclusion of the Gospel according to John yesterday, we read the conclusions of all three others today, with all three recounting one or both of the two events in the title of today's reading.

Matthew's conclusion flows perfectly from the last events and words in John, as the eleven Apostles proceed to Galilee with Jesus, and Jesus then gives them The Great Commission, in one of the most quoted passages in the Bible.

Mark's version of the Great Commission goes into some additional detail that Matthew omits, adding the "signs" that will accompany believers: casting out demons, speaking in tongues, and being able to pick up serpents and drink deadly poison without harm, among other things. Charismatics have seized on these two verses (Mark 16:17-18) as being particularly important in denominations like the Assemblies of God. Other Churches place less emphasis on these verses, partially because of their disputed authorship: Mark 16:9-20, including today's passage, is not found in several manuscripts including the most ancient ones. Despite this, most agree that verses 19-20 are authentic, and contain Mark's one-verse description of Jesus' ascension into Heaven.

Luke's conclusion doesn't have, formally, a Great Commission statement by Jesus, but does have several verses spoken by Him that are not found in either Matthew or Mark (Luke 24:44-49) that are, however, words of encouragement and understanding. He follows this with a somewhat more detailed version of the Ascension (24:50-51), but he reserves still more words of Jesus and an even more detailed version of the Ascension for his next letter to Theopolis, which we call The Acts of the Apostles, which begins tomorrow.

June 11, OT
Psalm 45:1-17; 1 Kings 5:1-12; 2 Chronicles 2:1; 2 Chronicles 2:3-16
Solomon Prepares to Build the Temple

Closing out the love songs surrounding King Solomon's marriage, Psalm 45 was written by the "sons of Korah". It is among the most overtly joyful Psalms ever written, celebrating the royal couple and praising God. It's style, being very similar to the Song of Solomon, is one of the reasons for the ongoing controversy regarding the authorship of the just-completed SoS.

The narrative then resumes in 1 Kings (and the parallel passages in 2 Chronicles) as Solomon contacts Hiram, king of Tyre (today a major ship port city in Lebanon), an ally of his father David's, and requests native cedar logs to begin construction of the Temple that the Lord denied David to build. Hiram joyously grants this request and sends servants to join the Israelite servants to deliver and begin to use them.

June 11, NT
Acts 1:1-14
Luke II

Our chronological reading plan began in Luke nearly 7 months ago. Matthew and Mark joined in before the New Year and John completed the New Testament picture on January 1, along with the Old Testament. Since then, the New Testament reading has come from one or more of those four Gospels as we tracked the life and ministry of Jesus while on earth. Now with Jesus' ascension into heaven, an event that is described again in today's NT reading (Acts 1:9), the first *outside* the Gospels, we begin a new era in salvation history. The opening verse refers to a "former book" and is addressed to a man named Theopolus (1:1). That former book is the Gospel according to Luke, and what Luke writes here to that same Theopolus provides a framework for nearly all the rest of the New Testament.

Because of its emphasis on the eleven (later 12) disciples closest to Jesus, along with other apostles added later, Luke's second magnum opus is called the Acts of the Apostles. Unlike his Gospel, Luke himself makes an appearance in the history he retells. These first 14 verses mainly cover two events: Jesus' ascension into heaven (this time with the aftermath, 1:11), and the Apostles' return to Jerusalem where they continued to spend time in the Upper Room.

June 12, OT
1 Kings 5:13-18; 2 Chronicles 2:2; 2 Chronicles 2:17-18; 1 Kings 9:15-16; 1 Kings 9:20-23; 2 Chronicles 8:7-10
The Laborers are Hired to Build the Temple

Once Hiram, king of Tyre, agreed to supply the wood, Solomon went about the actual hiring of the laborers to deliver the wood, as well as the stonemasons and other workers who would be needed, in the various short passages in 1 Kings and 2 Chronicles. Some of the passages are taken from a section subtitled "the Dedication of the Temple" *after* it was built, but only because this was the only place where some of these names were to be found.

June 12, NT
Acts 1:15-2:13
The Coming of the Holy Spirit

The number of believers was growing. Peter, taking the mantle of leader of the Apostles and the other believers, decided to make the Apostles a group of 12 again, recalling Judas Iscariot's betrayal of Jesus (Acts 1:16-17). Luke adds additional detail about Judas' suicide in verses 18-19. Then, Peter quotes two Psalms (#69 and #109) to make his case that they should choose a replacement for Judas (1:20-22). After deliberation narrows it down to two names, they cast lots and chose Matthias (1:23-26) to be the twelfth Apostle.

In a sense, this can be viewed as the first council of clergy in the new Church. Tradition, however, holds that the Church Age, as it is often called, did not begin until the coming of the Holy Spirit. Thus it happened on the Jewish feast of Pentecost (the "festival of weeks") that Peter and the rest of the Twelve were gathered "in one place" (2:1), presumably that same Upper Room, when a sound like a violent wind was heard (2:2), tongues of fire came to rest upon them (2:3), and thus came the Holy Spirit on them, allowing them to speak in other languages (2:4). The Church was born.

The crowd that gathered was from many countries and spoke many languages (2:5-11), and all were amazed.

Well, almost all. Some, as noted at the end of the passage, thought that the Apostles were drunk (2:13) and mocked the first preachers of the new Church.

June 13, OT
1 Kings 6:1-38; 2 Chronicles 3:1-17; Psalm 127:1-5; 1 Kings 7:1-12
The Building of the Temple and Solomon's Palace

In Solomon's 4th year as king, the Temple in Jerusalem began construction. In 1 Kings and 2 Chronicles, the Temple, which took 7 years to build, is described in great detail. It was huge and magnificent, and parts of it still stands today despite having been partially destroyed, twice rebuilt and buried under a Muslim Mosque. Solomon's next effort at Psalm writing, numbered as 127, was written in celebration of this amazing building, which was originally his father David's greatest desire.

The Temple's magnificence was exceeded only by one other piece of architecture: the king's palace (1 Kings 7:1-12) – an even larger effort. The wealth and prosperity of Israel's golden age was on display for everyone to see, as Solomon also had several other buildings made.

June 13, NT
Acts 2:14-36
Peter's Great Sermon

As promised by Jesus himself, the Holy Spirit had come upon the Apostles. Despite the reaction from a few in the crowd, Peter stood before them all and made the first great Christian sermon of the Church Age.

He begins by refuting the notion that he and the Apostles are drunk (Acts 2:14-15). Then, he uses a quote from the prophet Joel (Joel 2:28-32) to explain what just happened to him and the other Apostles (Acts 2:16-21). From this base, Peter recalls the life, death, and resurrection of Jesus, pointing out that Jesus rose from the dead despite their (meaning the crowd) putting Him to death. Peter quotes Psalm 16 in proving Jesus' resurrection as a fulfillment of prophecy from David (see reading for May 3) (2:25-28), and then goes on to show through another Psalm (110) that God has made Jesus both Lord and Savior (Messiah) (2:29-36), despite having been crucified.

The most amazing thing about this sermon was that Peter, a Galilean, spoke it. Galileans spoke primarily Aramaic, and knew perhaps a few words of Greek to be able to function in society. Yet as read yesterday, the crowd heard Peter and the others speaking in their native languages.

June 14, OT
1 Kings 7:13-51; 2 Chronicles 4:1-5:1; 1 Kings 8:1-21; 2 Chronicles 5:2-14
Completion and Dedication of The Temple, Part One

The first of the 3 main parts of today's OT reading is a detail of Hiram of Tyre's work in completing the Temple furnishings (1 Kings 7:13-51, 2 Chronicles 4:1-22). This is then followed by the bringing of the Ark of the Covenant into the Temple (2 Chronicles 5:1, 1 Kings 8:1-11), and finally by Solomon's address to the people in dedicating the now-completed Temple (1 Kings 8:12-21, 2 Chronicles 5:2-10). At the end of the dedication in 2 Chronicles, the glory of the Lord fills the Temple (5:11-14), just as it did the Tabernacle previously.

June 14, NT
Acts 2:37-3:10
The Church Grows to 3000 and Beyond

The people's response to Peter's sermon was swift. They immediately were moved by Peter's sometimes-harsh words and begged Peter to tell them what to do (Acts 2:37). Peter's response was to make the first "altar call" of the new Church (2:38-40). About 3000 people were saved and baptized that day. That growth continued "day by day" (2:46-47), though perhaps not at the same rate as that first day.

Some unknown days later, the Apostles Peter and John performed the first recorded miracle of the Church Age, and the first miracle that wasn't performed by Jesus in person: the healing of a lame beggar (3:1-10).

June 15, OT
2 Chronicles 6:1-11; 1 Kings 8:22-61; 2 Chronicles 6:12-7:3
Completion and Dedication of The Temple, Part Two

The passages from 2 Chronicles and 1 Kings today give further details to the last two parts of yesterday's OT reading, dominated by Solomon's prayers and Benediction before the Temple, and ending with the glory of the Lord filling the Temple, consuming the burnt offerings and sacrifices (2 Chronicles 7:1) and even preventing the priests from entering the House for a time (7:2).

June 15, NT
Acts 3:11-4:4
Peter's Second Sermon

Peter used the occasion of the first miracle of the Church Age (read yesterday) to speak to the observers with his second sermon. His words contained much of the same harshness of tone as his first sermon, chastising the people for having chosen to get a murderer released while executing the Prince of Peace (Acts 3:14-15). But Peter also lets it be known that the Israelites had acted in ignorance, and that their actions were foretold in prophecy (3:17-18). He concluded with another call for repentance, quoting Deuteronomy 18:15. The fact that this sermon took place just outside of the Temple and within hearing of the Sadducees resulted in their arrest and imprisonment (Acts 4:1-3). However, this second sermon resulted in even more converts, bringing the total number to about 5000 (4:4).

June 16, OT
1 Kings 8:62-66; 2 Chronicles 7:4-10; Psalm 132:1-18
The First Temple Sacrifices

In completing the dedication of the Temple, Solomon and all Israel offered sacrifices before the Lord: 22,000 cattle and over 120,000 sheep and goats, among other things (1 Kings 8:62-63). So massive was this event of sacrificial giving that some of it had to be conducted in the courtyard in front of the Temple (8:64), the first part of a festival that lasted two weeks. Psalm 132 was written during this time, though the author is not known (and most do not believe it was Solomon), in celebration of this monumental event.

June 16, NT
Acts 4:5-31
Peter and John Face the Court

The Sanhedrin (which included the Sadducees and elders) brought Peter and John before them after a night in jail, and demanded an explanation for the miracle that had occurred (in the June 14 reading). Peter's response, quoting Psalm 118:22 (Acts 4:11), was almost itself a mini-sermon. The Elders conferred in an effort to decide on an appropriate punishment, but couldn't agree on one, because of two main things: they were actually impressed with the boldness of Peter and John (4:13), and they could not debunk the actual miracle (4:14-16). It had happened; there was no doubt about it. They did, however, ask them to no longer spread this message in Jesus' name. They couldn't stop them from talking about the miracle itself, but they didn't want this "new Gospel" to spread any further than it already had. Then, they were released (4:21).

Of course, the result was the exact opposite of what the Sanhedrin intended. Peter and John rejoined the others, touching off another round of praise and thanks, quoting Psalm 2 (Acts 4:26). And, the Church thus continued to grow at an extremely rapid pace.

June 17, OT
1 Kings 9:1-9; 2 Chronicles 7:11-22; 1 Kings 9:10-14; 2 Chronicles 8:1-3; 1 Kings 9:24; 2 Chronicles 8:11; 1 Kings 9:25; 2 Chronicles 8:12-16; 1 Kings 9:17-19; 2 Chronicles 8:4-6; 1 Kings 9:26-28; 2 Chronicles 8:17-18; 1 Kings 10:22
Further Achievements of King Solomon

Despite the large amount of jumping around necessary to make this section of the OT make sense, the entirety of today's reading is contained within just two chapters of 1 Kings (a single verse from one of them) and one chapter of 2 Chronicles. In the two parallel accounts, the many achievements of Solomon during his first 20 years as king are chronicled (pardon the pun), following the construction and dedication of the Temple. Even though some of the details appear in just one place or the other and appear in a slightly different sequence, the agreement between the two different accounts, written more than 200 years apart, is remarkable.

The key passage in this reading is in 2 Chronicles 7:14, where God is speaking to Solomon. The passage is commonly used as a prayer for the "healing of our land", but it's actually part of a crucial 2-part message that God was delivering to the king. This part was the well known promise that if the people "humble themselves" and "turn from their wicked ways," the land would be healed. God continues the positive part of this message through verse 18. The flip side begins with verse 19, and carries equal weight: if the people turn away forsaking the decrees and commands of God, the people would be uprooted from the land and the Temple would be rejected. This is yet another proof that God's promises, though He always keeps them, are *conditional* promises based on our response to God's love and grace.

June 17, NT
Acts 4:32-5:16
The Generosity and the Hypocrisy of the Early Church

The level of unity that was shown by the early Church was, by any standards, incredible. Believers were of such a unified heart and mind (Acts 4:32) that they shared all of their material possessions with one another in a communal arrangement. Most did this with the spreading of the Gospel of Jesus Christ in mind, and the result was no needy persons amongst these believers (4:33-35). Some Pentecostal churches, in an attempt to emulate these early years of the Church, make these levels of giving a *requirement* for joining their local congregations. Some use Acts 4:32-36 (and, to some degree, the passage that follows in 5:1-11) to justify these standards, without realizing the context in which this passage relates this history. These first believers made their gifts voluntarily. No government or church organization was requiring the believers to perform these acts of generosity. People gave and shared according to their ability to do so. Some secular political discussions also cite this passage as being so-called "proof" that "Jesus was a Socialist," in order to advance a leftist political agenda. Here again, the proper context is necessary for the correct (plain) interpretation of the passage.

Of particular note is the contrast between two (actually three) people: Joseph Barnabas (4:36-37), mentioned here for the first of many times in the Acts of the Apostles, was a very generous giver, who gave the entire proceeds of a real estate sale to the Apostles, and the married couple of Ananias and Sapphira, who willfully held back on sharable resources when they had the means to share more (5:1). To make matters worse, both of them lied about it to Peter, and the result was their deaths (5:5, 5:10). It's a shocking passage, and it sounds as though the punishment is much more severe than the crime, but this was done to make one of the most important points in the New Testament: hypocrisy is among the most heinous of sins. Ananias was not obligated to give all of the money from his real estate sale like Barnabas did; in fact, he wasn't obligated to give anything. But it is obvious that Peter knew that Ananias had *pledged* these funds to the church, using the Greek word enosfisato (meaning to pilfer or embezzle, 5:2, normally translated as "kept back") to describe what Ananias did (and what Sapphira lied about to cover it up).

Despite the fear that came over the whole church because of this incident, the church continued to grow (5:12-16) as many more gatherings were held, and many more were healed like the earlier miracle.

June 18, OT
1 Kings 10:1-13; 2 Chronicles 9:1-12; 1 Kings 4:1-19; 1 Kings 4:29-34
The Visiting Queen of Sheba

Solomon's wealth and wisdom was so legendary that it reached the nation of Sheba, believed to be in the area where the modern nations of Ethiopia and Yemen exist today. In the parallel accounts in 1 Kings 10 and 2 Chronicles 9, Sheba and her entourage made the trip from Africa to not only verify what they had heard but to exchange gifts with King Solomon. Sheba even gave credit where credit was due in thanking The Lord for what Solomon had achieved.

In 1 Kings 4, Solomon's choices for his "cabinet positions" were another reflection of that wisdom, which he had asked the Lord to grant him. This wisdom would prompt Solomon to write his next book (the Song of Solomon was the first) from which we begin reading tomorrow.

June 18, NT
Acts 5:17-42
Persecution of the Apostles

The first incident of persecution in the early church involved only two of the Apostles, and was as brief as it was minor. They were warned to not spread this new Gospel any further. But holding the Great Commission to a higher standard than Jewish laws, Peter and the Apostles continued to spread the Good News and attract more and more believers. This infuriated the Jewish authorities (Acts 5:17) and their response was to have the Apostles (we're not told how many of them this time) thrown in jail again. But this time, an angel helped them make a jail break (5:19-20) and told the Apostles to go right on preaching in the Temple courts.

This puzzled the authorities more than it angered them, and they were brought in for further questioning the next day. The High Priest repeated their "strict orders" to not teach in this name (5:28), to which Peter told them the need to obey God rather than human beings (5:29). Peter once again brought the responsibility for Jesus' death down on the Jewish authorities in making his point, and this brought out their anger to the point of wanting to put the Apostles to death (5:33). But a Pharisee named Gamaliel argued for the release of the Apostles on the grounds that other movements had come and gone in the recent past, led by men who had died, thus marking the beginning of the end of their movements (5:34-39). In short, he dismissed this new Christian movement as just another activity of human origin, destined to fail and end – that is, unless it is truly from God. This argument proved persuasive, and the Apostles were flogged and then released again (5:40).

But being persecuted for His Name's sake is one of the greatest joys of being a believer, as Jesus himself taught in the Beatitudes, and the Apostles reflected this joy day after day, proclaiming the Good News (5:41-42).

June 19, OT
Proverbs 1:1-33
The Great Book of Solomon's Wisdom

There are two apocryphal books, one that is actually called the "Wisdom of Solomon" and the other, Ecclesiasticus, aka Sirach, that credit Solomon as the inspiration for the wisdom "in the manner of the Proverbs" found within each. Neither book was penned by Solomon and were, in fact, written more than 6 centuries later. But some time during Solomon's reign, a period sometimes referred to as a golden age in Israel, Solomon did write most of what we now know as the book of Proverbs.

The Proverbs are, as a whole, a collection of wise sayings, given as instructions as from a father to his son (Proverbs 1:8). Following this wisdom would lead to greater happiness and fulfillment. Failing to do so would not necessarily be sinful; just unwise, and therefore resulting in unhappiness or even personal danger. They cover a stunning variety of practical day-to-day topics. In each day's OT reading through June 30, the various themes covered by the Proverbs read that day will be listed. The first chapter serves mainly as an introduction to the wise sayings that follow, and identify the writer (Solomon) and emphasize the benefits of wise instruction. We will discover later that Solomon didn't write them all, but the first several days feature Solomon's Proverbs exclusively.

June 19, NT
Acts 6:1-15
Choosing the Seven; The Martyrdom of Stephen, Part One

As the Church continued to grow, it became increasingly necessary to delegate responsibility for certain duties to others besides the Twelve original Apostles. There were a number of practical reasons for this, including the one mentioned in Acts 6, where Hellenistic (Greek-speaking) Jewish converts felt neglected in certain areas of ministry. In response, the Twelve chose seven men to take on this responsibility. Their names were Stephen, Philip, Procorus, Nicanor, Timon, Parmenas, and Nicolas (Acts 6:5). They were formally ordained by the Apostles (6:6) and thus was the Word of God spread even further.

The first of those seven names is one which should be familiar to most readers, even if you have only made a casual reading of portions of the New Testament. Stephen was an extraordinary preacher and performer of miracles and signs (6:8). But just as it was with Peter and John earlier, Stephen's actions arose the opposition of the Jewish authorities (6:9-10). Being unable to speak against the actual wisdom of what he said, but rather, the person saying it, they accused Stephen of blasphemy, produced false witnesses against Stephen, and seized him (6:11-14).

But though we know how this particular incident of persecution would end, Stephen's face was "like the face of an angel" (6:15) as he began one of the greatest sermons ever preached, beginning in tomorrow's reading.

June 20, OT
Proverbs 2:1-4:27
Trust in God, Not in Yourself

The Proverbs, penned mostly by Solomon, cover a lot of ground. Without reading them all, one doesn't get a true perspective of just how many subjects are brought up. Today, we read what is possibly the best-known Proverb, 3:5-6, which reads "Trust in the Lord with all your heart and do not rely on your own understanding; In all your ways acknowledge him and He will make straight your paths." In addition to this gem about trust, the following Proverbs cover the following topics:

God, the source of wisdom – 2:5-9
Trust in God – 3:5-12
Becoming wise – 2:1-6
The spiritual life (and death) – 2:16-18, 3:18, 3:21-22
Avoiding sexual sin – 2:16-19
Parenting – 3:11-12

June 20, NT
Acts 7:1-23
The Martyrdom of Stephen, Part Two

After Stephen was accused of speaking "blasphemous words against Moses and God" (Acts 6:11, yesterday), Stephen defended himself by recounting the history of the Jewish people going all the way back to Abraham (7:2). From there, Stephen recounts the history of Abraham, Isaac, Jacob/Israel, and Joseph up through the Egyptian famine in verse 16. Starting in verse 17, Stephen recalls the Israelites in Egypt, and the first part of the story of Moses, through verse 23, with the remaining story in tomorrow's NT reading.

June 21, OT
Proverbs 5:1-7:27
Avoiding Sexual Indiscretion

Many Proverbs warn of the dangers of sexual sin, including some verses already read in chapter 2. In today's OT reading, warnings against sexual sin dominate the three chapters, along with just a few other topics as follows:

Sexual sin vs. marriage fidelity – 5:1-23, 6:30-35, 7:6-27
Choosing words carefully – 6:16-19
Laziness – 6:6-11

June 21, NT
Acts 7:24-43
The Martyrdom of Stephen, Part Three

Stephen's speech to the High Council continues with the history of Moses, mentioning Moses' encounter with the Burning Bush (Acts 7:30-34) and return to Egypt to liberate the Israelite people (7:35-36). It is here, as Stephen continues with the history lesson, that he changes the timbre of it to become more of a defense: Stephen recalls a prophecy made by Moses that "God will raise up a prophet for you from your own people…" (7:37), and how while Moses was receiving the law on Mount Sinai, the people had Aaron fashion a golden calf, driving home the point that God had turned away from them at that point (7:43). Stephen would continue this theme in the conclusion of chapter 7, tomorrow.

June 22, OT
Proverbs 8:1-10:32
Wisdom Personified

Both Wisdom and Folly (in 9:13-18) get *personified* in this section of Proverbs with the pronoun "she". "She" is then honored and exalted through chapters 8 and 9. Among others, these topics are covered:

God, the source of wisdom – 8:22-31, 9:10
Becoming wise – 9:1-10, 10:1, 10:5, 10:8, 10:14, 10:19, 10:23
God's blessing – 10:22, 10:27, 10:29
Money/finances – 10:4, 10:15, 10:22
The spiritual life (and death) – 10:11, 10:16, 10:21
Choosing words carefully – 10:19-20
Parenting – 10:1, 10:5
Laziness – 10:4, 10:26

June 22, NT
Acts 7:44-8:3
The Martyrdom of Stephen, Part Four

As Stephen makes his last few points in his history lesson to the High Council, he increasingly makes the point that Israel had, collectively, turned *their* backs on the promises of God. Picking up where he left off in yesterday's reading, Stephen recalls the aftermath of Moses' return from Mount Sinai, the building of the tabernacle (Acts 7:44), the conquest of the Promised Land from Joshua to David (7:45), and the construction of the Temple (7:46-47). He then makes the point that God doesn't dwell in houses made by human hands, and quotes Isaiah 66 to make the point (7:49-50).

This is the climax of Stephen's speech, as he then calls his accusers "stiff-necked people" (7:51), guilty of opposing the Holy Spirit "just as your ancestors used to do" and receiving the law but not keeping it. All of what Stephen had said was the truth in backing up his counter-accusation. Of course, the High Council was none too pleased about this. They were enraged (7:54) to the point of dragging him out of the city to be stoned (7:58).

It was thus that, though filled with the Holy Spirit and even "seeing the heavens opened and the Son of Man standing at the right hand of God" (7:55-56) that Stephen became the first Christian martyr, being stoned to death by the angry mob, even praying that the Lord would "not hold this sin against them" (7:59-60). Most notable is the brief mention of a young man named Saul (7:58, 8:1, 8:3), who wouldn't be mentioned for another whole chapter in Acts, yet became one of the most important people in the history of the Church.

Look for part three of Chronological Bible Commentary and Reading Guide, covering readings for June 23 through September 20, to be available for the first time on September 12, 2015.

June 23, OT
Proverbs 11:1-13:25
More General Maxims

Solomon continues in these 3 chapters with his poetic style of wise sayings on a wide variety of subjects:

Money/finances – 11:4, 11:16, 11:28, 13:8, 13:18, 13:22-23
Becoming wise – 11:2, 12:18, 13:10, 13:20
Choosing words carefully – 11:9, 11:12-13, 12:14, 12:18, 12:25
Parenting – 13:1, 13:24
Laziness – 12:24, 12:27, 13:4
Foolishness – 12:15-16, 12:23

June 23, NT
Acts 8:4-24
Philip in Samaria

The Church was now facing widespread persecution, spearheaded by the young man Saul (though he wouldn't be mentioned again until chapter 9). Despite this, the Word was proclaimed by the scattered Apostles "from place to place" (Acts 8:4). One of those evangelists was Philip, of whom we read in the first of two parts today. Philip was one of the seven Hellenistic Jews chosen to carry on the work of the Church (of which we first read about on June 19), and today we read the first of two evangelistic missions he was on. The first was in Samaria, and thus one of the first places outside of the Jewish nation to hear the Gospel. One of those who heard Philip preaching was a magician named Simon (8:9), who came to believe in the Lord and was baptized (8:13) but got overly impressed with the "spirit baptisms" performed by Peter and John who had joined them, and offered them money to *purchase* the power he saw them wield in the "laying on of hands" (8:18-19). Peter chastised Simon for his attempt to buy God's gifts with money, and implored him to repent. Simon asked for Peter to pray for him on his behalf.

June 24, OT
Proverbs 14:1-15:33
Two Chapters

Chapters 14 and 15 are slightly longer than the other chapters of Proverbs, thus giving us only 2 chapters to read today rather than 3. Despite the fewer chapters, the number of topics covered is about the same:

Trust in God – 14:26-27
God's blessing – 15:16

Becoming wise – 14:8, 15:7, 15:31
Spiritual life (and death) – 14:12, 14:27, 14:30, 14:32, 15:4, 15:10, 15:27
Choosing words carefully – 14:23, 15:1, 15:4, 15:23, 15:28
Parenting – 14:26, 15:20
Laziness – 15:19
Foolishness – 14:8-9, 14:16, 14:24, 15:14

June 24, NT
Acts 8:25-9:9
Philip and the Ethopian Eunuch; The Conversion of Saul, Part One

Despite this period of great persecution, one of the chosen seven, Philip, managed to first evangelize a Samaritan city, and is now pressed into service by an angel to do the same for a Eunich from Ethopia (Acts 8:26). The Eunuch was returning home from Jerusalem, reading a scroll from Isaiah that he could not interpret without Phillip's help (8:30-34). Philip used the scroll to give the Eunuch the Gospel, and stopped the chariot and found water in which to baptize the man (8:36-39). These two evangelistic efforts by Philip were the first recorded efforts to bring the Gospel outside of the immediate Judea/Galilee area; the Eunuch, in fact, would have been the first African Christian.

Believers at this time weren't yet called "Christians;" rather, they were referred to as a Jewish sect called "The Way" (9:2). There weren't yet any Gentile converts. Saul, who we first met at the stoning of Stephen, continued his murderous rampage against those who belonged to The Way (9:1). But while on his way to Damascus, he encountered Jesus in the form of a blindingly bright light and a voice (9:3-5). The men with Saul heard the voice as well but didn't see the blinding light. They led Saul the rest of the way to Damascus where he went 3 days without sight, and neither ate nor drank during that time (9:8-9). This encounter would become the most major turning point in the post-Resurrection spread of Christianity in history.

June 25, OT
Proverbs 16:1-18:24
Verbal Dynamite

Many Proverbs, some already read, concern the issue of what comes out of our mouths. It's the dominant topic of this 3-chapter section. A curious entry among these 3 chapters of Proverbs is one that appears, at first glance, to endorse *bribery* (17:8), but by reading further, one realizes that its other half is in verse 23.

Money/finances – 18:23
Becoming wise – 16:23, 17:24, 18:15
Choosing words carefully – 16:13, 16:23-24, 16:27-28, 17:10, 17:27-28, 18:8, 18:13, 18:21
Parenting – 17:6, 17:21
Foolishness – 17:10, 17:12, 17:16, 18:2, 18:6

June 25, NT
Acts 9:10-31
The Conversion of Saul, Part Two

Saul's dramatic encounter with Jesus on the road to Damascus left him blind for 3 days, praying that his sight would be restored. A man named Ananias was called by the Lord to go to the home where Saul was, lay hands on him, and restore his sight (Acts 9:10-12). But Ananias knew whom the Lord was talking about, and was reluctant to meet Saul (9:13-14), but the Lord reassured him that Saul was an "instrument" for bringing the Gospel to "Gentiles and kings" (9:15). Ananias complies, lays his hands on Saul, and prays for Saul, who regains his sight as something "like scales" fall from his eyes (9:17-18). Saul was then baptized, and ate his first meal in 3 days.

Saul's conversion was complete. Instead of seizing members of The Way, he began preaching the Gospel and gaining converts, but also thoroughly confusing local Jews. Some Jews, in fact, plotted to kill Saul, but he escaped (9:23-25). Saul returned to Jerusalem, but initially had difficulty joining the community of believers, until Barnabas took him in (9:27).

Most significantly, Saul's conversion brought the period of persecution to a virtual stop (9:31), and the Church began to increase in size again.

June 26, OT
Proverbs 19:1-21:31
Money Matters

The subject of wise handling of one's money comes up frequently in Proverbs (and elsewhere), and nowhere more so than in this 3-chapter section. That and other topics include:

Trust in God – 19:21, 21:31
Money/finances – 19:1, 19:4, 19:17, 20:13, 21:5, 21:17
Becoming wise – 19:11, 19:20, 20:1, 21:11
Spiritual life (and death) – 19:16, 19:23, 21:21, 21:25
Marriage/fidelity – 19:13-14, 21:9, 21:19
Parenting – 19:18, 19:26-27, 20:20
Laziness – 19:15, 19:24, 20:4, 21:25

June 26, NT
Acts 9:32-43
Miracles Performed by Peter

Saul, later to be renamed as Paul by the Lord, would become the principal evangelist to the Gentile world. Meanwhile, Peter was still the leader of the Church of Jerusalem, and thus the head of the world of Jewish believers at that time. Today's NT reading features an account of miracles performed by the Apostle Peter in Lydda and Joppa, including the healing of a paralytic named Aeneas (Acts 9:33-34) and the resurrection of Tabitha (9:36-41).

June 27, OT
Proverbs 22:1-24:22
Sayings of The Wise

Starting in Proverbs 22:17, we have a section titled "The Words of the Wise," which was presumably *not* written by Solomon. The style and subject matter are still, however, very much like the Proverbs in the first 21 chapters, though this section puts a lot more emphasis on money matters. Tomorrow's reading starts another section that IS identified as Solomon's writings.

God, the source of wisdom – 22:17-19
Money/finances – 22:1-2, 22:4, 22:7, 22:9, 22:16, 22:22-23, 23:5
Becoming wise – 23:4
Sexual sin – 23:26-28
Parenting – 23:13-16, 23:22-25

June 27, NT
Acts 10:1-23a
The First Gentile Conversion, Part One

In the readings for the past few days, we encountered Philip taking the Gospel message to Samaria and, via a Eunuch, to Ethiopia. In both cases, though, these people were already "of the circumcision". Saul was already a Jew before his dramatic conversion on the way to Damascus. But Ananias was told that Saul was an "instrument" for bringing the Gospel to "Gentiles and kings" (Acts 9:15). When Saul did his first preaching, he did it in synagogues (9:20), meaning that he, too, was concentrating on (Hellenistic) Jews. After Saul's escape (to Arabia, but we don't learn of that until he writes of this in Galatians 1:17) from the confused Jews, we read (yesterday) of miracles performed by Peter "among all the believers" (9:32), meaning that he was also ministering to Jews, not Gentiles. In today's NT reading, that all changes for the first time.

The first Gentile conversion was to a centurion named Cornelius. He was an uncircumcised Roman, but also a believer in God. Doubtless he had heard the Word of God from Jewish believers living in the area, and was thus moved by the Holy Spirit. An angel directed him to send men to (nearby?) Joppa, where Peter was staying (10:3-8).

The curious vision that Peter had in 10:9-16 can be interpreted as God's call to Peter to evangelize the Gentiles, who were unclean and even considered "profane" by the circumcised. One classic commentary described this as a way of breaking down Peter's prejudices against the Gentiles, which "would have prevented his going to Cornelius unless the Lord had prepared him for this service" (Matthew Henry Concise Commentary on Acts 10:9-18).

Today's reading ends with the arrival of Cornelius' men, who explain to Peter why they're there, while Peter invites them in and gives them lodging until tomorrow's journey back to Cornelius.

June 28, OT
Proverbs 24:23-27:27
Copied Proverbs

Today's OT reading starts by saying that "These also are sayings of the wise," indicating a possible non-Solomon authorship (Proverbs 24:23), but then comes the "other Proverbs of Solomon *that the officials of King Hezekiah of Judah copied"* (25:1). So, was Solomon the writer of these and they were "discovered later" (about 300 years) and copied by people in Hezekiah's time? Or were these written "in the manner of the Proverbs" like the Apocryphal books of Wisdom or Sirach, perhaps by Hezekiah himself? Were they written by one of those in Hezekiah's court, such as Isaiah or Micah? We'll never know for sure. The style is virtually indistinguishable from the earlier Proverbs we know were written by Solomon, so the first scenario seems the most likely, and it would allow these Proverbs to fit in this chronological sequence correctly. Among others, the topics include:

Spiritual life (and death) – 27:20
Choosing words carefully – 25:11-12, 25:15, 26:23-28
Marriage/fidelity – 27:15-16
Parenting – 27:11
Laziness – 26:13-16
Foolishness – 26:3, 26:11, 27:22

June 28, NT
Acts 10:23b-48
The First Gentile Conversions, Part Two

Peter went to the home of Cornelius, who was not alone when he arrived (Acts 10:24). Peter told them that it was unlawful for a Jew to associate with a Gentile, but came anyway when sent for (10:27-29). Cornelius spoke for the assembled group, explaining the angelic visit that led to his call for Peter (10:30-33) to "listen to all that the Lord has commanded you to say".

Peter took the opportunity, and delivered the Gospel message to the assembled Gentiles, showing "no partiality" (10:34-43). The Holy Spirit fell upon all who heard the Word, and then had the first Gentile Converts baptized.

June 29, OT
Proverbs 28:1-30:33
The Last of Solomon's Proverbs; The Sayings of Agur

Chapters 28 and 29 of Proverbs contain the last of those believed, by some, to be Solomon's. As mentioned yesterday, there is some doubt as to the authorship of the section that begins in chapter 25, but this chronology will assume that Solomon wrote the Proverbs in chapters 25 through 29, and that they were later "discovered" by Hezekiah.

With Chapters 30 and 31 (31 tomorrow), there is a radical shift in both style and focus, due primarily to the *un*disputed fact of their different authorship. Chapter 30 begins with "The words of Agur, son of Jakeh, an oracle." There is no other mention of Agur or Jakeh anywhere in the Bible, and we thus don't even know if he lived during the time of Solomon or, somewhat more likely, if he was one of "Hezekiah's officials" mentioned in Proverbs 25:1. Only one verse in Chapter 30 could be called a Proverb in the same sense as the rest of this book (30:10), because the rest of it is very clearly a prophecy. The style and substance, furthermore, feel very much like a portion of Isaiah 42, which makes its placement in Proverbs questionable. That it has been part of the Proverbs since at least the time of Hezekiah is of no doubt, and the chapter that follows (tomorrow), though also of disputed authorship, is likewise a worthwhile read of great quality, far higher in quality than any of the Apocryphal writings made in Solomon's name. Topics in both the section of Solomon's Proverbs and Agur's oracle include:

Sin (in general) – 28:9, 28:13
Trust in God – 29:25-26, 30:5-9
Money/finances – 28:3, 28:6, 28:8, 28:11, 28:19-20, 28:22, 28:27, 29:7, 29:14, 30:7-9
Becoming wise – 29:3, 29:8, 29:11, 29:15
Choosing words carefully – 28:23, 29:5
Parenting – 29:15, 29:17
Foolishness – 28:26, 29:11

June 29, NT
Acts 11:1-26
Believers Become Christians

Peter's trip to Joppa to help with the first Gentile conversions didn't go over particularly well with Jewish believers back home in Jerusalem. So when he returned, he had some serious explaining to do. But this he did (Acts 11:4-17), relating in detail the vision from God and the evangelization of Cornelius and his men. The Jews were satisfied with Peter's answer, and they praised God, and acknowledged that God has "given even to the Gentiles the repentance that leads to life" (11:18).

Peter's evangelization of Cornelius and the others may have been the first Gentile conversion, but it was by no means the last. Some Greek-speaking Jewish believers in Cyprus and Cyrene went to Antioch and proclaimed the Gospel to the Gentiles there (11:20), resulting in many new believers. News of this reached Barnabas in Jerusalem (11:22), who then went to Antioch, and rejoiced with the new believers. Barnabas went to Tarsus and got Saul, and brought him to Antioch as well, and they spent a year there teaching many people. It was here that the believers first began to call themselves by the title that we still use today: Christians (11:26).

June 30, OT
Proverbs 31:1-31
The Eisheth Ḥayil

Our final reading from Proverbs is given the Hebrew title of Eisheth Hayil, which means "ideal woman" or "noble wife". It is not known if it is an extension of the words of King Lemuel (Proverbs 31:1) or was actually written by Solomon. One interesting theory, particularly fascinating since the name Lemuel is otherwise completely unknown, is that Lemuel is actually an alias of Solomon, and the reference to Lemuel's mother would, then, be Bathsheba, effectively making her the author of this section.

Regardless of the authorship, the section, particular from verse 10 onwards, is an ode to a capable wife, resourceful and intelligent, skilled in many things. It is a message so positive and pro-woman that entire ministries for women have been built around its verses.

June 30, NT
Acts 11:27-12:25
Death of James, Imprisonment of Peter, and Death of Herod

There are 3 different men named James mentioned in the New Testament. Two of them are Apostles, the other is the half-brother of Jesus. If you're among those who believe that the Epistle of James (which begins in about 2 weeks) was written by James, the Apostle, the brother of John, then it would be necessary to insert that Epistle here before this reading, because that James is killed at the beginning of today's NT reading (Acts 12:1-2).

After this, Peter is once again thrown into prison (12:3-5), this time by Herod, and this time alone. But despite being heavily guarded, Peter is sprung from the prison by an angel (12:6-10). His first stop was the home of Mary (not Magdalene nor the mother of Jesus), the mother of a man named John Mark (12:12). That same John Mark, also mentioned in 12:25, would later become the first Gospel writer, using just the name Mark, about 20 years after these events.

The third event of which we read today is the death of Herod, struck down by the Lord himself (12:23) because he had not given glory to God. During this time, the Gospel continued to spread, as Barnabas and Saul returned to Jerusalem along with John Mark (12:25).

July 1, OT
1 Kings 4:20-28; 1 Kings 10:14-21; 2 Chronicles 9:13-21; 1 Kings 10:23-25; 2 Chronicles 9:22-24; 1 Kings 10:26-29; 2 Chronicles 1:14-17; 2 Chronicles 9:25-28
The Riches of King Solomon

After nearly 2 weeks of Proverbs, the narrative returns in 1 Kings and 2 Chronicles, consisting mostly of a detailed description of the opulent wealth accumulated by Solomon and by the nation of Israel during this "golden age". When Solomon's kingdom was first established, his only wish was to become wise. God was so pleased with that request that He not only granted wisdom, but riches as well. Solomon's wisdom was legendary, as evidenced by writing more than 3000 Proverbs (1 Kings 4:32, of which less than 25% of them actually were recorded as part of that book). But this wisdom made him outrageously wealthy, and that wealth was starting to go to his head. The mistakes he made as these riches started becoming a snare to him are told in tomorrow's OT reading.

July 1, NT
Acts 13:1-12
Saul Becomes Paul, Embarks on First Missionary Journey

The Church had spread as far as it could without sending missionaries on long journeys. Thus it was that Barnabas and Saul were commissioned and then sent off to spread the Gospel to new lands (Acts 13:1-3).

The First Missionary Journey began by having Barnabas and Saul sail to Cyprus, and preach in Jewish synagogues (13:5) along with John Mark. Then came the encounter with Sergius Paulus, the proconsul, and a magician named Bar-Jesus. Paulus was looking forward to hearing the word of God, but Bar-Jesus tried to stop it (13:6-8).

But it was at this point that we learn of Saul's name change. Some time on the journey, and as God had done several times before to men such as Abram (Abraham) and Jacob (Israel), Saul was given the new name of Paul. It was then Paul who strongly rebuked the magician Bar-Jesus (13:9-11) and even induced blindness in him. The proconsul was astonished at the teaching about God and believed (13:12).

July 2, OT
1 Kings 11:1-40
Solomon Turns Away From God

Two days ago, we read the final chapter of Proverbs. If that final chapter (31) was actually written by Solomon under the alias "King Lemuel," then the mother referred-to in the chapter is actually Solomon's mother Bathsheba. And if that's true, then that makes Solomon's bad choices in 1 Kings 11 all the sadder.

Proverbs 31:3, written possibly as advice from mother (Bathsheba) to son (Solomon) says "Give not thy strength unto women, nor thy ways to that which destroyeth kings." In 1 Kings 11:1-3, Solomon ignores this advice, and takes 700 wives from foreign lands, plus another 300 concubines. Besides being polygamous and adulterous, sins for which his father David was punished, it caused Solomon to do something his father never did: turn away his heart after foreign gods (11:4-8). The results were disastrous.

God became angry with Solomon (11:9), and told Solomon that the kingdom would be torn from him, though not in Solomon's lifetime (11:11-13). God raised adversaries to cause trouble for Solomon: Hadad the Edomite (11:14-22) and Rezon the Zobahite (11:23-25). Then, to complete Solomon's punishment in the exact manner prescribed by God, Jeroboam, a servant of Solomon, was given 10 of Israel's 12 tribes (11:26-39) in preparation for the divided kingdom to come after Solomon's death. Naturally, Solomon tried to stop this by having Jeroboam killed (11:40), but his effort failed. The fall of Solomon had begun.

Solomon's response, which we'll read over the course of the next 4 days, was to write a *third* great book of wise philosophy.

July 2, NT
Acts 13:13-31
The First Missionary Journey, Part Two: Paul and Barnabas in Antioch

Paul's and Barnabas' next stop on this First Missionary Journey was Pisidia Antioch, where they were invited to speak in a synagogue. There, Paul begins his longest recorded sermon, of which we read the first half in today's NT reading.

Paul's sermon begins by recounting the history of Israel starting with the Exodus (Acts 13:17-18), and the conquest of Canaan, through the time of the Judges (13:20), and then Israel's first kings, Saul (13:21), and David (13:22, quoting 1 Samuel 13:14).

From here, Paul jumps all the way to Jesus, skipping over all the generations after Solomon, and recalls Jesus' baptism by John (13:24-25), and then His death and resurrection (13:27-31), before getting to the real "point" of his sermon, as we will read tomorrow.

July 3, OT
Ecclesiastes 1:1-2:26
Vanity and Chasing After Wind

A correct understanding of the book of Ecclesiastes and its place in Scripture requires some knowledge of the words, originally in Hebrew, translated here as "vanity," and the book's title, "Ecclesiastes". The title, in Hebrew, is "Koheleth," which means "teacher" or "preacher," the same word as in Ecclesiastes 1:1 where the author identifies himself as "the son of David, king in Jerusalem." That author is, of course, Solomon.

Though it appears *before* the Song of Solomon in the Old Testament, it is quite obvious that this philosophical lament was written long after those joyful times. Though there is some dispute about Solomon's authorship, those that believe he wrote this also know that it would be his *third* book, with all 3 written while he was king. This final book would have been written some time after his taking of more than 700 wives, as read yesterday, thus placing this book chronologically near the end of his life.

The word, "vanity," forms the basis for the title of today's reading as well as the theme of the entire book. The Hebrew word is "hevel." Though "vanity" can also mean "foolish pride," it is used here to mean "meaninglessness" or "that which is empty, without permanent value, that which leads to frustration." The word appears 14 times in just these first two chapters alone (and several times thereafter), and reflects the tone of the writing, among the most melancholy of the entire Bible.

Another phrase that appears frequently in Ecclesiastes is "under the sun," and it forms the basis for Solomon's assertion that "all is vanity," which he "proves" in several sections. The first could be called "the never-ending cycle of creation" (Eccl 1:3-11), followed by "even wisdom cannot satisfy" (1:12-18). In chapter 2, this continues with a section on "the futility of self-indulgence" (2:1-11), and then a description of how wisdom is more valuable than wealth and riches, but even this is, as this reading concludes, vanity and chasing after wind (2:26).

July 3, NT
Acts 13:32-52
The First Missionary Journey, Part Three: Justification by Faith

Pauls' sermon to the Jews in Pisidia Antioch began with a history that no Jew would dispute. But when he got to the death and resurrection of Jesus, he was definitely preaching a Gospel with which the Jews would have a problem. Paul nevertheless was able to use Scripture (mostly Psalms), just as he did in yesterday's first half, to effectively proclaim justification by faith in Jesus (Acts 13:36-41). At first, it appeared that this message took hold, as they were invited to return on the next Sabbath and continue this preaching (13:42-43).

But, that's not what happened. The Jews, upon seeing the crowds gathered by Paul and Barnabas, became jealous (13:44-45) and began preaching *against* the very message they were gladly receiving before. Paul expected this, and explained to the crowd that the message had to be brought first to the Jews, but would now be brought to the Gentiles (13:46-47). The Gentiles welcomed this with joy, and the Gospel spread very quickly (13:48-49). The Jews didn't take this well, and drove Paul and Barnabas out of town (13:50). Acts even notes Paul and Barnabas doing exactly as the Apostles were told to do by Jesus, shaking the dust off their sandals in protest (13:51) as they made their exit and went to Iconium.

July 4, OT
Ecclesiastes 3:1-6:12
A Time for Everything Under Heaven

The first part of today's OT reading (Eccl 3:1-8) contains the words that are instantly recognizable as the lyrics to "Turn! Turn! Turn!" a song by Pete Seeger that The Byrds recorded and took to #1 in 1965. In the context of the rest of the reading, it shows the despair in Solomon of looking back at a life without meaning.

Solomon continues his "proofs" of the futility of life here in sections that could be called "life is not fair" (4:1-16), "religious practices cannot satisfy" (5:1-8), "the futility of riches" (5:9-20), and "the futility of life itself" (6:1-12).

July 4, NT
Acts 14:1-28
The First Missionary Journey, Part Four: Paul in Galatia

The last leg of Paul's First Missionary Journey took him and Barnabas through Iconium, Derbe, and Lystra, where several important encounters took place. In Iconium, they preached to both Jews and Gentiles ("Greeks" in most translations) and many of them believed (Acts 14:1). But some Jews there sought to dissuade these new believers, creating a division that resulted, again, in their ouster from a city (14:2-6).

Paul and Barnabas were not discouraged by this turn of events, and continued to preach wherever they went in the region known as Galatia. In Lystra, Paul performed the miracle of healing on a lame man (14:8-10), but the crowds completely misconstrued this as being the coming of the gods Zeus and Hermes in the form of the men Barnabas and Paul, respectively (14:11-12). Paul stopped the local priest of Zeus from turning the occasion into a pagan sacrificial ritual (14:14-17), but they still had to restrain the crowds from carrying it out anyway. When Jews from Antioch and Iconium showed up, having won over the crowds, they stoned Paul and dragged him out of town and left him for dead (14:19-20).

Paul wasn't dead, of course, and he and Barnabas began their return journey by going through Lystra, Iconium, and Antioch, preaching as they went, encouraging the believers, and appointing elders (14:21-28) in the still-young Church (between 10 and 15 years after Jesus' ascension).

July 5, OT
Ecclesiastes 7:1-10:20
Disillusioned Proverb Bookends

The first 13 verses of chapter 7 and all of chapter 10 serve as bookends to this section of Ecclesiastes, and are written in a very familiar style that reinforces the idea that Solomon was the writer of this book. The poetic style is very reminiscent of Proverbs, although the mood remains depressed in both sections. In between, Solomon speaks to the superiority of God's wisdom over man's (7:15-29, 8:10-16), observations regarding obedience to authority (8:1-9), and a lengthy section (9:1-18) about the certainty of death, despite wisdom or wealth. At least two verses in chapter 9 appear to have been inspired more by Satan than by God (9:2, 9:10), but this, too, is a by-product of the sadness being expressed by the king.

July 5, NT
Acts 15:1-35
The Council at Jerusalem

While Paul and Barnabas were returning from the First Missionary Journey, the dispute over whether or not Gentiles could or should be saved began to heat up (Acts 15:1). So much so, they were alerted of this while still as far away as Phoenicia (15:2-3), and made their way to Jerusalem quickly. The Apostles and elders greeted them warmly, and Paul and Barnabas reported to them all that had taken place, which included details of numerous Gentile conversions (15:4). But the Pharisees, in particular, took issue with this, stating that these new converts must be circumcised (15:5). The great debate was on.

Among those present at the Jerusalem council were the Apostle Peter, and James, the brother of Jesus. Peter's rebuttal to the Pharisees started by pointing out that he had been chosen first to bring the Gospel to the Gentiles (15:7-9). His position was articulated in the question "why do you put God to the test by placing on the neck of these disciples a yoke which neither our fathers… been able to bear?"

(15:10). He answered his own question in the next verse by stating that we are "saved through the grace of our Lord Jesus" (15:11).

The debate went on until Jesus' own half-brother, James, spoke up. James had become a member of the council, and was able to speak for the group, with authority. He acknowledged Peter's statement that Peter was called to bring the Gentiles to faith (15:14), and then uses a quote from Amos 9:11-12 to point out how this was in agreement with the prophets (15:15-18). James then concludes by saying that the council agrees to not burden the Gentiles with Jewish law and custom, but to caution them, in writing, to abstain from things contaminated by idols, from fornication, from blood and from things that are strangled (15:19-21). This decision pleased the Apostles and elders, and they drafted a letter to be sent with Paul, Barnabas, and two additional men (15:22-29), Judas and Silas, who delivered the message to an enthusiastic group of new believers in Antioch (15:30-35).

July 6, OT
Ecclesiastes 11:1-12:14
The End of the Matter

These two chapters bring Ecclesiastes, King Solomon's final written words, to a close. It becomes even more obvious in this last section that we are reading the words of someone old and wise, nearing the end of life, and knowing that the end is near. There is a slightly brighter tone to these words, as the "teacher" realizes that there are some things beyond understanding, no matter how much wisdom one possesses. Thus, even though he uses the word "vanity" to describe life here the largest number of times since chapter 1, he falls back on his own advice from the Proverbs: Fear God and obey Him, because that is the end of the matter (Eccl 12:13).

July 6, NT
Acts 15:36-16:10
The Second Missionary Journey Begins

With the Council in Jerusalem now past, and Paul, Barnabas, Judas, and Silas in Antioch, ready to bring the Gospel to even more people, the Second Missionary Journey is about to begin when a dispute broke out about who to take along on a trip through Galatia and surrounding areas (Acts 15:36). The dispute resulted in a split: Barnabas took Mark with him to Cyprus while Paul chose Silas (15:37-41). It would be the last time Barnabas is mentioned in Acts.

Once in Derbe and Lystra, Paul met Timothy (who would later become the addressee of Paul's final letters). Paul had Timothy circumcised because the Jews of the area knew that Timothy's father was a Greek (15:1-3). Together, they went through the region, delivering the decision of the church council in Jerusalem, and making more believers, planting more churches (15:4-5).

Forbidden to preach in Asia by the Holy Spirit, they went through Phrygian and Galatian regions. Paul had a vision of a man from Macedonia, asking to "come and help" (15:6-9), and so they immediately sought to go there, believing that God was calling them to preach to them.

July 7, OT
Psalm 73:1-28; Psalm 88:1-18; 1 Kings 11:41-43; 2 Chronicles 9:29-31; 1 Kings 14:21; 2 Chronicles 12:13-14
Solomon Dies; Rehoboam Takes the Throne

Solomon wrote neither of the two Psalms in today's OT reading, though both are believed to have been written during this period near the end of Solomon's life. Asaph, a court musician appointed by Solomon's father, David, some 40 years earlier, wrote the first of the two.

Despite reigning for the exact same number of years as his father (40), Solomon's biography is less than half the length of his father's in the Bible (due mostly to beginning his reign at a much younger age and dying at an age between 52 and 56, according to tradition). But where we don't get direct references to the other events in Solomon's life and reign, we get two other things: the writings of Solomon in 3 books of the Bible (Song of Solomon, Proverbs, and Ecclesiastes), and references to 3 other extra-biblical books that have been lost to history (1 Kings 11:41, 2 Chronicles 9:29). Solomon died and was buried in the city of David, Jerusalem.

Solomon's son Rehoboam then took the throne, but over a kingdom that would soon be divided.

July 7, NT
Galatians 1:1-24
The First Epistle

Since this chronological reading plan began almost 7 months ago, all of the New Testament has been presented in the order in which the *events* occurred, not the order in which the *books* were written, from books written a long time after the events occurred. The earliest NT events were written in Luke, who was also the writer of the Acts of the Apostles that we are now just past half way through. But Luke wasn't even the first Gospel writer, and the first Gospel writer (Mark) wouldn't write his account of the life of Jesus until about 10 years after the Council of Jerusalem. Matthew would follow about 5 years later, and then Luke would write his about 5 years after that. Luke would probably write Acts very shortly thereafter (John's Gospel would follow 25 to 35 years later). All this is to put into perspective an important quandary for anyone piecing together the New Testament in chronological order:

What about the Epistles? What was the actual first *writing* in New Testament times?

Approximately half of the New Testament consists of letters ("epistles" in Greek) written by Paul and others to the new, young Churches. They contain teachings and words of encouragement, but relatively little history. Thus, their placement in this reading plan is based mainly on when they were *written*, which begs the question of which one was written first? Looking through 2 chronological Bibles and 3 reading plans (including the one that was the foundation for this plan), there are 3 possibilities: one is Paul's First Letter to the Thessalonians, but it would seem far more likely for this to have been written *after* Paul's Second Missionary Journey, not near the beginning of it like we are at now. A second possibility, and the one from which most of this book came, is that James, the brother of Jesus, wrote his letter first. While it is likely that James' letter is among the earliest (see reading for July 13), the belief that his was first often stems from the mistaken notion that the writer of that Epistle was James the Apostle, not James the brother of Jesus.

In the end, the most likely possibility, and the only one acknowledged in 3 different places, is that Paul wrote his letter to the Galatians, which we begin today, first, near the beginning of his Second

Missionary Journey, to the people he had recently visited in his First Missionary Journey.

The biggest issue facing the early churches like those in Galatia had to do with whether or not it was necessary to continue the various Jewish observances, including circumcision, sacrifices, and the several holidays. In other words, did one have to first become Jewish before becoming Christian? So after one of Paul's shortest salutations (Galatians 1:1-5), Paul begins by chastising the Galatians for allowing others to confuse them or pervert the Gospel (1:6-9), which was clearly directed at the Jews in the region. Paul uses his own history, from his conversion through his First Missionary Journey, to justify his position (1:10-21).

July 8, OT
1 Kings 12:1-19; 2 Chronicles 10:1-19; 1 Kings 12:20-24; 2 Chronicles 11:1-4
The Northern Tribes Secede

When Solomon attempted to have Jeroboam killed for his rebellion, Jeroboam fled to Egypt (1 Kings 11:40, July 6). Now that Solomon had died, and Rehoboam (Solomon's son) was about to become king, Jeroboam returned from Egypt, gathered the people of Israel, and confronted the heir apparent with a harsh message about how Solomon had "made our yoke heavy" (12:1-4). Rehoboam didn't know how to respond to the charge, and sent everyone away for three days while he consulted the elder members of his father Solomon's staff (12:6-7). Ignoring the advice they gave him, he went on to the younger members of Solomon's staff (12:8-11). Their advice was to make the "yoke" even heavier than before. Unfortunately for the people of Israel, it is this advice that Rehoboam took.

After 3 days, Jeroboam and the people of Israel returned to hear the king's response (12:12-14), which he delivered, harshly, from the advice of the younger staff. As expected, the people rejected this message and rejected Rehoboam's kingship. Rehoboam fled to Jerusalem to take the throne over the cities of Judah (12:17-19) while Jeroboam took the throne as king over "all Israel" (12:20) *except* the tribe of Judah. Rehoboam assembled an army from two tribes: Judah and Benjamin, to go to war to reclaim the full kingdom, but was stopped from doing so by the word of God via a prophet named Shemaiah (12:21-24). All of these events are also written in 2 Chronicles 10 and 11, nearly verbatim.

July 8, NT
Galatians 2:1-21
Defending the Gospel of Grace

Paul continues his defense of the Gospel of Grace, by describing his own past and interaction with other Apostles, up to and including the First Missionary Journey and the Council of Jerusalem. He makes it quite clear that circumcision is *not* essential to be able "to enjoy the freedom we have in Christ Jesus" (Galatians 2:3-4). Paul also relates a part of the aftermath of the Jerusalem Council that Luke left out of the Acts account: a confrontation with Peter (listed here as Cephas, 2:11) over the latter's behavior with the Gentiles that Peter tried to hide from his fellow Jews, as if in shame. Paul called him out on this hypocrisy at the time and place where the Second Missionary Journey was about to begin (as read on July 6).

Paul then emphasizes that though he is a Jew addressing Gentiles, no one is justified by the Law but by faith in Jesus Christ (2:15-16). He even explains the apparent paradox that Jews are sinners, too (2:17), culminating in his assertion that he has been "crucified with Christ" (2:20). That verse and the one that follows formed the basis for the popular song recorded by Philips, Craig, and Dean.

July 9, OT
1 Kings 12:25-31; 2 Chronicles 11:13-17; 1 Kings 12:32-13:34
The Saga of the Kings of Judah and Israel Begins

With the kingdom now split into Northern (Israel) and Southern (Judah) kingdoms, only one of which (Judah) being in the line of David, the saga of the kings of Israel and Judah truly begins. The history would go for more than 200 years in the Northern kingdom, with not even one single "good" king, and over 400 years for Judah, with only a smattering of kings that *didn't* get listed as "doing evil in the sight of the Lord". Both kingdoms ended in foreign conquest and exile.

The first king of the North was Jeroboam, and among his first acts as king was to make two golden calves (1 Kings 12:25-30) and set them up as objects of worship. He even appointed priests (who weren't Levites) to lead worship in this new idolatry (12:31). Most Levites fled to Jerusalem to continue to serve the Lord in the Southern kingdom (2 Chronicles 11:13-17). Jeroboam enacted feast days and offered sacrifices on an altar he erected in Bethel (1 Kings 12:32-33).

Then came the curious events recorded in 1 Kings 13: an unnamed "man of God" arrives from Judah to condemn Jeroboam's idolatry (13:1-2) promising judgment from God for the altar to the false gods, and making a remarkable prophecy that would be fulfilled 340 years later. The altar was split as predicted, but the man of God extended a measure of grace to Jeroboam in healing Jeroboam's withered hand (13:3-6). The grateful king extended an invitation to dine with him, but the man of God declines, as per instructions he had received from the Lord (13:7-10). But both kingdoms' descent into sin became evident after this, when a prophet from the North convinces the man of God to join him at dinner (13:11-17) and lies about being a prophet of the true God (13:18-19). This causes the man of God to disobey the order to not break bread with the people in Bethel, and the prophet from Bethel predicts the man's doom (13:20-22), which is fulfilled when the man of God is killed by a lion on his return trip (13:23-25). The prophet makes sure he gets a proper burial, and requests that he be buried next to this man of God, too (13:25-32).

This was all done as an object lesson in obedience to the one, true God, but Jeroboam obviously didn't "get it," as he didn't turn from his evil ways (13:33-34). His sin became the example used throughout the books of the kings to describe the evil of each of his successors in the North and most of the kings of Judah, who "walked in the ways of Jeroboam." The lone exception was the one king (of whom we will read on July 14) of Judah who was described as being *even worse*.

July 9, NT
Galatians 3:1-22
Faith versus Works

Throughout Paul's Epistles, he makes numerous comparisons of the Law with the new covenant of grace. Today's reading marks the first of these comparisons. Besides the issue of Jews (or becoming Jews) and Gentiles is the issue of those laws (for Jews) vs faith in Jesus.

Paul begins by scolding the Galatians, asking if they thought that they received the Spirit by the works of the law or by faith (Galatians 3:1-6). He quotes Genesis 15:6 in proving his case that it was by faith, not the Law, that this Spirit came. He goes on to say that believers are, thus, "children of Abraham" (3:7-9) because of the promise made by God to Abraham (known as "The Covenant") that "all nations will be blessed through you," quoting Genesis 12:3 and 18:18. Paul then quotes Deuteronomy, Habakkuk, and Leviticus to make the point that the Law cannot save, but rather, *curse* (3:10-12), and that Jesus broke that curse by dying on the Cross, *becoming sin in our place* (3:13-14), thus permitting anyone to obtain the blessing of Abraham by faith.

Israel lost those blessings (but never the Promise) on numerous occasions. As read in this chronological reading plan, The Covenant, first given to Abraham, has never been broken by God, despite the numerous occasions where God allowed Israel to be punished (conquered, exiled, etc.) because they didn't keep up their end of the bargain. Paul explains that the law wasn't introduced until 430 years after Abraham, and thus, the Law was never supposed to be part of the promise given to the "seed of Abraham," (3:15-18) which the Galatians were now, metaphorically, part of.

Discussions, to this day, about how we now live under a *new* covenant, thus the name of the latter portion of the Christian Bible, often lead to questions about why the law was given in the first place, and whether or not the law is or was contrary to The Covenant. Paul artfully brings up both questions, and answers them with explanations that could only be inspired by God (3:19-22).

July 10, OT
1 Kings 14:1-18; 2 Chronicles 11:5-12; 2 Chronicles 11:18-23; 1 Kings 14:22-28; 2 Chronicles 12:1-12
Ahijah's Prophecy Against Jeroboam; Shemaiah's Prophecy Against Rehoboam

As was the case throughout nearly all 400 years of the "divided kingdom," events ran in parallel as God passed judgment on each king and nation for their evil. In the first part of today's OT reading, Jeroboam attempts to consult a blind prophet named Ahijah via his disguised wife, but instead receives a prophecy of doom, including the death of his son (1 Kings 14:1-18).

Meanwhile, in the Southern kingdom (Judah), Rehoboam fortified his cities against the North (2 Chronicles 11:5-12) and marries into his grandfather David's family, eventually taking 18 wives and more than 60 concubines (11:18-23), and names his son Abijah (a name often mixed up with Ahijah) the crown prince. But Rehoboam's sin, along with that of the tribes of Judah and Benjamin, made his fortifications meaningless, as God allowed Shishak, king of Egypt, to successfully attack the cities in Judah (1 Kings 22-28, 2 Chronicles 12:1-4). God then sent a prophet, Shemaiah, to Rehoboam (12:5) to explain God's actions. Rehoboam and his men humbled themselves (12:6) and this resulted in God *not* destroying the nation, but much of the temple treasure was stolen and God permitted this (12:7-12).

July 10, NT
Galatians 3:23-4:20
Being Children of God

In the first part of today's NT reading, Paul combines and concludes his discussions regarding having to first become Jews in order to become Christians (you don't) with the discussions regarding the Law vs. grace through faith in Jesus by telling the Galatians that they are now children of God, and thus heirs, because of their faith (Galatians 3:23-4:7). The key verse is 3:28, in which Paul states that all the things that divide us are irrelevant in light of our faith in Jesus. Paul would echo many of these themes again in other Epistles, most notably in Romans chapter 8.

As read on July 7, when this first Epistle began, the letters of Paul and others to the new churches contain relatively little in terms of history; thus they are placed in this chronology according to when they were written rather than any history that they contain. But just because they contain very little history doesn't mean that they don't contain any. Such was the case on July 8 when Paul tells of his encounter with Peter after the Jerusalem Council, and now here in this reading (4:8-20) as Paul relates some more details of his First Missionary Journey, when he visited the Galatians the first time and established the church there to whom he now writes. He uses this history of their past encounter to express his concern for the Galatians, whose faith seems to be teetering because of the influence of the Jews in the region that he first brought up in chapter 1 (on July 7).

July 11, OT
Psalm 89:1-52
Ethan's Psalm

In the title of the Psalm that makes up the entirety of today's OT reading, this Psalm's writer is identified (Ethan), and the type of Psalm (a "maskil") is described. We don't know much about Ethan except that this is his only Psalm, written (presumably) near the end of what was a very long career as a musician in Israel's (later Judah's) royal court. He was appointed as a court musician at either near the end of David's reign or the beginning of Solomon's, making his career nearly 50 years long at this point. Its placement here is due to references to David (Psalm 89:19-29) and the extension of God's covenant to him and to the people of Israel, followed by God's warning that was given to David (89:30-37) about the consequences of sin. Thus, the earliest this Psalm could have been written was near the beginning of the reign of Solomon, after the last of the usurpations and rebellions were done. But that period was a time of joy and peace in Israel, and the reign of Solomon is marked by having not one instance of being conquered (or even attacked) by any enemies or neighbors. Such things didn't begin to happen again until the kingdom was split, and the first such event was the one we read yesterday: the attack by Shishak, king of Egypt. Thus, the complaint raised by Ethan in the Psalm (89:38-52) and the plea for mercy that follows is most likely referring to this event. Thus, it is placed here during the reign of Rehoboam in Judah (the southern kingdom) at that time.

July 11, NT
Galatians 4:21-5:12
Freedom vs. Slavery (The Sarah vs. Hagar Analogy)

After contrasting Jewish works vs. grace by faith, Paul next uses the analogy of "slave vs. free" to describe the life of faith in Jesus. Paul uses the analogy of the first two sons (biologically) of Abraham: Ishmael, born to Hagar the servant, and Isaac, born to Abraham's wife Sarah (Galatians 4:22-26, 4:28-31) as a way of explaining how the Law effectively enslaves those who chose the way of circumcision (that is, become Jews as a way of becoming Christian) (5:2-6). Paul goes as far as to say that becoming circumcised is of no value at all, because becoming Jewish would require adherence to the whole Law, *and thus becoming alienated from Christ* (5:3-4).

Paul chastises the Galatians again, but more gently this time, by reminding them that the persuasion to become Jewish first does NOT come from the One who is calling them to faith (5:7), and adding the question that if he was still preaching circumcision, why then is he being persecuted? (5:11)

July 12, OT
1 Kings 14:29-31; 2 Chronicles 12:15-16; 1 Kings 15:1-8; 2 Chronicles 13:1-20
The Ends of Rehoboam, His Successor, and Jeroboam

http://www.vtaide.com/gleanings/Kings-of-Israel/kings.html

After two kings (David and Solomon) whose reign lasted about 40 years each, the end of Rehoboam came after just 18 years (1 Kings 15:1). He was succeeded by his son Abijah, whose reign was an even briefer 3-year period (2 Chron 13:2). References are made in multiple places in today's OT reading to extra-Biblical books that have been lost to antiquity. Fortunately, we still have the inspired works that we now know as the books of Kings and Chronicles to view this important history.

In the first two parts of today's OT reading, it is noted that Rehoboam and Jeroboam were continually at war during Rehoboam's reign. So after he died, his son Abijah likewise went to war against the Northern Kingdom. Like all of the kings of Israel and most of the other kings of Judah, Abijah's brief biography begins with a reference to the fact that he committed "all of the sins his father had done before him," (1 Kings 15:3), but for the sake of David's royal line, God "gave him a lamp" in Jerusalem to make Judah strong (15:4). The details of Abijah's death are not given, but during his brief reign he made a valiant attempt at reuniting the kingdoms (2 Chron 13:3-12), which fell on deaf ears. While Abijah was giving this speech, Jeroboam sent troops behind Abijah's army to ambush them (13:13) but Abijah's army cried out to the Lord, which not only resulted in their protection, but they were able to rout Jeroboam's army which was twice the size of Abijah's (13:14-18).

Abijah's next act was the pursuit of Jeroboam after the larger battle, and the taking of 3 cities in Ephriam, the southernmost part of the Northern Kingdom. It is noted there that Jeroboam never fully regained his throne during the life of Abijah, and the Lord struck Jeroboam down (13:19-20, 2 years later).

July 12, NT
Galatians 5:13-6:18
Life By the Spirit, Conclusion of Paul's Letter to the Galatians

Paul brings his first Epistle to a close by summing up the contrast that dominated the letter: that life in the Spirit is to faith in Christ as life "in the flesh" is to the circumcision. Key verses in this conclusion are: the repeat of Jesus' command to "love your neighbor as yourself" (Galatians 5:14) and the admonition that if you are "led by the spirit," you are not under the law (5:18).

Paul then lists the sins that make up the "acts of the flesh" (5:19-21). Some like to argue that the Old Testament law no longer applies. Some atheists use the "sexual morality" laws, found mainly in Leviticus, to justify their mockery of Christian moral values simply because the Old Testament version of these laws carries archaic punishments such as stoning. They don't realize that Jesus commuted the sentences for sinners who place their trust in Him for their salvation and repent of those sins, including those listed here by Paul. They're still as sinful as before, but that's not the issue anymore; the repentance and forgiveness of the sinner is. Besides, Paul goes on to contrast these sinful behaviors with the "fruits of the Spirit" (5:22-25), "against which there is no law".

Paul concludes the letter by putting it all together: he describes what it truly means to do good to one another (6:1-10), and using the term "a new creation" for the first time to describe what it means to be a Christian, repeating his admonition that one does not first have to become Jewish to become a Christian.

July 13, OT
2 Chronicles 13:21-14:1a; 1 Kings 15:9-11; 2 Chronicles 14:1b-7; 1 Kings 14:19-20; 1 Kings 15:12-15; 2 Chronicles 14:8-15:19
Good King Asa

Abijah reigned only 3 years in Jerusalem, but during that time he led the most successful battle against the Northern Kingdom (in yesterday's reading), married 14 wives and fathered 22 sons and 16 daughters (2 Chron 13:21). After yet another reference to an extra-Biblical history book, we next learn of one such son, Asa (14:1) who succeeded Abijah when he died. It is noted that this took place in the 20th year of Jeroboam (1 Kings 15:9).

Asa's reign as king in Judah is marked by two unique things: it lasted 41 years, the first to exceed 40 years since David and Solomon (9:10) and the notation that he did what was *right* in the eyes of the Lord (9:11), the first king of Judah for which this was true. II Chronicles goes into more detail about this, describing the 10 first years of peace enjoyed by Judah while Asa removed foreign altars and sparked a revival for the one true God (2 Chron 14:1b-7). In 1 Kings, the end of Jeroboam's reign in the North is recorded, marked at 22 years, and succeeded by his son Nadab (1 Kings 14:19-20) who, after just 2 years, would be murdered by his brother Baasha (15:12-15, see also tomorrow's reading). A proper understanding of 1 Kings 15:12, reading these sections in this sequence, can be made by substituting the name Asa where it begins "he" or "him". In some translations, the reference in that verse to "male prostitutes" or "temple prostitutes" is worded as "sodomites," meaning practitioners of homosexuality.

Just as was the case in yesterday's OT reading, today's reading ends with a more detailed look at a large portion of Asa's reign as king in 2 Chronicles, expanding on the brief section in 1 Kings 15. After 10 years of peace, Judah was attacked by Ethiopians (2 Chron 14:9) but after a sincere prayer by Asa (14:11), the Ethiopians were routed by the armies of Judah and Benjamin (14:12-15). A prophet named Azariah came to Asa after this success with both words of encouragement and words of warning from God (15:1-7), which then prompted Asa to enact numerous reforms, going even further than he had before the Ethiopian attack (15:8-18). After this, Judah once again enjoyed peace until Asa's 35th year (15:19).

July 13, NT
James 1:1-27
Becoming a Doer, Not Just a Believer

On July 7, we read the beginning of what is believed to be the first epistle, and completed that letter (Paul's Letter to the Galatians) yesterday. The next epistle to be written was not only written by someone else, but is believed to have been written a very short time after Paul wrote his first letter. So short of a time, in fact, that the two epistles could potentially be thought of as concurrent.

Like Paul's first epistle, the Epistle of James is placed here in this chronology based on when it was written, and not the history it contains. In this case, there are three key differences between the Epistle of James and Paul's letter to the Galatians: this Epistle was not addressed to a specific group or church (though we know it was sent to Jewish Christians, James 1:1), it contains no history to speak of at all (whereas Paul's letter contained an update regarding the Council of Jerusalem), and of course, it was written by someone other than Paul.

Depending on the denomination to which you belong, there is some debate as to the writer of the Epistle of James. At least part of the debate stems from the fact that the oldest manuscripts of this letter date from the late 3rd century, making it among the newest/youngest manuscripts used in the New Testament. But, the debate about later manuscripts aside, the main debate is about *which* James is the writer, and there are 3 men with that name that are potential candidates. If the writer was James the Apostle who was martyred in Acts 12:2 (read on June 30), then *this* would have been the first Epistle written, and our reading of it would have begun then. If the writer was James the Less, another Apostle, or (as Catholics suggest) a follower of a later James, the date of this writing would be impossible to know. But back on July 5, we read about the actions of James, the brother of Jesus at the Council of Jerusalem. There, among other things, he drafted a letter to Gentile believers in Antioch (Acts 15:30-35) that very closely matches the style of the writing here. Thus, it is believed that James the brother of Jesus penned this letter to Jewish believers as a sort of followup to the earlier effort.

Though the same 5 chapters in length as Paul's letter to the Galatians, the letter is, overall, slightly shorter, and will be covered over 5 days' time. The emphasis in this first chapter is on the need to put one's faith into *practice*, using the example of perseverance during life's trials and temptations. The key verse is 1:22 where James tells his audience to not merely *listen* to the Word but to *do* what it says. This passage is key to understanding and correctly interpreting a key verse in tomorrow's NT reading.

July 14, OT
1 Kings 15:33-34; 1 Kings 15:16; 1 Kings 15:32; 1 Kings 15:17-22; 2 Chronicles 16:1-10; 1 Kings 16:1-33
Asa vs. Baasha; From Baasha to Ahab

Nadab's successor in the North was Baasha, also son of Jeroboam, another in the line of kings of the North who "did evil in the eyes of the Lord" (1 Kings 15:33-34, 15:16, 15:32), and who was at war with Asa throughout his entire reign. Among the acts of war committed by by Baasha was, essentially, a blockade (15:17). Asa countered the blockade by forming an alliance with Ben-Hadad, king of Syria (15:18-22), who succeeded in breaking it (2 Chronicles 16:1-6).

But, for all the good done by Asa, this one thing was noted to not be that way. Specifically, Asa's actions in calling upon king Ben-Hadad were called out by a seer named Hanani because of Asa's *lack* of reliance on the Lord, comparing it to the earlier Ethiopian war where Asa *did* call upon God (2 Chron 16:7-9). Asa's response was even worse, as he imprisoned Hanani and oppressed his people (16:10).

After Baasha, the kings of the Northern Kingdom are given a few verses apiece for the brief reigns of Elah, son of Baasha (1 Kings 16:6-9), Zimri who murdered Elah after just 2 years, and then reigned for only a week himself (16:10-15), Omri who took over after Zimri's suicide (16:16-28), and finally, the king noted for being the worst of them all, Ahab (16:29-33), who did "more to arouse the anger of the Lord than any king of Israel before or since" (16:33).

July 14, NT
James 2:1-26
Faith Without Works is Dead

The Epistle of James is sometimes referred to as the "Proverbs of the New Testament" because of his emphasis on the practical application of the faith, or in other words, "true religion". In his first chapter (yesterday), he wrote of being "doers" of the word, not merely believers. In this second chapter, he starts by railing against the kind of country-club exclusivity found, unfortunately, in so many churches today (James 2:1-13). This is on the heels of his statement near the end of chapter 1 (1:26-27, yesterday) where he identified what true religion is.

But all this is NOT to say that James is trying to preach some form of works-based theology. The Catholic Church, in particular, likes to use the best-known verse in James, 2:26, to justify their position in which faith alone is NOT sufficient to be saved, contradicting Paul in Ephesians chapter 3 (to be read on October 7). But, this stems from a misinterpretation (and a partial quote) of the well-known verse. In the passage leading up to it, James emphasises the value of the faith of Abraham as an example of one whose faith was *completed* by his deeds. In other words, Abraham's deeds flowed FROM his faith because his faith was NOT dead.

One also has to remember James' audience in correctly interpreting this verse. James' audience was *already-saved believers* (the fact that they were Jewish converts is beside the point), so James' emphasis on the "works of the faith" was for the benefit of those who already believed. A lot of megachurches and televangelists would do well to learn this important lesson.

July 15, OT
1 Kings 15:23-24; 2 Chronicles 16:11-14; 1 Kings 22:41-46; 2 Chronicles 20:31-34; 2 Chronicles 17:1-18:1; 1 Kings 16:34
The Reign of Jehoshaphat

While all the chaos and corruption was going on in the Northern Kingdom from Baasha up to Ahab, only two kings in Judah overlapped their reigns: Asa and Jehoshaphat. All but the very last years of Asa have already been chronicled (pardon the pun), and his story as the first "good" king of the Southern Kingdom comes to an end in the first 2 parts of today's reading (1 Kings 15:23-24, 2 Chron 16:11-14). Both accounts give an extra detail about Asa's death, being the result of some sort of infection in his feet. In the 2 Chronicles account, it is further noted that he did NOT seek help from the Lord, but relied solely on physicians, thus further reinforcing the idea that Asa fell away from the Lord in his old age.

The accession of Jehoshaphat to the throne in Judah marks the second consecutive king listed as "good" in the list (1 Kings 22:43) but that very verse contains what some believe is also a blatant contradiction. Both there and in the recap of the reign of Jehoshaphat at the end of his life (2 Chron 20:31-33), it is mentioned that Jehoshaphat *failed* to take down the "high places," and that the people still burned incense and offered sacrifices. But jumping back to 2 Chronicles 17, which gives a much more detailed account of the life of Jehoshaphat, it says that he *did* remove the high places and Asherah poles from Judah (2 Chron 17:6). How do we reconcile this?

One classic commentary suggests that a Hebrew copying mistake resulted in dropping the word "not" from 2 Chronicles 17:6, which would make each account read the same, particularly considering the differences between two accounts *in the same book* by the same writer. But another commentary (Benson) suggests something else: that Jehoshaphat made a valiant attempt at removing the "high places" where the people worshipped pagan gods, and perhaps succeeded in taking down many of them (including the "Asherah poles") but failed to win over the *hearts* of the people, who largely continued their pagan worship practices despite losing the place of worship they used. Benson bases this mostly on a single verse (2 Chron 20:33) at the end of Jehoshaphat's reign, where it is the *hearts* of the people that he failed at, not the actual removal of the high places.

Despite this failure, Jehoshaphat is universally listed as having the Lord with him because he did what was right in His sight. There was one more error he made, though, mentioned near the end of the reading, where it states that he allied himself with Ahab in the North by marrying into the evil king's family (2 Chron 18:1). More about that alliance is found in future readings.

July 15, NT
James 3:1-18
Taming the Restless Evil

James continues his preaching of wisdom in a section commonly subtitled "Taming the Tongue." The tongue, he explains, though a small part of the body, has a huge influence (James 3:3-6). He likens the taming of various animals and birds to our taming of the tongue (3:7) and compares the tongue to a "restless evil" that cannot be tamed (3:8).

But lest anyone think that Jesus' brother is overemphasizing the role of a person's deeds, he quickly goes into a description of what it means to have earthly wisdom vs. Godly wisdom (3:13-18), which explains how a person's deeds stem *from* the type of wisdom a person has.

July 16, OT
1 Kings 17:1-19:21
The Coming of Elijah

http://www.vtaide.com/gleanings/Kings-of-Israel/kings.html

The Hebrew Bible, which we know today as the Old Testament (though the books are in a different sequence), was divided into 3 major sections: the Torah, the Prophets, and the Writings. In the Prophets section, you will not only find the major prophets like Isaiah, Jeremiah, and Ezekiel (Daniel is in the "Writings") and the 12 "minor" prophets, but also the "historical" books of Joshua, Judges, Samuel, and Kings. A big part of the reason for this is the subject of today's OT reading: a prophet of such great importance (despite not having a "book" of his own) that he is prophesied to return "before the great and terrible day of the Lord" in the final book of the OT (Malachi 3:19), is mentioned by Jesus multiple times in the three synoptic Gospels, was likened to John the Baptist in the Gospel of John, and appears in the Transfiguration, also in the three synoptic Gospels (as well as Peter's account of the event in his second Epistle). This prophet, along with Moses, (though neither is mentioned by name) is prophesied to return during The Tribulation as one of the "two witnesses" (Revelation 11:1-14) preaching in Jerusalem. This prophet is named Elijah.

The Bible jumps right in to the story of Elijah without any biographical data, other than that he was a "Tishbite" from Gilead (1 Kings 17:1), where he prophesies a multi-year drought to Ahab, the evil king of the North. After this announcement, the Lord protected Elijah (17:2-6), even having a raven bring Elijah food. During the drought, Elijah had an encounter with a poor widow and her son (17:7-24), promising them that the Lord would provide for them all the way through the drought.

In the third year of the drought (18:1), King Ahab (still upset with Elijah about the drought prophecy) sent his palace administrator Obadiah on a mission to find green grass for the horses. Obadiah was different: he was a devout believer in the Lord, despite working for Ahab (18:3-6). Elijah and Obadiah met while Obadiah was carrying out his mission, where Elijah wanted Obadiah to announce his arrival to Ahab (18:7-14). Obadiah, out of fear, declined Elijah's request for fear of being exposed as a believer to Ahab, but Elijah reassured him that it was Elijah who was going to be presented before the king (18:15). This was all a lead-up to one of the most dramatic miracles of the Old Testament, called Elijah's challenge to the Baal-worshipers of Mount Carmel (18:16-45). Though his challenge was successful, and God sent fire from heaven to consume the sacrifice, Elijah became distraught over not convincing *everyone*, and in particular, earning the wrath of the king and his wife Jezebel (19:1-9), and so he fled to the distant town of Horeb.

But, the Lord was having none of this. After communicating with Elijah using just a whisper (19:12) to help him overcome his fears, the Lord gave Elijah his next, great assignment: the anointing of the next prophet in Israel, Elisha (19:14-21).

July 16, NT
James 4:1-5:6
The Ten Commandments of the New Testament

There is a song we sing from time to time in our church called "Our Great God," written by Fernando Ortega. In the last part of the second verse, we sing "Our cold and ruthless enemy, His pleasure is our harm; Rise up, oh, Lord and he will flee, Before our sovereign God." The line often elicits actual cheering from enthusiastic members of our congregation - and why not? It's a beautiful application (and paraphrase) of James 4:7b, a centerpiece of a part of James' Epistle sometimes called the Ten Commandments of the New Testament.

After six verses in which James explains how conflicts can be conquered (by the proper application of the Commandment to "not covet"), he launches into his typically pithy manner of listing God's "new" Commandments. They are (quoted portions from the NIV):

1. Submit yourselves, then, to God (4:7a)
2. Resist the devil, and he will flee from you (4:7b)
3. Come near to God and He will come near to you (4:8a)
4. Wash your hands… ("get clean")(4:8b)
5. Purify your hearts… ("get sober") (4:8c)
6. Grieve, mourn, and wail... ("get serious") (4:9)
7. Humble yourselves before the Lord (4:10)
8. Do not slander one another (4:11)
9. There is only one lawgiver and judge (4:11-12)
10. Arrogant boasting is evil (4:13-17)

At the other end is James' commentary on those who have hoarded their wealth instead of sharing it (5:1-6). This, like several similar passages, isn't a condemnation of becoming rich; rather, it is a condemnation of what some rich people do (or fail to do) with their wealth, because of their mindset.

July 17, OT
Psalm 104:1-35; Psalm 114:1-8; Psalm 115:1-18; 1 Kings 20:1-43
Obeying The Lord *Completely*

Back on April 19, we read about Saul, the first king of Israel, and how he and the Israelites would incur the wrath of God by obeying the Lord only *partially*. Ahab, ruler of the northern kingdom of Israel, ruling from Samaria, is listed in several places as the *most* evil king of them all. Yet even Ahab partially obeyed the Lord, as we read today in 1 Kings. But, of course, what the Lord calls for is our *complete* obedience, not partial.

Following the incident at Mount Carmel, where Elijah called down fire from the Lord to prove His existence (read yesterday), 3 Psalms were written that sing the Lord's praises. Despite Elijah's melancholy over not winning over *everyone's* hearts, it is quite obvious from these joyous songs of praise that he won over *some* of their hearts.

Then, after 3 chapters in 1 Kings in which the focus was mainly on Elijah, we read of an incident involving Ahab and the king of Aram Damascus (aka Syria), Ben-Hadad (who we first read about on July 14). Ahab first appeases Ben-Hadad's messengers when they come to threaten him (1 Kings 20:1-4). But when those messengers return a second time with more demands (20:5), Ahab consults with the elders and tells the messengers that he refuses the new demands (20:6-9). After engaging in more saber-rattling (20:10-11), Ben-Hadad launches the threatened attack (20:12). Here is where the title of today's OT reading comes in, though: as the attack was being launched, a prophet (not named) of the Lord tells Ahab how he can defeat this enemy, and gives exact instructions for how to do it (20:13-21), which Ahab at first carried out and won a great victory. The prophet then warned of another attack by the same king (20:22) which happened as predicted (20:23-30), and Israel won an even greater victory. But when the king of Aram came offering terms of surrender to Ahab, Ahab allowed Ben-Hadad to live, accepting a treaty with the enemy king, instead of finishing the job he was given by the Lord (20:31-34). Another unnamed prophet then approaches Ahab, condemning the king for setting "a man free that [the Lord] had determined should die." (20:42a) In other words, Ahab's first act of obedience to the Lord was only a *partial* act, and he and his kingdom were going to be punished for it (20:42b).

July 17, NT
James 5:7-20
Patience Is Hope Rooted in Christ

At the beginning of James' Epistle, he wrote about perseverance in the face of life's trials and temptations (July 13). For the next 3 chapters, James packed a lot of wisdom in a relatively short letter about the practical application of the faith, including verses that have been nicknamed the "New Testament Proverbs" and even the "Ten Commandments of the New Testament." Here, James wraps things up by tying it all together, first using the analogy of a farmer waiting for his crop to grow (James 5:7), and leading to how unwavering faith in God was shown by the prophets and by Job (5:10-11) and how they were thus rewarded.

James' conclusion speaks of the power of prayer, and ties this to patience again. He makes reference to Elijah and his prayer for drought (5:17) and Elijah's later prayer that it would rain and nourish the crops again (5:18), both analogies bookended by how prayers for a person who is sick can make them well again.

July 18, OT
1 Kings 21:1-29; 1 Kings 22:1-35; 2 Chronicles 18:2-34; 1 Kings 22:51-53
The Evil of Jezebel; The End of Ahab

http://www.vtaide.com/gleanings/Kings-of-Israel/kings.html

It is said repeatedly, including a verse in today's reading (1 Kings 21:25), that Ahab not only did evil in the eyes of the Lord, but that he was the *most* evil king of Israel. That same verse also explains at least part of the reason why this was so: it mentions there that he was goaded into doing much of his evil deeds by his wife, Jezebel. Before that verse, we read the story of "Naboth's Vineyard" (21:1-16) where a combination of Ahab's greed and cowardice and Jezebel's evil was used to murder a man for his property. Then, in a scene strongly reminiscent of Nathan's confrontation of David (read on May 9), Elijah makes his next appearance, and condemns his actions and prophecies doom on the king and his offspring (21:17-22) and even promises that the royal couple will be "devoured by dogs" (21:23-24) like the rest of Ahab's followers. Ahab didn't make a full contrition like David did, but he did put on sackcloth and humble himself, causing the Lord to then hold off on the disaster that was promised, vowing instead that it would be inflicted on Ahab's son (21:27-29).

Following this, in the passages from 1 Kings 22 and 2 Chronicles 18 (including the only mention of Ahab in the Chronicles), another prophet makes an appearance as Ahab consults his southern rival Jehoshaphat, king of Judah. Jehoshaphat agrees to unite with Ahab in battle, but insists on first consulting the Lord (22:5). Ahab consults his prophets, and they recommend going forward with the attack, but Jehoshaphat sees through this and asks whether or not there is any prophet of the Lord remaining in Israel (22:6-7). Ahab introduces Jehoshaphat to a prophet named Micaiah, but also explains his reluctance to do so: Micaiah never prophesies anything good about him. Nevertheless, Micaiah is summoned, and despite being constantly prodded into agreeing with Ahab's "prophets," he delivers a cryptic prophecy of doom (22:9-28). It even prompted Ahab to make a sarcastic remark (22:18), and one of Ahab's men even slapped Macaiah's face over it (22:24). Micaiah was then thrown into prison (22:26-27) and Ahab decided to go to war anyway.

But so came the end of Ahab, when he still refused to listen to the Lord. He even tried a strategy in which he was disguised while Jehoshaphat was in his regal attire so that the enemy army would attack the king of Judah instead of himself. It didn't work, Ahab was later struck and wounded, and bled out in his chariot and died (22:29-35). All of this is also told in 2 Chronicles 18. We then read about the brief reign of Ahab's son Ahaziah at the end of the first book of the Kings.

July 18, NT
Acts 16:11-24
The Baptism of Lydia; Paul and Silas Imprisoned in Philippi (part one)

When we were last in Acts (July 6), Paul received a vision to go to Macedonia, and thus began the Second Missionary Journey. He wrote his letter to the Galatians en route, while James wrote from Jerusalem. Now in Acts again, Luke writes in the first person of their voyage to their first stop, the city of Philippi, officially Paul's first visit to Europe. Paul, along with Silas, Timothy, and Luke, prayed with a women's group (Acts 16:13), and even baptized one of their members, a woman named Lydia (16:14-15), with whom they stayed for a time afterwards.

During their time in Philippi, they met a slave girl who was a fortune teller. The girl would repeatedly "cry out" the message that "these men" were servants of the "most high God" (16:16-17). To the Jews in the area, they would have understood her message about the "Most High God" in terms of the one True God of the Bible. But to the pagans who dominated Philippi of that day, whose gods include many with the title "most high" or "highest," the message is ambiguous - and for Paul and his men, even potentially dangerous. Paul also recognized that this girl's profession and her message were at odds with each other, and drove the spirit from her (16:18). But the exorcism had the consequence of robbing the girl's masters of their fortune-telling profits, and so they had Paul and Silas arrested, beaten, and thrown in prison (16:19-24).

July 19, OT
1 Kings 22:36-40; 2 Chronicles 19:1-11; 2 Kings 1:1; 2 Chronicles 20:1-30; Psalm 46:1-11; Psalm 47:1-9; Psalm 48:1-14
Jehoshaphat Defeats Moab and Ammon

Today's OT reading begins with the immediate aftermath of the death of Ahab, when they had to wash his blood out of the chariot (1 Kings 22:38), and dogs licked it in fulfillment of prophecy. It is then mentioned again that Ahaziah, son of Ahab, became king.

In the southern kingdom, Jehoshaphat returns home and endures criticism for going to war alongside the evil king of the north (2 Chron 19:1-3). But, this is tempered by the fact that Jehoshaphat was continuously trying to do what was *right* by the Lord, including removal of the Asherah Poles (see reading for July 15). The king even went so far as to appoint judges (in the same manner as the Judges before the kingdom) to oversee the enforcement of the law of the Lord (19:4-11) to show his devotion to the Lord to his people, leading a mini-revival.

Despite Ahaziah's accession in the north, the power vacuum left after Ahab's death emboldened the Moabites and Ammonites (2 Kings 1:1), and they came to war against Israel. Coming, as they did, from Edom, they had to come up from the south, and thus, began by attacking Jehoshaphat in the southern kingdom. The passage from 2 Chronicles 20 records the events of this war, and makes a huge contrast with the way things were done under Ahab in the north. Jehoshaphat proclaimed a fast throughout Judah (2 Chron 20:3), prayed publicly and fervently (20:5-12), listened to *real* prophets of the Lord (20:13-17), and conducted open public worship (20:18-19). This led to a successful campaign against the invading armies, all the while singing the Lord's praises (20:20-28). The 3 Psalms numbered 46, 47, and 48 are believed to have been written at around this time, all of which sing the praises of the Lord in the same manner.

July 19, NT
Acts 16:25-40
Paul and Silas Imprisoned in Philippi (part two)

The Apostles (including Paul) were jailed fairly often, but their prison time was often cut short. Such was the case in the latest incident as Paul and Silas were the beneficiaries of an earthquake that broke open the Philippian jail while they were praying and singing hymns (Acts 16:25-26). The despondent prison keeper was about to commit suicide over the incident when Paul intervened (16:27-28). This obviously was the impetus to cause the jailer to ask the most important question of his life: "what must I do to be saved?" (16:29-30). Paul's answer is one of his best-known quotes: "Believe in the Lord Jesus and you will be saved, you and your household" (16:31). The new Christian and his family were all saved that day, and he treated Paul's and Silas' wounds and fed them (16:33-34).

The next morning, the city magistrates sought to release Paul and Silas silently, but Paul countered by exposing the fact that he was a Roman citizen (16:35-39) which scared the city officials into providing an escort out of the city. Paul and his group then stopped one more time at the home of Lydia before taking leave of Philippi (16:40). This wouldn't be Paul's last visit to the city.

July 20, OT
Psalm 49:1-20; Psalm 83:1-18; Psalm 91:1-16; 1 Kings 22:47-49; 2 Chronicles 20:35-37; 2 Kings 1:2-18; 2 Kings 3:1-3
The Brief Reign and End of Ahaziah

The mini-revival sparked by Jehoshaphat, king of Judah led to some great Psalm-writing, as shown in the 3 Psalms that start today's OT reading. Like yesterday's Psalms, they all are praise songs, one of which specifically mentions the events in yesterday's reading about the war against Moab.

The brief narrative in 1 Kings (the next-to-last time that we read anything from the first scroll) relates the fact that Edom was left without a king after the war, and that Jehoshaphat had a fleet of ships built that were wrecked, and that Ahaziah attempted to send help that Jehoshaphat refused. The extremely small amount of detail here is confusing unless you then read the section in 2 Chronicles 20, which uses a passage of the same length (3 verses) to relate the details: Jehoshaphat made an alliance with Ahaziah (2 Chron 20:35) to build the fleet, but a prophet came to Jehoshaphat warning that this alliance was evil, and that the fleet would be destroyed (20:36-37), which they were. It can then be presumed that it was Ahaziah's offer to "let my men sail with yours" that was refused in 1 Kings 22.

Two days ago (July 18), we read about an incident called "Naboth's Vineyard," in which Elijah prophesies doom on the family of Ahab. He made a cryptic reference to an "upper room" that would be part of his fate. Elijah was told, by the Lord, that Ahab's doom would be brought upon his son and not on Ahab because of Ahab's response in humbling himself after Elijah's confrontation. It is in this reading in the 2nd Book of the Kings (the second scroll of what was originally a single "book") that we learn of the fulfillment of both prophecies. Ahaziah is injured falling through a lattice in his "upper room," and calls upon "the god of Ekron" to determine if he's going to recover from this injury (2 Kings 1:2). But Elijah intercepts the message and repeats his earlier prophecy, which is then brought to the king of Israel just before he dies (1:3-17).

Because Ahaziah had no sons, his successor was his brother Joram (1:18, 3:1-3).

July 20, NT
Acts 17:1-15
The Second Missionary Journey Continues: A Tale of Two Cities

At each stop of his missionary journeys, Paul and his travel mates would stop first at the local synagogue, to preach the Gospel to Jews living in those areas. Thus, after departing Philippi, the missionaries' next stop was Thessalonica (Acts 17:1). At first, there were converts, including some Gentiles in the area (17:4). But, some Jews didn't take to the Gospel as well, forming a mob, starting a riot, and even dragging the man with whom they were staying (Jason) before the city council (17:5-8). Jason and some others had to post bail to get out of this situation, and Paul and Silas and their companions were forced to leave (17:9-10).

The contrast between the two cities becomes obvious when they arrive at the next destination, Berea. If the city name sounds familiar to you, it is because of what the Bereans did that many Thessalonians did not. They took to Paul's message with enthusiasm, and carefully studied scriptures (the Old Testament) and compared it to the Gospel to verify its Truth (17:11-12). Today, when you hear of a "Berean Baptist Church" or hear of a Bible study group called "Bereans," know that it comes from this event in Paul's Second Missionary Journey.

July 21, OT
2 Kings 2:1-25; 2 Kings 3:4-27; 1 Kings 22:50; 2 Chronicles 21:1-3
Chariots of Fire

The 1981 movie about 2 athletes competing in the 1924 Olympics took its title from the climax of the first segment of today's OT reading. In 2 Kings chapter 2, Elijah and his successor Elisha went to several places in and around the kingdom. Each time, Elisha was asked to stay behind while Elijah proceeded to the next destination, and each time Elisha refused, being fully aware that Elijah was going to be "taken from him" that day (2 Kings 2:3, 2:5). On the last of those, Elijah miraculously parted the waters of the Jordan river, allowing them to cross on dry land (2:7). Once across, Elisha requests a "double portion of [Elijah's] spirit" when he is to be taken (2:9). Elijah tells him that if he actually witnesses the taking, he will receive the request. Shortly afterward, a chariot of fire and a "flaming horse" swoop down and take Elijah to heaven, alive (2:10-12). Proving that Elisha inherited the requested double portion of spirit, he then repeated Elijah's earlier miracle of parting the waters of the Jordan (2:13-15).

The remainder of the reading shows several events surrounding the new chief prophet of Israel, Elisha. He performs more miracles, proves that his mentor has truly left earth (i.e. not just moved to a new location), and acted in the same role as Elijah and Micaiah had earlier with Ahab regarding an attack by Moab. Because the king (Jehoshaphat) listened whereas Ahab did not, the outcome of the attack was quite different this time (3:24-27).

After this, we read of the death of Jehoshaphat and the accession of his son, Jehoram.

July 21, NT
Acts 17:16-34
The Second Missionary Journey: Altar to an Unknown God

One of Paul's most famous speeches on any of his Missionary Journeys happened when he arrived in Athens, ahead of Timothy and Silas, after their time in Berea. Paul found Athens to be full of idols (Acts 17:16) but he nevertheless did his usual routine in preaching in local Synagogues. The great speech he gives, starting in verse 22, is in response to questions about Jesus, the Resurrection, and the Athenian perception that he was preaching about a "foreign God" (17:17-21).

Paul's speech starts with this observation: that he had found an altar bearing the inscription "to an unknown god" (17:23). He uses this observation, of the very thing the Athenian's were "ignorant of" yet "worshipped" as the basis for explaining who God really is (17:24-31). The main thrust of the speech is that the real God isn't one made by human hands, but rather, the exact opposite: since the real God, who we know by way of His son, is the creator, then we are therefore His offspring. He points out that God commands us to repent as a means of drawing closer to Him.

Some sneered at Paul's message, but others accepted it, and asked him to talk more on the subject (17:32-34).

July 22, OT
2 Kings 8:16-25; 2 Chronicles 21:4-20; 2 Chronicles 22:1-6; 2 Kings 8:26-29
Jehoram and Ahaziah of Judah

http://www.vtaide.com/gleanings/Kings-of-Israel/kings.html

If you have been paying attention to the names of kings in the last three days' Old Testament readings and/or if you look at the charts here and on July 18, you will notice that there are kings with both the names Jehoram and Ahaziah listed on both the Judah (southern kingdom) side as well as the Israel (northern kingdom) side. The confusion that can sometimes come from a straight reading (particularly KJV) of the Books of the Kings is made all the worse by the fact that the Jehoram from Judah reigned at the same as the Jehoram from Israel. Also note that where Ahaziah was Jehoram's successor in the south, Ahaziah was Jehoram's *predecessor* in the north. To help the reader, this chronology includes these charts which also note the other, most helpful thing: the "AKAs," or "also known as" markers. Although this chronology refers to Ahaziah in both the north and south with the same spelling and name, Jehoram is referred to as Joram in the north, and Jehoram in the south. Today's OT reading is the brief account of the relatively brief reigns of Jehoram and Ahaziah, both in the southern kingdom of Judah.

The most notable thing about each account is the detail about both Jehoram (2 Kings 8:18) and his *youngest* son (2 Chron 22:1) Ahaziah (22:3-4, 2 Kings 8:27) that they each "did evil in the sight of the Lord," thus breaking the long period of "good" kings of Judah (Asa, Jehoshaphat) that came before them.

July 22, NT
Acts 18:1-23
Paul in Corinth; Conclusion of the Second Missionary Journey

Paul's efforts at evangelization met with varying degrees of success. In some places, he met with little or no opposition to his message. In others, such as in Corinth, after spending time there working as a tentmaker, Paul started running into considerable resistance in the Synagogues (Acts 18:3-6), even becoming abusive to him to the point where he essentially gave up on the Jews and took his message to the Gentiles, exclusively (18:6-8). He was talked out of this (18:9-11) and made the second-longest stay in one location on any of his missionary journeys.

While still in Corinth, the Jews tried another tactic against Paul in much the same manner as Jesus was attacked before His crucifixion: they tried to get Paul in trouble with the secular authorities (18:12-13). The proconsul, Gallio, rejected the crowd's attempt (18:14-16), so the crowd took out their anger on the Synagogue leader without any retribution from the proconsul (18:17). The remainder of today's reading details Paul's voyage home to Jerusalem, back through the territory he had earlier visited on his First Missionary Journey (18:18-23). Details of replies to this Corinthian visit can be found in his letter to them, starting on July 31.

July 23, OT
2 Kings 9:1-37; 2 Chronicles 22:7-9
The End of Ahaziah in Judah and Joram in Israel

Yesterday's OT reading concerned itself with Jehoram and Ahaziah, both of Judah. Although we were told about Jehoram's death, Ahaziah's story yesterday ended as he joined Joram of Israel in battle. Today's reading doesn't pick up immediately where that one left off, but with a kind of "meanwhile."

Elisha, the new prophet of the Lord in Israel, sends one of his fellow prophets to anoint Jehu, an army captain, to be the new king of Israel (2 Kings 9:1-6) and gives him this task: to assassinate Joram, king of Israel, along with Joram's mother, Jezebel, the evil wife of former king Ahab (9:7-10). Jehu accepted the assignment (and the kingship) over the objections of some of his men who thought the prophet was a maniac (9:11), but when Jehu told them he was now the king, his men accepted this and cheered him (9:12-13).

Jehu (whose father's name was Jehoshaphat, but not to be confused with the former king of Judah, 9:14) went to the same site where Ahaziah of Judah was headed, to meet Joram. There, Jehu carried out the assassination of Joram (9:16-26), as commanded. Seizing an opportunity, he also mortally wounded Ahaziah, who later died in Migiddo (9:27-28). The new king of Israel then went to Jezreel to assassinate the Jezebel, former king Ahab's wife, in one of the more graphically violent passages in the books of the kings (9:29-37).

An important note for tomorrow's reading is found in the brief passage in 2 Chronicles, as Ahaziah, king of Judah, died without heirs.

July 23, NT
1 Thessalonians 1:1-2:12
Paul Writes Two Letters to the Thessalonians

On July 20, we read about Paul's visit to Thessalonica, an early (but not the first) stop on his Second Missionary Journey. A familiar pattern of events occurred there, when the Gentiles of the area became eager converts, while the Jews of the area showed more resistance. When Paul returned from the mission, one of his first acts was to pen two letters to the church he planted there. It would not be the last time he penned two letters to the same church back to back.

Paul spends the entire first chapter thanking the Thessalonians for their great show of faith (1 Thes 1:1-10), despite not reading about any of this in the Acts of the Apostles account, and then goes on to give his own account of it in the first 12 verses of the second chapter (2:1-12). The emphasis is on Paul's group's humility and work ethic, even in the face of strong opposition. The thought continues in tomorrow's reading, where we get to read exactly why we got little detail about the accomplishments in Thessalonica in Acts but read them now, here.

July 24, OT
2 Kings 10:1-27; 2 Kings 11:1-3; 2 Chronicles 22:10-12
Both Royal Families are Wiped Out

Jehu didn't stop after assassinating Jezebel. Though he was only told to do away with Joram the king and his mother Jezebel, Jehu had already assassinated Ahaziah, king of Judah. Now, in his zeal to do what he *thought* he had been told by the Lord, Jehu went on what amounts to a killing spree. Jehu's next target was the seventy sons of Ahab (2 Kings 10:1-8), which he explained to the people was the fulfillment of prophecy (10:9-10) before dispatching all of Ahab's remaining friends, chief men, and priests (10:11). Jehu then used some relatives of Ahaziah to track down the remainder of Ahab's family in Samaria before disposing of both (10:12-17).

Jehu used an elaborate deception to take out his next target. Posing as one who was a greater servant of Baal than Ahab, he gets all the Baal worshippers in the Northern kingdom to gather into one place, where he had them all killed by his officers (10:18-27), even destroying the "sacred stone" of Baal which, at the time of the writing of the Kings scrolls, was being used as a latrine. Baal worship wasn't completely wiped out, of course, as this sacred stone, a.k.a. "black moon rock" would become the object of worship by nomadic tribes living in the middle east to and through the time of Christ, and would be the spark that would later cause an Arab businessman named Mohammed to combine this with a twisted version of Judaism and form what is, today, the second largest religion in the world.

The brief passages in 2 Kings 11 and 2 Chronicles 22 describe the immediate aftermath of the killing of former king Ahaziah and most of his family in Judah: Athalia, mother of Ahaziah, finished the job that

King Jehu started, killing the rest of her son's family, and ruling as queen of Jehu for 6 years. One of Ahaziah's sons, Joash, was rescued from this carnage and was kept hidden while the young child's grandmother was on the throne in Jerusalem.

July 24, NT
1 Thessalonians 2:13-3:13
The Work of Timothy in Thessalonica

Luke, in writing the Acts, was very meticulous in his attention to detail, describing the events during Paul's missionary journeys and his eventual voyage to Rome. But for whatever reason, very little detail was given about Paul's visit to Thessalonica during the Second Missionary Journey. Very little, that is, except for an important detail we read on July 20: that Timothy and Silas remained in Thessalonica after Paul's departure. It was then Timothy who completed Paul's work there, and rejoining Paul some time later, gave those details to Paul who then recorded them in his letter to the Thessalonians. It may have even been the very impetus for writing them in the first place.

A key verse in this reading is the very first one: 1 Thessalonians 2:13 has Paul thanking the Thessalonians for receiving the word of God from them NOT as the words of men, but as the true words of God.

July 25, OT
2 Kings 11:4-21; 2 Chronicles 23:1-21
The Accession of Joash, King of Judah
http://www.vtaide.com/gleanings/Kings-of-Israel/kings.html

Judah's only female ruler, Athaliah, didn't get the typical byline reserved for kings that "did evil in the sight of the Lord" in either Judah or the Northern Kingdom of Israel. Nevertheless, it was she, and not Jehu of Israel, who was responsible for the slaughter of all but one member of her son's royal family. And in today's OT reading, two nearly identical accounts of what the Lord did about this evil are found, the first in 2 Kings 11, the other in 2 Chronicles 23.

Besides whatever other evil intent she had, Athaliah actually had a practical reason for taking over the kingdom following her son Ahaziah's death: Ahaziah's son was just a baby at that time. One could certainly argue that once he did get his chance to ascend to the throne, he was still far too young, being only 7 years old at the time (2 Kings 11:21). So it was when a priest named Jehoiada plotted with the armies of Judah to crown Joash, the true crown prince, king over the Southern Kingdom of Judah, and lure the new king's grandmother out of the temple and be killed by the sword, completing the transfer of power.

July 25, NT
1 Thessalonians 4:1-18
The Blessed Hope

Paul's First Letter to the Thessalonians contains mostly what one would call "salutation" for the first 3 chapters, just over half the length of the entire letter. It is here in the 4th chapter that Paul gets to the heart of the matter, with two sections of sound theological advice. The first, in verses 1-12, is sometimes called "how to live to please God". Like Paul's earlier letter to the Galatians and James' letter to new Christians, it must be emphasized here that Paul is writing to *believers* - people who have already heard and accepted the Gospel of Jesus Christ. By Gospel, of course, we are not referring to the written biographies of Jesus penned by Mark, Matthew, or Luke (though Mark may have written his Gospel by this time), but rather, the Good News of salvation by grace through faith. Paul emphasized in many places in his letters that one does not attain this salvation through good works; instead, the good works and ways of life he describes in 1 Thess 4:1-12 are our *response*, in gratitude, of the eternal life that God has given to us through His Son.

It is what follows this section filled with advice about how to "love one another" that brings the largest amount of attention to Paul's letter. These new believers were primarily Gentiles who did not know the Jewish law and custom, and know only what Paul and Timothy would have told them about Jesus. They would have, thus, most likely not even been aware of an afterlife and the ability to go to heaven with Jesus before Paul's Second Missionary Journey. Naturally, this would have caused some concern amongst them about the fate of those who were believers, though not in the Jewish faith, who have died. Paul answers this first by reassuring them that people who "fall asleep in Christ" will be with Him in heaven, crediting Jesus' Resurrection for this. Then, Paul turns to prophesy to inform the Thessalonians that there will be people who are still alive when Jesus comes again. These people won't be taken to heaven first, though, as those who died will be the first to meet Jesus "in the air," followed by the rest of those who are "caught up" in the air with the Lord. The words "caught up," as it translates directly from Greek to English, is rendered as "rapiemur" in Latin, from which we get the word RAPTURE.

The Rapture is actually mentioned in many other places besides this (though, oddly, *not* in Revelation), but only here are the words used that would actually translate that way. Dispensationalists, such as myself, view this verse as proof of not only a Rapture, a blessed hope for mankind as the End Times approach, but also of its timing: that it will occur *prior* to the Tribulation that will mark the last 7 years of man's rule of the Earth before Jesus comes in glory to reign on earth for a millennium. One thing's for sure, regardless of your stance on the timing of the rapture: Paul makes it clear that such an event *will* occur, and that there will be believers alive at the time of its occurrence. What a wonderful way of reassuring believers!

July 26, OT
2 Kings 12:1-16; 2 Chronicles 24:1-16; 2 Kings 10:28-36; 2 Kings 13:1-3; 2 Kings 13:22-23
Joash Repairs the Temple; The Death of Jehu; Jehoahaz of Israel

Joash, as a king, was a bit of a mixed bag. Certainly he started very young, and 2 Kings 12 lists him to be, at first, as a king that "did right in the eyes of the Lord," thus making him the 3rd king of Judah for whom this was true. But a qualifier in that very verse changes this picture, as 2 Kings 12:2 says he did right... "all the years Jehoiada instructed him". This issue comes up because we know that Jehoiada died before Joash did, at the end of the parallel passage in 2 Chronicles 24. He was an old man when he died, but his greatest achievement didn't come until Joash's 23rd year, when he took over the fundraising and contracting duties for the one positive thing for which Joash is known: the rebuilding of the Temple, which had fallen into disrepair after being abused by Baal worshippers, among others. Though he took this positive step, the book of the Kings also records that Joash did not remove the "high places," though it is not specified whether he failed in his attempt or never tried. (Further details in tomorrow's reading reinforce the fact that Joash is NOT be listed among the kings that "did good".)

Meanwhile, in the northern Kingdom, the Lord complimented Jehu on carrying out the executions of Ahab's family, and promised to keep Jehu's family on the throne through a fourth generation (2 Kings 10:30). But Jehu was a maverick king who had already gone well beyond what he was originally told to do, and has was not careful to follow the laws of the Lord. God's response was to allow enemy nations to pick away at Israel's territory including all of their land east of the river Jordan. Jehu died after 28 years on the throne and was succeeded by his son, Jehoahaz (10:35-36), who did evil in the sight of the Lord (13:2) and brought on oppression from neighboring king Hazael.

July 26, NT
1 Thessalonians 5:1-28
Children of the Light

Paul spends the last 28 verses of his first Letter to the Thessalonians giving instructions to the "children of the light," meaning, the Thessalonians. Paul's joy and delight with these people is more evident here than anywhere else, as the 5th chapter starts with a continuation of Paul's prophecy regarding the End Times.

Several often-quoted passages appear in just the first few verses, but they all have one thing in common: it is useless to try to predict "when" any of these things are going to occur; in fact, they will happen when the world least expects it. Given the known timing of events in the Tribulation, then 1 Thess 5:1-4 (along with 5:9) is absolute confirmation of a Rapture that will happen before the Tribulation. This is just an interpretation, and entire books have been written about this form of eschatology, but the basics are these: if the Rapture were to happen at either the midpoint of the Tribulation or just before "the wrath," then it would be possible to predict when this will occur in clear violation of Jesus' words in the Olivet Discourse. Only by placing it prior to the Tribulation do you get Paul's God-inspired ability to say that that day will come like a "thief in the night." Only by placing the Rapture before the Tribulation do you get a reconcilable, non-contradictory view of all the End Times events, particularly as described by Paul here.

Starting in verse 12, Paul wraps up with a burst of Proverbs-like advice for the new believers that we would be wise to follow today.

July 27, OT
2 Chronicles 24:17-25; 2 Kings 12:17-18; 2 Kings 4:1-44; 2 Kings 13:4-8; 2 Kings 8:1-6; 2 Kings 13:9-11
The Evil of Joash; Miracles of Elisha; Two More Kings of Israel

http://www.vtaide.com/gleanings/Kings-of-Israel/kings.html

Joash's evil didn't become apparent in the southern kingdom of Judah until after his "mentor," Jehoiada the priest, died in yesterday's reading. Today's OT reading begins by referencing the time as "after the death of Jehoiada," and what follows is the decline and fall of of the once "good" king of Judah. Joash took Judah down the path of idol worship (2 Chron 24:18) and this brought the wrath of the Lord down on them. Joash even plotted the murder of Jehoiada's son Zechariah (a prophet, but not to be confused with the prophet that later wrote a prophecy that is in the Bible, which we read starting November 22) when the latter tried to tell Joash that Judah would "not prosper" because of this (24:20-22). Later, after being wounded by an invading army, Joash is killed by his own men in his bed (24:23-25) and was buried.

Much of the rest of the OT reading for today is a detail of several miracles done by Elisha, the successor to Elijah, a prophet of the Lord in Israel. The jump-back to chapter 4 of 2 Kings is necessary because the account is told out of sequence, implying in its placement there that these events occurred during the reign of Jehoram of Israel. . But in fact, clues in one of the miracles (as well as the forthcoming reading for July 30) makes it necessary to move it up to the time of Jehoahaz, after the death of Jehu (in yesterday's OT reading). Elisha's miracles include the widow and the olive oil (2 Kings 4:1-7), the resurrection of the son of a Shunammite (4:8-37), decontamination of a pot of stew (4:38-41), and the feeding of one hundred people (4:42-44).
 Meanwhile, Jehoahaz was busy trying, unsuccessfully, to save Israel from the same invading army that attacked Judah, resulting in a devastating loss and his death (13:4-8). But before his death, according to the scholarship behind this chronology, he was

instrumental in restoring the Shunammite's land after their exile imposed by Elisha (8:1-6).

Either way, the Bible records here the death of Jehoahaz and the accession of Jehoash, his son, as the next king of Israel (13:9-11). There are, however, a few more things we hear about Jehoahaz before that chapter is closed.

July 27, NT
2 Thessalonians 1:1-2:12
The Antichrist

It is not known how much time passed after Paul wrote and sent his first letter to the Thessalonians and his writing of the second letter, nor do we know whether or not he wrote part or all of his first letter to the Corinthians, also visited on his Second Missionary Journey, before writing this second letter. It is assumed by this chronology, however, that both letters to Thessalonica were written between the Second and Third missionary journeys, so it would make sense to place the second letter immediately after the first.

Back in the 50s (and we're not talking the 1950s here) when Paul wrote these letters, there was no postal service with which to send them. A courier had to take the letter and deliver it in person. It can be assumed that either Silas or Timothy (or both) were involved with this delivery, and both are mentioned in the opening greeting (2 Thess 1:1). Paul then goes on for the rest of the first chapter giving thanks to God for the Thessalonian church, which has endured much persecution some time between the first and second letters (1:3-12). Embedded in this section, though, is another prophecy like the one Paul wrote in his first letter: this time speaking about another End Times event: the "Glorious Appearing" of Jesus (1:6-10) and the judgment that will take place thereafter, when justice is done, and the guilty (including Thessalonica's persecutors) are punished.

Somewhere along the way, the Thessalonians must have sent back questions as a reply to his first letter, because the next thing Paul goes into is yet another End Times prophecy: the nature of the "man of sin," or "man of lawlessness". That is, the man known in some other places as The Antichrist. The Apostle John would later clarify the difference between The Antichrist (as a singular person) and the Antichrists of the world (of which there will be many, in spirit), but for now, Paul gives some important information about this man, especially the *timing* of his arrival. The Thessalonians must have thought that they had already been left behind, i.e. that the "Day of the Lord" had already arrived (2:1-2), but Paul comforts them with the knowledge that the Antichrist must be revealed before this Day occurs (2:3-4). He then goes on to show that the Antichrist won't be revealed until after the One who is "holding him back" withdraws His hand of protection (2:6-8a). Though Paul doesn't mention Him by name, there is no doubt of Whom he is writing here: the Holy Spirit, whose hand of protection can't be removed from the earth until the church has been raptured. This is yet another piece of confirmation of the timing of End Times events which include a pre-tribulation rapture.

The first mention of this "man of lawlessness" goes back to Daniel's prophecies in the Old Testament, but Paul makes sure to confirm several details about what this Antichrist will do during his reign on earth (2:9-12), including a prophecy that also confirms Election by God: that unbelievers (in the Lord Jesus) will be sent a "strong delusion" (2:11-12) to believe that the Antichrist is actually God, and delight in their wickedness up to their own demise. The rapid rise of atheism in just the last few decades seems to foreshadow a fulfillment of this End Times prophecy.

July 28, OT
2 Kings 12:19-21; 2 Chronicles 24:25-27; 2 Kings 14:1-6; 2 Chronicles 25:1-10
Amaziah of Judah

One of the shortest OT readings since the saga of the kings of Israel and Judah began, today's reading starts with two segments that repeat the event of the death of Joash, assassinated by his own men (who, here in 2 Kings 12 and 2 Chronicles 24 are *named*), and succeeded by his son Amaziah. Amaziah proved to be the same kind of "mixed bag" as his father was - he started out "good" but later turned "evil". It is noted in two places (2 Kings 14:6, 2 Chronicles 25:4) that Amaziah made it a point to NOT have the children of his father's assassins executed, following a law found in Deuteronomy 24:16.

Still in the "good" phase of his reign, the reading concludes in 2 Chronicles as Amaziah amasses a large army that includes 100,000 troops hired out of the northern kingdom. When a prophet tells Amaziah that God does not approve of this troop hiring, Amaziah listens and backs down from this recruitment, sending the Israeli troops home (2 Chron 25:6-10)... in a *rage*.

July 28, NT
2 Thessalonians 2:13-3:18
Conclusion of Paul's Letter to the Thessalonians

Besides the great End Times prophecies, Paul spends the next-highest amount of space in both letters to the church in Thessalonica thanking God and singing the praises of a people that obviously showed amazing potential as new believers. Here in this conclusion, Paul refers to the Thessalonians as the "firstfruits" to be saved (2 Thess 2:13). He goes on to pray for the young church to be delivered from "wicked and evil men" (3:2), for "not all have faith". It's an important reality in the world today that some have faith while others don't. No one is beyond saving, but we must not ever forget that God already knows who is going to be saved and who is not. Paul's prayer is to direct their hearts (and thus, ours) to the love of God (3:5).

Using the example of his own experience in Thessalonica, Paul then gives his last warning to them, against idleness (3:6-15), before the closing Benediction (3:16-18).

July 29, OT
2 Kings 14:7-14; 2 Chronicles 25:11-24; 2 Kings 5:1-7:2
The Downfall of Amaziah; Elisha Makes an Enemy

After Amaziah sent home 100,000 purchased troops from the northern kingdom, he and his army accomplished a great victory over the Edomites (2 Kings 14:7). He next decided to try to take on Jehoahaz, king of Israel. Jehoahaz declined the challenge, but Ahaziah was insistent. It was then that the army of Judah was overrun by their neighbors to the north, and they were plundered and had part of the Jerusalem wall destroyed (14:8-14). The same two events are told in 2 Chronicles (2 Chron 25:11-13, 25:17-24), but with an important detail between them that 2 Kings doesn't record: after Amaziah's success against Edom but before his foolhardy challenge of Jehoahaz, Amaziah began worshiping false gods and idols (25:14-16), which would then account for why Amaziah, whose army was much larger than Jehoahaz's, was so easily defeated, as this was the Lord's doing.

Around this time, in Israel (in Samaria, the capital city), the general of the neighboring Syrian army, a man named Naaman, who was responsible for the Syrian victory over Jehoahaz some time earlier, requested that he go to Israel to seek a cure for his one major problem: Naaman was a leper (2 Kings 5:1-5). Naaman's quest eventually brought him to Elisha, who gave him instructions for removing the leprosy, which he eventually did (5:6-14). But Elisha's servant, Gehazi, sought to swindle Naaman out of the reward Naaman had offered Elisha (5:19b-23), but ended up paying for his theft by taking on Naaman's leprosy (5:24-27) himself.

Elisha performed another quick miracle after this (6:1-7) and then proceeded to stop a war by threatening to start it. He informed the king of Israel (who is never named in any of this) of the Syrian king's intentions, but stopped an invading army through the power of prayer, eventually getting the Syrian army in front of the Israeli king (6:8-20) but put a stop to all hostilities, eventually getting the king to send them all home (6:21-23). But all this action on behalf of the Lord didn't make Elisha any friends. In fact, he made an enemy of the king of Israel, as Elisha got blamed for the famine resulting from a siege by the Syrians to whom the king showed mercy (6:24-31), culminating in the king's threat to take off Elisha's head. But just as the king sent a captain to do the deed, Elisha promised an end to the famine that would come from the Lord (6:32-7:2). This story concludes in tomorrow's OT reading.

July 29, NT
Acts 18:24-19:20
The Third Missionary Journey Begins in Ephesus

Paul's first Epistle was addressed to a church he planted during his first Missionary Journey, Galatia. He wrote it during the beginning of his Second Missionary Journey, on which he visited the cities of Philippi, Thessalonica, and Corinth, among others. The Thessalonians were the addressees of his second Epistle, and he would later write letters to both of those other cities (see reading for two days from now). Now, as he begins his third (and longest) Missionary Journey, we first read about another evangelist, named Apollos, who visited Ephesus ahead of Paul (Acts 18:24-25). Paul would visit the city next, and much later write yet another of his Epistles to the new church there.

Apollos was an example of what was increasingly happening during the Church's 3rd decade, as more and more evangelists began to emerge who were not from the immediate circle of Apostles. But though Apollos was a bold speaker and loved the Lord dearly, even he needed instruction in the proper methods of spreading the Gospel among the new churches (18:26-19:1a) in Ephesus and then in Corinth.

Paul arrived in Ephesus next (19:1b), and found believers there that knew the Lord but didn't know the Holy Spirit (19:2-7). So Paul had them baptized and finished the job that Apollos had started, and stayed in the area for *two years*, preaching in the Synagogues, even in the face of some stubborn opposition (19:8-10).

Apollos wasn't the only Jewish leader to "turn Christian" and preach the Good News besides Paul. The "sons of Sceva," as they were known, were Jewish exorcists who, likewise, began to spread the real Gospel message through their own efforts in Ephesus (19:11-20).

July 30, OT
2 Kings 7:3-20; 2 Kings 8:7-15; 2 Kings 13:14-21; 2 Kings 13:24-25
Elisha Stops the Famine; Elisha's Final Prophecy

After Elisha's prediction that the famine (which was caused by a Syrian siege) would end, the next event recorded in the Bible *sounds* like it is not related to this prophecy - that is, until you read it to its conclusion. Today's OT reading, entirely in 2 Kings despite the 4 different sections, picks up where yesterday's left off, starting with the account of a group of lepers contemplating their next move. They reasoned that they'd be just as well off with the Syrians as they would be trying to get into the city (Samaria) (2 Kings 7:3-5a). But God made it sound to the Syrians as if there was an army invading them, rather than just a group of 4 lepers walking into their camp (7:5b-7), and fled. The lepers plundered some of the abandoned Syrian tents (7:8) but their guilt over this caused them to stop and return to Samaria to tell the king (7:9-10). At first, the king doubted the lepers' story, and sent two horsemen to check it out. It turned out that the lepers were telling the truth after all (7:11-16). And so the people plundered the rest of the Syrian camp, and the famine was over, exactly as was prophesied by Elisha, including the death of the king's captain at the gate (7:17-20).

Elisha went to Damascus and was involved in a prophecy there, predicting the accession of Hazael to the throne, replacing Ben-Hadad as king of Syria (8:7-15). Later, on his deathbed, Elisha makes a final prophecy to King Joash, predicting victory over the Syrians if only he'd do one thing: strike the ground with some arrows (13:14-18). When the king only struck the ground 3 times, Elisha bemoaned this, telling the king that he should have done this 5 or 6 times (13:19), because this would limit Israel to only 3 victories over Syria. Elisha died and was buried, and his last prophecy came to pass thereafter (13:20-21, 24-25).

July 30, NT
Acts 19:21-41
Artemis vs. The Way in Ephesus

From chapter 9 onwards, the Acts of the Apostles is dominated by the work of Paul on his Missionary Journeys. Yesterday began the third such journey, the longest of the three, yet it occupies the smallest amount of space in the Acts. At the beginning of today's reading, after the events in Ephesus yesterday, Paul resolves to go to Macedonia and eventually to Rome (Acts 19:21) but first sends a pair of helpers to Macedonia (19:22). Paul remains "in Asia," presumably meaning Ephesus, as the events described in the rest of the reading unfold, though Paul barely becomes involved in any of it,.

The remainder of today's NT reading is the account of an event that could be described as a riot. Believers, still being referred to as "The Way" were being challenged by the locals who believed in hand-made gods, including Artemis. In particular, a silversmith named Demetrius fired up a crowd over the fact that these new Christians were trying to take away their livelihoods by making their hand-made gods illegitimate (19:23-29). Paul tried to insert himself into the conflict that followed, but was prevented from doing so by other disciples (19:30-31), making these two verses the only two in which Paul is even mentioned. A Jew named Alexander tried to calm the crowd but was shouted down (19:32-34). It took a town clerk, who gave the townspeople a legal, secular solution to the problem, to finally end the riot (19:35-41), but we readers are left hanging at that point, as there is no further mention of Paul and what (if anything) he said or did in response to this in Ephesus.

But what we do know is this: some time during the period between Timothy and Erastus' departure for Macedonia and when Paul finally left Asia, he penned the first of two letters to one of his previous stops - on his *second* Missionary Journey, beginning in tomorrow's NT reading.

July 31, OT
2 Kings 13:12-13; 2 Kings 14:15-16; 2 Kings 14:23; 2 Kings 14:17-20; 2 Chronicles 25:25-28; 2 Kings 14:21-22; 2 Kings 15:1-5; 2 Chronicles 26:1-21
Clearing Up Name Confusion

http://www.vtaide.com/gleanings/Kings-of-Israel/kings.html

A combination of two things found in English translations of the Old Testament scriptures makes for a great deal of confusion amongst casual readers of the Bible. It is, in fact, an error in the original website that listed this chronology (and my correction of it) that resulted in a lot of this section which I call The Saga of the Kings of Israel and Judah. Of course, there are those who insist on using this reading as "proof" of the errors in the Bible, but nothing could be farther from the truth. There are no errors - only translation difficulties, which stem from one or both of those two things.

The first of those things is the fact that some kings are known by multiple names. Referring to the link above, which has appeared several times in this chronology already, five of the kings of Judah up to this point are known by more than one name, and two of the kings of Israel are likewise known. Thus 2 Kings 13 refers to the king of Israel as Joash, but in the very next chapter refers to him as Jehoash. Not only are these two passages referring to the same king, but one of those names also refers to an earlier king of Judah, of whom we read on July 27. That's the second thing that confuses casual readers: kings whose names appear on both sides of the ledger.

But if you read the passages in the prescribed chronological order (not to mention the passages about Elisha), things make at least a little more sense. Thus, today's OT reading begins with the death of

Joash/Jehoash of Israel, followed by accession of Jeroboam II (2 Kings 14:23) to that same throne (this time a repeated name), and then the accession and death of Joash *of Judah's* son Amaziah to the throne in Judah (14:17-20). After the same king appears in 2 Chronicles 25:25-28, we then go back to 2 Kings to read of Azariah (aka Uzziah), king of Judah after Amaziah's death. Known as Azariah in 2 Kings, he is known by the name Uzziah in 2 Chronicles 26, which also goes into much more detail about the king of Judah with the longest reign (52 years.) - a reign that overlaps portions of 6 kings of Israel, more than any other since Asa.

July 31, NT
1 Corinthians 1:1-25
Paul Writes to Corinth

Paul spent the longest portion of his Second Missionary Journey (as read on July 22) in a city that showed perhaps the greatest amount of resistance to the Gospel message of any he had visited. Corinth, with some 700,000 people, largest city in Greece, was second only to Rome as the largest city in the known world of the time. A true cosmopolitan seaport, it was the least likely place you would think that a church could be planted by Paul. But that's exactly what had happened; and despite some serious difficulties and hard hitting questions, the Corinthians' success at keeping a church going there led to Paul's desire to return to the city (as read yesterday) and to two Epistles, the first of which is Paul's second longest letter. Written from Ephesus during his Third Missionary Journey, we'll spend the next 18 days in what is, arguably, Paul's most passionate letter.

Paul's eloquence in answering their questions and making his case for the Gospel to the new, young church was so great, entire sermons or sermon series' have been made over just a few verses. Each day's reading will have a few of these "key verses" to point out. In this first section, the focal point is a topic he actually brings up in three separate places in just this letter alone: divisions in the church. After a greeting and thanksgiving (1 Cor 1:1-9), Paul launches into a virtual tirade against those who would use their disagreements and quarrels to divide the church. One of the sparks for writing the letter was obviously a report by one of "Chloe's people," reflecting the value of women in the early ministry (1:11). In a rare moment of sarcasm, Paul asks the Corinthians if Christ himself has been divided, or if Paul was crucified for them (1:13). He even thanks God that he only baptized a small number of people while there, lest this problem of division be even worse (1:14-16). But then Paul wraps it up by saying that his purpose was to proclaim the Gospel, not just to baptize, and emphasized the fact that it was not by his own wisdom that this was done (1:17).

The next section (part one of two, with part two tomorrow) addresses where the REAL power and wisdom of God lie: in Christ. The key points include the fact that the Cross is "foolishness" to those who are perishing (1:18), but the Cross has also made foolish the wisdom of the world (1:20), concluding with the statement that God's foolishness is greater than any human wisdom (1:25).

August 1, OT
Amos 1:1-3:15
The Prophets Speak

We've heard from prophets before. As far back as Joseph, son of Jacob, we've had prophecies made by several "major players" in salvation history. We've even read about prophets for other nations or other gods, such as Balaam at the time of the Exodus. Israel's first two prominent prophets, Elijah and Elisha, were described and made their prophecies in the second book of the Kings. But what hasn't happened until this point is an entire book (scroll) devoted to the writings of a single prophet. And though the first prophetic book in the Bible is Isaiah, the first one to be *written*, as the Saga of the Kings of Israel and Judah spirals down to its conclusion, comes from a country boy named Amos.

Reading the books of the prophets, particularly the "minor" ones like Amos, can be rather difficult, for a number of reasons. For the most part, the prophets wrote in a poetic style using a great deal of metaphor and symbolism. Amos is no exception, though his prophecy isn't the most difficult to understand. Like most of the other prophets, Amos pins down his place in the timeline at the beginning of his book, saying that it was during the reigns of Uzziah of Judah (where he actually lived) and Jeroboam of Israel, about 170 years after the kingdom was divided. You can imagine how the northern kingdom took his prophecy, coming from a farmer/shepherd in the South (Amos 1:1). It is obvious from the style that the book of Amos is a transcription of a speech or set of speeches made by Amos, written down by an unnamed scribe. Amos also mentions that his speech comes two years "before the earthquake." Though it is never described in any historical book of the Bible, and mentioned only in passing by two other prophets (Joel and Zechariah), scientific sources outside of the Bible have confirmed the occurrence of a magnitude 8+ quake that would have struck the region around the time of Uzziah and Jeroboam II.

Amos begins by establishing that the Lord's word, ROARED from Jerusalem, causes even the top of Mount Carmel (in the northern kingdom) to wither (1:2). He says this as he delivers a series of judgments from God against several neighboring nations, the first of which (Syria, 1:3-5) further confirms the timeline just after Elisha's prophecy about pushing back 3 attacks. Amos goes on to deliver scathing judgments against Gaza/Philistines (1:6-8), Tyre (1:9-10),

Edom (1:11-12), the Ammonites (1:13-15), and Moab (2:1-3), before going on to the two parts of the divided kingdom: Judah (2:4-5), and finally Israel (2:6-16). Each judgment starts with "Thus [says] the Lord". He spends the longest amount of time on Israel, despite the fact that this was not where he lived - Amos came from a small farming town in the South.

God's tirade against Israel continues in chapter 3, and culminates with verse 11, where Amos predicts the fall of the northern kingdom. Many more such predictions would be made by other prophets such as Isaiah, Hosea, and Micah.

August 1, NT
1 Corinthians 1:26-2:16
The Wisdom of the World vs. the Wisdom of Christ

Paul continues his contrast of the wisdom of the world with the real source of wisdom, Jesus Christ, starting with an almost startling display of humility. It is startling because Paul has been known since he was first introduced in the Acts of the Apostles to be a man who speaks very **boldly**, and very **boldly** pursues his passions, whether it was the work he did against Christians before his own conversion, to his Missionary Journeys (of which he was on his Third), to his Epistles to the cities where he had planted churches. His writing is eloquent and full of wisdom, yet he states in today's NT reading that he didn't come to Corinth to proclaim the word of God with "lofty speech or wisdom" (1 Cor 2:1). But, that's exactly what Paul did, though he does an eloquent job of explaining that this was all for the sake of "proclaiming Christ crucified" (2:2). Paul then goes on to explain how this wisdom comes to us, via the Holy Spirit, using two quotes from the prophet Isaiah to make his point: 1 Corinthians 2:9 quotes Isaiah 64:4, and 1 Corinthians 2:16 quotes Isaiah 40:13.

August 2, OT
Amos 4:1-6:14
The Lord Has About Had Enough

Yesterday's OT reading ended with a lengthy rant against the people of the northern kingdom of Israel, which is continued in this reading. Today's 3 chapters make for 3 distinct sections, all of which are directed against Israel. In chapter 4, Amos uses insults and sarcasm in the first few verses to let the Israelites know in no uncertain terms how angry the Lord is at them (Amos 4:1-5). He then uses a repeated cycle of pointing out how the Lord's actions were ignored by the people of Israel by stating that "did not return to Me" (4:6, 4:8, 4:9, et al).

Chapter 5 makes several points, but all of it contains an undertone of doom, in that the nation's fate has already been decided, but as individuals, survival is possible if they "seek the Lord" (5:1-17, 5:21-27). One section of Chapter 5 has the Lord asking the people, in essence, why on Earth would they want to be looking forward to the "Day of the Lord," for it is not a way out but a day of great darkness (5:18-20). In chapter 6, Amos goes back to the Lord's words from the first part of chapter 5, this time addressing the complacent and the comfortable, warning them of Israel's coming fate (6:1-14).

August 2, NT
1 Corinthians 3:1-23
The Cult of Personality, Part One

The word that came back to Paul about what had happened after he helped plant the church in Corinth must have made mention of this common human phenomenon: the cult of personality. It happens when a new, popular movement becomes associated with the people who *delivered* the movement rather than the movement itself or the person (in this case, Jesus) who is the foundation of the movement. It's obvious from the multiple mentions of Apollos, Paul himself, or even Peter (as Cephas, one of the few times he is mentioned by Paul after the First Missionary Journey, 1 Cor 3:22) that the Corinthians were dividing up into camps that were "of Apollos" or "of Paul" etc. Paul spends the entire 3rd chapter here, and thus the entire NT reading for today, passionately striking down this misinterpretation of what Christianity was supposed to be about. The key reminder here is that it is Christ, not any person, who is the foundation: Paul laid that foundation, and others are building on it, but it is Jesus Christ who, Himself, is that foundation. Today's numerous churches would do well to take this lesson to heart when getting into interdenominational squabbles.

August 3, OT
Amos 7:1-9:15; Hosea 1:1-3:5
The Destruction and The Restoration of Israel

The last words from Amos and the first words from Hosea share a common theme: the destruction of Israel which is to come, and the later *restoration* of the same. It isn't known whether the prophecies of Amos and Hosea were concurrent or if Hosea followed after a number of years, but Hosea's prophecies went on for a great deal longer period of time beyond Amos'. This is evidenced by the mention of the 4 kings of Judah, from Uzziah to Hezekiah, at the beginning of Hosea's prophecy (Hosea 1:1). It's interesting to note that Hosea's prophecy, like Amos', is directed almost entirely at the northern kingdom (Israel), not Judah, yet he positions himself in the timeline using kings of Judah. But, the most important thing to note there is that Hezekiah of Judah was on the throne in Judah when the northern kingdom was invaded and taken into exile.

In today's OT reading, the only such daily reading that encompasses 6 chapters of the Word, Amos describes 2 judgments from the Lord, one by locusts, another by fire, both of which Amos successfully convinced the Lord to show mercy and not do (Amos 7:1-6). Then, using the metaphor of a plumb line, the Lord shows that, despite His mercy, that the "sword will rise" against the house of Jeroboam and that the "high places" in Israel would be destroyed (7:7-9). In the verses that follow, we get almost the only actual history found in Amos' prophecy, as this message of Israel's destruction is delivered to Jeroboam, king of Israel, via a priest named Amaziah (not to be confused with the king of Judah of the same name). The dialog goes back and forth, with the king calling for Amos' departure (7:12), but Amos counters with a vivid description of the exact nature of the destruction of Israel: exile and death in a foreign land (7:17). Amos spends all of chapter 8 and the first 10 verses of chapter 9 delivering the message of the Lord, which contains even more violent imagery regarding the coming exile.

But then, Amos' prophecy takes a very sudden turn, with a positive message in the last 5 verses (9:11-15) describing the aftermath of the Assyrian exile to come: the restoration of Israel, and the bringing back of the people from exile. Interpretation of these verses varies wildly, because this restoration could refer to either the "10 Lost Tribes" of the northern kingdom, whose return from exile didn't occur until after

Israel became a nation again in 1948, or it could refer to the return to Jerusalem after the Babylonian exile of the southern kingdom, which had not yet been prophesied. However, other prophecies, notably Hosea's, makes the better case for the former than the latter.

Hosea's prophecy, after the introduction, shows how the Lord used Hosea's personal life to describe God's feelings for Israel. God viewed Israel's sin and coming exile the same way as a man would view an adulterous wife who, nevertheless, bore him children (Hosea 1:2-11). Chapter 2 paints further descriptive imagery of this adulterous relationship, but starts giving hints and clues that the punishment that will be given for this will not be a forever thing (2:7b, 2:16-17, 2:21-23) and that restoration will follow. Chapter 3 then uses the same metaphor, this time of the wife's restoration to her husband, to describe the eventual restoration of Israel.

August 3, NT
1 Corinthians 4:1-21
The Cult of Personality, Part Two; Humble Service to the Church

Paul concludes his admonition to stop squabbling among the various factions of the new Corinthian church here in chapter 4 by pointing out the arrogance of claiming any group as superior over another. Like a parent scolding a child, Paul repeats his explanation of how he and Apollos humbled themselves to deliver the Good News of Jesus Christ to the Corinthians when he last visited. He furthermore sent Timothy to continue this work (1 Cor 4:17), so that the church could focus on what is truly important rather than on the cult of personality that had developed after Paul's departure from Corinth. Paul concludes this section by expressing his desire to return, the Lord willing, to Corinth, for another visit, but asks them flat-out if they want him to return as a judging figure or with a spirit of gentleness (4:20-21).

August 4, OT
Hosea 4:1-5:7; 2 Kings 14:24-28
The Downward Spiral

http://www.vtaide.com/gleanings/Kings-of-Israel/kings.html

When you examine the chart of the kings of Israel and Judah, you note the fact that, with one *possible* exception, (and that was, frankly, a stretch), there wasn't even one single "good" king over Israel, the northern kingdom. That one exception (Jehu) wasn't even listed as "doing good in the sight of the Lord", though he did do *some* things against the house of Ahab that the Lord wanted done. But this is what Hosea meant in this continuation of his prophecy, when he brings the indictment from the Lord (Hosea 4:1-5:7) on Israel. The charges are harsh but absolutely true, and reflect the downward spiral in which Israel was on. Unlike Amos, Hosea's prophecies aren't believed to be a transcript of a speech or series of speeches; they are straight writings from what the Lord said to him, passed along to Israel, and specifically, Jeroboam II, the king. Most of the charges against Israel are likened to adultery and related sexual sins, but these are used as metaphors for the numerous and varied sins of Israel.

The passage in 2 Kings refers to the reign of Jeroboam II. During this time, and beyond, when Hosea was writing his oracles, another of the "minor" prophets appears on the scene (2 Kings 14:25), in tomorrow's OT reading.

August 4, NT
1 Corinthians 5:1-6:11
Sexual Sin Among the Corinthians

Chloe's (1 Corinthians 1:11, read on July 31) report about what happened in Corinth after Paul's visit must have contained some exceptionally lurid detail about their bad behavior. But Corinth was, after all, a very large city by 1st century standards, and had the cosmopolitan background to go with it. Thus, when Paul brings up the sin of incest in chapter 5 here, he speaks not only in terms of how this behavior violates Jewish law, but even that it violates the law of the Gentiles (specifically, Roman law). Though he doesn't directly quote anything from Leviticus 18, Paul makes the strong case against the guilty party, who was having sex with his stepmother, and pronounces very harsh judgment (5:1-5), the equivalent of excommunication. In verse 6, Paul uses a metaphor that Jesus once used against the Pharisees, of whom Paul once was one, to compare the acts of immoral men (such as the one guilty of incest) to leaven (yeast) that would cause the whole batch to rise. Paul preaches that what is needed is *new* leaven, spreading the influence of Godly behavior and removing and disassociating themselves from the Ungodly (5:6-13).

Because these immoral acts were against both Jewish and Roman law, there must have been at least some instances of people trying to bring these immoral men up on charges before Roman courts. This form of judgment is also discouraged by Paul (6:1-6); rather, these matters should be brought up among believers in the church, not the court of unbelievers. Paul even says that they're "already defeated" when they bring up such matters in the Gentile courts (6:7-8) and then lists the kinds of sexual sins that will prevent someone from getting into the kingdom (aka Heaven).

The list of sexual sins in 1 Corinthians 6:9 has been a matter of some considerable controversy, particularly recently, because of its mention of homosexuality. With the exception of idolaters, all of the sins in verse 9 are sexual in nature, and include the obvious (and easily translated) sins of adultery and fornication. Before the sentence continues in verse 10 (with several non-sexual sins listed and described), Paul's list of sexual sins concludes with two that are commonly translated as "effeminate" and "homosexual" in most newer word-for-word (Tyndale) translations. Even most older Tyndale-tradition translations used two separate terms, such as the KJV rendering using the word "effeminate" followed by a softened, less profane form of "sodomites" (the direct translation from the Greek) that says "abusers of themselves with mankind". Thought for thought translations, such as the NIV, combine the two terms into a single phrase such as "men who have sex with men". This combination creates some of the confusion we see today in the ongoing debate over homosexuality, as the original Word of God lists these as two separate sins, not just one.

But Paul doesn't leave the chapter on a negative, condemning them for their sins without bringing up the mercy of our Lord: in verse 11, Paul states that those who engag<u>ed</u> (*past tense*) in that long litany of sins have been "washed clean", sanctified, justified, by the Lord Jesus Christ before God, a clear statement of how God's mercy is available to all who turn to Jesus in faith.

August 5, OT
Jonah 1:1-4:11
A Most Reluctant Prophet

Open any children's Bible or "story Bible" for children, and you'll find Jonah, regardless of how many (or how few) other prophets are even mentioned (much less have their prophecies told) in those pages. Why Jonah? Certainly, the book of Jonah, which is read today in its entirety, is a "lighter" read than most other prophets, and actually contains much more history than prophecy. This is probably why the account is more palatable for children, the other being the most infamous part of the brief book, found in the first chapter.

Jonah is told in the 3rd person, which was a common practice in Hebrew writing, but it is therefore not certain if it was actually written by the prophet or by a scribe on Jonah's behalf. It starts with the familiar account of Jonah's call to go to Nineveh, a very long trip on foot from his home near Nazareth in the northern kingdom, and his futile attempt to escape this duty by setting sail on a cargo ship. Jonah ends up needing to be thrown overboard to quiet the storm that God set on them, where the grateful sailors give thanks to God for the deliverance, and Jonah is swallowed up by a "great fish" (or "whale" in some translations), only to be spit out on shore three days later. The passage is controversial (though always accepted by children) because of skeptics who say that it would not be possible for a man to survive inside a fish or whale for any length of time, much less three days. Of course, a God powerful enough to call up (and suddenly stop) a raging storm could easily sustain a man, particularly someone who was actually praying to God during that time.

And so in chapter 3, Jonah is again called by God to go to Nineveh, and this time he actually goes there, where he makes a *single line* of prophecy (3:4) that turns the people of Nineveh around (3:5-10), causing God to withdraw His threat of destruction. But this success actually displeased Jonah so much that he actually wished for death, all because Jonah could not comprehend God's mercy in sparing the people of Nineveh. In particular, Jonah was despondent over the fact that his prophecies (not recorded in the Bible) in his homeland (Israel) had fallen on deaf ears, whereas the people of Nineveh repented of their sin - a connection Jonah couldn't fathom. The book actually ends with God's question to Jonah in the aftermath: God asks (paraphrased) "why shouldn't I spare the 120,000 citizens of this town?" The writing ends abruptly after God's final question, and we never hear again about the fate of Israel's reluctant prophet.

August 5, NT
1 Corinthians 6:12-7:7
A Practical Explanation of "Why?"

Outside of the fact that Paul's writing in yesterday's NT reading was prompted by information he received from a Corinthian named Chloe, the question of "why" Paul placed so much emphasis on sexual sin in the last passage is a legitimate one. Paul writes a lot, in this letter and others, about how God's mercy is available to anyone who repents, and that this is all one has to do to attain salvation, a gift from God called "grace." But with that in mind, there seems to be an awful lot of writing in some parts of this letter on legalistic references to what sexual practices are and are not moral. So why is Paul so adamant about such things as yesterday's concluding verses? Because of what he says in the first part of today's: the metaphor of the "body" is used several times in several different ways by Paul, but here he means it more literally. Specifically, we are reminded that sexual sin and any immoral act is a sin against our own bodies, and our bodies are "members of Christ." Thus, the list of sins described in I Corinthians 6:9-10 is there because each one does damage to the Body of Christ - as a whole. That, for example, is why "gay marriage" in the U.S. is such a big issue. When asked why we (as Christians) object to the practice, we really should be referring to I Corinthians 6:12-20 and the need to glorify God in our bodies.

Chapter 7 continues this in his further response to "the things about which you wrote" (1 Cor 7:1) as Paul gives practical advice on marriage, including the fact that in a marriage setting a couple should not deprive one another except through mutual agreement (7:5) and that neither party's body belongs to themselves but to their spouse (7:4). Skeptics that accuse Paul of misogyny often cite verse 4 as proof but fail to read the whole verse which shows that this piece of advice works both ways. Paul even praises the ability of some men to remain celibate, which is interpreted by the Roman Catholic Church as a command for the clergy rather than the practical advice that it is (see reading for August 7).

August 6, OT
2 Kings 14:29; 2 Kings 15:8-16
From Jeroboam II to Menahem, Briefly

The saga of the kings of Israel and Judah resumes in this brief reading of the short reigns of 4 kings of the north starting with the death of Jeroboam II (2 Kings 14:29): Zechariah (spelled as Zachariah in some translations) (15:8-9), Shallum (15:10, 13), and Menahem (15:16), whose reign isn't yet chronicled, although his actions here set up tomorrow's OT reading. All of these kings came and went in the north while Uzziah reigned in Judah, and Uzziah is listed here as Azariah in some places (like 15:8) and Uzziah in others (like 15:13) in the same book.

August 6, NT
1 Corinthians 7:8-24
Your Status When You Are Called

There are many situations in which you must fill out a form where a checkbox indicates your status: married or single, renter or homeowner, income bracket, etc.. You indicate your status in many ways, and if that status changes, you have to make sure it is reported to whomever previously asked for the information, such as an employer. Here in Paul's first letter to the Corinthian church, Paul encourages believers to remain in their statuses, whatever they may be: the unmarried or widowed should stay that way (unless they can't control themselves, in which case they should then marry) (1 Cor 7:8-9), married couples should stay together regardless of whether or not both are believers (7:10-13), the uncircumcised should stay uncircumcised and the circumcised should stay circumcised (though I wasn't aware that circumcision could be reversed) (7:18-20). Along the way, Paul peppers his curious advice about the status quo with explanations, the bottom line of which is that the various statuses of a person are essentially *meaningless* in the face of the only status that does matter: being a **believer** in the Lord that assigned to you a condition (7:17, 7:24). The one exception to Paul's advice about keeping your status is when he speaks on slavery, starting with the advice to "not worry" about it (7:21b), as it, too, isn't the thing that's actually important. But he goes on to say that a slave called to be a believer is "Christ's freed man" and the free man who is a believer is "Christ's slave" (7:22). His explanation here echoes a line Paul wrote in yesterday's reading:

"you were bought with a price" (7:23a), and so one shouldn't become slaves of men.

August 7, OT
2 Kings 15:17-20; 1 Chronicles 5:23-26; 2 Kings 15:6-7; 2 Chronicles 26:22-23; 2 Kings 15:21-29
The Beginning of the End

Unlike the Babylonian exile that was to come for Judah (which is read in October), the Assyrian exile of the northern kingdom didn't happen as a single event. It happened much more gradually during the last years of Israel, starting with events during the reign of the last king mentioned in yesterday's OT reading: Menahem. His brief reign (though longer than any of those mentioned yesterday) included an attack by Pul, king of Assyria, that was thwarted only by paying off the enemy king with taxes levied against the citizens of the northern kingdom (2 Kings 15:19-20). In 1 Chronicles (that's right - First Chronicles, back in the middle of a skipped section of genealogical data), it is recorded that this same king, Pul, reneged on this deal by taking two and a half tribes (the ones that resided east of the Jordan) into exile anyway (1 Chron 5:23-26).

In Judah, the death of one of the southern kingdom's longest-reigning kings is recorded here, and then his succession by his son Jotham (2 Kings 15:6-7, 2 Chronicles 26:23). You may notice that Uzziah (recorded as Azariah in 2 Kings) doesn't get as much mention in the books of the Kings or Chronicles as did other long-reigning kings such as Asa before him, but 2 Chronicles 26:22 gives us what may very likely have been the reason why: the Chronicles were written down long after exiles (both of them) and the writer (likely Ezra) is putting together a compilation of historical facts from multiple sources, including many documents long lost to history. But one of those sources certainly could have been the writings of other prophets, and here we read the name Isaiah as the place where "the rest of the acts of Uzziah… Isaiah has written". This actually starts tomorrow, though not with Isaiah chapter 1 (you'll read why tomorrow).

And so back to 2 Kings, we read of the kings of the north from Menahem to Pekahiah to Pekah, the penultimate king in Samaria (2 Kings 15:21-29)

August 7, NT
1 Corinthians 7:25-40
The Case for Chastity

A dream find for a Biblical archaeologist today would be to find even a fragment of the letter written by Chloe of Corinth *to* Paul that prompted a large portion of Paul's First Letter back to them. As said before, for Paul to have written this much about a subject he couldn't have known much about (since he was unmarried his whole life), there had to have been a lot of conflict and confusion regarding the message Paul had delivered to these people on his Second Missionary Journey. Most of chapter 6 and all of chapter 7, which comes to a conclusion today, concerns the issues of sexual sin, marriage, and under what circumstances is celibacy preferable. The Roman Catholic Church even uses a portion of today's NT reading as justification for the mandate for celibate priests and nuns (1 Cor 7:32, 7:34). But the real message from God through Paul here is best considered when you 1) take in chapter 7 as a whole, and 2) carefully note the first verse of today's section of it. Paul starts here by saying that he doesn't have a command from the Lord regarding virgins, but has an opinion that can be considered trustworthy (7:25).

The overall message of the last 3 days can be summed up like this: being unmarried, one should be celibate, and that's good because you can concentrate more on the Lord; but there is nothing wrong with getting married, either, and it's actually a necessary thing if you burn with passion. Married people should stay married and thus avoid sexual sin, and unmarried people should avoid sexual sin by remaining chaste. Imagine how many of the problems we face today would be reduced or even eliminated if the vast majority of men and women actually lived by these principles!

August 8, OT
Isaiah 6:1-13; 2 Kings 15:32-38; 2 Chronicles 27:1-9; 1 Chronicles 5:11-17; 2 Kings 16:1-9; 2 Chronicles 28:1-21
Isaiah Preaches in Judah

Even though we don't get back to chapter 1 of Isaiah until nearly the end of this month, the Bible's second longest book begins today with its *6th* chapter. Why the 6th? Because the reference here to the death of Uzziah lines it up with the events read yesterday. We'll catch up with the history and background of Isaiah, one of the better-known or "major" prophets, including the controversy over whether or not the Book of Isaiah is the work of one man, on August 21. In the meantime, we get to read here about Isaiah's vision (Isaiah 6:1-7) and commission (6:8-13), which both formally occurred "in the year Uzziah died" (6:1). The key part is when Isaiah asks "how long" he is to continue preaching (6:11); and the Lord answered with what could only be a reference to an exile, when cities are "devastated and without inhabitant". The only question is: to which exile is the Lord referring? The soon-to-come Assyrian exile of the Northern Kingdom, or the later Babylonian exile of Judah, which is less known because they just finished with the long reign of a "good" king and were about to begin another?

That next "good" king was Jotham, whose biography is found in 2 Kings 15:32-38 and 2 Chronicles 27:1-9. The latter gives additional detail of a successful military campaign against the Ammonites, a war that was won because Jotham "ordered his ways to the Lord" (2 Chron 27:6). But the brief verses in both books are all we get about Jotham, and the account in 2 Kings ends with mention of how Pekah, king of Israel, teamed up with Rezin, King of Aram to begin attacking Judah (2 Kings 15:37). In the jump-back to 1 Chronicles, we read some genealogies that have been delayed until now because they were "published" during the time of Jotham.

With the death of Jotham and the accession of his son Ahaz, Judah saw the end of its last reign of two consecutive "good" kings that it would ever have. There would be other "good" kings, but in the meantime we read the biography of Ahaz who "did evil" in the Lord's sight. His abominations included putting his sons "through the fire," sacrificing to other gods and burning incense (2 Kings 16:3b-4, 2 Chronicles 28:2-4). Both books then give detail of an invasion of Judah - by Pekah of Israel! The account in 2 Chronicles is more detailed, and gives a clearer picture of how Ahaz of Judah actually enlisted the help of the Assyrians, the very nation that would invade the Northern Kingdom in just a few years, to stop the invasion.

August 8, NT
1 Corinthians 8:1-13
Knowing the One God

In chapter 8 of this Epistle, Paul takes on the question of what to do regarding food "sacrificed to idols" to debunk the idea that any other gods actually exist. It was obviously one of the many questions asked by the Corinthians after his time there on the Second Missionary Journey, but Paul nearly dismisses it as a non-issue. How? By pointing out the fact that we know the one, true God, and we know He is the *only* God; therefore, food sacrificed to idols aren't being sacrificed to anything *real*. What we eat (or not) doesn't matter to God. The only time that eating something would be an issue would be if it caused a non-believer, that is, someone who doesn't have the knowledge of God, to stumble.

August 9, OT
Isaiah 7:1-10:4; Isaiah 17:1-14
Two Great Messianic Prophecies and One End-Times Mystery

Ahaz's folly, detailed in yesterday's OT reading, in enlisting the help of the Assyrians to thwart an invasion of Judah by the northern kingdom, made many people in Judah very afraid. It didn't help that Ahaz wasn't a believer in God. But, God gave word to the prophet Isaiah to reassure the people of Judah that the double-cross feared by the people would not take place (Isaiah 7:3-9). It is also recorded in Isaiah that the Lord spoke directly to Ahaz (7:10-12) prompting the evil king to ask for a sign from the Lord, presumably to get him turned around and believing. Ahaz refused, and what was prophesied next though Isaiah became one of the most important prophecies of the Messiah to come.

Every year at Christmas time, we talk of the birth of Jesus as being the fulfillment of prophecy. Many prophecies were fulfilled when Christ was born, but one stands out in particular because of how skeptics seize on its scientific implausibility: the *virgin* birth of the Lord. On the second day of this chronological reading plan, we read in Luke of Gabriel's announcement to Mary that she would be the virgin mentioned as the Lord's response to Ahaz when he refused to see a sign from the Lord: that the virgin (not merely "young woman" as some suggest) would be with child (7:14) and that his name would be Immanuel, meaning "God with us". Though told in the context of the coming Assyrian invasion of Ahaz's neighbors to the north (7:16-25), this particular prophecy would be fulfilled with Jesus' birth about 700 years later.

Isaiah goes on to describe how the Assyrians would become an instrument of God in punishing Samaria for its rejection of God (8:1-10) but that this wasn't to be the end for Isaiah and his sons or for Judah (8:11-18). A promise of a savior to come makes for Isaiah's increasingly positive message, right up to where he mentions a place called "Galilee," "of the nations," "by the sea" (9:1), a place that, at that time, didn't exist with that name. He goes on to say that the people who have "lived in darkness" have "seen a great light" (9:2), and leads up to the second great Messianic prophecy: that a child will be born "unto us" who will have the government "on his shoulders" (9:6) and who will be called "wonderful counselor," "mighty God," "everlasting Father," and the "Prince of Peace."

Isaiah spends the rest of chapter 9 and the first part of chapter 10 reinforcing the case against the northern kingdom and the Lord's anger with those people. Damascus is mentioned several times throughout as being the instrument of God's justice against them, which is why this chronology also includes the passage from the 17th chapter: a cryptic prophecy from Isaiah that actually marks one of the very few prophecies made by him that have not yet come to pass. Damascus, now part of Syria (geographically almost the same territory as the ancient nation of Assyria), has the distinction of being the oldest *continuously* inhabited city in the world, yet the Lord is telling us via Isaiah that this will not last forever. There will come a day when Damascus will be a "heap of ruins" and will cease to be a city (17:1). Isaiah goes into his usual level of poetic detail and metaphor in describing this event, and ends with a very interesting description of those who will be destroyed, as the people whose "portion it is to loot us, the lot of those who plunder us". This doesn't seem like a terribly profound way of describing their Assyrian enemy, except that the phrase is also the name that Isaiah is commanded to give his son at the beginning of chapter 8: Maher-Shalal-Hash-Baz, which means "quick to the plunder, swift to the spoil", a reference to the fact that before his son would grow to be a man, Assyria would invade and carry off the people of the northern kingdom.

August 9, NT
1 Corinthians 9:1-27
The Gospel is Its Own Reward

One of the most difficult things about being an evangelical Christian in today's world, all issues of modern persecution aside, is dealing with skeptics and critics who (rightly) point out the hypocrisy of wealthy televangelists who have fleeced their congregations for tens of millions of dollars, all contributed voluntarily or in exchange for tiny material rewards, but that end up funding private jets and beachfront properties for the phony preachers. The critics who then say that they'll never become a Christian or never attend a church service blame their choice on these supposed-ministers of God who have abused their positions to the detriment of all seekers. No amount of skill on the part of *real* witnesses can overcome the entrenched attitudes of *some* to whom one tries to share the Gospel. This must have been an issue in Paul's time, as well, and he devotes the entire 9th chapter of this letter to how he did NOT use his time with the Corinthians to build his wealth.

It's not that people cannot or should not be able to make a living sharing the Gospel. Even Paul explained that he COULD have accepted pay for what he did, but he chose not to - that it was HIS choice, not the demand of any Corinthians. In Acts 18, it is mentioned that Paul was a tentmaker. That fact isn't repeated here in 1 Corinthians, but it can be presumed that Paul used this method, just as David sold his services as a shepherd, to make a living. Paul chose not to use the missionary journey to make a living by itself because he feels that the Gospel itself is reward enough, and he became quite good at it. The discipline needed to accomplish this is likened to that of an athlete (1 Cor 9:24-27) in one of 1 Corinthians' best known passages.

August 10, OT
Hosea 5:8-7:16
The Downward Spiral, Part Two; Israel and Judah's Restoration

Like his contemporary Amos (as well as his contemporary Isaiah, as we will read later), Hosea's prophecy consists mostly of the warnings, directed against the northern kingdom, of the destruction and exile that was soon to come due to their gross sin. This continues (after we last read from Hosea on August 4) in the first part of this reading, as Hosea delivers more harsh messages for the tribe of Ephriam in particular, which he then uses as a metaphor for the entire northern kingdom.

A change in tone comes in at the end of chapter 5 and the beginning of chapter 6, with a prophecy that could be interpreted as Messianic. In Hosea 5:17, the Lord explains through Hosea that He will "return to my place" after the exile but that a return is possible once the people acknowledge their guilt and "seek my face" and earnestly seek the Lord in their distress. He goes on to invite his audience to return to the Lord (6:1) and then uses a curious timeline metaphor: after saying that He has "torn us" in order to "heal us," the prophecy says that after two days He will "revive us" and "on the third day" He will raise us up (6:2). Knowing that the coming exile would certainly last more than three days, this prophecy sounds more like a prediction of the Resurrection of the Messiah yet to come.

After this, Hosea returns to the downward spiral of Israel's sins and the coming punishment, but with this twist: unlike Amos, these predictions of doom also include his native Judah (6:4, 6:11).

August 10, NT
1 Corinthians 10:1-11:1
Symbolism Yes, Not Idolatry

When one reads the account of the Exodus, when Moses led the Israelites out of Egypt to the Promised Land and received the Law from God, it's easy to miss the symbolism in some of the details of their journey. For example, as echoed here, the repeated references to "speaking to the rock" and Moses' striking of the rock to bring forth water are actually symbolized by the one Rock that is our Rock of salvation, our Lord Jesus Christ (10:1-4). Of course, the main reason for bringing up Moses and the Exodus is to point out how the Israelites made for an example of how NOT to live our lives in relationship to our Lord. Paul describes several of Israel's sins to make the point, focusing mainly on idolatry, and concluding with the simple admonition to "flee from idolatry" (10:14). Along the way, Paul offers one of the most important pieces of advice regarding sin and temptation: that no one is tempted beyond their ability to endure it if they are believers (10:13).

Catholics following this reading plan will instantly recognize verses 16-17 as the base for the lyrics to another popular John Michael Talbot hymn, "One Bread, One Body". Just as a rock is a symbol that represents Jesus Christ, so too are the bread and the wine used in the Lord's Supper. The comparison of the Lord's Supper to the sacrifices made by the Israelites and the sacrifices made by pagans to idols is a very important clarification of what Jesus meant when He broke bread with his disciples at the real Last Supper. It was obvious that some form of Lord's Supper was already in practice by this time.

Continuing then on an earlier point he made, Paul touches on the issues of eating meat sacrificed to idols by stating that what's important is to give God the glory in everything you eat, or drink… or do.

August 11, OT
2 Kings 16:10-18; 2 Chronicles 28:22-25; 2 Kings 15:30-31; 2 Kings 17:1-2; Hosea 8:1-9:17
The Last King of Israel

Most of the people mentioned at this point in 2 Kings, 2 Chronicles, or even the prophecies of Hosea (or Isaiah or Micah, see readings for the next few days) were only vaguely aware that the saga of the kings of Israel and Judah was about to come to an end. The prophets predicted that the northern kingdom would soon fall, and thus be the end of Israel for 10 of Israel's 12 tribes, but they didn't know *exactly* when or under which king this would occur. And with the exception of a few prophecies at this point (there would be many more later), there was little to indicate that anyone in Jerusalem and the surrounding area knew what would befall them many years after Israel's fall. Thus is was that Ahaz, king of Judah, was not aware that his idolatry described in 2 Kings 16:10-18 and 2 Chronicles 28:22-25 not only marked him as one of the worst kings of Judah, but that it also may have hastened the downfall of his northern neighbors. Nor was Ahaz aware that Hoshea, son of Pekah, came to power as the last king of Israel.

Hoshea's biography is nearly as brief as his reign in the North: 9 years, doing evil in the sight of the Lord, which was basically true of every king in Samaria, capital of the northern kingdom of Israel (2 Kings 17:1-2). Hosea's prophecies continue to point out the nature of the oncoming disaster about to befall Samaria, with two key verses in today's segment: Hosea 8:7, where Israel's sins are likened to "reaping the wind," and Hosea 9:17, where we are told that the people of Israel will be "wanderers among the nations," indicating how they will be dispersed, thus giving rise to the title the 10 "LOST" tribes of Israel.

August 11, NT
1 Corinthians 11:17-34; 11:2-16
The Lord's Supper and Practices of Worship

A better understanding of the two points made here in chapter 11 of Paul's First Letter to the Corinthians can be gained by reading them in the order specified, the reverse of how it is presented in the Epistle itself. Continuing from yesterday's discussion on the practice of the Lord's Supper, Paul acknowledges the divides that had taken place in Corinth and chastises them for it (1 Corinthians 11:17-22). We see similar disagreements about the Lord's Supper and liturgy and worship in general in our churches today. Catholics view the Eucharist completely differently than Protestants and Evangelicals do, though our practices are similar. The early church, and Corinth in particular, obviously practiced some primitive form of it and incorporated it into their worship ceremonies. Paul masterfully brings it all together by describing the proper method of partaking in the Lord's Supper (11:23-26), using quotes from Jesus and words that are in common with every denomination's version of the one ceremony Jesus himself taught us to do in His memory.

Paul goes on to describe the consequences of not receiving the Lord correctly in the breaking of the bread (11:27-32) and the correct mindset to engage in it. One of the more important differences between the modern liturgy of Communion and the way it was done back in the 1st century is that there was usually a full meal involved, of which the Lord's Supper was just one part. Paul's scolding of the Corinthians in verses 17-22 includes mention of this, as does verses

33-34, where he also mentions his desire to return to Corinth at some later date.

In the earlier section of the chapter (verses 2-16), Paul goes into considerable detail about the proper covering, or lack thereof, of people's heads, both men and women. Portions of this passage have been misinterpreted and misused for many years, but a correct interpretation actually answers many questions, and those answers *should* settle many matters. All that it takes to make a correct interpretation is to read the *entire* passage, and in the context of what came before (in yesterday's reading in particular) and after, which you should first. Remember: Paul's first letter to the Corinthians was written in *response* to at least one piece of correspondence he received from those people, which in turn was a followup to his visit during the Second Missionary Journey. We don't have the letter written *to* Paul, but we can infer from his responses what was in it: lots of detail about disagreements and divides that were created by the Corinthians after Paul planted a church there. The divisions largely concerned things that didn't much matter, as you have read in previous chapters. But when things regarding the order of worship, something we call a "liturgy", come up, Paul gets more specific in what should and should not be done. And in that regard, the last verse of yesterday's reading makes a terrific lead-in to this section: in our worship of the Lord, we are to be *like* the Lord; we are to attempt to *imitate* the Lord.

So we can draw certain conclusions from these 15 verses, all positive (or at least neutral) truths, without getting into any of the red herrings brought up by skeptics and atheists about how these truths make women out to be second class believers. Start with this question: is God male or female? God is male, as proven by these facts: Jesus is male and Jesus is God, and Jesus taught us to pray to "Our Father". As we imitate Jesus, we imitate the *man* he was and behave in a way that distinguishes the appearance of men from women. Does any of this mean that women can't be ministers/pastors? No, of course not (though the Catholic Church interprets this passage as saying just that). It does mean that we shouldn't be doing things that *blur the lines between what it means to be a man vs. what it means to be a woman*. Does any of this mean that women aren't equal to men? Not at all. God created men and women to be equal, just different. Men and women have different roles to play in life, and Paul's examples of "head coverings" (and double use of the word translated as "head") are merely a liturgical example of how these differences should be shown when gathering to worship the Lord.

August 12, OT
Hosea 10:1-12:14
The Destruction to Come from God's Viewpoint

Israel had been divided for a long time by the time Hosea wrote his prophecies. Hosea's writings aren't as long as some others, but it was spread out over the reigns of 4 kings in Judah, the last two of which reigned during the time of Samaria's last king, Hoshea. Though we have not yet read of the last of the 4 kings of Judah during Hosea's prophecies, Hezekiah, it can be assumed that Hezekiah's reign had begun by the time of the writing of this part of Hosea. The reason for this assumption can be found at the beginning and end of the middle chapter (11) of today's OT reading.

In chapter 10, Hosea continues his explanation of why the northern kingdom is about to be destroyed, citing mainly the idolatry and turning away from God that was taking place (Hosea 10:1-15), but then makes a very sharp change in tone as chapter 11 begins. In chapter 11, Hosea speaks for God in expressing how much He loves Israel, and how sad He now is because of what must come next. Allowing the events to unfold was extremely sad for God, but it couldn't be avoided: God's chosen people was about to be 10/12th destroyed, and the tribes of the northern kingdom would call an Assyrian their king (11:5). It's at the end of the chapter that we get a clue that this exile would occur and this prophecy was written during the reign of a good king in Judah, not the evil king Ahaz, as Hosea points out that Judah "still walks with God" and is faithful still (11:12).

After this, Hosea returns to his more negative tone, and prophesies that although Samaria's destruction is soon to come, Judah's punishment will also come... just later. God has an indictment against Judah too, and their time will also come (12:2-14).

August 12, NT
1 Corinthians 12:1-31
Spiritual Gifts, Part One: One Body, Many Members

It is frankly amazing how well, in the case of this chapter of Paul's First Letter to the Corinthians, Greek metaphors translate into the English language, with one in particular being very important to today's NT reading. The metaphor is "the body". Paul uses the various parts of the human body as a metaphor to describe how believers are members of the Body of Christ much the same way as a hand or a foot is a member of the human body. Paul starts by first going over the issue of spiritual gifts, of which all believers have at least one. No particular gift possessed by anyone is necessarily better or more important than any other (with one notable exception); the important thing is that we all get these gifts from the same Holy Spirit and they are used to worship the same Lord (I Cor 12:4-11). It's the same with the body: no one part of the body is necessarily better or more important than any other when they all work together (12:12-26). He even mentions, explicitly, the fact that both Jews and Gentiles are part of this Body.

So, thus, we all have spiritual gifts, though we don't all have the *same* gifts. But as members of the Body of Christ, we should all "desire" those greater gifts (12:27-31a). Paul leaves us, at the end of one of the most positive-toned chapters in his Epistles, with a great lead-in to the next, by telling us that he will show us the "most excellent way" of them all, in tomorrow's reading.

August 13, OT
Hosea 13:1-14:9; Micah 1:1-7
The Lord's Anger; The Lord's Mercy

The end of the book of Hosea and the first reading from Micah express several things in common. One is that the great sin of the northern kingdom must be punished; thus, the Lord's great anger is directed against them and results in their destruction. For all but one verse of chapter 13, Hosea graphically expresses the Lord's anger against Israel, and the tribe of Ephraim in particular. But in one verse (Hosea 13:14), a glimmer of hope is offered, in that God (the "I" mentioned twice) will deliver His people, a reference to a Savior yet to come.

Throughout Hosea's last chapter (14:1-9), a positive message is given, advising Israel to repent so that the Lord's blessings return.

Micah is another of the so-called "minor prophets" and a contemporary of Isaiah, Amos, and Hosea. Like Hosea, to which he is most similar, Micah lived in Judah and prophesied during the reigns of Jotham, Ahaz, and Hezekiah, overlapping the reigns of the last two kings of the north (Micah 1:1). But unlike Hosea, and though Micah predicts the fall of Samaria and the exile to the Assyrians, he spends considerably more time throughout the book on the fact that Judah is going to fall too, and for the same reason as Israel (1:2-7).

August 13, NT
1 Corinthians 13:1-13
Spiritual Gifts, Part Two: Complete, Mature Love

It's the subject of more popular song lyrics than any other topic. Shakespeare used it as the foundation of all of his comedic plays. Several verses regarding this word from this passage are frequently used in wedding ceremonies and vows. It is the basis for God's relationship with humans - the reason we were created, and the reason we were redeemed by a Savior. Yet it is also one of the most badly misused words in the English language, used as it is to justify all sorts of sexual sin. That word, in English, is *love*.

The most popular English translation of the Bible doesn't even translate the word as "love;" instead, it is translated in the KJV as "charity." The original Greek word "agape," as one particular *form* of love, appears 10 times in this 13-verse chapter, and is referred to indirectly an additional 8 times. All 10 times, it is translated as "charity" in the KJV, as the Latin Vulgate uses the word "caritas" in all 10 places. But this odd translation of "agape" isn't just in older translations, as the Geneva Bible of 1599, predating the KJV, translates the word "agape" as "love" in 9 of the 10 places where it appears.

There are actually 4 different words in Greek that English translators render as "love," each referring to a different *form* of love. As a direct continuation of Paul's discussion of Spiritual Gifts, Paul states that this form of love, the most pure form of caring compassion anyone can have for another, is not only another spiritual gift, but the *most superior* of them all. The Greek "agape" is a noun, but the form of love to which it refers is perhaps best thought of in the way DC Talk put it in their popular 1992 song: Love (spelled "Luv" in the song title) is a *Verb*. And it is this form of love, in its most complete and mature form, that is exalted here by Paul as the "greatest of these."

August 14, OT
2 Kings 17:3-23; 2 Kings 18:9-12; 2 Kings 17:24-41
The Fall of Israel

http://www.vtaide.com/gleanings/Kings-of-Israel/kings.html

Today's reading, technically, marks the end of the Saga of the Kings of Israel and Judah, because the first half of that statement comes to an end here. Though the kingdom of Judah would last for more than a century afterwards, and was headed for the same fate but with a different enemy, the fall of the northern kingdom of Israel occurs in this reading in 2 Kings exactly as prophesied by Isaiah, Amos, Hosea, and others. The Saga began after the death of Solomon, when Jeroboam took 10 of the 12 tribes and split the kingdom into northern and southern parts. The southern part maintained the Davidic line (Judah) while the northern part, which retained the name Israel, would see an unbroken string of kings listed as doing *evil* in the sight of the Lord, following in the ways of its first king, Jeroboam, on through to its last king, Hoshea.

The first 4 verses (2 Kings 17:3-6) describe the final corruption of Hoshea, and how the king of Assyria finally took the capital city of Samaria and dragged the people off to foreign exile. The writer of the books of the Kings (still unknown) then goes on to explain why this happened (17:7-23) in terms that sound almost exactly like the prophets of that day, such as Hosea in particular. The fall itself is described briefly again in 2 Kings 18:9-12. Then, back in the rest of 2 Kings 17, we read of how Israel's cities then were filled with the invading people, who brought their pagan customs with them, leaving the 10 "lost" tribes among the land of the Medes and elsewhere "even to this day" according to the writer. Certainly one of the saddest days in the history of God's Chosen People, and there were more sad days yet to come.

August 14, NT
1 Corinthians 14:1-40
Spiritual Gifts, Part Three: Speaking in Tongues

One of the most contentious topics in the Church today is the practice of speaking in tongues. Charismatics place a lot of emphasis on it while mainstream Protestants either ignore it or even condemn the practice. Even the very legalistic practices of the Catholic Church have no rule *against* glossolalia (from the Greek "glossa", meaning "a language"), at least not in one's private prayer life. All of the controversy surrounding this practice would, however, go away if people would just do two things: read today's passage from Paul's first Epistle to the Corinthians, and then carefully put it in the context of the last two days' readings as well as the mentions of "tongues" in Acts.

It should first be noted that *every* mention of "tongues" or "speaking in tongues" throughout the New Testament uses the exact same Greek word. It is thus important to understand that when the Apostles received the Holy Spirit in Acts chapter 2, and began to speak in "foreign tongues," these languages were *real, known* languages. Every reference thereafter, including here in 1 Corinthians 14, assumes that a real language is being spoken, although one that is not necessarily familiar to the person who is speaking. This means that the practice as is commonly seen and heard in some Pentecostal churches, where unintelligible gibberish appears to come from the speaker, stands in *clear violation* of what Paul recommends in this chapter. Apparently, the problem of "tongues" going uninterpreted in public isn't a new phenomenon that has only appeared since the beginning of the 20th century; the Corinthians were likewise perplexed by this and were doing the same thing as modern Charismatics are doing.

A proper interpretation of what God thinks of tongues stems from the *context* of what Paul writes in this chapter: tongues, like prophecy, like even *love*, is a **spiritual gift** we get from the Holy Spirit. Chapter 13 was not a break in the discussion of spiritual gifts on Paul's part; it was the *culmination* of it, as he wrote that even love itself (translated as "charity" in some places) is the greatest of all spiritual gifts. Here in chapter 14, Paul still has positive things to say about tongues, but he emphasizes that other gifts, especially prophecy, are *superior* to the ability to speak in a foreign language. Such conversations with God should be translated and correctly interpreted, not simply left as unintelligible utterances. For the sake of orderly worship, the number of people speaking in this manner should be limited, not like the complete chaos that sometimes ensues in Pentecostal worship services or prayer meetings. When someone speaks in tongues like this, it should be used as a way of building up the church ("edifying"), not simply some mystical experience in which the speaker can just turn off his/her brain and spout nonsense. Most of all, it's important to note the intended *audience* of speaking in tongues: *unbelievers*, not those who are already saved. Go on YouTube and search for "speaking in tongues" and watch a video of it happening, and then read some of the (mostly hostile) comments people write there. The unbelievers who ridicule the practice of tongues are the ones in the greatest need of the message being spoken, so it's that much more important that when speaking in tongues is taking place, that the guidelines put forth here by Paul are followed properly.

In the end, it's all about edification of the church and orderly worship, and marks the end of a 3-chapter-long discussion of spiritual gifts.

August 15, OT
Isaiah 5:1-30; 2 Kings 16:19-20; 2 Chronicles 28:26-27; 2 Kings 18:1-2; 2 Chronicles 29:1; 1 Chronicles 4:34-43
A Warning for Judah that Applies to Today

Lots of people today write "blogs" or other types of articles that are posted on websites for either anyone to read or for a specific group of people. My earliest experience with this actually predates what we now call the World Wide Web. In the late 1980s and early 1990s I used to write articles that were posted on BBSs (bulletin board systems), the equivalent of what we now do with social media like Facebook or Twitter. Once people started using browsers and public Web Log (blog) sites in the later 1990s, I joined up and started blogging too. I clearly remember my very first such article: it was called "The Isaiah 5:20 world". That verse is in today's OT reading.

Without going into detail about that original blog, suffice it to say that the key verse (Isaiah 5:20) in this reading is what makes the entire warning in Isaiah chapter 5 just as applicable to the world today, and the U.S. in particular, as it was in Judah just after the exile of the northern kingdom. If the prophecies of Isaiah are presented to us in their proper sequence in the Bible, then this warning for Judah was written prior to Isaiah's last warning to Samaria, and thus prior to the Fall of Israel, read yesterday. On the other hand, Isaiah may have written this warning, sometimes called the "Song of the Vineyard" due to its use of that metaphor to describe Judah, just *after* the Fall of Israel as he turned his attention (as he does for more than half of his entire book) to the Fall of Jerusalem/Judah which was to come. The latter seems more likely, despite reading chapters 6-10 before chapter 5, and both before reading Isaiah 1-4 a little over a week from now.

Regardless of which chronological interpretation is made, the warning ("woe") to the people of Judah was quite clear: if you're among those who call evil "good" and good "evil" (particularly the latter, which has become epidemic in recent years), you are in grave danger. The key verse describing the consequences of this sin is 5:26, which starts "He will raise a signal for nations far away" (ESV), referencing Babylon, a nation very far away, that would eventually do to Judah what Assyria did to Samaria: invade, conquer, and carry off the people into exile.

The remaining parts of today's OT reading wraps up the reign of Ahaz and begins the reign of Judah's next-to-last "good" king, Hezekiah, which synchronizes the chronology with the Assyrian exile following Israel's last king. A brief paragraph from *1* Chronicles describes the men in the time of Hezekiah who helped defeat an enemy, the most interesting verse noting the fact that these families "lived there to this day" (1 Chronicles 4:43). Noting that the Chronicles were written long after both exiles and even after Judah's return to Jerusalem, this indicates that at least some of the people of Judah were NOT exiled as Isaiah warned.

August 15, NT
1 Corinthians 15:1-34
The Central Tenet of all Hope

The longest chapter in Paul's first Letter to the Corinthians is not the 40-verses of chapter 14; rather, it is the 58 verses of chapter 15, which is broken into two day's readings.

One of my personal favorite music bands is named for two words - "Third Day" - in 1 Corinthians 15:4. Third Day refers to the fact that one of the central tenets of our faith is that not only did Jesus die, but he rose again on that third day. The verses on either side of this (15:3-5) are quoted almost verbatim in the Nicene Creed, first written about

275 years after Paul wrote this letter, as a profession of faith. But for all the emphasis on faith, that faith is said to be in *vain* if not for that one central tenet for the hopes of all mankind: the resurrection of the dead, including the fact that Jesus rose as well. Paul makes an impeccably logical argument in favor of Christ's Resurrection (15:12-26), about which whole books have been written. The last few verses of that section, and verse 26 in particular, not only solidify the case for Jesus' Resurrection, but also for Young Earth Creationism, as the last enemy to be defeated (death) was the result of the first man, who could not have lived much more than about 4000 years before Paul wrote this Divinely-inspired Epistle.

Paul's discussion of the Resurrection is bookended by verses that emphasize the importance of this tenet of faith above all others (15:1-3, 15:27-34).

August 16, OT
Isaiah 13:1-16:14
Oracles Concerning Babylon, Assyria, Philistia, and Moab

On numerous occasions throughout human history, God has made use of "evil" nations and people to accomplish His will. For example, the Godless nation of Assyria had just recently invaded the Northern Kingdom of Israel when Isaiah wrote the oracles that make up today's OT reading. Why would God allow this to happen? Because something had to be done to what had become the Godless nation of Israel a.k.a. the northern kingdom. Justice demanded that they be punished. Who else would accomplish this? Were there any other nations in the world of the time that *weren't* Godless? Well, we all know the answer to that.

Isaiah's prophecies weren't restricted to just Assyria, though. After warning Judah of the consequences of their rebellion, Isaiah starts this section by issuing a warning to the nation that would eventually dish out Judah's punishment: Babylon. There are some that read Isaiah 13:1-14:23 with the misinterpretation that the oracle is directed against Judah as was chapter 5, but this is not the case as evidenced mainly by Isaiah 14:1-23. There, after warnings of doom, Isaiah reassures the people of Judah that their nation will eventually be restored, and *Babylon* will be the one that gets punished.

Buried inside the prophecy against Babylon, specifically the part sometimes labeled "Israel's taunt of Babylon," is a passage that, if you read it using most of the newer translations of the Bible, you'll *miss*.

There are many references in both the Old and the New Testaments to The Devil. He appears as a serpent in Genesis 3. He is named as the accuser (English "Satan") first in Job 1, later in Zechariah 3, and then several times in the New Testament. So where does the reference come from that gives him the name "Lucifer?" It's right here in this passage: in Isaiah 14:12, Isaiah speaks from the point of view of the Remnant of Israel to the one who inspired (will inspire in future tense) the invasion and exile by Babylon. Isaiah addresses this being as the "morning star" or "day star", "son of the morning" or "dawn". In older translations and those that rely to any degree on the Latin Vulgate, the Latin name for morning star is used, which is Lucifer.

The Isaiah passage confirms that Lucifer was once in heaven and fell to earth (14:12-14). Later references confirm this identity in the New Testament as a being that can masquerade as an "angel of light".

He continues with oracles concerning Assyria (14:24-27), and two nations that Israel and Judah had to deal with in the past: Philistia (14:28-32) and Moab (15:1-16:14).

August 16, NT
1 Corinthians 15:35-58
Victory in the Lord

Paul's discussion of the Resurrection - both of Christ and of those who believe - continues here with an explanation of how the dead are raised, obviously in response to a question by the Corinthian people.

The question was obviously about what kind of body we were going to have in the kingdom of heaven (1 Corinthians 15:35), which Paul answers using the metaphor of a seed which dies when planted in the ground yet goes on to become a grain plant (15:36-49). He goes on to clarify the fact that our flesh and blood bodies do not inherit the kingdom of God, but rather, our imperishable spirits (15:50), but then makes a most interesting prophecy that he had previously made to the Thessalonians: the rapture (15:51-52). In making the prophecy, Paul uses it to explain the need to obtain new bodies for heaven, which even those who are raptured will obtain (15:53-55), and he quotes Isaiah 25:8 and Hosea 13:14 along the way.

Thus it is that faith that gives us the ability to say we have victory over death, a victory for which we give thanks - to the one who first obtained that victory, Jesus Christ.

August 17, OT
2 Chronicles 29:3-31:1; Psalm 66:1-20; Psalm 67:1-7
Hezekiah's Revivals, Part One

Hezekiah was the next-to-last "good" king of Judah, and successfully enacted the most-sweeping positive reforms in the history of the divided kingdom. Even before witnessing the fall of his northern neighbors in Israel ("...in the first month of the first year," 2 Chronicles 29:3), he started his campaign of reforms by repairing the damage to the temple and bringing in the priests to remove all the items of defilement, largely placed there by his father (29:3-16). He then had the temple re-consecrated and restarted the temple sacrifices and worship (29:17-36). He even accomplished something that previous "good" kings in Judah (Asa, Jehoshaphat, Uzziah) failed to do: he invited all of Judah and even the few remaining peoples left in Israel (mentioning Ephraim and Manasseh by name , 30:1) to celebrate Passover (30:1-12), and they gathered in Jerusalem for the re-institution of the most important feast on the Jewish calendar (30:13-27). When Passover was done, the pagan idols in Judah and Benjamin (which was also in the south) as well as the territories of Ephraim and Manasseh were destroyed (31:1). With the writing of two joyous praise Psalms, 66 and 67, at this time, it seemed as though Judah was about to enter a golden age. Tomorrow's reading also reflects this, but though the fall of Samaria and the coming fall of Jerusalem were 133 years apart, storm clouds were already gathering on the horizon.

August 17, NT
1 Corinthians 16:1-24
Paul Concludes the First Letter to the Corinthians

As will become increasingly apparent as other Epistles are read, as well as other history in the Acts of the Apostles, the Corinthian church that Paul helped plant on his Second Missionary Journey was a large and vibrant one, and Paul was particularly fond of them (despite the resistance he got). As was his custom in each of his letters, he concludes the letter on a personal note, mentioning other missionaries

(Timothy, 1 Corinthians 16:10; Apollos, 16:12), other churches (Galatia, 16:1), and even his then-current location in Ephesus (16:8), which we last read about on July 30, and confirming the timeline of this letter in Paul's mention of staying there at least through Pentecost. Paul's intention was to visit Corinth again on his way through Macedonia (16:5-7) on his current Missionary Journey, his third. He wanted to stay for "some time," perhaps the winter, but as will be read tomorrow and the next day, plans can quickly change.

August 18, OT
2 Chronicles 31:2-21; Isaiah 18:1-21:17
Hezekiah's Revivals, Part Two; More Oracles from Isaiah

The description of the main positive reforms enacted by King Hezekiah of Judah continues here in today's OT reading. The Temple had been refurbished, the pagan idols removed, Passover had been celebrated (at least once; it's not made clear in what year of his reign that this occurred), and now the work of the Levitical priests resumed in full measure (2 Chronicles 31:3-21).

Isaiah was still prophesying during this time (as he would throughout the reign of Hezekiah), and though he would have more to say about the future fate of Judah, the oracles here are directed towards Cush (Isaiah 18:1-7), Egypt (19:1-15), Babylon (21:1-10), Edom (21:11-12), and Arabia (21:13-17). In between two of these oracles, Isaiah makes a prophecy (the distinction being that of its predictive nature) about the future fate of Egypt, Assyria, and Israel (19:16-24) that is among the few predictions made by Isaiah that have not yet been fulfilled, and a prophecy against that same Egypt and Cush (20:1-6), in one of the Old Testament's shortest chapters.

August 18, NT
Acts 20:1-16
A Change of Plans

The first narrative of Paul's Third Missionary Journey since July 30 appears here after the lengthy reading of his first Letter to the Corinthians, picking up in the aftermath of the riots in Ephesus. In the epistle just completed yesterday, Paul expressed his desire to visit Corinth again, which he did for about 3 months (Acts 20:1-3a).

However, this second visit to Corinth in Greece is not documented in Acts (though it is in his next letter to the Corinthians, starting tomorrow), likely because his plans for his departure from Corinth were thwarted by a plot came against him that forced him to reroute his journey (20:3b-6). Along the way, and after 7 days in Troas, he participated in what appeared to be a resurrection miracle (20:7-12) and then resumed his journey. His now-changed plan avoided a second appearance at Ephesus, as he hastened his way to Jerusalem for Pentecost (20:13-16).

August 19, OT
Isaiah 22:1-23:18; 2 Kings 18:7b-8; Micah 1:8-3:12
Storm Clouds Gather on the Horizon

If anyone needed reminding that this *apparent* golden age in Judah would NOT last forever, it was the people of that southern kingdom. By this time, Israel (Samaria) was no more, and the fall of Jerusalem was more than a century away. King Hezekiah was enacting great reforms, and Isaiah was prophesying against every nearby nation you can possibly name. But Isaiah (and Micah, for that matter) was most definitely not done with Jerusalem, as today's OT reading starts with a chapter-long oracle on the city of David (Isaiah 22). The vision is as vague as it is ominous, with the one thing that is clear is the nature of the coming doom: exile in a foreign land. Then, in chapter 23, Isaiah resumes his oracles on foreign lands, with a pair concerning the port cities, now within Lebanon, of Tyre and Sidon.

The brief verse and a half that follows in 2 Kings 18 shows more of Hezekiah's positive achievements. We then read from Micah for the first time in nearly a week. In that earlier reading, Micah directed his prophecy against the now-gone northern kingdom. Most of the rest of the time, his prophecies are directed against Jerusalem, starting here in Micah 1:8. Throughout the remainder of chapter 1, and all of chapters 2 and 3, Micah echoes the same kinds of prophecy about the coming exile of Judah, and Jerusalem in particular, as did Hosea and Isaiah, both of whom were contemporaries. Though the entirety of today's reading from Micah can be interpreted as negative, Micah also offered some hope in his prophecies, such as in tomorrow's OT reading.

August 19, NT
2 Corinthians 1:1-14
Comfort In The Lord

Just as was the case with Paul's Second Letter to the Thessalonians, we don't know exactly how much time elapsed between the writing of his first letter and the second to the same church, as in the case of the Corinthians. There is evidence in both of these last two cases that the letters were, essentially, written "back to back" (i.e. there were no other Epistles written between these two) and we have a little bit more information, part of which is in this first chapter of the Second Letter to the Corinthians, as to how much time elapsed, even though we're not 100% sure of these details. Matthew Henry's commentary speculates that about one year had passed between the two letters, based on information in the Acts of the Apostles, and this seems to fit the timeline here.

But so begins another instance of Paul writing a second epistle to a church to which he previously wrote and had also visited earlier (in this case, twice). There is evidence to suggest that he received a reply from the Corinthian church after his first letter, as tomorrow's reading bears out. His departure from Corinth after his second visit was rerouted through Macedonia, because of the plot discussed yesterday. This resulted in some considerable suffering which he mentions early on as an explanation (2 Corinthians 1:8-14 and continued tomorrow, plus at the end of the letter starting August 29). Although it is early in the letter, it isn't the first thing Paul writes about. After a brief greeting (1:1-2), he preaches about one of the Lord's many attributes: comfort. In the face of suffering (which Paul had undergone in Asia), there is always comfort in the Lord. Paul uses the same word translated as "comfort" or one of its tenses 9 times in verses 3-7, and four of those times in a single verse (1:4) to show how much emphasis he wanted to place on this.

After this, he uses his message about comfort to explain his sufferings, and then (tomorrow) uses that to explain why he wasn't able to visit them *a third time.*

August 20, OT
Micah 4:1-7:20
The Restoration of Israel

Micah and Isaiah share a number of characteristics. Most notably, besides just the fact that they wrote their prophecies at about the same time, is the fact that both prophets place a great deal of emphasis on not just the destruction and exile of Jerusalem but also its future restoration. During the time of King Hezekiah, the fall of Jerusalem was still over a century away, and one can interpret the fact that the oracles against Jerusalem written here fell on deaf ears. But right away here in Micah chapter 4, the prophecies start by referencing the "mountain of the house of the Lord" that shall be established as the highest of places, to which people will flock so that he will "teach us His ways and walk in His paths" (Micah 4:1-2). Micah doesn't specify when any of these things will come to pass except that they will be in the "last days," (4:1) indicating a time even after the coming of the Messiah (see also tomorrow's reading in Isaiah). Knowing this, Micah even indicates that Judah should go to Babylon with their heads held high because of the rescue (salvation in some translations) to come (4:10), via a king who will reign forever.

That king, of course, is the Lord Jesus, and one of the things brought up here by Micah is His birthplace: Bethlehem (5:2), a prophecy that would be fulfilled with Jesus' birth. He goes on to provide other details about this new ruler (5:3-5a) and about the future remnant. But God, through Micah, makes very clear that the future restoration of Israel is the result of its punishment for its sins. The chosen people of God is, in short, being indicted (6:1-7:6) and sentenced, but Micah also ends his prophecy on a positive note (7:7-20), awaiting the salvation of the Lord.

August 20, NT
2 Corinthians 1:15-2:17
Paul's Reasons for Not Visiting a Third Time

Paul's first and longest visit to Corinth is documented in the Acts of the Apostles, and he comments on this in his first letter to them. At the end of that first letter, he tells them about his planned second visit. This did take place, and lasted about 3 months, but no details are given in Acts. In fact, the only evidence we have that this second visit took place is right here in *this*, second Letter to the Corinthians. And somewhere along the way, documented only here in this letter, Paul must have wanted to return for a third time but did not, instead sending Silvanus and Timothy (2 Corinthians 1:19).

The intended third visit must have been for some kind of disciplinary action, as Paul says he chose to "spare" them (1:23) a visit in "sorrow" (2:1-4). This must have been due to some great transgression that had taken place, resulting in a perpetrator being brought before the church for discipline. Paul admonishes the Corinthian church to forgive this person "who caused you pain" (2:5-11) so that we would "not be outwitted by Satan."

But again, not in a case of excuse-making, but rather, simply supplying the Corinthians with every possible explanation, Paul mentions the absence of Titus when he was in nearby Troas as one of the main reasons for his continuation to and through Macedonia (2:12-17) after his departure. But, as he further explains, it all turned out for good as the Gospel was further spread.

August 21, OT
Isaiah 1:1-4:6
First (?) Isaiah

Prior to today's reading of the *first* four chapters of Isaiah, we covered just under 17 chapters of Isaiah on 6 days' readings (August 8, 9, 15, 16, 18, 19) already. It is plainly obvious that when the writings of Isaiah were assembled into a single scroll that some of Isaiah's prophecies were placed there out of sequence. Isaiah 1:1 identifies the writer as the son of Amoz, a resident of Jerusalem, who prophesied during the reigns of 4 kings: Uzziah, Jotham, Ahaz, and Hezekiah, the last of whom we are currently reading about in this chronological reading plan. Isaiah's earliest prophecies were made in the year of Uzziah's death, and this is chronicled in Isaiah chapter 6 which we read back on August 8. Other prophecies are easily inserted into the timelines of the other 3 kings up to Hezekiah. The mention of Hezekiah in the first verse marks this section of Isaiah as having been written and/or compiled some time during or after the reign of Hezekiah. How much later? It's hard to tell, though the works of Isaiah were widely known during the time between the Testaments. But who wrote it? That question may, for some readers, sounds like a "duh" remark, but it's a serious question: was the Book of the Prophet Isaiah the work of *one* person, or were there (as some would put it) *multiple* Isaiahs?

The theory of a second Isaiah ("Deutero-Isaiah") is a relatively new idea, first brought forth in the late 18th century by liberal theologians who looked at the later chapters of Isaiah (particularly 40 onwards) and reasoned that it would have been impossible for a man living in the time of Hezekiah to have made explicit references to things like the Babylonian Exile, and particularly Israel's return from it by decree of King Cyrus of Persia. Others make the argument that names such as Cyrus would have had no meaning to the people of Judah during the time of Hezekiah, so the references were actually historical events to whoever wrote the last roughly 40% of the book. Still others cite the abrupt change in tone and style in chapters 40-55 compared to chapters 1-39, and then sometimes add a "*third* Isaiah" to the mix by claiming that the remaining chapters were written by yet another person.

However, if the later chapters of Isaiah were indeed written by a "student of Isaiah" (as two study Bibles I own state) or someone who, with no connection to the son of Amoz, wrote those prophecies during or after the Exile, their inclusion of that first verse in the compiled scroll would make the writer a *liar*. Just as the apocryphal writings of the Book of Wisdom and Ecclesiasticus were *inspired* by the writings of Solomon in Proverbs, so any such writings *inspired* by Isaiah would have been written as a separate scroll with a notation about the material that inspired it. And thus, Jesus would not have quoted Isaiah - by name - in places like Matthew 12:17, Matthew 8:16-17, or John 12:38-41, nor would Paul have quoted Isaiah in Romans 10:16 or in 2 Corinthians (see NT reading for August 23), if it were not for their assumption that Isaiah, son of Amoz, was the *sole* writer of the book that bears his name.

And so, with that assumption, we go back to the beginning of the Book of Isaiah, written during the reign of Hezekiah as was almost ⅔ of its 66 chapters, and starting out with an oracle against Judah and Jerusalem that actually compares it to the ancient, destroyed cities of Sodom and Gomorrah (Isaiah 1:9-10). Speaking for God, Isaiah points out how it is not animal sacrifices that the Lord wants, but for the people to "wash [themselves] clean...cease to do evil… let us reason together" (1:16-18). For the rest of chapter 1, Isaiah explains how Zion has been corrupted, but will nevertheless be redeemed.

Isaiah's second chapter carries another controversy with it: English translations of Isaiah 2:1-5 and Micah 4:1-5 (yesterday) are so similar that some think they were written word-for-word identically. Indeed, the original Hebrew in the two scrolls *is* quite similar, but it is not *exactly* the same. But, the fact is that these two prophecies were written very close to the exact same time; so close, in fact, that Micah and Isaiah may have received *simultaneous inspiration* to write these parts, with neither "copying" the other (as some skeptics like to claim). In both cases, the passage refers to the future restoration of Jerusalem, the "Mount Zion" that people will flock to.

The remainder of chapter 2, all of chapter 3, and the first part of chapter 4 set up the remainder of the Book of Isaiah with one of its overarching themes: that the restoration of Israel will constitute a **remnant** of God's people that will be preserved even during the End Times.

August 21, NT
2 Corinthians 3:1-4:6
The Ministry of the Spirit vs. The Ministry of the Law

With the preliminaries out of the way, Paul goes on to the main matter at hand. The Corinthian church was not only young, but the whole of Christianity - the whole Church (in capital letters) - was still a relatively new, young thing. It was plainly time for the churches to start realizing that *they* were the New Covenant in Christ, not the words of the Law that had been written down by Moses (or, as we now suspect, his scribe). Paul even goes so far as to describe the "old covenant" as a "ministry of death" (2 Corinthians 3:7), but also goes on to compare how much of a "glory" the old vs. new covenants really are (3:8-11).

Whereas Paul previously used the metaphor of "the body" for the church, he now extends this to say that the church is the "light that shines out of the darkness" (4:6), quoting the Lord in John chapter 1 - a work that wouldn't be written for another approximately 35 years.

August 22, OT
Isaiah 10:5-12:6; Isaiah 28:1-29
Prophecies of Many Different Times

When one reads Old Testament prophecies for the first time, it is often assumed that all such predictions made before Christ were fulfilled during the time of Christ or earlier. Isaiah, however, has prophecies that apply to many different eras of man, and even include End Times prophecies that have not yet come to pass. In today's reading, Isaiah gets back to the matter at hand, specifically the most recent event of significance, the Assyrian invasion and exile of the northern kingdom (Israel/Samaria). Isaiah pronounces God's judgment on Assyria despite the fact that Assyria was (and will again be) used as a tool by God to punish Israel (and later, Judah, Isaiah 10:5-19). This judgment is due primarily to Assyria's *pride*. Isaiah then spends the rest of that chapter (10:20-34) reassuring the people that a remnant of His people will return, but only after that next dose of punishment is doled out.

When Isaiah starts the next chapter, it is fairly obvious that this is a Messianic prophecy (11:1-5). The question gradually becomes one of timing: is Isaiah making reference to Jesus' first advent, or His *second*? Verses 6-9 seem to indicate the Second Advent, still in *our* future! This idea is further reinforced by verse 10, speaking of how the nations (that would be the *Gentile* nations) will "rally to him" (11:10, NIV), which didn't happen when He first came, and verse 11 which references a SECOND reaching out, by the Lord, to regather His people (11:11), which was fulfilled with the rebirth of the modern nation of Israel in **1948**. Isaiah was not the only one to predict this, but he was the first, and his description of the event (11:12-16) along with the song of praise that follows (12:1-6) make it all the more noteworthy that the time of which he is prophesying is the present day - right now.

Even in Isaiah's warning (28:1-15) to the leaders of Ephraim (what was left of the northern kingdom) and Judah (the southern kingdom), he offers words of reassurance and makes references to what it will be like after the Second Coming of the Messiah (28:16-29).

August 22, NT
2 Corinthians 4:7-5:10
Jars of Clay

Devotees of Contemporary Christian music, as a genre, will instantly recognize the first part of 2 Corinthians 4:7 as the name of the popular band Jars of Clay, especially if using the NIV translation for this reading plan. In most translations, this is listed as "earthen vessels," which actually refers to human beings - *us* - and not the pieces of pottery that most people envision when they hear the phrase "jars of clay". The use of this metaphor by Paul is a continuation from yesterday's reading: that the Church is the image of God in the world, the light that shines in the darkness, but that this light is contained within ordinary earthly bodies, our human bodies, to drive home the point that the power of the Gospel does NOT come from ourselves, but from God. So it is that in our fragile earthen vessels, we are "...afflicted in every way, but not crushed; perplexed, but not despairing; persecuted, but not forsaken; struck down, but not destroyed" (4:8-9, NASB). Paul uses these comparisons to get back to his more favored metaphor for the Church: the body (4:10). The message is that we carry the death of the body of Jesus with us but also the living spirit of that same Jesus.

In a very real sense, this passage is a passing of the torch to the Corinthians, and thus, to the Church as a whole. Paul recognizes here the ability for the Gospel to be spread further with the help of a church, willing and able to keep the message going, and he offers much in the way of encouragement to the Corinthians in the rest of chapter 4 and into chapter 5.

August 23, OT
Isaiah 29:1-32:20
Warnings and Blessings

Much of Isaiah's prophecies have both a warning, or "woe" component, along with a blessings component where reassuring words are given to the people of Judah. Isaiah starts this prophecy with a "woe" to the people of "Ariel" (Isaiah 29:1) which is identified as a city in which David lived (or "camped" in some translations). But if you go through a map of Biblical history, you won't find any such city, and there is no mention of Ariel in 1 Samuel, 2 Samuel, or 1 Chronicles where the life of David is chronicled. There is a modern city named Ariel in the West Bank, but it was founded in 1978 and has no recorded history prior to that time. So what is meant here when Isaiah writes "woe to you, Ariel"?

The answer lies in the apparently cryptic clue in that same verse along with a translation of the ancient Hebrew: Ariel means "lion of God" and is a word that was used to symbolize Jerusalem. It is similar in usage to "Zion," with the difference being that Zion refers to the actual mountain (hill) on which Jerusalem is built, and not the city itself; nevertheless, the alternate word is sometimes used for the actual city. But another meaning of "Ariel" is a "place [city] where things are burned in a temple," which also fits the warning given here to Jerusalem (29:1-16). This, though, is followed by a "blessing after discipline" (29:17-24). That pattern is repeated in the next chapter, as a warning against forming an alliance with Egypt is given (30:1-17) followed by a "blessing" to those who heed the warning (30:18-33). Isaiah revisits the issue of Egypt again in chapter 31 (31:1-9), but follows that with a bold Messianic prophecy (32:1-20), portions of which are quoted multiple times in the New Testament.

August 23, NT
2 Corinthians 5:11-6:10
A New Creation in Christ

Many times throughout Paul's letters, including this one, encouragement is given to the church in the context of the Gospel. In yesterday's NT reading, Paul referred to our bodies as "earthen vessels" that contain the treasure of eternal life. In today's reading, he explains more about how this has come to be. In a section sometimes called "the Ministry of Reconciliation," Paul starts with a word of encouragement to those Corinthians who were called "crazy" for their belief in the central Gospel message: that one person (Jesus) died for all of us, and that in Him we all died to a *new* life (2 Corinthians 5:11-15, 5:18-21)). The passage is bookended around the key verse here: that being reconciled to God means we are a "new creation in Christ" (5:17) and that the old life is gone, replaced by the new life. He thus calls the Corinthian church "God's co-workers" (6:1, NIV) and quotes Isaiah 49:8 (noting that he doesn't identify the prophet and doesn't say anything about this being a "second Isaiah," see OT reading for August 21) to further encourage (6:2).

In the remainder of the passage, Paul lays out some additional contrasts like the ones in yesterday's reading, to show the endurance of Christ's ministry even during difficult times (6:3-10).

August 24, OT
Isaiah 33:1-35:10
Prelude to an Invasion

A prelude, in music, refers to a (usually) brief work found at the beginning of a larger suite. It can be thought of as a sort of preface, like in literature. Labeling this section as a prelude to an invasion seems to place these prophecies out of sequence; that is, until you read tomorrow's OT reading. The most significant recent event in Isaiah's time was the Assyrian invasion and exile of the Northern Kingdom (Israel). The next event in his then-future seemed to be the prophesied "punishment" of Judah that would come at the hands of Babylon, more than a century into the future. Here in chapter 33, and unlike nearly all the rest of Isaiah's prophecies, there is no mention of the name of the nation (the "destroyer", Isaiah 33:1) being prophesied against. It would be odd for this section to be about Babylon since Isaiah had previously mentioned the nation by name and would do so again in the later chapters. Isaiah had also, by this time, prophesied for many chapters against Assyria, so why would he go on for 3 more chapters, without mentioning them by name? It's clear by Isaiah's descriptions of plunder, betrayal, and destruction that the "destroyer" here *is* Assyria, and the events being referenced are the recent events in Samaria. But then, in verses 5, 14, 20, and 24, the future punishment of Assyria will come after something that has to do with *Zion*. As previously mentioned, this is the hill upon which Jerusalem sits.

But Judah wasn't invaded; Samaria was. Is there another invasion being planned? We don't find out until tomorrow's reading, but in the meantime Isaiah continues on as he did in several other passages: rather than dwell on the coming doom (even to the extent of ALL nations being judged, 34:1-17), he emphasizes the fact that a remnant will remain faithful, and that Israel will be restored, using prophecies of many time periods, including even the End Times.

August 24, NT
2 Corinthians 6:11-7:16
The Purifying; Telling the Truth in Love

The first of the two parts in today's reading from Paul's Second Letter to Corinth is all about setting ourselves apart from the rest of the world through purity. Starting with the example of a parent applying loving discipline to their children, Paul goes into the oft-quoted (and for good reason) proverb to not be "yoked together with unbelievers" (2 Corinthians 6:14). He backs this up with no less than **5** comparisons (6:15-16a) which he further backs up with 3 paraphrases of Old Testament quotes: 2 Cor 6:16b paraphrases Leviticus 26:12, Jeremiah 32:38, and Ezekiel 37:27, 2 Cor 6:17 paraphrases Isaiah 52:11 and Ezekiel 20:34 and 41, and 2 Cor 6:18 paraphrases 2 Samuel 7:14 and 7:8. In every case, particularly the middle one, the emphasis is on our *pure* relationship with God, a relationship that "sets us apart" from others, a concept translated as being "holy" or being "pure" in various places in the Old and New Testaments.

The second part of the reading is a followup to the earlier parts of the letter, in which Paul speaks on a more personal level with the Corinthian people, citing examples from what was either some sort of reply to his first letter or his second visit (2 Cor 7:2-3), even being somewhat apologetic about its tone (7:8). But, the apparent harshness of tone that led at least some in Corinth to become saddened or hurt (7:9) is actually a source of joy for Paul because of what it produced in the Corinthians: repentance (7:9-11). It means the Corinthians "got it," and that means that many souls were saved through God's Word as written through Paul. The same is as true today as it was during the first century.

August 25, OT
2 Kings 18:13-19:37; 2 Chronicles 32:1-23
The Assyrian Invasion of Judah is Thwarted

Several times over the last few days, we read of oracles written by Isaiah against the nation of Assyria, who had just invaded the northern kingdom of Israel and carried off its people to exile. It would seem odd to write another oracle against Assyria when "the damage was done," and Israel was no more, **until you realize that the king of**

Assyria wasn't done yet. Sennacherib, king of Assyria, had every intention to keep going after conquering Samaria, and do likewise to Judah. Hezekiah first attempted to buy off the invading king (2 Kings 18:13-16), but that didn't work. And so, Sennacherib sent messengers to Jerusalem to try to persuade Hezekiah that the latter's resistance was futile (18:17-18). They tried to insist that Hezekiah couldn't be trusted, that the real God had abandoned them, and that their Egyptian allies were untrustworthy, among other things (18:19-25). After a sarcastic rebuke, Assyria's messengers continued their blasphemies, insults, and threats (18:28-35) but Hezekiah had instructed his people to not answer them (18:36).

Hezekiah's men brought back the message (18:37). Then, in one of the very few places where we read about a prophet in a book of history (see tomorrow's reading where history is included in a book of prophecy), Hezekiah consults Isaiah about the Assyrian threat (19:1-5), and Isaiah offers reassuring words to Hezekiah (19:6-7). After another series of threats (19:8-13), Hezekiah does the one thing (that he should have done in the first place) that solves the problem and breaks the siege: he takes the matter to the Lord in prayer (19:14-19). What follows is a detailed prophecy from Isaiah (repeated in tomorrow's reading, 19:20-37), predicting the fall of Sennacherib and the end of the siege.

The Chronicles tells of these same events in a more brief form (2 Chronicles 32:1-20), and without the Isaiah prophecy, but then finishes the account by explaining what happened afterwards (32:21-23).

August 25, NT
2 Corinthians 8:1-24
The Joy of Generosity, Part One

Bible passages can be used for either good or bad purposes, particularly in sections like this where the writer (Paul, in this case) is writing to people on a personal level. Continuing in this vein from yesterday's NT reading, Paul tells the Corinthians about how well some other churches in Macedonia are doing as far as putting their faith in action (2 Corinthians 8:1-7), ending by telling them to "abound in this gracious work also". Paul further explains that this isn't a command (8:8) but a way of testing how genuine their love is by making this comparison. The example of Jesus "becoming poor" that we may become rich (8:9) is the capstone of Paul's advice, and the entire section is correctly used by many churches today as a way to *encourage* giving. When used properly, and by emphasizing that the Macedonian churches that Paul was using as an example were increasing their giving out of their own accord, the emphasis on the *joy* of being generous and how this builds up the church results in obvious increases in revenue.

What is unfortunate is the extent to which positive passages such as this are abused by televangelists and unscrupulous ministers to *shame* people into giving beyond their means to do so, and then pocketing an inappropriate amount of this increased revenue in order to live an opulent lifestyle. Viewing even a short amount of time on "Christian" TV networks, it's easy to catch someone making reference to this passage in 2nd Corinthians as justification for some kind of funding drive. This is not, however, the fault of Paul or the translators of God's Word; it is, rather, the fault of people who don't take the time to read passages like this in their full context, including chronological and historical context. Paul wasn't shaming the Corinthians into increasing their giving, and you shouldn't let anyone shame you for the same reason. Give generously to your church. Lift up efforts to support your church's efforts to feed and clothe the poor, and to bring the Gospel message to those who lack it. But do it all with the same JOY expressed here in this letter.

August 26, OT
Isaiah 36:1-38:22; 2 Kings 20:1-11; 2 Chronicles 32:24-26; 2 Kings 20:12-19; 2 Chronicles 32:27-31; Isaiah 39:1-8
The Assyrian Invasion of Judah is Thwarted; Hezekiah's Illness

Just as there are prophecies in places in the "historical" books of the Bible, so too is history found in books of the prophets. It is by this method that the various parts of the Bible can be synchronized into a chronological format, which is the subject of this entire book. In today's OT reading, Isaiah chapters 36 and 37 are a near-exact repeat of 2 Kings 18 and 19, read yesterday. In some English-language translations, the two book's version of events is word-for-word identical; it shouldn't be - the original Hebrew for each is quite similar but is NOT identical (similar to the situation discussed earlier where Micah 4 and Isaiah 2 have a nearly identical prophecy), and this is reflected in the *better* translations, both old (KJV, GEN) and new (NASB, ESV).

The aftermath of these events is told, then, in Isaiah 38, with detail of the illness and near-death of King Hezekiah. Hezekiah was the next-to-last "good" king of Judah, primarily because he relied on the Lord. He was, by no means, perfect, and his flaws and sins are chronicled in much the same way as David's were. Hezekiah's reliance on the Lord resulted, first, in an additional 15 years added to his life (Isaiah 38:5, 2 Kings 20:5). The version of this event in 2 Kings 20 goes into much more detail regarding the conversation the king had with Isaiah, while the version in Isaiah 38 contains a prayer (Psalm?) of Hezekiah not recorded elsewhere. The event is also recorded in 2 Chronicles 32:24-26 but with neither of the above details.

The event called "Envoys from Babylon" found in 2 Kings 20:12-19 and in Isaiah 39:1-8 (with some other important details in 2 Chronicles 32) is a direct prophecy given to Hezekiah by Isaiah due to an error made by the king. Isaiah had previously prophesied about the Babylonian exile to come, and it was meant as a warning. Obviously, Hezekiah didn't think that a visit from the Prince of Babylon would be anything to worry about, but Isaiah made it clear that the future exile and plunder of Jerusalem would be precipitated by Hezekiah's naive move to let the envoy see his treasure.

August 26, NT
2 Corinthians 9:1-15
The Joy of Generosity, Part Two

Directly continued from yesterday's reading, Paul tells the Corinthians that he has been actively boasting to the Macedonians about their generosity, and that this is the main reason Paul sent Titus and others to Corinth to take up a collection (2 Corinthians 9:1-5). Paul then gives the all-important joy-based advice to the Corinthians, and by extension *us*, about what it really means to give to the Church; advice that would, if actually read and preached by more pastors, would stop unscrupulous televangelizing in its tracks.

The key is verses 6-11, which can be paraphrased as "you reap as you sow," meaning that the more of a giver you are, the more everyone - including YOU - benefits, thanks to your generosity. God loves a "cheerful giver," (9:7) and this should be the motivation for giving, not some kind of *compulsion* from the Church. Generosity will have a kind of snowball effect - the blessings received from your giving will allow you to be even more generous, and this will result in even more thanksgiving to God (9:11).

But there is a danger in preaching on these two chapters if the last 4 verses (9:12-15) aren't included. Besides the aforementioned televangelists, another big problem in the modern Christian Church is the Prosperity Gospel. The "Name It and Claim It" movement would love nothing more than to seize on passages like 2 Corinthians 9:6-11 and use it as justification for asking for more money. That is, and many of you reading this have probably already heard this, increasing your gift to [name a pastor or church] will result in YOU receiving magnificent benefits. The emphasis in the Prosperity Gospel circles is on YOU, not the work of the Church or the salvation of souls. Verses 12-15, though, put the emphasis back where it belongs: on those who are served by your gift, not on the giver.

August 27, OT
Psalm 75:1-10; Psalm 76:1-12; Psalm 77:1-20; Psalm 80:1-19; Psalm 87:1-7; Psalm 125:1-5
Four Psalms of Asaph, Plus Two More

The first four Psalms that make up today's OT reading are all listed as Psalms of Asaph. This Asaph is not to be confused with the Asaph who was a director of music under King David. Rather, Asaph here is the one mentioned as "Asaph the seer" during the description of Hezekiah's reforms in 2 Chronicles 29 (read on August 17). He, among others, was commanded to sing praises to the Lord as part of the restoration of Temple worship. These 4 Psalms were part of that effort, and may have been written over the course of several years in the first half of Hezekiah's reign as king. The first two seem to very clearly reflect the joy of having just escaped being invaded, thus their placement just after the end of that siege. Psalm 77, and to a lesser degree all 3 others (of Asaph), seems more pensive, and makes more references to saving "Ephriam" and "Benjamin," which would reflect having been written just *before* the fall of Samaria rather than just after. But, that would still place all 4 of these after Hezekiah announced his reforms at the beginning of his reign.

The two remaining Psalms are of unknown authorship. The common theme of praise to God for Zion would seem to stem from the same recent events of having escaped the siege by Assyria, leaving Jerusalem as the capital of what was left of Israel (that is, Judah).

August 27, NT
2 Corinthians 10:1-18
Paul Defends His Ministry

Multiple times in both his first and second Letter to the Corinthians, Paul takes a moment away from preaching or edification of the newly planted church to explain things that beg the question as to what, about Paul, these people were criticizing. For all the praises he lavishes on the the people in Corinth for being so receptive to the Gospel, it is obvious from his writings in both letters that there were many who weren't so receptive. Was it the message itself? Paul's evangelizing, throughout both letters and despite being written to believers, seems to indicate there were quite a few who resisted or just didn't "get it." Was it his past as an early persecutor of Christians? His statement about not wanting to use force (2 Corinthians 10:9-10, NASB) seems to indicate that this issue came up, at least briefly, when he visited Corinth in person (either the first or second time). Was it his outward appearance? Paul makes a couple of remarks in this passage (10:7, 10:10) that seem to say that there were people who criticized him for his appearance without regard to the message being delivered.

And that brings us to the point of this passage; more than merely a defense of his ministry (though this was needed to reassure the believers), this passage makes it plain that the whole message - the Gospel - is independent of the person delivering it. It's simply not about the *messenger*, it's about the *message*. He makes this point by using a paraphrase of something Jesus said to the Apostles just before the Crucifixion: that Paul and his fellow ministers of the Gospel were taking to them a message not "of the world" though they were "in the world" (10:3, 10:13-18) Despite the fact that this quote of Jesus (found in John 17:14-15) wouldn't be written down for another 35 years or so, Paul would use variations of this metaphor elsewhere in his letters, most notably in a letter not yet written to the place he wanted to visit the most: Rome (Romans 12:1-2).

August 28, OT
Isaiah 24:1-27:13
The Apocalypse of Isaiah

The beginning of this section, labeled "Judgment on the Earth" in most Bibles, is a subject of some considerable debate, even among the most scholarly. As mentioned previously, Isaiah's prophecies cover many different time periods, including even the End Times yet to come. The tone and language are definitely apocalyptic, and fits right alongside the New Testament book of Revelation with its images of horror, devastation, and doom. The word "earth," as it appears in numerous places in just Isaiah 24 alone, is the same Hebrew word used and translated as "earth" when referring to the *whole* earth in places like Genesis, where we read of the earth's creation. So, it would seem reasonable that Isaiah 24 refers to the End Times, still in our future.

The debate, however, concerns some English translations of this book that render the word "earth" as "country" instead, and thus turn this prophecy into an oracle concerning the coming exile of Judah by the Babylonians. Two days ago, we read of Hezekiah's welcome of envoys from Babylon, a naive error that he was "called out" for by Isaiah. With the very next reading from Isaiah going into such lurid detail about doom to come, who is not to say that this isn't a prediction of the exile? A casual reading of Isaiah 25 and 26, with its song of praise to God, and Isaiah 27, with its promise of eventual deliverance for Israel, seem to bear this out too.

But that's with a casual, not an in-depth, reading. Verses like Isaiah 24:21 indicate a judgment on all the kings of the earth that has not yet come to pass, and includes judgment on "the host of heaven," referring to the angels. The Lord reigning "on Mount Zion" in verse 23 is also a known End Times event, prophesied by many others besides Isaiah. A verse by verse expository of the songs in Isaiah 25 and 26 reveal prophecies regarding the resurrection of the dead and the restoration of Jerusalem that don't fit with the return from exile that Isaiah would prophecy later. But most of all, Isaiah concludes this section in 27:12-13 with a prophecy about how Israel will become a thriving and very large nation once again, stretching all the way from "the Wadi of Egypt" to the Euphrates river (27:12), gathered "one by one," and referencing both those suffering under Assyria (10 of the 12 tribes) as well as those "exiled in Egypt" (which could refer to the flight to Egypt by the family of Jesus, 27:13) as returning to worship the Lord on the "holy mountain of Jerusalem". Although partly coming true with the modern nation of Israel in 1948, the full measure of these prophecies have yet to come to pass.

August 28, NT
2 Corinthians 11:1-15
Father of the Bride

Most Bibles label this section as something like "Paul Defends His Apostleship" or similar, including the translation I most favor, the NASB. One of the reasons I favor the NASB, beyond its perceived level of accuracy, is a *measurable* part of that accuracy, in that the NASB translates each given word in Greek into the *same* word in English each time it appears. Not even the KJV can make that claim (although it comes closer than any other besides the NASB)! Thus, when Paul asks his readers to "bear with me," (2 Corinthians 11:1) the same word is used each time the word "bear" appears throughout the New Testament, not just Paul's 2nd Letter to Corinth, and it can be thought of as "tolerate" each time. In other words, Paul's defense of his ministry and his visit to Corinth a few years earlier ended with chapter 10, and now he's on to another point, asking us to "indulge" him for a while.

It would be easy to go on and on about the Biblical use of the word tolerance, as Paul uses it here, and apply it to issues of today, but that's not what this passage is all about. Rather, it is Paul's way of introducing this idea, not exactly new at the time, of the Church being the "bride of Christ," with Paul acting as a sort of "father of the bride." This metaphor (11:2), though not stated directly, is implied there to give warning to the young, naive, and vulnerable Church in the verses that follow. Paul would later use the metaphor of the Church being the bride of Christ in other Epistles, notably Ephesians (in chapter 5). Being young and inexperienced, just like a virgin bride, Paul saw the same problem then as many young people face today: being swayed by other influences that could pull them away from the Church, and away from God (11:3). For instance, Paul knew of his (apparently many) detractors, and freely admitted to being not as good of a speaker as some of these others (11:4-6). But having already defended his ministry, including the fact that he didn't take payment from the Corinthians as did some others, Paul goes on to say that the fact that other "gospels" have had some better preachers to deliver their messages just goes to show how the Corinthians are being "too tolerant" and should, instead, listen to the real Truth (11:7-13). The comparison is even made to Satan, who disguises himself as an "angel of light" (11:14-15). Obviously, as a kind of father figure to the Bride of Christ, Paul sought to protect these people from the kinds of influences that would lead them astray.

August 29, OT
Isaiah 40:1-42:25
The Savior to Come is The Lord Himself

The majority of the New Testament quotes of Isaiah come from the last roughly 40% of the book, that is, chapters 40 through 66, the first 3 of which are read today. Over the course of the next week, we will cover these last 27 chapters of the largest OT prophecy, uninterrupted, and in the sequence presented in the Bible. The jumping around that has been done so far, of the first 39 chapters, was due mainly to synchronize the prophecies with the events in the lives of 4 kings of Judah, and in particular, Hezekiah. In fact, only 7 of Isaiah's 66 chapters can be verified as being written prior to Hezekiah's reign. That means 59 chapters were written within the 29-year reign of Judah's next-to-last "good" king, of which 32 have been covered in this chronology.

It's important to note that many Bibles label this section as the beginning of a "Second Isaiah," though this chronology believes (as explained on August 21) that the Book of Isaiah is the work of a single prophet. The abrupt change in tone here, especially if you go back and read chapter 39 again before reading this (or yesterday's reading of chapters 24-27), has been used as the one of the bases for this theory. But there is another explanation: the 32 chapters of Isaiah already covered within the reign of King Hezekiah cover a period of roughly 15 years, or about half of Hezekiah's reign. Three days ago, we read about Hezekiah's illness that almost resulted in his death. God granted him an additional 15 years of which we are only about a year into that period. After the last recorded events in the life of Hezekiah, namely the visit from the Babylonian envoy, nothing more about Hezekiah's life is recorded anywhere in the Bible until his death. The only event of significance is the birth of his son Manasseh, the crown prince, but even this is not directly recorded; that is, we only learn about this from the fact that Manasseh was 12 when he became the next king. That means that the last 14 years of Hezekiah's life were a relatively quiet period, and plenty enough time for Isaiah to change his focus and shift everyone's attention to new areas of prophecy.

That new area of prophecy starts with one that doesn't sound, at first, like other Messianic prophecies he already made. But, a careful reading of 2 of the first 3 verses (Isaiah 40:2-3) show this as clearly pointing to a Savior who has removed the "iniquity" of Jerusalem, who has received "of the Lord's hand double for all her sins." This can only reference a Jerusalem that had been punished much harder than it had been up to that point, and for sins that were taken away by that Savior. The way for the Savior, identified as the Lord (40:3), needs to be prepared, which would only be necessary if the Lord *were to appear in human form*. That verse is quoted in each of the 4 Gospels and alluded to in at least 2 other places in the New Testament, referring to John the Baptist who did just exactly that.

The remainder of chapter 40 and all of chapters 41 and 42 can be much better understood in the context of a great Messianic prophecy. The reader of nearly any English language translation will quickly recognize numerous verses just in these 3 chapters that are either directly quoted (40:3, 42:1, 42:4, 42:6) or indirectly referenced (nearly too numerous to mention) in the New Testament, particular the Gospels and Paul's Letter to the Romans. **No greater declaration is made in the Old Testament that the Savior that is to come is the Lord Himself**, than right here; in fact, not until the Apostle John wrote the 4th Gospel.

But with Judah having just defeated its last enemy in Hezekiah's time, why would the Hebrew people need a savior, anyway? More on that question on future days in Isaiah.

August 29, NT
2 Corinthians 11:16-12:10
The Fool's Speech

In the 2010 movie, The King's Speech, Colin Firth plays the role of newly-crowned King George VI of England, faced with the daunting task of delivering a speech by radio at the dawn of World War II. The task was daunting not merely because of the weight of the subject matter at hand, but because the king's stuttering problem made it nearly impossible to give the speech. In the end, and with the help of a speech therapist, he comes through and delivers the essential words of encouragement for the British, giving them the resolve to face Hitler's Germany.

Here in his Second Letter to the Corinthians, Paul is faced with a similar task under similar circumstances. Not facing a war, unless you count the spiritual warfare faced by us all, Paul nevertheless had an important message to deliver. The roadblock for Paul was the way he was perceived by the Corinthians, which is what prompted the last 3 days' readings including today, in which each part is labeled in some way in some Bibles as Paul "defending" himself - his ministry, his Apostleship/position of authority in the Church, and today, his methods. Paul offers his "credentials" as part of that defense (2 Corinthians 11:22-23), but that's not really the point of any of these passages. The point is, rather, that his message shouldn't be rejected just because there are better speakers out there than he, delivering contrary messages. He wants to make his case without becoming like those others who deliver false messages, with their idle boasts. He decries the fact that he needs to be tolerated "as a fool" (2 Corinthians 11:16-17) and boast in much the same manner as the others who have come with messages.

And so, he makes a direct comparison: he is a Hebrew, an Israelite, a Son of Abraham (11:22) just like the others, but then he strikes a contrast by describing his sufferings: being in prison more frequently for his faith, being whipped, beaten, stoned, shipwrecked (11:23-27), and many more, all while maintaining his deep concern for the churches. He calls himself a fool (no fewer than 5 times in this passage) for having to boast of things that most people would not want to boast about: deprivation, anxiety, weakness (11:27-29), even describing an unusual vision that he had just before his First Missionary Journey ("14 years ago"), told in the third person so that he can say he is boasting of this man but not of himself (12:2-5). He was even given a "thorn in [his] flesh" in order that he would not boast from conceit (12:7-8). All of this leads up to the key verse of the entire passage: that rather than being removed from or relieved of any of these sufferings, God told him that His "grace is sufficient, [His] power is made perfect in weakness" (12:9).

A final note on the "third heaven" passage (12:2-5): this passage is another of the many that brings on the mockers and the atheists for its ambiguity and just, overall, weirdness. But if you pick it apart, it makes perfect sense to say it the way he did: his reason for describing this vision in the third person has already been stated, but he also found it important to distinguish the different meanings of the word "heaven" to make sure the Corinthians (and thus, us) understood his experience. The first heaven would be our atmosphere, the second heaven would refer to interstellar space and the rest of the universe.

Thus, the Third Heaven would refer to the domain of God and the angels, to which he was "caught up" (same word translated as "raptured" in some places) either in body or soul, he wasn't sure which. It's a powerful vision and one that should NOT be mocked.

August 30, OT
Isaiah 43:1-46:13
Israel's Need of a Savior

The people of this time, during the second half of the reign of Hezekiah, would have been almost totally unaware of the doom that would one day befall their nation. Thus, Isaiah's declaration that there would be a Savior to come, who would be the Lord Himself (which he repeats more than once in today's OT reading), would have left anyone hearing his prophecy scratching their heads in confusion. After all, they were living in a time when their last known enemy's (Assyria's) attempt to lay siege to Jerusalem had been thwarted. Hezekiah was known throughout the southern kingdom as a "good" king who made many positive reforms. They had many allies in neighboring nations like Egypt and Cush (aka Ethiopia). It may not have, exactly, been a "golden age," but it wasn't really a time of great tribulation, either. So why would Israel need a Savior?

One of the first things to note in Isaiah's last 27 chapters is his near-constant use of "Israel" as the name of the nation in which he lived and prophesied, instead of merely "Judah". The people of that time, however, would have recently witnessed the fall of that nation, more commonly referred to as Samaria (its capital) and known to us today as the "northern kingdom". So, when Isaiah starts this reading by declaring *Israel's* redemption (Isaiah 43:1), people had to wonder just what, exactly, was he talking about. Were the former two parts of the divided kingdom going to reunite? Isaiah does speak here of gathering His people from all compass directions (43:5-6), but that's not the point of this prophecy. Instead, he reiterates his prophecy that the Savior would be the Lord Himself (43:8-13) and then goes on to prophesy the destruction of a distant people (Babylon), not yet known to be an enemy (43:14-21). Without going into any more detail about that, Isaiah explains that it is Israel's sins and shortcomings, particularly in regards to the animal sacrifices in the Law, that would bring on the need for a Savior (43:22-28), in particular referring to the only means by which these sins can be taken away (43:25). This prophecy is Messianic as it makes the Savior the *sacrifice* that will take away sins in the same way as the burnt offering.

Isaiah goes on in chapters 44 - 46 to speak for God in most of the verses, starting with loving reassurance to Israel (44:1-8), explaining the folly of idolatry (44:9-20), and then showing His forgiveness (44:21-28). It is in the next chapter that many people mistakenly read this prophecy as having been written by someone much later on than Isaiah, as he makes repeated reference to Cyrus, the Persian king whose reign was at the *end* of the exile which wouldn't even *begin* until more than a century later (44:28-45:25), yet doesn't connect the not-yet-born king of that pagan nation with the exile, thus making this prophecy even more curious to the people of the time. He does, however, name two of Babylon's pagan gods in the final chapter of this reading (46:1-2) in the only real reference to a captivity in this reading, and he does refer to his own people as being from *Judah*, not Israel.

August 30, NT
2 Corinthians 12:11-13:14
Paul Concludes the Second Letter to the Corinthians

Paul comes full circle at the end of his last known written communication with the Corinthian Church, telling them of his intentions to visit them for a third time (and this time actually going there - 2 Corinthians 12:14-17) and making sure that Titus' visit went well in the interim. In verse 19, it is obvious that Paul loved the Corinthian people, calling them "beloved" and explaining that all of the writing that sounded like merely a defense of his previous ministry there is actually speaking the Truth in Christ for their edification.

He later repeats his intention to make that third visit, but also wants this to not be simply a disciplinary visit, by stating the case for every fact being confirmed "by the testimony of two or three witnesses"

(13:1), and then going on to tell the Corinthians how the coming visit will be different. Paul invites them to do some self-examination before his arrival (13:5-10), which later became a common practice in worship liturgies (opening with an examination of conscience and confession before worship begins). He then concludes the letter as he does his other ones, bestowing God's blessings on them all.

As much as Paul loved the people of this great city in southern Greece, it was on this visit to Corinth that Paul would write his magnum opus - a letter to another established church, one that he desperately wanted to also visit, that he didn't even plant - starting in tomorrow's NT reading.

August 31, OT
Isaiah 47:1-50:11
The Fall of Babylon, In Context

Isaiah's penchant for jumping around the prophetic timeline has, for centuries, brought confusion and even controversy to readers who can't or don't view it all from the Messianic point of view that we Christians do today. In yesterday's reading, Isaiah identifies an enemy (Babylon) and future king of another pagan nation (Cyrus, of Persia), who would come to Judah's aid at some future point, but goes into very little detail about what is going to happen. Isaiah still offers no other details as this passage begins, except to show its aftermath: likened to a virgin queen, Babylon is brought down in humiliation and defeat by the Lord Himself (Isaiah 47:1-15). Why a virgin queen? The metaphor would have been understood by the Israelites of the time as a nation or army that has never known defeat. So, the readers in Isaiah's day would have understood this as some future battle that, like those led by David years earlier, would end in victory for them because the Lord would be the one to lead them.

But Isaiah goes on to point out the stubbornness of the Israelites, and uses the name "Israel" instead of "Judah" to make his point (48:1-11) about their sins. To put it bluntly, the Lord is very angry with them, despite the relative calm of the time of Hezekiah, but will defer their punishment for an unknown period (48:9) so as not to "cut them off". The Lord's intention is not to destroy but to discipline His people, and his instrument of discipline (Babylon) will get their due, too (48:12-

22). The salvation that comes to Israel will be available to the whole world including the Gentile nations, and the bringer of this salvation will be someone who is despised by the people from whom he comes (49:1-26). In amongst the verses of chapter 49, Isaiah clarifies even further the identity of this Savior - not Cyrus of Persia as mentioned yesterday, but a redeemer who is a "mighty one of Jacob," meaning one of their own (49:26). This passage has led Jews to believe, to this day, that the Savior to come is a mighty, political and/or military leader, not the humble servant who we now know was and is the Savior of the world, described in Isaiah 50 and, especially, in tomorrow's reading.

August 31, NT
Romans 1:1-17
Not Ashamed of the Gospel

Paul was the chief evangelist of the early Church, and had planted numerous churches around the Mediterranean by the end of his Third Missionary Journey. Of the churches he planted himself, he was probably most fond of the Corinthian church, from which he wrote this Epistle during his last visit. Paul had not yet visited Rome, but he was, officially, a Roman Citizen, and he knew full well that Rome was essentially the capital of the world. Every place where Paul had visited was part of the Roman Empire. And, though he did not plant the church there (having not yet visited it), he was also aware that a church had already been planted by someone else (Catholics believe this was done by Peter though there is no evidence to either back it up or contradict it). Paul was made aware that the Roman church was large and vibrant one (Romans 1:8), and he expressed a longing to someday visit them (1:9-10). And so, in the meantime, Paul pens what many consider his magnum opus, his Epistle to the Romans.

The letter's position as the first book of the New Testament after the Gospels tells you all you need to know about the relative importance and esteem in which it is held. It was not Paul's first letter, but it is widely regarded as his greatest, mostly due to its densely packed content in which more points of Christian doctrine are made (and very well at that) here than in any other Epistle. By a narrow margin, it is his longest letter (only a few verses longer than 1 Corinthians), but there is very little in the way of "personal reflection" or history here when compared to any of his previous letters (particularly 2

Corinthians), as he focuses instead on The Gospel. And by "Gospel" here, we don't mean the books of the Bible we call Gospels, nor are we merely referring to biographical data about Jesus; we're talking about the central point and message of Jesus' appearance in person on earth: the good news of His salvation, available to all that believe in Him.

Everything in this first reading from Romans leads up to the key verse, that he is "not ashamed" of that Gospel (1:16), and it is available to both Jew and Greek, meaning everyone. With that in mind, we're going to spend the next almost 3 weeks in this great letter, with one or more key verses like that in every reading.

September 1, OT
Isaiah 51:1-55:13
The Suffering Servant

No clearer picture of the Messiah is made anywhere in the Old Testament than in these 5 chapters from Isaiah and, in particular, the middle chapter of this reading. Isaiah's vivid description of the Suffering Servant, who we all know to be our Lord Jesus Christ, points to a Savior who is most certainly NOT the military or political leader envisioned by Jews both then and now. Rather, the One who would come to save people from their *sins* is a man of modest appearance who would achieve this salvation by his suffering and death (Isaiah 53). It is not only the climax of this final section (chapters 40-66) of Isaiah, but the climax of the entire book.

Isaiah's description of the Messiah actually begins 2 chapters earlier, when Israel is exhorted to "look unto the Rock from which [you] are hewn" and look to "Abraham your father, and unto Sarah that bare you" (51:1-2). This is a clear picture of a Savior who would be one of their own: an Israelite born of the union of Abraham and Sarah, not Abraham and Ishmael. This precludes the Savior from coming from any other lineage such as Arab, and was fulfilled with Jesus' birth as son of Mary and adopted son of Joseph. This Savior would restore Israel to its former glory after Jerusalem is properly disciplined (51:3-52:12). This even includes references to the End Times.

Then starting in 52:13 and going verse by verse through chapter 53, Isaiah makes numerous specific prophecies that were ALL fulfilled with the arrest, trial, suffering, crucifixion, and death of Jesus, foretelling many very exact details about who He would be, what He would look like, how He would die, and what that death would do for the world. It is a stunning and beautiful picture of The Suffering Servant, and God inspired Isaiah to write it during the latter half of Hezekiah's reign as king, more than a century before the Babylonian Exile, which was 70 years before the Israelites' return to Jerusalem after the exile, and more than 686 years before Jesus was born.

September 1, NT
Romans 1:18-32
No Excuses

Not only was Paul aware of the church planted in the capital of the world (Rome), but he was also fully aware of what Rome and its people were really like. In answer to the obvious question someone must have asked, about how a culture such as Rome would have achieved such a preeminent position in the world while being so utterly pagan, Paul emphatically states that such ungodly people are basically without excuse (Romans 1:18-20). Even if they knew God, they chose not to honor God, and became fools (1:21-23), noting the many idols and mythological gods worshipped by these people. In short, they worship the *created* rather than the *Creator* (1:25).

There is nothing particularly controversial about that point, but the next point Paul makes is, mainly because of how one group of people today try to dismiss it or stretch the boundaries of interpretation to the breaking point. In his first Letter to the Corinthians, Paul spells out a virtual laundry list of sins of which the people were guilty, and among them were sexual sins such as homosexuality. Paul does it again here, as he tells his audience of Roman believers about how God "gave them over to degrading passions" because they turned their backs on Him (1:26). It's significant that homosexuality, both lesbianism (1:26) and male homosexuality (1:27), is not only the first sin listed but also the only one in which he goes into any detail. Advocates in the homosexual community dismiss this as being a result of the other sins listed here, in verses 29 and 30, often declaring that homosexuality isn't really a sin because it's not part of what it means to have a "depraved mind" (1:28) that Paul speaks of in the previous verse.

Nothing could be farther from the truth. All of Paul's writings are based on the idea that the existence of God is evident in His creation, and that there is no excuse (in any language) for people not to know and understand God's Word in matters such as sin. After he spells out some of these sins, he finishes this passage by warning them that even though some people know the "ordinances of God" and do these things that are "worthy of death" anyway, they advocate these sins as they "heartily approve" their practice (1:32). This should sound very familiar to anyone who keeps up with world and cultural affairs today, and the homosexual community in particular.

September 2, OT
Isaiah 56:1-60:22
Salvation For The Whole World

After a lengthy and quite astounding Messianic prophecy in chapter 53 (completely fulfilled with the crucifixion of Jesus), Isaiah returns to his previous form of jumping all around the prophetic timeline from near-future prophecies regarding future kings of Judah (Isaiah 56:9-12) and the idolatry of the people (57:1-13) to more Messianic prophecies (57:15-21), the return of the Israelites to the Law (58:1-14) and even End Times prophecies (60:1-22). Isaiah gives no names, though he was likely aware of the birth of the crown prince, Manasseh, and the evil that he would bring to Judah. Predictions concerning the Babylonian Exile and its aftermath are curiously absent from this 5 chapter section, the next to last in the Book of Isaiah (unless you count chapter 58 as being part of the post-exile timeline). But it's the beginning of this section and a part of chapter 59 that are the most significant here.

Isaiah starts with a prophecy that must have come as a bit of a shock to the Israelite readers of the day: that "foreigners" (meaning Gentiles as they came to be called, 56:3) could "join themselves to the Lord" (56:1-8). The very notion of anyone NOT part of God's Chosen People, Israel, having access to the Lord must have seemed quite preposterous. Isaiah just got done explaining how the Savior, who would be the Lord Himself, would be a descendent of Abraham just like them; so why would the Lord inspire Isaiah to write about salvation being extended others who weren't likewise Abraham's descendents?

The answer is found first in the unique way that Isaiah's prophecies of many different times seem to all flow together and make sense. That's part of Isaiah's style. The other, in this case, is found in chapter 59: the reason for the appearance of this Savior is not to save Israel from other nations as some kind of political or military leader but, rather, as a way of saving us from our *sins*. Since Gentiles share the same iniquities as Jews, they are equally separated from God (59:2) and just as much in need of a Savior. The nature of evil brings judgment, and judgment brings redemption that first comes "to Zion," and then to all (59:1-21).

September 2, NT
Romans 2:1-16
The Impartial Judge

There was a question on the minds of many new believers of Paul's day that is still an issue today: does one have to first become Jewish in order to become Christian? Believers of Paul's time, at least some of them, must have thought so as the Gospel message was further and further spread to the Gentile world. Paul refers to the distinction as the "circumcision" versus the "uncircumcision" in multiple places in Romans (tomorrow in particular), though he introduces the idea in today's reading.

Chapter 2 starts as a continuation from yesterday's "no excuses" statement; and in fact, he uses that exact phrase in Romans 2:1. But the attention is immediately shifted to the hypocrisy of judging people for certain sins that the person who judges commits himself (2:1-3). Paul rightly points out that the only impartial judge is the Lord, whose judgments are meant to bring repentance (2:4). All will be judged, first the Jew and then the Greek: the Jew within the Law, and the Greek without the Law (2:6-10, 2:12-14), but it makes no difference in the end, as the Lord shows no partiality in His righteous judgment (2:11).

September 3, OT
Isaiah 61:1-65:25
The Gospel is a Message of Deliverance

The word "gospel" comes from the Anglo-Saxon word "godspel" which literally means "good story". There are at least 99 instances in the New Testament of a Greek word translated as "gospel" or it's root phrase "good news". But in the Old Testament, written primarily in Hebrew and Aramaic, the term appears very seldom. The Israelites of the time probably didn't "get" the concept of needing a Savior - a deliverer - and so the concept of "good news" would have been confusing. More than 700 years after Isaiah wrote these 5 chapters near the end of the reign of Hezekiah, Jesus would start his ministry on earth by pointing out that He was the fulfilment of this very prophecy at the beginning of today's OT reading (Isaiah 61:1-2a).

The positive tone of this passage continues through chapter 61 and into chapter 62, as Isaiah prophecies the "vindication" of Zion. Many times in Isaiah, the then-future destruction of Jerusalem is prophesied. But more so than any other prophet, Isaiah also prophesies at great length about the restoration and rebuilding of Jerusalem. What isn't always clear is the timeline of which he is prophesying. Many of the prophecies speak of being held in high regard by all the nations of the world, a prediction that has not yet come to pass even today. Isaiah must have been referring to multiple times in which Jerusalem was destroyed, but for each prophecy, the question is "which one?" It turned out not to matter, really, as each lesson about future destruction was accompanied by the comforting word that the Lord was not abandoning them (63:9-17) but was chastising them.

It is interesting to note that for all the times in the Gospels (Matthew in particular) that Isaiah is quoted or referenced, the New Testament book that contains the largest number of Isaiah quotes or references is Paul's Letter to the Romans which is also currently being studied. It will be more than a week before the NT reading reaches chapter 10, but Isaiah 65:1-2 are both quoted, nearly verbatim, in Romans 10.

September 3, NT
Romans 2:17-3:8
To Be a Jew Or To Be a Gentile

A direct continuation of yesterday's NT reading, Paul continues his clarification of the role of Jews in the salvation of the world. Many of the new Christians in Rome were Jewish converts (and if Catholics are right about Peter establishing the church there, this would make sense), and they are the ones being addressed in this section. But, there were obviously problems: these new Jewish converts were acting with such hypocrisy, they were giving Christians everywhere a bad name (Romans 2:17-24).

Jews are held to a different standard than Gentiles because, having been entrusted with the Scriptures (today called the Old Testament, 3:2), they have always needed to follow the Law, too (2:25-29), else that person really isn't a Jew. They are, so to speak, uncircumcised. Then, Paul uses a technique for the first time that he would use quite often in this letter and later letters: sarcasm. He uses it to ask, in effect, to ask if just because of some Jews' unfaithfulness, does this mean that this nullifies God's faithfulness (3:3)? His answer ("by no means", 3:4) uses a quote from Psalm 51:4. Paul uses this technique of asking a sarcastic question and then answering it himself twice more in this passage, and would use this technique, familiar to Jews, many more times, including in tomorrow's reading.

September 4, OT
Isaiah 66:1-24; 2 Kings 18:3-7a; 2 Chronicles 29:2; 2 Kings 20:20-21; 2 Chronicles 32:32-33
Conclusion of Isaiah, Death of Hezekiah, Accession of Manasseh

Further support for the notion that Isaiah wrote all of the book that bears his name is found in the first real piece of history in this chronological reading plan in over a week, as 2 Chronicles 32:32 describes the other events in the life of Hezekiah as having been written in the book of the prophet Isaiah, son of Amoz. That verse, at the end of today's OT reading, comes after the next major event, chronologically, in the Bible: the death of King Hezekiah. The 15-year extension to his life had come to an end, and his 12-year-old son Manasseh became king.

But before we read that, we read the final chapter of Isaiah's incredible output of prophecy. It is likely that Isaiah wrote this last chapter either a short time before Hezekiah's death or very shortly afterwards as Manasseh rose to the throne. This is evidenced by the somewhat abrupt ending (and change in tone) at the end of the chapter. Isaiah 66 starts in a poetic style for 16 verses, and then switches to prose for verses 17-24, but all of it is a verbal quote from the Lord Himself. In one of the last things Stephen says before he is martyred, he quotes Isaiah 66:1-2. The Lord lists those who find favor in Him, and those things that don't please him, the latter being pretty much all of the animal sacrifices practiced by the Israelites of the day (66:3-4). But, the rest of the chapter describes how Israel, and Jerusalem in particular, will become a new nation, glorified in the Lord, as part of a new heaven and a new earth, whose enemies' bodies will be eaten by worms that never die and are consumed in a fire that never stops burning (66:24).

September 4, NT
Romans 3:9-31
The Romans Road

A popular and quite worthwhile technique for witnessing to seekers is called The Romans Road. It's an effective way of leading someone who is not sure about becoming a Christian to full faith in Christ and to their salvation. A tract that was very widely distributed back in the 1980s and 1990s, called the "Four Spiritual Laws," was loosely based on this same "Road." It's called The Romans Road because each of the parts are found somewhere in this, Paul's Letter to the Romans, and the first part is found in today's NT reading.

For the last two days in Romans, we have read Paul's overarching theme concerning the differences, or lack thereof, between Jews and Gentiles. That continues into today's reading, and culminates with one of the most important doctrines in all of Christianity, and the first step into the Romans Road: that we are *all* sinners. No exceptions. It doesn't matter if you are a Jew or Gentile, *all* have sinned and fall short of the glory of God (Romans 3:23). Before this, Paul builds up to this important conclusion by quoting Psalm 14:1-2, Psalm 53:1-3, Psalm 5:9, Psalm 140:3, and Psalm 10:7, all in a span of just 3 verses (Romans 3:12-14. The point would have been very clear to any Jew of the day, and is just as true to everyone today: your choice of religious practices is irrelevant, the family you were born into is irrelevant, and the region in which you were born is irrelevant. God loves everyone, despite the fact that everyone is a sinner.

But everyone is justified who put their faith in Jesus, thanks to the free gift of grace (3:24). The remaining verses of The Romans Road are all about this grace, and it becomes the overarching theme of Paul's entire letter to the Romans. Those other steps in the Romans Road are covered in future readings, and they are (following 3:23) 6:23, 5:8, 10:9, 10:13, 5:1, 8:1, and 8:38-39.

September 5, OT
2 Kings 21:1-17; 2 Chronicles 33:1-9; Psalm 82:1-8; 2 Chronicles 33:10-19; 2 Kings 21:18-26; 2 Chronicles 33:20-25; 2 Kings 22:1-2; 2 Chronicles 34:1-3
From Manasseh, To Amon, To Josiah

Despite being a boy of only twelve years of age, the death of his father Hezekiah thrust young Manasseh into the throne as king of Judah. The very first thing written about Manasseh besides his age is how much evil he did (2 Kings 21:2) and how he basically undid all of the good that his father had done (21:3-6) including even the sacrificing of his son in a fire. Isaiah's death is not recorded anywhere in the Bible, but part of the Talmud (Yevamot 49b) indicates that Isaiah was executed by being sawn in two under orders of the evil King Manasseh, and this may account for the abrupt ending of the book of Isaiah.

It was a very bad period for Judah, as also recorded in the first 9 verses of 2 Chronicles 33. In response to the return of the false gods, a Psalm was written as a prayer to the real God (Psalm 82), begging for judgment to put an end to these detestable practices put in place by Manasseh. God gave warnings through prophets (not named) that He would bring disaster on Jerusalem because of Manasseh's great sin (2 Kings 21:12-15) and then actually brought the Assyrian army to abduct King Manasseh (2 Chronicles 33:11).

That's when everything changed. In one of the most remarkable turnarounds in the history of the world, a king listed as more evil than even Ahab of Israel sought the Lord and repented (33:12-13). God had him returned to Jerusalem where he went on to make great positive reforms (33:14-16). There were still problems and issues in Jerusalem, but after one of Judah's longest reigns, he died and was buried with his ancestors (33:20, 2 Kings 21:18). His son Amon succeeded him as king, but turned back to his father Manasseh's earlier evils (2 Kings 21:20-21). After his father's long 55-year reign, Amon reigned only 2 years before being assassinated by his own officials (21:23), and never repented the way his father did.

And so, Josiah, an even younger boy (8 years old), acceded to the throne in Jerusalem and began a reign that would mark Judah's last "good" king. But as he was so young, he didn't really start with any positive reforms until his 8th year, when he would have been 16 (2 Chronicles 34:3). It was during the early part of his reign that a prophet wrote one of the darkest, doom-filled works in the entire Bible, in tomorrow's OT reading.

September 5, NT
Romans 4:1-25
Justification By Faith

Justification by faith, the idea that salvation was a free gift from God, called "grace", was an entirely new idea to the Jews of the day, and even to new believers who came from the Gentile world. But with his letter to the Romans being addressed primarily to recently-converted Jews, Paul needed to find an example that would be a familiar frame of reference, so that the new believers would truly get the idea about how the Gospel was NOT based on works or The Law, but on faith.

Paul found it in the first book of the Bible. No fewer than 4 times in this chapter, he quotes Genesis in describing Abraham, a figure familiar to all Jews, whose faith was "credited to him as righteousness." He uses the analogy of wages, and makes another Old Testament quote (Psalm 32:1-2), to explain how Abraham's justification was not "earned" by anything he actually *did*, but what he *believed* (Romans 4:4-13). Circumcision, or lack of it, doesn't matter. Paul keeps on going with the Abraham analogy through the rest of Chapter 4 to make the point that Abraham's justification is also for US - the Romans then, and us today.

September 6, OT
Zephaniah 1:1-3:20
Dies Irae

Dies Irae is a song, written in Latin, by a contemporary of Saint Francis in the 13th Century. For close to 700 years, it was sung in Roman Catholic, Orthodox, and later in several other Christian Churches' funeral liturgies. The melody is perhaps the best known in all of Gregorian Chant, and was used by several orchestral composers (notably Mozart, Brahms, and Berlioz) in their own works. The title means "Day of Wrath" and the lyrics are largely drawn from the Vulgate translation of the book of the prophet Zephaniah. Today, we will read that prophecy in its entirety.

Though it is largely an End Times (specifically, tribulation) prophecy, it's still important to understand the historical context in which it was written. Zephaniah was third cousin (once removed) from the then-current king, Josiah (Zephaniah 1:1). Josiah would have still been just a boy, having not yet begun the reforms that would make him Judah's last good king, which means that Zephaniah would have received this prophecy as a direct reaction to the evil reigns of Manasseh and Amon. Despite the turnaround in the last years of Manasseh's reign, there was still much idol worship and many pagan practices going on, even in Jerusalem. And so, after a brief introduction in which he identifies himself as the great-great-grandson of Hezekiah, Zephaniah launches into one of the most doom-filled, gloom-filled, darkest prophecies in the entire Bible.

It is immediately obvious that God's wrath in this prophecy is directed at the whole world, not just specifically Judah, and it even sounds at first like God threatening to break his promise to never again destroy the earth (Genesis 9:11). But it isn't a flood being threatened here as in the days of Noah; rather, it is *fire*, mentioned several times, so no promise is being broken here. The rest of chapter 1 is more specifically directed at Judah, but ends with yet another reference to a "terrible end" to "all the inhabitants of the earth" (1:18).

Besides fire, repeated references are made to the "day of the Lord" or the "day of the Lord's anger" (2:2-3 etc.), and thus the title given to this reading and to the song that draws from this book. After a chapter describing the great "day of the Lord," God (through the prophet) calls Judah to repentance (2:1-3) before going through an itemized list of judgments against other nations: Philistia (2:4-7), Moab (2:8-11), Cush (2:12) and Assyria (2:13-15) before returning attention to Jerusalem (3:1-8). But like bookends to the various judgments pronounced here, the section on Jerusalem doesn't focus so much on the destruction of the nation, but on the fact that the people are still not repentant, despite the judgment of so many other enemy nations. Zephaniah then finishes with a 2-verse change in tone along the same lines as other prophecies made earlier by Isaiah and Micah: the restoration of Israel's remnant.

September 6, NT
Romans 5:1-21
While We Were Still Sinners (Romans Road parts 6 and 3); Sin and Death

The sequence of steps in the Romans Road make it so that parts 6, then 3, are read before part 2 which is in tomorrow's reading. The key point here, as Paul makes clear throughout this letter to the Romans, is that we are all sinners in need of justification; but, we obtain that justification through faith in Jesus, who died for us *while we were still sinners* (Romans 5:8). In other words, at a time or point where our sins had completely separated us from God, Jesus made the ultimate sacrifice to atone for those sins, and thus bring us to "peace with God", i.e. reconciliation with Him (5:1).

In verse 12, Paul makes a point that not only solidifies the issue of Jesus' atoning death on our behalf, but also a point used by Young Earth Creationists (such as me) to make the point that God created the earth, the universe, and everything in it, in 6 real earth days about 6000 years ago. By linking death to sin (which Paul would do again several times in this Epistle) and the first sin to Adam, Paul, under the inspiration of God, makes it impossible for Adam to have NOT been a real person, who died (just as all humans eventually die) no more than about 3000 years before Jesus did. In other words, Genesis isn't/wasn't merely true in a spiritual sense, but in a historical sense as well. Another important point made here is that sin is the reason we die at all. Death itself didn't even exist before the sin of Adam, thus making it impossible for humans to have evolved from lower life forms, because evolution requires death as a mechanism. If death didn't exist before Adam, then evolution is impossible. Paul's use of the word translated as "death" here is used by virtually every writer in the New Testament, always in the context of physical death. A forthcoming book by yours truly contains an entire chapter on just this one topic, regarding Young Earth Creationism.

September 7, OT
2 Chronicles 34:4-7; Jeremiah 1:1-19
The Call of the Prophet Jeremiah

After the doom and gloom of the prophet Zephaniah, which followed the post-Hezekiah history of Judah through the evil reigns of Manasseh and Amon, we came to the start of the reign of the boy king, Josiah. In the brief few verses from 2 Chronicles, we get the first real history of Judah's last "good" king: an amazing effort at real reform, as still-young Josiah (probably about 16 years old at the time) travels all over Judah destroying Asherah poles and Baal altars, trying to restore Judah's faith in the real God.

At around the same time as this, another prophet came on to the scene, probably just as young as the boy king. This prophet, Jeremiah, would write prophecies through his scribe, Baruch, from the 8th year of Josiah's reign as king all the way through Judah's last king and the beginning of the exile in Babylon, about 40 years later. Despite the great reforms made by Josiah, God charged Jeremiah with the task of primarily doing what several other prophets did only partially: warn the people of Judah of the impending invasion and exile in a foreign land by the Babylonians, but also give them the hope of knowing how it will all end for those who turn their faith back to God.

The first chapter of Jeremiah doesn't show much of Jeremiah's feelings that led to his nickname, the "weeping prophet." But those things would appear later in this second-longest book of prophecy in the Old Testament, also the second-most quoted book of prophecy (fourth most overall) in the New Testament (both behind Isaiah; Psalms and Deuteronomy are both more frequently quoted in the NT than Jeremiah). In the first chapter, we mostly hear God's call to Jeremiah, the prophet's complaint of being too young and inexperienced, and eventually his reluctant acceptance of the role.

September 7, NT
Romans 6:1-23
Slaves to Righteousness, Not Sin (Romans Road part 2)

The metaphor of slavery is employed frequently by writers in the Bible, both the Old and the New Testaments. Paul actually calls himself a slave (literally "bond servant") in his introduction to several of his letters, including this one. In his continuation of his discussion of the link between sin and death from yesterday's reading, Paul uses the metaphor of slavery to describe our masters: either sin is our master, or righteousness is our master.

Paul builds up to this point, which includes the second step in the Romans Road (Romans 6:23) by first clarifying something he said at the end of chapter 5 (5:20-21, yesterday). When he made his point that the Law was designed to point out our own sin, that didn't and doesn't mean that we have a license to sin just because we are now under grace (6:1-2). A common complaint from non-Christians about our belief in grace is that since our sins are forgiven, we somehow have the ability to sin all we want and "get away with it," thus making us appear as hypocrites. Nothing could be farther from the truth, as Paul makes clear at the beginning of this reading.

But another point of contention, particularly with some people involved with Civil Rights in America (some of whom claim to be Christian), is Paul's use of the word "slavery" or "bondage" to describe our relationship to sin. Slavery during the first century bore no resemblance to the oppressive, racist, hideous practice that most of us think of today which wasn't outlawed until after the Civil War. Slavery then is closer in definition to what we, today, would call "employee". When you work for an employer, you expect to be paid, because your work creates a debt on the part of the employer. Substitute the word "master" for "employer" and "slave" for "employee" and suddenly Paul's point makes perfect sense: Jesus' substitutionary death on the Cross freed us from the slavery of sin (6:6-7). Sin, as a master, pays a cruel wage: *death* (6:23), but we need not be slaves to sin any more, but rather, slaves to righteousness (6:16-18).

Thus, a gap is now filled in the Romans Road, parts 1 to 3. Part 1 (3:23) states that all have sinned. Part 2 (6:23) states that the wages of sin is death. Part 3 (5:8, yesterday) states that Jesus took that death on Himself while we were still slaves to sin.

September 8, OT
Jeremiah 2:1-4:31
Faithless Israel

Despite everything positive that King Josiah did to reform the kingdom and bring people back to faith in God, God had clearly had enough with Judah's faithlessness. In what sounds much more like a mournful lament than a judgment, God pours His heart out to the people of Israel through Jeremiah's prophecy. The frequently used analogy of the bride that abandons her husband (Jeremiah 2:2, 3:1-10) is just one of the examples cited in the prophecy to point out how completely Israel has abandoned her God. Similar scoldings have been previously written by prophets like Micah, Isaiah, and Hosea, but seldom with this kind of emotion. And unlike Isaiah and Micah, in particular, the prophecy here doesn't end with a hopeful look into the distant future and a returning "remnant" of Israel. Rather, Jeremiah goes into the first of several prophecies of doom (4:5-31) for Judah, predicting the disaster to come for their faithlessness. This prophecy is nowhere near as dark - nor as far in the future - as Zephaniah's, but it is still doom, only this time it's more obvious that the disaster will take the form of an invasion and exile, still some 40 years in Judah's future.

Jeremiah would go into much deeper detail about this prediction, including several parts quoted by Jesus, in tomorrow's OT reading.

September 8, NT
Romans 7:1-25
Relationship of Believers to the Law and to Christ

In a very real sense, Romans chapter 7 is a bringing together of several points already made. There are no parts of the Romans Road to explore here, but Paul goes into much greater detail regarding the nature of sin, how it enslaves us, and how we can be released from that slavery. Paul uses the metaphor of marriage to explain how we must "die to sin" in order to be released from its bondage (Romans 7:1-3), just as a woman is not released from a marriage until she becomes a widow. Paul goes from that commandment (against adultery) to another (against coveting) to explain how he would not have known what sin even was were it not for the Law (7:7-11). In Paul's case, the use of the term "Law" refers to the whole of Jewish law, but includes nearly the only part of the Law quoted by Jesus: the Ten Commandments. But even with those examples of the Law, the emphasis here is that, as believers, the Law only serves to point out our sinful nature (7:13-14). We can't help but sin! It is in our very nature to do so, and we don't always even understand or want to do sinful things - but we do them anyway (7:15-20). That doesn't make them any less sinful, and we must not use this fact to deflect the blame or responsibility away from us, such as saying "the Devil made me do it". This is not a point of excuse-making; it's just a point of fact of human nature.

And it's this internal spiritual war (7:21-25) that makes it so crucial that we establish our relationship with Christ, and make Him our master instead of sin. We're all slaves to something; the key is to make ourselves slaves to the right thing.

September 9, OT
Jeremiah 5:1-6:30; Jeremiah 13:1-27
What's To Come for Jerusalem

Despite everything positive that King Josiah did to reform the kingdom and bring people back to faith in God, God had clearly had enough with Judah's faithlessness. In what sounds much more like a mournful lament than a judgment, God pours His heart out to the people of Israel through Jeremiah's prophecy. The frequently used analogy of the bride that abandons her husband (Jeremiah 2:2, 3:1-10) is just one of the examples cited in the prophecy to point out how completely Israel had abandoned her God. Similar scoldings have been previously written by prophets like Micah, Isaiah, and Hosea, but seldom with this kind of emotion. And unlike Isaiah and Micah, in particular, the prophecy here doesn't end with a hopeful look into the distant future and a returning "remnant" of Israel. Rather, Jeremiah goes into the first of several prophecies of doom (4:5-31) for Judah, predicting the *disaster* to come for their faithlessness. This prophecy is nowhere near as dark - nor as far in the future - as Zephaniah's, but it is still *doom*, only this time it's more obvious that the disaster will take the form of an invasion and exile, still some 40 years in Judah's future. To make this clear, Jeremiah quotes a dialog between him and God called "The Ruined Waistband", where the analogy is made (13:1-11). After this, God continues with more specific detail regarding the captivity to come (13:12-27).

September 9, NT
Romans 8:1-25
Life In The Spirit (Romans Road part 7)

The Romans Road, as has been discussed on several previous days' NT readings, is a string of verses from Paul's Epistle to the Romans, used as a witnessing tool. It is not, as is evident from the "parts" encountered each day, written in the same sequence as it is used as points along that Road. And so, as we've encountered them, we've gone through parts 1, 6, 3, 2, and now, 7 (with part 8 tomorrow) of the 8 parts of the Romans Road. The parts read today and tomorrow can be considered the climax, as well as the end, of the Romans Road.

The pastor of the church I attend did a 3-*month* long sermon series on just this one chapter of Romans, focusing each week on just a handful of verses, sometimes as little as 2 of them. The first 4 verses (Romans 8:1-4) neatly sum up the entire chapter, though, and the first verse (8:1, part 7 of the Romans Road) is the key. If you are "in" Christ Jesus (noting the reversal of the common name and title from "Jesus Christ"), you are no longer condemned. Paul went through more than 3 chapters linking sin with death, the need to die to sin, and other issues that leave us "condemned" to die in our sins. But there's always an out: accepting the ultimate sin offering (sacrifice) made by our Savior ("Messiah," "Christ"), Jesus (8:3) and living "in" the Holy Spirit.

The somewhat vague term of being "in" Christ or "in" the Holy Spirit is clarified by noting its opposite. If we're not living in Christ, we're living in (are enslaved to) our sinful nature. Instead, we live in the Spirit, meaning the Holy Spirit, as Paul explains in Romans 8:5-13. Living in the Spirit means being able to be called "children of God" (8:14-17) and therefore *heirs* of God's glory. For all the gloom of focussing on death in earlier parts of the Epistle, this section gives us the most positive, hopeful message of all, even given the fallen world in which we live, because of sin (8:18-25).

September 10, OT
Jeremiah 16:1-17:27; 2 Kings 22:3-20; 2 Chronicles 34:8-33
Foretellings of the Prophet Jeremiah and the Prophetess Huldah

Jeremiah gets a little darker in his predictions of doom to come (Jeremiah 16:1-10) but never gets quite as dark as, say, Zephaniah (or, for that matter, Nahum, from whom we read on September 12). Nevertheless, there are mighty consequences predicted for Judah, and all because their forefathers had forsaken the one, true God (16:11-12). That would result, eventually, in their captivity and exile (1:13), but the *return* from that exile (16:14-15) is also promised. Following this is an extension of that prophecy, which actually turns Messianic with its mention of "fishermen" who will come from the restored nation (16:16-21). As he further explains in chapter 17, the main problem is that our hearts are "desperately wicked" (17:9), in one of the most cited (though not directly quoted) verses from the prophet in the New Testament.

While Jeremiah made these prophecies, King Josiah continued his attempts at positive reform by having the temple rebuilt when he was about 26 years old (his "eighteenth year," 2 Kings 22:3, also in 2 Chronicles 34). Unlike the prophet Isaiah and his relationship with King Hezekiah, Jeremiah's relationship with King Josiah isn't nearly as intimate. Thus, it isn't known whether Josiah was even *aware* of Jeremiah's prophecies at this point in his reign. But Josiah did know Jeremiah's father, the High Priest Hilkiah, and it was Hilkiah that, then, found the book of the Law (probably Deuteronomy) in the Temple (2 Kings 22:8). The uproar that this caused was immense. Josiah, already well aware of his father's evil, was now confronted with the fact that the sins of Judah ran much deeper than he previously thought, and that Judah was facing impending doom (22:10-13). He sent Hilkiah and some others to inquire of the Lord about this; they, then, went to a prophetess named Huldah (22:14) who basically told them the same things that Jeremiah had been saying for several years already (22:15-20a). This word was then brought back to the king.

All of this is told with even more detail in the passage from 2 Chronicles 34.

September 10, NT
Romans 8:26-39
Nothing Can Separate Us from the Love of God (Romans Road part 8)

Though there is more to read in the Romans Road (because of the difference in the sequence of the Road versus the sequence in which Paul wrote it), it is here that we reach the end of that Road as commonly used as a witnessing tool. That final paving stone in the Romans Road is in the final two verses of today's NT reading, which also form the end of chapter 8. The parts in between are in Chapter 10, read on September 13, and so will be discussed in more detail then. But in the meantime, this very often quoted passage gives us one of the most comforting, reassuring promises that any believer could be given: that there is nothing that can separate us from the love of God (Romans 8:38-39). Nothing.

Leading up to it is quite possibly the most concentrated passage of verses quoted in songs and hymns out of the entire New Testament, certainly out of the Epistles. Every verse contains some important Christian doctrine, and quite a few different topics are covered. This writer plans to separately publish a list of the known songs and hymns that either quote, paraphrase, or cite at least one verse out of the 14 verses here. The amazing thing is that the list - SO FAR - contains more than 30 different songs. There are probably many more.

September 11, Old and New Testaments
Special Tribute on the Anniversary of the 9/11/2001 Terrorist Attacks

When I first started this project (way back in 2003), I promised to not get political in my commentary. With the exception of a few small points here and there, I have succeeded in that goal. But as I progressed in this project and particularly during the last 2 years, I have seen a level of deterioration of my home country's moral fabric that I never thought I'd see in my lifetime. Even when compared against the kinds of things I was writing about from the Bible, where whole nations and cities were *destroyed* as parts of God's judgment, I saw points in my life where I was seeing the Hand of God's judgment on the United States, and the need for this country to be judged even more, because it is plainly obvious that the bulk of the people still just don't "get it." The old expression that we're "going to Hell in a handbasket" has become much more than merely a profane joke. The sins of this nation are piling up to a point very far beyond the things described in the Bible for cities like Sodom, Gomorrah, Nineveh (see reading for September 12), Babylon, and Samaria. We are facing the same level of doom that was faced by Josiah of Jerusalem when Jeremiah's father found the book of the Law in the Temple. The United States has certainly been given up to its desires (Romans 1:26) in preparation for its judgment. The only real difference between the soon to come judgment and the judgments we read about in the Bible is that we are now much closer to (if not already inside of) the End Times, when a whole different set of prophecies will apply.

With all of that said, keep that in mind as you read this special commentary with no actual Bible reading today. September 11 is, of course, the anniversary of the worst attack on U.S. soil in its history, topping even Pearl Harbor that brought the United States reluctantly into World War II. But besides that, September 11 was a date when, all too briefly, the people of the U.S. came together - and came to God - in a show of unity not seen since the earlier attack. I believe it was a judgment from God, a wake-up call to get people to really come to the Lord and turn this nation back to Him. The problem was that it was far too brief. After turning to God, we went right back to our old ways, and things got even worse from there. After 2008 in particular, the moral fabric of this nation has deteriorated to a point where we must consider further judgment from God imminent.

As of this writing (2016), that hasn't yet happened. But the lack of a reading for September 11 (unless it is used as a catch-up day) is an opportunity to reflect on these points and use what you've already read in the Bible as a guide for how to deal with what's to come. Know that God is fully in control of what goes on. Learn more about how God deals with people and nations that turn their backs on Him. Lastly, know this: particularly as you reach the end of Part Four, both in the New Testament and the Old, God wins in the end. The future history has already been written, and we are living part of it today.

September 12, OT
Nahum 1:1-3:19
The Fall of Nineveh

The period around Josiah's 18th year was a very busy period in terms of geopolitics. It is interesting to note that the titular event for today's OT reading isn't actually recorded in the Bible. It is prophesied many times, however, and the last and most graphic of those prophecies is found here in the book of Nahum, read today in its entirety.

The mentions of the city of Nineveh in the Bible go all the way back to Genesis, when the city was founded by the warrior Nimrod. It later not only became part of the growing Assyrian Empire but actually became its capital city. Back on August 5, prior to the Assyrian invasion of Samaria (the Northern Kingdom), the prophet Jonah was called to bring God's message to Nineveh (in what is, today, northern Iraq) to prevent their destruction. It worked for a time - the original prophecy called for Nineveh's destruction in only 40 days. That didn't happen. Later, Assyria would invade Israel and carry off its people to exile (read on August 14), and attempt an invasion of Judah as well (August 25). But throughout several books of prophecy, notably Isaiah, Hosea, and Zephaniah, Assyria's destruction is also foretold, even though God used the nation as a tool of His judgment.

And so we come to Nahum, a prophet we know very little about except that he lived among the Elkoshites, a people who were geographically within the Assyrian Empire, though Nahum himself was a devout Hebrew (Nahum 1:1). Easily divided into 3 sections by chapter, the first chapter proclaims the awesomeness of God - His might, His justice - and then goes into a section warning the people of Nineveh. Chapters 2 and 3 go into more detail about the destruction about to befall the capital city. The tense is not clear despite the otherwise clear, poetic style in which Nahum writes, so it isn't known how far ahead of time this was written, or even if this is history rather than prophecy. This is the reason for placing it right at this point in the chronology: one of the few extra-biblical dates of which we know is the year in which Nineveh burned- 612 B.C. This also happens to be the 18th year of the reign of Josiah, thus placing the finding of the book of the Law, these prophecies, and the fall of Nineveh, all as nearly simultaneous events.

September 12, NT
Romans 9:1-33
The Potter and the Clay

In chapter 9 of Paul's letter to the Romans, he falls back on his Jewish roots (and Jewish history) to explain what is now known as the Doctrine of Election. Not to be confused with any discussion of "fate" or "predestination," Paul clarifies how certain people in the history of the Israelites were *chosen* - by God - to fulfill certain important roles. Back when we read the history of people like Isaac, Rebecca, Esau and Jacob, we brought up the fact that many times in passing the torch from one generation to the next, it was not the oldest son who was truly next in line. Here, Paul uses those facts to explain how God's choice is the Sovereign choice (Romans 9:4, 9:6-13), and that these choices are right and just (9:14-15). It culminates with the analogy of the potter and clay (9:20-21), and it wouldn't be the last time he used this way of explaining our relationship with God. In all, just in this 1 chapter, Paul quotes or references the prophets Malachi, Isaiah (4 times), and Hosea (2 times), and history from Genesis and Exodus, all as a familiar frame of reference for his largely Jewish convert audience.

September 13, OT
2 Kings 23:1-28; 2 Chronicles 35:1-19
The Passover is Restored

More so than any king of Judah before him, Josiah worked hard to get the people turned back to God. His efforts at reform included numerous acts of destroying pagan objects of worship from the Temple and from cities elsewhere in Judah and even in the territory of the former Northern Kingdom. And all because Jeremiah's father, the High Priest Hilkiah, had found the book of the Law (probably Deuteronomy) in the Temple, and their sin was exposed.

But perhaps the greatest reform he made was the re-institution of the Passover, the central and highest celebration of the Israelites (2 Kings 23:21-25, 2 Chronicles 35:1-19). He even used this as an opportunity for further reform. However, and though Josiah didn't realize it yet, the Lord's anger was never appeased (2 Kings 23:26-27) and all his reforms wouldn't matter, in the end. In short, the Lord had been pushed just a bit too far this time. And at the end of the 2 Kings 23 passage, we get the first hint that the end is near, both for Judah's last good king and for Judah itself, with the words often used to close the chapter on a king (23:28).

September 13, NT
Romans 10:1-21
The Way of Salvation (Romans Road parts 4 and 5)

The Romans Road, as a witnessing tool, has been touched on in the readings for 5 other days this month, and today is the 6th and final such reading. Some days have featured more than one of the 8 parts, or "steps" in the Road, and they have been presented in this chronology in the order in which Paul wrote them, not the order in which they're used when witnessing. The two parts we read today fit as the 4th (Romans 10:9) and 5th (10:13) steps in the Road, and Paul's point in these two statements (in the surrounding verses) is that it doesn't matter at all who you are or where or what religion you are born into - if you want to be saved, you have to call Jesus your Lord.

"Lord," in this sense, doesn't mean simply a royal title such as it is used in the UK. It means that Jesus Christ is the Lord of your life, not yourself. It means your life is run and guided by Jesus, not you. That doesn't mean you no longer have free will; it means that you have "called on the name of the Lord" - that is, you've made your choice in Who is truly in charge. Like in yesterday's reading, Paul uses several quotes or references from prophecy to back up these statements to his mostly Jewish convert audience, mostly from Isaiah again, but also from Joel in backing up verse 10:13.

And thus, the Way of Salvation is spelled out with the complete Romans Road, paraphrased with these verses and in this order:

- 3:23 Everyone's a sinner, no exceptions
- 6:23 Sin leads to death, both physical and spiritual
- 5:8 Christ died for us in spite of our sin, because he loves us
- 10:9 If we confess Jesus as Lord and believe in His Resurrection, we will be saved
- 10:13 Everyone who calls on the name of the Lord will be saved
- 8:1 There is no condemnation for those who are in Christ...
- 8:38-39 ...and no one can take that away

In a very real sense, this is the Gospel message, all in one letter. And yet, there is still more in Paul's magnum opus.

September 14, OT
Psalm 81:1-16; Jeremiah 47:1-48:47; 2 Kings 23:29-30; 2 Chronicles 35:20-36:1
Josiah Dies in Battle

Josiah's efforts at reform, including a restoration of Passover, resulted in, among other things, the joyful Psalm that opens today's OT reading. Listed as a Psalm "of Asaph," this was most likely *not* the same Asaph who wrote Psalms of praise during the reign of Hezekiah when that king engaged in similar reforms, simply because the earlier reforms of Hezekiah would have been at least 60 years earlier. Though still possible, and written in a remarkably similar style, the restoration of worship is Psalm 81's theme, and is one of the "Elohistic" Psalms (meaning the use of "Elohim" for the Name of God rather than the "unpronounceable" Yahweh) that are mostly attributed to Asaph, including a handful that were written after the Babylonian exile, making them less likely to have been written by the Asaph we learned about earlier.

It isn't known how much time passed between Josiah's restoration of Passover and Jeremiah's writing of a pair of judgments in Jeremiah 47 and 48, except to note that these occurred some time prior to Egypt's invasion of Gaza, then the southern part of Judah. The first judgment, in Jeremiah's 2nd shortest chapter, is against the Philistines (Jeremiah 47:1-7), and this is followed by Jeremiah's 2nd longest chapter which describes a judgment against Moab (Jeremiah 48:1-47). Both warn of destruction to come, but neither make direct reference to the soon-to-come death of Josiah or the coming exile of Judah to Babylon.

As it happened, the Egyptian assault was intended as a way of helping Assyria, an empire that still existed for a time after the fall of its capital, Nineveh. The brief account in 2 Kings 23, followed by a much more detailed account of the same in 2 Chronicles 35, was Josiah's attempt to stop Pharaoh Neco and engage him in battle. The attempt failed, and Josiah was killed, ending his 30 year reign as king, and ending the reign of the last good king of either Israel or Judah. His son

Jehoahaz (sometimes spelled Joahaz or, as we read tomorrow, Shallum) then became king.

September 14, NT
Romans 11:1-12
The Remnant of Israel

Many places in the Old Testament, usually as a followup to a prophecy of judgment, it is mentioned that there will someday be a "remnant" of Israel that remain faithful to the Lord, even in the End Times. This "remnant" is brought up in Isaiah, Jeremiah, Micah, Joel, and elsewhere, but interpretations vary as to what or who this actually refers to. Some actually take this, along with the frequently-used axiom that Israel is the "chosen people of God," to mean that there is some kind of special salvation that is only for the Jewish people (such as John Hagee), separate and distinct from the salvation just spoken of in Romans and elsewhere in the New Testament. In today's NT reading, Paul makes it clear that Israel is still God's chosen people (Romans 11:1-2a), but that even these chosen people must believe in Jesus as Lord, as he described in yesterday's reading.

Here again, Paul gives his mostly-Jewish audience a familiar frame of reference, by using Elijah's story from 1 Kings 19 (along with a Psalm and another quote from Isaiah) to explain how salvation has come to both the Gentiles and the Jews, and that there is no separate or special salvation that applies just to the Jews.

September 15, OT
Jeremiah 22:1-17; 2 Kings 23:31-37; 2 Chronicles 36:2-5
The First Conquest of Judah

The people of Judah may not have been aware that Josiah would be their last good king, but God certainly did. All 4 of Judah's remaining kings would go by multiple names, and 3 of these kings were sons of Josiah. We read of those first two in today's OT reading.

The first was actually the younger of the two, Jehoahaz, who also went by the names Joahaz in 2 Chronicles 36:2 and Shallum in Jeremiah 22:11. It is speculated that Jehoahaz was chosen over his older brothers because the eldest son was considered too submissive, and therefore more likely to submit to the Egyptian invaders who had killed Josiah. As it turned out, neither choice was correct: both brothers' reigns as king were marked by "doing evil in the sight of the Lord" (2 Kings 23:32), and the first brother to be crowned king is notorious for having the shortest reign of them all (3 months, 2 Chronicles 36:2). Jehoahaz was then carted off to exile in Egypt (as Jeremiah warned in Jeremiah 22:1-12), as Pharaoh Nico had his older brother, Jehoiakim, installed as king. Thus was Judah conquered for the first time; it wouldn't be the last.

Jehoiakim has the dubious distinction of being the first king of Judah to be installed by a foreign power. Though he was more willing to pay the tribute (tax) to Egypt than his younger brother, he practiced idol worship and lived an opulent lifestyle by enslaving his own people over the course of the next 11 years.

September 15, NT
Romans 11:13-36
A Word to the Gentiles About Jews

Paul's audience in Rome may have been mostly Jewish Christians, but there also certainly some Gentile believers there, too. He starts this part of the Letter to the Romans by directly addressing the Gentile believers there (Romans 11:13), reminding them that Christianity was essentially a branch of this originally Jewish root (11:14-24). But like he also told the Galatians and Corinthians, this didn't place the Jews above nor below other believers. In addition to the Remnant spoken of yesterday, Paul says that all of Israel will be saved eventually, but that this will not happen until the "fullness of the Gentiles" (11:25-32). That makes this an End Times prophecy, since this has not yet occurred, even in the modern nation of Israel.

But of course, the age of the Gentiles, according to dispensationalism, has not yet come to an end, either, and won't until the Rapture occurs to take away the Church. In the meantime, we are not to boast of the fact that the Jews rejected Jesus, because the Gospel will come to them just as it has come to Gentile believers.

September 16, OT
Habakkuk 1:1-3:19
The Just Shall Live By Faith

Habakkuk is another of the so-called "minor prophets" whose prophecy is brief enough to be read as one day's OT reading. Though his name is never mentioned in the New Testament, some very important passages - in three Epistles - quote the prophet, of whom we know very little. So little, in fact, that even the *timing* of his prophecies in the overall chronology is in question. Habakkuk offers no biographical data and doesn't align himself with any king, so speculation of his era has run from as early as Hezekiah (which would have aligned him with Isaiah) to as late as the Babylonian Exile after the fall of Jerusalem. The content of the scroll would seem to bear the latter out, given subject matter that references the "Chaldeans" multiple times, which is another name for "Babylonians". The first two of Habakkuk's three chapters was found as part of the Dead Sea Scrolls with the complete, intact scroll of Jeremiah, which confirms the consensus opinion that this was written either late in the reign of Josiah or, as this chronology places it, during the reign of one of Josiah's successors.

The prophecy itself consists of a dialog between the prophet and God in chapters 1 and 2. In the first dialog, specifically God's response to Habakkuk's first complaint, God tells the prophet about the rise of the Chaldeans (translated Babylonians in some Bibles), a nation that didn't begin to show itself to the world until after the fall of Nineveh and the crumbling of the Assyrian Empire (Habakkuk 1:6-11). This is the greatest evidence of its correct placement here, as a contemporary of Jeremiah and King Jehoiakim.

Almost buried inside God's response to Habakkuk's second complaint (1:12-2:1) is the key verse of the whole prophecy: in explaining the motives of the enemy, God makes a contrast with the enemy, whose desires are "not upright", with that of the righteous person ("just" person in many translations) who lives by faith (2:4). Paul would later quote this verse in Galatians 3:11 and Romans 1:17, and the writer of the Epistle to the Hebrews in Hebrews 10:38.

The third chapter of this brief book is hardly a prophecy; rather, it is a Psalm that would easily find its place alongside any of the other "Elohistic" Psalms such as was read 2 days ago. Its absence from the scroll found with the Dead Sea Scrolls has led some to believe that it was the work of a different writer, but it does still "feel" like the other two chapters despite the different content.

September 16, NT
Romans 12:1-21
Practical Instructions, Part One

Compared to some other Epistle writers (notably James), Paul isn't known particularly for showering his audience with practical advice for living their Christian faith. Paul spends far more time expressing deep theological truths than day to day types of advice. But Paul does it here in the first of two days' worth of readings from Romans, where all 21 verses of chapter 12 are quotable nuggets that read a lot like Proverbs. He even quotes one in verse 20 (Proverbs 25:21). Among other things, this chapter presents a call to pray in the Spirit (Romans 12:1-2), several items Paul had previously expressed to the Galatians and Corinthians (12:4-13, you should recognize several), and even advice that could have easily come straight from the Beatitudes (12:14-21). More to come, tomorrow.

September 17, OT
Jeremiah 8:4-9:15; Jeremiah 9:22-10:16; Jeremiah 26:1-24
Acquittal By Precedent

While Jehoiakim, king of Judah, was dealing with the Egyptian invasion, and Habakkuk was warning of a different invasion to come (from Babylon), Jeremiah was pointing out how both events (the one that just happened and the one soon to come) were a direct result of Judah's own treachery. Jeremiah spends most of chapter 8 telling the people of Judah that they essentially brought all this on themselves (Jeremiah 8:4-22). In one of the passages that gives Jeremiah the nickname of the "weeping prophet," he expresses this criticism as a lament (9:1-6), and goes on to give one of the clearest warnings ever delivered on the consequences of this evil - the coming desolation of Jerusalem when they are invaded and carted off to exile (9:7-15, 9:22-26). He even uses one of the Bible's most biting pieces of satire (10:1-16) to make a point about how Judah should not follow the idolatrous example of other nations.

His warnings to Judah continue in chapter 26 (26:1-6), which includes verses that pinpoint this section as having been written near the beginning of the reign of Jehoiakim. The writing then shifts from prophecy to history (and was probably written by Jeremiah's scribe Baruch, who we will read more about later) as we learn about a plot to have Jeremiah murdered (26:7-24). Jeremiah was saying a lot of negative things about Judah to the people of Judah, and the authorities were none too happy about this. Another prophet whose book doesn't appear in the Bible (Uriah, 26:20-23) was, in fact, put to death for similar prophecies. But it is by the precedent of another prophet who *does* appear in the Bible, namely Micah (26:17-19), that Jeremiah was spared.

September 17, NT
Romans 13:1-14
Proper Respect for Authority (Practical Instructions, Part Two)

Paul's practical applications of the Faith continue in chapter 13, with exhortations to stay out of debt (Romans 13:8), obey the commandments (13:9), and avoid sexual sin (13:13-14), among other things. But it is his advice regarding our relationship with the rulers under whom we are governed that dominates this chapter (13:1-7), and is also perhaps its most controversial part today.

It makes for some very interesting debate when considered on its face value. If taken literally, Romans 13:1-7 would clearly prohibit any Christian from engaging in civil disobedience. At the very least, and without extending the discussion of this to the length of a full book, the advice given here by God through Paul is a clear call to being a law-abiding citizen of whatever country you live in. Whether the individual leader (President, Prime Minister, Monarch, etc.) is "good" or not, in the eyes of individual people, it is important to respect the Office they hold, because people are put in that office only through the Will of God.

Let's not forget the fact that when Paul wrote this letter to the Romans, the Church planted there was basically *underground*, because the Roman authorities who ruled all of the known world of the day would have not allowed it. The Romans had their own gods and it was part of their own state religion to believe in and worship them. Christianity was essentially illegal in the Roman empire. Judaism was tolerated only to the extent that the citizens of Judea and other Jewish provinces continued to pay their taxes, and their religion wasn't seen as a threat. In that regard, Paul was doing little more than echoing the words of Jesus when He said to "render unto Caesar what is Caesar's…" in Mark 12:17. But, the main thrust of Paul's words here is that the law-abiding citizen truly has nothing to fear from the government, while the converse equally true.

September 18, OT
Jeremiah 7:1-8:3; Jeremiah 11:1-17; Jeremiah 15:10-21; Jeremiah 22:18-23
Falling on Deaf Ears

A problem that nearly all of the prophets, both major and minor, had in common was that their prophecies fell on largely deaf ears. Following the Egyptian invasion but prior to the Babylonian exile (in other words, during the reign of Jehoiakim), Jeremiah spent much of his time dictating the words he received from the Lord to his scribe, Baruch (we know of this because of something in tomorrow's OT reading), and passing along God's instructions to have these words proclaimed throughout all Jerusalem. The style of the passages in Jeremiah chapters 11, 15, and 22, in particular, indicate dictation of a dialog between the prophet and God, just as in several previous readings. Jeremiah made it a point in several places to mark where the Lord was speaking versus where Jeremiah himself was either responding to the Lord or expressing thoughts or feelings of his own (note Jeremiah 11:1-5a, 11:5b, and then 11:6 and beyond). Despite the amount of jumping around necessary to place these in the correct chronological order, each section of today's OT reading can be pinned to this period after the elder son of Josiah had taken the throne.

In Jeremiah 7:1-8:3, God goes well beyond merely warning of the invasion and desolation to come, telling the people that they have already been indicted, convicted, and sentenced, in some of Jeremiah's most graphic language. In chapter 11, God explains in detail the reason behind all this: how the Covenant, which always was supposed to be a two-way agreement, was broken because the Israelites had returned to the stubborn and wicked ways of their ancestors (11:10). In chapter 15, Jeremiah laments how everyone curses him for proclaiming these things, but then the Lord offers words of mercy - IF the people repent (15:19-21). But even the Lord knows that this will fall on deaf ears, as it is then clearly predicted that Jehoiakim would be exiled and would die outside of Jerusalem (22:18-23), the first major indicator of what would happen in tomorrow's OT reading.

September 18, NT
Romans 14:1-15:6
How, and How Not to Build Each Other Up

Back in Acts chapter 10 (read on June 27 and 28), the first Gentile conversion was made with the help of Peter, not Paul. Paul later took up the mantle of being the evangelist to the Gentile world, and embarked on three Missionary Journeys, of which he was just wrapping up the third, to parts of Europe and Asia Minor (northern Middle East) where many new churches were planted among both the Jewish and Gentile believers. In his Epistles, most of which up till now were written to churches he had visited in person, Paul spends a lot of time telling Gentiles that it isn't necessary to first become Jewish in order to become a Christian. Likewise, Paul has had to point out on several occasions, but especially here in Romans, that Jewish believers don't necessarily have to give up their customs and practices as they receive Grace, but that these customs and practices are *no longer necessary* to please God. Paul also needs to tell Jewish believers, which made up the larger part of the believers in Rome, that there was no basis for judging their fellow Gentile believers or discriminating against them for the fact that they don't follow Jewish customs. That's the central message of chapter 14 and part of 15 in today's NT reading.

Paul does this without once mentioning either Jews or Gentiles by name, at least not in this passage. Paul refers to all as merely "believers" and makes contrasts between those who eat certain things versus those who don't, referring to Jewish customs that were and are part of Jewish law. But those contrasts are designed to merely point out how new (and usually strong) believers should not quarrel over disputable matters with someone whose faith is less strong. Instead, we should focus on "not being a stumbling block" (Romans 14:13) in order to built up people's faith. Paul basically does away with practically everything in Jewish law having to do with prohibited foods, but he does it without specifying that it's Jewish law being replaced by grace. We should be seeking "mutual edification" (14:19) and peace and "bear with the failings of the weak" (15:1-2).

In some manuscripts of Paul's letter to the Romans, the closing of the letter (16:25-27) is actually at the end of chapter 14, and some others at the end of chapter 15.

September 19, OT
2 Kings 24:1-4; Jeremiah 35:1-36:32; 2 Chronicles 36:6-7
The Beginning of the End of the Kingdom

The observant reader will notice that today begins the next to last chapter of the books of the Kings. We're already in the last chapter of the Chronicles, and we take another 2 verses of it today. Despite being this close to the end of all this history, we're still nearly a month away from the events that mark the *complete* fall of Judah. Unlike the fall of Samaria, the fall of Jerusalem took more than 11 years to reach totality. But it is here that this fall begins.

Judah had already been conquered by Egypt, but only King Jehoahaz was exiled. Egypt installed Jehoahaz's older brother Jehoiakim as king, but Jehoiakim's reign was cut short when the first event in 2 Kings 24 takes place: the invasion of Judah by Nebuchadnezzar, king of Babylon, who turned Jehoiakim into little more than a regional governor (2 Kings 24:1). Jehoiakim attempted a rebellion, but this proved to be futile, as it was God who sent the armies of Babylon and its allies to destroy Jerusalem (24:2-4) and send Jehoiakim to exile (2 Chronicles 36:6-7), the first phase of a process that would leave Jerusalem desolate as predicted in prophecies by Zephaniah and Jeremiah.

Before Jehoiakim was exiled, the Lord called Jeremiah to get together with a family known as the Rechabites (or Rekabites; spelling differs in different translations). We know almost nothing of this clan besides what is written in Jeremiah 35. They had customs that closely mimicked Nazarites, of which John the Baptist was one. God used Jeremiah on this mission in order to point out a contrast between a family that obeys the word of their ancestors versus the whole of the people of Judah who have, obviously, not done so. He pronounces His sentence, promising to carry out the prophesied destruction (Jeremiah 35:17), but also has Jeremiah tell the Rechabites that their descendents will always be there to serve God (35:18-19).

At this same time, one of the most dramatic events recorded in Jeremiah's prophecy occurs, as Jehoiakim (who is still on the throne at this point) burned a copy of Jeremiah's prophecies after God had Baruch make a copy of them (36:1-26). The scroll was then replaced (36:27-32) with Baruch's help. This helps explain why there is even more jumping around within Jeremiah than there was in Isaiah.

September 19, NT
Romans 15:7-33
Paul Promises a Visit

Paul's letter to the Romans was distinct from those he had written before this (Galatians, 1 and 2 Thessalonians, 1 and 2 Corinthians) in two primary ways: he spends comparatively little time on personal matters and plans for the future, concentrating instead on doctrinal issues until this chapter. The other distinction is that he was writing to a place he had not yet visited, whereas he had visited Galatia, Thessalonica, and Corinth before writing to them. It is here in this next-to-last chapter that Paul decides to get personal and cover both bases.

Paul's admonition to "accept one another" (Romans 15:7) at the beginning of today's reading is a continuation of yesterday's, where Paul is making his role as Apostle to the Gentiles known to the Jewish-Christian audience. More in this Epistle than any other, he quotes Old Testament scripture to make his points, a technique that would make much more sense to his Jewish audience than to a Gentile crowd (15:9-12, verse by verse, quotes Psalm 18:49, Deuteronomy 32:43, Psalm 117:1, and Isaiah 11:10, respectively). Paul uses his success with Gentiles to inspire the Romans to spread the Gospel to anyone, not just Jews (Romans 15:14-22), ending this section with another quote from Isaiah.

But Paul also says that this emphasis on bringing the Gospel to the Gentiles is the reason why he had not yet visited Rome (15:22-23), a situation that he promised to rectify soon. He mentions how he must first return to Jerusalem (15:25), in one of his few mentions of surrounding events, confirming this Epistle's placement at this point, near the end of his Third Missionary Journey and after his visits and letters to Corinth.

September 20, OT
Jeremiah 25:1-38; Jeremiah 45:1-5
The Seventy-Year Exile Begins

With King Jehoiakim exiled, and having received the warning that Jerusalem was to be destroyed, Jeremiah decided it was now time (in "the first year of Nebuchadnezzar", Jeremiah 25:1) to complete the warning to all the people of Judah. Jeremiah points out that he's been prophesying about this since Josiah' was 30 years old (25:3) but, as pointed out 2 days ago, his prophecies have fallen on deaf ears (25:3, 25:7). Therefore, God was going to send the Babylonians to destroy the nation, making it a desolate wasteland, and the people will serve Nebuchadnezzar for a period of 70 years (25:11).

But then, like Micah and Isaiah (in particular) before him, Jeremiah notes what will happen at the end of those 70 years: Babylon will suffer the same fate as Judah (25:12-14), becoming desolate forever. He goes on to use the metaphor of a cup of wine to deliver the message that, eventually, *all* nations will suffer God's wrath (25:15-38), not just Judah. Jeremiah also makes it a point to pass along this message to his faithful scribe, Baruch, as a personal message from the Lord (45:1-5).

September 20, NT
Romans 16:1-27
Conclusion of Romans

Though it was mentioned yesterday that Paul spent relatively little time in personal matters, greetings, etc., in Romans vs. other letters he had written, that doesn't mean he didn't make mention of these things. In chapter 15, he mentioned among other things his desire to come to Rome on his way to Spain. Now, here in chapter 16, he devotes an entire (and fairly long) chapter to a series of "shout outs". As such, this chapter is often skipped when reading the entire Bible or entire New Testament on the basis that it's doctrinally unimportant. Perhaps it is less important than the Truths Paul spells out in chapters 1-14, but that doesn't make this an unimportant chapter from Paul's magnum opus. Several important clues are given to give us a very interesting picture of the early Church.

Having just told the Romans that he must first go to Jerusalem before paying the Romans a visit, he sends Phoebe, a deaconess from

Cenchrae, which is the Eastern part of Corinth (Romans 16:1-2) to them. This is proof, contrary to many critics who accuse Paul of misogyny, that women held important positions in the early Church. He also mentions Priscilla before her husband Aquila (16:3-5) among the other helpers. Several other women (and men) are mentioned in the closing greeting. It was obvious that it not only didn't matter whether you were Gentile or Jew, but it also didn't matter if you were male or female.

Some of the names mentioned here are people mentioned previously in Acts or in one of the letters to Corinth, but a few are new names never mentioned before. In these cases, they may have been people mentioned TO Paul that prompted the Epistle in the first place. In the midst of all the greetings, he echoes a verse he used in his second letter to Thessalonica (2 Thess 3:6, 3:14) in Romans 16:17-18 to take action to make sure to avoid those who cause divisions in the Church.

His closing prayer (16:25-27) mentions again the fact that Paul's primary role was bringing the Gospel to the Gentiles. With this letter, he extended an invitation for the new believers in Rome to do the same. It is interesting to note, amongst the names mentioned in this last chapter, the names of people who were *not* mentioned in this letter. Most notably, he never mentioned Peter in any form (Simon, Simon Peter, etc.), despite the fact that 1) Peter would mention Paul at the end of his last writing, known as 2nd Peter, 2) Catholics believe to this day that it was Peter who planted the church in Rome to which Paul then wrote, and 3) the Church in Rome would soon grow to be the largest Christian church in the world, thanks to the way it spread using Roman infrastructure, and despite being illegal until Constantine. It is assumed that both Peter and Paul were martyred there, and we are certain that Paul eventually did make that promised visit there, but Paul's lack of ever mentioning Peter in his writings has caused many to scratch their heads in wonder about this point of Christian history.

September 21, OT
Daniel 1:1-21; Jeremiah 46:1-28
Life Under Nebuchadnezzar (Introduction to Daniel)

For a variety of reasons, the Book of Daniel is among the most controversial but also most deeply studied books of the Bible. The apocalyptic nature of its prophecies is the most common reason for the controversy, but everything from the truth of the events related in the first 6 chapters to the uncertain authorship and timing add to the controversy. Daniel is never directly quoted in the New Testament except when mentioning the term "abomination of desolation". However, the prophecies of Daniel dovetail neatly into the apocalyptic prophecies in Revelation, though there are many who believe that Daniel's prophecies have already been fulfilled, during the time of the Maccabees (leaders of a Jewish revolt against Emperor Antiochus IV in about 165 BC), instead of being End Times prophecies as this chronology believes.

About the only thing that is universally agreed about Daniel is the timing of the *events* that are told in the first 6 chapters. The opening verse (Daniel 1:1) pins this near the beginning of the Babylonian Exile which we just read about yesterday. All scholarly debate about this aside, this chronology believes the following about the book to be true:

1. **Daniel wrote it himself**, most likely just after the end of the Babylonian Exile (Daniel would have been an old man of about 85-90 years of age at that time, Daniel 1:21), despite being written in the "third person" which is known to be a common technique in Hebrew writing.

2. It is **not a work of fiction** such as apocryphal books like Tobit and Judith or the additions to Daniel found in several Greek additions to the book, such as Bel and the Dragon, etc.

3. Prophecy is mixed with history in the first six chapters where Daniel interprets dreams, and appears as pure prophecy in chapters 7 onwards (though chronologically out of sequence in our Bibles), where **most of the prophecy is related to End Times events**.

4. Despite portions of Daniel for which only Aramaic scrolls are known (such as fragments that were found among the

Dead Sea Scrolls), this chronology assumes that the work was originally written entirely in Hebrew (such as Chapter 1 and Chapters 8 onward) for several reasons, not the least of which is the fact that the Aramaic language, from which the Hebrew language was later developed, was the primary language used by people living just before and during Jesus' lifetime, which is when the scrolls found in the Qumran caves would have been written.

In the first chapter, the story of how Daniel and 3 of his fellow officials (Daniel 1:3-7) are brought into Nebuchadnezzar's service is told, and they were given new names to go with their new roles. Daniel and the other 3 refused to "defile themselves" with the food and wine provided by the king, instead opting for a diet of vegetables only, thus sending a message to Nebuchadnezzar about how they would continue to obey their God, not the gods of Babylon (1:8-16). This not only earned God's favor but also impressed the Babylonian king (1:18-20).

Nebuchadnezzar didn't only invade Judah, but Egypt as well, as prophesied on several occasions. In the second part of today's two-part reading, Jeremiah begins a section of prophecies on various nations, starting with Egypt. The prophecies go on for several more chapters and concern other nations as well, but the entirety of chapter 46 is devoted to the nation that did all of the following things that we've read about during the past week:

1. Egypt attempted to assist in the defense of Assyria when Babylon invaded Assyria
2. King Josiah attempted to stop Egypt but not only failed but lost his life as well
3. Egypt installs Josiah's *youngest* son as king, and then exiles him to Egypt after just 3 months
4. Egypt then installs Jehoiakim, Josiah's oldest son, as king of Judah

Nebuchadnezzar, meanwhile, took Jehoiakim into exile along with many of the other high officials in Jerusalem, thus beginning the "Babylonian Exile" which would last for 70 years. Pharoah Nico was still in power in Egypt at this time (Jeremiah 46:2) even though Egypt was defeated by Babylon in the earlier battle during Jehoiakim's 4th year. Now, Jeremiah prophesies the conquest of Egypt at the hands of those same Babylonians (46:3-26a), but also foretells the restoration of Egypt (46:26b). Turning his attention back to Israel, Jeremiah reiterates the promise that all of the nations among which Judah will be scattered will be destroyed (46:27-28), a chilling prophecy in light of modern geopolitics in the Middle East.

September 21, NT
Acts 20:17-38
Paul Returns to Jerusalem, Part One

It's been more than a month since we last read any history from the Acts of the Apostles (August 18), due to the two Epistles written in between that time and now (2 Corinthians and Romans). So, when starting in verse 17, it would be easy to get a little lost as to who is narrating the events and where Paul is on his nearly completed Third Missionary Journey. But to recap briefly: after Paul paid another visit to Corinth, he planned to head straight back to Jerusalem in time for Pentecost (Acts 20:1-6) but his plans were thwarted due to a death threat. He spent 7 days in Troas (20:7-12) and then resumed his journey home with stops in Assos, Mitylene, Chios, Samos, and finally Miletus (20:13-16), from which he wrote the two Epistles mentioned earlier. From here, we read from the Acts of the Apostles uninterrupted for the next almost 2 weeks.

It is Luke, writer of the third Gospel as well as the Acts, who is doing the narrating of Paul's journey home, and it is picked up here in today's NT reading with Paul's call for the elders of Ephesus to join him in Meletus before embarking on the final leg of his trip to Jerusalem (20:17). He tells his plans to the elders, prays with them, and gives them a troubling parting prediction that he would never see them again (20:18-38) before boarding the ship that would bring him back to Judea.

September 22, OT
2 Kings 24:7; Daniel 2:1-49
Daniel, The Dream Interpreter

The kinds of foreshadowing that occur in the Bible is one of the most fascinating examples of how, ultimately, the author of the Bible as a whole is God. The individual writers put their own stamp on the history they record and the prophecies they make, but in the end it is God who is communicating to us through these events. Way back on January 30, the Old Testament reading for that day was called "Joseph, The Dream Interpreter." The event followed Joseph, an Israelite who was captive in Egypt, and his rise to a position of power in the Pharoah's court by interpreting dreams that the Pharoah's own mystics could not. In today's OT reading, the setting changes to Babylon instead of Egypt (now conquered by Babylon, 2 Kings 24:7), and the hero is Daniel instead of Joseph, but the events are very similar.

The events may be alike, but the nature of the dream interpreted by our hero is VERY different. In the earlier example with Joseph, the dream was interpreted to be a foretelling of near-future events concerning a time of plenty and a time of famine. Here, Nebuchadnezzar has a dream which troubles him so much that he threatens his astrologers with death if they can't correctly interpret it (Daniel 2:1-7). The king is so paranoid that he won't even let them *attempt* the interpretation until they can prove that they can do it (2:8-11). When the astrologers complained, the king set out to have them executed along with Daniel and his friends (2:12-15). But Daniel bought them all some time, consulted with his friends, prayed about the matter, and convinced the king's officials to let him make the attempt (2:16-24).

Daniel not only interpreted the dream, but was actually the one to describe it to Nebuchadnezzar instead of the other way around (2:25-35). The interpretation, which Daniel credits to God, concerns a great statue, made of several different materials, each representing the era of some different great world empire. The only one he names is the first: the then-current empire of Babylon, represented by the golden head (2:36-38). Each subsequent kingdom/empire is represented by other materials and lower parts of the body (silver, bronze, iron, and iron mixed with clay, 2:39-43). During that last kingdom, God will set up a kingdom that will never die (2:44-45), which makes this a Messianic prophecy.

The grateful king praised Daniel and even credits God for this, and elevates Daniel and his friends to high positions in his kingdom (2:46-48)

September 22, NT
Acts 21:1-14
Paul Returns to Jerusalem, Part Two; Conclusion of the Third Missionary Journey

Luke narrates the final stops along the way of Paul's return home to Jerusalem. With his arrival in Caesarea and a visit from a prophet from Jerusalem named Agabus (Acts 21:8-10), the Third Missionary Journey was officially brought to a close; Paul was home.

But before going to Jerusalem, Agabus gave Paul a warning, using Paul's belt as a prop to bind his hands and feet (21:11-12), no doubt because word of Paul's preaching among the Gentiles had reached the Jewish officials in Jerusalem, and they were none too happy about it (see tomorrow's reading for details). But Paul decided to ignore the warning, for reasons that are explained in more detail tomorrow, and with his companions' prayer that "the Lord's will be done," proceeded to Jerusalem (21:13-14).

September 23, OT
2 Kings 24:5-6; 2 Chronicles 36:8; 2 Kings 24:8-9; 2 Chronicles 36:9; 1 Chronicles 3:10-16; Daniel 3:1-30
Death of Jehoiakim; Accession of Jehoiachin; The Fiery Furnace Incident

The passages in 2 Kings and 2 Chronicles relate, briefly, the death of King Jehoiakim and his son's (Josiah's grandson's) ascent to the throne in Jerusalem, where we already know that he had the 2nd-shortest reign of any king of Judah, 3 months and 10 days (2 Chronicles 36:9). As we reach the near-conclusion of the kingdom, the succession of kings in Judah after Solomon is recorded in one last reading from *First* Chronicles, which shows all the names including the odd family tree from Josiah onwards. Josiah's youngest son, called Shallum here just as Jeremiah calls him, was his first successor, followed by Jehoiakim, Jehoiakim's son Jehoiachin, and finally Josiah's 3rd son, Zedekiah. Josiah's eldest son never becomes king and is not mentioned anywhere else in the Bible.

Meanwhile in Babylon, Nebuchadnezzar's praise of God was short-lived after Daniel's dream interpretation, as he had a great golden statue *of himself* erected, and decreed that everyone should bow down to worship the image (Daniel 3:1-7). Of course, Daniel and his friends wouldn't do any such thing, and the king's astrologers brought this to Nebuchadnezzar's attention (3:8-13a). The king was furious, and had Daniel's 3 friends, Shadrach, Meshach and Abednego, brought before him for interrogation (3:13b-18). Their refusal to bow down to the king's image resulted in a death sentence: he ordered the furnace stoked to 7 times its usual level, had the 3 of them bound up, and had them thrown alive into the furnace (3:19-21).

But Nebuchadnezzar's plans went south when two things happened. First, the over-fired furnace was so hot that the flames burned the soldiers that threw the 3 men into the furnace, killing them. Second, the king saw *four* men walking, alive and unharmed, inside the furnace. He did not know the identity of the 4th person (an angel, actually), but upon seeing that the 3 were unharmed ordered them removed from the furnace (3:22-27). Once again, just like with the dream interpretation by Daniel, Nebuchadnezzar gave credit to the God of Shadrach, Meshach and Abednego, even ordering a death sentence for anyone who speaks ill of the one, true God, and promoting the 3 to even higher positions in the kingdom (3:28-30).

This is the last we hear from the book of Daniel until November 5, due mainly to the events and prophecies of the early years of the Babylonian exile written by Jeremiah and Ezekiel.

September 23, NT
Acts 21:15-36
Paul is Welcomed, Then Arrested

Despite Agabus' warning, Paul's arrival in Jerusalem met with a warm welcome... at first (Acts 21:17). Paul told them about his Missionary Journeys, and visited James the brother of Jesus (21:18-19). They received this news warmly, but responded to the news about Paul's evangelization of Gentiles by suggesting that Paul join in a purification ritual with 4 other men (21:20-26).

There were some, though, that didn't think this whole Gentile thing was a particularly good idea. After Paul had been in Jerusalem for a week, some Jews from Asia saw Paul preaching, and started a riot over the issue of Paul's choice to bring Gentiles (called "Greeks" here) into the Temple (21:27-30), which was considered defilement. A Roman soldier stopped him from getting beat up, but at the insistence of the crowd took him away to a barracks (21:31-36) with the crowd still shouting at him all the way.

September 24, OT
Jeremiah 9:16-21; Jeremiah 10:17-25; Jeremiah 12:7-17; Jeremiah 19:14-20:18
The Diaspora

At this point in the Babylonian Exile, only the high officials and royalty of Judah had been taken into captivity. There would, however, soon come a time when Nebuchadnezzar would come for the rest of the people, leaving Jerusalem completely desolate, and the people scattered around the known world. The Northern Kingdom had also already suffered this fate, and the first line in today's OT reading completes a quote by the Lord in telling Judah that they will likewise be scattered, or "dispersed" as some translations say. This scattering of the people of Israel and Judah is named for the Greek word for dispersal, The Diaspora.

The readings in chapters 9 and 10 are mostly more such quotes from God. Chapter 10 ends with a prayer from Jeremiah, asking to only be disciplined "only in due measure," lest he be destroyed (Jeremiah 10:23-25). The section in chapter 12 is, likewise, God speaking, but the difference is that it is part of a response to Jeremiah in a section called "Jeremiah's complaint" which won't be read until October 2. Nevertheless, God's words here continue the theme of the scattering to come.

In Jeremiah 19:14 through 20:6,, we have yet another example of how Jeremiah got into trouble for bringing these prophecies to the people. Further proof of the stubborn, thick-headedness of the people of Judah is on display here, as even with the city under siege, the king and most of his officials carted off to exile, and the Temple plundered, Jeremiah's prophecy is met with scorn and ridicule. Once out, Jeremiah informs the priest Pashhur (his jailer) that he will share everyone else's fate too. Jeremiah then lifts his prayer to God, complaining about his continuous mistreatment, but praising the most high God (20:7-18).

September 24, NT
Acts 21:37-22:21
Paul Speaks to the Jerusalem Crowd

When Paul was being hauled to a barracks by a soldier, he asked to be able to speak to the stirred-up crowd. The soldier, surprised with Paul's use of the Greek language (thus making him a Roman citizen, see tomorrow's reading), gave him his chance (Acts 21:37-40). And so using the language of the common people, Aramaic (21:1-2), Paul addressed the crowd.

For the remainder of today's reading, Paul recalls the major events of his life and ministry, including his persecution of Christians, his presence at the stoning of Stephen, and most importantly, his conversion by Jesus himself on the road to Damascus, all in an effort to justify his ministry to the Gentiles, which came from God Himself (21:3-21). As you will read tomorrow, the crowd listened only up to the point where he mentions the Gentiles, the very thing that got him into trouble here on his return to Jerusalem.

September 25, OT
Jeremiah 22:24-23:8
The End of the Line; The New Beginning

Two days ago, we read of the accession of the next to last king of Judah, Jehoiachin: son of Jehoiakim, grandson of Josiah. The family tree of succession after Josiah didn't go particularly far, as the only king to follow Jehoiachin would be his *uncle*, Zedekiah, son of Josiah, in tomorrow's OT reading. We know this is where the family line ends in terms of royalty, because the kingdom ends when the Exile is complete. We also know this from a prophecy we read today from Jeremiah: after predicting Jehoiachin's soon to come exile (Jeremiah 22:24-27), the Lord says to "record this man as childless" and that "none will sit on the throne of David or rule anymore in Judah" (22:30). Jeremiah is marking the end of the line.

And then, after all of the predictions of exile, doom, and destruction for Judah and its kings, Jeremiah places a prediction of doom for the nations that the Israelites scattered to (23:1-4). The prediction that follows is one of Jeremiah's most strongly Messianic: that a righteous branch will rise from the house of David, a king who will reign wisely

(23:5), and will be called by the name "the Lord, Our Righteous Savior" (23:6). Israel will live in its original land in safety (23:8) and peace, a reference not only to Jesus Christ but also the return of the people of Israel to their homeland after the Exile - or it could even be further into the future, as in the rebirth of the modern nation of Israel in 1948.

September 25, NT
Acts 22:22-23:11
Roman Citizenship; Paul Meets with the Sanhedrin

Paul's attempt at defending his ministry to the Gentiles backfired in front of the Jerusalem crowd. For his safety, the Roman soldiers took him into protective custody in the barracks he was being led to (Acts 22:22-24). There, he was questioned about his Roman citizenship, since he had the ability to speak Greek (in yesterday's reading), and thus backed off from performing any interrogation (22:25-29). But curious about what had stirred up the crowd so much, they brought Paul before the Jewish religious leaders (the "Council," 22:30).

Paul went to mount a brave and bold defense before the divided (Sadducees and Pharisees) Council, only to be told by a bystander that he was insulting the High Priest for doing so (23:1-5), so he changed his tactic, using the fact that he was a Pharisee himself to get that side of the Council on his side (23:6-8). It worked; the Pharisaic side concluded that Paul was innocent of any charges (23:9), and the Roman soldiers (still fearing for Paul's life) had him taken away (23:10).

In this passage's last verse, God commands Paul to do what he always wanted to do anyway: bring the Gospel to Rome, in person. Paul's rejection by the Jewish authorities thus became the first step on the road to Rome.

September 26, OT
2 Kings 24:10-17; 2 Chronicles 36:10; Jeremiah 49:1-33
Deportation of Jehoiachin; Accession of Zedekiah

Just as prophesied, Jehoiachin's reign as king would mark the end of the royal line in Judah, as Nebuchadnezzar came to Jerusalem to lead the deportation of more than 10,000 people, including the king, to

Babylon. The king of Babylon then installed his *uncle* - not his brother or son - as king. In the account in 2 Kings, we learn that this son of Josiah was originally named Mattaniah, but Nebuchadnezzar gave him the new name of Zedekiah. Zedekiah would be listed as the last king of Judah.

Jeremiah's prophecies continue in chapter 49 with oracles against several of Judah's neighbors, given that they, too, had been conquered by Babylon: the nations listed include Ammon (Jeremiah 49:1-6), Edom (49:7-22), Damascus (49:23-27), and Kedar and Hazor (49:28-33). More such oracles follow in a few days, all of which prophecy some level of destruction or doom on all of these conquered nations.

September 26, NT
Acts 23:12-35
The Road to Rome, Part One: The Conspiracy to Kill Paul

Paul's life had been threatened before this, more than once, in fact. But this time, he had the whole Sanhedrin after him, waiting in ambush, while he was still under Roman guard in a barracks. The remaining portion of Acts chapter 23 (which was started yesterday) details the events surrounding the conspiracy of the Jewish religious leadership to have him tried and executed, all for the crime of bringing the Gospel message to the Gentiles.

Acts 23:12-22 tells of the conspiracy itself, and how Paul's nephew successfully got word to Paul and the Roman Commander, so that he could then be transferred out of there to Caesarea, which is told in verses 23-35. Paul was now in Herod's palace. He would never see Jerusalem again.

September 27, OT
Obadiah 1:1-21
The Future of Edom

The Old Testament's shortest book is the 21-verse vision of the prophet Obadiah, presented here in its entirety. After identifying himself by name in the first verse, no other biographical or chronological data is given. Thus, we know very close to nothing about the prophet, and can only speculate on the timing of his prophecy. The consensus opinion is that Obadiah's vision was written either during the early part of the Exile (as Zedekiah began his reign, as this reading plan believes) or just after the Exile ended. The prophecy is entirely against neighboring nation Edom, which actually dovetails perfectly with the passage read yesterday in Jeremiah 49.

Edom, you'll recall, was the nation founded by Jacob's brother Esau after the latter married into the family of Ishmael, Esau's grandfather Abraham's illegitimate son. The Edomites would go on to become the ancestors of modern-day Arabs. In this brief but succinct prophecy, Obadiah predicts that Edom will be conquered just like Judah has been, but *Judah* will be the nation that actually recovers afterwards, not Edom. The last verse promises deliverers who will go to Mount Zion (Jerusalem) to govern the mountains of Edom, and "the kingdom will be the Lord's", a fascinating prophecy in light of modern geopolitics: the nation of Jordan covers most of what once was Edom, and the city carved out of rock, Petra, will later play a role in the End Times.

September 27, NT
Acts 24:1-27
The Road to Rome, Part Two: The Trial Before Felix

Paul had been spirited away to Caesarea, but that didn't stop the Jewish authorities from tracking him down and sending a high priest and a lawyer (Acts 24:1) to take the case against Paul to the local Roman Governor, Felix. After opening arguments and Jewish testimony (24:2-9), Paul was granted time to speak in his defense (24:10-21), using his time to debunk all of the charges against him, and declare that the only reason for being put on trial was his belief in the resurrection of the dead (24:21).

Felix was well acquainted with The Way (which we would today call Christianity), and promised a quick ruling in the matter. He left Paul guarded under minimal security, and gave Paul additional opportunities to speak about faith in Jesus, privately, with him and his Jewish wife (24:24). But in the end, the Governor reneged on his promise of a quick ruling, leaving Paul still in prison after he left office and was succeeded by Porcius Festus (24:27).

September 28, OT
Jeremiah 14:1-15:9; Jeremiah 18:1-19:13; Jeremiah 24:1-10
Drought, Famine, Sword, and Plague

Today's reading (in 3 parts, all from Jeremiah) starts with a prediction from God of a drought to come (Jeremiah 14:1-6). As if the people of Judah didn't have enough to deal with already…

Jeremiah pleads for mercy (14:7-9), but the Lord has had quite enough. God answers Jeremiah's plea with a prediction of "sword, famine, and plague" (14:10-12). The dialog continues back and forth through the remainder of chapter 14 and into chapter 15, even including the statement by God that "even if Moses and Samuel were to stand before me, my heart would not go out to this people. Send them away from my presence! (15:1, NIV). Clearly, God had been pushed too far, and it was time for His wrath.

In chapter 18, God sends Jeremiah to a potter's house, to make a point about how the nation of Judah is like the potter's clay, molded by the potter into whatever shape he desires (18:1-10. This is followed by another declaration of disaster, which God knows will be stubbornly ignored or denied (18:11-17). Then, if you blink you'll miss it, verse 18 starts another complaint from Jeremiah, since he is being faced with having to deliver these prophecies to a hostile and uncaring audience (18:18-23). God answers with another example using the potter (19:1-13), that Jeremiah is to use in front of the elders and priests.

In the third segment, God uses the example of two baskets of figs, one good, one bad, to explain to Jeremiah how His relationship with the people of Judah: the exiles in the good basket, King Zedekiah and his evil officials in the bad basket (24:1-9) to whom God would send sword, famine, and plague (24:10).

September 28, NT
Acts 25:1-19
The Road to Rome, Part Three: Paul's Trials Before Festus and Agrippa

The next 3 days' NT readings are actually in regards to a single event; thus, parts 3, 4, and 5 are all parts of Paul's appearances before Governor Festus and then King Herod Agrippa, all on "The Road to Rome."

Paul's time in prison in Caesarea was more of a protective custody than it was a criminal sentence. That's not to say that he wasn't in chains - he was - but Paul's trial before Felix was supposed to prove that he had done nothing wrong according to Jewish law, and therefore, the Romans could not only dismiss the charges but protect him from the Jewish mob. But when Felix left him in prison for two years and then was succeeded by Porcius Festus, the effort to get to Rome and away from the Jews who wanted to kill him had to be started anew.

So, one of Festus' first acts was to go to Jerusalem to hear the charges against Paul (Acts 25:1-2). The Jews wanted Paul transferred back to Jerusalem for ulterior motives, but Festus was having none of it and set up the trial to commence in Caesarea instead (25:3-6). Paul was allowed to make his defense, but was also asked by Festus if he was willing to go to Jerusalem to face the charges there (25:7-9). At this point, Paul saw his opportunity and took it: declaring his innocence again, and using his status as a Roman citizen, he chose to bring his appeal directly to Caesar (25:10-11). Festus granted this appeal (25:12) and then went to consult the reigning monarch, named here as Agrippa (25:13-19). This king would have been the grandson of Herod the Great, and is thus Herod Agrippa, mentioned in several other places in the Bible under his full name.

September 29, OT
Jeremiah 29:1-32
A Message to the Exiles; A Message to Shemaiah

In response to God's words to Jeremiah (the two baskets of figs, yesterday) about the people already taken into Exile at this point (versus those who were yet to be taken), Jeremiah wrote a letter to the Exiles and had it delivered to Babylon (Jeremiah 29:1-3). The text of the letter (29:4-28) contains numerous pieces of practical advice for living in exile in Babylon. Through Jeremiah, the Lord tells the exiles to take root in the foreign land and live normal lives, because their stay there would be temporary but lengthy. The exiles were told to not listen to the false prophets and deceivers of that land, but to continue to pray to the Lord. Many other things were said in the letter, but the most important was another statement of the promise that this exile would last 70 years, and when it was done, they (their descendents) would be allowed to return and reclaim their land.

The letter strikes a contrast with those who were not yet exiled, including and especially King Zedekiah, Judah's last monarch, who would be slain by Nebuchadnezzar "before your eyes". One exile, though, that God told Jeremiah to call out by name was a false prophet named Shemaiah; he would be punished for preaching rebellion against God (29:29-32).

September 29, NT
Acts 25:20-26:11
The Road to Rome, Part Four: Paul's Trials Before Festus and Agrippa

When Festus went to Agrippa, his intention was only to make Paul's appeal to Caesar known, because Festus himself didn't know how to handle matters like this (Acts 25:20-21). Agrippa, however, wanted to hear from Paul himself (25:22).

Paul was introduced by Festus to Agrippa in open court (25:23-27), indicating the one main thing on the Roman officials' minds: the fact that a man being sent to Caesar for an appeal needed to know the charges being brought against him. So, Agrippa gave Paul his chance to speak, and Paul began his defense, this time with a greater emphasis on the works of Jesus Christ (25:28-26:11), and concluded in tomorrow's NT reading.

September 30, OT
2 Kings 24:18-20; 2 Chronicles 36:11-14; Jeremiah 49:34-39
The Reign of Zedekiah

Although the name of Zedekiah first came up a few days ago (changed from Mattaniah, as we read on September 26) as the name of the new king of Judah, we only now get to the modest amount of biographical data about him and his reign in 2 Kings and 2 Chronicles. Both passages list the 11-year length of his reign, the fact that he "did evil in the sight of the Lord", and that he began his reign at the age of 21. It also mentions that he attempted a rebellion against the real king of that day, Nebuchadnezzar of Babylon. More about that to come…

The brief passage in Jeremiah is a continuation of the passages, also from September 26, against neighboring nations, placed here only because Jeremiah 49:34 marks its place at the beginning of the reign of Zedekiah. The passage details the destruction of the nation of Elam, interesting mainly because the nation had already been mostly destroyed by the Assyrians just a few years earlier. Now, they would face complete destruction by Babylon. However, there is evidence that the nation still existed by this name (to some small extent) well into the time between the Testaments; that is, between 400 B.C. and the time of Christ.

September 30, NT
Acts 26:12-32
The Road to Rome, Part Five: Paul's Trials Before Festus and Agrippa

Paul concludes his (lengthy) defense of his ministry in front of the Roman court presided over by Agrippa the king and the regional governor, Festus. He recounts in detail the appearance by Jesus when he was on the Damascus road (Acts 26:12-18), and includes the fact that Jesus told him to preach to the Gentiles. He continues to use this defense as he recalls his subsequent missionary journeys (26:19-23), including to the Gentiles. At this point, Festus interrupts Paul, telling him that he's lost his mind (26:24); that his "great learning" has driven him mad. But Paul rebuts that too, even appealing to Agrippa about his belief in the prophets (26:25-27). Paul must have seemed very persuasive that day, as even Agrippa joked about Paul getting him converted to Christianity (26:28). Paul pointed out that this wasn't a joke, and that his hope was that all would come to this faith (26:29).

After conferring briefly, the court agreed that Paul was innocent of any crimes, and Agrippa told Festus that Paul would have been a free man had he not made his appeal to Caesar (26:30-32). Of course, we know the real reason Paul made this appeal, despite the fact that it would keep him in chains: the appeal would bring him to Rome, where God told him to preach next.

October 1, OT
Jeremiah 50:1-46
The Great Prophecy Against Babylon, Part One

Other prophecies by other prophets have appeared against Babylon and the Chaldean people, both before this and after, including some by Jeremiah. But of them all, this one stands out as a "great prophecy" because of the level of detail it goes into regarding the future of the very nation that had just conquered Judah, and it explains for all of the intended audience how the Exile that resulted from this would end.

The length of the Exile (70 years) had already been prophesied, multiple times, by Jeremiah. But until this chapter, we have not been given any actual detail as to how this would come about. The only clues were in two other books of prophecy (Isaiah and Daniel) which mention a king named Cyrus, wholly unknown to anyone of Jeremiah's time. The reason Cyrus was unknown, outside of the fact that he probably was not yet born, was that he was king of a Persian empire that would conquer Babylon. That conquest would end the Exile, and would result in the return to Jerusalem of its people in exile, and it is introduced in verses 2 and 3 of Jeremiah's 3rd longest chapter. Details about this punishment that would be delivered against Judah's punishers continue through chapter 51, tomorrow, which is Jeremiah's longest chapter.

Among the details given here by Jeremiah: Babylon's conqueror would come "from the North" (Jeremiah 50:3), and the people of *both* Israel and Judah (50:4) would then return, weeping, back to Zion (50:4-8). (We know from other prophecies that not all of Israel or Judah would return, as there are still some people in some tribes that are still "lost" to this day.) After the Jewish people leave and return, God will send a "hoard of nations" against Babylon (50:9-10). The whole point about how God will punish the punisher comes to a head in verses 17 through 20, which also includes an all-important clarification about the often-used term "remnant". Throughout the rest of the chapter, Jeremiah details the sometimes very violent imagery of God's vengeance on the people of Babylon.

October 1, NT
Acts 27:1-26
The Road to Rome, Part Six: The Voyage Begins

Roman citizens were free to move about within the Empire to whatever extent they wished back in the first century A.D. But Paul, who wanted to go to Rome anyway, found it necessary to get there in Roman chains in order to escape the Jews in Jerusalem. They had plotted to kill him for a number of reasons, not the least of which was his bringing the Gospel message to the Gentiles. Paul had written a letter to the church in Rome already, but the bulk of his audience there was Jewish converts - in other words, Jewish Christians. So even though he was not a free man going to Rome, his appeal to Caesar resulted in the voyage described in today's NT reading.

Luke, Paul's personal physician and the narrator of the Acts of the Apostles, gives a detailed account of the stops made as they set sail (Acts 27:1-8) in increasingly unfavorable conditions. Eventually, the voyage got to the point where proceeding any further would be too dangerous, and Paul admonished the Roman sailors (27:9-10) for it. But after looking over all the options, they decided to proceed anyway because the nearest harbor was not suitable for staying through winter (Acts 27:9-13).

A violent storm forced Paul, Luke, and the Roman crew to abandon ship, but they even had difficulty getting the lifeboat under control (27:14-20). After they ran out of food, and losing any hope of rescue, Paul gave them words of encouragement: they would be rescued by an angel, and there would be no loss of life; only the ship would be lost, because it was necessary for Paul to make it to Rome to meet Caesar (27:21-26). The aftermath of this speech is told in tomorrow's reading.

October 2, OT
Jeremiah 51:1-64; Jeremiah 11:18-12:6
The Great Prophecy Against Babylon, Part Two

Jeremiah could never be a politician in today's world; his messages are constantly negative. More than half of the book of Jeremiah consists of either warnings of doom for Judah or predictions of destruction, conquest, or punishment for neighboring nations. His 3rd longest (yesterday) and longest (today) two chapters are focussed on prophecies of that very type against just one nation: the nation that was in the process of conquering Judah and deporting its people into exile, Babylon.

The entirety of chapter 51 is about how Babylon will be punished for its sins against Israel, but there are a few key verses in there that need to be brought forth: Verse 5 is one of the most important statements ever made, by any prophet, to clarify what was really happening to what was left of the kingdom of Israel, in that this punishment (against Judah) was *not* a case of God forsaking his people; on the contrary, though the land is "full of guilt," the exile to Babylon is a disciplinary action, not a destruction. By contrast, Babylon would not only be disciplined but would be conquered *twice*: first by the Medes (Jeremiah 51:11) and later by Persia as we know from earlier prophecies, both by Jeremiah and by other prophets.

Verse 44 is the second reference Jeremiah makes to Bel, a false god/idol among the Chaldeans. This is the same Bel that is referenced in the apocryphal addition to the book of Daniel, "Bel and the Dragon," in which Bel is defeated by a hero named Daniel, not the prophet Daniel whose prophecies will return in this chronological plan on November 5, just before the Babylonian Exile comes to a close.

The chapter ends with the statement that "thus far are the words of Jeremiah" (51:64), indicating the end of the book. In fact, Jeremiah has 1 more chapter, but it was likely added by Baruch (or possibly Ezra; see reading for November 10) and contains history that parallels the end of 2 Kings and 2 Chronicles. The last section of today's reading is yet another example of Jeremiah being plotted against because of his prophecies, followed by a prayer to God about that plot.

October 2, NT
Acts 27:27-44
The Road to Rome, Part Seven: The Shipwreck

Paul's words of encouragement after their ship was wrecked by a storm on the way to Rome were successful in keeping them all alive, despite going 2 weeks without food. Paul gave further suggestions and help in today's NT reading as they drifted through the Adriatic Sea.
 All 276 people on board (Acts 27:37) took food and then lightened the load in the ship by throwing the remaining wheat overboard (27:38).

Eventually they reached land, though they did not recognize it, and let everyone including the prisoners (including Paul) swim ashore first and then bring everyone else ashore later (27:39-44). They would later discover that they had landed safely on the island of Malta, as detailed in tomorrow's NT reading.

October 3, OT
Jeremiah 23:9-40; Jeremiah 27:1-28:17
False Prophets

There were 3 "major" prophets active during the Babylonian exile: Jeremiah who prophesied from Jerusalem, and Daniel and Ezekiel, both of whom prophesied from Babylon (the latter of whom we hear from tomorrow). There was at least one other "minor" prophet active during this time, but his book (Obadiah) is very brief. At least, though, Obadiah is a book of true prophecy, in contrast to the prophets Jeremiah writes about in today's OT reading.

This had been a problem for a long time, based on the references going back to the Assyrian Exile of the Northern Kingdom (Jeremiah 23:13), but it had now become time to bring down punishment on these false prophets. The best conclusion one can draw from the section in chapter 23 is that these false prophets will be suffering a fate even worse than that of neighboring nations or of Babylon.

A very interesting contrast between the prophecy of a true prophet (Jeremiah, 27:1-22) and a false prophet (Hananiah, 28:1-17) is then made in adjacent chapters of the second part of today's reading. In Jeremiah's prophecy (chronologically marked at the beginning of the reign of Zedekiah, as is Hananiah's) in chapter 27, the Lord tells the remaining people in Jerusalem to not resist deportation, and to accept the nation's punishment and go willingly to Babylon when called upon to do so. Jeremiah further admonishes the king and the priests to not listen to the false prophets who were saying that the spoils of the Temple would very soon be brought back to Jerusalem; i.e. the Exile would soon be over, far earlier than Jeremiah had prophesied. A prophet named Hananiah makes that exact false prophecy (28:1-4), and then Jeremiah rebutted it (28:5-16) publically. In one of Jeremiah's most "in your face" prophecies, he declares to Hananiah that the latter was *not* sent by the Lord and that his words are lies. It is then recorded that Hananiah died later that same year (28:17).

October 3, NT
Acts 28:1-16
The Road to Rome, Part Eight: Paul Arrives in Rome

As we open the final chapter of the only New Testament book devoted exclusively to history (as opposed to doctrine, prophecy, or other theological matters), we find Paul and the rest of the shipwrecked crew landed safely at Malta, an island in the central Mediterranean Sea, south of Rome. The Malta natives welcomed them openly, but became suspicious of Paul when a snake wrapped itself around Paul's hand (Acts 28:3). The superstitious people then did a complete turnaround when Paul shook off the snake into a fire he was building, and instead believed him to be a god (28:4-6).

The leading man of the island (essentially "mayor"), a man named Publius, took in Paul and the ship's crew and treated them warmly. Publius' father was ill at that time, and Paul prayed for the man and laid hands on him, healing him from his sicknesses (28:7-10). Many then came to Paul to be healed in the same manner.

After 3 months, they set sail again for Rome in a ship with the image of the twin brothers Castor and Pollux, the sons of Zeus known in Latin as Gemini (28:11) as its figurehead. This voyage went much more smoothly and quickly than the earlier part of the journey, and they arrived at Puteoli, where they were met and were taken in by believers who had received Paul's letter, and thus had arrived in Rome (28:12-15)

Paul was allowed to have his own residence in Rome, along with his Roman guard, as opposed to being in a prison (28:16).

October 4, OT
Ezekiel 1:1-3:15
Introduction to Ezekiel

Many Bible passages have been turned into song lyrics, mostly from the New Testament or the Psalms. The major prophets don't fare quite as well in that regard, but one of them, introduced today, has not one but *two* popular or folk songs adapted from its verses. (The second song won't be discussed until we read Ezekiel 37 on October 28). That prophet is Ezekiel, who introduces himself in the third person in the opening verses, and sets the date and location of the book that bears his name (Ezekiel 1:1-3). The "fifth year of Jehoiachin's exile" could easily be written as the fifth year of Zedekiah, thus identifying Ezekiel as one of the exiles from the first deportation, along with Daniel.

Unlike all 3 of the other "major" prophets, Ezekiel's prophecies are in mostly chronological order as they appear in the Bible. The book can be divided up into 3 parts, the first part concerning itself with visions of the destruction of Jerusalem that was soon to come, in chapters 1-24, which we will read without interruption until October 12. The second part features prophecies against other nations in much the same manner as Jeremiah, in chapters 25-32. This section gets interrupted and its sequence is changed slightly, around the time of reading the destruction of Jerusalem itself. The final section, chapters 33-48, contain visions of the restoration of Israel, not just after the Exile, but also during the End Times. Although not quoted or even referenced in most of the New Testament, it is referenced extensively (second only to Daniel) in the Book of Revelation. Even fellow exile prophet Daniel and post-Exilic prophet Zechariah were influenced by the writings of Ezekiel in predicting far-future glory for Israel.

The vision he describes in the first chapter is the elaborate, bizarre, and even frightening vision of "four living creatures" resembling a man, a lion, an ox, and an eagle, riding a strange set of "wheels within wheels" (1:4-21), which became the inspiration for the folk song "Ezekiel Saw the Wheel." The song has been recorded by numerous artists, and includes a Gospel spin in its lyrics, but it's all based on this original vision by the prophet. The vision continues, describing a throne and a figure with the "appearance of a man" (1:22-27). Ezekiel identifies the man as the Lord (1:28), and the Lord speaks to the prophet, commissioning him (2:1-7). Throughout this reading and the entire book, Ezekiel is addressed repeatedly as "son of man" by the Lord. And in some sections, starting in chapters 2-3, he is given some truly bizarre instructions. For example, Ezekiel is handed a scroll by the Lord (2:8-3:3) and told to *eat* it. Of course, this can be taken as a metaphor for symbolically receiving the Word from God and then passing it along to the people in Exile.

October 4, NT
Acts 28:17-31
Conclusion of the Acts of the Apostles

Two of the longest books in the New Testament were written as a letter by a physician named Luke, who accompanied Paul on his Missionary Journeys and to Rome. Today, we read the last recorded words by this historian, which we call the Acts of the Apostles, featuring Paul under house arrest (in his own rented place) in Rome.
After this, there is no further recorded books of history in the New Testament. What follows the Acts consists of the several remaining Epistles of Paul and some others, and the Revelation to John that concludes the Bible with prophecy. There are a few tidbits of history along the way, but for the most part, today's NT reading concludes the history as found in the New Testament.

After landing near Rome and being received by some believers, Paul settles into a rented house (though still in chains) and calls some of the local Jewish leaders (Acts 28:17) and explains to them how and why he came to Rome (28:18-20). The leaders had not heard anything bad about Paul, and were therefore interested in hearing his viewpoint (28:21-22). So at another meeting, Paul goes into great detail regarding the Gospel, persuading them about Jesus, using what we would call Old Testament Scriptures (28:23-24). At one point, he quotes Isaiah 6:9-10 (Acts 28:25-27) to explain that he is compelled to bring the Gospel message to the Gentiles (28:28). He continued to preach from his home for at least 2 years after this (28:29-31).

The Acts of the Apostles ends at this point, somewhat abruptly. It is not known exactly when exactly he was transferred to an actual prison.
His arrival in Rome was somewhere around A.D. 60, and he was martyred (or so it is believed) some time in either 67 or 68 (just prior to Peter's martyrdom), so these words from Luke probably happened around A.D. 62, leaving an estimated 5 years of unrecorded history regarding Paul. Luke himself would be mentioned again multiple times in the letters written by Paul from Rome, including Paul's last letter (2 Timothy) which was written within weeks or perhaps days of his death. Tradition says that Luke died in Boeotia in Greece at the age of 84. If Luke was, indeed, a contemporary of Mary, the mother of Jesus, that would have meant that Luke died just a short time after Paul did. During those next few years, Paul would write 7 letters, starting with Ephesians, tomorrow.

October 5, OT
Ezekiel 3:16-4:17
The Watchman of Israel

For the next week, the readings each day from both the Old and New Testaments come exclusively from two of the six books of the Bible that begin with the letter "E:" Ezekiel (which was started yesterday) in the Old Testament, and Ephesians in the New Testament (see below).

The very first verse of today's OT reading gives the duration of the vision that Ezekiel experienced in yesterday's introduction (Ezekiel 3:16) and then goes on to God's next Word to "son of man," as Ezekiel is addressed through the book that bears his name. This next word is his appointment as "the Watchman of Israel," commanded to pass along warnings from God (3:17) in much the same way as Jeremiah was doing in Jerusalem. Ezekiel's task as "watchman" puts the liability on the prophet for making sure the Israelites (presumably the exiles that Ezekiel lived amongst) get properly warned (3:18-21). Ezekiel did as commanded (3:22-27) and then awaited his next set of instructions.

Those instructions consisted of a symbolic step-by-step walkthrough of the soon-to-come siege of Jerusalem, where the remaining people not already deported to Babylon would join Ezekiel and the rest of the exiles. The steps included the drawing of the city of Jerusalem on a block of clay and the "laying siege to it" (4:2) like one would do in mapping out a battle. Then, there is a symbolic laying down on his left side for "390 days" (4:4-5), representing the 390 year span from Jeroboam's rebellion that resulted in the divided kingdom until the final dethroning of Judah's last king, Zedekiah. The additional 40 day span on the right side (4:6-8) represents the last 40 years of Judah's existence, which spans from the beginning of Josiah's (Judah's last "good" king) reign to Zedekiah's deportation. This is despite Josiah's efforts at reform which fell flat with the people of Israel.

The remainder of this prophecy has the Lord giving Ezekiel a most curious bread recipe. It's curious not because of the ingredients (4:9-12a) but because of a cooking instruction that has Ezekiel using human dung for fuel (4:12b). This would defile the food, making it unclean, and therefore unfit for consumption by the Jewish people. But God knows this: it is another symbolic reference to the coming siege of Jerusalem, where the people will be forced to eat unclean food lest they starve to death (which many, in fact, did). God explains this to Ezekiel after the latter protests this instruction (4:13-14), and thus God backs off from the instruction to allow the bread to be cooked over cow dung instead (4:15) and then further explains the prophecy to Ezekiel (4:16-17).

October 5, NT
Ephesians 1:1-14
Greetings From Rome

The first of 7 letters Paul wrote from Rome was addressed to "the saints at Ephesus." Ephesus was his first stop on his Third Missionary Journey, and it was from there that he wrote the first Letter to the Corinthians. Now, Paul was in Rome, under house arrest, writing his letter back to the Ephesians. The opening verses make no mention of the chains he was in (that would come later), nor does it mention that Luke was still alive. It is believed that the Epistles to the Ephesians, Colossians (begins on October 12), and Philemon (read on October 16) were all written at about the same time, and so we will read them back to back as indicated.

There is a fair amount of debate as to whether this letter was actually written by Paul, or if instead by a student of Paul's some time in the 70s or even 80s A.D. This chronology will stick with the "traditional" belief that it was, indeed, Paul who wrote this, despite some of the anomalies that will be brought up. One of those it the matter of writing style: although most of the letter sounds exactly like Paul, as reflected in other Epistles, there are parts of the letter, including this opening section, that don't match Paul's style elsewhere. In most original Greek copies of this letter, Ephesians 1:3-14 is a single run-on sentence. Now, of course, English translations of the Bible tend to add punctuation marks to separate the verses into readable sentences, 3 in this case; and there is nothing unusual about long, run-on sentences in the Bible, Old Testament or New. The main note here is that Paul's previous letters, notably his then-most-recent letter (Romans), do very little of this. However, the most likely explanation (in this chronology, anyway) is that Paul had a scribe available to him, and the scribe wrote down the dictated text a slightly different way than what Paul would have wrote it himself. (Also see reading for October 13 in Colossians.)

This first reading from Ephesians introduces Paul and sets up the main overarching theme of the entire letter: that the Church (note the capital letter) is the Body of Christ, and should be One, unified body.

October 6, OT
Ezekiel 5:1-7:27
God's Wrath to be Unleashed on Jerusalem

The three chapters that make up today's OT reading consist of two chapters of prose (Ezekiel 5-6) followed by one of poetry (Ezekiel 7), all with the same overall theme: the coming destruction of Jerusalem. Speaking in the future tense throughout, and thus pegging this prophecy at close to the same time as the earlier chapters of Ezekiel (and thus, still near the half-way point of Zedekiah's reign as king), God lays out a plan for the punishment of Israel that shows His greatest display of anger since the destruction of Sodom and Gomorrah, all the way back in the time of Abraham. As mentioned yesterday, this is even despite King Josiah's attempts at reform. That is, Zedekiah's father, Judah's last good king, may have been a good king, but the people were largely unmoved, and thus the reason for God's most severe judgment on His people.

Chapter 5 largely deals with Jerusalem, while chapter 6 deals mainly with the surrounding countryside in Judah. The word is the same, though: God is "against" Israel, and will severely discipline the people, up to and including the deaths of about one third of the population. Chapter 7 reads like a Psalm, but is actually God's judgment on His people, in a poetic style.

October 6, NT
Ephesians 1:15-2:10
Grace Through Faith, Not By Works

Paul's Letter to the Ephesians has some of the most-quoted, most-frequently remembered verses in the entire New Testament, outside of the four Gospels. Some verses are actually quite controversial, too, and will be explored in the coming days. One verse, in particular, carries controversy with it only to the extent that Catholics and Protestants/Evangelicals have a strong disagreement on its meaning. That verse is near the end of today's NT reading.

Paul continues his greeting to the church in Ephesus with much thanksgiving and praise to God (Ephesians 1:15-23), emphasising the role Jesus himself had in creating the Church. From this point forward in this reading plan, the word Church will be capitalized when referring to the entire body of Christ (as Paul does in verse 23) as opposed to not capitalized ("church") when referring to a specific congregation, such as the Ephesians.

In chapter 2, Paul starts a section that is commonly labeled "Alive in Christ." This is a direct contrast to being "dead in our transgressions" or "dead in our sins" (depending on translation), following in the footsteps of the "prince of the power of the air," an oblique reference to Satan, the devil (2:1). In many ways, the section is a repeat of statements Paul has made in each of his letters to some degree: that our salvation is a gift from God that we obtain by faith. He actually says it twice in this passage (2:4, 2:8), but it is in the second instance, in particular, that Paul makes the statement that is most quoted and most controversial: that we are saved by grace through faith, "not of yourselves," it is the "gift of God", not a result of works, so that "no one can boast" (2:8). Besides being an indictment of works-based theologies (Roman Catholicism being the most obvious example), it is another of several examples in Paul's writings that solidify the doctrine of "once saved, always saved". Without going into more detail on this (it's discussed in several places in this reading plan, including the Gospels and the Epistle of James), the main point is that works aren't what brings the salvation; rather, our salvation brings the good works, as this is what we were created for (2:9-10).

October 7, OT
Ezekiel 8:1-9:11
The Lord Sees All

...and in His own way presents what He sees to His prophets. Such is the case in this continuation of God's presentation to Ezekiel of His wrath to be poured out on Jerusalem for her iniquities. Not since the book of Judges has the Bible readings contained so much graphic, violent imagery. Ezekiel's vision here is not unlike many other prophets, in which he felt as though he was plucked up off the earth and brought to a higher vantage point (or even, heaven) to be shown something hidden from the eyes of man but that is visible to God

(Ezekiel 8:1-4). Starting here, God starts directing the "son of man" (Ezekiel) to turn to the North and then look inside various places to see the abominations being committed by the Priests and other religious officials, including inside the soon-to-be-destroyed Temple (8:5-18), as if further justification for His wrath was needed.

The next part of this same vision was in regards to an angel (9:3, referred to as a "man in linen") charged with marking the foreheads of those (few) who wept over these abominations (9:4) but to strike those who do not (9:5-7) and expel them from the Temple. Ezekiel's response to this vision was in fear that God wouldn't leave any remnant after all this promised wrath (9:8), but God simply explains that the sins of Israel are "very very great" (9:9-10). The vision ends with the angel's report that he had done as he was commanded (9:11).

October 7, NT
Ephesians 2:11-3:21
The Two Became One

No, we're not talking about a wedding here. In fact, it is highly unlikely that this passage from Ephesians has ever been used in a wedding ceremony, despite the constant emphasis on how two groups of people have become one in Christ. Those two groups are identified first as the "uncircumcision" and the "circumcision" (Ephesians 2:11), of which Paul was one of the latter. The former are known as Gentiles while the latter are known as Jews. Paul points out the Gentiles' separation from Christ (2:12), but also brings up how the blood of Christ has brought them near (2:13). Paul speaks of barriers and dividing walls, and how all this is now *gone*, as the Gentiles have become co-heirs with God's chosen people, in one of the most upbeat and positive passages from any of Paul's Epistles.

It is notable that this letter, and this passage in particular, contains none of the scolding, correction, warning, or "putting out of fires" found in Paul's other letters to Gentile churches, notably Galatians. The positive tone in Ephesians belies the circumstances under which it was written, as Paul mentions for the first time here that he is a prisoner (3:1, 3:13).

October 8, OT
Ezekiel 10:1-13:23
God Leaves Jerusalem

More than 400 years before Ezekiel's prophecies, the "glory of the Lord" entered the newly-built Temple while Solomon was king. Through all of the ups and downs of the divided kingdom, that glory never left. That is, until this point in time during the reign of Zedekiah, Judah's last king, with the Exile in progress, and many already deported (including the prophets Daniel and Ezekiel). Today's 4-chapter OT reading (just under 100 total verses) describes a vision given to Ezekiel of God's glory leaving the Temple for the first time since He entered it.

The vision itself starts with a return of the "man in linen," (Ezekiel 10:2) that we encountered yesterday, and the "living creatures" riding the "wheels within wheels" that we first encountered at the beginning of Ezekiel's first chapter (10:9-17, 10:20-22). In the vision, they appear to escort the glory of the Lord out of the Temple and away (10:18-19). No doubt, this was done to make way for the destruction of that very Temple, one of the several things that was soon to happen when Nebuchadnezzar would lay siege to Jerusalem and subsequently destroy the Temple.

In the next chapter, God uses further extensions of that vision to speak judgment against false prophets (11:1-13), and reassure Ezekiel and his fellow exiles of the future restoration of Israel (11:14-25), which Ezekiel then passed along. Ezekiel is then given another set of instructions meant to symbolically represent an event to come. Previously, it was the starvation that would occur in the siege of Jerusalem; this time, the prophet was commanded to prepare for deportation as though he was still in Jerusalem (12:1-9), to symbolically represent a "prince in Jerusalem" (12:10-12) who will attempt an escape, only to be caught and delivered to Babylon (12:13-16). This would be literally fulfilled in just a few years by Zedekiah's dethronement. The remainder of the reading (12:17-13:23) repeats the judgment against false prophets.

October 8, NT
Ephesians 4:1-24
The Apostles' Creed

In many liturgical churches, worship services include a spoken creed or statement of belief that summarizes the faith. In the Orthodox churches and Roman Catholicism, the preferred form of this is the Nicene Creed, while mainstream Protestants (Lutherans in particular) use a shorter form known as the Apostle's Creed. There is some debate as to whether the origins of the Apostle's Creed predate the Nicene Creed or not, as we know the date of the latter but not the former. The Nicene form can be thought of as an expanded version of the Apostles' form, as all but one statement of the Apostles' Creed appears in the Nicene. That one statement that is unique to the Apostles' Creed is actually found in today's NT reading from Ephesians.

The statement has to do with what happened to Jesus after He died but before He rose again. Both creeds state that Jesus was "crucified, died, and was buried". But only the Apostles' Creed says that He "descended to the dead" (or "descended to hell" in the old form translated from Latin) before continuing with the statement that "on the third day, He rose from the dead" in both creeds. This reference to Christ "descending to the dead" is actually a very important doctrinal statement, as there were (and still are) those who believe that Jesus didn't really die, but merely entered a kind of fugue state or coma that He then rose from. Paul makes this clear in a blink-and-you'll-miss-it passage in Ephesians 4:9-10.

One other statement found in both creeds is the belief in the "holy catholic church". The word "catholic" in this usage is not capitalized, because it doesn't refer specifically and only to the Roman Catholic Church. Rather, it is the use of "catholic" that comes from the line in Latin: "sanctam Ecclesiam catholicam" which actually translates as the *One* holy Church. In this passage from Ephesians, Paul uses the word "one" in connection with the Church 8 times, more than in any other place in his letters, and continues from yesterday's reading in speaking to the Gentile audience who have become one with the Jews, united in Christ.

October 9, OT
Ezekiel 14:1-16:63
Israel, God's Faithless Bride

There are numerous places in the Bible where Israel or the Church is likened to an adulteress, faithless bride, or some similar metaphor. Most commonly, it is used as a condemnation of idolatry on the part of Israel. After all, the Israelites were the original "God's Chosen People," and so the comparison was both easy to understand and quite apt. In today's OT reading, after Ezekiel is instructed in how to respond to some idolatrous elders (Ezekiel 14:1-11) and is then told that God's mind is made up in the matter of Jerusalem's coming destruction (14:12-15:8), the Lord launches into some of the most sexually explicit language in the entire Bible to make a point about *why* Jerusalem is to be destroyed.

At 63 verses, Ezekiel 16 is by far the prophet's longest chapter. Being sexually explicit is largely a matter of opinion, but the tone and repeated references to Israel's "whoring" or "harlotry" (22 times starting with 16:15) make this a much harsher read than the Song of Solomon, for instance, which is actually a love song with lots of celebratory language. It's tame by today's standards, but would have been shocking to the point of nearly being obscene to readers of the 6th Century B.C. But it's all there to make a point about God's harsh but necessary disciplinary action. Although the city (Jerusalem) and the Temple that was there was going to be destroyed, and its people exiled, God makes it clear, though, that this is not the end of the nation. God promises that His covenant with His people is still in effect, and Israel would be punished but not destroyed (16:60-63).

October 9, NT
Ephesians 4:25-5:14
The Moral Life, Part One

Starting near the end of chapter 4, Paul turns from theology and doctrine to a section comprising almost 2 chapters of practical advice for the new believers, enough to divide up into two days' readings. The section is nearly as densely packed as his Epistle to the Romans. There is so many practical maxims here that a proper commentary would end up longer than the reading itself. Part Two (tomorrow) gets a longer commentary because of a controversial passage; Part One has its highlights, too, including: the best explanation in the Bible as to why you shouldn't use profanity (Ephesians 4:29, 5:4), not just the prohibition found in the Ten Commandments, a gorgeous 2-verse proverb telling us to put away anger and malice in exchange for kindness and forgiveness (4:31-32), and a treatise on exposing evil rather than participating in it (5:11-14) that culminates in the words "Awake, Sleeper: Arise from the Dead." This phrase, in German, is "Wachet Auf," and is the basis for a cantata of that name composed by J.S. Bach.

October 10, OT
Ezekiel 17:1-20:29
The Fate of a Rebellious King

A lot of the events that occurred in Jerusalem during the reign (if you can call it that) of its last king, Zedekiah, were first revealed to prophets like Ezekiel who were living in Exile and, most likely, never even met the king. This, though, would be why passages like two days ago (October 8, Ezekiel 12:12 in particular) and today's OT reading (17:1-24 in particular) never mention Zedekiah by name but were literally fulfilled in a reading yet to come (October 16). Using the metaphor of two eagles and a vine, God explains the two parts of the Exile to Ezekiel, and even gives a graphic picture of the future fate of that last king (17:1-24). Just as in the days immediately before the fall of Samaria, Judah and its king were in a downward spiral.

In chapter 18, God renounces a proverb regarding the shared guilt between a father and a son, using it to clarify His position against those who sin, thus making individual responsibility the new law of the land (18:1-32), all in an effort to get individual Israelites to repent and turn back to the Lord. Both chapters 18 and 19 are written in a poetic style that Ezekiel himself identifies at the end of chapter 19 as a Lament. This form, which may have actually been sung like a funeral dirge at some point, metaphorically mourns the nation of Israel, and in particular, its southern kingdom of Judah. Repeated references to lions makes it clear that this is God mourning the loss of the people of Judah, as they carried the nickname of the "Lion of God."

The next chapter marks the further progress of Ezekiel's prophecies in the timeline, now noting that we have reached the "seventh year, fifth month, and tenth day" (20:1) which would mean less than 2 years before Zedekiah's last act of rebellion would be the last straw for Nebuchadnezzar, and the latter would then lay siege of Jerusalem, nearly starving out its people, and finally destroying it. Ezekiel passes along all these predictions to some elders who were in Exile with him, directly chastising them for following in the same idolatrous ways that would be the downfall of their fellow Israelites (20:2-29).

October 10, NT
Ephesians 5:15-6:9
The Moral Life, Part Two

"Much more than a suggestion, yet not quite a command."

Sections like this, where a long list of Proverbs-like instructions are given, need to be viewed through the lens of the "plain interpretation" of the Bible. Different Christian denominations handle passages like this differently based on how literally it views the Bible in general (and, quite frankly, how much or how little "cherry picking" goes on in each church). The only type of interpretation this chronology assumes to be correct is the so-called "*plain* interpretation," where everything is taken in the Bible at its face value, carefully noting whether the passage is to be taken literally (as in historical passages), or as allegory (as in most prophecy) or doctrine; and when it's doctrine, whether the message from the Lord, through the prophet or evangelist, is intended as commandment, instruction, or example-setting. Three verses in today's NT reading are examples of doctrinal instruction, and they are: Ephesians 5:22, 6:1, and 6:5.

In telling wives to "submit to [their] husbands" in Ephesians 5:22, the evangelist Paul gets widely criticized for his *alleged* misogyny. Paul, after all, was never married, so many an atheist has asked "what business did he have in telling women that they must submit to men?" Were it not for the women's movement of the 1960s and 1970s, such verses would have likely been buried beneath the other verses in this second part of The Moral Life, the title given in this chronology to Ephesians 4:25-6:9, and gone unnoticed by all except those who study the Bible deeply, because most cultural norms aligned with this passage. But today, it's one of the most controversial verses in all of Scripture, and all because of a fundamental **MIS**understanding and **MIS**interpretation of this passage. The reason for this stems from the fact that far too many people fail to read the preceding verse (Ephesians 5:21) which exhorts us to submit *to one another* in the fear of God. The key words there are "to one another," and Paul then goes into a *pair* of explanations of this "submission". Not just as it applies to wives (5:22-24), but to husbands as well (5:25-31) including a quote from Genesis about how the two people in a marriage become "one flesh". Perhaps the best way to clear this up is to use a translation such as the NASB that uses the words "subject to one another" and "subject to your husband" instead of using the word "submission". And then, of course, is the matter of 5:32-33 where Paul explains that he is speaking of "Christ and the Church." Thus, Paul is making a doctrinal point about how Christ relates to His people, and is using the example of family life to tell us that if we want to truly emulate Christ, this is the way we need to run our families.

It does NOT mean that women can't work outside of the home. It does NOT mean that wives need to serve their husbands like some kind of slave, answering to their every whim. It does NOT mean that women are to be looked at or treated as second-class citizens in any way whatsoever. It does NOT mean that husbands have any role or right to try enforce this like a *law*, because it isn't a commandment - it is instruction in how to run a home in the manner that Christ runs His Church. It means that BOTH parties in the marriage put the needs of the other ahead of themselves. And it actually has more to do with orderly worship and the organization of the individual congregations than it does the nuclear family of father, mother, and their children.

Speaking of children, this controversy regarding the misinterpretation of the second half of The Moral Life extends into chapter 6 where Paul continues with his instruction for children to obey their parents (6:1). This time, though, Paul links this to an actual command (6:2) but also points out that this is the only of the Ten Commandments to come with "a promise" that it "may be well with you" (6:3), and even points out how this instruction is a two-way proposition, just like the one about husbands and wives (6:4).

The last of the three controversial verses concerns "slaves" (or "servants" in some translations) and their masters (6:5-8). There are a few in the civil rights community who view this, along with other passages that mention slavery, as an *endorsement* of slavery. This is complete nonsense. God knew then as He knows now that slavery exists in one form or another everywhere in the world. The fact that it was legal then in Ephesus (and throughout the Roman Empire) and in the United States, officially, until 1865, has nothing to do with the notion that someone who is a slave should be subject to their master. Paul merely used a cultural norm of his time (and made it another two-way relationship, 6:9) to explain The Moral Life to the Church. And despite being officially banned in many places like the United States, slavery does still exist in many parts of the world, and is still practiced in underground forms (like the sex trade) in the U.S. and elsewhere. The Bible's mention of this practice doesn't mean that slavery is something that God agrees with or endorses; it just means that God is aware that it exists.

The pastor I quote at the beginning of today's NT commentary was also the one to give a label ("plain interpretation") to what actually has always been my personal way of interpreting the Bible, and it is reflected throughout this chronological reading plan. That pastor was theologically liberal (and politically liberal as well), as is his denomination (Lutheran / ELCA), but it's a point that can and should be made to all believers in all Christian denominations, and there's no better place to bring it up than right here.

October 11, OT
Ezekiel 20:30-22:31
Then They'll Know That I Am God

Several times in Ezekiel (including several passages already read), God tells Ezekiel to pass along His Word, and ends the quote by telling the prophet, "...then they'll know that I am God." As the prophecies of Jerusalem's destruction hurtle towards fulfillment, these quotes from God become more frequent. In the first part of today's OT reading, God continues his dictation to Ezekiel about what to tell the elders of Israel (Ezekiel 20:30-44). This reading's title is quoted three times in that passage alone, including an ending section where God refers to the restoration of and return to Israel, as yet another example of how they will know that He is God.

After closing chapter 20 with a prophecy against a neighbor to the south, Negev (20:45-49), the next prophecy is sometimes titled "The Drawn Sword," referring to the way in which God has set Himself against Israel with His sword drawn, and will not put it back in its sheath (21:1-32) until the job of destroying the "dross of Israel" (22:17) is complete (22:1-31).

October 11, NT
Ephesians 6:10-24
The Full Armor of God; Conclusion of Ephesians

Spiritual warfare is a reality. We are constantly either at war with the forces of darkness or caught in the crossfire in the battle between good and evil. With that in mind, Paul gives the Ephesians (and therefore, us) a big final word of encouragement by telling us, *twice*, to put on the "full armor of God" (Ephesians 6:11, 6:13), one of Paul's most quoted verses, though with far less controversy than in yesterday's reading. Paul explains what this armor is by dividing it up into its component parts, each another metaphor for weapons and armor: the clothing of truth and the breastplate of righteousness (6:14), shoes made from the preparation of the Gospel of Peace (6:15), the shield of faith (6:16), the helmet of salvation (6:17a), and the sword of the Spirit (6:17b), aka the Word of God. All this to go against the "rulers and powers" (6:12) of spiritual darkness, not the flesh and blood.

Then, like every other Epistle he wrote, Paul closes in prayer (6:18-20) and greeting (6:21-24). Along the way, he makes another mention that he is an "Ambassador in chains," a reference to his confinement to a rented house in Rome. It was certainly better provisions than being in prison, but he was not a free man, and this by his own choice. It is hard to say if he knew the end was truly coming soon or not (I suspect "not" because of something he says in the next letter), but he used his time there wisely, and didn't take a break before writing his next letter, starting in tomorrow's reading.

October 12, OT
Ezekiel 23:1-49; Jeremiah 21:1-14; Ezekiel 24:1-27
The Siege of Jerusalem Begins; Death of Ezekiel's Wife

The actual event described in the title of today's OT reading won't be read from 2 Kings until October 16, but technically, it begins here in Ezekiel 24, the third section of the reading, where the prophet put another chronological marker in the book, per instruction from God.

But first, we get another example of a sexual metaphor to describe Israel and Judah, much like we read back on October 9 in Ezekiel chapter 16. The earlier reading was mainly about just Jerusalem; this time, God uses very similarly explicit language to describe the entire divided kingdom, giving the northern kingdom of Samaria the name "Oholah" and the southern kingdom of Judah the name "Oholibah" (Ezekiel 23:4). Ezekiel 23's 49 verses are arguably on the same level as Ezekiel 16's 63 verses as far as sexually explicit language, and in fact go into a greater degree of depth about the specifics of Israel's harlotry.

We then hear from Jeremiah for the first time in over a week, as God uses the prophet to respond to Zedekiah's request for mercy. Basically, the response to Zedekiah's request is "it's too late, the destruction of Jerusalem is inevitable and imminent." Zedekiah's rebellion against Nebuchadnezzar was a case of too little, too late before it even began, as God already had His mind made up.

After that, we go back to Ezekiel, where the opening verses have God telling Ezekiel to "mark the date" because it was the day that Nebuchadnezzar laid siege to Jerusalem (Ezekiel 24:2). God gives Ezekiel a parable about how Israel will not be made clean until His wrath is completely spent (24;3-13). In short, there will be no mercy until the punishment is truly complete (24:14). Then, just to drive home the point even further, God warned Ezekiel of the pending death of his wife and instructed the prophet not to mourn or weep over the loss (24:15-18). This did come to pass, and Ezekiel told the fellow Exiles about it (24:19-27), all in the name of a prophecy about the destruction of Jerusalem which will make them all "know that I am God," another reference like those read yesterday.

October 12, NT
Colossians 1:1-23
The Image of The Invisible God

Paul's letter to the Romans was the first of his Epistles to be written to a place that he had not visited. His letter to the Colossians would be his second. It is not that we know for certain that he never visited there; it is simply that there is no evidence, from the Acts of the Apostles or elsewhere, that he had ever gone any closer to Colossae than Laodicea, a place he *did* visit during his Second Missionary Journey, between the writing of his letters to the Galatians and the Thessalonians. Colossians is a shorter letter than Ephesians (95 vs. 155 verses), yet more than 80% of this letter (78 verses) consists of direct or near-direct repeats from his letter to the Ephesians. Thus,

Paul either wrote the letters concurrently or, as this chronology believes, back to back.

Paul's opening greeting includes Timothy, who we last heard about during that same Second Missionary Journey in the Acts of the Apostles (Colossians 1:1), referring to the two of them together, praying together and having heard about their (the Colossians') faith (1:3-4). It is obvious from the rest of the greeting that the news from Colossae is really good, and that a vibrant church has been established there.

Putting credit where credit is due, the praises continue for the One who "rescued us from the domain of darkness" (1:13), who is the "image of the invisible God" (1:15). Of course, Paul is speaking here of Jesus Christ, the Son of God who is, himself, God. Other attributes praised here include being the "firstborn of all creation" (1:15) and "by Him all things were created" (1:16), thus putting Jesus at the Creation! Few statements outside of the Gospels more definitely describe Jesus' divinity than right here.

October 13, OT
Ezekiel 25:1-17; Jeremiah 31:1-40
Post-Exilic judgment, Post-Exilic Restoration

After Ezekiel's last specific prophecies against Judah's last king, but before we read of the actual events occurring, the prophet received instructions from God to prophesy against 4 other nations who were neighbors of Babylon or Judah or somewhere else nearby. Those nations were the Ammonites (Ezekiel 25:1-7), Moabites (8-11), Edomites (12-14), and the Philistines (15-17). In each case, God is basically telling each nation that they're going to get theirs, too, so don't be gloating over the fall of Judah.

Besides being a bad thing (gloating) anyway, the reason for God's words to these nations can be summed up in Jeremiah's words in chapter 31 of that book. Jeremiah 31 is another of several chapters in which the emphasis is on the future restoration of Israel, not its pending destruction. Obviously, the destruction has to come first, as punishment for its many sins, but Jeremiah writes (from a dream, Jeremiah 31:26) in detail that this Exile is a temporary thing, and that the people will be returning from captivity. Not only is that promised, but a New Covenant will be made with Israel and Judah (31:31-34). No timeline is given for this, which means it could refer to the immediate aftermath of the Exile, the time of Christ, or the rebirth of the modern nation of Israel. It could, technically, mean all three, though the first scenario seems to fit best, given the last verse (31:38) about rebuilding the city (of Jerusalem).

October 13, NT
Colossians 1:24-2:19
Which Came First?

It was mentioned yesterday that 78 verses from Paul's previous letter (to the Ephesians, October 5-11) can be found here in Colossians as well, either as a direct quote, a paraphrase, or as a reference to the same topic or point (with different wording). Back when we began reading Ephesians (October 5), it was mentioned that there is a "fair amount of debate" as to whether or not Paul actually wrote that letter. Even though this chronology assumes that Paul was, indeed, the author of the Epistle to the Ephesians, the vast majority of study Bibles and documentation available online either declare outright that some "student of Paul's" was the author, or at least put forth both possibilities without favoring either one. Only one study guide that I've seen so far agrees fully with the traditional view that Paul was the author of Ephesians while there is nearly unanimous agreement of the Pauline authorship of Colossians. Considering the amount of overlap, why is there such discrepancy?

One would think that the overlap of verses (*a whopping 34 of today's 35 verses* are among the "quoted" verses from Ephesians) between these two letters would make it less of a debate. But, it actually has the exact opposite effect, because the 78 "common" verses could have easily been written, undisputedly, by Paul in Colossians *first*, and later copied by a "student of Paul's" in the 70s or 80s A.D., in the letter to the Ephesians. So, the question is: which came first? If Ephesians came first (as this guide believes), then Paul was just using the same points when he wrote to Colossae, and today's NT reading reflects almost half of that duplication. If Colossians came first, and Ephesians was written after Paul's death, then the writers somehow got hold of the Epistle to the Colossians and copied a large chunk of it.

The problem with the latter viewpoint is that it makes these unknown writers, in addition to being plagiarists, liars. The same problem cropped up when studying the authorship of the prophecies of Isaiah, with liberal theologians claiming a second or even third Isaiah writing under that name. In that case, just as this, the claim goes back to the more traditional viewpoint that preserves the integrity of the Bible in both the Old and New Testaments.

One last note: the 34 verses in today's reading that appear in some form or another in Ephesians (which would make for a very large chart) come from portions of all 6 chapters of the earlier letter.

October 14, OT
Ezekiel 29:1-16; Ezekiel 30:20-26
judgment Against Egypt

The timeline of these prophecies (actually two parts of a single prophecy) is mentioned at the beginning of each section of today's OT reading (Ezekiel 29:1, 30:20), marking them as just weeks before the actual fall of Jerusalem. This time, the target nation is Egypt, and the Pharaoh is the ruler being judged. In many ways, Ezekiel makes it sound as though Egypt will suffer nearly the exact same fate, and for the same length of time, as their neighbors in Judah: exile and scattering among the nations, followed by restoration 40 years later.

October 14, NT
Colossians 2:20-3:17
Things Above, Not Earthly Things

Christians living in the United States, unlike nearly any other nation that allows the practice of Christianity at all, enjoy a level of freedom regarding their religious practices that is unparalleled. Even among those nations that are officially a "Catholic" nation (like France, for instance) or a "Lutheran" nation (like Norway, for instance) codify their particular denomination's practices into law, such that Christians of other denominations have some restrictions placed upon them. Not so in the USA, where no Christian denomination is listed as official. But denominational differences are things of this earth, not of above. They don't matter to God any more now than did the differences between Jewish believers and Gentiles in the days when Paul wrote this Epistle.

For that reason, God (through Paul) drives home the point that we should keep our hearts and minds on things above (Colossians 2:20, 3:1-2) and not the things of the world (2:22-23, 3:5-6). In Christ, there is no distinction between Gentile or Jew (3:11, and so the human religious rules don't apply.

Two common misconceptions are drawn, however, from today's NT reading. One is the notion that we are not subject to any human laws because we are "in Christ". Those who believe this forget that this same Paul wrote to the Romans about being a good citizen in Romans 13, following the laws of the land and submitting to the proper early authorities. This doesn't contradict today's reading; in Colossians, Paul is speaking of religious mores and customs that don't mean anything in the big picture. The other misconception is called "Replacement Theology" which has been discussed before. It's the notion that the Church has replaced Israel as God's Chosen People, and that all of the promises made to Israel no longer apply to them, but to the Church instead. One of the verses (mis)used to justify this position is Colossians 3:12, where the Colossians, mostly Gentiles, are addressed as God's Chosen People. This, too, is nonsense, as God still will fulfill His promises to Israel, even in the End Times.

October 15, OT
Ezekiel 31:1-18; Jeremiah 32:1-33:26
Final Prophecies Before the Fall

Ezekiel's last prophecy before the Fall of Jerusalem comes within weeks of the event itself. But, the prophecy does not concern Judah or Jerusalem, but rather, a continuation of the prophecy against Egypt that began yesterday, written just 2 months later. In this prophecy, Ezekiel is tasked with passing along a warning to the Pharaoh of Egypt, that his nation and the recently-fallen nation of Assyria had a lot in common, particularly where Babylon was concerned. Assyria's conquest by Babylon was a secondary thing, not Babylon's primary target. Egypt would soon share their fate as a secondary target.

Jeremiah chapter 32 starts with a time marker that appears to be out of chronological sequence; that is, until you realize that Ezekiel wrote his prophecies in exile, near Babylon. From his point of view, the eleventh year and third month since the deportation of Jehoiachin would have actually coincided with what Jeremiah saw as the tenth year of King Zedekiah (Jeremiah 32:1). With no month being specified, it could have been anywhere during that tenth year, up to even the eleventh month, and news of the Fall that was about to come would have taken as many as 4 or 5 months to reach exiles living hundreds of miles away. Additionally, there is no doubt about exactly when this part of Jeremiah occurs, since the first part is history rather than prophecy, describing a city under siege and a king who had had quite enough of Jeremiah's predictions of doom (32:3-5), while the prophet himself was "shut up in the court of the guard" (32:2). Jeremiah's response to the king's complaint was to, essentially, ignore it.

Knowing what was about to happen, there would have been little point in trying to change Zedekiah for the inevitable was going to happen, regardless. So even with the pending destruction of Jerusalem, Jeremiah was then advised to make a land purchase within the land of Benjamin (32:6-15). He did this without questioning God; and since he was in prison (even if it was minimum security) he had his scribe Baruch handle the paperwork. He did, however, take the matter to the Lord in prayer (32:16-25), asking for an explanation. God gave him this explanation (32:26-35) but didn't really tell Jeremiah anything he didn't already know. What God does differently this time is go into great length and detail about the fact that the exiled people would later be re-gathered from all those places and restored to their homes in and around Jerusalem (32:36-44 and again in 33:1-13). Indeed, God makes a joyful prediction of restoration here, and takes it even further by setting up a Covenant: God promises a "righteous branch of David" that will rise up and execute "justice and righteousness on the Earth" (33:15). This can only be interpreted as a Messianic prophecy, not merely a prediction of the Israelites' return to Jerusalem after the Exile.

October 15, NT
Colossians 3:18-4:18
Conclusion of Colossians

The final 24 verses of Colossians begin with the easily recognized verses on family relations, a repeat of what was taught to the Ephesians (October 10, "The Moral Life," part two), but in a somewhat more condensed form (Colossians 3:18-4:1). After a few more verses of practical advice, all but one of which is, again, a repeat from Ephesians, Paul goes into his concluding greetings. Several names in the concluding section stand out: Onesimus (4:9) is mentioned here for the first time, but would feature prominently in Paul's next letter, tomorrow. Epaphras (4:12-13) may have been the one to actually found the church in Colossae, since Paul never got there in person. And of course, Luke (4:14), the "beloved physician," was still with Paul at this point. In the final verse, Paul once again tells them to "remember my imprisonment" (4:18). Paul would not have yet known how much longer he had or when he would be transferred to a real prison, but his "house arrest" still made him a prisoner, and he had not yet been able to take his case to Caesar.

It is believed at this point in the timeline that Mark (known as John-Mark) and Matthew had written their first drafts of the Gospels that bear their names, though Paul was probably not yet aware of the writings, certainly not Mark's, since he doesn't mention it in the parting greeting here (4:10). But knowing Luke who likely spent much time with him, would have been aware of Luke's likely start to his Gospel at this time, a work that wouldn't be completed until some time in the next decade.

October 16, OT
Jeremiah 34:1-22; 2 Kings 25:1-21
Too Little, Too Late; The Fall of Jerusalem, Part One

In the last prophecy by anyone prior to the Fall of Jerusalem, Jeremiah repeats the warning to Zedekiah, the king (Jeremiah 34:1-5), that he would not be killed in battle but would die in exile. He passed along this message while Jerusalem was deep into the siege by the Babylonian army (34:6-7). Zedekiah attempted to get God back on their side by having every slaveowner release a male and a female slave, according to Deuteronomy 15:12. However, the plan backfired when the people releasing the slaves immediately took them back (Jeremiah 34:8-11). Jeremiah then followed up on this by condemning the hypocritical attempt at re-gaining God's favor in the face of what was about to occur (34:12-22). It was too little, too late for the people of Jerusalem.

For the first time in over 2 weeks, we go back to 2 Kings to learn the history of what then happened. We briefly recap the siege (2 Kings 25:1-3), including the severe famine, and then read about the Babylonian army breaking through the walls and bringing the siege to a bloody conclusion (25:4-6). Just as was predicted by the prophets (Jeremiah in particular), Zedekiah was captured and carted off to Babylon, where he first had to endure watching his sons killed in front of him, and then his eyes gouged out (25:7).

The Fall of Jerusalem continued with the burning of the Temple and the destruction of many other important buildings (25:8-12), leaving behind only a few of the poorest of the poor to tend to the vineyards that were spared. What was left of the Temple was pillaged (25:13-17), and the few remaining priests were taken to the city of Riblah in Babylon and executed (25:18-20). The kingdom of Judah was, officially, over.

October 16, NT
Philemon 1-25
To The Slave Owner and The Slave

One of the shortest books in the New Testament (at 25 verses total, vs 20 and 21 verses, respectively, for 1 John and 2 John), Paul's letter to Philemon is Paul's shortest Epistle. Its placement here, immediately after Colossians, becomes quite obvious when you read the final verses, in particular. It's an easy read that can be accomplished in just a few minutes (in fact, in less time than this commentary). It starts with a greeting from Paul and Timothy, just as Colossians did, and ends with the same list of parting greetings except for one name (Philemon 1, 23-25). The one name that appears in Colossians that doesn't appear in the closing of Philemon is Onesimus, but that's because the bulk of this little letter is about him.

We can learn a great deal about what life was like in the early Church from just these brief verses. The letter is Paul's first to be addressed to an individual, but Paul also mentions another woman and another man, all of whom are part of a house church that is conducted in the home of Philemon (1-2). After a prayer of thanksgiving (3-7), Paul gets down to the "business" of his letter. That business is yet another example of how things said by Paul in the Epistles have caused a tremendous amount of controversy today, this time for the same reason as the readings for October 10 in Ephesians and yesterday in Colossians. The issue is that of slavery.

It is understandable that slavery, wherever it is depicted, is a sensitive issue, but none of the controversy about it changes the fact that slavery is an historical fact. Furthermore, the fact that the addressee of this letter was a slave owner should not be construed in any way as a Biblical endorsement of slavery. For one thing, the practice of slavery at that time was extremely different than what it was in America in the 19th century and earlier. These employees, such as Onesimus, were indentured, but they were also treated with a great deal more dignity than slaves of any other culture, then or now. There were rules (8-9) to follow, of course, in how slaves were to be treated, traded, and employed. There was even the equivalent of a "free agency" in the trade of slaves, and there is a hint of that in the letter when Paul tells Philemon that Onesimus had previously been "useless to you" (11) but had since become useful to both Paul and Philemon again. Paul urges Philemon to "take him back" (12) without the usual consequences, because Onesimus had become one of Paul's fellow evangelists. In short, Paul wants Philemon to welcome back Onesimus, not as a slave, but as he would Paul, an early evangelist of the new, young Church (13-21).

Paul must have assumed that, despite his own "old age" (9), which could not have been much more than perhaps 60 years of age at the time, he would someday get a chance to meet both of them in person again (22), as he asks Philemon to prepare a place for him. But Paul still mentions more than once in just this short letter that he is "in chains," indicating his imprisonment / house arrest in Rome.

October 17, OT
2 Chronicles 36:15-21; Jeremiah 39:1-18
The Fall of Jerusalem, Part Two

Much less of a second part than it is another account of the same event as brought up yesterday, the Fall of Jerusalem is told in the Second book of Chronicles as well as in Jeremiah 39. The account in 2 Chronicles is considerably more brief than the accounts found in either 2 Kings or in Jeremiah, but contains the same key details that bring the Chronicles very near its close. The event as told in Jeremiah chapter

39 is almost verse by verse identical to the account in 2 Kings 25 until you get to verse 11, where we learn of Jeremiah's fate. In the 2 Kings account, it sounds as if everyone except the poorest of the poor were exiled to Babylon, many of them executed. Here in Jeremiah, we learn that not only did the prophet survive, but his survival was the direct result of Nebuchadnezzar's orders (Jeremiah 39:11-14).

October 17, NT
Philippians 1:1-30
A Letter of Joy From a Prison Cell

The most common belief regarding Paul's time in Rome is that he lived under house arrest for approximately the first two years he was there, and wrote his Epistles to the Ephesians, Colossians, and Philemon during that early period. The timeline of history puts this (as discussed on October 4) 2-year span as most likely A.D. 60-61 or 62. It isn't known how long after that that he remained in house arrest, or if he made it to Spain as some speculate during that time. We do know that he wrote to the church in Philippi from Rome, and that he was "in chains" (Philippians 1:13-14) when he wrote it. What we don't know for certain is if this was after some time away from Rome and then, his return, or if he was still under the same house arrest as before, or if (with either scenario) that he was now in an actual prison instead of the "minimum security" incarceration he was in before. Whatever the case, this letter (just slightly longer than Colossians) is arguably the most joyous and positive Epistle written by Paul.

Paul's entire time in Rome was during the reign of Nero, one of Rome's most notorious Emperors. Rome had previously been, at least, tolerant of the Jews, some of whom lived freely in and around Rome. Christianity was another matter entirely. Under Nero, Christians suffered severe persecution. One historical account says that Nero had Christians dipped in oil and set on fire, used as human lamps. Another says that Nero continued the practice of one his predecessors (Caligula) of feeding Christians to the lions as part of the gladiator games. Either way, Paul's residence in Rome, whether under house arrest or actual prison, was officially an offense punishable by death. Paul's tone in describing his "chains" (1:19-24) is dramatically different than in other letters, which indicates some change in his circumstances and at least some passage of time. Since there is no mention of the great fire of A.D. 64 in Rome, this Epistle is believed to have been written before then, though some time after 61 or 62.

If Paul was indeed executed in either 67 or 68, he would still have had approximately 5 years left after writing this letter. Of course, he wouldn't know how much longer he had, though he believed that death could come at any time (1:27). The rest of the letter, though, reflects a kind of joy that is expressed in very few places elsewhere in the Bible much less in Paul's Epistles.

October 18, OT
Jeremiah 52:1-30; Psalm 74:1-23; Psalm 79:1-13; Psalm 85:1-13
The Fall of Jerusalem, Part Three

For the third straight day, we get an account of the Fall of Jerusalem, this time, just as yesterday, in Jeremiah. At the end of chapter 51, it is noted that the "words of Jeremiah are concluded". This part in chapter 52 sounds very much like someone else's writing that was later added to the book. All of the earliest manuscripts have it, including the intact copy found among the Dead Sea Scrolls. It was, perhaps, written by Ebed-Melek, the Cushite to whom Jeremiah wrote the prophecy recorded as chapter 39, read yesterday (Jeremiah 39:16), which is also an historical account of this event. This version reads very much like the version in 2 Kings, even more so than Jeremiah 39, and then adds some details not found in the 2 Kings, 2 Chronicles, or the earlier Jeremiah version: the statistic of 4600 total Jews exiled to Babylon (52:28-30).

The three Psalms are of unknown authorship. Two of them are subtitled as Psalms of Asaph while the third is "of the sons of Korah". Both Asaph and Korah lived much earlier, but the unknown author wrote under their names, and they're placed here because of the references found in each of them to God's anger directed against Jerusalem and against Judah.

October 18, NT
Philippians 2:1-30
The Nature of Christ

The doctrinal statements that would eventually coalesce into what is now recognized as Church Doctrine got their start first with the Epistles of Paul, and especially, this letter to the Philippians. At this point in approximately A.D. 62 or 63, two (at most) of the four Gospels had been written (Mark's, Matthew's), and Luke's wouldn't appear for probably a decade (though he probably started working on it around this time). The Gospel according to John wouldn't appear for more than 30 years, yet it is there that we get the most definitive statement regarding the dual nature of Christ, being fully God and fully man. Despite Catholic teaching to the contrary, Peter's office as the first Pope didn't actually make for any Church structure or governance to effectively start within the Roman Empire. The Church of that time was founded on the letters that Paul and James wrote to individual churches planted primarily by Paul while on his Missionary Journeys. Philippi was one of those churches, and Paul chose his letter to those Philippians to begin the theology of Christology, the study of the nature of Christ.

The key verses that began Christology start in chapter 2 verse 5, where he suggests having the same attitude as Christ Jesus "who, although He existed in the form of God" (Philippians 2:5-6) did not view equality with God as something to be grasped. Rather, He "humbled Himself, taking the form of a slave, and being made in the likeness of a man" (2:7). He continues from there, but it was a revolutionary idea for the time: Jesus was both God and man, and because of this, God (the Father) gave Jesus the "name above all names" (2:9). With Christ's divine status established, Paul confidently (and correctly) declares that "*every* knee will bow" and "*every* tongue will confess" that Christ Jesus is Lord (2:10-11). "Every" is the key word here, as this establishes a Lordship that does not depend upon whether or not any individual is a believer. This, then, is the heart of Christology.

October 19, OT
Psalm 102:1-28; Psalm 120:1-7; Psalm 137:1-9
After the Fall: Prayers for Mercy and Deliverance

The three Psalms for today are all anonymous. Unlike yesterday's three Psalms, which each had names (albeit historical names) attached to them, there are no such markings for these. But what these three all have in common is a theme of begging the Lord for mercy. Psalm 137, in particular, references Babylon and the Exile, placing its historical context right here. It's the most hopeful-sounding of the three, with its simpler request to tell the exiles how to worship the Lord in a foreign land. The other two have a tone much closer to the readings, starting tomorrow, that are more laments than anything else.

October 19, NT
Philippians 3:1-21
How To Gain Righteousness

How does one obtain righteousness? The question has already been answered in previous Epistles, and Ephesians in particular, where Paul continually emphasizes that we are saved by grace through faith in Jesus Christ. He actually says this same thing, usually with different wording or in different context, in every one of his letters to churches. Here in Philippians, the key verse on this topic comes in this chapter, when he says that he does not have a "righteousness of my own from the law" but instead "that which is through faith in Christ" (Philippians 3:9). Paul sets this up by describing his "no confidence" vote in earthly (or "in the flesh") methods of obtaining righteousness (3:3-6), describing all of his status points in being a Jew and a Pharisee. After making his statement in favor of righteousness by faith, he still says that such righteousness is goal that even HE is striving to obtain (3:10-14). This is one of the few places where Paul cites himself as an example to be followed (3:15-19), culminating in his statement that our citizenship is in heaven (3:20), a very different kind of statement than what he said to the Roman Centurion about his Roman citizenship, just before he left Jerusalem for the last time.

October 20, OT
Lamentations 1:1-2:22
After the Fall: The Lament over Jerusalem

A proper understanding of this 5-chapter book can only be made by first making sure you are up to speed on the recent historical events recorded in 2 Kings, 2 Chronicles, and the prophet Jeremiah. The prophet Jeremiah is believed to be the writer of this lament over the fallen city of Jerusalem. The book is anonymous, and the writer never identifies himself, but the writing style is similar enough to Jeremiah's to attribute it to him. There are some important differences, however, one of which is the fact that God never speaks at any point in this lament, whereas God is quoted as speaking directly to Jeremiah on numerous occasions in the prophet's book. Another important difference is the use of poetry or poetic forms in each chapter that Jeremiah uses only in a few places in his book of prophecy.

But what Lamentations does have in common with Jeremiah, very much so, in fact, is the obvious outpouring of emotion. Not since the recording in 2 Samuel of David's mournful wail over his son Absalom's death will you read such an expression of grief as right here. Jeremiah obviously loved his home city and its people very, very much, and relates a vivid image of its desolation after most of the rest of the people were exiled to Babylon. It is here, more likely than in his book of prophecy, that Jeremiah probably earned the nickname "the weeping prophet."

In Lamentations' first two chapters, we read a pair of "acrostic" poems. This means that each chapter is composed of 22 verses apiece, each verse starting with successive letters of the Hebrew alphabet. It's a shame that English-language translations can't capture the beauty of this structure.

October 20, NT
Philippians 4:1-23
Rejoice in the Lord Always; Conclusion of Philippians

In the office building where I work, there is a memorial plaque containing the names of members of our staff who have died. At the bottom of the memorial, it says: "...the peace of God, which surpasses all understanding, will guard your hearts and your minds in Christ Jesus". This is a quote of Philippians 4:7, found in this concluding section of Paul's Epistle to the young church he had visited years earlier. Taken in isolation like that, it becomes a comforting verse that nicely fits the memorial. Taken in context, it's the conclusion of another of Paul's most exuberant expressions of joy. Earlier in the same paragraph, Paul exhorts us to "rejoice in the Lord always, again I say, rejoice" (Philippians 4:4). He uses the word "joy" earlier in chapter 4, too. He sings the praises of some male - and *female* - co-workers in his ministry, showing that women have a valued place in ministry.

Paul goes on to thank the Philippians for their generosity, but gives credit where credit is really due with yet another often-quoted verse: "I can do all things through *God* who strengthens me" (4:13). The concluding verses are unique among Paul's Epistles in that he makes no direct mention of anyone by name (unless you count the workers he names in 4:2-3). But the tone remains the same throughout the 4th and final chapter of it, just as in the first 3 chapters: a joy-filled expression of enthusiasm even in his changed circumstances. There is little in the way of clues as to exactly what changed here, but Paul's next letter (if there actually was one, see tomorrow's reading) confirms the most drastic change in his circumstances.

October 21, OT
Lamentations 3:1-4:22
Jeremiah Continues the Lament

Though he remains anonymous into the 3rd and 4th chapters of Lamentations, chapter 3 begins with a statement of eyewitness to God's wrath (Lamentations 3:1). This, admittedly, only confirms that the writer lived in Jerusalem, survived the siege, and was left behind in the Exile; it doesn't confirm Jeremiah as the author. However, it is this chapter more than the other 4 that leads scholars to believe in Jeremiah's authorship here, primarily as he continues with descriptions of Jerusalem and complaints of his afflictions that sound very much like repeats from things Jeremiah said in his prophecies. There are a few changes in tone in the 2 chapters, notably the positive turn in 3:22 where Jeremiah takes some time to praise God for His mercy amidst the various complaints, and the first 20 verses of chapter 4, where Jeremiah offers a vivid, graphic description of the siege just before the final deportation.

Chapter 3 is a triple acrostic poem; that is, every *three* lines starts with successive letters of the Hebrew alphabet. Chapter 4 returns to the form of chapters 1 and 2, as single acrostic poetry.

October 21, NT
1 Timothy 1:1-20
Encouragement for a Young Pastor

Of the seven Epistles Paul wrote from Rome, this being the fifth (according to this chronology; see below), four of them have some questions regarding their Pauline authorship: Ephesians, this one, Titus (which we'll read on October 26-27), and the Second Letter to Timothy (November 6-9). The controversy over Paul's authorship of the letter stems primarily from two things: the fact that the writing style here (in 1 Timothy) lacks the joy of Philippians which would have been written just 2-3 years earlier, and the things that cause Paul to be accused of misogyny are prominently on display later in this letter just as they were in Ephesians (particularly chapter 5), in stark contrast to Paul's mention of women in ministry in Philippians. If liberal theologians are correct about which Epistles were or were not written by Paul, then Paul would have written only 3 letters from Rome: Colossians, Philemon, and Philippians, making yesterday's reading from Philippians Paul's last written words. This idea is further reinforced by the fact that 1 Timothy and Ephesians are addressed to the same people: Ephesians to the church there as a whole, and this letter to its pastor.

The problem with the theologically liberal position is the timeline in relation to other events, and the question of who was writing on Paul's behalf. You'll see this in more detail in the coming days and weeks as you read Paul's remaining letters, as well as both letters of Peter, the letter of Jude, and the letter to the Hebrews (which is of unknown authorship). But at this point, this much of the timeline of Rome in the 60s A.D. can be presented with confidence:

Event or book	Year (some approximate)
Paul arrives in Rome and is placed in house arrest	60
Epistles to Ephesians, Philemon, and	61-62

Colossians	
Epistle to the Philippians	63-64
The great fire in Rome	64
Paul is taken from rented house and placed in an actual prison. It is not known for certain if this event ever actually happened except for a handful of vague clues in a couple of letters, notably Philippians and 2 Timothy.	63-66 (This event is the one hardest to place with accuracy, most likely taking place in either late 64 just after the great fire, or in 66 or even early 67 just before Paul's last letter.)
First Epistle to Timothy	65
Epistle to Titus, First Epistle of Peter, Epistle of Jude	66
Second Epistle of Peter, Second Epistle to Timothy	67
Martyrdom of Paul	67
Martyrdom of Peter	68 (Catholics believe that Linus then took over as Bishop of Rome, a.k.a. Pope)
Death of Emperor Nero	68
Epistle to the Hebrews	69-70 (though some believe this was written as early as 63 while Paul was still alive).
Destruction of the Temple in Jerusalem	70

Taking the Epistles of controversial authorship out of this timeline and placing them some time after the death of Paul, death of Nero, or after the Epistle to the Hebrews (see readings for November 10-19) causes some of the things said in those letters to stop making sense. For these and other reasons, and there are too many to go into in this reading guide, this chronology will stick with the traditional position: that Paul wrote 7 letters in Rome, in the order and at the dates and times shown in the table, and the next such letter after Philippians was his first Letter to Timothy.

First Timothy wasn't Paul's first letter to an individual, rather than a church, but the difference in tone and content between this letter and his last previous letter to an individual (Philemon) is absolutely stunning. This letter was addressed to a young man who we've heard about multiple times before, Timothy. The last time we heard about him, Timothy was told to stay in Ephesus, the very same location as Paul's letter to that church, of which Timothy was acting as pastor. Here, after his greeting and self-identification, Paul recaps that suggestion (1 Tim 1:3), this time in an effort to stop some others in the young church from preaching various false doctrines (1:4-7). The false doctrine isn't exactly specified (liberal theologians speculate that is was Gnosticism, but this didn't become an issue until the 2nd century), but Paul makes several references to the Law and its role in our relationship with God (1:8-11, 18-20), bring up a similar list of sins that Paul did in 1 Corinthians, and telling Timothy to "fight the good fight" in keeping the false doctrines, presumably of Rabbinical teachers, away. Sandwiched between these two sections is a paragraph of Paul thanking God for His mercy in using Paul to proclaim the *real* Gospel (1:12-17).

October 22, OT
Lamentations 5:1-22; 2 Kings 25:22-26
A Prayer for Restoration; Governor Gedaliah

The final chapter of Lamentations shows yet another change in tone. It has 22 verses just like chapters 1, 2, and 4, and has a poetic style to it, but is not acrostic like those other chapters. It comes off as less of a melancholy lament, and more like a prayer for mercy, a prayer for God to look upon His people and see what has happened. At the end of the chapter, Jeremiah prays to God to "restore us to Yourself, Oh Lord, that we may be restored", the most quoted line from Lamentations (Lamentations 5:21), expressing the need for God to be the one Who saves us; an appeal for a Savior.

The 5 verses from 2 Kings tell of the first significant event to occur in Judah after the mass deportation. With the kingdom gone, even though the last 3 kings were all appointed by foreign leaders anyway, there had to be some kind of governance in the region. So, Nebuchadnezzar appointed Gedaliah as a regional governor (2 Kings 25:22) over the remaining people of Judah. But as the next few verses show, this didn't last long, and he was assassinated by some of his own men, who then fled to Egypt to escape Babylon's potential wrath (25:23-26).

October 22, NT
1 Timothy 2:1-3:16
The Church Chapters; Issues of Misogyny Debunked

Without going into a too-lengthy discussion of Church history, particularly the version that comes from the Catechism of the Catholic Church, the obvious needs to be stated here: the Church, at this point in history, was very young, had no central governing body, and had no real liturgy for worship or rules for conduct among its clergy. Even the very concept of an ordained clergy was very new. The concept of a priesthood was as old as the Jewish faith from which the new Christian Church drew much of its inspiration, but the old Jewish Law specified that priests be members of the tribe of Levi. In other words, you were born into it; you didn't become ordained into it. Despite all this, and also despite the fact that there wouldn't be any real governmental structure or standard liturgy until the time of Constantine in the 4th Century, there is no doubt about the *existence* of the Church already by this point in the 1st century.

But despite Catholic claims to the contrary, there were no "leaders" in the Church in the manner we think of them today. Individual congregations had a pastor of sorts, and some groups of these pastors may have coordinated their efforts to a small degree and chose bishops among themselves. Many had assistants that were called deacons. The Apostle Peter was the de facto leader of the Church by benefit of having been allegedly appointed to the role by Jesus Christ himself - Catholics mark this as the beginning of the Papacy, with Peter as the first Pope, from A.D. 32 until his martyrdom in 68. This means that Catholics believe Peter was Pope *while Paul was in Rome writing these final 7 letters*, though Paul was also appointed to his role by Jesus (on the road to Damascus). Peter *does* mention Paul in one of his letters (2 Peter 3:15-16), but Paul never mentions Peter or acknowledges him as Bishop of Rome.

What this all means is that young pastors like Timothy had no real guide for conducting worship or otherwise running their congregations, unless they were fortunate enough to have received instructions from someone like Paul, either directly (as in this Epistle) or indirectly (through other Epistles or just word of mouth). That, though, is exactly what today's NT reading represents: a very concise, 2-chapter (though only 31 total verses) summary of the things Timothy needed to know in order to be an effective pastor of the young Ephesian church. Every church today, of every denomination (including Catholic), draws their rules, bylaws, constitutions, or statements of faith, at least in part, from these two chapters in this Epistle.

It begins with instructions regarding prayer: Paul encourages prayers to be lifted up for *all* people, not just people in authority (1 Timothy 2:1-8), because God desires that all be saved. The qualifications to be an "overseer" or "bishop" are spelled out (3:1-7), and include requirements to be the husband of only one wife, which contradicts the rule in the Catholic Church that bishops and priests be celibate and unmarried. The qualifications for deacons are not as strict (3:8-10), but include a "test" for applicants to the position. Newcomers (like I once was) to an evangelical, non-denominational, or charismatic church sometimes marvel at the curious rules and procedures that appear from time to time with deacon and elder selections. They seem odd and out of place until you realize that they come right from here - Paul's first letter to Timothy.

At the end of the section on deacons (3:11-13), Paul ties in his teaching about the conduct of women (2:9-15) in the church, but it is here that many accusations of misogyny and much misinterpretation and misapplication of these instructions occur. Go back to the reading for Ephesians 5:22-6:5 ("The Moral Life, Part Two," October 10) and then come back here and apply the Plain Interpretation to this section of 1 Timothy. These instructions are clearly designed for the sake of orderly worship in a society that was highly patriarchal - at least at that time. Let us not forget that the purpose of this letter was to instruct Timothy on how to run a church that quite obviously was having some problems - perhaps not as bad as the Corinthian church, but a church that was certainly having some difficulties in acquiring some structure and order. False doctrines had crept in despite the best effort of Timothy and others. The women of that church were a very different lot than the women of the Philippian church, otherwise Paul would not have brought up these rules and would have, instead, sang the praises of those women.

But do these rules, therefore, mean that women in every church have a permanent glass ceiling with regards to their ministries? In short, are women forbidden from becoming pastors? It would seem that this passage tells us that, but that's only one out of ***three*** possible interpretations. Since Paul switches to speaking of "a woman" (singular) in verse 12 rather than speaking of "women" in the preceding verses, he could have been referring to an individual without naming her. Furthermore, he uses a word in Greek here that could be easily translated as "wife" rather than "woman," and he later uses the Greek word for "husband" where it is usually translated as "man" (2:12). In addition, and in all 3 possible scenarios, let's not forget that Paul's instruction here is in regards to teaching, which is only one part of what it means to be a pastor. Men and women are absolutely equal in God's eyes; we just have different roles to play, and this is what Paul is spelling out for us by using the Adam and Eve reference at the end of the section (2:13-15).

All debates about gender-based hierarchy and roles aside, Paul frames his reasoning for these instructions in his desire to get out of Rome (out of prison?) and visit them, but refers to a likely "delay" in getting there (3:14-15). This indicates that there had been some changes in Paul's circumstances (remember, Paul originally wanted to take the Gospel message to Caesar himself), and that he was either already in a prison, or just about to be transferred to one (the latter more likely). His closing poem (3:16b) is another statement of faith that has been used in creeds such as The Apostle's Creed.

October 23, OT
Jeremiah 40:1-42:22
A More Detailed Account of Governor Gedaliah

Several portions of the book of Jeremiah contain much more in the way of history than prophecy, and this is one of them. The narrative picks up where Jeremiah left off in chapter 39 ("The Fall of Jerusalem, Part Two," October 17), where Jeremiah was put into protective custody while the mass deportation was taking place. Nebuchadnezzar had given the order to Commander Nebuzaradan to make sure Jeremiah was not among the exiles, but instead was supposed to be released to Gedaliah (Jeremiah 39:11-14) whom we read about yesterday. In chapter 40, we read a much more detailed version of that, as the Commander releases Jeremiah and gives him the option to either go to Babylon where he would be taken care of, or go back to Jerusalem with Gedaliah (40:1-6). Jeremiah chose the latter.

From there, it seems as though the chronology is slightly out of sequence, but it is simply another account of the events in 2 Kings 25:22-26, also read yesterday. What took a mere 5 verses in 2 Kings takes most of 3 whole chapters (actually 5 when tomorrow's reading is counted) in Jeremiah, as the account written here goes into much deeper detail about the assassination (Jeremiah 40:7-41:3) of Gedaliah, other things the assassins did afterwards (41:4-15) and the plan to flee to Egypt (41:16-17). What Jeremiah (or, more likely, his scribe Baruch) adds to this narrative is the appeal to Jeremiah made by Johanan and the other army officers, asking his advice as to what to do next (42:1-3). Following this, the narrative details both the appeal and Jeremiah's response, a near-repeat of an earlier prophecy, but this time directed at the people who wanted to flee to Egypt to not do so (42:4-22). The story continues in tomorrow's OT reading.

October 23, NT
1 Timothy 4:1-16
Teach the Brethren Well

With much less controversy, Paul continues his instruction to young Timothy by first giving him a warning that some believe is an End Times prophecy. But unlike what he would later say about the coming apostasy (in 2 Timothy 3:1-5), he uses the term better translated as "later times" instead of "end times" (1 Timothy 4:1). Plus, as later verses indicate, he's speaking more about the false teachers who want to drag the young Christian community back to older Jewish practices (4:2-3).

Paul then returns to more positive instruction, basically telling Timothy what should be taught to "the brethren," which is a term in Greek that refers to all of the believers, both men and women (4:6-10). He encourages Timothy to not let the latter's youth cause a problem (4:12) and reiterates his expectation that he would visit some time in the future (4:13), telling Timothy to keep on reading Scripture (to us, the Old Testament) and preaching and teaching.

October 24, OT
Jeremiah 43:1-44:30; Psalm 71:1-24; Psalm 116:1-19
The Idolatrous Remnant and the Flight to Egypt

Jeremiah's words to Johanan and the others regarding their plans to flee to Egypt were met with arrogant denial (Jeremiah 43:1-7) and complete disregard. In other words, they went anyway. So, Jeremiah gets another prophecy in the aftermath of this, (43:8-13) detailing how Nebuchadnezzar will soon conquer Eqypt as well, including the Jews living there. Jeremiah passes this along as a warning (44:1-19), the key verse being 44:12, which predicts a final doom for all of the Remnant who fled to Egypt. God's anger shows in the further echoes of that warning, including some sarcasm (44:25 among others) as the rest of chapter 44 completes the last "venting" we hear in Jeremiah from God.

The two Psalms (71, 116) are both attributed, by most scholars, to David. But this chronology places them here for a number of reasons. For one, they're both anonymous, which is very rare for Davidic Psalms. The few Psalms of David that don't have his name attached to them speak of events that put them in obvious places in King David's timeline. Neither of these themes feature any such events. A few attribute them to Jeremiah, but the writing style doesn't sound very much like him. The subtitle commonly given to Psalm 71 is "Prayer of an Old Man for Deliverance." Jeremiah would have been getting up there in years at this point, so it is possible that Jeremiah wrote these. If it is, then these are the next to last words written by the prophet.

October 24, NT
1 Timothy 5:1-6:2
Widows, Elders, and Church Discipline

The code of conduct that Paul gives Timothy in this Epistle gets very specific in chapter 5 about how the different statuses of people should be handled, and it can all be summed up in the first two verses (1 Timothy 5:1-2). Essentially, Paul says that men and women of all ages should be treated like family, even in matters of church discipline: an older man should be treated like a father, younger men as brothers, older women as mothers, and younger women as sisters.

In modern legal terms, a widow is any woman whose husband died while they were married, regardless of their age, number of children, age of children, or whether or not the marriage was their first or later. But for the early church, Paul prescribes what amounts to a vetting process for defining a widow's status and place in the Church. For instance, a widow with children or grandchildren should be taken care of by that family (5:3-4). To be regarded as a "widow indeed," that is, to have that status in the Church, she should live alone (5:5), be at least 60 years old and married to only one man (5:9), and have a reputation of good works (5:10). Younger widows will likely want to remarry, or at least feel "sensual desires" in disregard of Christ (5:11) and should, thus, not be counted among the real widows. These rules are for the purpose of determining who is truly in need because of their widowed status and who, instead, would be an unnecessary burden on the church.

The office of Elder is described briefly (5:17-20) before Paul switches to more personal matters with Timothy (5:21-22), telling him, for example, to drink a little wine now and then to settle his chronic stomach problems (5:23) and speaking to him of the spiritual gift of discernment (5:24-25).

Chapter 6 then starts with 2 verses that echo what Paul wrote at least 3 previous times in the Epistles, regarding the conduct of slaves (6:1-2). It can't be said enough that verses like these do not, in any way, form an endorsement of slavery as a practice by God. Every time where such instructions appear, it is merely a reflection of the fact that slavery did exist, and that there is a code of conduct for the slave just as there is for the free man.

October 25, OT
Jeremiah 30:1-24; Ezekiel 26:1-21
Jeremiah's Last Messianic Prophecy; Judgment on Tyre

Ever since we began reading the prophecies of Jeremiah on September 8, we have been jumping forward and backward in the compiled chapters to a larger degree than with any other prophet. At one point, we passed the "last words of Jeremiah" at the end of chapter 51, and learned about how a Cushite named Ebed-Melek is most likely responsible for the final numbered chapter (52) in Jeremiah's book. After today, there is only one more reading from the book of Jeremiah, and it's from that very chapter. What that means is that chapter 30 can be considered as Jeremiah's last written words.

Unlike other "major" prophets like Isaiah, Daniel, and Ezekiel, Jeremiah's prophecies up to this point have stayed focused on events surrounding the Babylonian Exile. But here in chapter 30, the Word from God says that the "days are coming...when I will restore the fortunes of My people Israel and Judah" (Jeremiah 30:3). This isn't the first such prophecy from Jeremiah, and most of it references the return of the Jews to Jerusalem foretold by him before and also by Ezekiel. Towards the end, though, it takes a Messianic turn when he quotes God as saying that "their leader shall be one of them" (30:21) but makes no mention of a king or the restoration of the kingdom. The rest of the chapter, in fact, makes it more clear that He isn't talking about the nation of Israel, but rather, about God's People who first need to be chastised before a Savior would come. That is the clearest indicator that this final prophecy of Jeremiah is Messianic.

Ezekiel's first prophecy after the final mass deportation to Babylon is the first of several he makes against neighboring nations; in this case, Tyre, promising a level of destruction similar to that of Jerusalem when Nebuchadnezzar comes to conquer (Ezekiel 26:1-21).

October 25, NT
1 Timothy 6:3-21
The Love of Money; Conclusion of 1 Timothy

In the middle of Paul's final instructions to Timothy, at least in his first Epistle to him, is one of the Bible's most badly misused and frequently misquoted verses. Regardless of which translation you use or have previously read, you have doubtless heard the phrase "money is the root of all evil." By itself, that phrase is not a misquote, at least not from the KJV. But in every English translation, it's the ***love of*** money, not money itself, that is the root of all evil (1 Timothy 6:10). Furthermore, the vast majority of translations that use older Greek manuscripts say that the love of money is the root of "all kinds of evil," not just evil itself. The point is that the entire verse needs to be quoted and taken in context in order to be understood. It is not, contrary to many, a condemnation of riches; it is sound advice to a pastor (and by extension, to all of us) to not pursue after riches but to be content with what we have, lest money become a snare to us (6:8-9).

It is also best understood with the later instruction to pass along these instructions TO the rich to fix their hope on God (6:17) instead of money.

As Paul brings the letter to a conclusion, he does make one mention, in the next to last verse, of a heresy that would become a big problem in the 2nd century: gnosticism. In most translations, it is referred to as "what is falsely called 'knowledge'" (6:20). It's one of the verses that has led liberal theologians to believe that this letter was written much later than the mid 60s A.D. as this chronology believes. But although gnosticism didn't become a big problem for many years after Paul, it had to have its roots somewhere, and it is therefore the belief of this reading guide that it began right here.

October 26, OT
Ezekiel 27:1-28:26; Ezekiel 33:21-33
Lamentations Over Tyre; The Reason for the Exile

Ezekiel and Jeremiah were, in many ways, parallel prophets. They wrote their prophecies from different locations, but their subject matter was largely the same. They both prophesied at length about Judah's last 3 kings, the Fall, and the Exile. Both wrote in a style that included the phrase "thus says the Lord" dozens of times as they directly quoted God. Both wrote numerous prophecies against Judah's neighbor nations. There were, of course, some differences. Ezekiel was, himself, an early deportee, while Jeremiah remained in Jerusalem (presumably, for the rest of his life). Jeremiah was much more emotional in his writings while Ezekiel presented his visions from God in an almost stoic fashion. And although Jeremiah poured out his feelings and grief over the Fall of Jerusalem, Ezekiel never did this for Jerusalem, but with today's OT reading, we discover that he did do so for a different nation-state: Tyre. Yesterday's OT reading included a prophecy against Tyre; today, Ezekiel writes a lament (Ezekiel 27:1-36) over Tyre that shows nearly as much emotion as Jeremiah did over Jerusalem.

Following this is another prophecy, not lament, directed against the king of Tyre (28:1-19), and then a prophecy against a different neighbor nation, Sidon (28:20-26). All of the prophecies against neighbor nations mention a future restoration of Israel to its original land that nations like Tyre and Sidon will not enjoy.

The section in chapter 33 seems out of chronological sequence until you realize the news of the fall of Jerusalem would have taken a long time to actually reach exiles like Ezekiel living near Babylon. An escapee of Jerusalem brings the news which sparks a prophecy from God (33:21-23), in which the reasons for the fall are explained in detail (33:24-33).

October 26, NT
Titus 1:1-2:10
More Rules for the Early Church

About a year after writing to Timothy, Paul penned another Epistle to an individual. This time, the recipient of the letter is one who is not mentioned anywhere in the Acts of the Apostles like Timothy was; rather, the letter is written to a travel companion of Paul's whose only other mention is in the Epistle to the Galatians. The man is Titus, and the brief 3-chapter Epistle to him (today and tomorrow) reads very much like 1 Timothy in the sense that it contains instructions for an early Church pastor.

Besides being more brief, one of the other big differences between the letter to Timothy and this letter is in Paul's opening greeting, where he introduces himself as a "slave" or "bondservant" (depending on translation) of Jesus Christ (Titus 1:1). In 1 Timothy, Paul merely states that he is an "Apostle;" here he states both titles. This reflects an increase of devotion to a master; that is, Jesus, but also was quite possibly stated because of further problems and changes of circumstances, likely including Paul's transfer from a rented house to an actual prison.

His salutation goes on a bit longer than usual (1:2-4) before getting to the heart of the matter. Paul gives Titus the same instructions regarding elders as he gave to Timothy in regards to deacons (1:5-16). Since Paul separated the two in his letter to Timothy, it would seem odd to have combined the two offices, effectively, into one, but it can be easily explained by how similar the two offices are anyway, and by the fact that the Early Church was still a very unstructured body. After that, he repeats his instructions about how to treat older and younger men and older and younger women (2:1-8) like he did in 1 Timothy, and then uses the exact same word (translated as either slave or bondservant) as he did in verse 1 to instruct Titus to "urge bondservants to be subject to their own masters," yet another example of defining the role of slaves in the world of the new, young Church.

October 27, OT
Ezekiel 34:1-36:38
The Sheep and the Shepherds; The Future Restoration of Israel

Ezekiel was not the only prophet to promise a future restoration for Israel. But just like those other prophets, Jeremiah in particular, Ezekiel lays out some prerequisites in his prophecies, things God says must happen before these future happy times. One of those prerequisites is the removal of false shepherds, sometimes referred to as false teachers and false prophets, from among the people (Ezekiel 34:1-10). But then, Ezekiel uses the metaphor of sheep (also used by Jeremiah, Isaiah, Zechariah from whom we'll read in November, and others) in describing who the Good Shepherd will be (34:11-31) in an obvious Messianic prophecy (using the reference name of David, 34:23, implying that a descendent of David will be that shepherd).

Before getting on with more detail about what that restoration will look like, Ezekiel unleashes another judgment against a neighboring nation, this time against Mount Seir in Edom (35:1-15), once again ending the passage with the familiar line, "Then [the Edomites] will know that I am the Lord" (35:15). And so, Ezekiel goes into chapter 36 talking, likewise, about "the hills," this time the hills of Jerusalem instead of Edom, and makes the case *for* Israel using almost the exact same terms as was made *against* the neighboring nations (36:1-7).

A careful reading of the middle section of the chapter reveals, however, that Ezekiel isn't talking about a restoration of the *kingdom* of Israel. There is no mention of any king (after his earlier mention of David), only hopeful descriptions of more people living "on the land" (36:12). In fact, the whole section is addressed to "the mountains of Israel" (36:8-15), not necessarily to any group of people, though God refers to "my people Israel" as being those who will possess the land. God explains further that He had good reason to let the people be scattered, and that He will be the one responsible for bringing them back - but not for the people's sake, but for HIS sake (36:16-38), making the entire prophecy about the restoration of Israel, including the well-known part read tomorrow, a big case of promise fulfillment on God's part.

October 27, NT
Titus 2:11-3:15
Not Saved *by* Works, but Saved *to Do* Good Works; Conclusion of Titus

In every one of Paul's Epistles, a point is made somewhere in the letter that we no longer live under the law, but under grace. We are saved through God's grace and our only role is to accept that grace in faith. In different letters, he says it using different words, but the Gospel message is always essentially the same. Thus it is that this second half of his Epistle to Titus starts out as a direct continuation of yesterday's reading, giving advice that mostly echoes the same advice given to Timothy about how to run a church (Titus 2:11-15). After reminding Titus about being law-abiding citizens in the same manner as he wrote in Romans 13 (3:1), he gets to the part about what works really means in the life of the saved, noting that we are not saved by our works but instead we do good works *because* we are saved (3:3-11).

Paul wraps up this brief letter with an invitation for Titus to join him in a place called Nicopolis, a city in Western Greece (3:12). Given the traditionally accepted timeline (see reading for October 21), it isn't known if the invitation was merely wishful thinking on Paul's part (i.e. he was in prison and anticipated being released before winter) or if he was, in fact, out of his chains and able to travel freely. Given the lack of any recorded history (from Luke or anyone else, in or outside of the Bible) about this particular trip, it is entirely possible that the truth lies somewhere between, in that Paul was released for a time but never actually made it to Nicopolis. We simply don't know this history for sure. His parting greetings include mentions of two other people, one familiar (Apollos), in what likely was supposed to be an important early Church conference. All we do know for sure is that Paul would pen only one more letter, no more than about a year after this one to Titus, likely just days or a few weeks before his martyrdom. Before we read that letter, we read of 3 others by 2 other writers in between, starting tomorrow.

October 28, OT
Ezekiel 37:1-39:29
The Valley of Dry Bones; Gog and Magog

The best-known passage from Ezekiel is also the second prophecy from this book to be adapted into a song. The image of skeletons coming back to life was irresistible to songwriter James Weldon Johnson, who wrote the original version of "Dem Bones" in 1928. Since then, dozens of gospel and country singers have recorded the famous spiritual, the best-known versions done by "Tennessee" Ernie Ford, Rosemary Clooney, The Lennon Sisters, and even Alvin and the Chipmunks. The catchy lyrics include lines like "toe bone connected to the foot bone… foot bone connected to the heel bone…" etc., adapted from a scene right here in Ezekiel 37. The chapter describes another vivid and bizarre vision given to Ezekiel by God. The valley full of dry bones represents the *long-dead* nation of Israel (Ezekiel 37:11), and the picture of the bones coming together and then getting flesh on them is a clear representation of *rebirth*. The symbolism may be strange, but the message is actually quite clear: Israel will be regathered in its original land, and God isn't talking this time about merely the return of the Jews from the Exile. He's talking about the rebirth of the *nation* of Israel, a prophecy that would be literally fulfilled 2500 years later - on **May 15, 1948**.

The biggest clue here that Ezekiel isn't referring to the end of the Exile is, very simply, the vision of the bones being *dry*, symbolizing a people who have been dead a long time. Additionally, Ezekiel was as aware of the length of the Exile (70 years) as Jeremiah was, and therefore knew that some of his fellow exiles would still be alive to see them return to Jerusalem. That doesn't fit the image of a *long-dead* nation, so it must refer to a much later event. We know the history of the land where Israel is now, and we know that it wasn't actually called Israel at any point between the beginning of the Exile and its modern rebirth. Many people recognize the rebirth of Israel as a miraculous event. Just as many others deny the legitimacy of this newly-formed nation-state. But both sides of this debate must realize that what it really is, is the fulfillment of a prophecy that was written more than 2500 years ago, in Babylonian territory, by a prophet who once lived in that very nation, via a vision from God.

Another vision Ezekiel received from God, which immediately follows the Israel-rebirth prophecy, is among the Bible's most mysterious and controversial. It's mysterious because of the mention of "Gog" and "Magog," neither words of which appear anywhere else in the Bible. It's controversial because there are so many conflicting interpretations of this prophecy, with some saying that the prophecy was already fulfilled while others, including this writer, believes that this prophecy is yet to come. Among the reasons for believing in an End Times interpretation is simply the use of the name "Israel" in the references to the nation that gets invaded by a country "to the north". Ezekiel 38 and 39 goes into great depth about this future invasion, but during all of the time between the writing of this prophecy and the rebirth he predicts in the preceding chapter (just over 2500 years), there could have been no fulfillment of it because there was no nation called Israel. The land was, indeed, repossessed when the Jews returned after the Exile. Jews lived in the land after that, uninterrupted, for many centuries, and suffered multiple invasions and conquests thereafter, most notably the early Roman Empire that ruled the region during the time of Christ. But at no point was there his invader from the north. The only city or nation of any significance that lies straight to the north of Israel today is Moscow, the capital of Russia. This fact, along with references in Revelation 20:8 and Revelation chapters 21-22 to this part of Ezekiel, are the leading reasons to believe that this is an End Times prophecy, now partially fulfilled by the rebirth of Israel, and later to be fulfilled once it is known for certain if Gog and Magog refers to individuals, peoples, or nation-states. It is the only part of Ezekiel that is directly quoted in the New Testament, and only by John in Revelation.

The most significant aspect of the invasion prophecy concerns the fact that the invaders will not succeed, and that Israel will recover from this invasion because of God's protection. Those that believe that this prophecy was fulfilled with the Romans neglect the fact that Rome is much more west than north of Israel, and the prophecy clearly states that the invaders come from the "far north" (Ezekiel 38:6). This also rules out Syria, which now exists where Assyria once did, because the nation was and now is Israel's immediate neighbor to the north.

The point is this: even with the only correct ("plain") interpretation of this prophecy, it is still far too complex and vague to be treated dogmatically. Whole books have been written about just these 3 chapters, and spending more time than today would jeopardize the study of the whole Bible that this reading guide advocates.

Eschatology is a fascinating and worthwhile study, and there's more treasures related to this study in the Old Testament than most people think, and a big part of it is here in today's OT reading.

October 28, NT
1 Peter 1:1-21
Message to a Slowly Maturing Church

In today's NT reading, we turn away from either the Epistles of Paul or events in the life of Paul for the first time in more than two months, and hear from Peter, a man from whom we haven't heard about since July 5, when we read about the Council of Jerusalem in Acts 15. Paul and Peter knew each other at that time, which would have been between 15-18 years prior to Paul's just-completed letter to Titus. The first *written* mention of Peter would have actually been when Paul wrote his letter to the Galatians, describing Paul's rebuke of Peter (Galatians 2:11, July 8). All four Gospels, describing the life of Peter and his appointment as the leader of the Apostles by Jesus, would have been written later, as was the Acts of the Apostles. But that still means that we have not read from or about Peter for more than 3 and a half months.

The events of the preceding 18 (or so) years leading up to this Epistle are extensively recorded in the Acts and Paul's Epistles, but only with regards to *Paul's* activities and the churches that were founded during that period. There's nothing else in the Bible about the activities of Peter. The Catholic Church believes that Peter founded the church in Rome. Whether this is true or not, it's notable that when Paul wrote to the Roman church (in about 57 A.D.), he greets more than 50 people by name, but never mentions Peter. Nevertheless, the church in Rome was, indeed, in place prior to Paul's arrival, as were numerous other churches in what is now eastern and southern Europe, the Middle East, and northern Africa. Some were founded by Paul on his Missionary Journeys, some undoubtedly by Peter, and other churches founded by other early evangelists. The young Church was, as a whole, remarkably vibrant and widespread, but it was still very young and

going through some serious growing pains. There was no central governing body, and there was no structure ("liturgy") to worship.
 Young pastors needing help in the basic "how to" information in running a church looked to Paul - and Peter - for this. Peter opens his first Epistle by greeting those who reside "as aliens" in several places around the young Church area (1 Peter 1:1), with only one location having been previously mentioned by Paul (Galatia).

So regardless of what you believe about Peter's role in the Church (as first Pope or whatever title), he most definitely was an early Church leader, and he wanted the churches to which he wrote to thrive and grow. There is at least as much debate about whether or not he wrote these two Epistles (the second of which will be read on November 3-5) as there is about the Pauline authorship of the Epistles to Timothy and Titus. But like those Pauline Epistles, this chronology holds to the traditional position that Peter wrote these. Although the location *from* which he wrote them is unknown (some believe it was Rome but it is equally likely that this first one, at least, was written from Antioch), the locations *to* which he wrote are known locations of the early Church. The style is very different than Paul's, as is evident right from the beginning, but the message is very similar to Paul's later letters, in terms of instructions to leaders of the slowly maturing Church.

October 29, OT
Ezekiel 32:1-33:20
Lament Over Egypt; Duty of the Watchman

Today's OT reading is far less "flashy" than yesterday's grand visions of restoration, but it does divide up into 2 parts, this time consisting of a chapter apiece. In one of the few places where we read any part of Ezekiel out of the sequence in which it's presented, we drop back to chapter 32 to read Ezekiel's followup to his prophecy against Egypt (read on October 15), and read a lament over Pharaoh written in the "12th year, 1st day of the 12th month" (Ezekiel 32:1), or nearly the beginning of the 13th year of the Exile (the main reason for presenting it here in the chronology). Like the prophecy against Pharaoh, Ezekiel takes the word from God and writes the 15-verse lament in a poetic style (32:2-16) and even identifies it as such. Two weeks later (32:17), Ezekiel receives another call to "wail for the hordes of Egypt" (32:18), with comparisons between Egypt and other nations who have fallen or will soon fall (32:19-32).

The second part of today's reading constitutes a renewal of God's call to Ezekiel as the "Watchman" (33:1-20) of Israel, that introduces Ezekiel's final chapters and later prophecies, beginning tomorrow in chapter 40.

October 29, NT
1 Peter 1:22-2:17
The Rock

With all apologies to actor Dwayne Johnson, he is not The Rock. At least, he isn't the Rock of whom Peter writes in this second reading from his first Epistle. It was originally a play on words (in Greek) that Jesus used when Peter recognized Him as the Messiah that led to Simon Peter's nickname (remember, he was born *Simon* - Peter is the English version of the word "Petra" which means "rock" or "stone", thus "Peter" is actually a nickname). But in today's NT reading, Peter makes it clear that it is the "living Stone" that we believe in (1 Peter 2:4), and that we are like "living stones" (2:5) that are being built into a "spiritual house" - that is, the Church.

In this section, Peter quotes or references Isaiah no fewer than 3 times, starting with a quote of Isaiah 40:6-8 that he uses in 1 Peter 1:24-25 as he wraps up the practical instructions, started yesterday. He then goes on in 2:6 and 2:8, expanding on the metaphor of The Rock by quoting Isaiah 28:16 and 8:14. In between, he quotes a Psalm (118:22) in declaring "the Stone that the builders rejected has become the Cornerstone" (2:7). It is on this foundation that the Church is, thus, built.

One of the main reasons for writing this letter is expressed here, and it dovetails nicely with known history of the time. The young Church was born within the Roman Empire, and so long as Rome ruled the world, the Church spread only within those boundaries. But as previously mentioned, and although Judaism was officially tolerated (but not accepted or believed) by Rome, Christianity was not. Christianity was basically an underground movement and was officially illegal in the Roman Empire. It thus became important for the new Church to learn how to properly live within this pagan world

(2:11-17), and Peter's instructions here show the new churches exactly how to do that, much of which echoes similar teachings by Paul.

October 30, OT
Ezekiel 40:1-27
Vision of the Temple, Part One

The book of Ezekiel, from here on through chapter 48, consists of different parts of the same vision: the vision of a rebuilt Temple. By this time, 13 years after the fall of Jerusalem and 25 years into the Exile, Ezekiel would have been informed that the Temple in Jerusalem was destroyed. And so begins a lengthy and very detailed prophecy about a new Temple to be built in its place. Ezekiel is transported by a vision to Israel, and meets a man "like bronze," holding a measuring rod, and compelling Ezekiel to pay attention to these specifications and pass them along to the people of Israel (Ezekiel 40:1-4). The specs then begin with measurements for the walls from the east gate to the outer court (40:5-16), the outer court itself (40:17-19), the north gate (40:20-23), and the south gate (40:24-27).

The real question is: what Temple is being measured? The dimensions don't match Solomon's Temple which had just been destroyed, so it must refer to some future effort. When the Jews returned to Jerusalem after the Exile, they built a Temple. But, it was much smaller than either the original Solomon's Temple or the new Temple being described in the prophecy. That Temple went through a number of renovations and expansions, lastly by Herod the Great, and came to be known as Herod's Temple. But even that structure didn't match the dimensions and specifications given to Ezekiel in this vision. That, effectively, leaves only two possible choices as to the meaning of this vision: that the Temple being described is yet to be built, making this an End Times prophecy, or the Temple being described isn't a literal structure at all, but rather, is a reference to The Church in New Testament times, making this a Messianic prophecy. Which is right? Read on in this 5-part series for the answer.

October 30, NT
1 Peter 2:18-3:12
The Example of the Suffering Servant

The passage of Isaiah known as the "Suffering Servant" was read in this chronology back on September 1, and was literally fulfilled with the Crucifixion of Jesus Christ as told in the Gospels. Though we are now reading this months after we read about the Crucifixion, we must remember that, at this point, *at most* 2 of the 4 Gospels had been written. It's entirely possible that the Gospel according to Mark, believed to have been written with the help of Peter, was just recently completed at this point, if it had been completed at all. What that means is that the references to Christ's sufferings in today's NT reading as the fulfillment of Isaiah's prophecies may well have been the first written reference to this crucially important doctrine in New Testament times. Here, Peter uses an instruction, as continued from yesterday's reading, about slaves (1 Peter 2:18) to lead into his discussion of this suffering (2:19-25), updating it with direct references to Christ. Thus, Christ is our example, and the example Peter gave the new churches.

Then, in chapter 3, Peter goes into a section that reads very much like Paul's letter to the Ephesians that we read on October 10 called "the Moral Life," Just like Paul did, Peter opens it with the words "In the same way," (3:1) in order to lead the reader naturally from his description of the fulfillment of the Suffering Servant prophecy on into talking about wives being submissive to their husbands. Peter uses a slightly different explanation to justify this aspect of Godly living than what Paul did, but it carries the exact same message (3:2-6), including using the same counterpart argument about how the husband in the relationship should treat his wife (3:7). The similarities are notable in that it is widely accepted that Peter was a married man whereas Paul was not, yet Peter is seldom, if ever, accused of misogyny (while Paul is frequently accused). The point is, the message carries no misogyny at all, and is much more a description of how to use Christ as our example in living our lives.

October 31, OT
Ezekiel 40:28-41:20
Vision of the Temple, Part Two

The specs for a new Temple continue being given to Ezekiel in today's OT reading. First up are the measurements from the gates to the Inner Court (Ezekiel 40:28-37), then the rooms for preparing sacrifices (40:38-43), rooms for the priests (40:44-47), and then various other measurements ranging from individual door jambs to the thickness of the foundation (40:48-41:20), with more detail regarding some of these same things in tomorrow's OT reading.

October 31, NT
1 Peter 3:13-4:11
Living for God Amidst Persecution

In this part of Peter's first Epistle, we get a little bit more of an idea as to what, exactly, prompted Peter to write the letter. Peter seamlessly goes from describing Christ as the Rock to describing how Christ fulfilled the prophecy of the Suffering Servant in the last 2 days' readings. Now, he continues in using the "example of Christ" comparison, with His sufferings being that example, to speak to the young Church about conducting themselves amidst Christianity's latest problem: persecution. The Jews had gone through various periods of persecution over their history, but enjoyed a mostly tolerant attitude from the dominant Roman Empire of the first century. The regions to which Peter wrote in this letter were in an area once called "Asia Minor," and would be found today in the areas of modern-day Greece and Turkey. These areas once had a fairly large number of Hellenistic (Greek-speaking) Jews during the Roman Empire. Now, the Roman Empire was facing an increasing number of Jewish converts to the new Way, known as Christianity. Christianity did not enjoy the tolerance that Judaism did, no matter if the converts were mostly Jewish. In fact, Christians were severely persecuted in Rome itself, and the faith was declared illegal throughout the Empire. Thus, Peter's audience in this letter were new believers, formerly Jewish, learning how to build a Church where it was officially illegal to do so, and conduct themselves amongst people who might very well become their persecutors.

And so, Peter's words of encouragement here use examples going back to the family of Noah to drive the point home that suffering for the cause of Christ is a good thing, because Christ suffered for us in the flesh. He also, however, added a warning: that the "end of all things is near" (1 Peter 4:7), which sounds on the surface like he's talking about the end of the world. Obviously, the world did not end shortly after he wrote the Epistle, so Peter must have been referring to something else. Given the estimated timeline of A.D. 66 or 67 for the writing of this letter, it is believed that Peter became aware of the growing revolt by the Jews in Jerusalem, a revolt that would be crushed by the Romans in A.D. 70 with the destruction of the Temple in Jerusalem. Though Peter's audience consisted of converted Jews in Asia Minor, these rebels in Jerusalem would have been their kinsmen, and the coming retaliation from Rome would have certainly been the "end of all things" for their former culture and religion. (There is another possible interpretation of this that shows up in his Second Epistle, on November 3). Peter continues (and concludes) this message in tomorrow's reading.

November 1, OT
Ezekiel 41:21-43:27
Vision of the Temple, Part Three

Ever wonder why the main entrance to nearly all church buildings, particularly if they are Catholic and/or were built before 1960, faces East? An important clue to this tradition can be found right here in Ezekiel.

Ezekiel spends the rest of chapter 41 and all of chapter 42 finishing up the physical specifications of the Temple before then shifting gears for the first time in this vision. Chapter 42 is entirely a deeper detail of a part of the specs already mentioned in yesterday's OT reading, the rooms for the priests. Then, in chapter 43, the vision shifts to the return of God's glory to the Temple. Recall that, earlier, Ezekiel was allowed to witness the *departure* of God's glory from the Temple, prior to the final siege and invasion of Jerusalem by Nebuchadnezzar (Ezekiel 10:1-19, read on October 8). Now, God gives Ezekiel a chance to witness the opposite event: the *return* of God's glory, entering from the east, into the Temple again (43:1-2). Ezekiel alludes to that entrance facing east, and God's entrance from the east, no fewer than 3 times in the chapter. Ever since, and even though Herod's Temple was not built to the specs given here in Ezekiel, its main entrance faced east, as do the vast majority of Christian churches today.

November 1, NT
1 Peter 4:12-5:14
Resist the Adversary; Conclusion of Peter's First Epistle

In the first "General Epistle" ever written, by James (read at the end of June/early July), the brother of Jesus told his audience of believers to "resist the devil, and he will flee" (James 4:7). It is likely that Peter was aware of James' letter, and possibly was even aware of James' audience, which may have been the same as the addressees of this Epistle. In what is arguably the climax of the letter, Peter tells them that their "adversary, the devil, prowls around like a roaring lion, seeking someone to devour. But resist him, firm in your faith…" (1 Peter 5:8-9). Peter builds up to this by first continuing his encouragement of believers faced with having to suffer for their faith (4:12-5:7), telling them to keep on serving God, willingly and with diligence, and quoting a pair of Proverbs along the way (4:18 and 5:5 quote Proverbs 11:31 and 3:34, respectively). In much the same tone as James did, Peter tells the Church that they will be protected by God in the face of the real enemies (5:9-11).

Peter's final greetings at the end of the letter begin with a mention of a man named Silvanus (in Greek) or Silas (in Hebrew), likely the same Silas that also accompanied Paul on his First Missionary Journey. He then also mentions an unnamed woman "from Babylon" who sends greetings along with "my son Mark." The woman is completely unknown, and it is not known if Mark is Peter's literal son or if Peter was using a figure of speech referring to the young man. The reference to Babylon, however, is believed to be literal, and not a coded reference to Rome as the Apostle John would later use in Revelation. Peter would write another Epistle, but first we read from yet another first century writer, tomorrow.

November 2, OT
Ezekiel 44:1-46:24
Vision of the Temple, Part Four

The penultimate section of Ezekiel's "Vision of the Temple" continues to stay away from just building specifications and dimensions, focussing instead on the restoration of the Priesthood to go along with the new Temple. The Mosaic Covenant set up the original system of Priests in the books of Exodus and, especially, Leviticus, all of which was long before the kingdom. Multiple times during the divided kingdom after Solomon, kings had to work hard to restore the Law and worship. There were several periods of great reform by the "good" kings of Judah. But ultimately, their efforts failed because the people, as a whole, were not changed by the reform efforts of their kings. In other words, their changes in actions were little more than going through the motions while their hearts remained hardened, at least collectively. What Ezekiel is prophesying here is a return to the original Theocracy the Israelites had before the kingdom, and God gives Ezekiel nearly as much detail about it here (and in tomorrow's conclusion) as Moses got for inclusion in Leviticus.

November 2, NT
Jude 1:1-25
A Brief Warning

Like the Old Testament book of Obadiah and the New Testament book of Philemon, the 25-verse long Epistle of Jude, read today in its entirety, is so brief that the introduction/commentary found here is almost as long as the book itself. Though it contains the same number of verses as Paul's letter to Philemon, it is just a tiny bit longer in total words. It is the only work written by Jude, who is believed to be the younger brother of James who is, in turn, the younger half-brother of Jesus Christ. Though there is very little dispute about its authorship, the date of the letter and location from which it was written are unknown. Given several similarities between this letter and Peter's second letter (starting tomorrow), the consensus opinion is that the two Epistles were written about the same time, in about A.D. 66 or 67.

The message of Jude is very focussed on one topic: a warning against the teachings of certain "intruders" (Jude 1:4) who have "perverted the Gospel". Jude brings up "Balaam's error" (1:11) as a comparison, which would have been easily understood by a Jewish convert audience. Outside of that, there is no other real clue as to Jude's intended audience. Jude is also noted for two parts that quote or reference non-canonical scriptures: verse 9 refers to a dispute between the devil and Michael the Archangel, found in a work called the Assumption of Moses, a Jewish apocryphal work whose only existing manuscripts are some sixth-century fragments written in Latin. The work doesn't even contain the referenced conflict between Michael and Satan, but scholars believe that this would have been part of a lost ending passage in the book. Verses 14-15 make a direct quote from the first Book of Enoch, another apocryphal work that isn't even part of the Catholic deuterocanonical works. Enoch, however, is accepted as inspired by one part of one denomination (Ethiopian Orthodox), and it adds an apocalyptic flavor to the Epistle. It is also among the few works found in the Dead Sea Scrolls that isn't accepted as canon.

With this being Jude's only written work, and given the readings for the next week, it's notable that we're into a section of the New Testament that shows the last works of three different Biblical writers: Jude today, Peter tomorrow through November 5, and Paul (in his second letter to Timothy) on November 6-9. All three of these writers were martyred by Roman emperors: Peter and Paul both by Nero (and within the next year after this Epistle), and Jude by Trajan in roughly 99 A.D.

November 3, OT
Ezekiel 47:1-48:35
Vision of the Temple, Part Five (Conclusion)

Though today's OT reading brings us to the end of the book of Ezekiel, we actually have one more day's reading from Ezekiel tomorrow from earlier chapters that were skipped (and you'll find out why tomorrow). The question asked on October 30, at the beginning of this "Vision of the Temple," was whether or not the Temple being described here was a literal (and future) Temple, not yet even built in our time, or perhaps a symbolic description of the Church after the coming of the Messiah. Four chapters ago, Ezekiel's vision broke away from specifications of the physical structure of the Temple to describe the return of God's glory to the temple, and the restoration of pre-kingdom worship in that Temple. Chapter 47 then goes off in yet another direction, with a vision of water flowing from the Temple

(Ezekiel 47:1-12), which echoes more visions that other prophets would later see, notably John in Revelation. But this vision, along with the dividing up of the land of Israel into portions (different from the original divisions but still accounting for all 12 tribes of Israel), should put to rest any debate about what Ezekiel has been talking about for the last 4 days' OT readings.

As written earlier, the Temple in the vision could not refer to either the Temple built when the Exiles returned to Jerusalem, nor the structure it later became, known as Herod's Temple, due primarily to differences in dimensions. Thus, if it is referring to a structure at all, and since Herod's Temple was destroyed in 70 A.D. by the Romans and not rebuilt since, it would have to be a yet-to-be-built Temple, making it one of two major End Times events (the other being the 1948 rebirth of the nation of Israel) that must occur before the bulk of the rest of the Apocalypse.

What if it isn't a structure at all, but rather, is a vision of the Church? It's an easy interpretation to make, but is debunked by the references, especially in this final section, to the Twelve Tribes of Israel and a return to the land, referring to the nation of Israel (though not the kingdom). The details also don't metaphorically match up with the Church at any point in its history, and so we're left with the yet-to-be-built Temple that will become a focal point of some End Times events, one of which we'll read in Daniel in the coming days.

November 3, NT
2 Peter 1:1-21
A Call to the Elect

At first, the stark difference in tone between this Epistle and Peter's first one is enough to make you think that these were the works of two different writers. But as will become clearer later in the Epistle, Peter first introduced himself as not just a servant but an Apostle as well (2 Peter 1:1), identifies it as his second Epistle (3:1, November 5), mentions Paul by name (3:15-16, November 5), and makes clear his position as a leader (if not *the* leader) of the Church. It is thus very clear that if Peter wrote the first Epistle (as this chronology believes), he also wrote this second one.

Unlike the first one, though, Peter doesn't address the letter to any particular church or individual. His use of the word "friends" suggests that he is writing to a church or group of churches, and his identification of this being his "second letter to *you*" further suggests that this letter's audience is the same as the first. It would have been written somewhere between A.D. 66 when he wrote his first Epistle and Paul's martyrdom in 67. It was also no more than one year prior to his own martyrdom, which occurred in late 67 or early 68, and it was obvious that Peter knew that his death was coming soon (1:13-15). This gives the entire Epistle the tone of a farewell, and further may have been somewhat of a "passing of the torch" to his successor as Bishop of Rome, Linus. However, Peter never mentions Linus by name whereas Paul does (in 2 Timothy 4:21, November 9).

The Petrine authorship of this Epistle is of far less doubt than many other New Testament letters, however, and part of the reason is also his clear quotation of God's words at the Transfiguration to Jesus, "This is my Son, my beloved, in whom I am well pleased" (1:17). One could say he was merely quoting the Gospels of Mark or Matthew, but they would have been only recently completed if they had been completed at all by 67 A.D. It is therefore far more likely that this quotation is based on an eyewitness account. It is also believed that Mark got the bulk of his base material for the first written Gospel from Peter.

As a whole, Peter's second Epistle is about 2/3rds the length of his first, but is actually much more doctrinally dense (and more frequently quoted). The emphasis in the first chapter is on the reliability of God's Word, and the "confirmation of your calling" (1:3-11), which defines the doctrine of Election - being among those that God *chose* to spread the message of the Gospel.

November 4, OT
Ezekiel 29:17-30:19
One Last Lament

Though we read the end of the book of Ezekiel yesterday, there remains one last (relatively brief) reading from the book, placed here only because of where Ezekiel himself dated it: in the 27th year, which would make this the last thing actually written by the prophet. Now more than 2 decades into the Exile, Ezekiel receives a final prophecy from God about the fall of Egypt (Ezekiel 27:17-20), making the conquest of Judah/Israel and all of its neighbors (Tyre is mentioned in verse 18) complete. Nebuchadnezzar had successfully conquered the entirety of what is now known as the Middle East. This prompted one final lament over Egypt (30:1-19), which leaves the prophecies of Ezekiel with the familiar and often-repeat line "...they will know that I am the Lord".

November 4, NT
2 Peter 2:1-22
Rescue from False Prophets

When Christianity was brand new (between A.D. 33 and 67), the biggest concern facing the young Church was whether or not Gentiles should be allowed to join, and if so, whether they had to first "become Jewish" to do so. Paul's evangelical work during his Missionary Journeys and his Epistles before arriving in Rome were largely concerned with this issue. But by around 60, which would have been when Paul arrived in Rome, a shift had taken place, and it is reflected in the letters by Paul, Jude, and now Peter that were written during that decade. The shift was due to the fact that the Church was beginning to mature and become more established, despite the persecution (particularly in Rome) and the fact that it was officially illegal. But with any new but maturing and growing institution comes those who would take advantage of it for their own gain and agenda. These false teachers / false prophets were a growing problem then, and it's still a problem today.

Peter's emphasis here is that God will not tolerate these false prophets, and he uses the example of the fallen angels (2 Peter 2:4), Noah and his family (2:5), the cities of Sodom and Gomorrah (2:6), and Lot, the nephew of Abraham rescued from there (2:7-8), to point out God's judgment of them and how He will certainly rescue the Godly from temptation and unrighteousness (2:9-10). Peter continues with additional comparisons, including that of Balaam (2:15-16), that should sound quite familiar if you follow this reading plan, having read Jude two days ago. Second Peter quotes or paraphrases Jude six times in chapter 2 alone (there is an estimated 6 other quotes in chapters 1 and 3), suggesting that they either knew each other and received this as a prophecy at the same time (much like Isaiah and Micah did in Old Testament times), or that Peter read or was at least aware of Jude's letter and used some of the latter's material in writing this one. Either way, it's a powerful passage that culminates with a quote of Proverbs 26:11 (that Jude *didn't* do): "as a dog returns to its vomit, so fools repeat their folly."

November 5, OT
Daniel 4:1-37; 2 Kings 25:27-30; Jeremiah 52:31-34
Nebuchadnezzar's Dream of a Tree; Jehoiachin's Release

When we last read from Daniel, more than a month ago, we left off after Daniel's three Hebrew friends were thrown into the fiery furnace, only to be rescued by an angel of God. Nebuchadnezzar, the king, praised the God "of Shadrach, Meshach and Abednego" (Daniel 3:28) and decreed that no one could say anything against their God. He promoted the three men to high positions in Babylon, thus lifting them to Daniel's level in his kingdom. It would be, however, the last time we ever read about Daniel's friends.

Some years later, between the 27th and 37th year of the Exile, the king has another dream that requires Daniel's interpretation. The first 18 verses of chapter 4 are one long quote of Nebuchadnezzar, first praising the Most High God (4:2-3), then explaining how his dream had terrified him (4:4-5), and falling back on his pagan roots by identifying Daniel by his Babylonian name, Belteshazzar, the "name of my god and the spirit of the holy gods is in him" (4:8). Thus, the king was still a pagan at heart and had not truly converted to belief in the one true God, despite his early praises. The dream is then described (4:13-18), with his vision of a giant tree that he's told to cut down.

Daniel then interprets the dream, and it's not good news for Nebuchadnezzar. He tells Nebuchadnezzar that it is a decree from the Most High against the king, that the *king* is that tree that gets cut down, and that he will be driven away to live with wild animals and eat grass like an ox (4:24-25). He was given an "out," though, if he would repent and believe in God as the one God over all the kingdoms of the earth (4:26-27).

Everything, including the king's turnaround, was fulfilled exactly as Daniel interpreted it: he was driven away from his throne, but he repented and the kingdom was restored to him (4:28-37), with the last

2 verses being a quote from Nebuchadnezzar, just as were the first 18 verses of the chapter.

In the 37th year of the Exile, Nebuchadnezzar died, and his son Amel-Marduk (sometimes Anglicized as Evil-merodach) became king of Babylon. There are no more details in the Bible about the death of the king that conquered virtually the entire civilized world of the time, and there's even less info about Amel-Marduk, but we do know one of the new king's first acts: releasing the former king of Judah, Jehoiachin, whose deportation to Babylon 37 years earlier marked the beginning of the 70-year Exile. The event is told at the very ends of the books of 2 Kings and Jeremiah, marking the final time we read from either of those books in this chronology.

November 5, NT
2 Peter 3:1-18
The Day of the Lord; Conclusion of Second Peter

More than one writer in the Bible, in both the Old and New Testaments, refer to the End Times, and particularly the Day of Judgment, as the Day of the Lord. In the case of Epistle writers Paul (in 2 Timothy, starting tomorrow) and Peter, an End Times prophecy makes up the final written words of both of them. Peter begins his final chapter by reminding his audience that this is his second letter (2 Peter 3:1) to them, and that the scriptures from prophets and Apostles should be read and followed as their guide (3:2), before launching into his End Times predictions.

Paul would later go into more detail about this, but it is Peter who first mentions that the last days will see mockers and scoffers (3:3) who cast doubt on God and His promises by denying scripture. He brings up the facts that the Earth was formed with water and was once destroyed with water, but it now reserved for fire (3:4). But lest anyone think that we can predict exactly when the End will come, Peter lets us know that God exists *outside of time*, in one of the Bible's most frequently misused verses (3:8). Among the abuses of Peter's statement that "...with the Lord a day is like a thousand years, and a thousand years like a day" is the erroneous but very commonly-held belief that the universe was created billions of years ago in a "big bang" and that life on earth evolved from lower forms over millions of years. Even if the person believing this believes God is responsible for the "old earth" creation, this is still a form of "theistic evolution" that is debunked by a *plain interpretation* of the Bible.

Besides, Peter isn't making a statement about Creation here, but about the timing of End Times events. He even quotes Jesus in saying that the day of the Lord will come "like a thief" (3:10), though without using the term "in the night". He then continues with more details about how the world will end (3:11-13). Near the end of the letter and just before his final greeting, he mentions Paul by name, referring to him as "our beloved brother" and even refers to "his letters" (3:15-16), something which Paul never does.

Neither Peter nor Paul's martyrdom is recorded in the Bible; this, despite the writing of several more books after their deaths. It's not even known for certain whose martyrdom occurred first, though the consensus opinion is that Paul was first, then Peter. But Peter's last written words come first, as he closes his second Epistle with a brief parting that mentioned no one else.

November 6, OT
Daniel 7:1-28
Eschatology 101

The study of the End Times is known as Eschatology. It's a fascinating field, but unlike any other aspect of Bible studies, it is based solely on what various prophets have predicted about the *future* - from their point of view. Given how long ago some of these predictions were made, fulfilled prophecies have since become historical events. The question then becomes "what about prophecies that have not yet been fulfilled?" There are also situations where the prophecies contain a lot of symbolism or metaphor, and it can be difficult or even impossible to determine exactly what's being predicted; and therefore, it can't be determined if the prophecies are pointing to events yet to come or events that have already occurred.

Such is especially the case for prophets of the Old Testament that made End Times predictions. All four of the "major" prophets (including Daniel), along with at least three of the "minor" prophets (particularly Zephaniah) have at least a few verses that deal with the ultimate destiny of the world and its people, aka the End Times.
 Among them, Daniel is unique in two ways: although all four major

prophets are quoted by Jesus at least once in the Gospels, only Daniel has any of his End Times prophecies quoted or directly referenced by the Lord. And Daniel is also more often referenced than any other prophet in the New Testament's treasure trove of End Times prophecy, the book of Revelation.

But one problem, and it's a big one, with Daniel's prophecies is in the interpretation of them in light of the disagreement over exactly when they were written. With a large number of scholars believing that the bulk of the Book of Daniel was written in the 2nd century B.C., as opposed to the mid 6th century B.C., prophecies like here in chapter 7 become largely history instead of prophecy. For a variety of reasons, some of which are explored in later chapters of Daniel, this chronology will continue to hold on to the traditional view of this being written in the early to mid 6th century B.C., during the Babylonian Exile. One of those reasons stems from this observation: Daniel's first 6 chapters (of which we have yet to read two of the chapters) consist mainly of history and dream interpretation, not pure prophecy. Chapter 7 is the beginning of the visions Daniel receives but is also the last chapter of the book to be written in Aramaic. Even though chapter 8 and beyond was written in Hebrew, and not Aramaic, the prophecies there actually dovetail perfectly with the prophecies in chapter 7, *indicating that they were the work of the same writer.* It's the same Hebrew dialect that was used for the oldest known manuscripts of the Torah, but all this proves is that copies of Daniel's original work were made at roughly the same time as nearly all the rest of the Hebrew Bible, or Masoretic Text, which we now know as the Old Testament. And yet, with the references to Nebuchadnezzar, Evil-merodach, and now Belshazzar (Daniel 7:1), which are clearly in the 6th century B.C., these passages are dated in the Exile when we knew Daniel to have lived.

The prophecies themselves found in this chapter are far more intricate and detailed than what can be commented on in one day's OT reading, as prophecies like this whole books devoted to them. But in brief, the vision in this chapter can be summed up like this: during the first year of Belshazzar (about 550 B.C.), king of Babylon, Daniel received a vision of 4 beasts coming up from the sea: a winged lion, a bear, a four-headed four-winged leopard, and a terrifying beast with 10 horns (7:2-7), followed by a "little horn" that destroys 3 of the original 10 horns, and appears as a human (7:8). All of the beasts were placed under the judgment of the "Ancient of Days;" the little horn was executed while the others were merely stripped of their authority (7:9-12). Following this, one like a "son of man" appeared, approached the throne of the Ancient of Days, and was granted dominion over all of the kingdoms of the earth (7:13-14).

What makes this prophecy an End Times prophecy is its interpretation, received by Daniel as part of the vision (7:15-27). The beasts are each of 4 world empires that most people interpret as Babylon, Persia, Greece, and then Rome, with the little horn being a form of revived Roman empire, something that has yet to occur. There are some, however, who interpret this as the Papacy, casting the *Pope* as the little horn that tries to "change set time and laws," such as the doctrine of holding worship on Sundays instead of the original Saturday (Sabbath) that is observed by the Jews. The Ten Kingdoms that spring from the fourth beast has been widely interpreted of late as the 10 members of the original European Union council.

November 6, NT
2 Timothy 1:1-18
A Farewell Message to a Trusted Pastor

In 1796, George Washington decided to not seek a third term as U.S. President, and instead created a document (published September 19, 1796, in Philadelphia) designed to say goodbye to the American people. It is known as Washington's Farewell Address. Although he had no idea that he would die only 2 years after leaving the Presidency, George Washington felt it necessary to make a proper and complete farewell, with advice and warnings and everything else that comes with an epic passing of the torch. Approximately 1,730 years earlier, Paul wrote his Second Epistle to Timothy, which many consider to be his farewell address. In 67 A.D., Nero's Rome had stepped up its persecution of Christians, and Paul's house arrest had been converted into a genuine prison sentence. It is plainly obvious that Paul knew that the end was near (which, in fact, it was later that year, though Paul likely thought he had a little more time than that, see reading for November 9), and that there had to be a passing of the torch in the young Christian Church to those who would carry it forward. Paul was either unaware of Peter's presence in Rome (if, in fact, Peter was actually in Rome at this time) or chose not to pass the Church to him or Peter's successor, Linus (see reading for November

9), so he addressed the letter to his most trusted compatriot, the young Timothy who he had written to just a year earlier.

Paul's opening greeting includes a prayer of thanks for Timothy's extended family, including his mother and grandmother (2 Timothy 1:5), and then goes right into a reminder to keep the flame going in terms of spreading the Gospel (1:6-7). It's after this that Paul starts sounding like someone saying goodbye, as he mentions being a prisoner and calls Timothy to "join [him] in suffering for the Gospel"(1:8-10). Paul's position of leadership in the Church is stated in Paul's identification of himself as a "preacher, Apostle, and teacher," meaning that he's been charged with proclaiming the Gospel message, living with and like Jesus, and instructing others in doing the same (1:11). Timothy is called on to do the same (1:12-14).

Despite Paul's incarceration, it was obvious that he was kept aware of news from around the Church. All was not well in some parts of the Church, as Paul mentions at the end of today's NT reading (1:15-18), a warning to Timothy to not conduct his churches the same way.

November 7, OT
Daniel 8:1-27
The Ram and the Goat

Another of Daniel's strange visions of the End Times comes next, two years after the first (Daniel 8:1), and it is so disturbing and so bizarre that Daniel himself has no idea what it all means, even after the angel Gabriel helps him with it (8:15-17). Despite the subject matter being *the same as in chapter 7,* the imagery is completely different (not to mention more graphic, more violent, and with some completely different numbers). This may well be why Daniel, known for being an expert interpreter of dreams, was left exhausted and sick after this particular vision (8:27).

The setting of the vision is near the Persian city of Susa (8:2), where Daniel sees a ram with 2 horns, one longer than the other, though the longer horn emerged after the shorter one (8:3-4). The angel Gabriel would later identify the ram as representing the kings of Media and Persia, the latter being one of the kingdoms represented by one of the four beasts in chapter 7 (8:20). This ram was attacked by a male goat coming from the west, distinguished by having one large horn (8:5-7).

Once the goat became "mighty," the large horn was broken but was then replaced by four smaller ones (8:8), one of which sprouted another, smaller horn that "grew exceedingly great" (8:9-10). This goat was identified as Greece by Gabriel (8:21-26), and the four horns and the Little Horn that replace the one that is broken represent four other, unnamed, kingdoms that appear after that. We know from history that the Roman Empire was the next major world empire after Greece, but the other empires are then not identified, not even by Gabriel. The fact that this is a prophecy of the End Times is made plain 3 times in the chapter (8:17, 8:19, 8:26), all as part of Gabriel's attempt to help Daniel interpret the vision.

About the only thing that isn't in any doubt is the tyrannical nature of the rule of the empire under the Little Horn (8:11-14). Jesus quotes this as part of the Olivet Discourse in Matthew 24 when He answers the Apostles' question about the End Times. This fact alone should dispel the notion that these prophecies were fulfilled during the time of the Jewish rebellion against Antiochus IV, led by the Maccabees, and that these prophecies refer to events yet to come even in our time.

November 7, NT
2 Timothy 2:1-26
Be a Strong and Unashamed Workman

Paul's words to Timothy in chapter 2 can be summed up in one phrase: *be strong.* Be strong in spite of hardships and imprisonment (2 Timothy 2:2-3, 2:9-10). Be strong in spite of the injustice of not being able to be the first to receive the fruits of your labor (2:6-7). Be strong even though there are rules that you did not make that must be followed (2:4-5). The trustworthy saying Paul uses to encourage Timothy in these matters (2:11-13) is not a known quote from any other part of Scriptures such as a Psalm or a prophet but it neatly sums up the message Paul is trying to express.

Most of the rest of the chapter seems to center on this idea of not being "quarrelsome" and about how "irreverent babble" leads to "ungodliness" (2:14, 2:16). At the time Paul wrote this, the Church was still young and didn't have a unified structure or liturgy. The various churches, of which Timothy was Pastor to one, still had their different factions whose main differences had to do with how much, if any, of the Jewish laws and customs were still applicable. When applied to the Church of today, it's clear that Paul's advice to Timothy about avoiding quarrel and division is just as relevant today as then.

The bickering and infighting that goes on between the denominations, and particularly between Catholics and the entire rest of the Church, is an absolute scandal. If every church would simply follow the advice given here (particularly 2:14-26), the Church would see a real revival, a real resurgence, and real growth of the Body of Christ again.

November 8, OT
Daniel 5:1-31
The Handwriting on the Wall

The final mention of Belshazzar in Daniel comes a couple of chapters prior to the two prophecies we just read about in chapters 7 and 8. Here, we learn of a great feast held by the king, using some of the gold and silver stolen by Nebuchadnezzar (Belshazzar's great-grandfather) from the Temple in Jerusalem (Daniel 5:2-3). It was a great pagan party. But then, a frightening vision appeared: an apparition of a hand wrote an inscription on the wall of the palace, and no one in the king's court could interpret its meaning (5:5-9). Even the queen had no idea what it meant, but she did have an idea for who should be asked - Daniel, who had previously interpreted things for Nebuchadnezzar (5:10-12).

Belshazzar then called Daniel to the palace and offered him a position ("third ruler") in the kingdom is he could interpret the writing on the wall (5:13-16). Daniel's response was to tell the king to "keep it" (5:17) but that he would interpret it anyway. Daniel's ability to interpret the writing stems from the fact that it was written in Daniel's native language of Aramaic, but he first reminds the king about his great-grandfather's turnaround to belief in the one, true God, which Belshazzar has not yet done (5:18-23). The inscription read "Mene, Mene, Tekel, Upharsin." The meaning is spelled out as being "the days of the Babylonian kingdom are numbered, you [Belshazzar] have been weighed and have come up short, and the kingdom has been divided and given to the Medes and Persians" (5:25-28). Belshazzar accepts this and elevates Daniel to third ruler (5:29). But Belshazzar is killed that same night (5:30) and is succeeded by a Mede named Darius (5:31)...

...who, according to many historians, never existed. More about this tomorrow.

November 8, NT
2 Timothy 3:1-4:8
How To Deal With the Difficult Times to Come

Paul's last written words before making final greetings make up a great End Times prophecy. Besides predicting what the future would be like (including two sections that sound frighteningly like *today*), Paul gives what many Bible-believing Christians believe to be his number one piece of advice.

Paul makes a vivid description of the difficult times coming in the "last days" (2 Timothy 3:1), and it is stunning to read how much this describes the people of today (3:2-5). Paul's description is used as a comparison with two people named Jannes and Jambres, magicians in the Pharoah's court when Moses and Aaron confronted them just prior to the Exodus (3:6-9), but the comparison is for the purpose of warning about people in the future. Just how close to the End Times we really are can be realized by reading these descriptions and asking yourself how closely this describes today's world versus the world of your parents or grandparents. Peter mentioned these kinds of people too, in his Second Epistle, so God obviously found it important to give both of these leaders of the early Church the same prophecy. These people would someday not "listen to sound doctrine" (4:3-4) and would turn instead to myths. Does that not sound exactly like the New Age movement and/or the fringe denominations that focus their attention too narrowly on just one book or passage in the Bible? Or, worse yet, those that denounce the Bible as a book of myths written by men and not God?

The Lord's solution to all these problems is embedded within Paul's description of the End Times. His direct advice to Timothy applies to all preachers: stick to the teachings given previously by Paul, endure the sufferings and persecutions (3:10-14), and be ready "in season and out" to tell the Truth with patience (4:2). But most of all, and this applies to everyone (not just ministers), preach the word (4:2a) knowing that "ALL Scripture is inspired by God and is profitable for teaching, for reproof, for correction, for training in righteousness (3:16, NASB). This one piece of advice - to live and preach according to what we now call the Bible - is the single most important thing to remember. When Paul wrote this, Scriptures consisted only of what we now have as the Old Testament, or Hebrew Bible. He may or may not have known that his letters and those of others, along with 4 detailed biographies of Jesus (the Gospels, of which 1 or 2 had been written by this time) would be compiled into a New Testament. But he did say "ALL," and he knew he had to get this word to Timothy, partly because he knew his own time was almost up (4:6-8), making the oft-quoted passage that he has "fought the good fight, finished the course, ...kept the faith." This would be Paul's last words of prophecy or instruction, but he wasn't quite finished with the letter….

November 9, OT
Daniel 9:1-27
As the Exile Ends; The Prophecy of Seventy Weeks

When recorded history *outside* of the Bible seems not to jibe with events and dates *inside* the Bible, what is one supposed to do? Bible-believing Christians (and, in fact, all people) are called to view the Bible as the Word of God, inspired into about 40 writers over a 1500-year period, inerrant in its original manuscripts, and completely true in all matters of doctrine. Some, like me, take all events as being historically true as well, just as other Young Earth Creationists do.
 The claim from non-believers is that some things in the Bible (such as the Creation) have actually been disproved by scientific discovery. **This is not possible** if Genesis is part of the inspired Word of God!
 In other words, and without getting into a potentially lengthy treatise on Biblical Apologetics, wherever the Bible and extra-Biblical sources differ or even contradict each other, it's the *Bible* and not the other sources that should be believed as Truth, and other sources of information should be interpreted as being adapted into it, not the other way around.

Sometimes, this is easy to do, but other times (such as here in Daniel) it can be rather difficult, reconciling the Bible with recorded history outside of it. At the end of yesterday's OT reading, the beginning of today's, and portions of tomorrow's as well, Daniel writes about Belshazzar's successor as ruler over Babylon: Darius, from Media (Daniel 9:1). It's mentioned in passing, only to give a timeline of perspective to the prophecies in this chapter through chapter 12, along with the last major event in Daniel's life, told in chapter 6 (tomorrow).

It's also used to set up the prayer of Daniel that takes up over half of this chapter, in response to his discovery of the writings of Jeremiah, showing that the Exile would end after 70 years (9:2-19). This event coming up very soon, and the hopeful tone of the prayer is tempered by Daniel's contrition in admitting that the Jewish people got what they deserved. There's just one problem - there is no historic record of a man named Darius the Mede outside the Bible. Everyone else - from Belshazzar to Cyrus of Persia (who is listed in most places as Belshazzar's successor) to Daniel himself is mentioned in some historical account outside the Bible. So accurate are some of these extra-Biblical accounts that we can positively date much of the Old Testament because of its relation to the known date of the fall of Babylon - October 13, 539 B.C. But without Darius the Mede, how do we reconcile the Bible with known history?

There are several solutions to this, though we don't know which one, if any, is truly correct. One thing to keep in mind is that the Persians and Medes were allies, and there would later come a man named Darius who was a Persian (a later king of Persia, in fact), and is well known in history. The problem with the assumption of Darius the Persian and Darius the Mede being the same man is that this messes up the timeline rather badly. Another possible solution comes from an appointee of King Cyrus, named Gubaru, a Mede, who was made regional governor at this time over the area where Daniel lived.

Gubaru was born in 601 B.C. and would have, thus, been 62 years of age when Daniel first mentions the man, the exact age Daniel puts forth. The problem here is that the name Gubaru is never mentioned in the Bible, and simply using the name Darius for Gubaru doesn't make sense in light of the frequent use of the full title "King Darius" in Daniel and elsewhere. A third possibility, though the least likely, is that the word "darius" is also a title, much like referring to someone as "Governor" or, perhaps, "Commander". The problem with this solution is similar to the second one above, that several places (notably in Daniel 6, tomorrow) feature the full title "King Darius" where Darius cannot be anyone but a person, and his title is king.

Going on the assumption that original manuscripts were inerrant in their inspiration from God, as was all of the Bible, and further that Daniel was actually written by the prophet Daniel in the 6th century during and just after the Exile, this chronology believes that Darius the Mede refers to the man Gubaru, who may have gone by the name

Darius when Persia conquered Babylon, was appointed as a regional governor before the formal arrival of Cyrus, and would have thus acted as a king even if his title didn't formally bear this out. He may never have mentioned his real name to the Exiles, and even gets mentioned by his adopted name of Darius by an angel when giving another prophecy of the End Times to Daniel in the reading for November 16 (in Daniel 10).

And so, the next such prophecy after the quick fulfillment of the "Handwriting on the Wall" prophecy is among the Old Testament's most mysterious, because of its use of numbers, notably the number 70. Because of its partial fulfillment, it is considered a foundational prophecy of Eschatology, and in particular, Dispensationalism. Again, without going into a lengthy explanation, Dispensationalism is the belief that God has divided up human history into eras or stages that reveal Himself and His plan of salvation. Or, in other words, salvation history as shown in the Bible can be divided up into separate "dispensations" that can be seen in all of history as well as prophecies of the future. Here in Daniel 9, a brief 4-verse passage (9:24-27) at the end of the chapter spells out dispensations for centuries to come.

Daniel gets assistance from the angel Gabriel again (9:20-23) in declaring that there will be "seventy weeks" for the Jewish people to "finish the transgression, to make an end of sin" (9:24). Seventy weeks, if interpreted as regular 7-day weeks, would only be a little over one year, so it is obvious that something else is meant by this. And, in fact, the next verses clarify this: from the decree to restore Jerusalem to the coming of the Messiah is "seven weeks and sixty-two weeks" (9:25). Seven weeks of years would be 49 years, which is exactly the length of time it took, as recorded in Ezra and Nehemiah, for the Jews to return to Jerusalem and rebuild a Temple. The sixty-two additional weeks would be 434 years which brings us to the time of Christ, the Messiah. Verse 26 then prophesies the "cutting off" of that Messiah, which refers to Jesus' Crucifixion… but then in the same verse is a reference to a "prince who is to come [who] will destroy the city and the sanctuary" (9:26). The latter event would refer to Rome and the destruction of the Temple in 70 A.D. But this "prince" that is referred to in verse 26 takes on a completely different characteristic in verse 27.

The last verse of this prophecy is the only part of it that is not yet fulfilled, because it speaks of someone powerful enough to "make a firm covenant with the many for one week," a seven year period known as the Tribulation (9:27). The reference in that verse to the Tribulation being divided into 2 parts fits perfectly with other prophecies in both the Old and New Testaments, including those made by Jesus, of an Antichrist who will rule the world, make this covenant, but break it by setting up the "abomination of desolation". What is all means is that we are living between Daniel's 69th week and his 70th, and that the yet-to-come 70th marks the beginning of the Apocalypse. This period, or dispensation, is the Church Age, which will come to an end when that Tribulation period begins.

November 9, NT
2 Timothy 4:9-22
End of an Era

The last 14 verses of Paul's last chapter of written Word is notable for not containing any new prophecy, doctrine, or instruction, and only includes a few tidbits of historical note. But it does mark a very important "end of an era". Within a year of writing this letter, both Paul and then Peter would be martyred in Rome, and the Church would then have to be officially passed along to Timothy (by Paul) Linus (by Peter), and the rest of the "brethren". Paul mentions more people by name in this final parting than in any other place besides his Epistle to the Romans, and not all of them are mentioned for good reasons. He starts by asking Timothy to "make every effort to come to me soon" (2 Timothy 4:9), indicating Paul's belief that he would, in fact, live long enough for this to happen even though he knew the end was near. Paul laments the departures of Demas, Crescens, and Titus, the latter being the addressee of his Epistle, and notes only the presence of Luke (4:10-11) who, at this time, would have been just starting to write the Gospel (and then Acts) that bears his name. Also mentioned is Mark, but it is not known if this is the same John-Mark who wrote that Gospel (assisted by Peter) or some other Mark.

Paul goes on to ask for the return of some of his belongings, and gives Timothy warnings to avoid a certain few people who "did me much harm" (4:13-15). But he also thanks the Lord who "stood with me and strengthened me" throughout his ministry, which was focussed on the Gentiles (4:16-18). He then brings everything to a close, asking Timothy once again to come, adding "before winter" (4:20) to mark the urgency of the visit. Two names among those mentioned in a positive light at the end stand out as significant: Priscilla (Prisca in some translations), and Linus. Linus is significant because of the belief in the Catholic Church that he became the second Pope after Peter's martyrdom. Linus was not a common name, and he is mentioned as being in Rome as was Paul, so it is very likely that Linus here refers to that same person. Priscilla is significant for a reason that will be explained in tomorrow's NT reading.

And so the era of Peter and Paul came to an end less than a year later; Paul, by beheading, and Peter, by crucifixion upside down. But with the end of one era, another then began.

November 10, OT
Daniel 6:1-28; Ezra 1:1-4; 2 Chronicles 36:22-23
Daniel in the Lion's Den; Cyrus Lets the Israelites Return

While the king (Cyrus) was trying to set up a government and a society in Babylon, we open today's OT reading with the governor (Darius) appointing "satraps" including Daniel over the kingdom. These would be sub-governors who would each rule over a small region. Apparently, Daniel was pretty good at politics, and his fellow satraps became jealous (Daniel 6:1-5), jealous enough to plot his demise by conspiring with Darius to enact a law that Daniel would be forced to break (6:6-9). The penalty? Being thrown into the lion's' den where death was assured.

Daniel heard about the new law, and prayed to God about it (6:10). His prayers were reported to Darius in violation of that law, and the conspirators then pointed out that it was Daniel who was violating the law (6:11-13). This bothered Darius (referred to as "the king" throughout the chapter, when he was, in fact, the governor) very much, and he made an effort to deliver Daniel from this, but failed (6:14-15). When it came time to give the order, he told Daniel that God would rescue him (6:16). The rest of the familiar story went as expected: Daniel was sealed in the lion's den but was found unharmed the next day, and Darius had Daniel's accusers thrown into the den where they were immediately consumed (6:17-24).

The use of the name Darius, unknown to history outside of the Bible, including its pairing with the title of king (i.e. King Darius) has led many scholars to believe this to be a fictitious story, written in the

second century B.C. as possibly a teaching tool for children. The apocryphal additions to Daniel found in Catholic Bibles are believed to be part of the same set of stories. However, the last 4 verses of Daniel 6, along with the 2 brief readings that follow from Ezra and 2 Chronicles, seem to clarify things, and make the story more credible.
 You see, the end of the Babylonian Empire was prophesied many times by many prophets, most notably Jeremiah, and every man of God knew exactly when it would occur, too. It made sense that the conquering Persians and Medes would set up a system of city-states very much like they had done throughout Asia Minor. Each city-state would have a governor who represented the king and would, for all intents and purposes, *be* the king for that region. Thus, references to "King Darius" simply were made to note his place in the new governmental system. He had the same power as the king, and therefore was able to write and enforce laws and issue decrees, and though he is never mentioned in the Bible by his (presumed) name of Gubaru, he was a real person separate and distinct from Cyrus the Persian, who *is* mentioned by name.

It is obvious that both Darius/Gubaru and Cyrus were believers in God, as Darius issued a decree declaring the God of Daniel as the one, true God (6:25-27), and Daniel lived on during the reigns of both of them (6:28). The fact that they "reigned" at the same time is another clue that Darius was the local ruler while Cyrus was the king. Cyrus then made another, much bigger, and much more important declaration: the Exiles were told they could go back to Jerusalem and rebuild the Temple. **The Exile was over**, as prophesied. It is the first thing told in the book of Ezra and the last thing told in the Chronicles, and they're read in this order only because of the order in which the two scrolls would have been written - and both by the same Ezra that we'll learn more about in tomorrow's OT reading.

November 10, NT
Hebrews 1:1-14
An Epistle to Jerusalem

At the same time as Peter and Paul were writing their final Epistles to the Church, Jewish Christians living in the very city where Jesus was crucified were embroiled, along with their more orthodox brethren, in a revolt against their Roman oppressors. Rome would eventually crack down on the rebellious Jews, destroy the Temple, and most of the rest of the city of Jerusalem. The siege of the city started in 66 A.D. and lasted until the final destruction in 70 A.D. Some time during this period, an Epistle was written to the Jews there as a means of both encouragement (to the Jewish Christians) and evangelization (to the unconverted Jews). That Epistle is known as the Letter to the Hebrews.

The exact date the letter was written is not known, nor is the location from which it was written. In one of the few cases where this chronology breaks from tradition, the long-held belief that Paul wrote this Epistle is dismissed. Though the style is similar to Paul's, there are many things that debunk the notion that this is another of his Epistles. For one, and unlike *every* other letter of Paul's, there is no identification of himself as the writer anywhere in the letter. Other issues include the different theological focus of the letter, even when compared to his other Epistle to a largely Jewish audience (Romans). These doubts date all the way back to the 2nd century, even though Jerome's translation of the Bible into Latin in 400 A.D. (the "Vulgate") gives this Epistle the title of "Paul's Epistle to the Hebrews". Other names that have been suggested as this letter's author include Clement (3rd Pope), Barnabas, Apollos, and even Luke, but each of these is easily dismissed (though each for different reasons). But one intriguing suggestion has been made that this chronology has adopted: an increasing number of scholars attribute the Epistle to the Hebrews to Priscilla, a woman addressed by Paul in more than one of his letters. It would have been necessary in the society of the day for a female writer, particularly a writer whose focus was Christian theology, to remain anonymous. All the way up to even the 20th century, many women authors wrote under pen names to hide their gender from their audiences, and so it is reasonable to conclude that the lack of known authorship for this Epistle is a case of deliberate censorship, in order to protect the letter and make sure it got to its intended audience.

As for date and location, some scholars place this letter as early as 63 A.D. while Paul was still alive in Rome, while others date this as late as the late 70s. However, this chronology will assume that it was written, or at least completed, some time between the death of Paul and the destruction of Jerusalem, thus putting it somewhere in 68 or 69 A.D. Paul's reference to Priscilla, if she is indeed the author, makes it likely that it was written in Rome just as were Paul's letters.

And so begins one of the greatest works in the field of Christology, a vivid picture of Jesus Christ in all of his many attributes, and quoting or referencing more of the Old Testament (Hebrew Bible) than any other work in the New Testament except for Paul's letter to the Romans. In the first chapter alone, focussing on how the Son was God's "final Word" spoken to us (Hebrews 1:1-2), she quotes 5 different Psalms, and portions of 2 Samuel, 1 Chronicles, and Deuteronomy. On the latter point, it is noted that this Epistle was found among the Dead Sea Scrolls, and that the quote of Deuteronomy 32:43 found in Hebrews 1:6 is word-for-word exactly the same as the Septuagint version of that part of the Torah.

November 11, OT
Ezra 1:5-2:20
A New Beginning

Ezra was a priest, scribe, musician, historian, and Psalmist, and writer of two major two-part scrolls in what is now our Old Testament. The obvious one is the one that bears his name, which we started reading yesterday and continue today. But the books of Ezra and Nehemiah (which we start reading tomorrow) were actually *both* written by Ezra and were originally part of the same scroll. In addition, it is believed (though not known for certain) that this same Ezra wrote the just-completed book of history known as the Chronicles, which later got divided into the two parts that we now know as 1st and 2nd Chronicles in the Bible. Ezra is revered by both Jews and Christians today; he is credited with establishing the "Great Assembly," the forerunner of the Sanhedrin; and he is credited by Christians as having laid down the largest portion of Old Testament history in the Bible.

Despite his apparent emphasis on putting things into chronological order (thus, the Chronicles), the books of Ezra and Nehemiah aren't laid down in the order of events. Nevertheless, our first readings from Ezra do start at the beginning of the book while Nehemiah is started tomorrow in its 7th chapter for reasons that will become apparent then. Today's reading centers on two parts of the "new beginning" for the Jewish people: the return of 5,400 stolen items from the Temple which had been carried away by Nebuchadnezzar when Jerusalem was destroyed (Ezra 1:5-11), and a census of men returning to Jerusalem from several families that had been exiled (2:1-20). As mentioned back in January when we first started reading the Chronicles, these lists of names and family trees may make for boring reading, but are an essential part of what it means to understand God's salvation history.

November 11, NT
Hebrews 2:1-4:13
Focus on the Lord

The entire Bible has the Lord as its focus; the expression is generally that everything "points to the Lord" in both the Old and New Testaments. Of course, the New Testament gives us the details on the life of Jesus, and the Epistles and other writings that follow Jesus' time on earth then focus on how His life, death, and resurrection changed everything for everyone on earth. In the early Church, and particularly the Jewish Christians in Jerusalem where it all began, people needed some reminding. They needed to be told, with more repetition, how Jesus accomplished this work and how we must keep our focus on the Lord going forward.

The writer of Hebrews (Priscilla, as is believed here) starts today's 3-chapter reading with a dense 4-verse summary of why we must pay attention, maintaining our focus (Hebrews 2:1-4) on Jesus' salvation of those who believe. She explains at length how Jesus was made a human, not an angel (2:5-18), and was thus one of us, being both fully God and fully man, one of the major doctrines of Christianity. Then, in perfectly logical succession, she goes on to note that Jesus was greater than Moses (3:1-6). Though both were men, it was Jesus who became our great High Priest, and a great comparison is made to show how He is above Moses and the angels too. The comparison continues as a warning against unbelief (3:7-19). Continuing to use even more references in chapter 4 to Moses, and then Joshua, as leaders of the Hebrew people, Priscilla quotes or references Psalm 8:4-6, Psalm 22:22, Isaiah 8:17-18, Numbers 12:7, Psalm 95:7-11 (twice), and Genesis 2:2, all known passages to the Hebrew people, to make the point about how different the new leadership of Jesus is compared to that of Moses (in particular), the most revered figure in all of Judaism.

November 12, OT
Nehemiah 7:4-25
The Exiles Returning to Jerusalem

Nehemiah, like Ezra, is another important figure in post-Exile history, and is the central figure of the Biblical book that bears his name (though it was written as the second half of a scroll by Ezra). It contains much of the same history as Ezra and also explains the chronology of events somewhat better than in Ezra itself. It is believed that Nehemiah went to Judah before Ezra did, though they both eventually resided there, and that he is more directly responsible for the rebuilding of the walls of Jerusalem. Noticeable in the lists of people returning to Jerusalem (yesterday in Ezra, today in Nehemiah 7:4-25, nearly identical) is the absence of either men. When Cyrus proclaimed the return of the Jewish people to their homeland, neither Ezra nor Nehemiah were among the first wave of people to go - they waited until Artaxerxes, one of Cyrus' descendants, later took the throne.

November 12, NT
Hebrews 4:14-6:20
Jesus, The Promised Great High Priest

The themes of Jesus as being our "Great High Priest" as well as His being promised by God are combined in this frequently-quoted passage from the Epistle to the Hebrews. The whole concept of being a High Priest is defined and described to show how Jesus became and is, for us, the *ultimate* such example (Hebrews 4:14-5:10). Twice in this passage, the name of an obscure figure who is mentioned only twice in the Old Testament, is brought up as a point of comparison: Jesus' status as High Priest is part of the "order of Melchizedek, and Priscilla uses two Psalms (Psalm 2:7 and 110:4, the latter being one of the two places that mention Melchizedek in the OT) to make the point. She would later use the connection between Melchizedek and Abraham from Genesis 22 to show how this is the fulfillment of a promise - a promise we now know as the Abrahamic Covenant (Hebrews 6:13-20).

In between, another warning against "falling away" is made, in an appeal to become more mature in faith, and to gain real understanding of this new salvation (5:11-6:12).

November 13, OT
Ezra 2:21-70
More Details of the Census of the Returned

When we read of the "returned," that is, the men of various position and rank returning to Jerusalem from their Babylonian Exile, it almost sounds like something you would see in a science fiction movie. But, the returned simply refers to the men, all ordinary people like you and me, whose families spent as many as 70 years hundreds of miles from their original homes as part of a captivity foretold by numerous prophets of God. Today's OT reading consists of a continuation of a list of those who returned, broken down not only by family, but also by position and rank: priests, Levites, musicians, and Temple gatekeepers and servants, among others. In addition, more detail is given about their possessions: their slaves, other singers, horses, camels, and donkeys. The number of people and animals that made this trek was well into the tens of thousands.

November 13, NT
Hebrews 7:1-9:22
Jesus' Priesthood, The Ultimate Sacrifice

Besides being the ultimate example of High Priest (see yesterday's NT reading), Jesus and the mysterious Old Testament figure of Melchizedek share a number of other things in common, and this becomes the focus of the first chapter of today's almost-3 chapter reading. Priscilla, writer of this Epistle, points out that Melchizedek was "without genealogy," and that we don't know his birth and death dates, thus resembling the Son of God, and is therefore a "priest forever" (Hebrews 7:2-3). Melchizedek, like Jesus, did not descend from Levi (or course, he lived well before Israel and Levi), yet collected a tithe from Abraham and the other Israelites as would a High Priest (7:4-10). The whole point of the section is brought out with the statement that when the "order" of the priesthood changed, so the Law must change also; that Jesus is the guarantor of a new, better covenant, supplanting the old (7:11-22). This would have been well understood by the Jewish readers of this Epistle. Jesus' resurrection then gave Him something that no other priest could attain: a permanent priesthood (7:23-24) that meets everyone's needs. God still requires a sacrifice for sin; Jesus, the High Priest of the New Covenant thus became the ultimate such sacrifice too (7:25-8:13).

Jesus has made the old Law obsolete, and therefore the old form of worship obsolete. Priscilla states that we used to have an earthly tabernacle with strict regulations for worship (9:1-7), where only the High Priest, and only with blood, and only once a year, would enter. The old way of worship thus applied only until that blood was replaced by the Blood of Christ, brought in by the new High Priest himself (9:8-22). The doctrine of substitutionary atonement is made more clear here than perhaps anywhere else in the New Testament.

November 14, OT
Nehemiah 7:26-73a
More Details of the Census of the Returned

Today's OT reading is almost an echo of yesterday's from Ezra, and for good reason: Ezra wrote both passages, one was merely part of the same scroll as the other. Notable in the census data in both places is the similarity in style between these lists and similar lists presented in First Chronicles, further reinforcing the idea that these were all written by Ezra. The note at the end says that the reading ends with verse 73a, meaning the first half of that verse. In most Bibles, reading all the way through verse 73 shows that 73b opens a new section where Ezra reads the Law in the seventh month. This chronology believes this event to have happened after several other events occurred, as chronicled (pardon the pun) elsewhere in Ezra, Nehemiah, and the works of three prophets: Daniel, Zechariah, and Haggai.

November 14, NT
Hebrews 9:23-10:18
Once And For All, and No Purgatory

The NT readings from the last 4 days from Hebrews has followed a logical pattern that most readers will notice. Each day's reading expands upon the main point from the previous day, and then leads up to yet another main point that would make the most sense to a Rabbinical Jew; this, too, if you have read the Old Testament readings up to this point. Yesterday's reading, for instance, led up to the idea that Jesus' sacrifice on the Cross was the ultimate substitutionary sacrifice, replacing all of the former laws regarding Temple worship and sacrifice. Today expands on that, by first emphasizing that the sanctuary entered by Jesus was not made by human hands, not a copy of the true sanctuary as was The Temple in Jerusalem (which still stood at this time, which gives further credibility to the notion that this Epistle was written before 70 A.D.), but heaven itself, in God's presence (Hebrews 9:23-24). Therefore, unlike the Temple sacrifices made annually by the High Priest, Christ didn't have to and doesn't have to suffer over and over again, repeating this sacrifice, but rather, once and for all, doing away with sin by sacrificing himself (9:25-28).

An important doctrine against the notion of a Purgatory or the existence of ghosts or spirits of the dead is buried in this section: in 9:27, the comparison is made with Jesus that "just as people are destined to *die once*, and after that to face judgment..." (9:27, NIV). The statement is there to emphasize Jesus' one time sacrifice for all, but it is deeper than even that. The notion of an afterlife was held only by some Jews, not all, and those that did believe in a heaven and a hell often also believed in an additional place where some dead resided. The place, called Purgatory by Catholics, is never named in the Bible, and is only alluded to in a few places in the Bible. Most notable is the apocryphal 2 Maccabees 12:46, where it says that the dead may be freed from sin. A couple of misinterpreted passages in Matthew, Luke, and even Revelation seem to say that there "must be" such a place, but these are misinterpretations and suppositions. The great reformer Martin Luther caught on to this apparent inconsistency and condemned the Church for its practices related to this supposed Purgatory in his 95 Theses: the sale of "indulgences" so that the dead imprisoned in Purgatory could be freed. This implies the exact kind of sacrifices that Priscilla, writer of Hebrews, condemns - once you have died, you have either paid for you sins in full and go to heaven (possible only through the grace of God through the ONE TIME sacrifice of Jesus Christ) or you haven't and you go instead to hell. There is no intermediate step or afterlife prison - as this verse says, you die and then you are judged.

All this is listed as the fulfillment of a prophecy in Jeremiah, as explained in Hebrews 10:1-18, quoting Jeremiah 31:33-34 along the way.

November 15, OT
Ezra 3:1-13; Psalm 92:1-15; Psalm 126:1-6
Restoration Begins

In the overall chronology of events, it is fairly well known that Ezra didn't, himself, return to Judah with the Exiles until nearly 80 years had passed. During Ezra's continued time in Babylon (which came under Persian rule), he would have had plenty of time to write both scrolls of The Chronicles, and he most likely received some news about the goings-on in Jerusalem over that period. He may have started the book that bears his name and/or the book of Nehemiah as well, but he didn't finish either work until after he arrived in Jerusalem. When he did go there, he found a town that had been largely rebuilt. What he never saw with his own eyes was the ghost town it had become during the Exile.

Some 50,000 Exiles did (not all at once), and the first wave of them would have found a city in utter ruin, uninhabited, and virtually uninhabitable. Other parts of Judah were largely still populated because they hadn't been deported, but the capital city, which accounted for about a third of the population, was almost completely gone. The people of Judah in Babylon discovered people from other tribes of Israel, deported in the Assyrian Exile too, before the Assyrians were conquered by Nebuchadnezzar. Yet for all of this, their first major act upon their return wasn't the rebuilding of the outer walls or the residence buildings, but instead they built an altar (Ezra 3:2) in order to resume worship ceremonies according to the Law of Moses (3:1-3). They were a united people, though they had no king; they were a people without a leader, but they had God, and with the green light from King Cyrus of Persia, they laid the foundation for a new Temple and began construction (3:7-13). It was a time of great joy despite the desolation they found when they first arrived. Two joyful Psalms of thanksgiving were also written at this time, of unknown authorship (Psalms 92 and 126).

November 15, NT
Hebrews 10:19-39
Persevering in the Lord

The Jewish nature of this Epistle's audience is never more evident than when direct comparisons are made between significant parts of the Law and Jesus Christ. In the first part of today's NT reading, Jesus'

Body becomes the metaphor for the veil or curtain that separated the Holy of Holies from the rest of the Temple (Hebrews 10:19-20). Building on that metaphor, Jesus' status as High Priest is used to give the main emphasis scattered through several parts of the reading: that since we have the ability to approach God through Jesus, draw near Him and keep on drawing near Him, persevering in our faith (10:21-23, 10:35-39). The point is made using quotes from Isaiah 26:20 and Habakkuk 2:3-4, both of whom would have been quite familiar to the Jews.

In between are two power pieces of advice for the believer, also related to the idea of perseverance: many believers fall away from their local congregations by not "going to church," that is, not worshipping in fellowship with others, "giving up" on fellow believers for whatever reason. Priscilla says here to not do that; to NOT give up "meeting together" (10:24-25), which was obviously a problem then just as today. The other idea related to perseverance is a warning about the reality of hell: that we need to particularly not do deliberate sin in the face of receiving the knowledge of Truth - that is, once we become believers, we don't have any more excuse for sin, in fact it is more of an issue for the believer than for the unbeliever (10:26-31). But, perseverance will keep us from falling into the hands of the Lord in this particular way.

November 16, OT
Daniel 10:1-11:35
The Shape Of Things to Come, Part One

Prophecy, by its very nature, involves prediction of future events. Some prophecies involved events in the prophet's immediate, or at least near, future. Others range anywhere from decades to centuries in the prophet's future. Daniel's last 3 chapters, divided up into 2 readings, cover 2 broad periods of future events - to the prophet Daniel, anyway. The split isn't at the "halfway point" of the 3 chapters, but rather, it is at the point where Daniel's prophecies of his future change from fulfilled prophecies (today) to End Times prophecies, yet to be fulfilled (tomorrow).

Daniel had already, by this point, made predictions concerning his immediate and near future (chapters 7 and 8) along with End Times prophecies (chapter 9). Chapters 10 and most of 11 concern the same subject matter as chapters 7 and 8 - the future of the Persian, then Greek, and then Roman empires, including the coming of a Messiah during that last period. In many ways, it's written in a way that is a simultaneously more detailed yet more vague version of the earlier prophecies. These last 3 chapters make for some of the Bible's most difficult reading. Yet, scholars are in remarkable agreement on the interpretation of the prophecies found here. One of the easier-to-read translations, such as the New Living Translation, is helpful here to make sense of it.

One of the most remarkable things about this prophecy is its fulfillment. Despite never once mentioning any names of individuals, kings, or even nations (except for vague mentions of being in the "north" or the "south", etc.), every single detail found in this reading can be linked to a person or nation, and it can be noted as 100% fulfilled. As there is much more to the reading than what will fit in a commentary in a one-year reading plan, I invite you to check out https://www.wake-up.org/end-times-prophecy/daniel-prophecy/daniel-101-1135-israels-prophetic-destiny.html and similar websites that do an excellent job tying prophecies to world events. Of course, this can't yet be said to be the case with prophecies that have not yet been fulfilled...

November 16, NT
Hebrews 11:1-16
Heroes of the Faith, Part One

In an odd coincidence, both the Old and New Testament readings for today are parts one of two. Here in the Epistle to the Hebrews, we begin a two-part section commonly called the Heroes of the Faith, containing as it does the most quoted verse from Hebrews, in verse 1. Before embarking on a most remarkable list of Old Testament heroes to look up to, we get a clear definition of faith itself: the assurance of things hoped for, the conviction of things not seen (Hebrews 11:1). This simple statement is as beautiful as it borders on being obvious. When coupled with other statements, in this Epistle and elsewhere, about how faith is a gift from God, it reinforces just how important faith really is.

The Jewish and Jewish-Christian audience of this Epistle would have been very interested in examples from their history to show where faith has been rewarded, and that's exactly what Priscilla, presumed writer of Hebrews, serves up here. Heroes mentioned here include Abel (11:4), Enoch (11:5-6), Noah (11:7), Abraham (11:8-10), along with Sarah (11:11-12). Before continuing with more heroes and what they accomplished "by faith," it is explained that none of these people lived to see the promise from God, that is, the reward for their faith, yet they nevertheless remained faithful (11:13-16).

November 17, OT
Daniel 11:36-12:13
The Shape Of Things to Come, Part Two (Conclusion of Daniel)

Pretty much any prophecy that hasn't yet come to pass would have to either be an End Times prophecy or be a false prophecy, and the only way in which a prophecy can be proven false is if it becomes *no longer possible* for it to ever be fulfilled. That's the remarkable thing about Biblical prophecy, and Daniel's End Times prophecies in particular: these Old Testament prophecies dovetail perfectly with prophecies made by Jesus himself in the Gospels, as well as Revelation, the New Testament's greatest treasure trove of End Times prophecy. For comparison, just try looking at the track record of people like Nostradamus or more modern "prophets" like Edgar Cayce or Jeanne Dixon.

In 1995, the first book in the Left Behind series, by Jerry Jenkins and Tim LaHaye, was written and published, starting a 9-year, 13-volume series of apocalyptic fiction based on Biblical End-Times prophecy. What many, including some who have read the entire series, fail to notice is that more of the framing details about the End Times events, including the length of the Tribulation Period and the actions of the Antichrist, are found here in Daniel than in the book credited with providing most of Left Behind's material, Revelation. Daniel does this at chapter 11 verse 36 when he makes an abrupt change in the narrative of describing kings and nations and conflicts and wars, and shifts attention to a "king" who will "exalt and magnify himself above every god" (Daniel 11:36) and, among other things, will go to war with many following a three and a half year period (a time, times, and half a time, 12:7, or 1290 days, 12:11), or exactly half of the Tribulation. Like all the rest of the kings and rulers mentioned by

Daniel, this person isn't given a name or a title. Yet, there's little doubt as to his identity, called in various places in the New Testament as the Man of Perdition, Man of Sin, or even the Son of Satan, but he is best known as the Antichrist, and he would dominate the affairs of men in the End Times.

Partly because it was further away in the future than it would be for the Apostle John in Revelation, and partly because of the terrifying nature of the vision itself, Daniel is twice told in this concluding prophecy that these visions are to be sealed up until the time of the End (12:4, 12:13). This means that at the appropriate time, God will open our eyes to the Truth contained in these prophecies, and allow us to interpret them. I firmly believe that part of this has already happened, in the form of 13 books in the series Left Behind. And that also means that we are very close to the fulfillment of these End Times prophecies.

November 17, NT
Hebrews 11:17-40
Heroes of the Faith, Part Two

The Epistle to the Hebrews continues its exploration of Old Testament heroes as examples of the importance of faith in today's NT reading. Today's part of the reading starts where yesterday's left off, with Abraham and Isaac (Hebrews 11:17-19), including Abraham's willingness to sacrifice his son and validating Isaac as the legitimate heir of the Hebrew people. The letter goes on to credit the accomplishments of Jacob and Esau (11:20-21) and then Joseph (11:22), before going into a larger amount of detail, understandably, about the central figure of Judaism, Moses (11:23-29). Every accomplishment here, just like yesterday, is preceded by the phrase "by faith" to drive home the point that none of these great works were simply done for their own sake, but by faith in the One True God.

Joshua and Rahab get a verse apiece (11:30-31), even though Joshua is not mentioned by name. Named without going into detail about their accomplishments by faith are Gideon, Barak, Samson, Jephthah, David and Samuel, though they along with "the prophets" get a full paragraph about how they suffered for their faith (11:32-38). Along the way, and though he is not mentioned by name, the traditional view that Isaiah was martyred by being sawed in two is brought up (11:37). The reading ends the same way as its first half ended yesterday:

Priscilla (presumed writer of this Epistle) summarizes all of this history by explaining that they all gained approval through their *faith*, and never received the promises of God (11:38-40), yet remained faithful anyway.

November 18, OT
Psalm 93:1-5; Psalm 94:1-23; Psalm 95:1-11; Psalm 96:1-13
Shout To The Lord, Part One

While the prophet Daniel wrote his final apocalyptic End Times prophecies in his final days on Earth (he would have been in his 80s or possibly even 90s at the time he wrote the last 3 chapters), the young priest Ezra wrote (it is believed) his lengthy and detailed history of the world known as the Chronicles. He did this while a large group of his fellow Jews left Babylon for Jerusalem in a massive return home that was granted by the Persian King Cyrus. Ezra also recorded much of this great event, and would later join his Israelite brethren to re-establish the Law and worship. The return to Jerusalem would appear in his other major 2-part scroll, named Ezra and Nehemiah in the Bible.

During this same time, 8 Psalms were written, numbered from 93 through 100, that share a common theme of praise and thanksgiving to the Lord, particularly highlighting His "mightiness" and "majesty". Four of them are read today, and the other four tomorrow. All 8 are anonymous, but the very similar style and wording of each of them, not to mention their consecutive appearance in every scroll containing Psalms, indicates that they were almost certainly the work of one person. Though it is nowhere near a universal belief, many believe that the writer was Ezra. Portions of all 8 of them (but especially Psalm 100 in tomorrow's reading) have been adapted into modern hymns and contemporary Christian music, thus the title of this two-part reading. With the exception of Psalm 94, they are very positive, joyful proclamations of praise, Psalm 94 standing out because of its vengeful tone.

November 18, NT
Hebrews 12:1-29
The Discipline of God's Children

When we hear the word "discipline," we often picture only the punishment end of that concept, therefore equating "discipline" with "chastising". But a careful reading of the Bible, and the Epistle to the Hebrews in particular, gives the word a different perspective. Here, you not only get the "chastising" aspect of it, but also the "skill" connotation, i.e. the discipline of learning how to play a musical instrument or learning a foreign language. That theme of discipline comes through loud and clear in chapter 12 of Hebrews.

Like an athlete in training, Priscilla (presumed writer of Hebrews) writes of throwing off that which hinders us and the sin that entangles (Hebrews 12:1). The atmosphere of practical advice is enhanced by the use of two quotes from Proverbs: Proverbs 3:11-12 in Hebrews 12:6, and Proverbs 4:26 in Hebrews 12:13. She uses the word "discipline" in past or present tense 8 more times outside of the Proverbs quote (10, total, when counting the Proverb), making it clear that the second meaning, that of a strived-for skill, is what she's talking about, especially in the first 13 verses.

Despite mentioning Esau in a positive light in the Heroes of the Faith section (yesterday), Esau is mentioned here as "godless" (12:16), and adding details from his history, to make the point of contrast with the undisciplined. Then, addressing the Jewish audience directly, she references Mount Zion and makes the contrast with that mountain and a "mountain of fear" (12:18-27), but finishes by using the metaphor of a "consuming fire" to describe God (12:28-29), which is also a common metaphor for refinement - or discipline.

November 19, OT
Psalm 97:1-12; Psalm 98:1-9; Psalm 99:1-9; Psalm 100:1-5
Shout To The Lord, Part Two

Lots of Psalms get set to music; after all, they are meant to be sung. One of the most popular songs in Contemporary Christian Music is "Shout to the Lord," written and recorded by Darlene Zschech. The title and often-repeated line comes from the first verse of Psalm 100, in today's OT reading. The rest of the lyrics come from several other

Psalms also part of this two-day reading, bookended by short 5-verse-long Psalms of thanksgiving and praise that appear to all be the work of the same writer.

Devotees of Contemporary Christian Music, and particularly worship music, will also recognize the first 7 verses from Psalm 97. In the live recording of the song "Let it Rain," on the Michael W. Smith CD "Worship," a man with a thick Scottish accent does a dramatic reading of Psalm 97:1-7, causing the audience to get completely fired up, shouting with excitement. One wonders if this is the way the Jews returning to Jerusalem felt and acted during this joyful period of time!

November 19, NT
Hebrews 13:1-25
Entertaining Angels; Conclusion of Hebrews

With this chapter of this Epistle, the Pauline era of Christianity comes to an end. This chronology believes it to have been written by a woman named Priscilla, addressed by Paul in more than one of his letters; but even if you believe that Paul wrote this letter, remaining anonymous for unknown reasons, this letter would have been the last one written before the destruction of the Temple in Jerusalem by the Roman Emperor Titus. The next part of the Bible we would read would come between 15 and 20 years later (and starts tomorrow).

During the gap between this Epistle and the first Epistle of John, the Church would see explosive growth in spite of continued oppression by the Roman Empire, but it would also have to deal with heresies and controversies within itself. The purpose of these Epistles in the Church's early days was to thwart as much of this as possible.

Priscilla's charge to the "Hebrews" was for them to become aware of how Christ's Jewish heritage is what led to the then-modern Christian Church; that the heroes of the Old Testament were heroes not because of what they did, but what they *believed* - that is, their faith.

In the final chapter, Priscilla brings it all together with a flourish of practical advice and words of encouragement. There are no quotes of Proverbs in the final chapter, but the chapter does have that kind of feel to it, and it starts with the advice to show hospitality to strangers for a reason that brings another whole realm of creation into the picture: to paraphrase the verse, we could be entertaining angels (Hebrews 13:2). Indeed, there are many more documented encounters with angels in the Bible than what many people think. Most likely, these encounters still happen today, and with frequency.

The practical advice continues, with many verses that sound almost exactly like the kinds of things found in Paul's Epistles. This is probably the most likely reason that the Pauline authorship of this Epistle was believed for so many centuries. When the letter wraps up, only one person is actually named in the closing Benediction and greetings: Timothy, the addressee of Paul's last written work (13:23). Outside of that, the Epistle to the Hebrews closes on a positive but very generic note.

November 20, OT
Ezra 4:1-5; Ezra 4:24; Nehemiah 1:1-4:23
Restoration Hits a Roadblock

As mentioned back on November 12 and 15, neither Ezra or Nehemiah were among those to return to Jerusalem when the Exile was officially terminated by Cyrus of Persia. The Jews that did return found a ghost town that was almost totally destroyed. They set out to rebuild the walls of Jerusalem, and laid the foundation for a new Temple. We know about these events, during the reigns of 3 Persian emperors, largely from extra-Biblical sources; however, Ezra (writing in both the books of Ezra and Nehemiah) provides a great deal of information about the rebuilding effort when he wrote the scrolls following his own return to Jerusalem, some time after Nehemiah did likewise, decades after the first Jews made their return.

The difficulty in zipping up the history of this era is the simple fact that Ezra didn't write everything down in exact chronological order - in either of his scrolls. This is a stark contrast from Ezra's earlier written work, known as the First and Second Books of the Chronicles, but the likely reason for this was simply the location of the earlier writing (Babylon) and the fact that Ezra's priestly duties took center stage when he returned to Jerusalem.

Thus we have the history of the point where Jerusalem had been largely rebuilt except for the Temple, but the effort to do that was met with a strong and unexpected opposition. The brief 6 verses from Ezra 4 recount that opposition and what was done about it (for we know the Temple did indeed get built). The passage from Nehemiah recounts a more detailed version of events going all the way from the post-Exile's early days, through the early reign of Artaxerxes, when Nehemiah made his return, and then the event in Ezra where restoration efforts met with opposition.

Of historical note is the fact that during this period, the reign of Artaxerxes' father Xerxes I occurred, where the Persian empire was, arguably at its peak. Its one (and only, really) failure occurred when the attempt was made to invade Greece and were stopped by the Spartans at Thermopylae, an event immortalized in the motion picture "300". More and more as the Old Testament continues from here, we read of events that have both a Biblical and an Extra-Biblical source.

November 20, NT
1 John 1:1-2:6
The Apostle Jesus Loved

Six times during the Gospel According to John, one of the Apostles is referred to as the "disciple Jesus loved" or "the beloved disciple". He is never actually identified. Some modern scholars think that it refers to James, the brother of Jesus. Others, including this chronology, believe the more traditional view that John, the same as the writer of that Gospel, is the "beloved disciple," and this person later became known as John the Evangelist. Though this chronology has long since read the entirety of the Gospel according to John, this is due to when the events occurred in the earthly life of Jesus, not when it was written (such as is the case with the Epistles). In fact, the Gospel According to John would have most likely been written some time shortly *after* John wrote his 3 Epistles, the first of which is begun today.

Between 15 and 20 years is estimated to have passed since the destruction of the Temple in Jerusalem in 70 A.D., placing this first Epistle of John somewhere between 85 and 90 A.D. (the Gospel was likely written around 92-95, and Revelation, his later work, followed shortly thereafter). According to the Catholic Church, 4 different Popes would have led the Church during that span. John would have been a young man, possibly a teenager, when he was one of the Twelve, and thus was an old man at the time all of his written work was done. His Epistle does not have an addressee, either a church or an individual, and is thus meant for the Church as a whole. The theology and writing style are identical to that of the Gospel According to John, and there is very little dispute about the authorship.

The brief first reading from John's first Epistle looks back on what must have been decades of early Church history, and emphasizes the need to be obedient to our Lord in order to show our love for the Lord.

November 21, OT
Haggai 1:1-2:23
Rebuild The Temple!

If the first four chapters of Nehemiah are viewed as a summary of events between the reigns of Cyrus and Artaxerxes, then the works of two minor prophets, the first of which is read today, can be viewed as the detail. The book of the prophet Haggai (pronounced "hey, guy") consists of only 2 chapters, and it fits perfectly into this period after the Exile, with the Jews back in a rebuilt Jerusalem, preparing to rebuild the Temple, later given the designation of the Second Temple.

The Temple that would eventually be built would stand, in one form or another, until 70 A.D. when it would be destroyed by the Roman Emperor Titus. At no point would the Temple conform to the specifications given by exilic prophet Ezekiel in his final chapters. Furthermore, Haggai's prophecy concerning the Temple contains no building specifications; rather, it is a message from God to get going on the Temple, to break the opposition that was happening at the time. The detail of the prophecy concerned contacting the then-governor of Judah, Zerubbabel, to get thing moving, offering encouragement and blessings.

November 21, NT
1 John 2:7-29
A Study of Contrasts

It's easy to see the similarities in style between the Gospel According to John and this Epistle, particularly with the repeated references to the contrast between the light and the darkness. Back on January 1, we read from John 1, where 3 verses there (John 1:9-11) likened Jesus to the Light. Noting that the Gospel was written after this Epistle, it's therefore notable that this Epistle, and particularly chapter 2, contains so many of the same references. The metaphors of "light" is used in 1 John 2:9, 2:10, and 2:11.

Throughout chapter 2, John uses contrasts like "light and dark" to tell several deep theological Truths. Verse 7 opens with a "new, old command". He poetically bounces back and forth between fathers and sons in verses 12-14 to contrast knowing God and overcoming the Evil One. John contrasts love of the world with love of God in verses 15-17. And in one of the New Testament's starkest contrasts, the many antichrists, or spirits of the antichrist, are contrasted with the anointing of the Holy One (2:18-27).

November 22, OT
Zechariah 1:1-2:13
The Post-Exilic Ezekiel

While Haggai and Zechariah both wrote their prophecies around the same time (during the reign of Darius I of Persia, after the Exile), their books couldn't be more different. Although both prophets concerned themselves with the building of the new Temple, Zechariah uses strange visions and angelic encounters, much like Ezekiel did *during* the Exile, where Haggai did neither. Haggai wrote the second shortest scroll among the so-called "minor prophets," while Zechariah wrote the longest. Most of all, where Haggai's prophecies were really on just one subject - the Temple - Zechariah's prophecies cover a wide range of subjects and eras, from Messianic prophecies to End Times visions, and back to the Temple again. The influence of Ezekiel on Zechariah is very obvious.

Also unlike Haggai, Zechariah includes a small dose of biographical information (Zechariah 1:1), and a couple of yet-to-be-read passages in Ezra add some more detail. Zechariah's style is considered very similar to that of Ezekiel primarily because both prophets were also priests. There is some scholarly debate about this primarily because the Ezra passages, along with a quote from Jesus in the Gospel According to Matthew (Matthew 23:35), give some different, seemingly contradictory, biographical data, making it possible that more than one person named Zechariah is being described. However, this debate isn't nearly as heated as some other Biblical controversies, and this chronology will assume that all of the references to Zechariah refer to the same post-Exilic prophet.

The first two chapters of Zechariah consist of a set of angelic encounters very much like Ezekiel's visions - except the angel goes unnamed in this prophecy. Each encounter is marked with a date, such as the "24th day of the 11th month, Shebat, in the second year of Darius" (1:7), referring to Darius I of Persia. The first encounter does like many other prophets, referring to the angel as a man "standing among the myrtle trees" (1:11). What is most interesting about the first vision, which serves to deliver the message from the Lord that Jerusalem and the Temple will both be restored, is that the angel is seen on a horse with 3 other horses, a vision God would use with John in Revelation as well.

The visions, delivered by the same angel, continue with "four horns and four craftsmen" (1:18-20), referring to the four nations that first scattered, and then will regather, the people of Israel, and then the "man with the measuring line" (2:1-13), likely another angel, sent to measure Jerusalem in preparation for the return of the people from the many scattered places.

November 22, NT
1 John 3:1-24
As The World Hates You, Love Each Other

All of John's writings carry two strong themes with them: the spiritual separation of God's people from the rest of the world, and the emphasis on God's love for us, more so than any other Gospel writer, or even any other New Testament writer (Paul's "love chapter" in 1 Corinthians 13 notwithstanding). There are other attributes of note, but these are the two that stand out, here in chapter 3 in particular, as John delivers a message of love from God. More like a prophet than an evangelist, all that's missing is a declaration of "thus says the Lord" at the end of each paragraph. If the first verse of this chapter sounds familiar, it's probably because of songs such as Chris Tomlin's "How Great is Our God" and Third Day's "How Great," which both quote the verse (1 John 3:1).

The love God has for us, His children, gives us both special status and special attributes, and John expresses this in both positive and negative terms, such as when he describes and defines sin (3:4-10) and then further shows what love is by describing its opposite (3:11-12). But in this setting apart, he asks us not to be surprised when the "world hates you" (3:13), but to remember how much God loves us, and specifically what Jesus did to show us that love (3:16-18), setting for us the ultimate example of how we should love one another, that is, obeying the greatest commandment (3:23-24).

November 23, OT
Zechariah 3:1-6:15
Six Visions

After yesterday's introduction to both Zechariah and the angel delivering the messages, the first 6 chapters, of which we read 2 yesterday, consist of a series of 8 visions, and 6 of them are found in today's OT reading. They range, topically, from prophecies of Judah's immediate future to fascinating Messianic and even End Times prophecies, all delivered to Zechariah over the course of a single night.

The first of today's readings reveals the character Joshua, not to be confused with the Israelite leader who took over after the death of Moses, who is a high priest chosen to be the first such priest of the new Temple (Zechariah 3:1-10). He is mentioned in both Haggai and Zechariah, but his name is, significantly, spelled *Yeshua* in Ezra and Nehemiah. It is significant because the Epistle to the Hebrews gives Jesus the same title, as our Great High Priest, the ultimate successor to Joshua, but with the further note that the name Jesus is the Greco-Latin translation of the Hebrew name *Yeshua*. Thus, this vision is both a prophecy of the near-future regarding Temple restoration, as well as being symbolically Messianic.

In the next vision, called "the Gold Lampstand and the Two Olive Trees" in most Bibles, Zechariah is introduced to Zerubbabel, the person responsible for much of the rebuilding of Jerusalem, and the laying of the foundation of the new Temple (4:1-14). The vision of the huge, flying scroll (5:1-4) follows this, as a curse that enters the houses of the thieves and of those who swear falsely by the Lord's name. The strange vision of the "woman in a basket" (5:5-11) may be a foretelling of the story later told in the book of Esther (which we will begin to read on November 29).

The visions in chapter 6 are, however, the ones that get the most attention here in Zechariah, as the first is another vision of four horses, which foretells the "four horsemen of the apocalypse" in Revelation (6:1-8), and the bookend of this reading, the vision of the crowning of

Joshua (6:9-15) which, particularly when using the Hebrew spelling of Yeshua, forms a strong symbolism of the Messiah to come.

November 23, NT
1 John 4:1-21
God Is Love

When I was in Catholic elementary school, one of the first songs we learned was a simple little ditty that had just one line, repeated again and again in a round-like fashion. I remember it very clearly: "God is love, and he who abides in love, abides in God, and God in him". What we weren't taught, but I found out much later when doing a complete read-through of the Bible, is that this is a direct quote of 1 John 4:16, the climax of this chapter and this reading on who God truly is.

John starts the chapter by first making sure the readers understand something that would become the central theme of his next major work after the Epistles, the Gospel According to John: that **Jesus is God**, that is, God in the flesh (1 John 4:1-6). Immediately afterward, John launches into what is arguably the greatest exposition of God as "love" in the entire Bible (4:7-21). As explained when we last encountered a chapter like this (Paul's First Epistle to the Corinthians, chapter 13), love is the basis for God's relationship with humans - the reason we were created, and the reason we were redeemed by a Savior (see reading for August 13). The word translated here as "love" is the same word that is, sometimes, translated as "charity" in some older translations, and it appears in 1 John 4 more times than in any other single chapter in the entire Bible: **27 times** (and that's if you don't count the 3 appearances of the word "beloved" that are also in this chapter). The point of the chapter is that not only is Jesus the embodiment of God, but God is the embodiment of *agape* - the word translated variously as "charity" (from the Latin "caritas") and "love". God *is* love.

November 24, OT
Zechariah 7:1-8:23
To Mourn No More

Two years after the angelic encounter and visions that Zechariah recorded in his first 6 chapters, the prophet records his next prophecies which have a completely different tone to them, being direct quotes of God delivered to the people responsible for the rebuilding of the Temple (Zechariah 7:1-2). Zechariah's priestly duties come through here as he answers a question by two other priests, regarding the mourning that had continued for the last 70 years "in the fifth month" (7:3), presumably commemorating the beginning of the Exile. God's answer, delivered through Zechariah, can be paraphrased as follows: the observation that was conducted in the fifth and seventh months was a ritual of man, not a command of God, and is therefore no longer needed, in fact it never was (7:4-7).

Zechariah uses this opportunity to then deliver more advice from God for how to perform their duties as priests (7:8-10). The other priests, however, were stuck on their rituals and had hardened their hearts "like flint" against any change, earning the wrath of God (7:11-14). In chapter 8, the prophet expands on this idea of "mourning no more" with more words of comfort and encouragement.

November 24, NT
1 John 5:1-21
The Three are One; Our Confidence in the Lord (Conclusion of 1 John)

John brings it all together as he wraps up his first Epistle. Linking our faith in God with God's love for us, he explains how this is the means by which we "overcome the world" (1 John 5:1-12). Of course, this is a well-known quote of Jesus himself that John would later record in the Gospel (John 16:33). Along the way, John makes mention of the Spirit, meaning the Holy Spirit, and so brings together the whole Trinity: Father, Son, and Spirit who together make one God.

The emphasis of most of the Epistle was on the tangibility of one of those 3 parts, that is, the incarnation of God as Jesus Christ. John uses this to explain the purpose of his letter (1 John 5:13-20), repeating some of the earlier theological Truths he brought up. That purpose is the confidence that we, believers, have in the Lord, that our faith in

Him and His love for us is exactly how we obtain eternal life. It's guaranteed to all believers, and believers were and are the audience of this Epistle.

John's final words in this Epistle have led some to believe that this letter is actually *un*finished. The simple message to "my children" to stay away from idols (5:21) is such an abrupt change of topic but also an abrupt ending, that some think there may have been more to this letter at one time. The second and third letters, though believed to be the work of the same writer, are not believed to be additional parts to this same letter.

November 25, OT
Ezra 5:1-6:18
And So It Goes

After reconstruction of the Temple had ground to a halt, the prophets Haggai and Zechariah wrote words of encouragement to get the process moving again. A Psalmist even wrote ten Psalms of praise thanking God for giving the Israelites their pass to return to Jerusalem and rebuild it. Now as we resume the narrative in Ezra, our chronicler records 2 communications and another snippet of history in today's OT reading.

The first communication is a report written by one Tattenai, a regional governor, to King Darius of Persia, showing the construction in progress, and going very well (Ezra 5:3-17). The second is Darius' response: he dug into his archives to find a scroll containing Cyrus' original decree, not only allowing the Jews to return home but mandating it (6:1-5), and turning it into a decree of his own that no one should interfere with the construction and that it should all be paid for out of the Persian treasury (6:6-12).

And so it goes, as the Temple was indeed completed, dedicated, and Temple worship was re-established (6:13-18) according to the law of Moses.

November 25, NT
2 John 1-13
To The Chosen Lady and Her Children

John's second Epistle is not merely an extension of the first one, because it starts with a specific greeting. He identifies himself as "the elder" (2 John 1:1a) and the addressee as the "chosen lady and her children" (1:1b). Neither John nor the addressee are given actual names at any point; in fact, no names of people are mentioned in 2 John at all. The brief 13 verses of this Epistle form the shortest book in the entire Bible, and the repetition of themes, such as loving one another, obeying the commandments, and how this all ties together, makes it very obvious that this is the work of the same writer as the First Epistle of John. It is not known whether the chosen lady was also part of the audience of the first letter; but the re-explanation of the same major points as there suggest that she was not.

Near the end, John expresses his desire to visit her in person (1:12), but it is not known whether this visit ever took place. The letter would have been written shortly after the first, some time between A.D. 85 and 90, prior to the writing of the Gospel According to John and the book of Revelation, the latter of which was written from the prison island of Patmos. Since we don't know the exact date of John's imprisonment, it could easily have been as early as shortly after the writing of this Second Epistle, or perhaps the Third.

November 26, OT
Psalm 118:1-29; Psalm 129:1-8; Psalm 148:1-14; Psalm 149:1-9; Psalm 150:1-6
Priestly Psalms of Praise

We once again read a set of 5 Psalms, likely written by the same person just as was the set of 10 we read a week ago. But there are some important differences: these 5 are not presented consecutively, though the last 3 are, and they have a structure that suggests that they were written by a priest. In particular, the call and response of Psalm 118 sounds like something that would be recited or sung in worship, and the instructions to praise the Lord with a variety of musical instruments in Psalm 150 sound like someone who leads worship.

What is entirely possible is that these 5 Psalms were written by Ezra, in response to the wonderful news that the Temple had been rebuilt.

Though the end of the book of Psalms is reached at this point, many Psalms are yet to be read.

November 26, NT
3 John 1-14
The Last Epistle

About 50 years before John wrote his 3rd Epistle, Paul wrote his first Epistle to the Galatians during his Second Missionary Journey. At this point, a lot has happened in God's salvation history: the Church had spread to cover all of what we now call the Middle East, most of northern Africa, and most of Europe, even though the Church was up against the Roman Empire, dead set against its further spread. All of Paul's Epistles had been written, along with those of Peter, and both Peter and Paul had been martyred. An infrastructure had been built to carry on the Church through a hierarchy called the Papacy, now into its 4th or 5th Pope. Gospels had been written by John Mark, Matthew the Apostle, and Luke the Physician and companion of Paul by this time. John, the "Apostle that Jesus loved," was the last writer to receive inspiration from God to write works that would later be compiled into our Bible. Three Epistles, the 4th Gospel, and finally, the great prophecy known as Revelation would bring Biblical writing to a close at the end of the 1st century.

His first Epistle was sent to an unknown audience in the Church, his second sent to an unnamed woman. This 3rd, the second shortest book of the Bible, is addressed to a man named Gaius. The letter's theme is different from his 2nd letter, focussing more on crediting Gaius for good work in helping spread the Gospel to Gentile territory (3 John 1:1-8) than any new theological truths. John's reference to something he wrote to the church may have been his First Epistle, and his earlier message had been rejected by a man named Diotrephes (1:9-10). John uses this to give his only real piece of advice in the short letter: to not imitate what is evil, but what is good (1:11).

John's last Epistle, but certainly not his last writing, ends nearly the exact same way as his Second Epistle, with the hope of a future in-person visit (1:13-14), though we don't know if this ever happened.

November 27, OT
Ezra 6:19-22; Zechariah 9:1-17
Passover is Celebrated; The Restoration is Complete

Israel's days as a kingdom, divided or otherwise, were long gone. It had been more than 500 years since David had united Israel and passed this golden age along to his son Solomon. Since that time, they went through a divided kingdom and many ups and downs. They were taunted and attacked by neighboring nations. The Northern Kingdom eventually fell to Assyria, and the Southern Kingdom of Judah later fell to Babylon. When Babylon was conquered by Persia, the Persian king allowed them to return home, which thousands did, and those that returned were tasked with rebuilding a city and a Temple that had been destroyed 70 years earlier. So, when they finally completed the repairs and reconstruction efforts of the Temple, what did they then do? Nothing less than restore the most important celebration in all of Hebrew life: they observed the Passover for the first time in decades (Ezra 6:19-22).

Ezra noted that even the king of Assyria helped in getting the Temple rebuilt (6:22), likely due to the way Babylon had swallowed up Assyria years earlier. Technically, there was no longer an Assyrian Empire like there once was, but there was, presumably, a kingdom still there. Israel, on the other hand, did not have a king, as it was never re-established. They chose instead to keep God as their king by making it a point to observe the Passover. This was presumably a move that pleased God very much, and this pleasure was passed along to the prophet Zechariah in the form of a prophecy *against* a long list of neighboring nations (Zechariah 9:1-8). It's at the end of that prophecy that we get the most important part: a 2-part prophecy that is both Messianic and related to the End Times.

Israel had no king, but God's promise to them is that there *will* be one, and He will arrive mounted on a donkey (9:9), a prophecy fulfilled when Jesus rode into Jerusalem on what we now celebrate as Palm Sunday. In the next verse, God promises that this King would bring peace and rule the whole world (9:10), but we know this to be a prophecy not yet fulfilled. What we do know is that this will happen when God decides the world is going to come to an end, a time that will be described in great detail in the NT book that starts today.

November 27, NT
Revelation 1:1-20
Introduction To The Apocalypse

The Bible contains many examples of "apocalyptic literature," in both the Old and New Testaments. To fully understand what "apocalyptic" means, note that many older Bibles have "The Apocalypse of Jesus Christ to John" as the title of this final book of the Bible, more commonly known as Revelation. The same Greek root word is the basis for "apocrypha," a part of the Bible that is hidden from, or left out of, Scriptures because it is not considered inspired. The words "apocrypha" and "apocalypse" are, in fact, opposites: the former refers to something that is hidden, the latter refers to something that is *revealed*. And thus, we come to the conclusion of the Bible with the largest collection of End Times prophecy in all of Scriptures.

No book in the Bible is the subject of more controversy than Revelation. It was the last book to be accepted as "canon," that is, to be included with the rest of Scriptures. There is a wide range of possible interpretations, ranging from Preterism (the belief that Revelation refers mainly to events that occurred in the first century) and Idealism (the belief that everything in Revelation is symbolic of the ongoing struggle between good and evil) to Amillennialism (the belief that the prophesied millennium has already begun and we're in it today) and Futurism (the belief that Revelation is mostly prophecy of events yet to come even in *our* time). **This chronology holds to the Futurist eschatology**, which best goes with a Plain Interpretation of the Bible, as has been discussed many times previously.

Revelation is such a lofty, heady, and difficult work to read (over the next 3 ½ weeks) that a daily chronological reading plan such as this can just barely do it any justice. Nevertheless, it is very important to read all of it just as it is important to read the entire Bible. Of particular note in Revelation are the numerous places where it echoes prophecies that were already made by prophets such as Daniel and Ezekiel, and where the prophecies dovetail neatly with those made by Isaiah, Zephaniah, Zechariah, and most of all, Jesus himself in the Gospels (Matthew 24 in particular, but also elsewhere). Of additional note is the fiction series called Left Behind, which takes an even more literal view of Revelation than a Plain Interpretation would dictate. I do, personally, recommend the books because they do the best job of any writers outside of the Bible of tying together the End Times prophecies of the various sources, besides just Revelation, into one cohesive exposition of what is likely to come in the near future. It's not perfect, but it's the closest anyone has come to date. The fiction series even uses an event NOT found in Revelation as its focal point: the Rapture of the Church, prophesied by Jesus and by Paul in 1 Thessalonians.

John identifies himself (Revelation 1:1) by name, which has led to some speculation as to whether this John is the same writer as the 3 Epistles and a Gospel that also bear the name John. One thing of note is that John never identifies himself by name in the other works. References to John in the Gospel are to John The Baptist (John 1:6), and the opening greeting of two of the Epistles of John state only that he is "the elder" (2 John 1:1, 3 John 1:1). If the "Apostle Jesus loved" is the writer of all of these works, as this chronology believes, then some time between the writing of the fourth Gospel and the writing of this work, John was exiled to the Greek island of Patmos (Revelation 1:9). But, the numerous references to Jesus in Revelation using the exact same words as were used in the Gospel According to John mean he must have been aware of the writing of the fourth Gospel. It is reasonable to conclude that, at the very least, the fourth Gospel and Revelation were written by the same John, even if you hold to the notion that the Epistles were written by someone else.

The first chapter of Revelation is therefore, primarily, an introduction. As Jesus stated that no one knows the day or the hour of the End Times taking place, John would have had no idea how far into the future the events would be, and so he says that the "time is near" (1:3) just as many other prophets have done. John also introduces at least part of the purpose of the prophecy: to send a message to the "seven churches in Asia" (1:4) which will make up the readings for the next 3 days. It is in this intro that we learn that Jesus, when He returns, will be seen by everyone in the world "in the clouds" (1:7). The seven churches are named (1:11), all locations in what is, today, western Turkey (thus referring to the Roman province of Asia, not the continent). And then, we get the first of the numerous symbolic visions that numerologists have examined for centuries, as he explains how he received the "Patmos vision" from an angel holding seven stars, standing among seven lampstands that represent the seven churches that we'll learn more about starting tomorrow (1:12-20).

November 28, OT
Zechariah 10:1-11:17
Promises and Warnings

Zechariah's 9th chapter centers largely on a Messianic prophecy, delivered in response to the decision to restore the Passover and Temple worship. Chapter 10 continues this positive outlook of the future of Israel from the time of the building of the Second Temple up to the coming of the Messiah. There are even some additional, though more vague, references to that coming Savior dotted in the chapter. But once this chapter ends, the promises of blessings end and a much more bleak outlook emerges.

There are relatively few prophecies in the Old Testament that give any real detail about the Crucifixion of the Messiah or the destruction, 40 years later, of the Temple that was just completed in Jerusalem. Zechariah chapter 11 has both, and it can be summed up in one sentence: disaster is in store for Israel. Despite all the "feel good" words in chapters 9-10, Israel's future will not be so bright as all that. Of course, we know from history that Israel (never again named that way until its rebirth in 1948) was effectively wiped out after the destruction of the Temple in 70 A.D. That event is foretold here with the description of the "cedars of Lebanon," the construction material used to build the Temple, being burned (Zechariah 11:1-2). What's most interesting here is the reference to Who will bring it about: the 3rd verse speaks of a "shepherd's wail" and the sound of a "young lion's roar" as the "pride of the Jordan," that is, the Temple, is ruined (11:3). The "young lion" is a clear reference to the tribe of Judah, still the dominant tribe after the return from Exile, and all the way up to the time of Christ, and the tribe from which Jesus himself came. The shepherds are the future leaders of the people of Israel, whose attempt at shepherding their flock will fail because of this Messiah. They are later identified as the "three shepherds" (11:8) that would, arguably, refer to the Pharisees, Sadducees, and Herodians of Jesus' time. The most important detail here is the prediction that the "good" shepherd would be sold to the "evil" shepherds for thirty pieces of silver, the exact amount paid to Judas to betray Him to the authorities (11:12). Even the prediction that this blood money would later be used to buy the "Potter's field" (11:13) is fulfilled in Matthew 27:7.

In summary, Zechariah 11 forms one of the darkest, but also most important, prophecies of the Messiah to come, especially when it is added to Isaiah 53, in the entire Old Testament.

November 28, NT
Revelation 2:1-17
The Seven Churches, Part One: Ephesus, Smyrna, Pergamum

The "Seven Churches" refer to real places in what is now Turkey. They represented only a small portion of the new Christian Church at the end of the first century, but their geographic proximity to Patmos and to each other, and the order they are presented here in Revelation, is what makes them important. A courier delivering John's writings, though not an Epistle but a prophecy, would have sailed from Patmos to the nearest church to begin delivering the message. That nearest church is Ephesus, and the rest are shown on the map below. Ephesus is the only one known to have been visited by Paul, and is one of only three (the other two being Sardis and Laodicea) that are mentioned at all elsewhere in the New Testament.

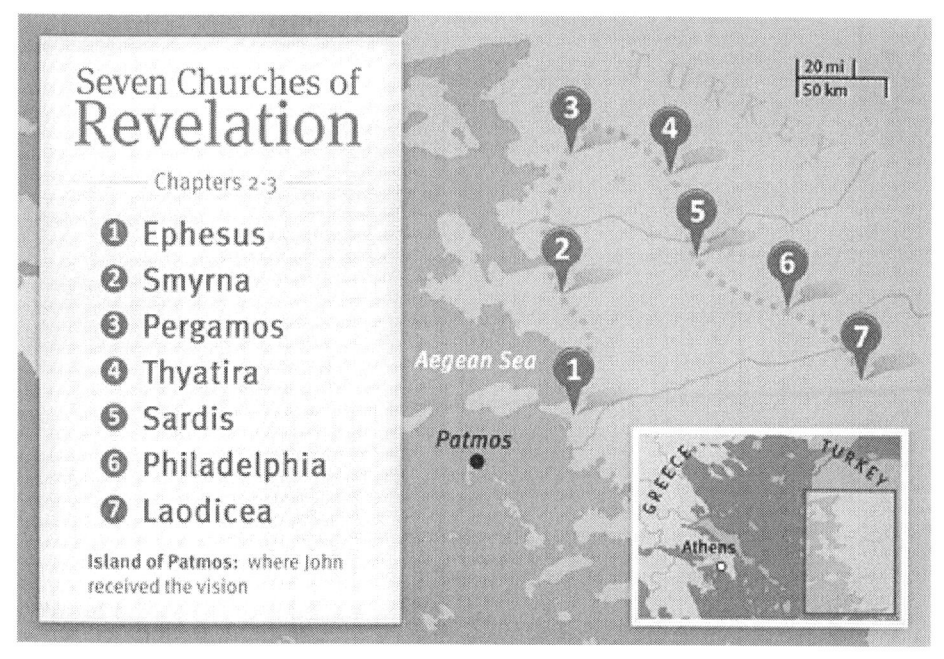

Seven Churches of
Revelation
Chapters 2-3

❶ Ephesus
❷ Smyrna
❸ Pergamos
❹ Thyatira
❺ Sardis
❻ Philadelphia
❼ Laodicea

Island of Patmos: where John received the vision

Though the messages were first intended for real, first century churches, each church represents future eras and churches of the so-called Church Age, and is thus a message for us all to see. In other words, each message is both a message to a local church and to a church era "which will take place after this" (Revelation 1:19). The common pattern of each message is this: the church is addressed by the Lord, and the main, usually positive, characteristics of the church are pointed out; this is followed by some kind of admonition or criticism, and is sometimes followed by some kind of positive promise.

To the church in Ephesus, which could be thought of as representative of nearly all first century churches, the message points out their hard work in separating themselves from the wicked, but they're then scolded for losing sight of their "first love" (2:1-7). But, by turning back to the Lord, the church can "eat of the tree of life" again.

To the church in Smyrna, the message is one of encouragement in the face of persecution (2:8-11), which could easily be viewed as the Church as a whole, during its next era from roughly 100 A.D. until Christianity was legalized in the Roman Empire, about 316 A.D.

To the church in Pergamum, the message is mainly about the need to repent of allowing false teachers to creep in to the church (2:12-17), a message that vividly describes the early days (at least) of the Catholic Church in the Middle Ages following the Council of Nicea.

The future history of the Church continues in tomorrow's reading.

November 29, OT
Zechariah 12:1-14:21; Esther 1:1-22
Israel In The End Times; Israelites in Persia

At first glance, the four chapters of today's OT reading look like a very lengthy read, but with Zechariah 12 and 13 both being very short chapters, the total length is about average. Zechariah's prophecies have gone from priestly advice while the Temple was being rebuilt, to a celebration of the completion of that work, to Messianic visions and beyond. Here in his last 3 chapters, Zechariah leaps ahead to the End Times, and gives us a picture of the fate of Israel when the Messiah makes His triumphant return.

At an unspecified time during the Tribulation, Jerusalem will be attacked, but God himself will come to their defense (Zechariah 12:6-9). They'll look back on what they had done to the Messiah and, by the power of the Holy Spirit, repent (12:10-14). False teachers will be shamed away, but a third of the people will be refined as through a fire and call the Lord their God (13:1-9).

Chapter 14, and thus the book of Zechariah, wraps up with the most vivid description of the Glorious Appearing of Jesus found in the Old Testament, as the final battle is said to end when He sets foot on the Mount of Olives and splits it in two (14:1-5). After this, the prophecy shifts to visions that would later be echoed by John in Revelation, as we get the Bible's first pictures of the river of living waters (14:8) and the establishment of the Kingdom by the Messiah (14:9-21).

Lots of prophets make End Times predictions, but few besides Zechariah make prophecies of such a wide range, or so vividly. But while these prophecies were being inspired, and Temple worship and a new Jewish community was being established in Jerusalem, more than half of the people exiled from Judah, not to mention the thousands exiled from what once was the Northern Kingdom, were living out their lives in various parts of the Persian empire. Such was the case during the reign of Ahasuerus, a.k.a. Xerxes, and the events recorded in the book called Esther.

Esther is a fascinating book and a fascinating story. Considerable controversy exists regarding its writing, though, as there is widespread belief that it is a work of fiction, a parable like those told by Jesus in the Gospels or were written as books such as Tobit and Judith, both apocryphal. Part of the reason for this stems from portions of an "expanded" version of Esther that are considered apocryphal (Catholics include them as part of the Deuterocanonical books), and found only in the Greek translation of Esther included in the Septuagint. The version is written in Hebrew is the version that will be read as part of this chronology, and the first chapter is covered today. One curiosity remains regarding this familiar story of God's providence: God is never actually mentioned anywhere in the story, at least not in the Hebrew version of the story.

November 29, NT
Revelation 2:18-3:6
The Seven Churches, Part Two: Thyatira, Sardis

The fourth and fifth of the "Seven Churches" are given messages here. Refer to yesterday's reading for a summary and map of all seven churches, and the messages to the first three, then return here to read about the next two.

To the church in Thyatira, the message is first one of gratitude for the love and faith and service of the church, but then a message of criticism for being tolerant of the teachings of a prophetess named Jezebel (Revelation 2:18-29). It isn't known if Jezebel was the name of a real woman living in the first century, but whether it does or does not, it easily describes the Church during the mid to late Middle Ages up to just before the Reformation. Church history during this time is full of false teachings that crept their way in, slowly and gradually, mostly due to the lack of printed Bibles, as the Church spread more quickly than they could be printed, even after the invention of the printing press. Catholic doctrines such as the devotion to Mary were developed during this period, including a small sect that elevates her to the level of goddess, which some still believe today. Other Catholic doctrines developed during the "Thyatiran" period include the sale of indulgences to release souls from Purgatory and other abuses that Martin Luther criticized in his "95 Theses". God's message to this church also mentions the people who wisely didn't follow the "deep things of Satan" (2:24) and therefore have no burden placed on them.

To the church in Sardis, the message refers to a dead church that needs to wake up and strengthen the "things that remain" for the sake of not being erased from the book of life (3:1-6). The warning includes a repeat of Jesus' words of warning about coming "like a thief in the night" at an hour they will not know (3:3), which could be translated as a threat of being left behind at the Rapture if they do not awaken. But by pointing out the "few that have not soiled their garments" and will thus walk with the Lord in white (3:4-5). This picture of the church dovetails perfectly with the Protestant Reformation, particularly in its early days. All of the major players of the early Reformation were converts from Catholicism who either had theological (Luther) or political (Henry VIII) differences with the Roman Papacy, like the ones of Sardis who would not go along with the rest of the "dead" church.

The two remaining churches addressed here are covered tomorrow.

November 30, OT
Esther 2:1-4:17
A Jewess Becomes Queen of Persia

Where yesterday's reading in Esther was mainly an introduction to the setting of the events, the title person is never mentioned. In fact, the only people mentioned in yesterday's first chapter of Esther were the king (Artaxerxes), the queen (Vashti), and a handful of the royal court's officials in Susa, the Persian capital. No Jews are mentioned, much less Esther, and nothing in the first chapter seems to indicate that this is a story that even belongs in Scripture. But, the historical background is a necessary thing to understand the how and why of the events that come next.

Those events center around first finding a replacement for the deposed queen. The method that was suggested was to gather young virgins for the king and, essentially, conduct a beauty contest (Esther 2:1-4). Meanwhile, we learn of the Benjaminite Mordecai, great-grandson of an exile from Jerusalem, and his young cousin who became his adopted daughter, Esther (2:5-7). After lengthy preparations, which included Mordecai's instructions to Esther to not reveal her nationality, her beauty charmed the king and she became queen (2:8-18). She kept her Jewish background a secret, even as she received a warning from Mordecai that there was a plot to assassinate the king (2:19-21). She passed the warning along to Artaxerxes and credited Mordecai, and the plot was stopped, saving the king's life (2:22-23), but instead of giving Mordecai any credit, a promotion was given instead to a man named Haman (3:1-2).

The rest of chapters 3 and 4 make up the familiar story of how Haman, angered that Mordecai wouldn't bow down to him, plotted to kill not only Mordecai but all of his kind, the Jews. The conspiracy went all the way to the king, and everything was set up for what could have been a massive holocaust. Mordecai and Esther sent messages back and forth about the coming disaster, ending with Esther's brave resolve to go to the king herself and speak to him about this. Notable at this point is that the king was still unaware of his queen's Jewish background.

November 30, NT
Revelation 3:7-22
The Seven Churches, Part Three: Philadelphia, Laodicea

The last two of the Seven Churches of Revelation are described in today's NT reading. They're presented in the order shown for more reasons than just their positions on a path in Asia Minor, of which Patmos was just off the shore. They're in this order because of what they represent in the future of the Church from John's point of view. And with these prophecies, we get a capsule history of Church eras, starting with the First Century Church that John was, himself, part of, on up through the pre-Constantine Church, the Church of the Middle Ages, the Renaissance period just before the Reformation, and the Reformation itself. Here, the visions of the "future Church" conclude with Philadelphia (not the city in Pennsylvania) and Laodicea, representing the the multi-denominational Church that has gone through many revivals and has spread to all parts of the world, and then the final apostate Church just prior to the Rapture, respectively.

The Philadelphian Church could be thought of as representing the numerous denominations that sprung up after the Reformation and prior to the 21st Century. A study of Church history would be far longer than what could be covered in this reading guide, but it's easy to look at the fact that, at one time, there really was only one denomination prior to Luther, and that the rich period after he was excommunicated from it led to the more than 20,000 that exist today. At the time of the Reformation, or the beginning of the Philadelphian period, Bibles existed almost exclusively in Latin; after Luther (and Wycliffe, and many others), the Bible was translated into hundreds of other languages. The picture of the "Church of Philadelphia" is certainly a positive one.

But, a single verse in the midst of this description has led to this all-important questions: are we in the Philadelphian Church today, or are we in the Laodicean Church? That verse is Revelation 3:10, which praises Philadelphia for keeping "my word of perseverance", and promising that the Church will be "kept from the hour of testing". This line seems to be an obvious reference to the Rapture, which means that it is the Philadelphian Church that will be raptured, but this implies that the final Church, that of Laodicea, will be the "lukewarm" Church during the Tribulation. This could also mean that the Rapture does not happen at the beginning or just before the Tribulation, but some time *during* that 7-year period.

Either way, the seventh and final Church, of Laodicea, is not a desireable thing to be part of, as its "lukewarm" nature will lead to being "spit out" by God (3:16). They, however, like all of the Churches, are given the opportunity to repent. Because they're told to seek out "gold refined by fire" and "white garments to clothe yourselves" (3:18), there is a belief (of which I concur) that this refers to the Tribulation Saints post-Rapture who, without benefit of the Holy Spirit, have to come to God of their own accord.

The section on the Seven Churches takes us all the way through the Church Age, leaving us on the doorstep of the Tribulation period (starting tomorrow), with a familiar quote of the Lord: "Behold, I stand at the door and knock…" (3:20), a call to evangelism for all people, not just the people who belong to these 7 first-century Churches.

December 1, OT
Esther 5:1-9:16
The Brave Queen and The Jewish Triumph

The plot to assassinate Artaxerxes was thwarted by a Jew, yet Mordecai was not honored for it. Artaxerxes had a Jewish queen, yet he wasn't aware of it. The man mistakenly honored in Mordecai's place, Haman, had plotted to massacre the entire Jewish population within Persia, yet Esther didn't know if she could find a way of saving her people without exposing the fact that she, too, was a Jew. This precursor to the Jewish Holocaust of the 20th Century was a disaster in the making, and a prime example of how, over the many centuries, God's Chosen People have been oppressed, discriminated against, and even attempted to be exterminated. But God's intent has always been to chastise, not destroy, His people when they need to be disciplined, such as the Babylonian Exile that was now ended, thanks to these very Persians.

Esther, however, was as smart and clever as she was brave, and she came up with the perfect solution to the looming problem of Haman's treachery. Today's 5-chapter OT reading is among this reading guide's longest, but it's an engaging read that shows exactly how

God's providential care is extended to His people wherever they are. Through a combination of Esther's wise choices, King Artaxerxes' sleepless night, and then Esther's confession of her true heritage, the massacre was averted and justice was done.

December 1, NT
Revelation 4:1-11
The Throne in Heaven

From this point forward in Revelation, the focus shifts from things on Earth to things in Heaven. John is told to "come up here" (Revelation 4:1) to see "what must take place after this". What follows is a glorious picture of heaven, and specifically, a throne, with a being on it, surrounded by 24 other thrones occupied by elders (4:2-4) with thunder and lightning and other spectacular displays. Though John doesn't identify the person, it is obvious that it is The Lord, Jesus seated there, and being praised by the "4 living creatures" (4:5-8a) with words that have been adapted into numerous hymns and songs over the years. Most recently, devotees of Contemporary Christian Music will instantly recognize song lyrics such as:

Clothed in rainbows of living color
Flashes of lightning rolls of thunder
Blessing and honor strength and glory and power be
To You the only wise King
Holy, holy, holy is the Lord God Almighty
Who was and is and is to come
With all creation I sing praise to the King of kings
You are my everything and I will adore You

This is the second verse and chorus from "The Revelation Song" written by Jennie Lee Riddle and recorded most famously by Gateway Worship with Kari Jobe. These lyrics are direct quotes of several verses from today's reading from Revelation.

December 2, OT
Esther 9:17-10:3
The Celebration of Purim

The saving of the Jewish people throughout the Persian empire (which, incidentally, included Judah) thanks to Queen Esther was cause for celebration. To this day, Jews celebrate this day as a national holiday called "Purim". Like Hanukkah, Purim is not a religious holiday in the same sense as Passover, but it is celebrated every year on the 14th day of the Jewish month of Adar, which is usually some time during March.

This final reading from Esther shows the origins of the holiday, and how Mordecai was given his due honor.

December 2, NT
Revelation 5:1-14
The Lamb and the Seven-Sealed Scroll

The scene in heaven continues with many of the same elements as were described in yesterday's reading, but with one important addition, and one big change. The "seven spirits of God" (Revelation 5:6), the throne itself (5:7), the four living creatures and the 24 elders (5:8) all appeared yesterday in "The Throne in Heaven". But in today's reading, the "man" in the throne is replaced by a "lamb, looking as though it was slain" (5:6), completing the image first given to us by John the Baptist, when he proclaimed "Behold, the Lamb of God who takes away our sins". It is interesting to note that it was the Gospel according John that contained the only other such reference, and that John is also the writer of Revelation.

The addition is in the form of what is being held by the Lamb: a scroll with seven seals, seals that can only be broken by the Lamb, as He is the only One who is worthy (5:1-5), and the thousands of angels who joined in the chorus of praise (5:11-14). The casual reader will note that there has been very little in the way of "action" or any "violence" at all in Revelation. Readers of the popular fiction series Left Behind have probably been disappointed by lack of anything in Revelation showing up in the book series so far.

That's all about to change, and the action centers on those same seven seals on the scroll.

December 3, OT
Ezra 4:6-23; Psalm 105:1-45
Another Round of Opposition

The king's wife, a Jew (Esther), had just saved the Jewish people from a holocaust brought on by discrimination and hate. The Temple in Jerusalem was rebuilt, and Temple worship had been restored. But the city itself still needed a lot of work, and though they had workers able and ready to keep going in the reconstruction efforts, word of this got back to the king (Artaxerxes) in the form of an exchange of letters recorded in Ezra chapter 4. Artaxerxes agreed with the reasons given by Rehum (Ezra 4:8-9) and ordered the men to stop the work.

At around this time, a pair of Psalms (#105 today, #106 tomorrow) of unknown authorship was written, likely as a result of the king's response, that contains praises for His miracles and His promises, and recounts the history of Israel from the time of Abraham up to Moses. Obviously, these men in Jerusalem saw God's promises as a good reason to ignore the king's orders and continue the rebuilding of Jerusalem.

December 3, NT
Revelation 6:1-17
The Four Horsemen of the Apocalypse; The Wrath of the Lamb Earthquake

The most difficult thing in the study of Eschatology is putting together the various pieces of the puzzle into one, cohesive whole. End Times prophecies were made by several Old Testament prophets, most notably Daniel, Ezekiel, Zephaniah, and Zechariah. Jesus himself made several End Times predictions when prompted by His own Apostles. Paul reassured his readers in Thessalonica that before any of these terrible things would come to pass that the body of believers, that is, the Church, would be Raptured to heaven. This is the basis for the pre-Tribulation, pre-Millenium belief of most Dispensationalists, such as the writer of this reading guide. But that doesn't change the fact that there are a LOT of events prophesied to occur in the End Times that aren't in Revelation, and even the events in Revelation are in chronological order, we don't know how they dovetail with the other prophesied events.

Believe it or not, one of the best resources for putting it all together is a work of fiction called Left Behind, written by Tim LaHaye and Jerry Jenkins. Their sequence of End Times events is not the only sequence ever put together, but it is one that makes a lot of sense, and doesn't violate or contradict any passages of Scripture. The first book chronicles the Rapture, the thwarted attack on Jerusalem, and the rise of the Antichrist. The prophecies leading up to the events of Left Behind are in 1 Thessalonians, Ezekiel, and this chapter of Revelation, respectively. The second book of the Left Behind series, called Tribulation Force, builds up to a climax of war, famine, and death. The third book, Nicolae, has the Wrath of the Lamb earthquake as its climax. These events, in addition to their appearance in a different sequence in Zephaniah, can be matched up with the first 6 of the 7 seals opened by Jesus in today's NT reading from Revelation.

The first 4 seals comprise the prophecy commonly known as the Four Horsemen of the Apocalypse. They represent the Antichrist, War, Famine, and Death respectively, all of which happen during the early part of the Tribulation. Daniel prophesied the length of the Tribulation period and Zechariah was actually the first to prophecy the Four Horsemen, but it's here in Revelation that we get these prophecies in the form of the seven-sealed scroll opened by Jesus himself. The 5th seal recalls all the martyrs - those who died for the faith through the centuries. It is then the 6th seal that brings an event more easily associated with Revelation: the Wrath of the Lamb earthquake, a devastating worldwide event that actually causes the sky to darken and "every mountain and island is moved from its place". Kings and rulers everywhere in the world attempt to hide in caves, and some even wish for the mountains to "fall on them" in desperation as God pours out his anger on the earth.

December 4, OT
Psalm 106:1-48; Ezra 7:1-8:14
Ezra Arrives in Jerusalem

Psalm 106 feels like a followup to 105, and was likely written by the same, unknown author. Similar in structure too, it begins with praises (Psalm 106:1-3), prayer (106:4-5), and repentance (106:6) before embarking on a history of God's chosen people, this time starting with Moses and the Exodus, through the entry into the Promised Land, and then jumping forward to the Exile and the mercy shown to Israel when the Exile was over.

Artaxerxes may have given in to the opposition as far as the city walls were concerned, but he had no problem with the Temple or with God, so when Ezra decided it was time to go to Jerusalem himself, he carried with him a letter from the king that spelled out how he should bring treasures from Persia and use them to purchase bulls, goats, and other animals to sacrifice to the one, true God. We first get a detailed genealogy of Ezra (Ezra 7:1-5), and then his date of arrival in Jerusalem (7:8-10). After this comes the letter from Artaxerxes (7:11-28) showering praises on God and on the Temple. Ezra did not travel alone; in fact, hundreds more of Israel's people went with him, and they are listed by family in chapter 8.

December 4, NT
Revelation 7:1-17
144,000 Evangelists

The early Christians were Jewish converts, and the early evangelists were, originally, Jewish. As bookends to this, 12,000 from each of the 12 tribes of Israel were appointed, just after the Wrath of the Lamb earthquake, to finish evangelizing what was left of the world (Revelation 7:1-8). The first 6 seals unleashed a devastating disaster on the people remaining on earth, but there were many who became believers before they died. These are the people who "came out of the Tribulation" and appeared in John's vision wearing white robes and holding palm branches (7:9), standing around the throne and singing their praises to God (7:10-12). John is asked by one of the elders if he knows who these people are; John can only say "Sir, you know" (7:13-14), and so he gets a detailed explanation from the elder about the great multitude in heaven (7:15-17).

December 5, OT
Ezra 8:15-10:44; 1 Chronicles 3:17-24
The Issue of Intermarriage in Jerusalem

Ezra's return to Jerusalem wasn't all celebrations and pleasantries. As shown in Ezra's last 3 chapters, his trip to Jerusalem was about business - the business of getting the Levite priesthood up and running again. On the final leg of the trip, Ezra was informed that there were no Levites available to do worship correctly, and so gathered up many of them from surrounding areas to join him in Jerusalem (Ezra 8:15-20). He then called a fast, and set them up with an offering for the Temple (8:20-34), and finally offered burnt sacrifices with them (8:35-36).

Then came the discovery that not only were they conducting Temple worship without Levite priests, but there were other, more serious problems going on. Apparently, there were many Israelite men who were taking women from neighboring, pagan nations as wives (9:1-2). The issue of national purity makes Ezra's reaction (9:3-15) and, especially, the solution the people came up with (10:1-17) sound like a bigoted, even racist issue. But it is neither of those things. It's the Law of Moses, and Ezra would know that, being a priest who has spent nearly his entire long life to that point living in a foreign land under the rule of pagan kings. Purity in marriage is something first brought up in Exodus and Leviticus as God was bring His Chosen People to the Promised Land (and echoed in Joshua as well). Paul would later emphasise this as being "equally yoked" in marriage, for the exact same reason, in his Second Letter to the Corinthians. It is a God thing, not a human construct born of racism. And it is so big a deal that the men guilty of this infraction are listed (10:18-44) to conclude this scroll by Ezra.

Ezra's penchant for genealogies and his meticulous attention to historical detail shows up in another way, as we jump back into (presumably) his earlier scroll known as 1 Chronicles, and view the continued royal line of Judah from the beginning of the Exile up to the then-present day (1 Chronicles 3:17-24).

December 5, NT
Revelation 8:1-13
The Seventh Seal and the First Four Trumpets

After the huge events of the first 6 seals of the scroll being broken, the breaking of the 7th seal seems quite anti-climactic. But, it serves as a pause between the first set of judgments being rained down on the earth, and the second. The second set has 7 events just like the first, only this time they are marked by trumpet blasts, the first four of which we read today.

A Plain Interpretation of the Bible isn't exactly the same as the Literal Interpretation, but it is quite a bit more literal than many casual studies. Despite the frightening visions shown here, there isn't any reason to take them as anything other than literal, with the sole exception of the Third Trumpet (Revelation 8:10) which describes a "star" falling to earth. Obviously, this can't happen with a star of any size, but as a vision it works the same way as when one calls a meteor a "shooting star".

The seventh seal results in a period of silence (8:1). But even this silence can't remain, as between this and the first Trumpet, there's more thunder and lightning and another earthquake (8:5). Then comes the Trumpets: the first burns up a third of the earth with hail mixed with fire (8:7). The second kills a third of the living creatures in the seas and destroys a third of the ships with a "giant mountain" that falls from the sky, obviously a type of meteor (8:8). The third Trumpet is the "star" (another meteor) known as "Wormwood," turning a third of the fresh water on earth bitter (poisonous) and killing many (8:10-11).
 The fourth Trumpet finds the sun (and thus, the moon since it reflects the sun's light) darkened by a third, along with a third of other stars (8:12). It is not stated "how" this is accomplished; only that it happens, and it isn't clear from the language used whether a third of all the stars go dark or if all the stars lose a third of their luminosity (the latter seems more likely, since it goes with what happens to our own sun). What may not be apparent at first reading is that this is most certainly the most devastating of the judgments from God so far.
 What's worse is that an angel appearing as an eagle warns us that there is even more - and even worse - devastation to come (8:13).

December 6, OT
Nehemiah 5:1-7:3
The Walls of Jerusalem are Completed

The scroll bearing the name of Ezra may be done, but his writings continue in other scrolls like Nehemiah. The events of Nehemiah 5 sound like a direct continuation of the just-completed scroll, but are told from Nehemiah's point of view rather than Ezra's. In addition to the issue of the Israelite men taking "foreign wives," they were charging "usury" (interest) of each other during some tough economic times (Nehemiah 5:1-13) in clear violation of the Law of Moses

(Nehemiah was also a priest, like Ezra). The issue was resolved in much the same way as was the "foreign wives" issue.

After this, we read further about additional opposition to the completion of the walls of Jerusalem (6:1-15), which continued even through the actual completion and long afterwards (6:16-7:3). But this type of human opposition is no obstacle for a task such as this, born out of the fear of God.

December 6, NT
Revelation 9:1-12
Apollyon, The Destroyer

Though it is assumed that the events described in Revelation are in chronological order, it is not known how far apart they are or where we would, thus, find ourselves within the seven-year period known as the Tribulation. Tim LaHaye and Jerry Jenkins make a number of Biblically-acceptable assumptions about the timeline of End Times events, including fitting the events in other books (Daniel, Ezekiel, Zephaniah, etc.) into the chronology of Revelation. The assumption is that the Trumpet Judgments, of which the fifth Trumpet is the subject of today's NT reading, take place in the months leading up to the midpoint of the Tribulation, a significant turning point in End Times events, particularly given things predicted elsewhere. That fifth Trumpet is also the central event of the fifth novel in the Left Behind series, Apollyon.

Apollyon is the Greek form of the name "Abaddon," in Hebrew, and means "destroyer" in both languages. It refers to the "king of the Abyss" that emerges from the earth after yet another devastating fallen object comes to earth, this time opening up a "shaft to the Abyss" (Revelation 9:1-2) which could refer to an active volcano. The main difference here is that this shaft to the abyss unleashes flying creatures so frightening in both their appearance as well as their actions that unbelievers being tortured by these locust-like beings wish for death, but cannot attain it (9:3-11). This is the first of any of the judgments to discriminate between believers remaining on earth and unbelievers. All of the other seals and trumpets so far have been either directed at the earth itself or were events that pertained to all the people of the earth regardless of their faith.

December 7, OT
Psalm 1:1-6; Psalm 107:1-43
Priestly Psalms, Part One

For the next 7 days, the OT reading consists of Psalms or portions of Psalms written in celebration of the last great event in the recorded history of the Hebrew people in Old Testament times. All are anonymous, but have in them a tone and a theology that is clearly priestly. That is, it's obvious from the content, particularly of some of them, that they were written by one of the priests of the newly built Temple in Jerusalem, and meant for Temple worship. The odd thing about some of them is that a few are attributed to David (including #107, today) in some Bibles, despite there being no mention of this in the original Hebrew.

Many Bibles divide up the Psalter into five "books" of Psalms of roughly equal length:

11. Book 1 - Psalms 1-41
12. Book 2 - Psalms 42-72
13. Book 3 - Psalms 73-89
14. Book 4 - Psalms 90-106
15. Book 5 - Psalms 107-150

The divisions themselves have no meaning, particularly in light of the fact that there is at least one Psalm of David in each of the 5. But it is interesting to note that both of today's Psalms are at the beginning of these sections, book 1 and book 5, respectively. Both sound like they were written in response to the response of the people who had made a pair of crucial errors in breaking the Law of Moses, but repented and reformed their ways of life to not follow the "ways of the wicked".

December 7, NT
Revelation 9:13-10:11
The Sixth Trumpet; The Mighty Angel with the Edible Scroll

World War III or World War IV? History has recorded the first two World Wars, and a third is believed to occur near the beginning of the Seal Judgments with the appearance of the Four Horsemen of the Apocalypse. But, we get almost no detail about that war - who fires the first shot?, what are the relative strengths of the armies?, how quickly is it over? These questions make it difficult to identify whether that war is truly WWIII or if, instead, WWIII refers to the Sixth Trumpet judgment. Either way, the frightening picture of an army of two hundred million, unleashed (so to speak) from the other side of the Euphrates River, to kill a third of what remains of mankind (Revelation 9:13-19), would be the biggest World War the world had ever seen to that point, and it matters little if you would number it as the third or the fourth. As part of the explanation of this event, John reveals for us the purpose of these increasingly devastating disasters, plagues, and wars: God is trying to get our attention, to give us one last opportunity to repent. The problem is that the "rest of mankind" didn't do so, at least not at this point (9:20-21).

The issue of whether or not anyone can actually repent and be saved during the first half of the Tribulation period has been debated for centuries. Much of the debate centers on the timing of the Rapture relative to these events, other controversy exists because of that timing, such as whether or not one can come to Christ without the presence of the Holy Spirit, who would be absent during this part of the End Times. Whichever is the truth of this matter, part of the problem is simply the way in which End Times events are scattered across many different prophets, and that even John, being given this longest and most complete vision of the Tribulation period, is not given every detail. In fact, some of the details are deliberately censored by God himself! In the second half of today's reading, a mighty angel appears, speaking like thunder, when another voice from heaven (God?) tells John to "seal up the things which the seven peals of thunder have spoken and *do not write them*" (10:4). The same voice later tells John told to eat the small scroll in the mighty angel's hand (10:8-10), which isn't the first time that the odd act of actually eating (which may be a metaphor for "taking in") a scroll was commanded of a prophet (see, for example, Ezekiel 3:3).

December 8, OT
Psalm 111:1-10; Psalm 112:1-10; Psalm 117:1-2
Priestly Psalms, Part Two

Today's 3 Psalms all start with the Hebrew "Hallelujah!," meaning "praise the Lord". All 3 are brief, anonymous, joyful songs of praise. Psalms 111 and 112 are both acrostic poems, in that their brief 10 verses apiece begin with successive letters of the Hebrew alphabet. Psalm 117 is not only the shortest Psalm at only 2 verses, but is the shortest "chapter" in the entire Bible as a result. This is in stark contrast to the readings for the next 2 days.

December 8, NT
Revelation 11:1-19
The Third Temple, the Two Witnesses and the Seventh Trumpet

The ministry, death, and resurrection and ascension into heaven of the Two Witnesses is one of Revelation's most mysterious yet spectacular events. Proof that Jerusalem will be a key part of End Times events is found at the beginning of this chapter, as John is given a measuring rod and commanded to measure the Temple. Given that the Temple in Jerusalem had been destroyed more than 20 years before John received these visions, the Temple to which John is referring must be a Temple yet to be built, and is referred to as the "Third Temple" by dispensationalists. But this Temple's exact location is not known.

The site of the current Temple Mount in Jerusalem is topped with the Dome of the Rock Mosque, and this might be the people referred to as Gentiles in Revelation 11:2. But refuting this is the fact that this "trampling" on the holy city is supposed to last for 42 months, or 3 and a half years, and the al-Aqsa mosque has been there for much longer than that.

Much more significant is the fact that 3 ½ years is exactly half the length of the Tribulation period, prophesied on multiple occasions as lasting 7 years. There are also multiple prophecies of a Great Tribulation period, being distinct from the rest of the Tribulation, being of that same length. If the Two Witnesses prophesied here make their first appearance near the beginning of the Tribulation period, then their assassinations (Revelation 11:7-10) and subsequent resurrections (11:11-12) would occur almost right at the midpoint. Revelation does not identify the Two Witnesses, but speculation has been made through the centuries that these two are Moses and Elijah (as depicted in the Left Behind book series, especially in Apollyon and Assassins, the last two books to take place before the midpoint of the Tribulation), while others think the Two are Enoch and Elijah, being the only two figures of the Old Testament who never died. The former idea is justified by the fact that Moses and Elijah were the only two to

perform the miracles attributed here to the Two Witnesses (11:6).
 Either way, it is shown that this event, not associated with any of the Seal or Trumpet Judgments (falling in between the 6th and 7th Trumpet), is referred to as the Second Woe (the 6th Trumpet was the First Woe), and ends with another great earthquake that destroyed a 10th of Jerusalem, followed by a warning of the Third Woe.

When George Frideric Handel composed the oratorio Messiah in 1741, he took the lyrics of each of the 53 sung parts directly from Scripture. In the case of its most famous part, the Hallelujah chorus (Part 2, Scene 7, song 44), God's ultimate victory is praised by using the words from right here in Revelation 11:15 (along with other parts of Revelation already read). What many people listening to this great work don't necessarily realize is that this is the first part of the Seventh Trumpet, which is also the last trumpet, which ends with an earthly vision of the Ark of the Covenant in heaven (11:15-19), along with lightning, thunder, rumblings, and a severe hailstorm. It is also believed by some (and, in fact, was the dominant belief for centuries until the Pre-Tribulation Rapture was first preached) that this is the moment of the Rapture of the Church. But whether the Rapture occurred just prior to the Tribulation or right here, the climax of the first half of the Tribulation is about to occur, centering on the person most directly responsible for the misery suffered by those that are left behind: the Antichrist.

December 9, OT
Psalm 119:1-88
Priestly Psalms, Part Three: The Longest Psalm

Where we read, yesterday, the shortest Psalm and shortest chapter of the Bible, today and tomorrow we read Psalm 119, the longest Psalm and the longest single chapter of the entire Bible. It is the only Psalm of sufficient length to be broken into two days' reading, and is longer by itself than 14 of the books of the Old Testament and 17 of the books of the New Testament. The Psalm's 176 verses are divided into 22 stanzas of 8 verses apiece, each stanza starting with successive letters of the Hebrew alphabet, thus making this another acrostic Psalm. This one uses all 22 letters of the Hebrew alphabet, as opposed to just the small portion that we get in the Psalms read yesterday. The themes of praise to the Law and the Torah that run throughout the

Psalm make this another that fits perfectly with the other priestly Psalms believed to have been written during this time. It is anonymous, and is even believed to have been written by David by the Eastern Orthodox Church, but this is a very small minority. Some believe that this may have been written by Ezra or Nehemiah.

December 9, NT
Revelation 12:1-13:1a
The Woman, The Child, and the Dragon

Most of Revelation is laid out in a chronological fashion, or so it can be assumed. Reconciling the events seen by John and recorded here with other prophecies isn't always easy; in fact, it is sometimes very difficult as yesterday's reading will attest. But in between the last Trumpet judgment and the events surrounding the Antichrist, John gets a different kind of vision that, if viewed by a person today, would probably be referred to as a flashback. John records signs from heaven that depict a symbolic history of the three major players of all human history in the forms of a woman, a Child, and a dragon. What they each represent can be interpreted largely from the context of the writing, and is one of the few areas in Revelation in which there is almost universal agreement.

The woman represents God's people. At first, this is more specifically Israel, as she is depicted as having a crown of twelve stars on her head, presumably a reference to the Twelve Tribes of Israel (Revelation 12:1). Later, this is a more generalized reference to all who "keep God's commands and hold fast their testimony about Jesus" (12:17), which refers to the Church. The woman, back in the first part where she represents Israel, gives birth to a male Child, who is in danger from the moment of birth of being devoured by the dragon, but who will "rule all the nations" (12:2, 12:4b-5). The various references to the Child are references to Jesus Christ. The enormous red dragon is the third major player, and his identity is the easiest to understand, because John's vision explains it to us: the dragon is Satan, the Devil (12:3-4a, 12:7-9) who was expelled from Heaven after conducting a war there against the leader of the angels, Michael, taking a third of the angels with him, who we know as demons.

When, exactly, did this take place? We know from earlier Scriptures that the Devil had full access to both Heaven and earth, freely going back and forth between the realms. Those angels that were, eventually, expelled with him had the same freedoms. Thus, Satan and his angels have been roaming the earth (and heaven) for quite a long time. The war in heaven, however, takes place during the first half of the Tribulation: the 1260 day period (12:6) in which the woman ("God's people") is protected from the Devil corresponds with the 3 ½ year first part of the Tribulation where the Church has been Raptured, but would be in need of protection if war broke out in heaven (12:7). It is thus at this point that the war in heaven *results* in Satan's expulsion from it at the midpoint of the Tribulation, and he is furious - because he knows "his time is short" (12:12).

The imagery that follows indicates further conflict between Satan and God's people, though the people enjoy protection in their new locale for a "time, times, and half a time" (12:14), another reference to a 3 ½ year period, this time being the Great Tribulation. This protection just keeps infuriating Satan all the more, though, as this part of the vision ends with an even more troubling scene: Satan standing at the edge of the sea, anticipating the arrival of something even more evil.

December 10, OT
Psalm 119:89-176
Priestly Psalms, Part Four: More of The Longest Psalm

Psalm 119, the longest Psalm and longest chapter in the Bible, is concluded in today's OT reading. Yesterday we read the first 11 stanzas, today the last 11 stanzas, each labeled and beginning with successive letters of the Hebrew alphabet, making for a very large acrostic poem, praising the Law, the Torah, and the author of that law.

December 10, NT
Revelation 13:1b-18
The Unholy Trinity

He is never given a name, yet nearly everyone knows about him. In various places in the Bible, he gets the title of "man of perdition," "son of Satan," and here, of course, "beast". He is responsible, more than any other single person, for bringing on the "time of Jacob's Trouble." His place of origin has been a topic of debate for centuries. Paul writes about him and those who have "his spirit," in his Epistles, even saying that there are multiple such beings. He is to the devil as Jesus is to God the Father. He is assassinated at the midpoint of the Tribulation but rises again (Revelation 13:3, 13:14), and carries out Satan's work on earth during the time of the End.

He is the Antichrist.

The "sea" from which the beast comes is not any literal ocean. A Plain Interpretation of this difficult chapter would view the "sea" as the sum total of all the Gentile nations, and so the beast that comes out of it is the final leader of all the nations of the world (except Israel). It can be surmised that he came to power during the war that happened at the beginning of the Tribulation. He could be alive today, as he would have to be an adult at the time of the Rapture and of the beginning of the Tribulation. Besides the prophecy here, he is predicted by Daniel as the "little horn" in Daniel 7:8, 7:20-21, and 7:24-25) and the coming prince (Daniel 9:26). His appearance here, with seven heads, ten horns, ten crowns, etc., is also a symbolic description of the system of world government that would exist at this midpoint of the Tribulation. His scary appearance with characteristics of a leopard, a bear, and a lion ties him to Satan as well as the "fourth beast" in Daniel 7:7 and 7:23. The vision of having "his deadly wound healed" could be either a reference to the death and resurrection of the Antichrist, or it could refer to the fall of the old Roman Empire and its subsequent revival in the End Times - it could actually be both.

The 42 additional months the Antichrist is given to blaspheme God (Revelation 13:4-6) is the Great Tribulation period, or the second half of the Tribulation. This would fit with this vision being presented here at the midpoint. It would have taken most of the first half of the Tribulation for the unbelievers of the world to turn their worship toward him, while believers in God are protected by having their names in the "book of life" (13:7-8). The Power of the Beast comes from Satan himself, indwelt in the Antichrist. But this will not last forever, and he and Satan will be defeated in the end (13:9-10).

Then, as if we needed another manifestation of evil, another beast comes "up from the earth" (which could indicate Israel as his origin, thus making him a Jew) and causes everyone to worship the first beast (the Antichrist) "whose deadly wound was healed" (13:11-12), which seems to reinforce the idea that the Antichrist is assassinated at the midpoint of the Tribulation, but is miraculously resurrected in an exact counterfeit of the Resurrection of Christ. Like the Antichrist, this second beast will be given Satanic powers. He is known as the False Prophet, and he completes the unholy trinity, representing the Holy Spirit's part just as the Antichrist represents Jesus. The False Prophet will construct a giant statue of the slain Antichrist and "bring it to life" (13:14-15), and order all those who do not worship the image to be killed (20:4, December 17).

But perhaps the most terrifying characteristic of the False Prophet comes when people are forced to take a mark in their "right hand or in their foreheads" in order to buy or sell anything (13:16-17). This mark is the equivalent of a "branding," such as what happens with slaves. Thus, taking the mark makes you a slave to Satan, and is thus a *permanent disqualification from heaven* (more about this tomorrow). It is a permanent, irreversible rejection of Jesus. Many today live in great fear of technological innovations that make you, as a customer, a number in a system, and they fear using things like credit cards and other tools of commerce for fear of accidentally taking the Mark of the Beast. But here, a plain interpretation of the Bible will help put your mind at ease: the Mark of the Beast is a *visible* mark on the forehead or right hand, so invisible systems or systems that aren't permanently branded onto those parts of your body can't be the Mark.

Furthermore, acceptance of the Mark also comes with worship of the Beast, and that means that only a willful acceptance, not an accidental one, of the Mark would condemn you.

As for the meaning of the number 666 (13:18), there are whole volumes of works that speculate about its exact meaning; here is the only important thing you must know about it: there is no place in the Bible where the answer (or even any meaningful clues) is found. So, rather than read anything into it from outside of Scripture, we are left with the patience and faith to know that when the time does come, some of those left behind will have the wisdom and discernment to know what it means when they see it.

December 11, OT
Psalm 121:1-8; Psalm 122:1-9; Psalm 123:1-4; Psalm 128:1-6
Priestly Psalms, Part Five

All four of today's Psalms, plus two of tomorrow's, are listed as a "Song of Ascents" in their titles. This means they were written to be sung by worshippers as they ascended the road to Jerusalem, presumably for Temple worship. There are 15 of them in all, numbered from 120 to 134, and four of them (122, 124, 131, and 133) are listed as Psalms of David. Indeed, Psalms 124, 131, and 133 have all been read already, and are attributed to David correctly, but one of them (122, today) appears to actually be an error on the part of the scholars that gathered the Psalms into the book we know today. Inside Psalm 122 is a reference to the "thrones of the house of David," a reference to David's descendants who make up the "royal line" of Judah, something David could not have known about.

Far more likely is that all four of the Psalms we read today and the four tomorrow were written in celebration of Nehemiah's completion of the reconstruction of the walls of Jerusalem, here during this post-Exilic period, by unknown authors.

December 11, NT
Revelation 14:1-13
The 144,000 Again?

Back in Revelation chapter 7, we were introduced to a group of 144,000 Jewish converts to Christianity who were tasked with evangelizing the world as a kind of "bookend" to the first Christians in the First Century who were, likewise, Jewish converts to Christianity. Here in chapter 14, following the vivid descriptions of the Antichrist and the False Prophet at the midpoint of the Tribulation, we appear to encounter this group again. Some scholars believe that the references are to two different groups, but there are many things arguing against that possibility. For one is the unusual number, being exactly 12 x 12000, which fits perfectly with the idea of the 12 Tribes of Israel, and being a bit too much of a coincidence to be the exact size of two different groups. The fact that there is no mention of their Jewish roots in chapter 14 is nearly the only clue that there might be two different groups here. Still others believe the setting to be different, believing that this encounter with the 144,000 takes place in heaven, not earth. But this chronology accepts the more traditional view that the two encounters, in chapter 7 and in chapter 14, refer to the same group of people.

Even though there is a lot of good to say about these 144,000 evangelists, it quickly becomes obvious that their efforts are simply not enough. The reason we know this is what happens next, as God sends 3 angels to do a job that was previously exclusively the duty of humans, never angels: to evangelize, spreading the "eternal Gospel" to all people on earth (Revelation 14:6-7). After the first angel's message warning of the hour of judgment, the second angel's message on the fall of "Babylon the Great" (14:8) seems confusing. Is this referring to the city of Babylon, whose empire had fallen centuries earlier to the Persians? The city never stopped being inhabited, and even became a center for trade and culture as predicted by both Isaiah and Jeremiah, even though the empire was gone. But if this chapter marks the fall of "Babylon the Great," what, then, is being described 2 days from now in chapter 16, when the city of Babylon is destroyed?
 The far better explanation is that "Babylon the Great" isn't the literal city, but a symbolic title for the system of world government that had, essentially, outlawed Christianity. It makes more sense this way given the wording as well as the context, sandwiched between a warning to turn away from the Antichrist and the third angel's warning to avoid taking the Mark of the Beast at all costs (14:9-12).

December 12, OT
Psalm 130:1-8; Psalm 134:1-3; Psalm 135:1-21; Psalm 136:1-26
Priestly Psalms, Part Six

Two of today's four Psalms are part of the set of "Songs of Ascents" from which we read yesterday. The other two, which follow by number, continue the set of "priestly Psalms" meant for Temple worship in the newly rebuilt facility. Both Psalms 135 and 136 do something seen very commonly in Psalms written by Priests: recount the history of Israel with an emphasis on Moses and the Exodus. In particular, Psalm 136 contains one of the best known call and response formats found in the Bible, with every verse ending with the phrase "His love endures forever."

December 12, NT
Revelation 14:14-16:1
The Great Harvest and Winepress; Preparing for the Seven Bowl Judgments

With the first half of the Tribulation past, and the major events of the midpoint involving the Antichrist seen, the vision revealed to John turns its attention to the second half of the Tribulation, known as the Great Tribulation. It's already obvious from descriptions in chapters 13 and 14 that the Great Tribulation is going to be a very different period than the earlier half. Even though the Great Tribulation sees only 7 judgments from God, vs. 14 of them in the first half of the Tribulation, their severity is ramped up to a point that the vast majority of those that remain will not survive them. Unbelievers, in particular, are in for a very bad time as things get underway, with John seeing one "like a son of man" seated on a cloud and engaging in a great harvest of the earth (Revelation 14:14-16), which is followed by a great pressing of grapes which symbolically represent followers of the Antichrist (14:17-20). John Steinbeck's The Grapes of Wrath takes its title from verse 19, while musicians who know the entire song "Battle Hymn of the Republic" will recognize verses 19-20 in part of the song's first verse.

The Seven Bowl Judgments that are "poured out" on the earth are so immense and so severe that an entire chapter is devoted to just the introduction of them by seven angels (15:1-8). In the chapter's brief 8 verses, we learn that these are the last seven plagues, because with them God's Wrath is completed. And with this very big introduction, the buildup to the Seven Bowl Judgments, starting tomorrow, is complete too.

December 13, OT
Psalm 146:1-10; Psalm 147:1-20
Priestly Psalms, Part Seven

Besides being the last two of the so-called "Priestly Psalms," the two Psalms that make up today's OT reading are the last two, chronologically, in the Bible. Like all of the Priestly Psalms, they are anonymous, but likely written by either Nehemiah, Ezra, or one of the other Priests charged with restoring Temple worship during the post-Exilic period.

December 13, NT
Revelation 16:2-21
Seven Bowls of God's Wrath

The judgments of God that dominate the Tribulation period, both before and after the midpoint, are the dominant events of the End Times, along with the Battle of Armageddon. The Rapture is believed by many to occur just *before* the Tribulation, and the Glorious Appearing of Christ occurs just *after* the Tribulation, leaving a total of 21 judgments, at least 2 worldwide wars, and the ultimate final battle between good and evil at Armageddon as the major events of the time. The judgments, in particular, are a focal point because of how each one has some catastrophic worldwide effect, and each one gets more and more severe than its predecessor (with the exception there of the seventh "seal" judgment, which serves mainly to introduce the trumpet judgments that follow). What at least the first 14 have in common is the desire on God's part to reach out to humanity one last time to get their attention, giving mankind a chance to repent, turn away from the Antichrist, and instead turn towards the Lord. But after the midpoint of the Tribulation, which features the death and resurrection of the Antichrist, the worldwide system of government changes to include a required "Mark of the Beast", which makes a clear, visible distinction between those who can still be saved vs. those who are forever condemned. That, then, changes the purpose of God's judgments, from attempts to reach out to humanity, to statements of His Wrath - punishment for the unbelievers that remain.

The seven bowls of wrath that are, symbolically, poured out onto the earth by each of seven angels (whom we met yesterday) and are increasingly severe judgments that affect the whole world; but even though only the first one is designed specifically and only for those loyal to the Antichrist who have taken the Mark, it can be rightly assumed that believers that remain on earth will continue to have some protection from these judgments. The first bowl produces sores and boils on the skin of those who have taken the Mark (Revelation 16:2). The second turns the seas into blood and kills all the creatures within (16:3). The third does likewise to the fresh water rivers and springs (16:4-7), taking away all drinkable water.

The fourth bowl judgment turns the sun scorching hot, likely a huge solar flare or storm (16:8-9). The fifth is a plague of darkness such as has never happened in world history (16:10-11). The sixth has two parts to it, the first of which relates back to a Trumpet Judgment: the drying up of the Euphrates river, allowing the massive army of 200 million strong to cross the river on dry land, setting up the Battle of Armageddon to come. The second part of the same bowl judgment is the appearance of "3 unclean spirits," which come from Satan and represent each of the parts of the unholy trinity (16:12-16). These demons help to gather up the kings of the world in preparation for the Battle named in verse 16.

The seventh and final bowl judgment features multiple calamities, including lightning, thunder, and the most severe earthquake ever seen, even more severe than the Wrath of the Lamb earthquake that happened as one of the Seal judgments earlier in the Tribulation. Babylon (the city, this time) is destroyed, most of the rest of the cities in the world are leveled, and even Jerusalem is split into 3 parts. Hailstones weighing 100 pounds fall on the earth, and still there are those who curse God for these judgments (16:17-21).

December 14, OT
Nehemiah 7:73b-9:37
Ezra Reads the Book of the Law

It is not known how many, if any, of the Psalms that we read over the course of the last 7 days were written by Ezra, the Priest. We do know that the scroll that bears his name was completed 9 days ago, and that the Book of Nehemiah is actually the second part of the same scroll written by him; we also believe that Ezra was the writer of the books we now know as the Chronicles. The main reason for this belief, besides some extra-Biblical evidence, is actually in the reading for 2 days from now from 1 Chronicles (more about this on December 16). In the meantime, the next major event of history is recorded by Ezra in Nehemiah, and it centers on Ezra himself.

Many things happened after Cyrus of Persia had released the Israelites to return home after the Exile. Keeping in mind that the entire region of Israel was still under Persian rule, the Israelites basically did everything except crown a new king: they rebuilt the Temple and the walls of Jerusalem, and the priests, Levites, gatekeepers, musicians, and servants and the rest of the people settled in their towns (Nehemiah 7:73**a**). Passover had been celebrated, and the priestly system of worship was reinstituted. But what hadn't yet been done, at least not in public, was a formal reading of The Law; that is, until Ezra's arrival in Jerusalem and being asked to bring it out on the "first day of the seventh month" (7:73b-8:2).

It is likely that the book of The Law from which Ezra read was Deuteronomy, but could have been the entire Torah, or everything from Genesis through Deuteronomy (8:3-8). At any rate, the reading actually frightened many of the listeners, who thought that The Law, exposing their sins, was cause for mourning and weeping (8:9-11), but Nehemiah set them straight, and turned the event into a celebration of what The Law really meant (8:12-18). The Israelites' guilty consciences still forced them to come before the priests on the 24th day of the same month to confess their sins (9:1-3), but even this was turned into a great worship service led by a group of Levites (9:4-37).

December 14, NT
Revelation 17:1-18
Who is the Whore of Babylon?

Chapter 16 of Revelation, read yesterday, takes us chronologically very close to the end of the Tribulation period. Thus, chapter 17 is actually a little bit of a step back - not so much back in time, but back to chapter 14, where the fall of "Babylon the Great" was first read - but not fully explained. As is revealed to John by one of the seven angels that poured a bowl of judgment (Revelation 17:1a), Babylon the Great doesn't refer literally to the city of Babylon, but the explanation of what it really means doesn't come until here in this chapter. Here, Babylon the Great is referred to, depending on Bible translation, as the "great prostitute," "great harlot," "whore of Babylon," or any number of other names (17:1-2) that refer to the system of world government led by the Antichrist. This is verified by the description of her, being carried by a scarlet beast whose description closely matches that of the "beast from the sea," or the Antichrist, now indwelt by Satan himself (17:3-4, 17:8, 17:11-13). The fact that this description is symbolic and not literal is actually stated in the text of verse 5, that on her forehead was written "a mystery" (17:5). So although the world government of the Antichrist is personified as female, it should not be taken literally that either the Antichrist, the False Prophet, or the leader or deputy leader of the world government is a woman.

Nor should this be interpreted as anything to do with the Roman Catholic Church, the Pope, or their devotion to Mary, the mother of Jesus. Over the centuries since the Reformation, there has been widespread misinterpretation of the symbols and visions presented to John in this part of Revelation. Preterists, in particular, have believed that Babylon is a code name for Rome, and that mentions of the city and of the world government it symbolizes refer to Rome and to the Papacy, respectively. Part of this stems from the idea that the "harlot who sits on many waters" (17:1b) and "the seven hills on which the woman sits" (17:9) can be interpreted as Rome, which does sit on seven hills by the Mediterranean Sea, with a tie-in to the Catholic zeal for Mary. The Roman Catholic over-devotion to Mary is an error, but it is not a heresy unless it goes all the way to actual worship of Mary as some kind of co-redemptrix. Part of the Catholic Church's reasoning for believing that Mary remained "ever virgin" stems from the notion that she needs to be identified as separate from the Whore of Babylon, and thus anyone who *doesn't* believe Mary to have been "ever virgin" is guilty of the heresy of believing in the harlot "with whom the kings of the earth committed immorality… and made drunk with the wine of her immorality" (17:2). This is, at worst, a bad misinterpretation of this chapter, and at worst, circular reasoning.

But, the correct interpretation, like so much else in the Bible but especially in Revelation, can be found through a Plain Interpretation which is only possible by reading the *entire* Bible; or, in this case, the rest of the chapter. The further explanation in 17:14-18 of the identity of the woman solidifies the interpretation of the woman as Babylon the Great, which "reigns over the kings of the earth" (17:18) which must refer to the world government implemented by the Antichrist, and is actually further explained in the next chapter, in tomorrow's NT reading.

December 15, OT
Nehemiah 9:38-11:36
The Post-Exilic Covenant

Throughout human history, starting all the way back from Adam, God and His people, have been brought into covenants (agreements, contracts) with varying obligations on the part of the people and promises on the part of God. Adam and Eve broke the first covenant between God and man. The Abrahamic, Mosaic, and Davidic covenants were among the others, each one eventually broken by the people, and resulting in some kind of punishment dealt out by the Lord. After the Exile, Israel had neither a king nor a covenant with God, though God's promises - in ALL of the covenants - were and still are binding. As such, when the Jews returned to Israel and to Jerusalem, and the Law was read to them, they repented of their sins and decided to make a new covenant with God - in writing - and seal the document with the names of their spiritual and political leaders (Nehemiah 9:38). Thus, the post-Exilic covenant was signed by Nehemiah and the priests (notably not including Ezra) (10:1-27), and described the obligations of the people of Israel which were, mostly, echoes of specific Laws found in Deuteronomy (10:28-39).

And so, with Jerusalem set up as the seat of government (11:1-2) and the other leaders dispersed throughout Judah (11:3-19) and the rest of Israel (11:20-36), life after the Exile went on without a king.

December 15, NT
Revelation 18:1-20
Lament Over Babylon

Confusion over the identity of Babylon as well as Babylon the Great is confounded by the fact that Babylon was and is a real city in addition to its identity as the system of world government instituted by the Antichrist. Widespread belief in the notion that Babylon is a code word for Rome led to the shocking discovery that Babylon had been rebuilt sometime before the 2003 invasion of Iraq by US-led forces. It had been long believed that the city was destroyed and that there was nothing left of the ruins. Admittedly, there has been serious damage done to the ruins, making archaeological study of the ancient city difficult or even impossible, but just the fact that it was discovered to still exist at all came as a shock. It opened the door to the possibility that the Babylon referred to in the End Times would be a real city, not

Rome, situated on or near the ancient city, as the center of the Antichrist's seat of government.

There are still some, however, who believe that Babylon is code for yet another location, the United States of America. In John Price's The End of America, the case is laid out for Babylon referring to *America*, and that the warning in this chapter to "flee her" (Revelation 18:4) means for believers to leave the U.S. before it is too late to do so. However, this is at best of leap of logic in that there is no direct mention of the U.S.A. in the Bible, and Babylon can't symbolically be linked to any other great world power. A Plain Interpretation of the Bible, though, coupled with the modern rebuilding of Babylon, Iraq and known archaeology, make is easier to understand what's being described here in Revelation and elsewhere in the Bible: a real city, and the real seat of government for the forces of evil in the End Times, which eventually falls (18:1-3) and is destroyed by fire (18:8).

People all over the world will lament the fall of Babylon when it happens (18:9-20), and it serves as a perfect bookend to the history of the founding of the ancient city, back when it was called Babel (in Hebrew) and had in it a tower that was built by Nimrod in an attempt to reach heaven before God had it destroyed and their languages confused (Genesis 11:4-9).

December 16, OT
1 Chronicles 9:1b-34; Nehemiah 12:1-47
Living in Post-Exilic Israel

Many times throughout this Bible-reading guide, it is speculated that Ezra was the writer of a great deal more of the Old Testament than just the one book that bears his name. One of the reasons that he is believed to be the writer of the Chronicles is found in this last section from either 1st or 2nd Chronicles to be read as part of this chronology. Basically, if Ezra wrote the book of Nehemiah, which is almost universally believed, since it's the second part of the same scroll as the book of Ezra, then chapter 9 of 1 Chronicles was written by the same person who wrote Nehemiah, and is therefore Ezra, because the list there of priests, Levites, Temple Servants, and the rest found in 1 Chronicles 9:1b-34 is almost identical to the list found in yesterday's and today's readings from Nehemiah. Certainly, it could not have been written any earlier than some time after the return from the Exile and the rebuilding of the Temple. This leaves only two chapters, one today (Nehemiah 12:1-47) and one tomorrow, of actual history of the Old Testament recorded by Ezra left in this chronology.

December 16, NT
Revelation 18:21-19:21
Antichrist Defeated; The Glorious Appearing of Christ

Back on December 13 during the reading of Revelation 16 and the Bowl Judgments, the location of the final battle between good and evil - or between those people loyal to the Antichrist and those loyal to Jesus - was presented to us: the plains of Megiddo, about 60 miles north of Jerusalem in present-day Israel, known as Armageddon.

From Revelation 16:16 up to this point, our attention has been focussed on the fact that the forces of evil, led by the Antichrist and known as Babylon the Great, was going to be defeated. Today's NT reading starts with a "mighty angel" announcing the final doom of Babylon (Revelation 18:21-24). Its complete destruction is a cause for celebration and of praise (19:1-10). Once again, those readers who are musically inclined will recognize more verses that were used as lyrics in George Frederick Handel's Hallelujah Chorus from Messiah, particularly verses 6 and 16.

The heavenly multitudes singing Hallelujah (meaning Praise the Lord) then become soldiers in the final battle itself, led by none other than Jesus Christ (19:11-16), the King of Kings and Lord of Lords. This is the true Second Coming. This is the Glorious Appearing of Christ. It is at this point that the prophecy in Zechariah 14 is fulfilled, as Jesus sets foot on the Mount of Olives and completes His return to earth in human form. The Antichrist and the False Prophet are captured and thrown alive into the Lake of Fire (19:17-21), and the Tribulation that marks the End Times as prophesied is over

Just as Jesus promised.

December 17, OT
Nehemiah 13:1-31
The Last of the Old Testament History

The Old Testament is nearly done, but the remaining 3 days' of readings are made up of prophecy, not history, which makes today's OT reading the last of the Old Testament history that we read. This last chapter of Nehemiah contains neither his name nor Ezra's name, even once, yet both these men figure prominently in these last events.

Some Bibles list this chapter as "Nehemiah's Last Reforms". It starts with a reading of the book of the Law (Nehemiah 13:1) where they made the discovery that foreigners weren't supposed to be part of the Temple assembly. So, Nehemiah (as governor of the land) led an effort to have them removed (13:2-3). Further reforms included the expulsion of Tobiah and the cleansing of the Temple (13:4-9), the restoration of tithes (13:10-14), and the restoration of the Sabbath (13:15-22). In the midst of these reforms are places where the writer, Ezra, speaking in the first person, prays to be remembered by God (13:14).

The last of the reforms concerns the mixed marriages again (13:23-31), completing a lengthy and difficult purification of the Temple and of Jerusalem in an attempt to bring things back into accord with The Law of Moses. Historically, we are left at approximately 400 BC, and a gap between this time and the first appearance of Christ that is sometimes called the "time between the Testaments." The Old Testament books of the Maccabees appear during this time, but inconsistencies and outright errors in them taint their ability to be used as Biblical history, and are consigned to be called Apocrypha. Two books of prophecy follow this reading, over the course of the next 3 days, but they contain no historical detail (and one of them, in fact, is actually difficult to place in the chronology because of this lack of historical detail).

December 17, NT
Revelation 20:1-10
The Millennium

Just exactly what is a "millennium"? Simply defined, a millennium is a 1000 year period. Y2K was a big deal because it was the end of a 1000 year period that began in the year 1000. But that's all any of this

was - a coincidence of dates involving 1000 year periods. The Bible predicts a very important 1000 year period, the importance of which is enough to give it the definitive article in the title: The Millennium.
What happens during The Millennium?

The Millennium is bookended by the imprisonment (Revelation 20:1-3a) and subsequent release (20:3b, 20:7-8) of Satan, the devil. In between is a 1000 year period of Christ reigning on earth (20:4-6), in person, along with all those who "stuck it out" and didn't take the Mark of the Beast. After Satan's release at the end of The Millennium, his doom is sealed and he is thrown into the Lake of Fire just as were the Antichrist and the False Prophet (20:9-10).

In other words, God wins in the end.

December 18, OT
Joel 1:1-2:32
From The Threat of Locusts to The Coming of the Holy Spirit

The last two books from which we read in the Old Testament as part of this chronological reading plan are both works of minor prophets: first Joel (today and tomorrow), and lastly, Malachi (December 20). Of all the minor prophets, Joel is the most difficult to date with precision, and is arguably the most difficult to interpret. Joel gives us no biographical data outside of listing his father's name (Joel 1:1), and neither Joel nor Pethuel are mentioned in any books of history or by other prophets. Along the way, Joel appears to quote several other prophets (including Isaiah, Ezekiel, Zephaniah, Jonah, and Obadiah), but this could be interpreted two different ways: some scholars believe that Joel wrote these prophecies as early as the 9th century B.C., during the reign of King Joash of Judah, which would mean that all of the above prophets were actually quoting *Joel*, instead of the other way around. Others place Joel near the end of the kingdom of Judah, making him a contemporary of Jeremiah (with whom he shares no quotes) or immediately after the end of the Exile, making him a contemporary of Zechariah (with whom he also shares no quotes).
  The modern consensus, and the interpretation used by this reading plan, is the placement of Joel as the next-to-last prophet of the Old Testament, writing right around 400 B.C.

The reason for the difficulty in dating Joel stems not just from the lack of references to any kings or rulers, though that's certainly a factor. The main reason is the prophecy itself: Joel 1:2-20 describes a locust plague and a severe famine and drought. Much of the prophecy centers on the impact of these disasters on the ability to harvest things used as sacrifices in the Temple. This pretty much eliminates the theory that Joel was a contemporary of Jeremiah, as the Temple was destroyed near the beginning of the Exile and not rebuilt until after their return. But there's still another problem: if the Temple Joel refers to is the one built in the 5th century B,C,, then this prophecy was never fulfilled because there was no such plague and famine between the building of the Second Temple and its destruction in 70 A.D. This isn't to say that it can't still be fulfilled during the time of a Third Temple, but that would make this an End Times prophecy that doesn't exactly dovetail with other End Times prophecies found in Zephaniah, Zechariah, Daniel, or Revelation.

One interpretation, however, seems to shed some light on this mystery, and it is made by simply going into the next chapter and interpreting the locusts as being symbolic rather than literal. The symbolism, in this case, would liken the locusts to an army, and the famine and drought to the ravages of war. The war itself may symbolically refer to any number of the wars during the Tribulation period described in Revelation, even the Battle of Armageddon (Joel 2:1-11), particularly with Joel's description of this being "the day of the Lord" (2:11) much as Zephaniah does. Joel goes on to describe the deliverance to be bestowed on Israel if the nation would repent of her sins and turn back to the Lord (2:12-27), up to and including the promise of pouring out "My Spirit on all mankind" (2:28) which foretells the coming of the Holy Spirit.

December 18, NT
Revelation 20:11-21:8
The Great White Throne Judgment; The New Heaven and the New Earth

Two great post-Millennium events are described in today's NT reading; as different as are the two events, they actually both end the same way with a reference to and description of the Second Death.

The first event is sometimes titled the Great White Throne Judgment. This is actually the third of the Judgments to take place after the

Tribulation, but the only one to be described in detail in Revelation. The first post-Tribulation judgment is sometimes called "The Sheep and the Goats," and is described in Matthew 25:31-36 by Jesus himself, which picks those who will and will not enter the Millennial kingdom. The second judgment is sometimes called the "Bema Judgment" of "Bema Seat of Christ," described in 2 Corinthians 5:10, where believers who have already begun their eternal lives in heaven receive different degrees of reward for their service to God. This third judgment, which must take place after the Millennium, is the final separation of believers who get to live with God for eternity, and unbelievers who are cast into the Lake of Fire (Revelation 20:11-15) which John defines here as the Second Death.

Some believe that one or both of the earlier judgments takes place at the same time as the Great White Throne Judgment, and there is some merit to that belief, but some other problems are also created by believing that the Sheep and Goats judgment and/or Bema Judgment occur before the Millennium. But regardless of the timing of the events, there is no doubt about which one occurs last, and the final outcome for unbelievers who stand before God at that time. The Second Death is what most people think of when they refer to Hell or Eternal Damnation. If you are an unbeliever at the time of your death, your fate is sealed - you will stand before the Great White Throne and be judged, unsaved, for your sins. And this is all done just before what most people know of as the End of the World.

The End Times includes all of the events including the Tribulation, the Rapture, the Glorious Appearing/Second Coming of Christ, the Millennium, and the Judgments, regardless of the sequence or duration of any of the parts. Some mistakenly refer to the Battle of Armageddon as the End of the World, but this error is caused by not reading the rest of Revelation and putting things together with other End Times prophecies. Once the judgments are done, God sends away both the old earth and the old heaven and creates a new heaven and a new earth (21:1) and a new Jerusalem (21:2) to be the new eternal home for God and mankind, the eternal Bride of Christ. The description is joyous and comforting (21:3-4) and effectively constitutes a second Creation (21:5a). With this new Creation, God pronounces that He is finished. It is done. Those that believe will inherit this new Creation, while those that don't will join the unbelievers in the Lake of Fire, a.k.a. The Second Death (21:6-8), leaving no gray area in this final matter.

December 19, OT
Joel 3:1-21
Judgment of the Enemies of God

Part of the reason that a consensus of scholars believe that Joel's prophecies refer to the End Times stems from this third chapter. One issue of confusion comes from the very numbering of chapters and verses in Joel. The numbering of verses didn't really take place until the translation of the Old Testament scrolls from Hebrew into Greek that we call the Septuagint, but "chapters" as we now think of them were already in place. The earliest manuscripts of Joel's prophecy actually divide what we now think of as chapter 2 into 2 parts, with chapter 2 going from verse 1 through 27, and then what we now know as 2:28-32 being numbered as 3:1-5, making today's reading a fourth chapter instead of a third. The tone of this final chapter, whether you number it as 3 or 4, is quite different from the rest of the work, though it's unmistakably the work of the same writer. The final chapter is all about how Israel's neighboring nations will be judged: how God will restore the fortunes of Judah and Jerusalem (Joel 3:1), and neighbors will be punished, some very severely (3:4-8), even destroyed in war (3:9-10). Part of the prophecy refers to gathering the nations before the Lord at a seat of judgment to take place in the "valley of Jehoshaphat" (3:12), which refers to the site of King Jehoshaphat's victory over the invading armies of Moab and Edom, not far from Jerusalem in what is present-day Jordan. There are some who believe that this is the location of the Last Judgment, or Great White Throne Judgment, as prophesied in Revelation 20 (in yesterday's *New Testament* reading), which would make Joel's prophecies in all 3 (or 4) chapters make much more sense.

December 19, NT
Revelation 21:9-22:5
The New Jerusalem; The River of Life

One of the most glorious visions given to John to write down comes from one of the angels that held one of the Bowls of Judgment (though it's not specific about which one, Revelation 21:9). With the appearance of a "new heavens and new earth" and a "new Jerusalem" yesterday, we now get a detailed preview of the most glorious dwelling place ever created. The angel refers to it as the "bride, the wife of the Lamb" (21:9b), and it is the holy city, Jerusalem (21:10) having come down out of heaven from God. Its glory and brilliance is vividly described (21:11-21) and its dimensions given, with walls of jasper and streets of gold and gates made from precious gems, 12 of them, 1 for each of the 12 tribes of Israel. There was no Temple (21:22-27), and no sun or moon because none were necessary - the glory of God is the only illumination needed.

The same angel then reveals the River of Life, flowing past the Tree of Life, from the throne of God and of the Lamb (22:1-2). This is the ultimate bookend to the Bible, as this Tree and River represent the new Eden - the new Creation of God, where there will be no more Curse (22:3) and the people will be marked with the name of God (22:4-5).

December 20, OT
Malachi 1:1-4:6
Looking To The Future

In a way, all prophecy, both in the Old and the New Testament, is a look into the future. But as the closing book of the Old Testament, the mysterious prophecy of Malachi holds a special place. Its four chapters are brief enough to fit into a single day's reading, though its mysteries are broad and deep enough to make for an entire multi-week sermon series (the church where I worship spent an entire Summer in this one book). Its tone is harsh and difficult to read in places, but is actually an optimistic view of the future - for Israel and for all mankind.

Malachi provides even less biographical data than Joel did, yet this scroll is much easier to date than Joel's. Since the word Malachi, in Hebrew, simply means "my messenger," it isn't even known if Malachi is a person's name or simply a title for an unknown author. Roman Catholic scholarship even claims dogmatically that Malachi is an abbreviation of the term "Málakhîyah," which means "Messenger of Elohim". The use of Elohim as the name of God, particularly when coupled with the term "the word of God" instead of using the Yahweh abbreviation, is a priestly convention that is used in only a handful of other places in the Old Testament, but most notably in Zechariah and in Ezra, which has led some to believe that Malachi was either written by the prophet Zechariah or by the priest Ezra. The former is a slight possibility, while the latter seems unlikely if only because of the known dates: If this was written by Ezra, he would have been a very old man, likely in his mid 120s, but this may account for the very different tone than in the other known works of Ezra.

A couple of places in Malachi are quoted in the Gospels and/or Paul's Epistles to show the fulfillment of the prophesies. The basic premise of Malachi is a message from God chastising Israel for doubting His love. God promises that even if Edom (Esau) rebuilds, it's Israel, not Edom, that will be protected by Him (Malachi 1:1-5). But that's not to say that Israel is blameless. The priests, in particular, are guilty of many wrongs that, effectively, break the covenant between God and Israel: blemished sacrifices (1:6-2:9), divorces (2:10-16), and other injustices (2:17-3:5). In that section, Malachi mentions a messenger who will "prepare the way before me," (3:1), a reference to John the Baptist who eventually came before Christ to do just that. Each of the wrongs that God points out are argued by the people (3:6-15), but in the end there is a faithful remnant that will be spared from judgment when God separates the righteous from the wicked (3:16-18).

And so the final chapter of the Old Testament looks to this final judgment, with an eye towards the final fate of those who don't believe - a fate of fire that is also described in Revelation as the Second Death or Lake of Fire (4:1-3). One of the last two verses makes a prediction that, depending on interpretation, was either fulfilled at the Transfiguration or will later be fulfilled as one of the Two Witnesses that preaches during the first half of the Tribulation: the sending of Elijah before the "great and dreadful day of the Lord" (4:5). The latter seems more likely, as God promises destruction ("a curse") as the "or else" condition to the turning of hearts and minds to The Lord (4:6).

December 20, NT
Revelation 22:6-21
The End

When John received these visions, he had no idea how much time would pass before the events would occur. But, having heard the Doctrine of Imminency straight from the mouth of Jesus as an Apostle years earlier, John came to the conclusion that these End Times events were going to happen very soon. At least 3 times in these final verses (Revelation 22:6-7, 22:10, 22:20), John mentions that these things must come "soon". The fact that the events have not yet happened isn't an error on his part - John simply did not know, and he was taught this by Jesus himself. Two of the quotes come from Jesus in this reading as well. But as Peter said in his First Epistle, God views a thousand years as a day, existing outside of time, so the difference in the perception of time by God vs. by man is completely understandable.

Much of Revelation was delivered to John by angels; but when he bowed down to worship at the feet of the angel telling these things, he was told the true nature of them - that the angels were fellow servants of God (22:8-9), just like John. The angel had other instructions for John as well (22:10), the exact opposite of the instructions given to Daniel when he received a similar set of apocalyptic visions. The authenticity of the visions is declared, and John makes a statement that carries the dual interpretation of applying to the book of Revelation, as well as the whole Bible: that if anyone adds to or takes away from the words of the book, they will suffer the plagues described in the book (22:18-19)

And so with these closing words, the Revelation to John, and thus the Bible itself, comes to an end. It was the last book to be written (estimated to be just before the end of the first century) and the last to be accepted as part of the "canon" of Scripture. But in the end, and regardless of its interpretation, it provides the proper conclusion to the story of God's relationship with man. The visions, though sometimes frightening, often confusing, and subject to multiple interpretations, carry the unmistakable message to the reader: that God is the victor in the end. The final battle between good and evil is won by the good side. Satan's rebellion is quashed, and the created being who was ultimately behind every bit of human suffering in all of history, is destroyed. Jesus Christ, the Son of God, came to earth once before in human form, saved us from our sin by dying on a cross and rising again, and he's going to come back to earth in human form once again!

Are you on His side? Are you going to be on the winning side? If you have not been saved from your own sins by this very Jesus who is the focal point of the entire Bible (including Revelation), then there is no better time than right now to quote Revelation 22:20b, the next to last verse of the Bible, and add the phrase "into my heart". That is,

Amen, Come, Lord Jesus, into my heart.

If you just completed a reading of the entire Bible, congratulations on completing one of the most rewarding experiences you will ever have. If you reach this point but started at a different time and have more reading to do, please continue for the exact same reason. In fact, regardless of whether or not reading this means you have completed this reading of the entire Bible, you are encouraged most strongly to do two things: read it again once you have completed it, and tell everyone you know - family, friends, classmates, social media - about this remarkable journey through the Bible.

To quote the very last verse of the Bible, the Grace of the Lord Jesus be with all. Amen.

Printed in Great Britain
by Amazon